Second
Edition
Self and World
Readings in Philosophy

Second Edition
Self and World
Readings in Philosophy

Edited by
JAMES A. OGILVY

Under the General Editorship of Robert J. Fogelin,
Dartmouth College

Harcourt Brace Jovanovich, Inc.

New York / San Diego / Chicago / San Francisco / Atlanta / London / Sydney / Toronto

Preface

Self and World is organized around the path toward self-knowledge. Its argument leads from the immediate locale of the self, where inquiry is always interesting to the inquirer, outward toward the perhaps unsuspected social origins of individuality. By arranging the readings around the theme of self-knowledge and by structuring the readings into a kind of running argument, I have tried to achieve something more than a mere representation of major thinkers on a range of topics. While major thinkers are well represented, this book seeks to relate those thinkers to one another and to the reader's own growing self-awareness.

In the eight years since the first edition of *Self and World* was published, its primary themes have become ever more pressing. Preoccupations with selfhood have reached narcissistic proportions. A sense of world citizenship has spread with a growing ecological concern. This second edition remains faithful to the basic structure of the first edition. The changes include the addition of several essays specifically related to ecology and medical ethics and the deletion of several essays that seemed dated or too difficult. Kant and Marcuse are gone, but Aristotle, Hobbes, and Rousseau are now represented. I have happily abandoned the stance of editorial neutrality. The selections cover a range of views on each topic, so the reader will hardly experience indoctrination. Respect for thought, reflected in honesty about one's own beliefs and one's reasons for holding them, is the surest guard against indoctrination. A well-informed doubt is discernibly different from a confused or dishonest neutrality.

By pursuing an argument concerning the nature of self-knowledge, the coherence of the book as a whole avoids the cynical relativism often bred by anthologies presenting an assortment of loosely related essays. The differing needs of many instructors, however, demand a collection that can be used in different ways. Consequently this book is divided into eight sections, each with its own introduction orienting that section to the whole. If these introductions serve as joints articulating the separate parts of the organism, the "transitions" are the circulatory system within each part and within the whole. Between introductions and transitions, groups of essays in each subsection function together and in opposition, rather like extensor and flexor muscles. Following nature's guide in providing stronger bones for heavier loads, headnotes, introductions, and the transitions to the more difficult texts offer more detailed analyses, so that all sections and readings may be clearly accessible to the student. The internal structure of the various parts achieves the coherence of the whole, but invites flexible use of the book.

The quest for self-knowledge is eminently philosophical, for its faithful pursuit inevitably leads through all the major questions posed by philosophers past and present. The juxtaposition of both contemporary and classical readings in a pattern of ever-expanding circles of self-awareness invites readers to locate themselves in relation to issues both timely and timeless. In the first part, for example, Voltaire and the very contemporary Tom Wolfe set the stage with a provocative standoff over the virtues and vices of our sometimes narcissistic preoccupations with self.

René Descartes was among the first to reflect on the subject of consciousness. Part Two, "The Self," begins with Descartes's account of his solitary meditations. Gilbert Ryle, a twentieth-century philosopher, questions Descartes's conclusions. The next exchange again crosses the centuries, with St. Augustine and Jean-Paul Sartre discussing free will. Finally, empiricist David Hume and contemporary psychologist Erik Erikson address the question of self-identity. Part Two as a whole, with its reflections on the subject of consciousness, free will, and identity, remains close to what might be considered the core of the self. The reader will find this concentrated self-centeredness both fascinating and ultimately unsatisfactory. The inner path itself leads inevitably outward toward a world that gives selfhood its substance.

Part Three, "Knowledge and Other Selves," begins with one of the most famous images of the philosophical quest from an interior to a brighter exterior— Plato's myth of the cave. Epicurus then adds some insights on pleasure and pain and on the profits to be gleaned from meditating "by yourself, and with a companion like to yourself." The remainder of Part Three deals with two questions and their interrelation: first, What is knowledge?; second, How do we know other selves? In the first essays, Henri Bergson and A. J. Ayer discuss knowledge by intuition and knowledge by concepts derived from sense-experience; both essays examine the self as the object of knowledge. Michael Polanyi and Erving Goffman explore the subtle signs that weave the tapestry of interpersonal perception. And finally, George Herbert Mead summarizes: "to be self-conscious is essentially to become an object to one's self in virtue of one's social relations to other individuals."

With social relations established as the necessary presupposition for self-knowledge, Part Four, "From Family to Society," expands the horizons of investigation to the first and smallest unit of social organization, the family. Beginning with the classic statements of Aristotle and John Locke, the opening essays examine fatherhood, or patriarchy, as the primal form of authority. Wilhelm Reich and R. D. Laing then articulate the repressive mechanisms sometimes found in the family structure and some modern attempts to challenge and overcome those mechanisms. Finally, Plato, John Stuart Mill, and Karl Marx address the question of the legitimacy of authority not based on the biological claim of paternity.

Part Five, "Politics and the Environment," takes up the role of the State in determining social relations. Following influential statements by Hobbes and Rousseau, the discussion jumps forward two centuries to statements by two contemporary thinkers who appeal to the anarchistic tradition, Martin Buber and Gary Snyder. A third contemporary, Benjamin Barber, defends politics against those who think we can do without it. The final two essays relate politics to ecology: Gregory Bateson describes the kind of thinking necessary for our dealings with nature, and William Ophuls relates the ecological crisis to the political philosophies of Hobbes and Rousseau.

Parts Six and Seven, with essays by Arthur Schopenhauer, Germaine Greer, Judith Jarvis Thompson, Daniel Callahan, Frantz Fanon, Hannah Arendt, Paolo Freire, John Dewey, George Leonard, Plato, and André Breton, take up a series of more specific problems that cut across the ever-widening circles of self-awareness defined in the first five parts. The issues in Part Six, "Ethics," move across contexts relating the individual to others and finally back to further dimensions of self-knowledge. The first four essays address the image of women and the moral issues that surround abortion. The last two essays discuss the inducement of a negative self-image among the oppressed of the third world—oppression has an uncanny way of generating its own "truth"—and the role of violence in throwing off that negative self-image.

Providing an alternative to violence, Part Seven, "Tradition and Upheaval: Esthetics and Education," begins with Paolo Freire's "The Pedagogy of the Oppressed," an essay on learning with which some learners may wish to begin their reading. Part Seven represents a return to the theory of knowledge first addressed in Part Three, but now the question of learning is enriched by the addition of a social and historical context. The historical dimension is underscored by the contrast between Plato and André Breton on the role of art in human experience. The questions of esthetics and artistic representation serve as a transition to the widest and perhaps most mysterious context of self-knowledge— our relation to the divine.

In Part Eight, "The Community of Man and Cosmos," essays by Søren Kierkegaard, Friedrich Nietzsche, W. K. Clifford, William James, Daisetz T. Suzuki, W. T. Stace, and John Findlay continue to examine the nature of knowledge, while investigating the philosophy of religion. Questions about the nature of truth and the warrants for belief are inseparable from any serious discussion of the sacred. The final three essays stretch toward the ineffable in their attempts to define the place of mystical insight in human experience.

The trend in Anglo-American philosophy during this century has been toward tidier topics than those addressed in Self and World. Questions about psychology, art, and religious mysticism sometimes seem intractable to the finely honed tools of symbolic logic and linguistic analysis. The effort to come up with a few clear answers, however inconsequential, has led to an abandonment of many of the questions that perennially preoccupied philosophers of earlier centuries. In this book I have chosen unabashedly to return to the issues that once gave philosophy its vitality. While philosophy in general, and Self and World in particular, may offer precious few answers to the questions it raises, we could do worse than to follow Socrates' injunction to pursue our inquiries whether or not we come up with clear answers. For the self that we come to know in the path toward self-knowledge may not be the sort of self that admits of finality or precision. Instead the wonder so characteristic both of philosophy and of deep self-knowledge may be a function of the fact that human life, unlike long division, is not a soluble problem but something more like an adventure or an art work that we continue to alter creatively as we go along.

I would like to thank again those who helped years ago and thank anew those who have assisted with the second edition. John McDermott has been especially helpful in giving form to what follows. His painstaking remarks on the first edition and his enthusiastic support of the second are especially appreciated. I would also like to thank Ellen Black, Robin Evans, Cathy Gross, Nancy Kaplan, Heather Ogilvy, Richard Probst, Judy Solomon, and Susan Tuttle for their help in preparing the manuscript for press; Joan Levinson for her perceptive and intelligent editing of the first edition; Juliana Koenig for her equally scrupulous editing of the second; Patrick Hill and several anonymous referees for their helpful comments; and finally Robert J. Fogelin, Bill McLane, and William Pullin for both the initial suggestion to undertake the project and their constant encouragement toward its completion.

JAMES A. OGILVY

Contents

4/FROM FAMILY TO SOCIETY   147

5/POLITICS AND
THE ENVIRONMENT   219

6/ETHICS   293

7/TRADITION AND UPHEAVAL: ESTHETICS AND EDUCATION   357

8/THE COMMUNITY OF MAN AND THE COSMOS   421

Second
Edition
Self and World
Readings in Philosophy

1/Introduction: Philosophy and Self-Knowledge

Story of a Good Brahmin
VOLTAIRE *(1694–1778)*

On my travels I met an old Brahmin, a very wise man, of marked intellect and great learning. Furthermore, he was rich and, consequently, all the wiser, because, lacking nothing, he needed to deceive nobody. His household was very well managed by three handsome women who set themselves out to please him. When he was not amusing himself with his women, he passed the time in philosophizing. Near his house, which was beautifully decorated and had charming gardens attached, there lived a narrow-minded old Indian woman: she was a simpleton, and rather poor.

Said the Brahmin to me one day: "I wish I had never been born!" On my asking why, he answered: "I have been studying forty years, and that is forty years wasted. I teach others and myself am ignorant of everything. Such a state of affairs fills my soul with so much humiliation and disgust that my life is intolerable. I was born in Time, I live in Time, and yet I do not know what Time is. I am at a point between two eternities, as our wise men say, and I have no conception of eternity. I am composed of matter: I think, but I have never been able to learn what produces my thought. I do not know whether or no my understanding is a simple faculty inside me, such as those of walking and digesting, and whether or no I think with my head as I grip with my hands. Not only is the cause of my thought unknown to me; the cause of my actions is equally a mystery. I do not know why I exist, and yet every day people ask me questions on all these points. I have to reply, and as I have nothing really worth saying I talk a great deal, and am ashamed of myself afterward for having talked.

"It is worse still when I am asked if Brahma was born of Vishnu or if they are both eternal. God is my witness that I have not the remotest idea, and my ignorance shows itself in my replies. 'Ah, Holy One,' people say to me, 'tell us why evil pervades the earth.' I am in as great a difficulty as those who ask me this question. Sometimes I tell them that everything is as well as can be, but those who have been ruined and broken in the wars do not believe a word of it—and no more do I. I retire to my home stricken at my own curiosity and ignorance. I read our ancient books, and they double my darkness. I talk to my companions: some answer me that we must enjoy life and make game of mankind; others think they know a lot and lose themselves in a maze of wild ideas. Everything increases my anguish. I am ready sometimes to despair when I think that after all my seeking I do not know whence I came, whither I go, what I am nor what I shall become."

The good man's condition really worried me. Nobody was more rational or more sincere than he. I perceived that his unhappiness increased in proportion as his understanding developed and his insight grew.

The same day I saw the old woman who lived near him. I asked her if she had ever been troubled by the thought that she was ignorant of the nature of her soul. She did not even understand my question. Never in all her life had she reflected for one single moment on one single point of all those which tormented the

Brahmin. She believed with all her heart in the metamorphoses of Vishnu and, provided she could obtain a little Ganges water wherewith to wash herself, thought herself the happiest of women.

Struck with this mean creature's happiness, I returned to my wretched philosopher. "Are you not ashamed," said I, "to be unhappy when at your very door there lives an old automaton who thinks about nothing, and yet lives contentedly?"

"You are right," he replied. "I have told myself a hundred times that I should be happy if I were as brainless as my neighbor, and yet I do not desire such happiness."

My Brahmin's answer impressed me more than all the rest. I set to examining myself, and I saw that in truth I would not care to be happy at the price of being a simpleton.

I put the matter before some philosophers, and they were of my opinion. "Nevertheless," said I, "there is a tremendous contradiction in this mode of thought, for, after all, the problem is—how to be happy. What does it matter whether one has brains or not? Further, those who are contented with their lot are certain of their contentment, whereas those who reason are not certain that they reason correctly. It is quite clear, therefore," I continued, "that we must choose not to have common sense, however little common sense may contribute to our discomfort." Everyone agreed with me, but I found nobody, notwithstanding, who was willing to accept the bargain of becoming a simpleton in order to become contented. From which I conclude that if we consider the question of happiness we must consider still more the question of reason.

But on reflection it seems that to prefer reason to felicity is to be very senseless. How can this contradiction be explained? Like all the other contradictions. It is matter for much talk.

introduction: satire as self-revealing– from Voltaire to Tom Wolfe

"Philosophy begins in wonder," said the Greek philosopher Aristotle over twenty-three centuries ago. Philosophy ends in confused despair, seems to be the message of Voltaire's Good Brahmin. Either way more questions than answers accompany the philosopher.

What is time? Why is there evil? Surely there is something funny about such questions. Comedian Dick Gregory asks, "Why is there air?" and answers, "To pump up basketballs, of course!" There's something comical about the entire enterprise of philosophy. Steve Martin quips that he took just enough philosophy in college to confuse him for the rest of his life.

Ludwig Wittgenstein, among the greatest minds of this century, considered philosophy something of a disease, something whose conclusion was a cure; it was not a body of secure knowledge. Whether some kind of curse, or a disease to be cured, philosophy does not sound like an entirely good thing. Perhaps Voltaire's question is well taken. Perhaps felicity is to be preferred to reason. And perhaps not....In any case, "It is matter for much talk."

John Stuart Mill wondered whether it was better to be a pig satisfied or a Socrates unsatisfied. His answer: Socrates.

Like Voltaire and Mill, most of us would probably choose the life of a Socrates rather than the life of a pig if the choice were posed so starkly. But why? Socrates, after all, was sentenced to death by the citizens of Athens in 399 B.C. After a long life of questioning, in which he often reduced fellow Athenians to profound doubts about their claims to knowledge, Socrates was condemned to drink the poisonous hemlock. The official charge was impiety. He lacked sufficient respect for the local deities: too many questions, too few safe and satisfying answers.

In his final defense before the citizens of Athens, Socrates quoted the famous Oracle at Delphi, who said that Socrates was the wisest man in Athens—a curious remark given that Socrates himself claimed to have no knowledge of the most important things in life. His inquiries into the nature of the virtues end with no firm conclusions about the subjects they cover. Yet something is gained through the course of the Socratic dialogues. Over the portal of the Delphic Oracle's temple are inscribed the words *know thyself.* Socrates, it was said, knew himself better than any man in Athens. Though he claimed no special knowledge about most matters of importance, his wisdom consisted in his self-knowledge of the nature of his ignorance. Though philosophy provokes more questions than answers about most matters of importance, philosophy—*philo-sophia,* Greek for the *love* of *wisdom*—promises some progress along the path toward self-knowledge.

The path toward self-knowledge involves more than narcissistic navel-gazing. Narcissus, according to Greek myth, fell in love with his own image reflected in a pool of water. Totally uninterested in others or the rest of the world, he would not bestir himself from the bank of the pool. Eventually he starved to death. There on the bank, where his body nourished the soil, grew the flower with a golden heart we now call the Narcissus. The myth of Narcissus is not only a myth of self-love, it is a myth of self-transformation, of death and rebirth.

Recently there has been much talk of narcissism as a problem in our society. In his book of the same name, social critic Christopher Lasch labels our society "the culture of narcissism." To listen to Lasch one might think that a preoccupation with self-knowledge were an unmitigated evil. Others, too, have called attention to increased self-involvement as a growing problem in recent decades. Following the wave of social conscience in the sixties, Tom Wolfe wrote an influential essay describing the seventies as the Me Decade. The essence of his insight appears in the following essay from *The Pump House Gang* (1965) in which he describes *Playboy* magnate Hugh Hefner as a hero for our times and a harbinger for others who would "split from communitas" to start their own leagues.

We begin with Tom Wolfe because he is the Voltaire of our times. Though neither Voltaire nor Wolfe engages in philosophical arguments, strictly speaking, both succeed in reflecting their times in the mirrors of their satires. Voltaire, like Socrates, evoked the wrath of people in high places. For his satirical insights he was rewarded with exile from Paris and more than a few months in the Bastille. He maintained a life-long battle with the Church. In his most famous book, *Candide* (1759), he satirized the optimism of the German rationalist philosopher, Leibniz (1646-1716), who had claimed, "This is the best of all possible worlds."

Like Voltaire's *Candide,* Wolfe's essays carry their points to ironic and often amusing extremes. And like Socratic irony, the results reveal a great deal about the times they portray. We begin with Wolfe because the path toward self-knowledge must begin wherever we happen to be. And Wolfe, more than any other social commentator I know, is a master at portraying the subtleties of late twentieth-century pretensions.

On Ego Extension and Overjoy
TOM WOLFE *(b. 1931)*

It was a strange time for me. Many rogue volts of euphoria. I went from one side of this country to the other and then from one side of England to the other. The people I met—the things they did—I was entranced. I met Carol Doda. She blew up her breasts with emulsified silicone, the main ingredient in Silly Putty, and became the greatest resource of the San Francisco tourist industry. I met a group of surfers, the Pump House Gang. They attended the Watts riot as if it were the Rose Bowl game in Pasadena. They came to watch "the drunk niggers" and were reprimanded by the same for their rowdiness. In London I met a competitive 17-year-old named Nicki who got one-up on her schoolgirl chums by taking a Kurdish clubfoot lover. I met a £9-a-week office boy named Larry Lynch. He spent his lunch hour every day with hundreds of other child laborers in the crazed pitchblack innards of a noonday nightclub called Tiles. All of them *in ecstasis* from the frug, the rock 'n' roll, and God knows what else, for an hour—then back to work. In Chicago I met Hugh Hefner. He revolved on his bed, offering scenic notes as his head floated by—

Now, about Hefner. I was heading for California from New York and I happened to stop off in Chicago. I was walking down North Michigan Avenue when I ran into a man from the Playboy organization, Lee Gottlieb. Something he said made me assume that Hefner was out of town.

"Out of town?" said Gottlieb. "Hef never leaves his house."

"Never?"

Never, said Gottlieb. At least not for months at a time, and even then only long enough to get in a limousine and go to the airport and fly to New York for a TV show or to some place or other for the opening of a new Playboy Club. This fascinated me, the idea that Hefner, the Main Playboy himself, was now a recluse. The next afternoon I went to the Playboy offices on East Ohio Street to see about getting in to see him. In the office they kept track of Hefner's physical posture in his Mansion, which was over on North State Parkway, as if by play-by-play Telex. He was flat out in bed asleep, they told me, and wouldn't be awake until around midnight. That night I was killing time in a dive in downtown Chicago when a courier materialized and told me Hefner was now on his feet and could see me.

Hefner's Playboy Mansion had a TV eye at the front portals and huge black guards or major-domos inside. *Nubian slaves*, I kept saying to myself. One of the blacks led me up a grand staircase covered in red wall-to-wall, to a massive carved-wood doorway bearing the inscription, *Si Non Oscillas, Noli Tintinnare*, "If you don't swing, don't ring." Inside were Hefner's private chambers. Hefner came charging out of a pair of glass doors within. He was wound up and ready to go. "Look at this!" he said. "Isn't this fantastic!" It was an issue of *Ramparts* magazine that had just come. It had a glossy foldout, like the one in *Playboy*. Only this one had a picture of Hefner. In the picture he was wearing a suit and smoking a pipe. "Isn't this fantastic!" Hefner kept saying. Right now he was wearing silk pajamas, a bathrobe, and a pair of slippers with what looked like embroidered wolf heads on them. This was not, however, because he had just gotten up. It was his standard wear for the day, this day, every day, the uniform of the contemporary recluse.

There were several people in attendance at the midnight hour. The *dame d'honneur* of the palace, who was named Michele; Gottlieb; a couple of other Playboy personnel; the blacks: they were all dressed, however. Hefner showed me through his chambers. The place was kept completely draped and shuttered. The only light, day or night, was electric. It would be impossible to keep track of the days in there. And presently Hefner jumped onto . . . the center of his world, the bed in his bedroom. Aimed at the bed was a TV camera he was very proud of. Later on *Playboy* ran a cartoon showing a nude man and woman in a huge bed with a TV set facing them, and the man is saying, "And now, darling, how about an instant replay." Hefner hit a dial and the bed started revolving . . . *

All I could think of at that moment was Jay Gatsby in the Fitzgerald novel. Both were scramblers who came up from out of nowhere to make their fortunes and build their palaces and ended up in regal isolation. But there was a major difference between Hefner and Gatsby. Hefner no longer dreamed, if he ever did, of making the big social leap to East Egg. It was at least plausible for Gatsby to hope to make it into Society. But Hefner? He has made a fortune, created an empire, and the Playboy Beacon shines out over the city and the Great Lakes. But socially Hefner is still a man who runs a tit magazine and a string of clubs that recall the parlor floor—not the upper floors but the parlor floor—of a red-flock whorehouse. There is no Society in Chicago for Hugh Hefner.

So he has gone them one better. He has started his own league. He has created his own world, in his own palace. He has created his own statusphere. The outside world comes to him, including the talented and the celebrated. Jules Feiffer stays awhile in his scarlet guest suite. Norman Mailer skinnydips in his Playboy swimming pool. He has his courtiers, his girls, and his Nubian slaves. Not even God's own diurnal light rhythm intrudes upon the order that Hefner has founded inside.

What a marvelous idea! After all, the community has never been one great happy family for all men. In fact, I would say the opposite has been true. Community status systems have been games with few winners and many who feel like losers. What an intriguing thought—for a man to take his new riches and free time and his machines and *split* from *communitas* and start his own league. He will still have status competition—but he invents the rules.

Why has no one ever done it before? Well, of course, people have. Robin Hood did it. Spades, homosexuals, artists, and street gangs have done it. All sorts of outlaws, and outcasts, by necessity or choice. The intriguing thing today, I was to find, is that so many Americans and Englishmen of middle and lower incomes are now doing the same thing. Not out of "rebellion" or "alienation"—they just want to be happy winners for a change.

---

*The ellipses in this essay are Wolfe's own. In later selections ellipses indicate the omission of a portion of text.—J.A.O.

What is a California electronics worker making $18,000 a year supposed to do with his new riches? Set about getting his son into Culver Military and himself and the wife into the Doral Beach Country Club? Socially, he is a glorified mechanic. Why not, à la Hefner, put it all into turning his home into a palace of technological glories—and extend that abroad in the land with a Buick Estate Wagon and a Pontiac GTO—and upon the seas with an Evinrude cruiser and even into the air with a Cessna 172? Why not surround the palace with my favorite piece of landscaping of the happy worker suburbs of the American West, the Home Moat. It is about three feet wide and a foot and a half deep. Instructions for placing rocks, flowers, and shrubs are available. The Home Moat is a psychological safeguard against the intrusion of the outside world. The Home Moat guards against the fear that *It* is going to creep up in the night and press its nose against your picture window.

Southern California, I found, is a veritable paradise of statuspheres. For example, the move to age segregation. There are old people's housing developments, private developments, in which no one under 50 may buy a home. There are apartment developments for single persons 20 to 30 only. The Sunset Strip in Los Angeles has become the exclusive hangout of the 16 to 25 set. In 1966 they came close to street warfare to keep it that way, against the police who moved in to "clean up."

And...the Pump House Gang. Here was a group of boys and girls who had banded together in a way that superficially resembled a street gang's. They had very little of the street gang's motivation, however. They came from middle-class and upper-middle-class homes in perhaps the most high-class beach community in California, La Jolla. They had very little sense of resentment toward their parents or "society" and weren't rebels. Their only "alienation" was the usual hassle of the adolescent, the feeling that he is being prodded into adulthood on somebody else's terms. So they did the latest thing. They split off—*to the beach! into the garages!*—and started their own league, based on the esoterica of surfing. They didn't resent the older people around them; they came to pity the old bastards because they couldn't partake of this esoteric statusphere.

The day I met the Pump House Gang, a group of them had just been thrown out of "Tom Coman's garage," as it was known. The next summer they moved up from the garage life to a group of apartments near the beach, a complex they named "La Colonia Tijuana." By this time some were shifting from the surfing life to the advance guard of something else—the psychedelic *head* world of California. That is another story. But even the *hippies*, as the heads came to be known, did not develop *sui generis*. Their so-called "dropping out" was nothing more than a still further elaboration of the kind of worlds that the surfers and the car kids I met— "The Hair Boys"—had been creating the decade before.

The Pump House Gang lived as though age segregation were a permanent state, as if it were inconceivable that any of them would ever grow old, i.e., 25. I foresaw the day when the California coastline would be littered with the bodies of aged and abandoned *Surferkinder*, like so many beached whales.

In fact, however, many of these kids seem to be able to bring the mental atmosphere of the surfer life forward with them into adulthood—even into the adult world where you have to make a living. I remember going to the motorcycle races at Gardena, California, which is just south of Watts, with a surfer who is now about 30 and has developed a large water-sport equipment business. This was a month after the Watts riots. We were sitting in the stands at Gardena. The motorcycles were roaring around the half-mile track below and flashing under the lights. Just beyond the track from where we sat were Watts and Compton.

"Tom," he said to me, "you should have been here last month."

"Why?"

"The riots," he said. "You should have been here. We were all sitting here right where we are now and the bikes were going around down below here. And over here"—over to the left you could look over the edge of the stands and see the highway—"the National Guard units were pulling and jumping off the trucks and getting into formation and everything with the bayonets and all. It was terrific. And then, there"—and his gaze and his voice got a far-off quality, going beyond the track and toward Watts—"and there, there in the distance, was Los Angeles . . . *burning!*"

A few minutes later ten motorcycles came into the first turn, right in front of where we were sitting. Five went down in a pile-up. Bodies shot through the air every which way. I saw one, a rider in black and white racing leathers, get hit in midair by one motorcycle and run over by the one behind it. This was a kid named Clemmie Jackson. He was dead. Everybody could see that. His neck was broken like a stick. Two other riders were seriously injured. The p.a. announcer didn't mention those who were lying there, however. He only mentioned those who got up. "There's No. 353, Rog Rogarogarog, he's up and his bike looks O.K. . . ." As soon as the bodies were removed, the race resumed. Luckily they hadn't had to take both the ambulances. They have two ambulances at the track, and if both have to leave, the races have to stop until one returns. They were able to get the three worst bodies into one ambulance. The ambulance, a big white Cadillac, left very quietly. It didn't even flash a light. About three minutes later you could hear the siren start up, way down the highway. Off in the distance, as they say. It was a freaking ghastly sound, under the circumstances. Within seconds, however, the race was on again, with five bikes instead of ten, and all was forgotten. As usual, there were only a couple of paragraphs in the papers about the death.

I don't think that is a very morbid incident, taken in context. The half-mile racers are the wildest and most suicidal crowd in the motorcycle life, but all the motorcycle crowds get a lot of their juice out of the luxury of risking their necks. The motorcycle life has been perfect as a statusphere. It is dangerous and therefore daring. It is as esoteric as surfing. It can liberate you physically from the *communitas.*

When you mention the motorcycle life, people tend to think—again—of outlaws. Namely, the Hell's Angels. The Angels and other motorcycle outlaws, however, make up only a small part of the people who have started their own league with their bikes. I'll never forget the Harley-Davidson agency in Columbus, Ohio. A guy came in the back there dragging a big Harley. It was all bent and mashed, the spokes, the headers, the cylinder heads, the sprocket, the drive chain. Everybody said, You had a wreck! The guy said, Naw, it was my wife. Everybody said, Was she hurt bad! The guy said, Naw, she took a block of cement about this big and she—well, it seems she had smashed the hell out of it. He had first bought the Harley just for a little recreation away from the wife and kids. Then he had discovered hundreds of motorcyclists around Columbus—all drifting away from the wife and kids. Pretty soon he was meeting the boys every day after work at a place called Gully's and they would drink beer and ride up to Lake Erie before coming home, a mere 200-mile trip. By and by they had a whole new life for themselves—blissful liberation!—based on the motorcycle. Until his wife decided to sort that little situation out...

Columbus is the world capital of the motorcycle life. This statement, I find, comes as a surprise and an annoyance—the damnable Hell's Angels again—to a lot of people in Columbus, despite the fact that the American Motorcycle Association has its headquarters there. On the surface, Columbus could not be more conservative and traditional. A few big property-owning families seem to control everything. Well, they don't control the motorcycle life, which has proliferated in and around the town over the past ten years in full rich variety, from half-mile racing daredevils to Honda touring clubs. They also have a local version of the Hell's Angels, the Road Rogues. The vast majority of Columbus motorcyclists, however, are perfectly law-abiding citizens who happen to have found an infinitely richer existence than being a standard wage-mule for whoever does run Columbus.

The two great motorcyclists of Columbus are Dick Klamforth, a former half-mile racing champion and now owner of the Honda agency there, the biggest in the country, and Tom Reiser. Reiser is truly one of the greats. He built "Tom's Bomb." He achieved an ultimate. He flew through the air of the American Midwest, astride a 300-horsepower Chevrolet V-8 engine... riding bareback...

Now, this is not exactly what the great Utopian thinkers of the nineteenth century, the Saint-Simons, the Fouriers, and the Owens, had in mind when they envisioned a world of the future in which the ordinary working man would have the time and the money to extend his God-given potential to the fullest. The old Utopians believed in industrialism. In fact, it was Saint-Simon who coined the word. Yet the worker paradise industrialism would make possible was to take a somewhat more pastoral form. They saw it as a kind of Rousseauvian happy-primitive village with modern conveniences. In short, a community, with everyone, great and small, knit together forever after, grateful as spaniels. More recently, in the 1920's and 1930's, the vision was amended. It now put the happy workers into neat lead-white blocks of Bauhaus apartments and added Culture. Every night, in this vision, the family would gather around the hearth and listen to Dad read from John Strachey or Mayakovsky while WQXR droned in the background. The high point of the week would be Saturday afternoon, when Dad would put on his electric-blue suit—slightly gauche, you understand, but neat and clean and pressed, "touching," as it were—and the whole family would hold hands and walk up to the Culture Center to watch the Shock Workers of the Dance do a ballet called "Factory." Well, today, in the 1960's, the Culture Centers have sprouted up, sure enough. We have them in most of the metropolises of America. But where have all the happy workers gone? These temples to breeding and taste are usually constructed at great cost, in the name of "the people." But the people, the happy people, have left them to the cultivated, educated classes, the "diploma elite," who created them.

And even the cultivated classes—the term "upper classes" no longer works—are in a state of rather amusing confusion on the subject. When great fame—the certification of status—is available without great property, it is very bad news for the old idea of a class structure. In New York, for example, it is done for, but no one has bothered to announce its death. As a result, New York "Society" is now made up of a number of statuspheres—all busily raiding the old class order for trappings to make their fame look genuine. Business and other corporate statuspheres have been so busy cannibalizing the old aristocratic modes, I have had to write an entire new gull's handbook on the subject ("Tom Wolfe's New Book of Etiquette"). The great hotel corporations now advertise Luxury (equals "class") to the same crowd who used to go to those durable second-raters, the commercial or businessman's hotel. It is a pretty amusing invention, this second-class *class*, unless you happen to stay at The Automated Hotel without knowing the name of the game. Meanwhile, individual climbers are busy moving into separate little preserves that once made up the happy monolith of "the upper class"—such as charities and *Yes!* Culture—and I offer the golden example of Bob and Spike Scull for those who want to make it *Now*, without having to wait three generations, as old fashioned sorts, such as the Kennedy family, had to do. Of course, with so many statuspheres now in operation, and so many short cuts available, there is a chronic chaos in Society. People are now reaching the top without quite knowing what on earth they have reached the top of. They don't know whether they have reached *The* Top or whether they have just had a wonderful fast ride up the service elevator. But as Bob Scull himself says: "Enjoy!"

What struck me throughout America and England was that so many people have found such novel ways of doing just that, *enjoying*, extending their egos way out on the best terms available, namely, their own. It is curious how many serious thinkers—and politicians—resist this rather obvious fact. Sheer ego extension—especially if attempted by all those rancid proles and suburban petty burghers—is a perplexing prospect. Even scary, one might say. Intellectuals and politicians currently exhibit a vast gummy nostalgia for the old restraints, the old limits, of the ancient egocrusher: *Calamity*. Historically calamity has been the one serious concern of serious people. War, Pestilence—Apocalypse! I was impressed by the profound relief with which intellectuals and politicians discovered poverty in America in 1963, courtesy of Michael Harrington's book *The Other America*. And, as I say, it was *discovered*. Eureka! We have found it again! We thought we had lost it! That was the spirit of the enterprise. When the race riots erupted—and when the war in Vietnam grew into a good-sized hell—intellectuals welcomed all that with a ghastly embrace, too. War! Poverty! Insurrection! Alienation! O Four Horsemen, you have not deserted us entirely. The game can go on.

One night, in the very middle of the period when I was writing these stories, I put on *my* electric-blue-suit—it is truly electric blue—and took part in a symposium at Princeton with Günter Grass, Allen Ginsberg, and Gregory Markopoulos, who is an "underground" filmmaker, before 1,200 students. The subject was "The

Style of the Sixties." Paul Krassner was the moderator, and Krassner has a sense of humor, but the Horsemen charged on. Very soon the entire discussion was centered on police repression, Gestapo tactics, the knock on the door, the Triumph of the Knout. I couldn't believe what was happening, but there it was.

"What are you talking about?" I said. "We're in the middle of a ...Happiness Explosion!" But I didn't know where to begin. I might as well have said let's talk about the Fisher King. Happiness, said Saint-Just a century ago, is a new concept in Europe. Apparently it was new here, unheard-of almost. Ah, *philosophes!*—if we want to be *serious,* let us discuss the real apocalyptic future and things truly scary: ego extension, the politics of pleasure, the self-realization racket, the pharmacology of Overjoy...

But why discuss it now. I, for one, will be content merely to watch the faces of our leaders, political and intellectual, the day they wake up and look over their shoulders and catch the first glimpse of their erstwhile followers—streaking— *happy workers!*—in precisely the opposite direction, through God's own American ozone—*apocalyptic riders!*—astride their own custom versions—*enjoy!*—of the 300-horsepower Chevrolet V-8 engines of this world...riding bareback...

2/The Self

introduction:
the metaphysics of self-identity

Individualism is as much a theory about collectivities as about individuals: the individualist claims that the best society puts the fewest limits on the liberty of the individual. Conversely, anti-individualism is as much a theory about individuals as about society: the anti-individualist claims that individualism sets the self adrift from its natural social context and thereby inhibits the development of selfhood. Both individualism and its critics affirm the existence of individual self and social collectivities; they differ in their accounts of the nature of that self and its relation to society. Even the strongest opponent of individualism as a social theory may acknowledge a private part of the self, removed from historical flux and social determination. He may grant that even after the question "Who am I?" has been answered with public titles like "student" or "teacher," "male" or "female," "lover" or "spouse," even after all the public titles have been determined in countless questionnaires, a sense of incompleteness may remain. The public titles say *what* I am, but do they determine *who* I am? Is there an inner core that bears these titles? Is there a nonsocially defined "me" who determines the choice of one title rather than another? Is there a part of me that defines me uniquely and not merely as one among many bearing the same title?

Efforts to answer these questions take many forms. Where philosophers speak of the quest for self-knowledge and psychologists speak of identity crises, frustrated parents and teachers sometimes speak of adolescents' attempts to find themselves. Adolescence seems to provoke this difficult inner quest, since growth away from one's parents forces one to come to grips with life on one's own, but the quest for self-knowledge ought not be regarded as a "stage" that one passes through and leaves behind. Finding and maintaining self-identity can be a lifelong process. While it makes sense to expect that we can carry on the process without the pain and desperation often experienced in adolescence, it is a mistake to assume that once the pain has stopped the process is over. Rather than suffer the doubts and uncertainties of growth toward an indeterminate destination, many people fix a destination very early in life and then define themselves in terms of that destination: "I am a good parent"; "I am an engineer"; "I am a dropout." Many people imagine they can settle the account of self-identity once and for all and then live in the security of their certainty. But that premature decision is a subtle form of suicide. It amounts to opting out of life, for to live is to grow and change.

How, then, to live? How to find one's self and, once found, avoid petrifaction? The task can be performed well or poorly. Philosophy is largely about following the quest well rather than poorly. It is possible to make mistakes in the way we think about ourselves, not only in the public titles we ascribe to ourselves, but about the kind of thing a self is. We may be amused when someone treats a car as if it were an animate being by talking to it or kicking it when it fails to start. It is less amusing when people are treated like machines, yet this is precisely the kind of mistake people make when they prematurely settle on a destination and transform themselves into machines for getting there. But if the self is not a machine, if it is not a mechanism with a clearly describable structure and function, then what is it?

Metaphysics is the branch of philosophy that deals with the question of kinds of being. The name was first assigned in a quite arbitrary way around 70 B.C. to one of Aristotle's books. He had written a *Physics* and then another book, scholars thought, *after* that, which they named the *Metaphysics;* in Greek *meta* means "after." But since then the name metaphysics has been used to describe any attempt to answer the questions posed by Aristotle in his *Metaphysics.* Aristotle described his inquiry as the science of being, meaning that he was not asking about particular beings and their properties, but about what it is in general "to be": what is it to be something rather than nothing? Although metaphysics does not describe particular beings, it does inquire into *ways* of being. Are there different ways of being—physical being on the one hand and nonspatiotemporal being on the other—or is there only one mode of being—the physical, material mode?

Metaphysics is necessary to the quest for self-knowledge because if the self cannot be located with a scalpel, if the self is not like physical entities that have a simple location in space and time, then we want to know what other kind of being it can have, if any. If we are mistaken about the kind of being the self exhibits, then we can hardly help making mistakes when it comes to defining and determining the nature and identity of particular selves, including one's own self. Once again, it may be amusing when someone mistreats a car, but the subtle suicide involved in mistreating one's self is not. We can take the car to a mechanic, but can we take the self to a metaphysician? The quest for self-knowledge is necessarily a do-it-yourself enterprise, but the philosophical tradition contains priceless aids for exploring the metaphysics of self-identity.

The six essays that follow include representative samples from very different branches of the philosophical tradition, but the sampling is hardly random. Beginning with Descartes' argument for the self as "a thing which thinks," and Ryle's contemporary critique of the Cartesian metaphysics, we move to the problem of free will and determinism, a metaphysical problem in that it turns partially on the concept of causality as such rather than an examination of particular causes. Further, the denial of freedom is a denial of any autonomy for the self and hence a denial of an ongoing, self-identical, responsible agent. The two essays by Hume and Erikson then discuss the process character that distinguishes the being of this ongoing self from the being of inanimate entities.

RENÉ DESCARTES *(1596–1650)*

Descartes' influence on modern philosophy would be hard to overestimate. His Meditations *(1641) and his* Discourse on Method *(1637) mark the beginning of a major concern with the* methods *of philosophy. How can we know whatever we do know? How can we know when we are being deceived? How, for example, can we tell whether we are asleep or awake? The most frightening nightmares are often those in which one dreams that one has awakened only to find the horror continuing: you dream that you wake up, reach for the light, and feel a slimy hand.*

If objects provide no indubitable marks of their reality, then perhaps we can find certainty in subjective states; perhaps the subjective quality of an experience provides more proof of its truthfulness than its objective contents. In his inauguration of what we now refer to as the "Subjective Turn," Descartes singled out as most important the subjective qualities of clarity and distinctness.

Whatever the limitation of his method, we owe Descartes a great debt for focusing on the importance of method. Whether or nor philosophy can provide prepackaged answers to anyone asking a given question, at least we should expect philosophy to assist us in knowing how to go about asking and answering questions that do not merely increase confusion. Descartes presents us with a clear method: doubt everything you can until you get down to what is clear and distinct. But how much can you doubt? Descartes admits that his method imposes upon him a "laborious wakefulness." The labors of meditation are not always easy, but the fruits of those labors can be worth the effort.

Meditations I and II

Meditation I

OF THE THINGS WHICH MAY BE BROUGHT WITHIN THE SPHERE OF THE DOUBTFUL.

It is now some years since I detected how many were the false beliefs that I had from my earliest youth admitted as true, and how doubtful was everything I had since constructed on this basis; and from that time I was convinced that I must once for all seriously undertake to rid myself of all the opinions which I had formerly accepted, and commence to build anew from the foundation, if I wanted to establish any firm and permanent structure in the sciences. But as this enterprise appeared to be a very great one, I waited until I had attained an age so mature that I could not hope that at any later date I should be better fitted to execute my design. This reason caused me to delay so long that I should feel that I was doing wrong were I to occupy in deliberation the time that yet remains to me for action. To-day, then, since very opportunely for the plan I have in view I have delivered my mind from every care [and am happily agitated by no passions] and since I have procured for myself an assured leisure in a peaceable retirement, I shall at last seriously and freely address myself to the general upheaval of all my former opinions.

Now for this object it is not necessary that I should show that all of these are false—I shall perhaps never arrive at this end. But inasmuch as reason already persuades me that I ought no less carefully to withhold my assent from matters which are not entirely certain and indubitable than from those which appear to me manifestly to be false, if I am able to find in each one some reason to doubt, this will suffice to justify my rejecting the whole. And for that end it will not be requisite that I should examine each in particular, which would be an endless undertaking; for owing to the fact that the destruction of the foundations of necessity brings with it the downfall of the rest of the edifice, I shall only in the first place attack those principles upon which all my former opinions rested.

All that up to the present time I have accepted as most true and certain I have learned either from the senses or through the senses; but it is sometimes proved to me that these senses are deceptive, and it is wiser not to trust entirely to any thing by which we have once been deceived.

But it may be that although the senses sometimes deceive us concerning things which are hardly perceptible, or very far away, there are yet many others to be met with as to which we cannot reasonably have any doubt, although we recognise them by their means. For example, there is the fact that I am here, seated by the fire, attired in a dressing gown, having this paper in my hands and other similar matters. And how could I deny that these hands and this body are mine, were it not perhaps that I compare myself to certain persons, devoid of sense, whose cerebella are so troubled and clouded by the violent vapours of black bile, that they constantly assure us that they think they are kings when they are really quite poor, or that they are clothed in purple when they are really without covering, or who imagine that they have an earthenware head or are nothing but pumpkins or are made of glass. But they are mad, and I should not be any the less insane were I to follow examples so extravagant.

At the same time I must remember that I am a man, and that consequently I am in the habit of sleeping, and in my dreams representing to myself the same things or sometimes even less probable things, than do those who are insane in their waking moments. How often has it happened to me that in the night I dreamt that I found myself in this particular place, that I was dressed and seated near the fire, whilst in reality I was lying undressed in bed! At this moment it does indeed seem to me that it is with eyes awake that I am looking at this paper; that this head which I move is not asleep, that it is deliberately and of set purpose that I extend my hand and perceive it; what happens in sleep does not appear so clear nor so distinct as does all this. But in thinking over this I remind myself that on many occasions I have in sleep been deceived by similar illusions, and in dwelling carefully on this reflection I see so manifestly that there are no certain indications by which we may clearly distinguish wakefulness from sleep that I am lost in astonishment. And my astonishment is such that it is almost capable of persuading me that I now dream.

Now let us assume that we are asleep and that all these particulars, e.g. that we open our eyes, shake our head, extend our hands, and so on, are but false delusions; and let us reflect that possibly neither our hands nor our whole body are such as they appear to us to be. At the same time we must at least confess that the things which are represented to us in sleep are like painted representations which can only have been formed as the counterparts of something real and true, and that in this way those general things at least, i.e. eyes, a head, hands, and a whole body, are not imaginary things, but things really existent. For, as a matter of fact, painters, even when they study with the greatest skill to represent sirens and satyrs by forms the most strange and extraordinary, cannot give them natures which are entirely new, but merely make a certain medley of the members of different animals; or if their imagination is extravagant enough to invent something so novel that nothing similar has ever before been seen, and that then their work represents a thing purely fictitious and absolutely false, it is certain all the same that the colours of which this is composed are necessarily real. And for the same reason, although these general things, to wit, [a body], eyes, a head, hands, and such like, may be imaginary, we are bound at the same time to confess that there are at least some other objects yet more simple and more universal, which are real and true; and of these just in the same way as with certain real colours, all these images of things which dwell in our thoughts, whether true and real or false and fantastic, are formed.

To such a class of things pertains corporeal nature in general, and its extension, the figure of extended things, their quantity or magnitude and number, as also the place in which they are, the time which measures their duration, and so on.

That is possibly why our reasoning is not unjust when we conclude from this that Physics, Astronomy, Medicine and all other sciences which have as their end the consideration of composite things, are very dubious and uncertain; but that Arithmetic, Geometry and other sciences of that kind which only treat of things that are very simple and very general, without taking great trouble to ascertain whether they are actually existent or not, contain some measure of certainty and an element of the indubitable. For whether I am awake or asleep, two and three together always form five, and the square can never have more than four sides, and it does not seem possible that truths so clear and apparent can be suspected of any falsity [or uncertainty].

Nevertheless I have long had fixed in my mind the belief that an all-powerful God existed by whom I have been created such as I am. But how do I know that He has not brought it to pass that there is no earth, no heaven, no extended body, no magnitude, no place, and that nevertheless [I possess the perceptions of all these things and that] they seem to me to exist just exactly as I now see them? And, besides, as I sometimes imagine that others deceive themselves in the things which they think they know best, how do I know that I am not deceived every time that I add two and three, or count the sides of a square, or judge of things yet simpler, if anything simpler can be imagined? But possibly God has not desired that I should be thus deceived, for He is said to be supremely good. If, however, it is contrary to His goodness to have made me such that I constantly deceive myself, it would also appear to be contrary to His goodness to permit me to be sometimes deceived, and nevertheless I cannot doubt that He does permit this.

There may indeed be those who would prefer to deny the existence of a God so powerful, rather than believe that all other things are uncertain. But let us not oppose them for the present, and grant that all that is here said of a God is a fable; nevertheless in whatever way they suppose that I have arrived at the state of being that I have reached—whether they attribute it to fate or to accident, or make out that it is by a continual succession of antecedents, or by some other method— since to err and deceive oneself is a defect, it is clear that the greater will be the probability of my being so imperfect as to deceive myself ever, as is the Author to whom they assign my origin the less powerful. To these reasons I have certainly nothing to reply, but at the end I feel constrained to confess that there is nothing in all that I formerly believed to be true, of which I cannot in some measure doubt, and that not merely through want of thought or through levity, but for reasons which are very powerful and maturely considered; so that henceforth I ought not the less carefully to refrain from giving credence to these opinions than to that which is manifestly false, if I desire to arrive at any certainty [in the sciences].

But it is not sufficient to have made these remarks, we must also be careful to keep them in mind. For these ancient and commonly held opinions still revert frequently to my mind, long and familiar custom having given them the right to occupy my mind against my inclination and rendered them almost masters of my belief; nor will I ever lose the habit of deferring to them or of placing my confidence in them, so long as I consider them as they really are, i.e. opinions in some measure doubtful, as I have just shown, and at the same time highly probable, so that there is much more reason to believe in than to deny them. That is why I consider that I shall not be acting amiss, if, taking of set purpose a contrary belief, I allow myself to be deceived, and for a certain time pretend that all these opinions are entirely false and imaginary, until at last, having thus balanced my former prejudices with my latter [so that they cannot divert my opinions more to one side than to the other], my judgment will no longer be dominated by bad usage or turned away from the right knowledge of the truth. For I am assured that there can be neither peril nor error in this course, and that I cannot at present yield too much to distrust, since I am not considering the question of action, but only of knowledge.

I shall then suppose, not that God who is supremely good and the fountain of truth, but some evil genius not less powerful than deceitful, has employed his whole energies in deceiving me; I shall consider that the heavens, the earth, colours, figures, sound and all other external things are nought but the illusions and dreams of which this genius has availed himself in order to lay traps for my credulity; I shall consider myself as having no hands, no eyes, no flesh, no blood, nor any senses, yet falsely believing myself to possess all these things; I shall remain obstinately attached to this idea, and if by this means it is not in my power to arrive at the knowledge of any truth, I may at least do what is in my power [i.e. suspend my judgment], and with firm purpose avoid giving credence to any false thing, or being imposed upon by this arch deceiver, however powerful and deceptive he may be. But this task is a laborious one, and insensibly a certain lassitude leads me into the course of my ordinary life. And just as a captive who in sleep enjoys an imaginary liberty, when he begins to suspect that his liberty is but a dream, fears to awaken, and conspires with these agreeable illusions that the deception may be prolonged, so insensibly of my own accord I fall back into my former opinions, and I dread awakening from this slumber, lest the laborious wakefulness which would follow the tranquility of this repose should have to be spent not in daylight, but in the excessive darkness of the difficulties which have just been discussed.

Meditation II

OF THE NATURE OF THE HUMAN MIND; AND THAT IT IS MORE EASILY KNOWN THAN THE BODY.

The Meditation of yesterday filled my mind with so many doubts that it is no longer in my power to forget them. And yet I do not see in what manner I can resolve them; and, just as if I had all of a sudden fallen into very deep water, I am so disconcerted that I can neither make certain of setting my feet on the bottom, nor can I swim and so support myself on the surface. I shall nevertheless make an effort and follow anew the same path as that on which I yesterday entered, i.e. I shall proceed by setting aside all that in which the least doubt could be supposed to exist, just as if I had discovered that it was absolutely false; and I shall ever follow in this road until I have met with something which is certain, or at least, if I can do nothing else, until I have learned for certain that there is nothing in the world that is certain. Archimedes, in order that he might draw the terrestrial globe out of its place, and transport it elsewhere, demanded only that one point should be fixed and immoveable; in the same way I shall have the right to conceive high hopes if I am happy enough to discover one thing only which is certain and indubitable.

I suppose, then, that all the things that I see are false; I persuade myself that nothing has ever existed of all that my fallacious memory represents to me. I consider that I possess no senses; I imagine that body, figure, extension, movement and place are but the fictions of my mind. What, then, can be esteemed as true? Perhaps nothing at all, unless that there is nothing in the world that is certain.

But how can I know there is not something different from those things that I have just considered, of which one cannot have the slightest doubt? Is there not some God, or some other being by whatever name we call it, who puts these reflections into my mind? That is not necessary, for is it not possible that I am capable of producing them myself? I myself, am I not at least something? But I have already denied that I had senses and body. Yet I hesitate, for what follows from that? Am I so dependent on body and senses that I cannot exist without these? But I was persuaded that there was nothing in all the world, that there was no heaven, no earth, that there were no minds, nor any bodies: was I not then likewise persuaded that I did not exist? Not at all; of a surety I myself did exist since I persuaded myself of something [or merely because I thought of something]. But there is some deceiver or other, very powerful and very cunning, who ever employs his ingenuity in deceiving me. Then without doubt I exist also if he deceives me, and let him deceive me as much as he will, he can never cause me to be nothing so long as I think that I am something. So that after having reflected well and carefully examined all things, we must come to the definite conclusion that this proposition: I am, I exist, is necessarily true each time that I pronounce it, or that I mentally conceive it.

But I do not yet know clearly enough what I am, I who am certain that I am; and hence I must be careful to see that I do not imprudently take some other object in place of myself, and thus that I do not go astray in respect of this knowledge that I hold to be the most certain and most evident of all that I have formerly learned. That is why I shall now consider anew what I believed myself to be before I embarked upon these last reflections; and of my former opinions I shall withdraw all that might even in a small degree be invalidated by the reasons which I have just brought forward, in order that there may be nothing at all left beyond what is absolutely certain and indubitable.

What then did I formerly believe myself to be? Undoubtedly I believed myself to be a man. But what is a man? Shall I say a reasonable animal? Certainly not; for then I should have to inquire what an animal is, and what is reasonable; and thus from a single question I should insensibly fall into an infinitude of others more difficult; and I should not wish to waste the little time and leisure remaining to me in trying to unravel subtleties like these. But I shall rather stop here to consider the thoughts which of themselves spring up in my mind, and which were not inspired by anything beyond my own nature alone when I applied myself to the consideration of my being. In the first place, then, I considered myself as having a face, hands, arms, and all that system of members composed of bones and flesh as seen in a corpse which I designated by the name of body. In addition to this I considered that I was nourished, that I walked, that I felt, and that I thought, and I referred all these actions to the soul: but I did not stop to consider what the soul was, or if I did stop, I imagined that it was something extremely rare and subtle like a wind, a flame, or an ether, which was spread throughout my grosser parts. As to body I had no manner of doubt about its nature, but thought I had a very clear knowledge of it; and if I had desired to explain it according to the notions that I had then formed of it, I should have described it thus: By the body I understand all that which can be defined by a certain figure: something which can be confined in a certain place, and which can fill a given space in such a way that every other body will be excluded from it; which can be perceived either by touch, or by sight, or by hearing, or by taste, or by smell: which can be moved in many ways not, in truth, by itself, but by something which is foreign to it, by which it is touched [and from which it receives impressions]: for to have the power of self-movement, as also of feeling or of thinking, I did not consider to appertain to the nature of body: on the contrary, I was rather astonished to find that faculties similar to them existed in some bodies.

But what am I, now that I suppose that there is a certain genius which is extremely powerful, and, if I may say so, malicious, who employs all his powers in deceiving me? Can I affirm that I possess the least of all those things which I have just said pertain to the nature of body? I pause to consider, I revolve all these things in my mind, and I find none of which I can say that it pertains to me. It would be tedious to stop to enumerate them. Let us pass to the attributes of soul and see if there is any one which is in me? What of nutrition or walking [the first mentioned]? But if it is so that I have no body it is also true that I can neither walk nor take nourishment. Another attribute is sensation. But one cannot feel without body, and besides I have thought I perceived many things during sleep that I recognised in my waking moments as not having been experienced at all. What of thinking? I find here that thought is an attribute that belongs to me; it alone cannot be separated from me. I am, I exist, that is certain. But how often? Just when I think; for it might possibly be the case if I ceased entirely to think, that I should likewise cease altogether to exist. I do not now admit anything which is not necessarily true: to speak accurately I am not more than a thing which thinks, that is to say a mind or a soul, or an understanding, or a reason, which are terms whose significance was formerly unknown to me. I am, however, a real thing and really exist; but what thing? I have answered: a thing which thinks.

And what more? I shall exercise my imagination [in order to see if I am not something more]. I am not a collection of members which we call the human body: I am not a subtle air distributed through these members, I am not a wind, a fire, a vapour, a breath, nor anything at all which I can imagine or conceive; because I have assumed that all these were nothing. Without changing that supposition I find that I only leave myself certain of the fact that I am somewhat. But perhaps it is true that these same things which I supposed were non-existent because they are unknown to me, are really not different from the self which I know. I am not sure about this, I shall not dispute about it now; I can only give judgment on things that are known to me. I know that I exist, and I inquire what I am, I whom I know to exist. But it is very certain that the knowledge of my existence taken in its precise significance does not depend on things whose existence is not yet known to me; consequently it does not depend on those which I can feign in imagination. And indeed the very term *feign* in imagination[1] proves to me my error, for I really do this if I image myself a something, since to imagine is nothing else than to contemplate the figure or image of a corporeal thing. But I already know for certain that I am, and that it may be that all these images, and, speaking generally, all things that relate to the nature of body are nothing but dreams [and chimeras]. For this reason I see clearly that I have as little reason to say, 'I shall stimulate my imagination in order to know more distinctly what I am,' than if I were to say, 'I am now awake, and I perceive somewhat that is real and true: but because I do not yet perceive it distinctly enough, I shall go to sleep of express purpose, so that my dreams may represent the perception with greatest truth and evidence.' And, thus, I know for certain that nothing of all that I can understand by means of my imagination belongs to this knowledge which I have of myself, and that it is necessary to recall the mind from this mode of thought with the utmost diligence in order that it may be able to know its own nature with perfect distinctness.

But what then am I? A thing which thinks. What is a thing which thinks? It is a thing which doubts, understands, [conceives], affirms, denies, wills, refuses, which also imagines and feels.

[1]Or 'form an image' (effingo).

Certainly it is no small matter if all these things pertain to my nature. But why should they not so pertain? Am I not that being who now doubts nearly everything, who nevertheless understands certain things, who affirms that one only is true, who denies all the others, who desires to know more, is averse from being deceived, who imagines many things, sometimes indeed despite his will, and who perceives many likewise, as by the intervention of the bodily organs? Is there nothing in all this which is as true as it is certain that I exist, even though I should always sleep and though he who has given me being employed all his ingenuity in deceiving me? Is there likewise any one of these attributes which can be distinguished from my thought, or which might be said to be separated from myself? For it is so evident of itself that it is I who doubts, who understands, and who desires, that there is no reason here to add anything to explain it. And I have certainly the power of imagining likewise; for although it may happen (as I formerly supposed) that none of the things which I imagine are true, nevertheless this power of imagining does not cease to be really in use, and it forms part of my thought. Finally, I am the same who feels, that is to say, who perceives certain things, as by the organs of sense, since in truth I see light, I hear noise, I feel heat. But it will be said that these phenomena are false and that I am dreaming. Let it be so; still it is at least quite certain that it seems to me that I see light, that I hear noise and that I feel heat. That cannot be false; properly speaking it is what is in me called feeling; and used in this precise sense that is no other thing than thinking.

From this time I begin to know what I am with a little more clearness and distinction than before; but nevertheless it still seems to me, and I cannot prevent myself from thinking, that corporeal things, whose images are framed by thought, which are tested by the senses, are much more distinctly known than that obscure part of me which does not come under the imagination. Although really it is very strange to say that I know and understand more distinctly these things whose existence seems to me dubious, which are unknown to me, and which do not belong to me, than others of the truth of which I am convinced, which are known to me and which pertain to my real nature, in a word, than myself. But I see clearly how the case stands: my mind loves to wander, and cannot yet suffer itself to be retained within the just limits of truth. Very good, let us once more give it the freest rein, so that, when afterwards we seize the proper occasion for pulling up, it may the more easily be regulated and controlled.

Let us begin by considering the commonest matters, those which we believe to be the most distinctly comprehended, to wit, the bodies which we touch and see; not indeed bodies in general, for these general ideas are usually a little more confused, but let us consider one body in particular. Let us take, for example, this piece of wax: it has been taken quite freshly from the hive, and it has not yet lost the sweetness of the honey which it contains; it still retains somewhat of the odour of the flowers from which it has been culled; its colour, its figures, its size are apparent; it is hard, cold, easily handled, and if you strike it with the finger, it will emit a sound. Finally all the things which are requisite to cause us distinctly to recognise a body, are met with in it. But notice that while I speak and approach the fire what remained of the taste is exhaled, the smell evaporates, the colour alters, the figure is destroyed, the size increases, it becomes liquid, it heats, scarcely can one handle it, and when one strikes it, no sound is emitted. Does the same wax remain after this change? We must confess that it remains; none would judge otherwise. What then did I know so distinctly in this piece of wax? It could certainly be nothing of all that the senses brought to my notice, since all these things which fall under taste, smell, sight, touch, and hearing, are found to be changed, and yet the same wax remains.

Perhaps it was what I now think, viz. that this wax was not that sweetness of honey, nor that agreeable scent of flowers, nor that particular whiteness, nor that figure, nor that sound, but simply a body which a little while before appeared to me as perceptible under these forms, and which is now perceptible under others. But what, precisely, is it that I imagine when I form such conceptions? Let us attentively consider this, and, abstracting from all that does not belong to the wax, let us see what remains. Certainly nothing remains excepting a certain extended thing which is flexible and movable. But what is the meaning of flexible and movable? Is it not that I imagine that this piece of wax being round is capable of becoming square and of passing from a square to a triangular figure? No, certainly it is not that, since I imagine it admits of an infinitude of similar changes, and I nevertheless do not know how to compass the infinitude by my imagination, and consequently this conception which I have of the wax is not brought about by the faculty of imagination. What now is this extension? Is it not also unknown? For it becomes greater when the wax is melted, greater when it is boiled, and greater still when the heat increases; and I should not conceive [clearly] according to truth what wax is, if I did not think that even this piece that we are considering is capable of receiving more variations in extension than I have ever imagined. We must then grant that I could not even understand through the imagination what this piece of wax is, and that it is my mind alone which perceives it. I say this piece of wax in particular, for as to wax in general it is yet clearer. But what is this piece of wax which cannot be understood excepting by the [understanding or] mind? It is certainly the same that I see, touch, imagine, and finally it is the same which I have always believed it to be from the beginning. But what must particularly be observed is that its perception is neither an act of vision, nor of touch, nor of imagination, and has never been such although it may have appeared formerly to be so, but only an intuition of the mind, which may be imperfect and confused as it was formerly, or clear and distinct as it is at present, according as my attention is more or less directed to the elements which are found in it, and of which it is composed.

Yet in the meantime I am greatly astonished when I consider [the great feebleness of mind] and its proneness to fall [insensibly] into error; for although without giving expression to my thoughts I consider all this in my own mind, words often impede me and I am almost deceived by the terms of ordinary language. For we say that we see the same wax, if it is present, and not that we simply judge that it is the same from its having the same colour and figure. From this I should conclude that I knew the wax by means of vision and not simply by the intuition of the mind; unless by chance I remember that, when looking from a window and saying I see men who pass in the street, I really do not see them, but infer that what I see is men, just as I say that I see wax. And yet what do I see from the window but hats and coats which may cover automatic machines? Yet I judge these to be men. And similarly solely by the faculty of judgment which rests in my mind, I comprehend that which I believed I saw with my eyes.

A man who makes it his aim to raise his knowledge above the common should be ashamed to derive the occasion for doubting from the forms of speech invented by the vulgar; I prefer to pass on and consider whether I had a more evident and perfect conception of what the wax was when I first perceived it, and when I believed I knew it by means of the external senses or at least by the common sense as it is called, that is to say by the imaginative faculty, or whether my present conception is clearer now that I have most carefully examined what it is, and in what way it can be known. It would certainly be absurd to doubt as to this. For what was there in this first perception which was distinct? What was there which might not as well have been perceived by any of the animals? But when I distinguish the wax from its external forms, and when, just as if I had taken from it its vestments, I consider it quite naked, it is certain that although some error may still be found in my judgment, I can nevertheless not perceive it thus without a human mind.

But finally what shall I say of this mind, that is, of myself, for up to this point I do not admit in myself anything but mind? What then, I who seem to perceive this piece of wax so distinctly, do I not know myself, not only with much more truth and certainty, but also with much more distinctness and clearness? For if I judge that the wax is or exists from the fact that I see it, it certainly follows much more clearly that I am or that I exist myself from the fact that I see it. For it may be that what I see is not really wax, it may also be that I do not possess eyes with which to see anything; but it cannot be that when I see, or (for I no longer take account of the distinction) when I think I see, that I myself who think am nought. So if I judge that the wax exists from the fact that I touch it, the same thing will follow, to wit, that I am; and if I judge that my imagination, or some other cause, whatever it is, persuades me that the wax exists, I shall still conclude the same. And what I have here remarked of wax may be applied to all other things which are external to me [and which are met with outside of me]. And further, if the [notion or] perception of wax has seemed to me clearer and more distinct, not only after the sight or the touch, but also after many other causes have rendered it quite manifest to me, with how much more [evidence] and distinctness must it be said that I now know myself, since all the reasons which contribute to the knowledge of wax, or any other body whatever, are yet better proofs of the nature of my mind! And there are so many other things in the mind itself which may contribute to the elucidation of its nature, that those which depend on body such as these just mentioned, hardly merit being taken into account.

But finally here I am, having insensibly reverted to the point I desired, for, since it is now manifest to me that even bodies are not properly speaking known by the senses or by the faculty of imagination, but by the understanding only, and since they are not known from the fact that they are seen or touched, but only because they are understood, I see clearly that there is nothing which is easier for me to know than my mind. But because it is difficult to rid oneself so promptly of an opinion to which one was accustomed for so long, it will be well that I should halt a little at this point, so that by the length of my meditation I may more deeply imprint on my memory this new knowledge.

transition: mind, matter, and philosophic method

Was Descartes true to his method? His doubts are certainly radical, but are they radical enough? He showed the way into the introspective well of doubt, but did he plumb its depths? To see how difficult his method is to master, let us examine some of the questions raised by other philosophers.

First, is Descartes correct in his estimation of the point at which the drill of doubt meets the bedrock of certainty? For example, in his analysis of the identity of the piece of wax, is he correct in his description of what is left behind when all the changeable qualities are removed? Other philosophers have tried the same thought experiment and have come up with different answers. Aristotle (384–322 B.C.), in his *Metaphysics* (Book Zeta, Chapter 3), attempts the same metaphysical undressing and in his estimation the "length and breadth and depth" of a thing can be stripped away just as easily as its color and weight. In that passage Aristotle identifies matter as the ultimate substratum (bedrock) of identity, but he does not define matter in terms of extension as Descartes does. Similarly, Kant shows us a metaphysical striptease in his *Critique of Pure Reason* (B xxxv/A xxi): "if I take away from the representation of a body that which the understanding thinks in regard to it, substance, force, divisibility, etc., and likewise what belongs to sensation, impenetrability, hardness, colour, etc., something still remains over from this empirical intuition, namely, extension and figure." But Kant attributes this extension and figure not to the object in itself but to the cognitive faculties of the subject. For Kant, space and time are not objective realities but subjective forms of the way we see things. Thus the bedrock of identity is located even more subjectively than Descartes had imagined. On the basis of these passages from Aristotle and Kant we can see that the metaphysical striptease is not easy to perform. Even with a careful articulation of the method of doubt, what is certain to one person is not always certain to another.

This leads us to a second and even more radical objection to Descartes' method: what if we should doubt the method of doubt itself? Is subjective certainty a reliable criterion of truth? Perhaps the whole metaphor suggested by Descartes' method is a mistake; perhaps there is no bedrock. Or to use another metaphor, perhaps philosophic inquiry is more like peeling an onion than an orange. Descartes' method presupposes that beneath the rind of illusion one will find the fruit of truth. What if the truth is simply the totality of all the layers our doubt so briskly peels away? This is not to say there is no truth any more than the lack of a differentiated center denies the existence of an onion. The onion theory of reality, to coin a phrase, simply denies the notion that truth is to be found in a bedrock of reality that lies separate from and beneath appearances. According to the onion theory, reality is the totality of the appearances, not something separate from appearances. The distinction between reality and appearance still makes sense, however, because as long as one remains preoccupied with a single layer one is necessarily cut off from the totality, and hence cut off from reality and truth. Descartes' method remains helpful in encouraging us to doubt the finality of any "truth" we apprehend. Whether or not we reach bedrock, the method of doubt spurs us on to regard each successive layer as another level of appearance. Thus the method of doubt leads to a totality in which each of the appearances is reclaimed as a part of the whole and not dismissed as a simple falsehood.

This method of totalizing (the method I embrace) has as its major exponent in the western tradition Georg Hegel (1770–1831). Hegel's writings, not surprisingly, rely so heavily on the relatedness of their various parts that no single part can be justly excerpted for an anthology. Readers will get a taste of the method of totalizing as they see that method inform the organization of the rest of this anthology.

Gilbert Ryle limits the use of the metaphor of interior layers to the simple distinction of inside and outside. He accuses Descartes of having bifurcated a person into a mental inside and physical outside. Without anticipating the details of Ryle's argument, it should be noted that Ryle's essay, too, can be read as a discourse on method. Just as Descartes' *Meditations* bear not only on the content of the mind-body problem but also on the method of the Subjective Turn, so Ryle's essay combines reflection on the mind-body problem with an application of the Linguistic Turn. That is, just as Descartes turned from a reflection on objects to a reflection on subjective experience, so Ryle turns from the method of introspection to an examination of the language we use in articulating our puzzlements. Ryle was not the first to make the Linguistic Turn. Perhaps its most famous initiators were Bertrand Russell (1872–1970), Ludwig Wittgenstein (1889–1951), and Rudolph Carnap (1891–1970). Through an examination of language we use in talking about mind, matter, and existence, they showed how we are deceived by surface similarities among certain types of sentences. The sentence, 'She insists,' may look very like the sentence, 'She exists,' but a closer examination shows that the word 'exists' functions very differently from 'insists,' and if we insist on treating existence as a predicate that ascribes a particular property or activity to a subject, then our reliance on superficial linguistic similarities will end in confusion. The surface similarity of the two words muddies the distinction between *what* a thing is and *that* it is; the surface similarity between the sentences above leads us to think that 'exists,' since it is located in the predicate position, tells us something in particular about *what* the subject is or is doing, whereas in fact the word 'exists' only reasserts *that* there is a subject to which we may ascribe particular properties. The point may seem insignificant if regarded merely as an esoteric observation about our language, but when we realize that proofs for the existence of God as well as discussions of the existence of values turn on such points, then the results of linguistic analysis may seem more important. (For a full representation of this important movement in twentieth-century philosophy Richard Rorty's anthology, appropriately titled *The Linguistic Turn,* is excellent.)

The transition from Descartes to Ryle is a big transition. While Ryle places himself in a direct dialogue with Descartes, more than three hundred years passed between the publication of Descartes' *Meditations* and Ryle's *Concept of Mind* (1949). During that time many philosophers not only followed Descartes' footsteps around the Subjective Turn but broke new paths in their own investigations of mind, matter, and philosophic method. Throughout the long transition from Descartes to Ryle the history of philosophy teaches the lesson that *what* we see depends on *how* we look: philosophic method influences the resultant metaphysics. Conversely, a commitment to a given metaphysics influences the method of inquiry most appropriate to expounding that metaphysics: if we are convinced that reality is nothing but matter and motion in space and time, then a Cartesian mathematical physics is the most appropriate method of inquiry. If, instead, we regard the logical space of discourse as the most significant reality for philosophical inquiry, then an examination of the logic of our language will be the most appropriate method of inquiry. And once we have taken the Linguistic Turn, its method not only replaces the method of the Subjective Turn, the metaphysics of Cartesianism comes under attack as well. Descartes' pictures of mind and matter fall under the charge that the Cartesian metaphysics follows from linguistic confusions.

GILBERT RYLE *(1900–1976)*

Gilbert Ryle is one of the most important of the contemporary British philosophers interested in examining our ordinary language, and as professor at Oxford and former editor of the philosophical journal Mind, *Ryle has influenced the course of philosophical debate in the English-speaking world for almost a generation. Since the publication of* The Concept of Mind *and the posthumous publication of Wittgenstein's* Philosophical Investigations *in 1953, a whole tradition known as the "philosophy of mind" has centered around the issues raised in these two books. This tradition is characterized not only by its primary object, mind, but also by its method of inquiry, the examination of ordinary language. The same tradition is often referred to as "ordinary language philosophy."*

In the following essay, the first chapter of his Concept of Mind, *Ryle shows how the Cartesian view of mind is the result of what Ryle calls a "category-mistake." Ryle finds it easiest to use examples to show the meaning of the term "category-mistake," but he generalizes from the examples to claim that category-mistakes are generated by an "inability to use certain items in the English vocabulary." A close reading of Ryle's analysis of category-mistakes is well worth the effort, for the analytic tool of identifying category-mistakes proves helpful in contexts other than the philosophy of the mind.*

Descartes' Myth

The Official Doctrine

There is a doctrine about the nature and place of minds which is so prevalent among theorists and even among laymen that it deserves to be described as the official theory. Most philosophers, psychologists and religious teachers subscribe, with minor reservations, to its main articles and, although they admit certain theoretical difficulties in it, they tend to assume that these can be overcome without serious modifications being made to the architecture of the theory. It will be argued here that the central principles of the doctrine are unsound and conflict with the whole body of what we know about minds when we are not speculating about them.

The official doctrine, which hails chiefly from Descartes, is something like this. With the doubtful exceptions of idiots and infants in arms every human being has both a body and a mind. Some would prefer to say that every human being is both a body and a mind. His body and his mind are ordinarily harnessed together, but after the death of the body his mind may continue to exist and function.

Human bodies are in space and are subject to the mechanical laws which govern all other bodies in space. Bodily processes and states can be inspected by external observers. So a man's bodily life is as much a public affair as are the lives of animals and reptiles and even as the careers of trees, crystals and planets.

But minds are not in space, nor are their operations subject to mechanical laws. The workings of one mind are not witnessable by other observers; its career is private. Only I can take direct cognisance of the states and processes of my own mind. A person therefore lives through two collateral histories, one consisting of what happens in and to his body, the other consisting of what happens in and to his mind. The first is public, the second private. The events in the first history are events in the physical world, those in the second are events in the mental world.

It has been disputed whether a person does or can directly monitor all or only some of the episodes of his own private history; but, according to the official doctrine, of at least some of these episodes he has direct and unchallengeable cognisance. In consciousness, self-consciousness and introspection he is directly and authentically apprised of the present states and operations of his mind. He may have great or small uncertainties about concurrent and adjacent episodes in the physical world, but he can have none about at least part of what is momentarily occupying his mind.

It is customary to express this bifurcation of his two lives and of his two worlds by saying that the things and events which belong to the physical world, including his own body, are external, while the workings of his own mind are internal. This antithesis of outer and inner is of course meant to be construed as a metaphor, since minds, not being in space, could not be described as being spatially inside anything else, or as having things going on spatially inside themselves. But relapses from this good intention are common and theorists are found speculating how stimuli, the physical sources of which are yards or miles outside a person's skin, can generate mental responses inside his skull, or how decisions framed inside his cranium can set going movements of his extremities.

Even when 'inner' and 'outer' are construed as metaphors, the problem how a person's mind and body influence one another is notoriously charged with theoretical difficulties. What the mind wills, the legs, arms and the tongue execute; what affects the ear and the eye has something to do with what the mind perceives; grimaces and smiles betray the mind's moods and bodily castigations lead, it is hoped, to moral improvement. But the actual transactions between the episodes of the private history and those of the public history remain mysterious, since by definition they can belong to neither series. They could not be reported among the happenings described in a person's autobiography of his inner life, but nor could they be reported among those described in some one else's biography of that person's overt career. They can be inspected neither by introspection nor by laboratory experiment. They are theoretical shuttlecocks which are forever being bandied from the physiologist back to the psychologist and from the psychologist back to the physiologist.

Underlying this partly metaphorical representation of the bifurcation of a person's two lives there is a seemingly more profound and philosophical assumption. It is assumed that there are two different kinds of existence or status. What exists or happens may have the status of physical existence, or it may have the status of mental existence. Somewhat as the faces of coins are either heads or tails, or somewhat as living creatures are either male or female, so, it is supposed, some existing is physical existing, other existing is mental existing. It is a necessary feature of what has physical existence that it is in space and time, it is a necessary feature of what has mental existence that it is in time but not in space. What has physical existence is composed of matter, or else is a function of matter; what has mental existence consists of consciousness, or else is a function of consciousness.

There is thus a polar opposition between mind and matter, an opposition which is often brought out as follows. Material objects are situated in a common field, known as 'space,' and what happens to one body in one part of space is mechanically connected with what happens to other bodies in other parts of space. But mental happenings occur in insulated fields, known as 'minds,' and there is, apart maybe from telepathy, no direct causal connection between what happens in one mind and what happens in another. Only through the medium of the public physical world can the mind of one person make a difference to the mind of another. The mind is its own place and in his inner life each of us lives the life of a ghostly Robinson Crusoe. People can see, hear and jolt one another's bodies, but they are irremediably blind and deaf to the workings of one another's minds and inoperative upon them.

What sort of knowledge can be secured of the workings of a mind? On the one side, according to the official theory, a person has direct knowledge of the best imaginable kind of the workings of his own mind. Mental states and processes are (or are normally) conscious states and processes, and consciousness which irradiates them can engender no illusions and leaves the door open for no doubts. A person's present thinkings, feelings and willings, his perceivings, rememberings and imaginings are intrinsically 'phosphorescent'; their existence and their nature are inevitably betrayed to their owner. The inner life is a stream of consciousness of such a sort that it would be absurd to suggest that the mind whose life is that stream might be unaware of what is passing down it.

True, the evidence adduced recently by Freud seems to show that there exist channels tributary to this stream, which run hidden from their owner. People are actuated by impulses the existence of which they vigorously disavow; some of their thoughts differ from the thoughts which they acknowledge; and some of the actions which they think they will to perform they do not really will. They are thoroughly gulled by some of their own hypocrisies and they successfully ignore facts about their mental lives which on the official theory ought to be patent to them. Holders of the official theory tend, however, to maintain that anyhow in normal circumstances a person must be directly and authentically seized of the present state and workings of his own mind.

Besides being currently supplied with these alleged immediate data of consciousness, a person is also generally supposed to be able to exercise from time to time a special kind of perception, namely inner perception, or introspection. He can take a (non-optical) 'look' at what is passing in his mind. Not only can he view and scrutinize a flower through his sense of sight and listen to and discriminate the notes of a bell through his sense of hearing; he can also reflectively or introspectively watch, without any bodily organ of sense, the current episodes of his inner life. This self-observation is also commonly supposed to be immune from illusion, confusion or doubt. A mind's reports of its own affairs have a certainty superior to the best that is possessed by its reports of matters in the physical world. Sense-perceptions can, but consciousness and introspection cannot, be mistaken or confused.

On the other side, one person has no direct access of any sort to the events of the inner life of another. He cannot do better than make problematic inferences from the observed behaviour of the other person's body to the states of mind which, by analogy from his own conduct, he supposes to be signalised by that behaviour. Direct access to the workings of a mind is the privilege of that mind itself; in default of such privileged access, the workings of one mind are inevitably occult to everyone else. For the supposed arguments from bodily movements similar to their own to mental workings similar to their own would lack any possibility of observational corroboration. Not unnaturally, therefore, an adherent of the official theory finds it difficult to resist this consequence of his premises, that he has no good reason to believe that there do exist minds other than his own. Even if he prefers to believe that to other human bodies there are harnessed minds not unlike his own, he cannot claim to be able to discover their individual characteristics, or the particular things that they undergo and do. Absolute solitude is on this showing the ineluctable destiny of the soul. Only our bodies can meet.

As a necessary corollary of this general scheme there is implicitly prescribed a special way of construing our ordinary concepts of mental powers and operations. The verbs, nouns and adjectives, with which in ordinary life we describe the wits, characters and higher-grade performances of the people with whom we have do, are required to be construed as signifying special episodes in their secret histories, or else as signifying tendencies for such episodes to occur. When someone is described as knowing, believing or guessing something, as hoping, dreading, intending or shirking something, as designing this or being amused at that, these verbs are supposed to denote the occurrence of specific modifications in his (to us) occult stream of consciousness. Only his own privileged access to this stream in direct awareness and introspection could provide authentic testimony that these mental-conduct verbs were correctly or incorrectly applied. The onlooker, be he teacher, critic, biographer or friend, can never assure himself that his comments have any vestige of truth. Yet it was just because we do in fact all know how to make such comments, make them with general correctness and correct them when they turn out to be confused or mistaken, that philosophers found it necessary to construct their theories of the nature and place of minds. Finding mental-conduct concepts being regularly and effectively used, they properly sought to fix their logical geography. But the logical geography officially recommended would entail that there could be no regular or effective use of these mental-conduct concepts in our descriptions of, and prescriptions for, other people's minds.

The Absurdity of the Official Doctrine

Such in outline is the official theory. I shall often speak of it, with deliberate abusiveness, as 'the dogma of the Ghost in the Machine.' I hope to prove that it is entirely false, and false not in detail but in principle. It is not merely an assemblage of particular mistakes. It is one big mistake and a mistake of a special kind. It is, namely, a category-mistake. It represents the facts of mental life as if they belonged to one logical type or category (or range of types or categories), when they actually belong to another. The dogma is therefore a philosopher's myth. In attempting to explode the myth I shall probably be taken to be denying well-known facts about the mental life of human beings, and my plea that I aim at doing nothing more than rectify the logic of mental-conduct concepts will probably be disallowed as mere subterfuge.

I must first indicate what is meant by the phrase 'Category-mistake.' This I do in a series of illustrations.

A foreigner visiting Oxford or Cambridge for the first time is shown a number of colleges, libraries, playing fields, museums, scientific departments and administrative offices. He then asks 'But where is the University? I have seen where the members of the Colleges live, where the Registrar works, where the scientists experiment and the rest. But I have not yet seen the University in which reside and work the members of your University.' It has then to be explained to him that the University is not another collateral institution, some ulterior counterpart to the colleges, laboratories and offices which he has seen. The University is just the way in which all that he has already seen is organized. When they are seen and when their co-ordination is understood, the University has been seen. His mistake lay in his innocent assumption that it was correct to speak of Christ Church, the Bodleian Library, the Ashmolean Museum *and* the University, to speak, that is, as if 'the University' stood for an extra member of the class of which these other units are members. He was mistakenly allocating the University to the same category as that to which the other institutions belong.

The same mistake would be made by a child witnessing the march-past of a division, who, having had pointed out to him such and such battalions, batteries, squadrons, etc., asked when the division was going to appear. He would be supposing that a division was a counterpart to the units already seen, partly similar to them and partly unlike them. He would be shown his mistake by being told that in watching the battalions, batteries and squadrons marching past he had been watching the division marching past. The march-past was not a parade of battalions, batteries, squadrons *and* a division; it was a parade of the battalions, batteries, and squadrons *of* a division.

One more illustration. A foreigner watching his first game of cricket learns what are the functions of the bowlers, the batsmen, the fielders, the umpires and the scorers. He then says 'But there is no one left on the field to contribute the famous element of team-spirit. I see who does the bowling, the batting, and the wicket-keeping; but I do not see whose role it is to exercise *esprit de corps.*' Once more, it would have to be explained that he was looking for the wrong type of thing. Team-spirit is not another cricketing-operation supplementary to all of the other special tasks. It is, roughly, the keenness with which each of the special tasks is performed, and performing a task keenly is not performing two tasks. Certainly exhibiting team-spirit is not the same thing as bowling or catching, but nor is it a third thing such that we can say that the bowler first bowls *and* then exhibits team-spirit or that a fielder is at a given moment *either* catching *or* displaying *esprit de corps*.

These illustrations of category-mistakes have a common feature which must be noticed. The mistakes were made by people who did not know how to wield the concepts *University, division* and *team-spirit*. Their puzzles arose from inability to use certain items in the English vocabulary.

The theoretically interesting category-mistakes are those made by people who are perfectly competent to apply concepts, at least in the situations with which they are familiar, but are still liable in their abstract thinking to allocate those concepts to logical types to which they do not belong. An instance of a mistake of this sort would be the following story. A student of politics has learned the main differences between the British, the French and the American Constitutions, and has learned also the differences and connections between the Cabinet, Parliament, the various Ministries, the Judicature and the Church of England. But he still becomes embarrassed when asked questions about the connections between the Church of England, the Home Office and the British Constitution. For while the Church and the Home Office are institutions, the British Constitution is not another institution in the same sense of that noun. So inter-institutional relations which can be asserted or denied to hold between the Church and the Home Office cannot be asserted or denied to hold between either of them and the British Constitution. 'The British Constitution' is not a term of the same logical type as 'the Home Office' and 'the Church of England.' In a partially similar way, John Doe may be a relative, a friend, an enemy or a stranger to Richard Roe; but he cannot be any of these things to the Average Taxpayer. He knows how to talk sense in certain sorts of discussions about the Average Taxpayer, but he is baffled to say why he could not come across him in the street as he can come across Richard Roe.

It is pertinent to our main subject to notice that, so long as the student of politics continues to think of the British Constitution as a counterpart to the other institutions, he will tend to describe it as a mysteriously occult institution; and so long as John Doe continues to think of the Average Taxpayer as a fellow-citizen, he will tend to think of him as an elusive insubstantial man, a ghost who is everywhere yet nowhere.

My destructive purpose is to show that a family of radical category-mistakes is the source of the double-life theory. The representation of a person as a ghost mysteriously ensconced in a machine derives from this argument. Because, as is true, a person's thinking, feeling and purposive doing cannot be described solely in the idioms of physics, chemistry and physiology, therefore they must be described in counterpart idioms. As the human body is a complex organised unit, so the human mind must be another complex organised unit, though one made of a different sort of stuff and with a different sort of structure. Or, again, as the human body, like any other parcel of matter, is a field of causes and effects, so the mind must be another field of causes and effects, though not (Heaven be praised) mechanical causes and effects.

The Origin of the Category-mistake

One of the chief intellectual origins of what I have yet to prove to be the Cartesian category-mistake seems to be this. When Galileo showed that his methods of scientific discovery were competent to provide a mechanical theory which should cover every occupant of space, Descartes found in himself two conflicting motives. As a man of scientific genius he could not but endorse the claims of mechanics, yet as a religious and moral man he could not accept, as Hobbes accepted, the discouraging rider to those claims, namely that human nature differs only in degree of complexity from clockwork. The mental could not be just a variety of the mechanical.

He and subsequent philosophers naturally but erroneously availed themselves of the following escape-route. Since mental-conduct words are not to be construed as signifying the occurrence of mechanical processes, they must be construed as signifying the occurrence of non-mechanical processes; since mechanical laws explain movements in space as the effects of other movements in space, other laws must explain some of the non-spatial workings of minds as the effects of other non-spatial workings of minds. The difference between the human behaviours which we describe as intelligent and those which we describe as unintelligent must be a difference in their causation; so, while some movements of human tongues and limbs are the effects of mechanical causes, others must be the effects of non-mechanical causes, i.e. some issue from movements of particles of matter, others from workings of the mind.

The differences between the physical and the mental were thus represented as differences inside the common framework of the categories of 'thing,' 'stuff,' 'attribute,' 'state,' 'process,' 'change,' 'cause' and 'effect.' Minds are things, but different sorts of things from bodies; mental processes are causes and effects, but different sorts of causes and effects from bodily movements. And so on. Somewhat as the foreigner expected the University to be an extra edifice, rather like a college but also considerably different, so the repudiators of mechanism represented minds as extra centers of causal processes, rather like machines but also considerably different from them. Their theory was a para-mechanical hypothesis.

That this assumption was at the heart of the doctrine is shown by the fact that there was from the beginning felt to be a major theoretical difficulty in explaining how minds can influence and be influenced by bodies. How can a mental process, such as willing, cause spatial movements like the movements of the tongue? How can a physical change in the optic nerve have among its effects a mind's perception of a flash of light? This notorious crux by itself shows the logical mould into which Descartes pressed his theory of the mind. It was the self-same mould into which he and Galileo set their mechanics. Still unwittingly adhering to the grammar of mechanics, he tried to avert disaster by describing minds in what was merely an obverse vocabulary. The working of minds had to be described by the mere negatives of the specific descriptions given to bodies; they are not in space, they are not motions, they are not modifications of matter, they are not accessible to public observation. Minds are not bits of clockwork, they are just bits of not-clockwork.

As thus represented, minds are not merely ghosts harnessed to machines, they are themselves just spectral machines. Though the human body is an engine, it is not quite an ordinary engine, since some of its workings are governed by another engine inside it—this interior governor-engine being one of a very special sort. It is invisible, inaudible and it has no size or weight. It cannot be taken to bits and the laws it obeys are not those known to ordinary engineers. Nothing is known of how it governs the bodily engine.

A second major crux points the same moral. Since, according to the doctrine, minds belong to the same category as bodies and since bodies are rigidly governed by mechanical laws, it seemed to many theorists to follow that minds must be similarly governed by rigid non-mechanical laws. The physical world is a deterministic system, so the mental world must be a deterministic system. Bodies cannot help the modifications that they undergo, so minds cannot help pursuing the careers fixed for them. *Responsibility, choice, merit* and *demerit* are therefore inapplicable concepts—unless the compromise solution is adopted of saying that the laws governing mental processes, unlike those governing physical processes, have the congenial attribute of being only rather rigid. The problem of the Freedom of the Will was the problem how to reconcile the hypothesis that minds are to be described in terms drawn from the categories of mechanics with the knowledge that higher-grade human conduct is not of a piece with the behaviour of machines.

It is an historical curiosity that it was not noticed that the entire argument was broken-backed. Theorists correctly assumed that any sane man could already recognise the differences between, say, rational and nonrational utterances or between purposive and automatic behaviour. Else there would have been nothing requiring to be salved from mechanism. Yet the explanation given presupposed that one person could in principle never recognise the difference between the rational and the irrational utterances issuing from other human bodies, since he could never get access to the postulated immaterial causes of some of their utterances. Save for the doubtful exception of himself, he could never tell the difference between a man and a Robot. It would have to be conceded, for example, that, for all that we can tell, the inner lives of persons who are classed as idiots or lunatics are as rational as those of anyone else. Perhaps only their overt behaviour is disappointing; that is to say, perhaps 'idiots' are not really idiotic, or 'lunatics' lunatic. Perhaps, too, some of those who are classed as sane are really idiots. According to the theory, external observers could never know how the overt behaviour of others is correlated with their mental powers and processes and so they could never know or even plausibly conjecture whether their applications of mental-conduct concepts to these other people were correct or incorrect. It would then be hazardous or impossible for a man to claim sanity or logical consistency even for himself, since he would be debarred from comparing his own performances with those of others. In short, our characterisations of persons and their performances as intelligent, prudent and virtuous or as stupid, hypocritical and cowardly could never have been made, so the problem of providing a special causal hypothesis to serve as the basis of such diagnosis would never have arisen. The question, 'How do persons differ from machines?' arose just because everyone already knew how to apply mental-conduct concepts before the new causal hypothesis was introduced. This causal hypothesis could not therefore be the source of the criteria used in those applications. Nor, of course, has the causal hypothesis in any degree improved our handling of those criteria. We still distinguish good from bad arithmetic, politic from impolitic conduct and fertile from infertile imaginations in the ways in which Descartes himself distinguished them before and after he speculated how the applicability of these criteria was compatible with the principle of mechanical causation.

He had mistaken the logic of his problem. Instead of asking by what criteria intelligent behaviour is actually distinguished from non-intelligent behaviour, he asked 'Given that the principle of mechanical causation does not tell us the difference, what other causal principle will tell it to us?' He realised that the problem was not one of mechanics and assumed that it must therefore be one of some counterpart to mechanics. Not unnaturally psychology is often cast for just this role.

When two terms belong to the same category, it is proper to construct conjunctive propositions embodying them. Thus a purchaser may say that he bought a left-hand glove and a right-hand glove, but not that he bought a left-hand glove, a right-hand glove and a pair of gloves. 'She came home in a flood of tears and a sedan-chair' is a well-known joke based on the absurdity of conjoining terms of different types. It would have been equally ridiculous to construct the disjunction 'She came home either in a flood of tears or else in a sedan-chair.' Now the dogma of the Ghost in the Machine does just this. It maintains that there exist both bodies and minds; that there occur physical processes and mental processes; that there are mechanical causes of corporeal movements and mental causes of corporeal movements. I shall argue that these and other analogous conjunctions are absurd; but, it must be noticed, the arguments will not show that either of the illegitimately conjoined propositions is absurd in itself. I am not, for example, denying that there occur mental processes. Doing long division is a mental process and so is making a joke. But I am saying that the phrase 'there occur mental processes' does not mean the same sort of thing as 'there occur physical processes,' and, therefore, that it makes no sense to conjoin or disjoin the two.

If my argument is successful, there will follow some interesting consequences. First, the hallowed contrast between Mind and Matter will be dissipated, but dissipated not by either of the equally hallowed absorptions of Mind by Matter or of Matter by Mind, but in quite a different way. For the seeming contrast of the two will be shown to be as illegitimate as would be the contrast of 'she came home in a flood of tears' and 'she came home in a sedan-chair.' The belief that there is a polar opposition between Mind and Matter is the belief that they are terms of the same logical type.

It will also follow that both Idealism and Materialism are answers to an improper question. The 'reduction' of the material world to mental states and processes, as well as the 'reduction' of mental states and processes to physical states and processes, presuppose the legitimacy of the disjunction 'Either there exist minds or there exist bodies (but not both).' It would be like saying, 'Either she bought a left-hand and a right-hand glove or she bought a pair of gloves (but not both).'

It is perfectly proper to say, in one logical tone of voice, that there exist minds and to say, in another logical tone of voice, that there exist bodies. But these expressions do not indicate two different species of existence, for 'existence' is not a generic word like 'coloured' or 'sexed.' They indicate two different senses of 'exist,' somewhat as 'rising' has different senses in 'the tide is rising,' 'hopes are rising,' and 'the average age of death is rising.' A man would be thought to be making a poor joke who said that three things are now rising, namely the tide, hopes and the average age of death. It would be just as good or bad a joke to say that there exist prime numbers and Wednesdays and public opinions and navies; or that there exist both minds and bodies. In the succeeding chapters I try to prove that the official theory does rest on a batch of category-mistakes by showing that logically absurd corollaries follow from it. The exhibition of these absurdities will have the constructive effect of bringing out part of the correct logic of mental-conduct concepts.

Historical Note

It would not be true to say that the official theory derives solely from Descartes' theories, or even from a more widespread anxiety about the implications of seventeenth century mechanics. Scholastic and Reformation theology had schooled the intellects of the scientists as well as of the laymen, philosophers and clerics of that age. Stoic-Augustinian theories of the will were embedded in the Calvinist doctrines of sin and grace; Platonic and Aristotelian theories of the intellect shaped the orthodox doctrines of the immortality of the soul. Descartes was reformulating already prevalent theological doctrines of the soul in the new syntax of Galileo. The theologian's privacy of conscience became the philosopher's privacy of consciousness, and what had been the bogy of Predestination reappeared as the bogy of Determinism.

It would also not be true to say that the two-worlds myth did no theoretical good. Myths often do a lot of theoretical good, while they are still new. One benefit bestowed by the para-mechanical myth was that it partly superannuated the then prevalent para-political myth. Minds and their Faculties had previously been described by analogies with political superiors and political subordinates. The idioms used were those of ruling, obeying, collaborating and rebelling. They survived and still survive in many ethical and some epistemological discussions. As, in physics, the new myth of occult Forces was a scientific improvement on the old myth of Final Causes, so, in anthropological and psychological theory, the new myth of hidden operations, impulses and agencies was an improvement on the old myth of dictations, deferences and disobediences.

transition: free will and determinism

Ryle calmly affirmed, "The problem of the Freedom of the Will was the problem how to reconcile the hypothesis that minds are to be described in terms drawn from the categories of mechanics with the knowledge that higher-grade human conduct is not of a piece with the behaviour of machines." In his "Historical Note," he identified "Stoic-Augustinian theories of the will" as playing a supporting role in the "official doctrine" of the ghost in the machine. Let us now take a longer look at the problem of the Freedom of the Will, and let us see what Augustine has to say about it. Not everyone will agree with Ryle's description of the problem. If we do, and if we further agree with Ryle in rejecting "the hypothesis that minds are to be described in terms drawn from the categories of mechanics," and if we consequently *dissolve* the problem by eliminating the need to reconcile that rejected hypothesis with "the knowledge that higher-grade human conduct is not of a piece with the behaviour of machines," we may still want to know something about how higher-grade human conduct does in fact differ from that of machines. In short, there is not just one problem of the Freedom of the Will, there are many; and Ryle's dissolution of one of them, admirable as it may be, does not answer all our doubts about the Freedom of the Will. Even if Ryle is right in attacking the notion of an inner will that not only causes overt behavior but also suffers the effects of other causes, and even if he dissolves the problem of the freedom of the *Will,* has he dissolved the problem of freedom? True, the Will as it is described in the "official doctrine" may be a mythical entity, a mere name that refers to nothing behind voluntary acts, but we still do distinguish between voluntary acts and involuntary acts. Is the distinction legitimate? How is it made?

Clearly, there seem to be differences between going downstairs to get the mail, falling down the stairs, and being dragged down the stairs by the police. In the first case I intentionally do what I want to do. In the second my act is involuntary, an accident. The third case may be no accident, but my descent is still involuntary. And we can see the need for distinguishing among various kinds of involuntary behavior: accidents, behavior influenced by the active constraint of others, or the beating of one's heart, which seems to be another kind of involuntary behavior. Among voluntary actions we may want to distinguish between those actions we do consciously, like getting the mail, and those we do unconsciously, like balancing a bike while riding. The latter is hardly involuntary like a heartbeat; it is a learned behavior, and during the process of learning is most certainly conscious. But once learned it becomes quite unconscious and thus a candidate for a different species of the voluntary.

Such proliferation of distinctions could, and indeed does, go on without limit. Without seeking any finality that qualifies any particular set or subset of distinctions between the voluntary and the involuntary, let us examine the kinds of distinctions swept aside by the claims of the determinist.

The determinist may choose to make one of several different possible claims. If he claims that *no* distinctions can be made between voluntary and involuntary actions, he is clearly wrong. We have just seen that some distinctions can be made. The question is, then, their legitimacy. If the ultimate court of appeals is ordinary linguistic usage, then the determinist is wrong unless he is making some particular claim about the *significance* of the distinctions. He may, for example, be saying something analogous to the claim that you can distinguish among fishes, horses, flies, snakes, and people, but in the end they're all animals. In other words, the determinist may admit that there are grounds for making certain distinctions, but he will claim that in the end all behavior is *caused*. There are no violations of the laws of causality. Your thought processes may be quite different when you go down to get the mail and when you are dragged down the stairs by the police, but *finally*, says the determinist, all your actions can be explained through an analysis of interlocking, never-ending chains of cause and effect.

At this point the determinist has shifted the ground of the argument. He has moved from an analysis of the distinctions we find useful in our experience to an analysis of principles he claims to be operative beneath our experience. In short, he has shifted into metaphysics. Now I, for one, am not an enemy of metaphysics, the quest for those fundamental principles we can use to make sense of what we find around us. To disown metaphysics as many twentieth-century philosophers have done is to discount the possibility that our ordinary way of looking at things could be simply wrong. The metaphysician will not take ordinary linguistic usage as the ultimate court of appeals. Like Aristotle, the metaphysician will go to the trough of ordinary language to make sure he is not simply engaging in idle fancy. But he will not discount the possibility that unanimity of usage might still hide falsehood. After all, there was a time when everyone thought the earth was flat. Was that theory adequately verified, given the currency of expressions like, "I would go to the edge of the earth for you"?

No, the metaphysician may be right with some of his claims. But he may be wrong, too. If he claims infallibility he may be mad, or the truth he is espousing may be a disguised tautology—that is, a less obvious case of such a statement as "All bachelors are unmarried." The truth of a tautology is guaranteed by the fact that the predicate is contained in the definition of the subject. Thus, if the determinist makes the statement, "All behavior is subject to causal laws," the statement may be true but empty if he defines behavior as motion in space and time. Signing one's name is a motion in space and time, and as such it is subject to causal laws. But what is the determinist to say about the differences between writing one's name for the fun of it and signing a contract? If behavior is defined not merely in terms of motion in space and time but as action in the world of persons and legal statutes, then his claim that all behavior is subject to causal laws becomes somewhat vacuous. The law of gravity is of much less interest than the law of torts where signing a contract is concerned.

A further claim that the determinist might make is that all action is in principle predictable. This is a curious claim for at least two reasons. First, the phrase "in principle": what does it mean? If it means that the determinist thinks he *will* be able to find a way around any obstacle to prediction, then his claim is a mere hope and deserves no more attention than we accord other yet-to-be-realized hopes. But second, even if someone could predict a person's future behavior, were that behavior anything like the person's past behavior it would include all sorts of distinctions between voluntary and involuntary acts. So the determinist might find his claim of predictability entailing a prediction of freedom—not exactly what he set out to prove.

If this second claim of determinism—predictability in principle—sounds a bit too peculiar to be consumed without further question, then the following piece by St. Augustine may increase its digestibility. Augustine knew nothing of nineteenth-century physicalistic determinism, but freedom was an issue for him as he struggled with the problem of predestination in God's omniscience. As Ryle noted, "the bogy of Predestination reappeared as the bogy of determinism." Such reappearances of philosophical problems is an important feature of the history of philosophy. The fact that the same problems keep coming up in different guises speaks for the need to identify a guise as a guise and at the same time appreciate the thinking of earlier philosophers who dealt with our problems in their earlier incarnations.

ST. AUGUSTINE *(354–430 A.D.)*

In the following passage from On Free Will, *Augustine establishes an argument not too different from the one traced above. Just as modern courts of law distinguish between the voluntary and the involuntary in order to attribute responsibility for punishable acts, so Augustine begins by discussing "culpable" acts—that is, acts that are blameworthy in the sight of God. The initial problem concerns God's omnipotence: isn't God responsible for the evil done? The modern lawyer might argue that society in its omnipotence is responsible for the action of the criminal. In both cases a fairly subtle argument is required to identify properly the agent of an action. Next, the argument moves to "predictability in principle" on the basis of God's omniscience. Here the modern correlate is the physical determinist. Consider whether it is significant that people have always been able to find some sense in which they seemed to be involuntarily determined, whether by God, physical causality, unconscious instincts, economic and social determinants, technology, or whatever. What if we are, in fact, determined in all these different ways? How does that reflect on the apparent bindingness of any one form of determinism?*

On Free Will

(i, 1)EVODIUS. It is sufficiently evident to me that free will is to be numbered among the good things, and, indeed, not among the least of our good things. We are, therefore, compelled to confess that it has been given us by God, and that he has rightly given it to us. But now, if you think a suitable time has come, I want to learn from you whence arises the movement by which the will itself turns from the unchangeable good, which is the common property of all, to its own interests or to the interests of others or to things beneath it, and so turns to mutable goods.

AUGUSTINE. Why must you know this?

EVODIUS. Because if free will is so given that it has that movement by nature, it turns of necessity to mutable goods; and no blame attaches where nature and necessity prevail.

AUGUSTINE. Do you like or dislike that movement?

EVODIUS. I dislike it.

AUGUSTINE. So you find fault with it?

EVODIUS. I do.

AUGUSTINE. Then you find fault with a movement of the mind though it is faultless.

EVODIUS. No, I do not. But I do not know whether there is any fault in abandoning the unchangeable good and turning towards the mutable goods.

AUGUSTINE. Then you are finding fault with something which you do not know.

EVODIUS. Don't insist on a verbal point. I said that I did not know whether there was any fault, but I meant to be understood really as having no doubt about it. Certainly I said I do not know, but obviously I was being ironical in suggesting that there could be any doubt about so clear a matter.

AUGUSTINE.   Just consider what is that truth you hold to be so certain that it has caused you so soon to forget what you said a moment ago. If that movement of the will exists by nature or necessity, it is in no way culpable. And yet you are so firmly convinced that it is culpable that you think fit to wax ironical about hesitation over a matter so certain. Why did you think it right to affirm, or at least to say with some hesitation, what you yourself show to be obviously false? You said: "If free will has been given in such fashion that it has that movement by nature, then it turns to mutable things of necessity and, no fault can be found where nature and necessity rule." But you ought to have had no doubt that it was not given in that fashion, since you do not doubt that that movement is culpable.

EVODIUS.   I said that the movement is culpable, and that therefore it displeases me, and that I cannot doubt that it is reprehensible. But I hold that a soul which is thereby drawn from the unchangeable good to mutable goods is not to be blamed if its nature is such that it is so moved by necessity.

(2) AUGUSTINE.   To whom belongs the movement which you admit is blameworthy?

EVODIUS.   I see that it is in the soul, but to whom it belongs I know not.

AUGUSTINE.   You do not deny that the soul is moved by that motion?

EVODIUS.   No.

AUGUSTINE.   Do you then deny that the motion by which a stone is moved is the motion of the stone? I don't mean the motion that we give to it, or that is given to it by some other force, when it is thrown upwards, but that by which of its own accord it falls back to earth.

EVODIUS.   I do not deny that the motion you refer to, by which it turns and falls downward, is the motion of the stone, but it is its natural motion. If the motion of the soul is like that, it too is natural, and it cannot rightly be blamed for a motion that is natural. Even if it moves to its own destruction, it is compelled by the necessity of its own nature. Moreover because we have no doubt that the soul's motion is culpable we must absolutely deny that it is natural, and therefore not like the motion of the stone, which is natural motion.

AUGUSTINE.   Did we achieve anything in our two previous discussions?

EVODIUS.   I am sure we did.

AUGUSTINE.   No doubt you remember that in the first discussion we discovered that the mind can become the slave of lust only by its own will. No superior thing and no equal thing compels it to such dishonour, because that would be unjust. And no inferior thing has the power. It remains that that must be the mind's own motion when it turns its will away from enjoyment of the Creator to enjoyment of the creature. If that motion is accounted blameworthy—and you thought anyone who doubted that deserved to be treated ironically—it is not natural but voluntary. It is like the motion of the falling stone, in so far as it is a motion of the soul as the former is the motion of the stone. But it is dissimilar in this, that it is not in the power of a stone to arrest its downward motion, while if the soul is not willing it cannot be moved to abandon what is higher and to love what is lower. Thus the stone's motion is natural, the soul's voluntary. Hence anyone who says that a stone sins when it is carried downwards by its own weight is, I will not say more senseless than the stone but, completely mad. But we charge the soul with sin when we show that it has abandoned the higher things and prefers to enjoy lower things. What need is there, therefore, to seek the origin of the movement whereby the will turns from the unchangeable to the changeable good? We acknowledge that it is a movement of the soul, that it is voluntary and therefore culpable. And all useful learning in this matter has its object and value in teaching us to condemn and restrain that movement, and to convert our wills from falling into temporal delights to the enjoyment of the eternal good.

(3) EVODIUS.   I see, and in a sense grasp that what you say is true. There is nothing that I feel more certainly and more personally than that I have a will, and that it moves me to enjoy this or that. I know nothing I could call my own if the will by which I will "yea" or "nay" is not my own. If I use it to do evil, to whom is the evil to be attributed if not to myself? Since a good God has made me, and I can do nothing right except by willing, it is clearly evident that it was to this end that the will has been given to me by God who is good. Moreover, unless the movement of the will towards this or that object is voluntary and within our power, a man would not be praiseworthy when he turns to the higher objects nor blameworthy when he turns to lower objects, using his will like a hinge. There would be no use at all in warning him to pay no attention to temporal things and to will to obtain the eternal things, or to will to live aright and to be unwilling to live an evil life. But whoever thinks that man is not to be so warned ought to be cut off from membership in the human race.

(ii, 4) That being so, I have a deep desire to know how it can be that God knows all things beforehand and that, nevertheless, we do not sin by necessity. Whoever says that anything can happen otherwise than as God has foreknown it, is attempting to destroy the divine foreknowledge with the most insensate impiety. If God foreknew that the first man would sin—and that anyone must concede who acknowledges with me that God has foreknowledge of all future events—I do not say that God did not make him, for he made him good, nor that the sin of the creature whom he made good could be prejudicial to God. On the contrary, God showed his goodness in making man, his justice in punishing his sin, and his mercy in delivering him. I do not say, therefore, that God did not make man. But this I say. Since God foreknew that man would sin, that which God foreknew must necessarily come to pass. How then is the will free when there is apparently this unavoidable necessity?

(5) AUGUSTINE.   You have knocked vigorously. May God in his mercy grant us his presence and open the door to those who knock. But I verily believe that the vast majority of men are troubled by that question for no other reason than that they do no ask it in a pious fashion. They are swifter to make excuses for their sins than to make confession of them. Some are glad to hold the opinion that there is no divine providence presiding over human affairs. They commit themselves, body and soul, to fortuitous circumstances, and deliver themselves to be carried about and tormented by lusts. They deny that there is any divine judgment, and deceive human judges when they are accused. They imagine that they are driven on by the favour of fortune. In sculpture or painting they are wont to represent Fortune as blind, either because they are better than the goddess by whom they think they are

ruled, or because they confess that in their sentiments they are afflicted with that same blindness. In the case of such people it is not absurd to admit that they do everything by chance, seeing that they stumble in all that they do. But against this opinion, so full of foolish and senseless error, we have, I think, sufficiently spoken in our second disputation. Others do not venture to deny that the providence of God presides over human affairs, but they would rather indulge in the wicked error of believing that providence is weak or unjust or evil than confess their sins with suppliant piety. If all these would suffer themselves to be persuaded to believe that the goodness, justice and power of God are greater far, and far superior to any thought they can have of goodness, justice or might, if they would but take thought to themselves, they would know that they owe thanks to God, even if he had willed them to be somewhat lower in the scale of being than they actually are, and with all that is within them they would exclaim with the Psalmist: "I have spoken: Lord have mercy upon me; heal my soul for I have sinned against thee" (Ps. 41:5). So by stages the divine mercy would bring them to wisdom. They would be neither inflated by what they discover, nor rebellious when they fail to find the truth; by learning they would become better prepared to see the truth, and by recognizing their ignorance they would become more patient in seeking it. I am quite sure that these are your views too. Now first answer a few questions I am going to put to you, and you will see how easily I can find a solution to your tremendous problem.

(iii, 6) Your trouble is this. You wonder how it can be that these two propositions are not contradictory and incompatible, namely that God has fore-knowledge of all future events, and that we sin voluntarily and not by necessity. For if, you say, God foreknows that a man will sin, he must necessarily sin. But if there is necessity there is no voluntary choice in sinning, but rather fixed and unavoidable necessity. You are afraid that by that reasoning the conclusion may be reached either that God's foreknowledge of all future events must be impiously denied, or, it that cannot be denied, that sin is committed not voluntarily but by necessity. Isn't that your difficulty?

EVODIUS.   Exactly that.

AUGUSTINE.   You think, therefore, that all things of which God has fore-knowledge happen by necessity and not voluntarily.

EVODIUS.   Yes. Absolutely.

AUGUSTINE.   Try an experiment, and examine yourself a little, and tell me what kind of will you are going to have to-morrow. Will you want to sin or to do right?

EVODIUS.   I do not know.

AUGUSTINE.   Do you think God also does not know?

EVODIUS.   I could in no wise think that.

AUGUSTINE.   If God knows what you are going to will to-morrow, and foresees what all men are going to will in the future, not only those who are at present alive but all who will ever be, much more will he foresee what he is going to do with the just and the impious?

EVODIUS.   Certainly if I say that God has foreknowledge of my deeds, I should say with even greater confidence that he has foreknowledge of his own acts, and foresees with complete certainty what he is going to do.

AUGUSTINE.   Don't you see that you will have to be careful lest someone say to you that, if all things of which God has foreknowledge are done by necessity and not voluntarily, his own future acts will be done not voluntarily but by necessity?

EVODIUS.   When I said that all future events of which God has foreknowledge happen by necessity, I was having regard only to things which happen in God himself. Indeed, in God nothing happens. Everything is eternal.

AUGUSTINE.   God, then, is not active within his creation?

EVODIUS.   He determined once for all how the order of the universe he created was to go on, and he never changes his mind.

AUGUSTINE.   Does he never make anyone happy?

EVODIUS.   Indeed he does.

AUGUSTINE.   He does it precisely at the time when the man in question actually becomes happy.

EVODIUS.   That is so.

AUGUSTINE.   If, then, for example, you yourself are happy one year from now, you will be made happy at that time.

EVODIUS.   Exactly.

AUGUSTINE.   God knows to-day what he is going to do a year hence?

EVODIUS.   He eternally had that foreknowledge, but I agree that he has it now, if indeed it is to happen so.

(7) AUGUSTINE.   Now tell me, are you not God's creature? And will not your becoming happy take place within your experience?

EVODIUS.   Certainly I am God's creature, and if I become happy it will be within my experience.

AUGUSTINE.   If God, then, makes you happy, your happiness will come by necessity and not by the exercise of your will?

EVODIUS.   God's will is my necessity.

AUGUSTINE.   Will you then be happy against your will?

EVODIUS.   If I had the power to be happy, I should be so at once. For I wish to be happy but am not, because not I but God makes me happy.

AUGUSTINE.   The truth simply cries out against you. You could not imagine that "having in our power" means anything else than "being able to do what we will." Therefore there is nothing so much in our power as is the will itself. For as soon as we will [*volumus*] immediately will [*voluntas*] is there. We can say rightly that we do not grow old voluntarily but necessarily, or that we do not die voluntarily but from necessity, and so with other similar things. But who but a raving fool would say that it is not voluntarily that we will? Therefore though God knows how we are going to will in the future, it is not proved that we do not voluntarily will anything. When you said that you did not make yourself happy, you said it as if I had denied it. What I say is that when you become happy in the future it will take place not against your will but in accordance with your willing. Therefore, though God has foreknowledge of your happiness in the future, and though nothing can happen otherwise than as he has foreknown it (for that would mean there is no foreknowledge) we are not thereby compelled to think that you will not be happy voluntarily. That would be absurd and far from true. God's foreknowledge, which is even to-day quite certain that you are to be happy at a future date, does not rob you of your will to happiness when you actually attain happiness. Similarly if ever in the future you have a culpable will, it will be none the less your will because God had foreknowledge of it.

(8) Observe, pray, how blind are those who say that if God has foreknowledge of what I am going to will, since nothing can happen otherwise than as he has foreknown it, therefore I must necessarily will what he has foreknown. If so, it must be admitted that I will, not voluntarily but from necessity. Strange folly! Is there, then, no difference between things that happen according to God's fore-knowledge where there is no intervention of man's will at all, and things that happen because of a will of which he has foreknowledge? I omit the equally monstrous assertion of the man I mentioned a moment ago, who says I must necessarily so will. By assuming necessity he strives to do away with will alto-gether. If I must necessarily will, why need I speak of willing at all? But if he puts it in another way, and says that, because he must necessarily so will, his will is not in his own power, he can be countered by the answer you gave me when I asked whether you could become happy against your will. You replied that you would be happy now if the matter were in your power, for you willed to be happy but could not achieve it. And I added that the truth cries out against you; for we cannot say we do not have the power unless we do not have what we will. If we do not have the will, we may think we will but in fact we do not. If we cannot will without willing, those who will have will, and all that is in our power we have by willing. Our will would not be will unless it were in our power. Because it is in our power, it is free. We have nothing that is free which is not in our power, and if we have something it cannot be nothing. Hence it is not necessary to deny that God has foreknowledge of all things, while at the same time our wills are our own. God has foreknowledge of our will, so that of which he has foreknowledge must come to pass. In other words, we shall exercise our wills in the future because he has foreknowledge that we shall do so; and there can be no will or voluntary action unless it be in our power. Hence God has also foreknowledge of our power to will. My power is not taken from me by God's foreknowledge. Indeed I shall be more certainly in possession of my power because he whose foreknowledge is never mistaken, foreknows that I shall have the power.

EVODIUS.   Now I no longer deny that whatever God has foreknown must necessarily come to pass, nor that he has foreknowledge of our sins, but in such a way that our wills remain free and within our power.

(iv, 9) AUGUSTINE.   What further difficulty do you have? Perhaps you have forgotten what we established in our first disputation, and now wish to deny that we sin voluntarily and under no compulsion from anything superior, inferior or equal to us.

EVODIUS.   I do not venture to deny that at all. But I must confess I do not yet see how God's foreknowledge of our sins and our freedom of will in sinning can be other than mutually contradictory. We must confess that God is just and knows all things beforehand. But I should like to know with what justice he punishes sins which must necessarily be committed; or how they are not necessarily committed when he knows that they will be committed; or how the Creator is to escape having imputed to him anything that happens necessarily in his creature.

(10) AUGUSTINE. Why do you think our free will is opposed to God's foreknowledge? Is it because it is foreknowledge simply, or because it is God's foreknowledge?

EVODIUS. In the main because it is God's foreknowledge.

AUGUSTINE. If you knew in advance that such and such a man would sin, there would be no necessity for him to sin.

EVODIUS. Indeed there would, for I should have no real foreknowledge unless I knew for certain what was going to happen.

AUGUSTINE. So it is foreknowledge generally and not God's foreknowledge specially that causes the events foreknown to happen by necessity? There would be no such thing as foreknowledge unless there was certain foreknowledge.

EVODIUS. I agree. But why these questions?

AUGUSTINE. Unless I am mistaken, you would not directly compel the man to sin, though you knew beforehand that he was going to sin. Nor does your prescience in itself compel him to sin even though he was certainly going to sin, as we must assume if you have real prescience. So there is no contradiction here. Simply you know beforehand what another is going to do with his own will. Similarly God compels no man to sin, though he sees beforehand those who are going to sin by their own will.

(11) Why then should he not justly punish sins which, though he had foreknowledge of them, he did not compel the sinner to commit? Just as you apply no compulsion to past events by having them in your memory, so God by his foreknowledge does not use compulsion in the case of future events. Just as you remember your past actions, though all that you remember were not actions of your own, so God has foreknowledge of all his own actions, but is not the agent of all that he foreknows. Of evil actions he is not the agent but the just punisher. From this you may understand with what justice God punishes sins, for he has no responsibility for the future actions of men though he knows them beforehand. If he ought not to award punishment to sinners because he knew beforehand that they would sin, he ought not to reward the righteous, because he knew equally that they would be righteous. Let us confess that it belongs to his foreknowledge to allow no future event to escape his knowledge, and that it belongs to his justice to see that no sin goes unpunished by his judgment. For sin is committed voluntarily and not by any compulsion from his foreknowledge.

JEAN-PAUL SARTRE *(1905–1980)*

Jean-Paul Sartre carries the argument for freedom even further than Augustine. Augustine said, "we charge the soul with sin when we show that it has abandoned the higher things and prefers to enjoy the lower things." The soul's freedom extends to choosing between what Christian doctrine fixes as higher and lower. Sartre argues that the denominations of higher and lower are not fixed. Our freedom extends to the determination and creation of 'higher values.'

Sartre's radicalization of the argument for freedom extends so far that we begin to question whether Evodius was right when he said, "free will is to be numbered among the good things." Freedom becomes an almost impossible burden. Freedom is anguished, says Sartre, so difficult to bear that we are inclined to fall into what he calls "bad faith." We are inclined to view ourselves as things, as not free, because it is easier that way; we no longer bear the burden of responsibility for our acts, or for determining the values by which we judge our acts. Note the difference between these two responsibilities. Augustine affirmed the first, but anguish follows from the combination of the first with the second. It is easier to accept only the first responsibility, and then acknowledge guilt before a table of values we are not responsible for. To accept the burden of responsibility for both the act and the criteria of judgment is to accept the role of a creator of values. And that is hard. To take on the role of the creator is to end all possibility of scapegoating. You cannot say, "Oh, it was the devil in me." Nor can you even take credit for doing the "right thing," where "right" is determined by some other. As Sartre says, you cannot justify your actions. All you can do is accept the fact that whatever happens, you did it, even if what you did was try to get out of a responsibility for your acts and values.

Here it is worth introducing another theme that reappears in later discussions. One easy way to misread Sartre is to interpret him as espousing a shallow form of subjective relativism. That is, one can jump to the simple conclusion, "Whatever I do is all right because there are no objective values, only subjective tastes. I like what I like and you like what you like and there's no point in discussing values because they're all relative." True, Sartre is denying the objective givenness of absolute values, but between the security of objective absolutes and the simplicity of subjective relativism there lies a position we can call objective relativism: roughly put, one can deny objective values but one cannot deny certain objective facts, and the process of valuation is relative to both the personal subject and the objective facts. We are creators, but we are not creators in a void. To ignore the nature and being of the materials we have to work with is to fore-doom the product of creation—namely, ourselves.

Freedom and Self-creation

Value derives its being from its exigency and not its exigency from its being. It does not deliver itself to a contemplative intuition which would apprehend it as *being* value and thereby would remove from it its right over my freedom. On the contrary, it can be revealed only to an active freedom which makes it exist as value by the sole fact of recognizing it as such. It follows that my freedom is the unique foundation of values and *nothing*, absolutely nothing, justifies me in adopting this or that particular value, this or that particular scale of values. As a being by whom values exist, I am unjustifiable. My freedom is anguished at being the foundation of values while itself without foundation. It is anguished in addition because values, due to the fact that they are essentially revealed to a freedom, cannot disclose themselves without being at the same time "put into question," for the possibility of overturning the scale of values appears complementarily as *my* possibility. It is anguish before values which is the recognition of the ideality of values.

Ordinarily, however, my attitude with respect to values is eminently reassuring. In fact I am engaged in a world of values. The anguished apperception of values as sustained in being by my freedom is a secondary and mediated phenomenon. The immediate is the world with its urgency; and in this world where I engage myself, my acts cause values to spring up like partridges. My indignation has given to me the negative value "baseness," my admiration has given the positive value "grandeur." Above all my obedience to a multitude of tabus, which is real, reveals these tabus to me as existing in fact. The bourgeois who call themselves "respectable citizens" do not become respectable as the result of contemplating moral values. Rather from the moment of their arising in the world they are thrown into a pattern of behavior the meaning of which is respectability. Thus respectability acquires a being; it is not put into question. Values are sown on my path as thousands of little real demands, like the signs which order us to keep off the grass.

Thus in what we shall call the world of the immediate, which delivers itself to our unreflective consciousness, we do not first appear to ourselves, to be thrown subsequently into enterprises. Our being is immediately "in situation"; that is, it arises in enterprises and knows itself first in so far as it is reflected in those enterprises. We discover ourselves then in a world peopled with demands, in the heart of projects "in the course of realization." I write. I am going to smoke. I have an appointment this evening with Pierre. I must not forget to reply to Simon. I do not have the right to conceal the truth any longer from Claude. All these trivial passive expectations of the real, all these commonplace, everyday values, derive their meaning from an original projection of myself which stands as my choice of myself in the world. But to be exact, this projection of myself toward an original possibility, which causes the existence of values, appeals, expectations, and in general a world, appear to me only beyond the world as the meaning and the abstract, logical signification of my enterprises. For the rest, there exist concretely alarm clocks, signboards, tax forms, policemen, so many guard rails against anguish. But as soon as the enterprise is held at a distance from me, as soon as I am referred to myself because I must await myself in the future, then I discover myself suddenly as the one who gives its meaning to the alarm clock, the one who by a signboard forbids himself to walk on a flower bed or on the lawn, the one from whom the boss's order borrows its urgency, the one who decides the interest of the book which he is writing, the one finally who makes the values exist in order to determine his action by their demands. I emerge alone and in anguish confronting the unique and orginal project which constitutes my being; all the barriers, all the guard rails collapse, nihilated by the consciousness of my freedom. I do not have nor can I have recourse to any value against the fact that it is I who sustain values in being. Nothing can ensure me against myself, cut off from the world and from my essence by this nothingness which I am. I have to realize the meaning of the world and of my essence; I make my decision concerning them—without justification and without excuse.

Anguish then is the reflective apprehension of freedom by itself. In this sense it is mediation, for although it is immediate consciousness of itself, it arises from the negation of the appeals of the world. It appears at the moment that I disengage myself from the world where I had been engaged—in order to apprehend myself as a consciousness which possesses a preontological comprehension of its essence and a pre-judicative sense of its possibilities. Anguish is opposed to the mind of the serious man who apprehends values in terms of the world and who resides in the reassuring, materialistic substantiation of values. In the serious mood I define myself in terms of the object by pushing aside *a priori* as impossible all enterprises in which I am not engaged at the moment; the meaning which my freedom has given to the world, I apprehend as coming from the world and constituting my obligations. In anguish I apprehend myself at once as totally free and as not being able to derive the meaning of the world except as coming from myself.

We should not however conclude that being brought on to the reflective plane and envisaging one's distant or immediate possibilities suffice to apprehend oneself in *pure* anguish. In each instance of reflection anguish is born as a structure of the reflective consciousness in so far as the latter considers consciousness as an object of reflection; but it still remains possible for me to maintain various types of conduct with respect to my own anguish—in particular, patterns of flight. Everything takes place, in fact, as if our essential and immediate behavior with respect to anguish is flight. Psychological determinism, before being a theoretical conception, is first an attitude of excuse, or if you prefer, the basis of all attitudes of excuse. It is reflective conduct with respect to anguish; it asserts that there are within us antagonistic forces whose type of existence is comparable to that of things. It attempts to fill the void which encircles us, to re-establish the links between past and present, between present and future. It provides us with a *nature* productive of our acts, and these very acts it makes transcendent; it assigns to them a foundation in something other than themselves by endowing them with an inertia and externality eminently reassuring because they constitute a permanent game of *excuses*. Psychological determinism denies that transcendence of human reality which makes it emerge in anguish beyond its own essence. At the same time by reducing us to *never being anything but what we are,* it reintroduces in us the absolute positivity of being-in-itself and thereby reinstates us at the heart of being.

But this determinism, a reflective defense against anguish, is not given as a reflective *intuition.* It avails nothing against the *evidence* of freedom; hence it is given as a faith to take refuge in, as the ideal end toward which we can flee to escape anguish. That is made evident on the philosophical plane by the fact that deterministic psychologists do not claim to found their thesis on the pure givens of introspection. They present it as a satisfying hypothesis, the value of which comes from the fact that it accounts for the facts—or as a necessary postulate for establishing all psychology. They admit the existence of an immediate consciousness of freedom, which their opponents hold up against them under the name of "proof by intuition of the inner sense." They merely focus the debate on the *value* of this inner revelation. Thus the intuition which causes us to apprehend ourselves as the original cause of our states and our acts has been discussed by nobody. It is within the reach of each of us to try to mediate anguish by rising above it and by *judging* it as an illusion due to the mistaken belief that we are the real causes of our acts. The problem which presents itself then is that of the degree of faith in this mediation. Is an anguish placed under judgment a disarmed anguish? Evidently not. However here a new phenomenon is born, a process of "distraction" in relation to anguish which, once again, supposes within it a nihilating power.

By itself determinism would not suffice to establish distraction since determinism is only a postulate or an hypothesis. This process of detachment is a more complete activity of flight which operates on the very level of reflection. It is first an attempt at distraction in relation to the possibles opposed to *my* possible. When I constitute myself as the comprehension of a possible as *my* possible, I must recognize its existence at the end of my project and apprehend it as myself, awaiting me down there in the future and separated from me by a nothingness. In this sense I apprehend myself as the original source of my possibility, and it is this which ordinarily we call the consciousness of freedom. It is this structure of consciousness and this alone that proponents of free-will have in mind when they speak of the intuition of the inner sense. But it happens that I force myself at the same time to *be distracted* from the constitution of other possibilities which contradict *my* possibility. In truth I can not avoid positing their existence by the same movement which generates the chosen possibility as mine. I cannot help constituting them as *living* possibilities; that is, *as having the possibility of becoming my possibilities.* But I force myself to see them as endowed with a transcendent, purely logical being, in short, as things. If on the reflective plane I envisage the possibility of writing this book as *my* possibility, then between this possibility and my consciousness I cause a nothingness of being to arise which constitutes the writing of the book as a possibility and which I apprehend precisely in the permanent possibility that the possibility of not writing the book is *my* possibility. But I attempt to place myself on the other side of the possibility of not writing it as I might do with respect to an observable object, and I let myself be penetrated with what I wish to see there; I try to apprehend the possibility of not writing as needing to be mentioned merely as a reminder, as not concerning me. It must be an external possibility in relation to me, like movement in relation to the motionless billiard ball. If I could succeed in this, the possibilities hostile to *my* possibility would be constituted as logical entities and would lose their effectiveness. They would no longer be threatening since they would be "outsiders," since they would surround my possible as purely *conceivable* eventualities; that is, fundamentally, conceivable *by* another or as *possibles of another who might find himself in the same situation.* They would belong to the objective situation as a transcendent structure, or if you prefer (to utilize Heidegger's terminology)—*I* shall write this book but *someone* could also not write it. Thus I should hide from myself the fact that the possibles are *myself* and that they are immanent conditions of the possibility of my possible. They would preserve just enough being to preserve for my possible its character as gratuitous, as a free possibility for a free being, but they would be disarmed of their threatening character. They would not *interest* me; the chosen possible would appear—due to its selection—as my only concrete possible, and consequently the nothingness which separates me from it and which actually confers on it its possibility would collapse.

But flight before anguish is not only an effort at distraction before the future; it attempts also to disarm the past of its threat. What I attempt to flee here is my very transcendence in so far as it sustains and surpasses my essence. I assert that I *am* my essence in the mode of being of the in-itself. At the same time I always refuse to consider that essence as being historically constituted and as implying my action as a circle implies its properties. I apprehend it, or at least I try to apprehend it as the original beginning of my possible, and I do not admit at all that it has in itself a beginning. I assert then that an act is free when it exactly reflects my essence. However this freedom which would disturb me if it were freedom before myself, I attempt to bring back to the heart of my essence—i.e., of my self. It is a matter of envisaging the self as a little God which inhabits me and which possesses my freedom as a metaphysical virtue. It would be no longer my being which would be free *qua* [as] being but my Self which would be free in the heart of my consciousness. It is a fiction eminently reassuring since freedom has been driven down into the heart of an opaque being; to the extent that my essence is not translucency, that it is transcendent in immanence, freedom would become one of its properties. In short, it is a matter of apprehending my freedom in my self as the freedom of another. We see the principal themes of this fiction: My self becomes the origin of its acts as the other of his, by virtue of a personality already constituted. To be sure, he (the self) lives and transforms himself; we will admit even that each of his acts can contribute to transforming him. But these harmonious, continued transformations are conceived on a biological order. They resemble those which I can establish in my friend Pierre when I see him after a separation. Bergson expressly satisfied these demands for reassurance when he conceived his theory of the profound self which endures and organizes itself, which is constantly contemporary with the consciousness which I have of it and which can not be surpassed by consciousness, which is found at the origin of my acts not as a cataclysmic power but as a father begets his children, in such a way that the act without following from the essence as a strict consequence, without even being foreseeable, enters into a reassuring relation with it, a family resemblance. The act goes farther than the self but along the same road; it preserves, to be sure, a certain irreducibility, but we recognize ourselves in it, and we find ourselves in it as a father can recognize himself and find himself in the son who continues his work. Thus by a projection of freedom—which we apprehend in ourselves—into a psychic object which is the self, Bergson has contributed to disguise our anguish, but it is at the expense of consciousness itself. What he has established and described in this manner is not our freedom as it appears to itself; *it is the freedom of the Other.*

Such then is the totality of processes by which we try to hide anguish from ourselves; we apprehend our particular possible by avoiding considering all other possibles, which we make the possibles of an undifferentiated Other. The chosen possible we do not wish to see as sustained in being by a pure nihilating freedom, and so we attempt to apprehend it as engendered by an object already constituted, which is no other than our self, envisaged and described as if it were another person. We should like to preserve from the original intuition what it reveals to us as our independence and our responsibility but we tone down all the original nihilation in it; moreover we are always ready to take refuge in a belief in determinism if this freedom weighs upon us or if we need an excuse. Thus we flee from anguish by attempting to apprehend ourselves from without as an Other or as *a thing*. What we are accustomed to call a revelation of the inner sense or an original intuition of our freedom contains nothing original; it is an already constructed process, expressly designed to hide from ourselves anguish, the veritable "immediate given" of our freedom.

Do these various constructions succeed in stifling or hiding our anguish? It is certain that we can not overcome anguish, for we *are* anguish. As for veiling it, aside from the fact that the very nature of consciousness and its translucency forbid us to take the expression literally, we must note the particular type of behavior which it indicates. We can hide an external object because it exists independently of us. For the same reason we can turn our look or our attention away from it—that is, very simply, fix our eyes on some other object; henceforth each reality—mine and that of the object—resumes its own life, and the accidental relation which united consciousness to the thing disappears without thereby altering either existence. But if I *am* what I wish to veil, the question takes on quite another aspect. I can in fact wish "not to see" a certain aspect of my being only if I am aquainted with the aspect which I do not wish to see. This means that in my being I must indicate this aspect in order to be able to turn myself away from it; better yet, I must think of it constantly in order to take care not to think of it. In this connection it must be understood not only that I must of necessity perpetually carry within me what I wish to flee but also that I must aim at the object of my flight in order to flee it. This means that anguish, the intentional aim of anguish, and a flight from anguish toward reassuring myths must all be given in the unity of the same consciousness. In a word, I flee in order not to know, but I can not avoid knowing that I am fleeing; and the flight from anguish is only a mode of becoming conscious of anguish. Thus anguish, properly speaking, can be neither hidden nor avoided.

Yet to flee anguish and to be anguish can not be exactly the same thing. If I am my anguish in order to flee it, that presupposes that I can decenter myself in relation to what I am, that I can be anguish in the form of "not-being it," that I can dispose of a nihilating power at the heart of anguish itself. This nihilating power nihilates anguish in so far as I flee it and nihilates itself in so far as *I am anguish in order to flee it*. This attitude is what we call *bad faith*. There is then no question of expelling anguish from consciousness nor of constituting it in an unconscious psychic phenomenon; very simply I can make myself guilty of bad faith while apprehending the anguish which I am, and this bad faith, intended to fill up the nothingness which I *am* in my relation to myself, precisely implies the nothingness which it suppresses. . . .

. . . We should examine more closely the patterns of bad faith and attempt a description of them. This description will permit us perhaps to fix more exactly the conditions for the possibility of bad faith; that is, to reply to the question we raised at the outset: "What must be the being of man if he is to be capable of bad faith?"

Take the example of a woman who has consented to go out with a particular man for the first time. She knows very well the intentions which the man who is speaking to her cherishes regarding her. She knows also that it will be necessary sooner or later for her to make a decision. But she does not want to realize the urgency; she concerns herself only with what is respectful and discreet in the attitude of her companion. She does not apprehend this conduct as an attempt to achieve what we call "the first approach": that is, she does not want to see possibilities of temporal development which his conduct presents. She restricts this behavior to what is in the present; she does not wish to read in the phrases which he addresses to her anything other than their explicit meaning. If he says to her, "I find you so attractive!" she disarms this phrase of its sexual background; she attaches to the conversation and to the behavior of the speaker, the immediate meanings, which she imagines as objective qualities. The man who is speaking to her appears to her sincere and respectful as the table is round or square, as the wall coloring is blue or gray. The qualities thus attached to the person she is listening to are in this way fixed in a permanence like that of things, which is no other than the projection of the strict present of the qualities into the temporal flux. This is because she does not quite know what she wants. She is profoundly aware of the desire which she inspires, but the desire cruel and naked would humiliate and horrify her. Yet she would find no charm in a respect which would be only respect. In order to satisfy her, there must be a feeling which is addressed wholly to her *personality*—i.e., to her full freedom—and which would be a recognition of her freedom. But at the same time this feeling must be wholly desire; that is, it must address itself to her body as object. This time then she refuses to apprehend the desire for what it is; she does not even give it a name; she recognizes it only to the extent that it transcends itself toward admiration, esteem, respect and that it is wholly absorbed in the more refined forms which it produces, to the extent of no longer figuring anymore as a sort of warmth and density. But then suppose he takes her hand. This act of her companion risks changing the situation by calling for an immediate decision. To leave the hand there is to consent in herself to flirt, to engage herself. To withdraw it is to break the troubled and unstable harmony which gives the hour its charm. The aim is to postpone the moment of decision as long as possible. We know what happens next; the young woman leaves her hand there, but she *does not notice* that she is leaving it. She does not notice because it happens by chance that she is at this moment all intellect. She draws her companion up to the most lofty regions of sentimental speculation; she speaks of Life, of her life, she shows herself in her essential aspect—a personality, a consciousness. And during this time the divorce of the body from the soul is accomplished; the hand rests inert between the warm hands of her companion—neither consenting nor resisting—a thing.

We shall say that this woman is in bad faith. but we see immediately that she uses various procedures in order to maintain herself in this bad faith. She has disarmed the actions of her companion by reducing them to being only what they are....

...We have seen also the use which our young lady made of our being-in-the-midst-of-the-world—i.e., of our inert presence as a passive object among other objects—in order to relieve herself suddenly from the functions of her being-in-the-world—that is, from the being which causes there to be a world by projecting itself beyond the world toward its own possibilities. Let us note finally the confusing syntheses which play on the nihilating ambiguity of these temporal ekstases, affirming at once that I am what I have been (the man who deliberately *arrests himself* at one period in his life and refuses to take into consideration the later changes) and that I am not what I have been (the man who in the face of reproaches or rancor dissociates himself from his past by insisting on his freedom and on his perpetual re-creation). In all these concepts, which have only a transitive role in the reasoning and which are eliminated from the conclusion, (like hypochondriacs in the calculations of physicians), we find again the same structure. We have to deal with human reality as a being which is what it is not and which is not what it is.

transition: the self's being as a process of becoming

Descartes identifies man as a thinking thing, but Ryle cautions against locating the thinker as a ghost inside a machine. He gives us reasons to reject the hypothesis that "minds are to be described in terms drawn from the categories of mechanism." His argument introduces the problem of free will. In their efforts to articulate man's freedom, Augustine and Sartre show us a picture of man as a process in time. Sartre's description takes us beyond the categories of mechanism. A refrigerator is a refrigerator, but "we have to deal with human reality as a being which is what it is not and which is not what it is." Sartre's paradoxical plunge into nonmechanistic categories threatens to leave us in confusion. What kind of being is he talking about?

If there is any such thing as a self, its kind of being is not the kind of being we are used to dealing with when we talk about the being of physical entities in space and time. This is not to say that the self is a nonphysical, immaterial thing. The self, as is later argued, is eminently physical. The point is rather to imagine a way of being that is different from the way many physical things are.

Many things exist in such a way that their properties are never separated from each other. Even though the properties of Descartes' piece of wax may change when it is held near the heat, the color is always found where the shape is, and the smell and taste go together as well. Consequently, Descartes is led to suppose that there is something *in which* all these properties inhere, something that accounts for the substantiality, the unity and togetherness of the various properties. Extension is his answer.

Ryle, however, points to the category-mistake involved in immediately assuming that everything is like the piece of wax in that it can be located in one extension. The university is nonetheless existent even though it cannot be located as its separate buildings can. Ryle's example of a category-mistake pertains to the existence of things in space. Just because a thing cannot be located in one continuous portion of space, it does not follow that the thing does not exist. Nor does it follow that it is nonspatial and mystical. Similarly, we make category-mistakes with respect to time. Just because something cannot be located in a specific stretch of time, it does not follow that it does not exist, nor does it follow that it is mystically nontemporal.

The problem with examples like the piece of wax, or chairs, or tables, is not that they are spatiotemporal, but rather that they present us with a paradigm of existence in which continuity and simplicity are the criteria for existence. If the space occupied by the properties of the wax becomes discontinuous, then we say there are two pieces of wax and not one. There are many other kinds of examples. The university shows the being of something discontinuous in space. A game is an example that can show discontinuity in time. If you break off playing a game of Monopoly and return to it the next day, you return to the same game. You have one game, not two. Or you could end one game and start another during a continuous stretch of time. Try to think of other examples.

In any case, the point is that the self may be a kind of process rather than a complete and underlying continuous thing. The following two essays reflect on the nature of that process.

DAVID HUME *(1711–1776)*

The name David Hume is inseparable from the school known as British Empiricism. Following John Locke (1632–1714) and Bishop Berkeley (1685–1753), Hume developed a philosophy whose main points stand in almost diametrical opposition to the philosophy of the Continental rationalists Descartes, Leibniz, and Spinoza (1632–1677). Where the rationalists founded knowledge on innate ideas and the functions of understanding, the empiricists denied the existence of innate ideas and trusted rather to the evidence of the senses. Where Leibniz sees perceptions as confused ideas, Hume sees complex ideas as combinations of simple sensations. Where the rationalists see the world as a vast pattern of necessary connections, all similar in kind from the truths of mathematics down to the tiniest details of historical fact, the empiricists distinguish sharply between the logical necessity of truths of reason and the empirical contingency of truths of fact. It was Hume above all who attacked the rationalist idea that causal connections exhibit the same necessity found in logic or mathematics.

In the following selection from The Treatise of Human Nature *Hume attacks the concept of identity as it was developed by Descartes, among others. Compare Hume's analysis with Descartes'* Meditations *concerning the differences between rationalists and empiricists. And most important, compare Hume's analysis with your own meditations. Try to follow his directions for introspection just as you followed Descartes' method of doubt. Hume reports that he never finds his self on his inner quest, but only bundles of perceptions connected by relations of resemblance, contiguity, or causation. Those perceptions, he argues, are not connected by any underlying identity, and our tendency to import some substratum of identity is a mistaken attempt to account for the felt continuity of our experience. Sometimes, of course, our experience does not feel terribly continuous. Sometimes we experience an identity crisis, as the psychologist Erik Erikson puts it. We come to doubt just who it is that we are. How would you relate Hume's discussion of self-identity to the experience of an identity crisis?*

On Self-identity

There are some philosophers, who imagine we are every moment intimately conscious of what we call our *self;* that we feel its existence and its continuance in existence; and are certain, beyond the evidence of a demonstration, both of its perfect identity and simplicity. The strongest sensation, the most violent passion, say they, instead of distracting us from this view, only fix it the more intensely, and make us consider their influence on *self* either by their pain or pleasure. To attempt a farther proof of this were to weaken its evidence; since no proof can be derived from any fact, of which we are so intimately conscious; nor is there any thing, of which we can be certain, if we doubt of this.

Unluckily all these positive assertions are contrary to that very experience, which is pleaded for them, nor have we any idea of *self*, after the manner it is here explained. For from what impression could this idea be derived? This question 'tis impossible to answer without a manifest contradiction and absurdity; and yet 'tis a question, which must necessarily be answered, if we would have the idea of self pass for clear and intelligible. It must be some one impression, that gives rise to every real idea. But self or person is not any one impression, but that to which our several impressions and ideas are supposed to have a reference. If any impression gives rise to the idea of self, that impression must continue invariably the same, through the whole course of our lives; since self is supposed to exist after that manner. But there is no impression constant and invariable. Pain and pleasure, grief and joy, passions and sensations succeed each other, and never all exist at the same time. It cannot therefore be from any of these impressions, or from any other, that the idea of self is derived; and consequently there is no such idea.

But farther, what must become of all our particular perceptions upon this hypothesis? All these are different, and distinguishable, and separable from each other, and may be separately considered, and may exist separately, and have no need of any thing to support their existence. After what manner therefore do they belong to self; and how are they connected with it? For my part, when I enter most intimately into what I call *myself*, I always stumble on some particular perception or other, of heat or cold, light or shade, love or hatred, pain or pleasure. I never can catch *myself* at any time without a perception, and never can observe any thing but the perception. When my perceptions are removed for any time, as by sound sleep; so long am I insensible of *myself*, and may truly be said not to exist. And were all my perceptions removed by death, and could I neither think, nor feel, nor see, nor love, nor hate after the dissolution of my body, I should be entirely annihilated, nor do I conceive what is farther requisite to make me a perfect nonentity. If any one upon serious and unprejudiced reflection, thinks he has a different notion of *himself*, I must confess I can reason no longer with him. All I can allow him is, that he may be in the right as well as I, and that we are essentially different in this particular. He may, perhaps, perceive something simple and continued, which he calls *himself*; though I am certain there is no such principle in me.

But setting aside some metaphysicians of this kind, I may venture to affirm of the rest of mankind, that they are nothing but a bundle or collection of different perceptions, which succeed each other with an inconceivable rapidity, and are in a perpetual flux and movement. Our eyes cannot turn in their sockets without varying our perceptions. Our thought is still more variable than our sight; and all our other senses and faculties contribute to this change; nor is there any single power of the soul, which remains unalterably the same, perhaps for one moment. The mind is a kind of theatre, where several perceptions successively make their appearance; pass, re-pass, glide away, and mingle in an infinite variety of postures and situations. There is properly no *simplicity* in it at one time, nor *identity* in different; whatever natural propension we may have to imagine that simplicity and identity. The comparison of the theatre must not mislead us. They are the successive perceptions only, that constitute the mind; nor have we the most distant notion of the place, where these scenes are represented, or of the materials, of which it is composed.

What then gives us so great a propension to ascribe an identity to these successive perceptions, and to suppose ourselves possessed of an invariable and uninterrupted existence through the whole course of our lives? In order to answer this question, we must distinguish betwixt personal identity, as it regards our thought or imagination, and as it regards our passions or the concern we take in ourselves. The first is our present subject; and to explain it perfectly we must take the matter pretty deep, and account for that identity, which we attribute to plants and animals; there being a great analogy betwixt it, and the identity of a self or person.

We have a distinct idea of an object, that remains invariable and uninterrupted through a supposed variation of time; and this idea we call that of *identity* or *sameness*. We have also a distinct idea of several different objects existing in succession, and connected together by a close relation; and this to an accurate view affords as perfect a notion of *diversity*, as if there was no manner of relation among the objects. But though these two ideas of identity and succession of related objects be in themselves perfectly distinct, and even contrary, yet 'tis certain, that in our common way of thinking they are generally confounded with each other. That action of the imagination, by which we consider the uninterrupted and invariable object, and that by which we reflect on the succession of related objects, are almost the same to the feeling, nor is there much more effort of thought required in the latter case than in the former. The relation facilitates the transition of the mind from one object to another, and renders its passage as smooth as if it contemplated one continued object. This resemblance is the cause of the confusion and mistake, and makes us substitute the notion of identity, instead of that of related objects. However at one instant we may consider the related succession as variable or interrupted, we are sure the next to ascribe to it a perfect identity, and regard it as invariable and uninterrupted. Our propensity to this mistake is so great from the resemblance above-mentioned, that we fall into it before we are aware; and though we incessantly correct ourselves by reflection, and return to a more accurate method of thinking, yet we cannot long sustain our philosophy, or take off this bias from the imagination. Our last resource is to yield to it, and boldly assert that these different related objects are in effect the same, however interrupted and variable. In order to justify to ourselves this absurdity, we often feign some new and unintelligible principle, that connects the objects together, and prevents their interruption or variation. Thus we feign the continued existence of the perceptions of our senses, to remove the interruption; and run into the notion of a *soul*, and *self*, and *substance*, to disguise the variation. But we may farther observe, that where we do not give rise to such a fiction, our propension to confound identity with relation is so great, that we are apt to imagine something unknown and mysterious, connecting the parts, beside their relation; and this I take to be the case with regard to the identity we ascribe to plants and vegetables. And even when this does not take place, we still feel a propensity to confound these ideas, though we are not able fully to satisfy ourselves in that particular, nor find any thing invariable and uninterruped to justify our notion of identity.

Thus the controversy concerning identity is not merely a dispute of words. For when we attribute identity, in an improper sense, to variable or interrupted objects, our mistake is not confined to the expression, but is commonly attended with a fiction, either of something invariable and uninterrupted, or of something mysterious and inexplicable, or at least with a propensity to such fictions. What will suffice to prove this hypothesis to the satisfaction of every fair inquirer, is to shew from daily experience and observation, that the objects, which are variable or interrupted, and yet are supposed to continue the same, are such only as consist of a succession of parts, connected together by resemblance, contiguity, or causation. For as such a succession answers evidently to our notion of diversity, it can only be by mistake we ascribe to it an identity; and as the relation of parts, which leads us into this mistake, is really nothing but a quality, which produces an association of ideas, and an easy transition of the imagination from one to another, it can only be from the resemblance, which this act of the mind bears to that, by which we contemplate one continued object, that the error arises. Our chief business, then, must be to prove, that all objects, to which we ascribe identity, without observing their invariableness and uninterruptedness, are such as consist of a succession of related objects.

In order to this, suppose any mass of matter, of which the parts are contiguous and connected, to be placed before us; 'tis plain we must attribute a perfect identity to this mass, provided all the parts continue uninterruptedly and invariably the same, whatever motion or change of place we may observe either in the whole or in any of the parts. But supposing some very *small* or *inconsiderable* part to be added to the mass, or subtracted from it; though this absolutely destroys the identity of the whole, strictly speaking; yet as we seldom think so accurately, we scruple not to pronounce a mass of matter the same, where we find so trivial an alteration. The passage of the thought from the object before the change to the object after it, is so smooth and easy, that we scarce perceive the transition, and are apt to imagine, that 'tis nothing but a continued survey of the same object.

There is a very remarkable circumstance that attends this experiment; which is, that though the change of any considerable part in a mass of matter destroys the identity of the whole, yet we must measure the greatness of the part, not absolutely, but by its *proportion* to the whole. The addition or diminution of a mountain would not be sufficient to produce a diversity in a planet; though the change of a very few inches would be able to destroy the identity of some bodies. 'Twill be impossible to account for this, but by reflecting that objects operate upon the mind, and break or interrupt the continuity of its actions not according to their real greatness, but according to their proportion to each other: and therefore, since this interruption makes an object cease to appear the same, it must be the uninterrupted progress of the thought, which constitutes the imperfect identity.

This may be confirmed by another phænomenon. A change in any considerable part of a body destroys its identity; but 'tis remarkable, that where the change is produced *gradually* and *insensibly* we are less apt to ascribe to it the same effect. The reason can plainly be no other, than that the mind, in following the successive changes of the body, feels an easy passage from the surveying its condition in one moment to the viewing of it in another, and at no particular time perceives any interruption in its actions. From which continued perception, it ascribes a continued existence and identity to the object.

But whatever precaution we may use in introducing the changes gradually, and making them proportionable to the whole, 'tis certain, that where the changes are at last observed to become considerable, we make a scruple of ascribing identity to such different objects. There is however another artifice, by which we may induce the imagination to advance a step farther; and that is, by producing a reference of the parts to each other, and a combination to some *common end* or purpose. A ship, of which a considerable part has been changed by frequent reparations, is still considered as the same; nor does the difference of the materials hinder us from ascribing an identity to it. The common end, in which the parts conspire, is the same under all their variations, and affords an easy transition of the imagination from one situation of the body to another.

But this is still more remarkable, when we add a *sympathy* of parts to their *common end,* and suppose that they bear to each other the reciprocal relation of cause and effect in all their actions and operations. This is the case with all animals and vegetables; where not only the several parts have a reference to some general purpose, but also a mutual dependance on, and connexion with each other. The effect of so strong a relation is, that though every one must allow, that in a very few years both vegetables and animals endure a *total* change, yet we still attribute identity to them, while their form, size, and substance are entirely altered. An oak, that grows from a small plant to a large tree, is still the same oak; though there be not one particle of matter, or figure of its parts the same. An infant becomes a man, and is sometimes fat, sometimes lean, without any change in his identity.

We may also consider the two following phænomena, which are remarkable in their kind. The first is, that though we commonly be able to distinguish pretty exactly betwixt numerical and specific identity, yet it sometimes happens, that we confound them, and in our thinking and reasoning employ the one for the other. Thus a man who hears a noise, that is frequently interrupted and renewed, says, it is still the same noise; though 'tis evident the sounds have only a specific identity or resemblance, and there is nothing numerically the same, but the cause, which produced them. In like manner it may be said without breach of the propriety of language, that such a church, which was formerly of brick, fell to ruin, and that the parish rebuilt the same church of free-stone, and according to modern architecture. Here neither the form nor materials are the same, nor is there any thing common to the two objects, but their relation to the inhabitants of the parish; and yet this alone is sufficient to make us denominate them the same. But we must observe, that in these cases the first object is in a manner annihilated before the second comes into existence; by which means we are never presented in any one point of time with the idea of difference and multiplicity; and for that reason are less scrupulous in calling them the same.

Secondly, we may remark, that though in a succession of related objects, it be in a manner requisite, that the change of parts be not sudden nor entire, in order to preserve the identity, yet where the objects are in their nature changeable and inconstant, we admit of a more sudden transition, than would otherwise be consistent with that relation. Thus as the nature of a river consists in the motion and change of parts; though in less than four and twenty hours these be totally altered; this hinders not the river from continuing the same during several ages. What is natural and essential to any thing is, in a manner, expected; and what is expected makes less impression, and appears of less moment, than what is unusual and extraordinary. A considerable change of the former kind seems really less to the imagination, than the most trivial alteration of the latter; and by breaking less the continuity of the thought, has less influence in destroying the identity.

We now proceed to explain the nature of *personal identity*, which has become so great a question in philosophy, especially of late years in England, where all the abstruser sciences are studied with a peculiar ardour and application. And here 'tis evident, the same method of reasoning must be continued, which has so successfully explained the identity of plants, and animals, and ships, and houses, and of all the compounded and changeable productions either of art or nature. The identity which we ascribe to the mind of man, is only a fictitious one, and of a like kind with that which we ascribe to vegetables and animal bodies. It cannot therefore have a different origin, but must proceed from a like operation of the imagination upon like objects.

But lest this argument should not convince the reader; though in my opinion perfectly decisive; let him weigh the following reasoning, which is still closer and more immediate. 'Tis evident, that the identity, which we attribute to the human mind, however perfect we may imagine it to be, is not able to run the several different perceptions into one, and make them lose their characters of distinction and difference, which are essential to them. 'Tis still true, that every distinct perception, which enters into the composition of the mind, is a distinct existence, and is different, and distinguishable, and separable from every other perception, either contemporary or successive. But as, notwithstanding this distinction and separability, we suppose the whole train of perceptions to be united by identity, a question naturally arises concerning this relation of identity; whether it be something that really binds our several perceptions together, or only associates their ideas in the imagination. That is, in other words, whether in pronouncing concerning the identity of a person, we observe some real bond among his perceptions, or only feel one among the ideas we form of them. This question we might easily decide, if we would recollect what has been already proved at large, that the understanding never observes any real connexion among objects, and that even the union of cause and effect, when strictly examined, resolves itself into a customary association of ideas. For from thence it evidently follows, that identity is nothing really belonging to these different perceptions, and uniting them together; but is merely a quality, which we attribute to them, because of the union of their ideas in the imagination, when we reflect upon them. Now the only qualities, which can give ideas an union in the imagination, are these three relations above-mentioned. These are the uniting principles in the ideal world, and without them every distinct object is separable by the mind, and may be separately considered, and appears not to have any more connexion with any other object, than if disjoined by the greatest difference and remoteness. 'Tis therefore on some of these three relations of resemblance, contiguity, and causation, that identity depends; and as the very essence of these relations consists in their producing an easy transition of ideas; it follows, that our notions of personal identity proceed entirely from the smooth and uninterrupted progress of the thought along a train of connected ideas, according to the principles above-explained.

The only question, therefore, which remains is, by what relations this uninterrupted progress of our thought is produced, when we consider the successive existence of a mind or thinking person. And here 'tis evident we must confine ourselves to resemblance and causation, and must drop contiguity, which has little or no influence in the present case.

To begin with *resemblance;* suppose we could see clearly into the breast of another, and observe that succession of perceptions, which constitutes his mind or thinking principle, and suppose that he always preserves the memory of a considerable part of past perceptions; 'tis evident that nothing could more contribute to the bestowing a relation on this succession amidst all its variations. For what is the memory but a faculty, by which we raise up the images of past perceptions? And as an image necessarily resembles its object, must not the frequent placing of these resembling perceptions in the chain of thought, convey the imagination more easily from one link to another, and make the whole seem like the continuance of one object? In this particular, then, the memory not only discovers the identity, but also contributes to its production, by producing the relation of resemblance among the perceptions. The case is the same whether we consider ourselves or others.

As to *causation;* we may observe, that the true idea of the human mind, is to consider it as a system of different perceptions or different existences, which are linked together by the relation of cause and effect, and mutually produce, destroy, influence, and modify each other. Our impressions give rise to their correspondent ideas; and these ideas in their turn produce other impressions. One thought chases another, and draws after it a third, by which it is expelled in its turn. In this respect, I cannot compare the soul more properly to any thing than to a republic or commonwealth, in which the several members are united by the reciprocal ties of government and subordination, and give rise to other persons who propagate the same republic in the incessant changes of its parts. And as the same individual republic may not only change its members, but also its laws and constitutions; in like manner the same person may vary his character and disposition, as well as his impressions and ideas, without losing his identity. Whatever changes he endures, his several parts are still connected by the relation of causation. And this view our identity with regard to the passions serves to corroborate that with regard to the imagination, by the making our distant perceptions influence each other, and by giving us a present concern for our past or future pains or pleasures.

As memory alone acquaints us with the continuance and extent of this succession of perceptions, 'tis to be considered, upon that account chiefly, as the source of personal identity. Had we no memory, we never should have any notion of causation, nor consequently of that chain of causes and effects, which constitute our self or person. But having once acquired this notion of causation from the memory, we can extend the same chain of causes, and consequently the identity of our persons beyond our memory, and can comprehend times, and circumstances, and actions, which we have entirely forgot, but suppose in general to have existed. For how few of our past actions are there, of which we have any memory? Who can tell me, for instance, what were his thoughts and actions on the first of January, 1715, the eleventh of March, 1719, and the third of August, 1733? Or will he affirm, because he has entirely forgot the incidents of these days, that the present self is not the same person with the self of that time; and by that means overturn all the most established notions of personal identity? In this view therefore memory does not so much *produce* as *discover* personal identity, by shewing us the relation of cause and effect among our different perceptions. 'Twill be incumbent on those who affirm that memory produces entirely our personal identity, to give a reason why we can thus extend our identity beyond our memory.

The whole of this doctrine leads us to a conclusion, which is of great importance in the present affair, viz. that all the nice and subtile questions concerning personal identity can never possibly be decided, and are to be regarded rather as grammatical than as philosophical difficulties. Identity depends on the relations of ideas; and these relations produce identity, by means of that easy transition they occasion. But as the relations, and the easiness of the transition may diminish by insensible degrees, we have no just standard by which we can decide any dispute concerning the time, when they acquire or lose a title to the name of identity. All the disputes concerning the identity of connected objects are merely verbal, except so far as the relation of parts gives rise to some fiction or imaginary principle of union, as we have already observed.

What I have said concerning the first origin and uncertainty of our notion of identity, as applied to the human mind, may be extended with little or no variation to that of *simplicity*. An object, whose different coexistent parts are bound together by a close relation, operates upon the imagination after much the same manner as one perfectly simple and indivisible, and requires not a much greater stretch of thought in order to its conception. From this similarity of operation we attribute a simplicity to it, and feign a principle of union as the support of this simplicity, and the centre of all the different parts and qualities of the object.

ERIK ERIKSON *(b.1902)*

Erik Erikson was trained in psychoanalysis in Vienna, close to the influence of Freud's genius. Since then he has practiced psychoanalysis, taught at Harvard, and written several books, including Childhood and Society *(1950),* Young Man Luther *(1958), and* Ghandhi's Truth *(1969). Followed by younger men like Robert Jay Lifton and Kenneth Keniston, Erikson has pioneered the application of psychological insights to biography, history, and social change. In the following selection from the Prologue to his* Identity, Youth and Crisis *(1968) Erikson examines the history of the term 'identity-crisis,' a phrase he first used some twenty-five years ago. His self-conscious application of historical perspective to his own achievements, and their influence on others and, finally, on himself makes Erikson a model of the phenomenon he is discussing: the changing patterns not only of one's own identity, but of the very nature of the identity problem itself.*

Certainly Erikson's formulation of the problem of self-identity is different from Hume's, but the two are not necessarily opposed. Rather, Erikson's formulation can be regarded as a set of directions for the concrete application of Hume's relatively abstract insights. Hume and Ryle argue that the identity of the self is not established by some inner, substantial, unalterable core. Relations of contiguity, resemblance, and causation constitute one's feelings of continuity. But what criteria are we to use for resemblance? As Hume noted in closing, simplicity is a relative concept requiring choices in its application. Similarly, resemblance is a relative concept requiring the application of specific criteria of resemblance. For example, if you are presented with a green square, a green circle, and a blue circle and then asked which two resemble one another most, you would have to choose whether you regarded sameness of shape or of color as the more important criterion of resemblance. This example is very simple. We can clearly see the difference between the typologies of color and shape, and we know how to use both. But now substitute typologies of individual selfhood based on social or solitary definitions of continuity. For the self that is engaged in and dependent on the community, the important criteria for resemblance derive from the values and norms set by the social group. People feel themselves growing continuously from childhood to adulthood if their experiences resemble each other, cause each other, and remain contiguous with each other on a socially defined curriculum, for example grades in grammar school and the familiar sequence from freshman to senior in high school or college. For Wolfe's individual in a technological fortress, however, a different source of criteria for resemblance must be found or created, such as a familiar set of private fantasies.

By relating issues of individual identity to the historically changing patterns of social organization, Erikson brings together the issues of this and the preceding section. As Erikson makes perfectly clear, the metaphysics of self-identity must be made concrete and specific in terms of one's own historical time. Furthermore, his argument points ahead to the rest of this book: since it is true that the quest for self-identity requires, as Erikson calls it, an ever renewed "consolidation" of self and world, the wider circles of self-awareness reflect back into the constitution of self-identity. As he says of the process of realizing self-identity, "the process described is always changing and developing: at its best it is a process of increasing differentiation, and it becomes ever more inclusive as the individual grows aware of a widening circle of others significant to him, from the maternal person to 'mankind.'"

Identity, Youth and Crisis

To review the concept of identity means to sketch its history. In the twenty years since the term was first employed in the particular sense to be discussed in this book, its popular usage has become so varied and its conceptual context so expanded that the time may seem to have come for a better and final delimitation of what identity is and what it is not. And yet, by its very nature, what bears such a definitive name remains subject to changing historical connotations.

"Identity" and "identity crisis" have in popular and scientific usage become terms which alternately circumscribe something so large and so seemingly self-evident that to demand a definition would almost seem petty, while at other times they designate something made so narrow for purposes of measurement that the over-all meaning is lost, and it could just as well be called something else. If, to give examples of the wider use of the term, the papers run a headline "The Identity Crisis of Africa" or refer to the "identity crisis" of the Pittsburgh glass industry; if the outgoing president of the American Psychoanalytic Association titles his farewell address "The Identity Crisis of Psychoanalysis"; or if, finally, the Catholic students at Harvard announce that they will hold an "Identity Crisis" on Thursday night at eight o'clock sharp, then the dignity of the term seems to vary greatly. The quotation marks are as important as the term they bracket: everybody has heard of "identity crisis" and it arouses a mixture of curiosity, mirth, and discomfort which yet promises, by the very play on the word "crisis," not to turn out to be something quite as fatal as it sounds. In other words, a suggestive term has begun to lend itself to ritualized usage.

Social scientists, on the other hand, sometimes attempt to achieve greater specificity by making such terms as "identity crisis," "self identity," or "sexual identity" fit whatever more measurable item they are investigating at a given time. For the sake of logical or experimental maneuverability (and in order to keep in good academic company) they try to treat these terms as matters of social roles, personal traits, or conscious self-images, shunning the less manageable and more sinister—which often also means the more vital—implications of the concept. Such usages have, in fact, become so indiscriminate that the other day a German reviewer of the book in which I first used the term in the context of psychoanalytic ego theory called it the pet subject of the *amerikanische Populaerpsychologie*.

But one may note with satisfaction that the conceptualization of identity has led to a series of valid investigations which, if they do not make clearer what identity is, nevertheless have proved useful in social psychology. And it may be a good thing that the word "crisis" no longer connotes impending catastrophe, which at one time seemed to be an obstacle to the understanding of the term. It is now being accepted as designating a necessary turning point, a crucial moment, when development must move one way or another, marshaling resources of growth, recovery, and further differentiation. This proves applicable to many situations: a crisis in individual development or in the emergence of a new elite, in the therapy of an individual or in the tensions of rapid historical change.

The term "identity crisis" was first used, if I remember correctly, for a specific clinical purpose in the Mt. Zion Veterans' Rehabilitation Clinic during the Second World War, a national emergency which permitted psychiatric workers of different persuasions and denominations, among them Emanuel Windholz and Joseph Wheelwright, to work together harmoniously. Most of our patients, so we concluded at that time, had neither been "shellshocked" nor become malingerers, but had through the exigencies of war lost a sense of personal sameness and historical continuity. They were impaired in that central control over themselves for which, in the psychoanalytic scheme, only the "inner agency" of the ego could be held responsible. Therefore, I spoke of a loss of "ego identity."[1] Since then, we have recognized the same central disturbance in severely conflicted young people whose sense of confusion is due, rather, to a war within themselves, and in confused rebels and destructive delinquents who war on their society. In all these cases, then, the term "identity confusion" has a certain diagnostic significance which should influence the evaluation and treatment of such disturbances. Young patients can be violent or depressed, delinquent or withdrawn, but theirs is an acute and possibly passing crisis rather than a breakdown of the kind which tends to commit a patient to all the malignant implications of a fatalistic diagnosis. And as has always been the case in the history of psychoanalytic psychiatry, what was first recognized as the common dynamic pattern of a group of severe disturbances (such as the hysterias of the turn of the century) revealed itself later to be a pathological aggravation, an undue prolongation of, or a regression to, a normative crisis "belonging" to a particular stage of individual development. Thus, we have learned to ascribe a normative "identity crisis" to the age of adolescence and young adulthood.

Referring to the first use of the term "identity crisis," I said, "if I remember correctly." Perhaps one should be able to remember such things. But the fact is that a term which later becomes so distinctive is often first used as something one takes, and thinks others take, for granted. This brings to mind one of the innumerable stories with which Norman Reider could be counted on to lighten those often weary war days. An old man, he recounted, used to vomit every morning, but he showed no inclination to consult a doctor about it. His family finally prevailed on him to go to Mt. Zion for a general checkup. When Dr. Reider approached him cautiously, "How are you?" he was told promptly, "I'm fine. Couldn't be better." And, indeed, on further examination the constituent parts of the old man seemed to be in as good shape as could be expected. Finally, Dr. Reider

---

[1]Erik H. Erikson, "A Combat Crisis in a Marine," *Childhood and Society,* Second Edition, New York: W. W. Norton, 1963, pp. 38–47.

became a bit impatient. "But I hear you vomit every morning?" The old man looked mildly surprised and said, "Sure. Doesn't everybody?"

In telling this story, I am not implying that "identity crisis" is a symptom of mine that I simply assumed everybody else had also—although there is, of course, something to that too. But I did assume that I had given the most obvious name to something that everybody had had at one time and would, therefore, recognize in those who were having it acutely.

Judged by the clinical origin of these terms, then, it would seem reasonable enough to link the *pathological* and the *developmental aspects* of the matter and to see what might differentiate the identity crisis typical for a case history from that of a life history. This emphasis on individual lives, however, would make the other and wider uses of the terms "identity" and "identity crisis" appear all the more suspect as mere analogies not admissible in any court of definition. That Catholic students would try to pool their individual crises, enjoy them together, and get them over with in one evening makes at least humorous sense. But what possible connection could adolescence as such have with the state of an African nation or of a scientific body? *Is* this a mere analogistic usage such as is employed, with a mixture of boastfulness and apology, when a nation is said to be in its historical and economic "adolescence," or to have developed a "paranoid political style"? And if a nation cannot be said to be "adolescent," can a type of individual identity crisis be shared by a significant section of the young population? And further, to return to the faddish use of the term "identity confusion," would some of our youth act so openly confused and confusing if they did not *know* they were *supposed* to have an identity crisis?

The history of the last twenty years seems to indicate that there are clinical terms which are taken over not only by diagnosticians, but also by those who have been overdiagnosed, and, in this case, by a section of a whole age group who echo our very terms and flamboyantly display a conflict which we once regarded as silent, inner, and unconscious.

. . . Today when the term identity refers, more often than not, to something noisily demonstrative, to a more or less desperate "quest," or to an almost deliberately confused "search" let me present two formulations which assert strongly what identity feels like when you become aware of the fact that you do undoubtedly *have* one.

My two witnesses are bearded and patriarchal founding fathers of the psychologies on which our thinking on identity is based. As a *subjective sense* of an *invigorating sameness* and *continuity*, what I would call a sense of identity seems to me best described by William James in a letter to his wife:[2]

> A man's character is discernible in the mental or moral attitude in which, when it came upon him, he felt himself most deeply and intensely active and alive. At such moments there is a voice inside which speaks and says: *"This* is the real me!"

[2]*The Letters of William James,* edited by Henry James (his son), Vol. I, Boston: The Atlantic Monthly Press, 1920, p. 199.

Such experience always includes

> an element of active tension, of holding my own, as it were, and trusting
> outward things to perform their part so as to make it a full harmony, but
> without any *guaranty* that they will. Make it a guaranty... and the
> attitude immediately becomes to my consciousness stagnant and sting-
> less. Take away the guaranty, and I feel (provided I am *ueberhaupt*
> [totally or generally] in vigorous condition) a sort of deep enthusiastic
> bliss, of bitter willingness to do and suffer anything... and which,
> although it is a mere mood or emotion to which I can give no form in
> words, authenticates itself to me as the deepest principle of all active and
> theoretic determination which I possess...

James uses the word "character," but I am taking the liberty of claiming that
he describes a sense of identity, and that he does so in a way which can in principle
be experienced by any man. To him it is both mental and moral in the sense of
those "moral philosophy" days, and he experiences it as something that "comes
upon you" as a recognition, almost as a surprise rather than as something
strenuously "quested" after. It is an active tension (rather than a paralyzing
question)—a tension which, furthermore, must create a challenge "without
guaranty" rather than one dissipated in a clamor for certainty. But let us
remember in passing that James was in his thirties when he wrote this, that in his
youth he had faced and articulated an "identity crisis" of honest and desperate
depth, and that he became *the* Psychologist-Philosopher of American Pragmatism
only after having experimented with a variety of cultural, philosophic, and
national identity elements: the use in the middle of his declaration of the
untranslatable German word *"ueberhaupt"* is probably an echo of his conflictful
student days in Europe.

One can study in James's life history a protracted identity crisis as well as the
emergence of a "self-made" identity in the new and expansive American civilization. We will repeatedly come back to James, but for the sake of further definition,
let us now turn to a statement which asserts a unity of *personal and cultural*
identity rooted in an ancient people's fate. In an address to the Society of B'nai
B'rith in Vienna in 1926,[3] Sigmund Freud said:

> What bound me to Jewry was (I am ashamed to admit) neither faith nor
> national pride, for I have always been an unbeliever and was brought up
> without any religion though not without a respect for what are called the
> "ethical" standards of human civilization. Whenever I felt an inclina-
> tion to national enthusiasm I strove to suppress it as being harmful and
> wrong, alarmed by the warning examples of the peoples among whom we
> Jews live. But plenty of other things remained over to make the
> attraction of Jewry and Jews irresistible—many obscure emotional
> forces, which were the more powerful the less they could be expressed in

---

[3]Sigmund Freud, "Address to the Society of B'nai B'rith" [1926], *Standard Edition*, 20:273, London:
Hogarth Press, 1959

words, as well as a clear consciousness of inner identity, the safe privacy of a common mental construction. And beyond this there was a perception that it was to my Jewish nature alone that I owed two characteristics that had become indispensable to me in the difficult course of my life. Because I was a Jew I found myself free from many prejudices which restricted others in the use of their intellect; and as a Jew I was prepared to join the Opposition, and to do without agreement with the "compact majority."

No translation ever does justice to the distinctive choice of words in Freud's German original. "Obscure emotional forces" are *"dunkle Gefuehlsmaechte"*; the "safe privacy of a common mental construction" is *"die Heimlichkeit der inneren Konstruktion"*—not just "mental," then, and certainly not "private," but a deep communality known only to those who shared in it, and only expressible in words more mythical than conceptual.

These fundamental statements were taken not from theoretical works, but from special communications: a letter to his wife from a man who married late, an address to his "brothers" by an original observer long isolated in his profession. But in all their poetic spontaneity they are the products of trained minds and therefore exemplify the main dimensions of a positive sense of identity almost systematically. Trained minds of genius, of course, have a special identity and special identity problems often leading to a protracted crisis at the onset of their careers. Yet we must rely on them for formulating initially what we can then proceed to observe as universally human.

This is the only time Freud used the term identity in a more than casual way and, in fact, in a most central ethnic sense. And as we would expect of him, he inescapably points to some of those aspects of the matter which I called sinister and yet vital—the more vital, in fact, "the less they could be expressed in words." For Freud's "consciousness of inner identity" includes a sense of bitter pride preserved by his dispersed and often despised people thoughout a long history of persecution. It is anchored in a particular (here intellectual) gift which had victoriously emerged from the hostile limitation of opportunities. At the same time, Freud contrasts the *positive identity* of a fearless freedom of thinking with a *negative* trait in "the peoples among whom we Jews live," namely, "prejudices which restrict others in the use of their intellect." It dawns on us, then, that one person's or group's identity may be relative to another's and that the pride of gaining a strong identity may signify an inner emancipation from a more dominant group identity, such as that of the "compact majority." An exquisite triumph is suggested in the claim that the same historical development which restricted the prejudiced majority in the free use of their intellect made the isolated minority sturdier in intellectual matter. To all this, we must come back when discussing race relations.

And Freud goes farther. He admits in passing that he had to suppress in himself an inclination toward "national enthusiasm" such as was common for "the peoples among whom we Jews live." Again, as in James's case, only a study of Freud's youthful enthusiasms could show how he came to leave behind other aspirations in favor of the ideology of applying the methods of natural science to the study of psychological "forces of dignity." It is in Freud's dreams, incidentally, that we have a superb record of his suppressed (or what James called "abandoned," or even "murdered") selves—for our "negative identity" haunts us at night.

The two statements and the lives behind them serve to establish a few dimensions of identity and, at the same time, help to explain why the problem is so all-pervasive and yet so hard to grasp: for we deal with a process "located" *in the core of the individual* and yet also *in the core of his communal culture*, a process which establishes, in fact, the identity of those two identities. If we should now pause and state a few minimum requirements for fathoming the complexity of identity we should have to begin by saying something like this (and let us take our time in saying it): in psychological terms, identity formation employs a process of simultaneous reflection and observation, a process taking place on all levels of mental functioning, by which the individual judges himself in the light of what he perceives to be the way in which others judge him in comparison to themselves and to a typology significant to them; while he judges their way of judging him in the light of how he perceives himself in comparison to them and to types that have become relevant to him. This process is, luckily, and necessarily, for the most part unconscious except where inner conditions and outer circumstances combine to aggravate a painful, or elated, "identity-consciousness."

Furthermore, the process described is always changing and developing: at its best it is a process of increasing differentiation, and it becomes ever more inclusive as the individual grows aware of a widening circle of others significant to him, from the maternal person to "mankind." The process "begins" somewhere in the first true "meeting" of mother and baby as two persons who can touch and recognize each other,[4] and it does not "end" until a man's power of mutual affirmation wanes. As pointed out, however, the process has its normative crisis in adolescence, and is in many ways determined by what went before and determines much that follows. And finally, in discussing identity, as we now see, we cannot separate personal growth and communal change, nor can we separate (as I tried to demonstrate in *Young Man Luther*) the identity crisis in individual life and contemporary crises in historical development because the two help to define each other and are truly relative to each other. In fact, the whole interplay between the psychological and the social, the developmental and the historical, for which identity formation is of prototypal significance, could be conceptualized only as a kind of *psychosocial relativity*. A weighty matter then: certainly mere "roles" played interchangeably, mere self-conscious "appearances," or mere strenuous "postures" cannot possibly be the real thing, although they may be dominant aspects of what today is called the "search for identity." . . .

It must be confessed that at least those of us who are occupied with making sense of case histories or of biographies (which so often superficially resemble case histories) and who are teaching either young psychiatrists or the humanisti-

---

[4]Joan M. Erikson, "Eye to Eye," *The Man Made Object*, Gyorgy Kepes (ed.), New York: Braziller, 1966.

cally privileged college youth, are often out of touch with the resources of identity available to that majority of youths whose ideology is a product of the machine age. That youth, on the whole, does not need us, and those who do assume the "patient role" created by us. Nor do we seem to think that our theories need to include them. And yet we must assume that masses of young people both here and abroad are close enough both by giftedness and by opportunity to the technological trends and the scientific methods of our time to feel at home in it as much as anybody ever felt at home in human life. I, for one, have never been able to accept the claim that in mercantile culture or in agricultural culture, or indeed, in book culture, man was in principle less "alienated" than he is in technology. It is, I believe, our own retrospective romanticism which makes us think that peasants or merchants or hunters were less determined by their techniques. To put it in terms of what must be studied concertedly: in every technology and in every historical period there are types of individuals who ("properly" brought up) can combine the dominant techniques with their identity development, and *become* what they *do*. Independently of minor superiorities or inferiorities, they can settle on the *cultural consolidation* which secures them what joint verification and what transitory salvation lies in doing things together and in doing them right—a rightness proven by the bountiful response of "nature," whether in the form of the prey bagged, the food harvested, the goods produced, the money made, or the technological problems solved. In such consolidation and accommodation a million daily tasks and transactions fall into practical patterns and spontaneous ritualizations which can be shared by leaders and led, men and women, adults and children, the privileged and the underprivileged, the specially gifted and those willing to do the chores. The point is that only such consolidation offers the coordinates for the range of a period's identity formations and their necessary relation to a sense of inspired activity, although for many or most it does so only by also creating compartments of pronounced narrowness, of enforced service, and of limited status. Each such consolidation, by dint of its very practicality (the fact that "it works" and maintains itself by mere usage and habituation), also works for entrenched privileges, enforced sacrifices, institutionalized inequalities, and built-in contradictions, which become obvious to the critics of any society. But how such consolidation leads to a sense of embeddedness and natural flux among the very artifacts of organization: how it helps to bring to ascendance some style of perfection and of self-glorification; and how it permits man at the same time to limit his horizon so as *not* to see what might destroy the newly won familiarity of the world and expose him to all manner of strangeness and, above all, to the fear of death or of killing—all of this we have hardly approached from the point of view of depth psychology. Here the discussion of the "ego" should take on new dimensions.

The history of cultures, civilizations, and technologies is the history of such consolidations, while it is only in periods of marked transition that the innovators appear: those too privileged in outlook to remain bound to the prevailing system; too honest or too conflicted not to see the simple truths of existence hidden behind the complexity of daily "necessities"; and too full of pity to overlook "the poor" who have been left out. As therapists and ideologists, we understand the uppermost and the lowest fringe better, because of our own therapeutic ideology.

Thus we often take for granted the vast middle which, for reasons of its own, maintains us. Yet insofar as we aspire to contribute to "normal psychology" we must learn to understand cultural and technological consolidation, for it, ever again, inherits the earth.

And always with it comes a new definition of adulthood, without which any question of identity is self-indulgent luxury. The problem of adulthood is how to *take care* of those to whom one finds oneself committed as one emerges from the identity period, and to whom one now owes *their* identity.

Another question is what the "typical" adult of any era's consolidation is able and willing to renounce for himself and demand of others, for the sake of a style of cultural balance and, perhaps, perfection. Judging from the way Socrates, the philosopher, in his Apologia, exposed the fabric of Athenian consolidation, it was probably not only for himself that, at the very end, he pronounced death to be the only cure for the condition of living. Freud, the doctor, revealed for the mercantile and early industrial period what havoc the hypocritical morality was wreaking, not only in his era, but in all of human history. In doing so, he founded what Philipp Rieff has described as the *therapeutic orientation*, which goes far beyond the clinical cure of isolated symptoms. But we cannot know what technological conformity does *to* man unless we know that it does *for* him. The ubiquitous increase in mere number, of course, at first transforms many erstwhile problems of quality into matters of mere quantitative management.

If the majority of young people, therefore, can go along with their parents in a kind of fraternal identification, it is because they jointly leave it to technology and science to carry the burden of providing a self-perpetuating and self-accelerating way of life. This would make it plausible that the young are even expected to develop new values-as-you-go. But the fact is that the values associated with indefinite progress, just because it strains orientation as well as imagination, are often tied to unbelievably old-fashioned ideas. Thus technological expansion can be seen as the sure reward of generations of hard-working Americans. No need is felt to limit expansionist ideals, as long as—together with technical discipline— old-fashioned decencies and existing political machineries survive, with all their hometown oratory. There is always hope (a hope which has become an important part of an implicit American ideology) that in regard to any possible built-in evil in the very nature of supermachines, appropriate brakes and corrections will be invented in the nick of time, without any undue investment of strenuously new principles. And while they "work," the supermachineries, organizations, and associations provide a sufficiently "great," or at any rate adjustable, identity for all those who feel actively engaged in and by them.

Thus, also, the major part of youth which sees no reason to oppose the war in Vietnam is animated by a combination of a world-war patriotism, anticommunism, obedience to the draft and to military discipline, and finally by that unshakable solidarity, the highest feeling among men, which comes from having renounced the same pleasures, facing the same dangers, and having to obey the same obnoxious orders. But there is a new element in all this which comes from the technological ideology and makes a soldier an expert whose armament is mechanized and whose fidelity is an almost impersonal technical compliance with a policy or strategy which puts a certain *target* into the range of one of the admirable weapons at hand. No doubt certain "character structures" fit such a world view better than others, and yet, on the whole, each generation is prepared to participate in a number of consolidated attitudes in one lifetime.

But until a new ethics catches up with progress, one senses the danger that the limits of technological expansion and national assertion may not be determined by known facts and ethical considerations or, in short, by a certainty of identity, but by a willful and playful testing of the range and the limit of the supermachinery which thus takes over much of man's conscience. This could become affluent slavery for all involved, and this seems to be what the new "humanist" youth is trying to stop by putting its own existence "on the line" and insisting on a modicum of a self-sustaining quality of living.

3/Knowledge and Other Selves

introduction: the modes of cognition

The quest for self-knowledge now turns from the nature of the self that is known to the nature of knowledge itself. What is knowledge? How do we know? How to distinguish true knowledge from mere opinion?

Epistemology is the name for the theory of knowledge. Pursued as an academic discipline, epistemology sometimes devolves into abstract debates over how to describe a sensation of redness or some other triviality. If we substitute the self for a sense-datum of redness as the object of knowledge, epistemology becomes as vital as it is inescapable. For we do not, by and large, know ourselves very well. And part of the reason lies in our confusion about what knowledge is.

We may think we know ourselves well because we are, after all, the closest and most permanent witnesses to our experiences. But mere familiarity is not the same as knowledge. The stars were familiar to humankind long before we knew their composition. And even while we are now slightly more familiar with their composition, who is to say that we *know* the stars in a way that will reveal no further breakthroughs? Likewise, with our knowledge of ourselves we might undergo unsuspected revelations.

The first of the following selections deals with the shock of revelation through the use of imagery. A man who had been looking at shadows is forcefully turned around to look toward the light, at the things whose shadows it had cast. As Plato notes, the experience can be painful. Plato's images of the quest for knowledge have an experiential richness. For Plato it is always clear that knowledge occurs in a context. The context for the purely cognitive may be the experience of pleasure and pain, about which Epicurus writes. Or the context may be the physical gestures and social relationships discussed in the essays by Polanyi, Goffman, and Mead. In either case it is worth recalling the importance of the noncognitive and the constraints it places on the will to know, especially where the object of knowledge is one's self. Where else do we see the capacity for self-deception exercised more patently than in the case of self-knowledge? Our ability to deceive ourselves about ourselves should be a warning against overestimating our knowledge regarding everything else.

Some theorists ask the question "What is knowledge?" in a way that allows one to expect only one correct answer. One mode of cognition will deserve our respect, and all others will be dismissed as delusion. Bergson and Ayer debate the correct route toward knowledge of the self—metaphysical intuition or empirical perception combined with logical inference.

The final verdict on the nature of knowledge will not emerge at the end of this section. It is enough if the issues are clearer and at least some of the more obvious pitfalls pointed out. A fuller treatment of epistemology must await an appreciation of social and historical context, the role of educational institutions, and, finally, religious belief.

PLATO *(428–347 B.C.)*

Plato's philosophy, written during the fourth century B.C. in Athens, is the first of the major western philosophies. The twentieth-century philosopher Alfred North White-head has even gone so far as to suggest that the entire history of western philosophy can be regarded as a series of footnotes to Plato. Plato had some important predecessors. The pre-Socratic philosophers Thales, Anaximander, Anaxagoras, Heraclitus, and Parmenides each had profound influences on Greek thought in the century preceding Socrates. The Sophists were a group of teachers who trained young Athenians in rhetoric and who also claimed expertise in other matters from military prowess to domestic affairs. And there was, of course, Socrates, who wrote nothing but was Plato's teacher and model in the way he demonstrated to the Sophists and others that they did not in fact know what they thought they knew. Socrates was a great talker, a brilliant man whose wit and will to get to the bottom of things, to play the gadfly stinging the soft underbelly of some "proper" Athenians, eventually earned him a condemnation to death in 399 B.C. A public court of more than five hundred Athenians voted him guilty on charges of corrupting the youth, not believing in the public gods, and introducing divinities of his own making. The details of the charges are obscure, but clearly Socrates was a severe embarrassment to the Athenian establishment. Aristophanes' play The Clouds *(423 B.C.) draws a picture of what many of his countrymen thought of Socrates: a strange old man who talked about silly things, in such a way that his young listeners lost respect for their fathers and opposed them in matters sacred and profane. Plato wrote his dialogues, many of which are understood to be fairly close accounts of conversations between Socrates and his fellow Athenians, partly to clear his teacher by showing his conviction to be unjust, and partly to continue his teacher's quest. The two aims go well together, for in pursuing the first Plato was showing the Athenians that they did not know what they thought they knew, as Socrates had done before him.*

Plato's dialogues are written substitutes for the living person of Socrates. Keeping this fact in mind facilitates a just reading of the dialogues. Otherwise one is liable to dismiss the dialogues as many dismissed Socrates: he angered them by his apparent simplicities, by his continual questioning, by his irony, by not coming out with the truths they always suspected he was holding up his sleeve, by putting what he knew in the form of myths or parables that obviously couldn't represent the literal truth. Similarly, Plato's dialogues taunt the reader, not merely by representing Socrates at work, but by the way the dialogues themselves work even when Socrates is not present. Often they end without explicitly answering the question they set out to answer. Plato purposely hides certain lines of inquiry beneath the literal or surface level of the dialogue, and the reader has to go back and dig to a deeper level of interpretation to find what lies hidden. Interestingly enough, in the dialogue called the Symposium *Plato has Alcibiades describe Socrates as like the Silenus figures: statuettes that reveal one thing on the surface but can be opened up to disclose an inner beauty. Such are Plato's dialogues. And consequently they are sometimes frustrating, but purposely so. Readers must supply their own resources. Reading a Platonic dialogue is not at all like watching television, but then neither was talking to Socrates. The pedagogy of the Platonic dialogue (or the Socratic conversation) is one that demands participation.*

These two selections are excerpted from one of Plato's longest and best known dialogues, the Republic. *Although neither selection can really be interpreted in its full significance apart from surrounding passages, both are such classic passages in the history of philosophy that they reward study even in truncated form. One has to begin reading Plato somewhere, and these excerpts provide at least a good beginning.*

The following passage comes from the end of Book Six and the beginning of Book Seven of the Republic *(Benjamin Jowett translation) and offers a picture (but only a picture) of Plato's ideas about knowledge. Four different kinds of knowing correspond to four different kinds of objects of knowledge. Each kind of object is known by the corresponding capacity for knowledge. The objects themselves are ranked in an order from appearance to reality. Finally, the idea of the Good, symbolized by the sun, renders possible both knowledge and its objects. It is worth thinking a long time about why this principle of supreme value is located on neither side of the divided line, neither merely subjective nor wholly objective. It is also worth thinking about what is involved in the scene down in the cave. (Plato's description of watching the shadows on the wall bears an uncanny resemblance to watching television.) And what does he mean by "when any of them is liberated and compelled suddenly to stand up and turn his neck round and walk towards the light, he will suffer sharp pains"? What does he mean by each detail of the tale? And how, precisely, does the ascent from the cave parallel the course of the divided line?*

The Divided Line and the Myth of the Cave

... Let us not at present ask what is the actual nature of the good, for to reach what is now in my thoughts would be an effort too great for me. But of the child of the good who is likest him, I am ready to speak, if I could be sure that you wished to hear—otherwise, not.

By all means, he said, tell us about the child, and you shall remain in our debt for the account of the parent.

[507][1] I do indeed wish, I replied, that I could pay, and you receive, the account of the parent, and not, as now, of the offspring only; take, however, this latter by way of interest,[2] and at the same time have a care that I do not pay you in spurious coin, although I have no intention of deceiving you.

Yes, we will take all the care that we can: proceed.

Yes, I said, but I must first come to an understanding with you, and remind

---

[1] [The numbers in brackets refer to the pages of the Stephanus edition of the Greek text of Plato's works. Scholarly editions in all languages bear these numbers, making it easy to go from one edition or translation to another.—J. A. O.]

[2] A play upon τόκος which means both 'offspring' and 'interest.'

you of what I have mentioned in the course of this discussion, and at many other times.

What?

The old story, that there are many beautiful things and many good. And again there is a true beauty, a true good; and all other things to which the term *many* has been applied, are now brought under a single idea, and, assuming this unity, we speak of it in every case as *that which really is*.

Very true.

The many, as we say, are seen but not known, and the Ideas are known but not seen.

Exactly.

And what is the organ with which we see the visible things?

The sight, he said.

And with the hearing, I said, we hear, and with the other senses perceive the other objects of sense?

True.

But have you remarked that sight is by far the most costly and complex piece of workmanship which the artificer of the senses ever contrived?

Not exactly, he said.

Then reflect: have the ear and voice need of any third or additional nature in order that the one may be able to hear and the other to be heard?

Nothing of the sort.

No, indeed, I replied; and the same is true of most, if not all, the other senses—you would not say that any of them requires such an addition?

Certainly not.

But you see that without the addition of some other nature there is no seeing or being seen?

How do you mean?

Sight being, as I conceive, in the eyes, and he who has eyes wanting to see; colour being also present in the objects, still unless there be a third nature specially adapted to the purpose, sight, as you know, will see nothing and the colours will be invisible.

Of what nature are you speaking?

Of that which you term light, I replied.

True, he said.

[508] Then the bond which links together the sense of sight and the power of being seen, is of an evidently nobler nature than other such bonds—unless sight is an ignoble thing?

Nay, he said, the reverse of ignoble.

And which, I said, of the gods in heaven would you say was the lord of this element? Whose is the light which makes the eye to see perfectly and the visible to appear?

I should answer, as all men would, and as you plainly expect—the sun.

May not the relation of sight to this deity be described as follows?

How?

Neither sight nor the organ in which it resides, which we call the eye, is the sun?

No.

Yet of all the organs of sense the eye is the most like the sun?

By far the most like.

And the power which the eye possesses is a sort of effluence which is dispensed from the sun?

Exactly.

Then the sun is not sight, but the author of sight who is recognized by sight?

True, he said.

And this, you must understand, is he whom I call the child of the good, whom the good begat in his own likeness, to be in the visible world, in relation to sight and the things of sight, what the good is in the intellectual world in relation to mind and the things of mind:

Will you be a little more explicit? he said.

Why, you know, I said, that the eyes, when a person directs them towards objects on which the light of day is no longer shining, but the moon and stars only, see dimly, and are nearly blind; they seem to have no clearness of vision in them?

Very true.

But when they are directed towards objects on which the sun shines, they see clearly and there is sight in them?

Certainly.

And the soul is like the eye: when resting upon that on which truth and being shine, the soul perceives and understands, and is radiant with intelligence; but when turned towards the twilight and to those things which come into being and perish, then she has opinion only, and goes blinking about, and is first of one opinion and then of another, and seems to have no intelligence?

Just so.

Now, that which imparts truth to the known and the power of knowing to the knower, is, as I would have you say, the Idea of good, and this Idea, which is the cause of science and of truth, you are to conceive as being apprehended by knowledge, and yet, fair as both truth and knowledge are, you will be right to [509] esteem it as different from these and even fairer; and as in the previous instance light and sight may be truly said to be like the sun and yet not to be the sun, so in this other sphere science and truth may be deemed to be like the good, but it is wrong to think that they are the good; the good has a place of honour yet higher.

What a wonder of beauty that must be, he said, which is the author of science and truth, and yet surpasses them in beauty; for you surely cannot mean to say that pleasure is the good?

God forbid, I replied; but may I ask you to consider the image in another point of view?

In what point of view?

You would say, would you not, that the sun is not only the author of visibility in all visible things, but of generation and nourishment and growth, though he himself is not generation?

Certainly.

In like manner you must say that the good not only infuses the power of being known into all things known, but also bestows upon them their being and existence, and yet the good is not existence, but lies far beyond it in dignity and power.

Glaucon said, with a ludicrous earnestness: By the light of heaven, that is far beyond indeed!

Yes, I said, and the exaggeration may be set down to you; for you made me utter my fancies.

And pray continue to utter them; at any rate let us hear if there is anything more to be said about the similitude of the sun.

Yes, I said, there is a great deal more.

Then omit nothing, however slight.

I expect that I shall omit a great deal, I said, but shall not do so deliberately, as far as present circumstances permit.

I hope not, he said.

You have to imagine, then, that there are two ruling powers, and that one of them is set over the intellectual world, the other over the visible. I do not say heaven, lest you should fancy that I am playing upon the name. May I suppose that you have this distinction of the visible and intelligible fixed in your mind?

I have.

Now take a line which has been cut into two unequal parts, and divide each of them again in the same proportion, and suppose the two main divisions to answer, one to the visible and the other to the intelligible, and then compare the subdivisions in respect of their clearness and want of clearness, and you will find that the first section in the sphere of the [510] visible consists of images. And by images I mean, in the first place, shadows, and in the second place, reflections in water and in solid, smooth and polished bodies and the like: Do you understand?

Yes, I understand.

Imagine, now, the other section, of which this is only the resemblance, to include the animals which we see, and every thing that grows or is made.

Very good.

Would you not admit that both the sections of this division have different degrees of truth, and that the copy is to the original as the sphere of opinion is to the sphere of knowledge?

Most undoubtedly.

Next proceed to consider the manner in which the sphere of the intellectual is to be divided.

In what manner?

Thus:—There are two subdivisions, in the lower of which the soul, using as images those things which themselves were reflected in the former division, is forced to base its enquiry upon hypotheses, proceeding not towards a principle but towards a conclusion; in the higher of the two, the soul proceeds *from* hypotheses, and goes up to a principle which is above hypotheses, making no use of images as in the former case, but proceeding only in and through the Ideas themselves.

I do not quite understand your meaning, he said.

Then I will try again; you will understand me better when I have made some preliminary remarks. You are aware that students of geometry, arithmetic, and the kindred sciences assume the odd and the even and the figures and three kinds of angles and the like in their several branches of science; these are their hypotheses, which they and everybody are supposed to know, and therefore they do not deign to give any account of them either to themselves or others; but they begin with them, and go on until they arrive at last, and in a consistent manner, at the solution which they set out to find?

Yes, he said, I know.

And do you not know also that although they make use of the visible forms and reason about them, they are thinking not of these, but of the ideals which they resemble; not of the figures which they draw, but of the absolute square and the absolute diameter, and so on—the forms which they draw or make, and which themselves have shadows and reflections in water, are in turn converted by them into images; for they are really seeking to behold the things themselves, which can only be seen with the eye of the mind?

[511] That is true.

And this was what I meant by a subdivision of the intelligible, in the search after which the soul is compelled to use hypotheses; not ascending to a first principle, because she is unable to rise above the region of hypothesis, but employing now as images those objects from which the shadows below were derived, even these being deemed clear and distinct by comparison with the shadows.

I understand, he said, that you are speaking of the province of geometry and the sister arts.

And when I speak of the other division of the intelligible, you will understand me to speak of that other sort of knowledge which reason herself attains by the power of dialectic, using the hypotheses not as first principles, but literally as hypotheses—that is to say, as steps and points of departure into a world which is above hypotheses, in order that she may soar beyond them to the first principle of the whole; and clinging to this and then to that which depends on this, by successive steps she descends again without the aid of any sensible object, from Ideas, through Ideas, and in Ideas she ends.

I understand you, he replied; not perfectly, for you seem to me to be describing a task which is really tremendous; but, at any rate, I understand you to say that that part of intelligible Being, which the science of dialectic contemplates, is clearer than that which falls under the arts, as they are termed, which take hypotheses as their principles; and though the objects are of such a kind that they must be viewed by the understanding, and not by the senses, yet, because they start from hypotheses and do not ascend to a principle, those who contemplate them appear to you not to exercise the higher reason upon them, although when a first principle is added to them they are cognizable by the higher reason. And the habit which is concerned with geometry and the cognate sciences I suppose that you would term understanding and not reason, as being intermediate between opinion and reason.

You have quite conceived my meaning, I said; and now, corresponding to these four divisions, let there be four faculties in the soul—reason answering to the highest, understanding to the second, faith (or conviction) to the third, and perception of shadows to the last—and let there be a scale of them, and let us suppose that the several faculties have clearness in the same degree that their objects have truth.

I understand, he replied, and give my assent, and accept your arrangement. . . .

Book VII

[514] And now, I said, let me show in a figure how far our nature is enlightened or unenlightened:—Behold! human beings housed in an underground cave, which has a long entrance open towards the light and as wide as the interior of the cave; here they have been from their childhood, and have their legs and necks chained, so that they cannot move and can only see before them, being prevented by the chains from turning round their heads. Above and behind them a fire is blazing at a distance, and between the fire and the prisoners there is a raised way; and you will see, if you look, a low wall built along the way, like the screen which marionette players have in front of them, over which they show the puppets.

I see.

And do you see, I said, men passing along the wall carrying all sorts of vessels, and statues and figures of animals made of wood and stone and various materials, which appear over the wall? While carrying their burdens, some of them, as you would expect, are talking, others silent.

You have shown me a strange image, and they are strange prisoners.

Like ourselves, I replied; for in the first place do you think they have seen anything of themselves, and of one another, except the shadows which the fire throws on the opposite wall of the cave?

How could they do so, he asked, if throughout their lives they were never allowed to move their heads?

And of the objects which are being carried in like manner they would only see the shadows?

Yes, he said.

And if they were able to converse with one another, would they not suppose that the things they saw were the real things?[3]

Very true.

And suppose further that the prison had an echo which came from the other side, would they not be sure to fancy when one of the passers-by spoke that the voice which they heard came from the passing shadow?

No question, he replied.

To them, I said, the truth would be literally nothing but the shadows of the images.

---

[3] [Text uncertain: perhaps 'that they would apply the name *real* to the things which they saw.'—J. A. O.]

That is certain.

And now look again, and see in what manner they would be released from their bonds, and cured of their error, whether the process would naturally be as follows. At first, when any of them is liberated and compelled suddenly to stand up and turn his neck round and walk and look towards the light, he will suffer sharp pains; the glare will distress him, and he will be unable to see the realities of which in his former state he had seen the shadows; and then conceive someone saying to him that what he saw before was an illusion, but that now, when he is approaching nearer to being and his eye is turned towards more real existence, he has a clearer vision,—what will be his reply? And you may further imagine that his instructor is pointing to the objects as they pass and requiring him to name them,—will he not be perplexed? Will he not fancy that the shadows which he formerly saw are truer than the objects which are now shown to him?

Far truer.

And if he is compelled to look straight at the light, will he not have a pain in his eyes which will make him turn away to take refuge in the objects of vision which he can see, and which he will conceive to be in reality clearer than the things which are now being shown to him?

True, he said.

And suppose once more, that he is reluctantly dragged up that steep and rugged ascent, and held fast until he is forced into the presence of the sun himself, is he not likely to be pained [516] and irritated? When he approaches the light his eyes will be dazzled, and he will not be able to see anything at all of what are now called realities.

Not all in a moment, he said.

He will require to grow accustomed to the sight of the upper world. And first he will see the shadows best, next the reflections of men and other objects in the water, and then the objects themselves; and, when he turned to the heavenly bodies and the heaven itself, he would find it easier to gaze upon the light of the moon and the stars at night than to see the sun or the light of the sun by day?

Certainly.

Last of all he will be able to see the sun, not turning aside to the illusory reflections of him in the water, but gazing directly at him in his own proper place, and contemplating him as he is.

Certainly.

He will then proceed to argue that this is he who gives the seasons and the years, and is the guardian of all that is in the visible world, and in a certain way the cause of all things which he and his fellows have been accustomed to behold?

Clearly, he said, he would arrive at this conclusion after what he had seen.

And when he remembered his old habitation, and the wisdom of the cave and his fellow-prisoners, do you not suppose that he would felicitate himself on the change, and pity them?

Certainly, he would.

And if they were in the habit of conferring honours among themselves on those who were quickest to observe the passing shadows and to remark which of them went before and which followed after and which were together, and who were best able from these observations to divine the future, do you think that he would be eager for such honours and glories, or envy those who attained honour and sovereignty among these men? Would he not say with Homer, "Better to be a serf, labouring for a landless master," and to endure anything, rather than think as they do and live after their manner?

Yes, he said, I think that he would consent to suffer anything rather than live in this miserable manner.

Imagine once more, I said, such a one coming down suddenly out of the sunlight, and being replaced in his old seat; would he not be certain to have his eyes full of darkness?

To be sure, he said.

And if there were a contest, and he had to compete in measuring the shadows with the prisoners who had never [517] moved out of the cave, while his sight was still weak, and before his eyes had become steady (and the time which would be needed to acquire this new habit of sight might be very considerable), would he not make himself ridiculous? Men would say of him that he had returned from the place above with his eyes ruined; and that it was better not even to think of ascending; and if anyone tried to loose another and lead him up to the light, let them only catch the offender, and they would put him to death.

No question, he said.

This entire allegory, I said, you may now append, dear Glaucon, to the previous argument; the prison-house is the world of sight, the light of the fire is the power of the sun, and you will not misapprehend me if you interpret the journey upwards to be the ascent of the soul into the intellectual world according to my surmise, which, at your desire, I have expressed—whether rightly or wrongly God knows. But, whether true or false, my opinion is that in the world of knowledge the Idea of good appears last of all, and is seen only with an effort; although, when seen, it is inferred to be the universal author of all things beautiful and right, parent of light and of the lord of light in the visible world, and the immediate and supreme source of reason and truth in the intellectual; and that this is the power upon which he who would act rationally either in public or private life must have his eye fixed.

I agree, he said, as far as I am able to understand you.

Moreover, I said, you must agree once more, and not wonder that those who attain to this vision are unwilling to take any part in human affairs; for their souls are ever hastening into the upper world where they desire to dwell; which desire of theirs is very natural, if our allegory may be trusted.

Yes, very natural.

And is there anything surprising in one who passes from divine contemplations to the evil state of man, appearing grotesque and ridiculous; if, while his eyes are blinking and before he has become accustomed to the surrounding darkness, he is compelled to fight in courts of law, or in other places, about the images or the shadows of images of justice, and must strive against some rival about opinions of these things which are entertained by men who have never yet seen the true justice?

Anything but surprising, he replied.

[518] Anyone who has common sense will remember that the bewilderments of the eyes are of two kinds and arise from two causes, either from coming out of the light or from going into the light, and, judging that the soul may be affected in the same way, will not give way to foolish laughter when he sees anyone whose vision is perplexed and weak; he will first ask whether that soul of man has come out of the brighter life and is unable to see because unaccustomed to the dark, or having turned from darkness to the day is dazzled by excess of light. And he will count the one happy in his condition and state of being, and he will pity the other; or, if he have a mind to laugh at the soul which comes from below into the light, this laughter will not be quite so laughable as that which greets the soul which returns from above out of the light into the cave.

That, he said, is a very just distinction.

But then, if I am right, certain professors of education must be wrong when they say that they can put a knowledge into the soul which was not there before, like sight into blind eyes.

They undoubtedly say this, he replied.

Whereas our argument shows that the power and capacity of learning exists in the soul already; and that just as if it were not possible to turn the eye from darkness to light without the whole body, so too the instrument of knowledge can only by the movement of the whole soul be turned from a world of becoming to that of being, and learn by degrees to endure the sight of being, and of the brightest and best of being, or in other words, of the good.

Very true.

And must there not be some art which will show how the conversion can be effected in the easiest and quickest manner; an art which will not implant the faculty of sight, for that exists already, but will set it straight when it has turned in the wrong direction, and is looking away from the truth?

Yes, he said, such an art may be presumed.

And whereas the other so-called virtues of the soul seem to be akin to bodily qualities, for even when they are not originally innate they can be implanted later by habit and exercise, the virtue of wisdom more than anything else contains a divine element which never loses its power, and by this conversion is rendered useful and profitable; or, by conversion of another [519] sort, hurtful and useless. Did you never observe the narrow intelligence flashing from the keen eye of a clever rogue—how eager he is, how clearly his paltry soul sees the way to his end; he is the reverse of blind, but his keen eye-sight is forced into the service of evil, and he is mischievous in proportion to his cleverness?

Very true, he said.

But what if such natures had been gradually stripped, beginning in childhood, of the leaden weights which sink them in the sea of Becoming, and which, fastened upon the soul through gluttonous indulgence in eating and other such pleasures, forcibly turn its vision downwards—if, I say, they had been released from these impediments and turned in the opposite direction, the very same faculty in them would have seen the truth as keenly as they see what their eyes are turned to now.

Very likely.

Yes, I said; and there is another thing which is likely, or rather a necessary inference from what has preceded, that neither the uneducated and uninformed of the truth, nor yet those who are suffered to prolong their education without end, will be able ministers of State; not the former, because they have no single aim of duty which is the rule of all their actions, private as well as public; nor the latter, because they will not act at all except upon compulsion, fancying that they are already dwelling apart in the islands of the blest.

Very true, he replied.

Then, I said, the business of us who are the founders of the State will be to compel the best minds to attain that knowledge which we have already shown to be the greatest of all, namely, the vision of the good; they must make the ascent which we have described; but when they have ascended and seen enough we must not allow them to do as they do now.

What do you mean?

They are permitted to remain in the upper world, refusing to descend again among the prisoners in the cave, and partake of their labours and honours, whether they are worth having or not.

But is not this unjust? he said; ought we to give them a worse life, when they might have a better?

You have again forgotten, my friend, I said, the intention of our law, which does not aim at making any one class in the State happy above the rest; it seeks rather to spread happiness over the whole State, and to hold the citizens together by persuasion and necessity, making each share with others any benefit [520] which he can confer upon the State; and the law aims at producing such citizens, not that they may be left to please themselves, but that they may serve in binding the State together.

True, he said, I had forgotten.

Observe, Glaucon, that we shall do no wrong to our philosophers but rather make a just demand, when we oblige them to have a care and providence of others; we shall explain to them that in other States, men of their class are not obliged to share in the toils of politics: and this is reasonable, for they grow up spontaneously, against the will of the governments in their several States; and things which grow up of themselves, and are indebted to no one for their nurture, cannot fairly be expected to pay dues for a culture which they have never received. But we have brought you into the world to be rulers of the hive, kings of yourselves and of the other citizens, and have educated you far better and more perfectly than they have been educated, and you are better able to share in the double duty. Wherefore each of you, when his turn comes, must go down to rejoin his companions, and acquire with them the habit of seeing things in the dark. As you acquire that habit, you will see ten thousand times better than the inhabitants of the cave, and you will know what the several images are and what they represent, because you have seen the beautiful and just and good in their truth. And thus our State, which is also yours, will be a reality and not a dream only, and will be administered in a spirit unlike that of other States, in which men fight with one another about shadows only and are distracted in the struggle for power, which in their eyes is a great good. Whereas the truth is that the State in which those who are to govern have least ambition to do so is always the best and most quietly governed, and the State in which they are most eager, the worst.

EPICURUS *(341–270 B.C.)*

Epicurean philosophy stresses the importance of pleasure as a guide for right action. Epicurus is quick to add: "When we maintain that pleasure is the end, we do not mean the pleasures of profligates and those that consist in sensuality." What, then, does he mean?

As the following passage, Letter to Menoeceus, *suggests, Epicurus was writing in hard times. The old order, the classic height of Periclean Athens, suffered tumultuous decline. Social discord raised doubts about the future. In a manner perhaps appropriate to the times, both Stoic and Epicurean schools of philosophy advertised ideals that were therefore far less ambitious than Plato's* Republic. *In place of social justice, they stressed individual survival. The best one could hope for would be "freedom from disturbance"—an insular vision.*

For better or for worse, Epicurus' philosophy may once again be appropriate to the times. It is worth returning to his words, both to set the record straight by freeing him from the false caricature of hedonism and to test the subtleties of ancient wisdom against our contemporary experience.

Letter to Menoeceus

Let no one when young delay to study philosophy, nor when he is old grow weary of his study. For no one can come too early or too late to secure the health of his soul. And the man who says that the age for philosophy has either not yet come or has gone by is like the man who says that the age for happiness is not yet come to him, or has passed away. Wherefore both when young and old a man must study philosophy, that as he grows old he may be young in blessings through the grateful recollection of what has been, and that in youth he may be old as well, since he will know no fear of what is to come. We must then meditate on the things that make our happiness, seeing that when that is with us we have all, but when it is absent we do all to win it.

The things which I used unceasingly to commend to you, these do and practise, considering them to be the first principles of the good life. First of all believe that god is a being immortal and blessed, even as the common idea of a god is engraved on men's minds, and do not assign to him anything alien to his immortality or ill-suited to his blessedness: but believe about him everthing that can uphold his blessedness and immortality. For gods there are, since the knowledge of them is by clear vision. But they are not such as the many believe them to be: for indeed they do not consistently represent them as they believe them to be. And the impious man is not he who denies the gods of the many, but he who attaches to the gods the beliefs of the many. For the statements of the many about the gods are not conceptions derived from sensation, but false suppositions, according to which the greatest misfortunes befall the wicked and the greatest blessings the good by the gift of the gods. For men being accustomed always to their own virtues welcome those like themselves, but regard all that is not of their nature as alien.

Become accustomed to the belief that death is nothing to us. For all good and evil consists in sensation, but death is deprivation of sensation. And therefore a right understanding that death is nothing to us makes the mortality of life enjoyable, not because it adds to it an infinite span of time, but because it takes away the craving for immortality. For there is nothing terrible in life for the man who has truly comprehended that there is nothing terrible in not living. So that the man speaks but idly who says that he fears death not because it will be painful when it comes, but because it is painful in anticipation. For that which gives no trouble when it comes, is but an empty pain in anticipation. So death, the most terrifying of ills, is nothing to us, since so long as we exist death is not with us; but when death comes, then we do not exist. It does not then concern either the living or the dead, since for the former it is not, and the latter are no more.

But the many at one moment shun death as the greatest of evils, at another yearn for it as a respite from the evils in life. But the wise man neither seeks to escape life nor fears the cessation of life, for neither does life offend him nor does the absence of life seem to be any evil. And just as with food he does not seek simply the larger share and nothing else, but rather the most pleasant, so he seeks to enjoy not the longest period of time, but the most pleasant.

And he who counsels the young man to live well, but the old man to make a good end, is foolish, not merely because of the desirability of life, but also because it is the same training which teaches to live well and to die well. Yet much worse still is the man who says it is good not to be born, but 'once born make haste to pass the gates of Death.' For if he says this from conviction why does he not pass away out of life? For it is open to him to do so, if he had firmly made up his mind to this. But if he speaks in jest, his words are idle among men who cannot receive them.

We must then bear in mind that the future is neither ours, not yet wholly not ours, so that we may not altogether expect it as sure to come, nor abandon hope of it, as if it will certainly not come.

We must consider that of desires some are natural, others vain, and of the natural some are necessary and others merely natural; and of the necessary some are necessary for happiness, others for the repose of the body, and others for very life. The right understanding of these facts enables us to refer all choice and avoidance to the health of the body and the soul's freedom from disturbance, since this is the aim of the life of blessedness. For it is to obtain this end that we always act, namely, to avoid pain and fear. And when this is once secured for us, all the tempest of the soul is dispersed, since the living creature has not to wander as though in search of something that is missing, and to look for some other thing by which he can fulfill the good of the soul and the good of the body. For it is then that we have need of pleasure, when we feel pain owing to the absence of pleasure; but when we do not feel pain, we no longer need pleasure. And for this cause we call pleasure the beginning and end of the blessed life. For we recognize pleasure as the first good innate in us, and from pleasure we begin every act of choice and avoidance, and to pleasure we return again, using the feeling as the standard by which we judge every good.

And since pleasure is the first good and natural to us, for this very reason we do not choose every pleasure, but sometimes we pass over many pleasures, when greater discomfort accrues to us as the result of them: and similarly we think many pains better than pleasures, since a greater pleasure comes to us when we have endured pains for a long time. Every pleasure then because of its natural kinship to us is good, yet not every pleasure is to be chosen: even as every pain also is an evil, yet not all are always of a nature to be avoided. Yet by a scale of comparison and by the consideration of advantages and disadvantages we must form our judgement on all these matters. For the good on certain occasions we treat as bad, and conversely the bad as good.

And again independence of desire we think a great good—not that we may at all times enjoy but a few things, but that, if we do not possess many, we may enjoy the few in the genuine persuasion that those have the sweetest pleasure in luxury who least need it, and that all that is natural is easy to be obtained, but that which is superfluous is hard. And so plain savours bring us a pleasure equal to a luxurious diet, when all the pain due to want is removed; and bread and water produce the highest pleasure, when one who needs them puts them to his lips. To grow accustomed therefore to simple and not luxurious diet gives us health to the full, and makes a man alert for the needful employments of life, and when after long intervals we approach luxuries, disposes us better towards them, and fits us to be fearless of fortune.

When, therefore, we maintain that pleasure is the end, we do not mean the pleasure of profligates and those that consist in sensuality, as is supposed by some who are either ignorant or disagree with us or do not understand, but freedom from pain in the body and from trouble in the mind. For it is not continuous drinkings and revellings, nor the satisfaction of lusts, nor the enjoyment of fish and other luxuries of the wealthy table, which produce a pleasant life, but sober reasoning, searching out the motives for all choice and avoidance, and banishing mere opinions, to which are due the greatest disturbance of the spirit.

Of all this the beginning and the greatest good is prudence. Wherefore prudence is a more precious thing even than philosophy: for from prudence are sprung all the other virtues, and it teaches us that it is not possible to live pleasantly without living prudently and honourably and justly, nor, again, to live a life of prudence, honour, and justice without living pleasantly. For the virtues are by nature bound up with the pleasant life, and the pleasant life is inseparable from them. For indeed who, think you, is a better man than he who holds reverent opinions concerning the gods, and is at all times free from fear of death, and has reasoned out the end ordained by nature? He understands that the limit of good things is easy to fulfil and easy to attain, whereas the course of ills is either short in time or slight in pain: he laughs at destiny, whom some have introduced as the mistress of all things. He thinks that with us lies the chief power in determining events, some of which happen by necessity and some by chance, and some are within our control; for while necessity cannot be called to account, he sees that chance is inconstant, but that which is in our control is subject to no master, and to it are naturally attached praise and blame. For, indeed, it were better to follow the myths about the gods than to become a slave to the destiny of the natural philosophers: for the former suggests a hope of placating the gods by worship, whereas the latter involves a necessity which knows no placation. As to chance, he does not regard it as a god as most men do (for in a god's acts there is no disorder), nor as an uncertain cause of all things: for he does not believe that good and evil are given by chance to man for the framing of a blessed life, but that opportunities for great good and great evil are afforded by it. He therefore thinks it better to be unfortunate in reasonable action than to prosper in unreason. For it is better in a man's actions that what is well chosen should fail, rather than that what is ill chosen should be successful owing to chance.

Meditate therefore on these things and things akin to them night and day by yourself, and with a companion like to yourself, and never shall you be disturbed waking or asleep, but you shall live like a god among men. For a man who lives among immortal blessings is not like a mortal being.

transition: metaphysics and logical positivism

Ancient philosophers were inclined to be generous in their appraisals of the ways we come to know both ourselves and the world around us. Whether by recognizing a series of different states of consciousness occupied successively or by acknowledging different faculties of cognition operating simultaneously, philosophers spoke of several kinds of cognition well into the nineteenth century. Earlier in this century one dominant branch of Anglo-American philosophy turned toward an exclusive recognition of strictly logical inferences based on sense-contents as the only admissible form of cognition. All else, including metaphysics, began to look a little like heresy. This new school of philosophy was known as logical positivism. Its proponents included Moritz Schlick, Rudolph Carnap, and A. J. Ayer, among others. The driving motive of this new school was to clean up the mess of metaphysics by paying closer attention to language.

The Linguistic Turn taken by contemporary philosophy is in many ways comparable to the subjective turn taken by Descartes centuries ago. In both cases the turn pulls us back from unmediated access to the objects of knowledge toward the means of cognition. Where Descartes doubted the veracity of his senses, the logical positivists doubted the veracity of the language we use in articulating claims of truth. According to logical positivism, most philosophical problems are the results of confusions in our language. The abstract language of metaphysics came in for particularly savage attacks.

The following two essays represent extreme poles in a long-standing argument. Bergson defends metaphysical intuition and attacks the adequacy of concepts represented by symbols. Ayer defends the usefulness of what he calls "sense-contents," and attacks what he regards as the vagaries of metaphysics. It can be argued that neither position is entirely viable. Taken alone, the usefulness of either of these essays is doubtful, but together they sharpen some issues that deserve to be aired.

The central issue is not new. Plato's description of what he called "a battle of gods and giants" gives us an excellent introduction to the debate between Bergson and Ayer:

> One party is trying to drag everything down to earth out of heaven and the unseen, literally grasping rocks and trees in their hands, for they lay hold upon every stick and stone and strenuously affirm that real existence belongs only to that which can be handled and offers resistance to the touch. They define reality as the same thing as body, and as soon as one of the opposite party asserts that anything without a body is real, they are utterly contemptuous and will not listen to another word.... Accordingly their adversaries are very wary in defending their position somewhere in the heights of the unseen, maintaining with all their force that true reality consists in certain intelligible and bodiless forms. In the clash of argument they shatter and pulverize those bodies which their opponents wield, and what those others allege to be true reality they call, not real being, but a sort of moving process of becoming. (*The Sophist* 246a-c)

HENRI BERGSON *(1859–1941)*

Bergson is more than eager to talk about what Plato calls "a sort of moving process of becoming." The following passage from An Introduction to Metaphysics *(1903) describes the self in terms of a series of different metaphors attempting to express "pure mobility" and the duration of a process. Taken together with other representations of selfhood, Bergson's essay adds to our sense of selfhood. But Bergson's manner is, it must be confessed, more evocative than argumentative. He suggests much more than he proves; he invites more than he demonstrates. Indeed there remains some doubt about the possibility of any philosophical demonstration once Bergson has completed his critique of concepts.*

Rather than relying on argument and demonstration, Bergson asks each of us to make the effort of introspection to see for ourselves. The trouble with this invitation to private intuitions is that none of us can possibly know whether our experience is the same or different from anyone else's in certain of its felt qualities. We can try to describe them, but, as Bergson will be the first to argue, our use of general terms will fail to capture the specific and unique character of our experience. Bergson tries to tell us what he intuits. And with the aid of his suggestive description, his readers might agree that their experiences correspond to his descriptions. But then again, some of us might not agree, and then where would we be? Since the object of our disagreement is inaccessible to any third party who might apply a neutral criterion for judgment, we would be reduced to a difference of opinion with no reasonable means of resolving the conflict. Though we purport to be discussing entities in everyday experience—selves—our disagreement would quickly take on a theological tone, as if we were discussing otherworldly beings unavailable to empirical validation. Does the self require faith?

Metaphysical Intuition and the Self

... By intuition is meant the kind of *intellectual sympathy* by which one places oneself within an object in order to coincide with what is unique in it and consequently inexpressible. Analysis, on the contrary, is the operation which reduces the object to elements already known, that is, to elements common both to it and other objects. To analyze, therefore, is to express a thing as a function of something other than itself. All analysis is thus a translation, a development into symbols, a representation taken from successive points of view from which we note as many resemblances as possible between the new object which we are studying and others which we believe we know already. In its eternally unsatisfied desire to embrace the object around which it is compelled to turn, analysis multiplies without end the number of its points of view in order to complete its always incomplete representation, and ceaselessly varies its symbols that it may perfect the always imperfect translation. It goes on, therefore, to infinity. But intuition, if intuition is possible, is a simple act.

Now it is easy to see that the ordinary function of positive science is analysis. Positive science works, then, above all, with symbols. Even the most concrete of the natural sciences, those concerned with life, confine themselves to the visible form of living beings, their organs and anatomical elements. They make comparisons between these forms, they reduce the more complex to the more simple; in short, they study the workings of life in what is, so to speak, only its visual symbol. If there exists any means of possessing a reality absolutely instead of knowing it relatively, of placing oneself within it instead of looking at it from outside points of view, of having the intuition instead of making the analysis: in short, of seizing it without any expression, translation, or symbolic representation —metaphysics is that means. *Metaphysics, then, is the science which claims to dispense with symbols.*

There is one reality, at least, which we all seize from within, by intuition and not by simple analysis. It is our own personality in its flowing through time—our self which endures. We may sympathize intellectually with nothing else, but we certainly sympathize with our own selves.

When I direct my attention inward to comtemplate my own self (supposed for the moment to be inactive), I perceive at first, as a crust solidified on the surface, all the perceptions which come to it from the material world. These perceptions are clear, distinct, juxtaposed or juxtaposable one with another; they tend to group themselves into objects. Next, I notice the memories which more or less adhere to these perceptions and which serve to interpret them. These memories have been detached, as it were, from the depth of my personality, drawn to the surface by the perceptions which resemble them; they rest on the surface of my mind without being absolutely myself. Lastly, I feel the stir of tendencies and motor habits—a crowd of virtual actions, more or less firmly bound to these perceptions and memories. All these clearly defined elements appear more distinct from me, the more distinct they are from each other. Radiating, as they do, from within outwards, they form collectively, the surface of a sphere which tends to grow larger and lose itself in the exterior world. But if I draw myself in from the periphery towards the center, if I search in the depth of my being that which is most uniformly, most constantly, and most enduringly myself, I find an altogether different thing.

There is, beneath these sharply cut crystals and this frozen surface, a continuous flux which is not comparable to any flux I have ever seen. There is a succession of states, each of which announces that which follows and contains that which precedes it. They can, properly speaking, only be said to form multiple states when I have already passed them and turn back to observe their track. Whilst I was experiencing them they were so solidly organized, so profoundly animated with a common life, that I could not have said where any one of them finished or where another commenced. In reality no one of them begins or ends, but all extend into each other.

This inner life may be compared to the unrolling of a coil, for there is no living being who does not feel himself coming gradually to the end of his role; and to live is to grow old. But it may just as well be compared to a continual rolling up, like that of a thread on a ball, for our past follows us, it swells incessantly with the present that it picks up on its way; and consciousness means memory.

But actually it is neither an unrolling nor a rolling up, for these two similes evoke the idea of lines and surfaces whose parts are homogeneous and super-posable on one another. Now, there are no two identical moments in the life of the same conscious being. Take the simplest sensation, suppose it constant, absorb in it the entire personality: the consciousness which will accompany this sensation cannot remain identical with itself for two consecutive moments, because the second moment always contains, over and above the first, the memory that the first has bequeathed to it. A consciousness which could experience two identical moments would be a consciousness without memory. It would die and be born again continually. In what other way could one represent unconsciousness?

It would be better, then to use as a comparison the myriad-tinted spectrum, with its insensible gradations leading from one shade to another. A current of feeling which passed along the spectrum, assuming in turn the tint of each of its shades, would experience a series of gradual changes, each of which would announce the one to follow and would sum up those which preceded it. Yet even here the successive shades of the spectrum always remain external one to another. They are juxtaposed; they occupy space. But pure duration, on the contrary, excludes all idea of juxtaposition, reciprocal externality, and extension.

Let us, then, rather, imagine an infinitely small elastic body, contracted, if it were possible, to a mathematical point. Let this be drawn out gradually in such a manner that from the point comes a constantly lengthening line. Let us fix our attention not on the line as a line, but on the action by which it is traced. Let us bear in mind that this action, in spite of it duration, is indivisible if accomplished without stopping, that if a stopping point is inserted, we have two actions instead of one, that each of these separate actions is then the indivisible operation of which we speak, and that it is not the moving action itself which is divisible, but, rather, the stationary line it leaves behind it as its track in space. Finally, let us free ourselves from the space which underlies the movement in order to consider only the movement itself, the act of tension or extension; in short, pure mobility. We shall have this time a more faithful image of the development of our self in duration.

However, even this image is incomplete, and, indeed, every comparison will be insufficient, because the unrolling of our duration resembles in some of its aspects the unity of an advancing movement and in others the multiplicity of expanding states; and, clearly, no metaphor can express one of these two aspects without sacrificing the other. If I use the comparison of the spectrum with its thousand shades, I have before me a thing already made, whilst duration is continually in the making. If I think of an elastic which is being stretched, or of a spring which is extended or relaxed, I forget the richness of color, characteristic of duration that is lived, to see only the simple movement by which consciousness passes from one shade to another. The inner life is all this at once: variety of qualities, continuity of progress, and unity of direction. It cannot be represented by images.

But it is even less possible to represent it by *concepts*, that is by abstract, general, or simple ideas. It is true that no image can reproduce exactly the original feeling I have of the flow of my own conscious life. But it is not even necessary that I should attempt to render it. If a man is incapable of getting for himself the intuition of the constitutive duration of his own being, nothing will ever give it to him, concepts no more than images. Here the single aim of the philosopher should be to promote a certain effort, which in most men is usually fettered by habits of mind more useful to life. Now the image has at least this advantage, that it keeps us in the concrete. No image can replace the intuition of duration, but many diverse images, borrowed from very different orders of things, may, by the convergence of their action, direct consciousness to the precise point where there is a certain intuition to be seized. By choosing images as dissimilar as possible, we shall prevent any one of them from usurping the place of the intuition it is intended to call up, since it would then be driven away at once by its rivals. By providing that, in spite of their differences of aspect, they all require from the mind the same kind of attention, and in some sort the same degree of tension, we shall gradually accustom consciousness to a particular and clearly-defined disposition—that precisely which it must adopt in order to appear to itself as it really is, without any veil. But, then, consciousness must at least consent to make the effort. For it will have been shown nothing: It will simply have been placed in the attitude it must take up in order to make the desired effort, and so come by itself to the intuition. Concepts, on the contrary—especially if they are simple—have the disadvantage of being in reality symbols substituted for the object they symbolize, and demand no effort on our part. Examined closely, each of them, it would be seen, retains only that part of the object which is common to it and to others, and expresses, still more than the image does, a *comparison* between the object and others which resemble it. But as the comparison has made manifest a resemblance, as the resemblance is a property of the object, and as a property has every appearance of being a *part* of the object which possesses it, we easily persuade ourselves that by setting concept beside concept we are reconstructing the whole of the object with its parts, thus obtaining, so to speak, its intellectual equivalent. In this way we believe that we can form a faithful representation of duration by setting in line the concepts of unity, multiplicity, continuity, finite or infinite divisibility, etc. There precisely is the illusion. There also is the danger. Just in so far as abstract ideas can render service to analysis, that is, to the scientific study of the object in its relations to other objects, so far are they incapable of replacing intuition, that is, the metaphysical investigation of what is essential and unique in the object. For, on the one hand, these concepts, laid side by side, never actually give us more than an artificial reconstruction of the object, of which they can only symbolize certain general and, in a way, impersonal aspects; it is therefore useless to believe that with them we can seize a reality of which they present to us the shadow alone. And, on the other hand, besides the illusion there is also a very serious danger. For the concept generalizes at the same time as it abstracts. The concept can only symbolize a particular property by making it common to an infinity of things. It therefore always more or less deforms the property by the extension it gives to it. Replaced in the metaphysical object to which it belongs, a property coincides with the object, or at least molds itself on it, and adopts the same outline. Extracted from the metaphysical object, and presented in a concept, it grows indefinitely larger, and goes beyond the object itself, since henceforth it has to contain it, along with a number of other objects. Thus the different concepts that we form of the properties of a thing inscribe round it so many circles, each much too large and none of them fitting it exactly. And yet, in the thing itself the properties coincided with the thing, and coincided consequently with one another. So that if we are bent on reconstructing the object with concepts, some artifice must be sought whereby this coincidence of the object and its properties can be brought about. For example, we may choose one of the concepts and try, starting from it, to get round to the others. But we shall then soon discover that according as we start from one concept or another, the meeting and combination of the concepts will take place in an altogether different way. According as we start, for example, from unity or from multiplicity, we shall have to conceive differently the multiple unity of duration. Everything will depend on the weight we attribute to this or that concept, and this weight will always be arbitrary, since the concept extracted from the object has no weight, being only the shadow of a body. In this way, as many different *systems* will spring up as there are external points of view from which the reality can be examined, or larger circles in which it can be enclosed. Simple concepts have, then, not only the inconvenience of dividing the concrete unity of the object into so many symbolical expressions; they also divide philosophy into distinct schools, each of which takes its seat, chooses its counters, and carries on with the others a game that will never end. Either metaphysics is only this play of ideas, or else, if it is a serious occupation of the mind, if it is a science and not simply an exercise, it must transcend concepts in order to reach intuition. Certainly, concepts are necessary to it, for all the other sciences work as a rule with concepts, and metaphysics cannot dispense with the other sciences. But it is only truly itself when it goes beyond the concept, or at least when it frees itself from rigid and ready-made concepts in order to create a kind very different from those which we habitually use; I mean supple, mobile, and almost fluid representations, always ready to mold themselves on the fleeting forms of intuition. . . .

A. J. AYER *(b. 1910)*

As in the previous essay, two different points are at issue in the following selection from Ayer's Language, Truth and Logic *(1936). The first point is "How do we know?" The second, "What is the self?" Ayer's essay makes a good transition to the essays by Polanyi, Goffman and Mead because Ayer concludes his discussion by addressing the issue of how we know other selves.*

Ayer describes his epistemology as phenomenalism. *The term has sometimes been used to describe the skeptical view that we cannot know things in themselves, but only their appearances as phenomena within our sense-experience. But Ayer rejects the view that a phenomenalist epistemology must give a causal account of the way "real things" give rise to phenomenal appearances "in the mind." Ayer's phenomenalism is designed to avert metaphysical puzzles about the causal relationships between things that are somehow supposed to be behind experience and ideational events within our experience. Ayer's phenomenalism is linguistic rather than causal. Thus, "What we hold is that the self is reducible to sense-experiences, in the sense that to say anything about the self is always to say something about sense-experiences; and our definition of personal identity is intended to show how this reduction could be made." Reduction is then a kind of translation whose reverse direction is the "logical reconstruction" of statements about the self from statements about sense-experiences. The analysis of the logical relationships among statements should not be confused with the analysis of causal relationships among things or events.*

In trying to come to some conclusions about the disagreements between Bergson and Ayer, readers might want to reflect on the relationships between epistemologies and theories of the self. How does each epistemology lead to a theory of the self? How does each theory of the self support its corresponding epistemology? Or can we decouple the theory of the self from the theory of knowledge in our quest for self-knowledge?

Philosophical Analysis and the Problem of Other Minds

Language and Sense-Contents

A factor which complicates the structure of a language such as English is the prevalence of ambiguous symbols. A symbol is said to be ambiguous when it is constituted by signs which are identical in their sensible form, not only with one another, but also with signs which are elements of some other symbol. For what makes two signs elements of the same symbol is not merely an identity of form, but also an identity of usage. Thus, if we were guided merely by the form of the sign, we should assume that the "is" which occurs in the sentence "He is the author of that book" was the same symbol as the "is" which occurs in the sentence "A cat is a mammal." But, when we come to translate the sentences, we find that the first is equivalent to "He, and no one else, wrote that book," and the second to "The class of mammals contains the class of cats." And this shows that, in this instance, each "is" is an ambiguous symbol which must not be confused with the other, nor with the ambiguous symbols of existence, and class-membership, and identity, and entailment, which are also constituted by signs of the form "is."

To say that a symbol is constituted by signs which are identical with one another in their sensible form, and in their significance, and that a sign is a sense-content, or a series of sense-contents, which is used to convey literal meaning, is not to say that a symbol is a collection, or system, of sense-contents. For when we speak of certain objects, *b*, *c*, *d* . . . as being elements of an object *e*, and of *e* as being constituted by *b*, *c*, *d* . . . we are not saying that they form part of *e*, in the sense in which my arm is a part of my body, or a particular set of books on my shelf is part of my collection of books. What we are saying is that all the sentences in which the symbol *e* occurs can be translated into sentences which do not contain *e* itself, or any symbol which is synonymous with *e*, but do contain symbols *b*, *c*, *d* . . . In such a case we say that *e* is a logical construction out of *b*, *c*, *d* . . . And, in general, we may explain the nature of logical constructions by saying that the introduction of symbols which denote logical constructions is a device which enables us to state complicated propositions about the elements of these constructions in a relatively simple form.

What one must not say is that logical constructions are fictitious objects. For while it is true that the English State, for example, is a logical construction out of individual people, and that the table at which I am writing is a logical construction out of sense-contents, it is not true that either the English State or this table is fictitious, in the sense in which Hamlet or a mirage is fictitious. Indeed, the assertion that tables are logical constructions out of sense-contents is not a factual assertion at all, in the sense in which the assertion that tables were fictitious objects would be a factual assertion, albeit a false one. It is, as our explanation of the notion of a logical construction should have made clear, a linguistic assertion, to the effect that the symbol "table" is definable in terms of certain symbols which stand for sense-contents, not explicitly, but in use. And this, as we have seen, is tantamount to saying that sentences which contain the symbol "table," or the corresponding symbol in any language which has the same structure as English, can all be translated into sentences of the same language which do not contain that symbol, nor any of its synonyms, but do contain certain symbols which stand for sense-contents; a fact which may be loosely expressed by saying that to say anything about a table is always to say something about sense-contents. This does not, of course, imply that to say something about a table is ever to say the same thing about the relevant sense-contents. For example, the sentence, "I am now sittting in front of a table" can, in principle, be translated into a sentence which does not mention tables, but only sense-contents. But this does not mean that we can simply substitute a sense-content symbol for the symbol "table" in the original sentence. If we do this, our new sentence, so far from being equivalent to the old, will be a mere piece of nonsense. To obtain a sentence which is equivalent to the sentence about the table, but refers to sense-contents instead, the whole of the original sentence has to be altered. And this, indeed, is implied by the fact that to say that tables are logical constructions out of sense-contents is to say, not that the symbol "table" can be explicitly defined in terms of symbols which stand for sense-contents, but only that it can be so defined in use. For, as we have seen, the function of a definition in use is not to provide us with a synonym for any symbol, but to enable us to translate sentences of a certain type.

The problem of giving an actual rule for translating sentences about a material thing into sentences about sense-contents, which may be called the problem of the "reduction" of material things to sense-contents, is the main philosophical part of the traditional problem of perception. It is true that writers on perception who set out to describe "the nature of a material thing" believe themselves to be discussing a factual question. But, as we have already pointed out, this is a mistake. The question "What is the nature of a material thing?" is, like any other question of that form, a linguistic question, being a demand for a definition. And the propositions which are set forth in answer to it are linguistic propositions, even though they may be expressed in such a way that they seem to be factual. They are propositions about the relationship of symbols, and not about the properties of the things which the symbols denote.

It is necessary to emphasise this point in connection with the "problem of perception," since the fact that we are unable, in our everyday language, to describe the properties of sense-contents with any great precision, for lack of the requisite symbols, makes it convenient to give the solution of this problem in factual terminology. We express the fact that to speak about material things is, for each of us, a way of speaking about sense-contents, by saying that each of us "constructs" material things out of sense-contents: and we reveal the relationship between the two sorts of symbols by showing what are the principles of this "construction." In other words, one answers the question, "What is the nature of a material thing?" by indicating, in general terms, what are the relations that must hold between any two of one's sense-contents for them to be elements of the same material thing. The difficulty, which here seems to arise, of reconciling the subjectivity of sense-contents with the objectivity of material things will be dealt with in a later chapter of this book.

The solution which we shall now give of this "problem of perception" will serve as a further illustration of the method of philosophical analysis. To simplify the question, we introduce the following definitions. We say that two sense-contents directly resemble one another when there is either no difference, or only an infinitesimal difference, of quality between them; and that they resemble one another indirectly when they are linked by a series of direct resemblances, but are not themselves directly resemblant, a relationship whose possibility depends on the fact that the relative product[1] of infinitesimal differences in quality is an appreciable difference in quality. And we say that two visual, or tactual, sense-contents are directly continuous when they belong to successive members of a series of actual, or possible, sense-fields, and there is no difference, or only an infinitesimal difference, between them, with respect to the position of each in its own sense-field; and that they are indirectly continuous when they are related by an actual, or possible, series of such direct continuities. And here it should be explained that to say of a sense-experience, or a sense-field which is a part of a sense-experience, or a sense-content which is part of a sense field, that it is possible, as opposed to actual, is to say, not that it ever has occurred or will occur in fact, but that it would occur if certain specifiable conditions were fulfilled. So when it is said that a material thing is constituted by both actual and possible

---

[1]"The *relative product* of two relations R and S is the relationship which holds between x and z when there is an intermediate term y such that x has the relation R to y and y has the relation S to z." *Principia Mathematica*, Introduction, Chapter I.

sense-contents, all that is being asserted is that the sentences referring to sense-contents, which are the translations of the sentences referring to any material thing, are both categorical and hypothetical. And thus the notion of a possible sense-content, or sense-experience, is as unobjectionable as the familiar notion of a hypothetical statement.

Relying on these preliminary definitions, one may assert with regard to any two of one's visual sense-contents, or with regard to any two of one's tactual sense-contents, that they are elements of the same material thing if, and only if, they are related to one another by a relation of direct, or indirect, resemblance in certain respects, and by a relation of direct, or indirect, continuity. And as each of these relations is symmetrical—that is to say, a relation which cannot hold between any terms A and B without also holding between B and A—and also transitive—that is, a relation which cannot hold between a term A and another term B, and between B and another term C, without holding between A and C—it follows that the groups of visual and tactual sense-contents which are constituted by means of these relations cannot have any members in common. And this means that no visual, or tactual, sense-content can be an element of more than one material thing....

The Self and Other Minds

To begin with, we must make it clear that we do not accept the realist analysis of our sensations in terms of subject, act, and object. For neither the existence of the substance which is supposed to perform the so-called act of sensing nor the existence of the act itself, as an entity distinct from the sense-contents on which it is supposed to be directed, is in the least capable of being verified. We do not deny, indeed, that a given sense-content can legitimately be said to be experienced by a particular subject; but we shall see that this relation of being experienced by a particular subject is to be analysed in terms of the relationship of sense-contents to one another, and not in terms of a substantival ego and its mysterious acts. Accordingly we define a sense-content not as the object, but as a part of a sense-experience. And from this it follows that the existence of a sense-content always entails the existence of a sense-experience.

It is necessary, at this point, to remark that when one says that a sense-experience, or a sense-content, exists, one is making a different type of statement from that which one makes when one says that a material thing exists. For the existence of a material thing is defined in terms of the actual and possible occurrence of the sense-contents which constitute it as a logical construction, and one cannot significantly speak of a sense-experience, which is a whole composed of sense-contents, or of a sense-content itself as if it were a logical construction out of sense-contents. And in fact when we say that a given sense-content or sense-experience exists, we are saying no more than that it occurs. And, accordingly, it seems advisable always to speak of the "occurrence" of sense-contents and sense-experiences in preference to speaking of their "existence," and so to avoid the danger of treating sense-contents as if they were material things.

The answer to the question whether sense-contents are mental or physical is that they are neither; or rather, that the distinction between what is mental and what is physical does not apply to sense-contents. It applies only to objects which are logical constructions out of them. But what differentiates one such logical construction from another is the fact that it is constituted by different sense-contents or by sense-contents differently related. So that when we distinguish a given mental object from a given physical object, or a mental object from another mental object, or a physical object from another physical object, we are in every case distinguishing between different logical constructions whose elements cannot themselves be said to be either mental or physical. It is, indeed, not impossible for a sense-content to be an element both of a mental and of a physical object; but it is necessary that some of the elements, or some of the relations, should be different in the two logical constructions. And it may be advisable here to repeat that, when we refer to an object as a logical construction out of certain sense-contents, we are not saying that it is actually constructed out of those sense-contents, or that the sense-contents are in any way parts of it, but are merely expressing, in a convenient, if somewhat misleading, fashion, the syntactical fact that all sentences referring to it are translatable into sentences referring to them.

The fact that the distinction between mind and matter applies only to logical constructions and that all distinctions between logical constructions are reducible to distinctions between sense-contents, proves that the difference between the entire class of mental objects and the entire class of physical objects is not in any sense more fundamental than the difference between any two subclasses of mental objects, or the difference between any two subclasses of physical objects. Actually, the distinguishing feature of the objects belonging to the category of "one's own mental states" is the fact that they are mainly constituted by "introspective" sense-contents and by sense-contents which are elements of one's own body; and the distinguishing feature of the objects belonging to the category of "the mental states of others" is the fact that they are mainly constituted by sense-contents which are elements of other living bodies; and what makes one unite these two classes of objects to form the single class of mental objects is the fact that there is a high degree of qualitative similarity between many of the sense-contents which are elements of other living bodies and many of the elements of one's own. But we are not now concerned with the provision of an exact definition of "mentality." We are interested only in making it plain that the distinction between mind and matter, applying as it does to logical constructions out of sense-contents, cannot apply to sense-contents themselves. For a distinction between logical constructions which is constituted by the fact that there are certain distinctions between their elements is clearly of a different type from any distinction that can obtain between the elements.

It should be clear, also, that there is no philosophical problem concerning the relationship of mind and matter, other than the linguistic problems of defining certain symbols which denote logical constructions in terms of symbols which denote sense-contents. The problems with which philosophers have vexed themselves in the past, concerning the possibility of bridging the "gulf" between mind and matter in knowledge or in action, are all fictitious problems arising out of the senseless metaphysical conception of mind and matter, or minds and material things, as "substances." Being freed from metaphysics, we see that there can be no *a priori* objections to the existence either of causal or of epistemological connections between minds and material things. For, roughly speaking, all that we are saying when we say that the mental state of a person A at a time *t* is a state of awareness of a material thing X, is that the sense-experience which is the element of A occurring at time *t* contains a sense-content which is an element of X, and also certain images which define A's expectation of the occurrence in suitable circumstances of certain further elements of X, and that this expectation is correct: and what we are saying when we assert that a mental object M and a physical object X are causally connected is that, in certain conditions, the occurrence of a certain sort of sense-content, which is an element of M, is a reliable sign of the occurrence of a certain sort of sense-content, which is an element of X, or vice versa. And the question whether any propositions of these kinds are true or not is clearly an empirical question. It cannot be decided, as metaphysicians have attempted to decide it, *a priori*.

We turn now to consider the question of the subjectivity of sense-contents—that is, to consider whether it is or is not logically possible for a sense-content to occur in the sense-history of more than a single self. And in order to decide this question we must proceed to give an analysis of the notion of a self.

The problem which now confronts us is analogous to the problem of perception with which we have already dealt. We know that a self, if it is not to be treated as a metaphysical entity, must be held to be a logical construction out of sense-experiences. It is, in fact, a logical construction out of the sense-experiences which constitute the actual and possible sense-history of a self. And, accordingly, if we ask what is the nature of the self, we are asking what is the relationship that must obtain between sense-experiences for them to belong to the sense-history of the same self. And the answer to this question is that for any two sense-experiences to belong to the sense-history of the same self it is necessary and sufficient that they should contain organic sense-contents which are elements of the same body.[2] But, as it is logically impossible for any organic sense-content to be an element of more than one body, the relation of "belonging to the sense-history of the same self" turns out to be a symmetrical and transitive relation. And, from the fact that the relation of belonging to the sense-history of the same self is symmetrical and transitive, it follows necessarily that the series of sense-experiences which constitute the sense-histories of different selves cannot have any members in common. And this is tantamount to saying that it is logically impossible for a sense-experience to belong to the sense-history of more than a single self. But if all sense-experiences are subjective, then, all sense-contents are subjective. For it is necessary by definition for a sense-content to be contained in a single sense-experience.

To many people, the account of the self, on which this conclusion depends, will no doubt appear paradoxical. For it is still fashionable to regard the self as a

---

[2]This is not the only criterion. Vide *The Foundations of Empirical Knowledge*, pp. 142–44.

substance. But, when one comes to enquire into the nature of this substance, one finds that it is an entirely unobservable entity. It may be suggested that it is revealed in self-consciousness but this is not the case. For all that is involved in self-consciousness is the ability of a self to remember some of its earlier states. And to say that a self A is able to remember some of its earlier states is to say merely that some of the sense-experiences which constitute A contain memory images which correspond to sense-contents which have previously occurred in the sense-history of A.[3] And thus we find that the possibility of self-consciousness in no way involves the existence of a substantive ego. But if the substantive ego is not revealed in self-consciousness, it is not revealed anywhere. The existence of such an entity is completely unverifiable. And accordingly, we must conclude that the assumption of its existence is no less metaphysical than Locke's discredited assumption of the existence of a material substratum. For it is clearly no more significant to assert that an "unobservable somewhat" underlies the sensations which are the sole empirical manifestations of the self than it is to assert that an "unobservable somewhat" underlies the sensations which are the sole empirical manifestations of a material thing. The considerations which make it necessary, as Berkeley saw, to give a phenomenalist account of material things, make it necessary also, as Berkeley did not see, to give a phenomenalist account of the self.

Our reasoning on this point, as on so many others, is in conformity with Hume's. He, too, rejected the notion of a substantive ego on the ground that no such entity was observable. For, he said, whenever he entered most intimately into what he called himself, he always stumbled on some particular perception or other—of heat or cold, light or shade, love or hatred, pain or pleasure. He never could catch himself at any time without a perception, and never could observe anything but the perception. And this led him to assert that a self was "nothing but a bundle or collection of different perceptions."[4] But, having asserted this, he found himself unable to discover the principle on which innumerable distinct perceptions among which it was impossible to perceive any "real connection" were united to form a single self. He saw that the memory must be regarded not as producing, but rather as discovering, personal identity—or, in other words, that, whereas self-consciousness has to be defined in terms of memory, self-identity cannot be; for the number of my perceptions which I can remember at any time always falls far short of the number of those which have actually occurred in my history, and those which I cannot remember are no less constitutive of my self than those which I can. But having, on this ground, rejected the claim of memory to be the unifying principle of the self, Hume was obliged to confess that he did not know what was the connection between perceptions in virtue of which they formed a single self.[5] And this confession has often been taken by rationalist authors as evidence that it is impossible for a consistent empiricist to give a satisfactory account of the self.

For our part, we have shown that this charge against empiricism is unfounded. For we have solved Hume's problem by defining personal identity in terms of bodily identity, and bodily identity is to be defined in terms of the

[3]cf. Bertrand Russell, *Analysis of Mind*, Lecture IX.
[4]*Treatise of Human Nature*, Book I, Part IV, section vi.
[5]*Treatise of Human Nature*, Appendix.

resemblance and continuity of sense-contents. And this procedure is justified by the fact that whereas it is permissible, in our language, to speak of a man as surviving a complete loss of memory, or a complete change of character, it is self-contradictory to speak of a man as surviving the annihilation of his body.[6] For that which is supposed to survive by those who look forward to a "life after death" is not the empirical self, but a metaphysical entity—the soul. And this metaphysical entity, concerning which no genuine hypothesis can be formulated, has no logical connection whatsoever with the self.

It must, however, be remarked that, although we have vindicated Hume's contention that it is necessary to give a phenomenalist account of the nature of the self, our actual definition of the self is not a mere restatement of his. For we do not hold, as he apparently did, that the self is an aggregate of sense-experiences, or that the sense-experiences which constitute a particular self are in any sense parts of it. What we hold is that the self is reducible to sense-experiences, in the sense that to say anything about the self is always to say something about sense-experiences; and our definition of personal identity is intended to show how this reduction could be made.

In thus combining a thoroughgoing phenomenalism with the admission that all sense-experiences, and the sense-contents which form part of them, are private to a single self, we are pursuing a course to which the following objection is likely to be raised. It will be said that anyone who maintains both that all empirical knowledge resolves itself on analysis into knowledge of the relationships of sense-contents, and also that the whole of a man's sense-history is private to himself, is logically obliged to be a solipsist—that is, to hold that no other people besides himself exist, or at any rate that there is no good reason to suppose that any other people beside himself exist. For it follows from his premises, so it will be argued, that the sense-experiences of another person cannot possibly form part of his own experience, and consequently that he cannot have the slightest ground for believing in their occurrence; and, in that case, if people are nothing but logical constructions out of their sense-experiences, he cannot have the slightest ground for believing in the existence of any other people. And it will be said that even if such a solipsistic doctrine cannot be shown to be self-contradictory, it is nevertheless known to be false.[7]

I propose to meet this objection, not by denying that solipsism is known to be false, but by denying that it is a necessary consequence of our epistemology. I am, indeed, prepared to admit that if the personality of others was something that I could not possibly observe, then I should have no reason to believe in the existence of anyone else. And in admitting this I am conceding a point which would not, I think, be conceded by the majority of those philosophers who hold, as we do, that a sense-content cannot belong to the sense-history of more than a single self. They would maintain, on the contrary, that, although one cannot in any sense observe the existence of other people, one can nevertheless infer their existence with a high degree of probability from one's own experiences. They would say that my observation of a body whose behaviour resembled the

---

[6]This is not true if one adopts a psychological criterion of personal identity.
[7]c.f. L. S. Stebbing, *Logical Positivism and Analysis*.

behaviour of my own body entitled me to think it probable that that body was related to a self which I could not observe, in the same way as my body was related to my own observable self. And in saying this, they would be attempting to answer not the psychological question, What causes me to believe in the existence of other people? but the logical question, What good reason have I for believing in the existence of other people? So that their view cannot be refuted, as is sometimes supposed, by an argument which shows that infants come by their belief in the existence of other people intuitively, and not through a process of inference. For although my belief in a certain proposition may in fact be causally dependent on my apprehension of the evidence which makes the belief rational, it is not necessary that it should be. It is not self contradictory to say that beliefs for which there are rational grounds are frequently arrived at by irrational means.

The correct way to refute this view that I can use an argument from analogy, based on the fact that there is a perceptible resemblance between the behaviour of other bodies and that of my own, to justify a belief in the existence of other people whose experiences I could not conceivably observe, is to point out that no argument can render probable a completely unverifiable hypothesis. I can legitimately use an argument from analogy to establish the probable existence of an object which has never in fact manifested itself in my experience, provided that the object is such that it could conceivably be manifested'in my experience. If this condition is not fulfilled, then, as far as I am concerned, the object is a metaphysical object, and the assertion that it exists and has certain properties is a metaphysical assertion. And, since a metaphysical assertion is senseless, no argument can possibly render it probable. But, on the view which we are discussing, I must regard other people as metaphysical objects; for it is assumed that their experiences are completely inaccessible to my observation.

The conclusion to be drawn from this is not that the existence of other people is for me a metaphysical, and so fictitious, hypothesis, but that the assumption that other people's experiences are completely inaccessible to my observation is false: just as the conclusion to be drawn from the fact that Locke's notion of a material substratum is metaphysical is not that all the assertions which we make about material things are nonsensical, but that Locke's analysis of the concept of a material thing is false. And just as I must define material things and my own self in terms of their empirical manifestations, so I must define other people in terms of their empirical manifestations—that is, in terms of the behaviour of their bodies, and ultimately in terms of sense-contents. The assumption that "behind" these sense-contents there are entities which are not even in principle accessible to my observation can have no more significance for me than the admittedly metaphysical assumption that such entities "underlie" the sense-contents which constitute material things for me, or my own self. And thus I find that I have as good a reason to believe in the existence of other people as I have to believe in the existence of material things. For in each case my hypothesis is verified by the occurrence in my sense-history of the appropriate series of sense-contents. . . .

transition: epistemology and interpersonal perception

The selection from Sartre concluded, "We have to deal with human reality as a being which is what it is not and which is not what it is." In terms of the traditional opposition between essence and existence—the distinction between what a thing *is* (in its very essence) and what it *does* (how it happens to exist)—we could say that human reality is constituted through its existence, not given through an original essence. Human reality is not what it is (essentially), rather it is what it is not; it is what it becomes; it is what it is not now but what it comes to be through its existence. Hence the name 'Existentialism' for a philosophy that argues the primacy of existence to essence.

The following selections hold that the existence of the self is largely constituted by its relations to other selves. You may object that you don't cease to exist as a self when you go off into the woods away from other selves. And, where did the first self come from if it needed other selves to become a self? To the first objection: the reason you don't cease to exist apart from other selves is that selves, once constituted, do not decompose that quickly. A mountain lake does not disappear as soon as the rain stops; yet the water level is clearly not independent of the rainfall. A complex ecology relates the lake to the weather: without sun no trees would grow, no roots would hold the soil, and erosion might empty the mountain lake into the plains below. Both rain and sun preserve the lake, just as society and solitude nourish the self. The relation between the self and others is more complex than a simple moment-to-moment dependence for preservation, and your survival in the woods alone does not discount the possibility that your self depends for its existence on the existence of other selves. So much for the first objection.

But what about the other selves? To return to the second objection, if each self depends on other selves, where did the first self come from? This objection is in a way more difficult but less damaging. After all, if we know that selves are interdependent *now,* why must we speculate on how they got that way? To argue from the lack of an account of the first self to the independence of contemporary selves is like arguing that since we cannot describe the first language user we can claim that contemporary language users do not learn from others but make up their language all by themselves. Though we lack an accurate account of its first beginnings, it is clearly possible for selfhood, as well as language, to have a distinctively social genesis.

If, nevertheless, we want a theory of the first beginnings of selfhood, we can turn to Hegel, who posits the mutual genesis of self-conscious selves in a life-and-death struggle ending in a master-slave relationship. Without going into the details of his analysis, suffice it to say that for the struggle that issues in selfhood, it takes at least two to play. No one can do it alone. *Utterly* alone one is "no one." This is not a sentimental point; it is an ontological point (*ontos,* Greek for "being"; *logos,* "logic" or "science"; hence ontology as the science of being). The being of the self is constituted by its relations to others, just as others in turn are constituted in their being by their relations.

Let us pause on a structural point concerning the relationship of whole to part and the ways we often misconstrue that relationship. Because we must focus on parts, because we need to identify particular instances in their individuality if we are to get along at all, we often tend to overemphasize their individuality, their apparent self-sufficiency and nonrelatedness. I want to know Charlie "as he really is" and not merely as I sometimes see him, or as Jane sees him. Rather than deal with the impossible complexity of acknowledging that Charlie "as he really is" is a complexity of countless relationships other than his relationships to me and Jane, I tend to distinguish between his relatedness to me and Jane on the one hand, and an autonomous Charlie-as-he-really-is on the other. And once again a false dichotomization suggests that if relatedness qualifies one term of the distinction, then nonrelatedness must qualify the other. In fact, Charlie as independent of me and Jane is simply (or rather very complexly) Charlie as dependently related to slews of other entities, animate and inanimate. Failing to see this, I absolutize Charlie the particular and lose sight of Charlie as related to the whole. I absolutize a relative. I make a simple substance out of what is really a complex nexus of relations.

We frequently simplify by drawing false dichotomies between the relative and some absolute, and philosophical inquiry often turns out to be a struggle against our absolutizings. The specific form of absolutizing with respect to part and whole often goes something like this: we see the part out of relation to the whole, and then, when it comes to talking about the whole, see it as a mere sum of the parts, or think about it the same way we think about the parts. Knowing that it makes sense to infer from some parts to other parts, we think we can infer from part to whole. For example, knowing what it means to say that the desk is upside-down, we can infer what it would mean for the whole room to be upside-down: not just the desk, but everything in the room, including the walls, would be topsy-turvy. Extrapolating beyond the inference from desk to room, I might think that the following question makes sense: "What if *everything* were upside down?" But a little reflection will show that this question makes no sense at all since the concept 'upside-down' is a relational concept: desk relative to room, or room in relation to the rest of the house or the earth. Because we are able to attribute upside-downness without explicitly or consciously referring to that in relation to which something is upside-down, we slip into thinking of upside-downness as nonrelational, and then imagine that we can attribute it to anything. But our error becomes apparent when we try to attribute upside-downness to the whole—everything—for there is nothing else relative to which everything together could be said to be upside-down.

Nor will it do to say everything is upside-down relative to space. *If* space were absolutized into a self-subsistent thing, relative to which everything *else* could be upside-down, we must include that thing called space in the "everything" that gets turned upside-down. But space is not a thing, even though 'space' is a noun. Rather, spatiality is something about the relations among things. Indeed, the nonabsolute character of space is a key doctrine of *relativity* theory in physics.

The following selections are steps toward a relativity theory in philosophy. The comparison with Einstein's theory is apt, for it helps forestall misplaced fears about relativism. When people object to the horrors of so-called modern relativism, they may be objecting to the position that can be described as *subjective* relativism: a position that says I can say whatever I like, and you can say whatever you like, and what I say is true only relative to me, and what you say is true only for you, and so on. A totally subjective relativism reduces to absurdity: truth presupposes intersubjective validity, so the concept of 'true for me' is empty. If there be no intersubjectively shared criteria for truth, then truth becomes indistinguishable from mere opinion. So subjective relativism is a total skepticism in which there is no truth, only a vast multiplicity of opinions, none better than any other.

But one can evade the skepticism of subjective relativism without recourse to a positing of absolutes. Einstein's relativity theory rests on more than Einstein's opinion. Similarly a philosophy that exposes the structures relating part to part and part to whole may qualify as what could be called an *objective* relativism. We understand parts of our experience by their relationships to other parts. We understand ourselves not only *through* our relationships to others, but *as being* our relationships to others.

MICHAEL POLANYI *(b.1891)*

Michael Polanyi is a contemporary scientist turned philosopher. In The Tacit
Dimension *(1966) he shows that we can know more than we can tell. Here we will
stress only three of the many ways his thesis is relevant to our concerns. First, we need
an epistemology of interpersonal perception. Goffman's essay places such stress on the
subtlety of communication that we must first be convinced that we can master that
subtlety before we can take Goffman seriously. Polanyi establishes an epistemological
foundation for the claim that we need not know* that *we are projecting messages about
ourselves or* how *we do so in order to be able to project those messages. Similarly, we
may be able to read all sorts of things from the behavior of others without being able to
say how it is that we read their behavior.*

*Second, Polanyi's essay is one of the several essays in this volume bearing on the
question of women's liberation. Although he does not make the case explicit himself, his
argument begs for interpretation as an analysis of so-called women's intuition. In
Polanyi's analysis women's intuition is no myth; rather it is a natural capacity
available to any humans who do not constrain themselves to know only what they can
tell. As Polanyi points out, and Germaine Greer will underscore, "an unbridled lucidity
can destroy our understanding of complex matters."*

*Third, and finally, Polanyi articulates the role of personal investment in inquiry.
He argues that the ideal of objectivity can be a mistake. The ramifications of this
complex point may remain tacit for the moment, but readers should ruminate on
Polanyi's remarks.*

How I Know Others

Some of you may know that I turned to philosophy as an afterthought to my
career as a scientist. I would like to tell you what I was after in making this change,
for it will also explain the general task to which my present lecture should
introduce us.

I first met questions of philosphy when I came up against the Soviet ideology
under Stalin which denied justification to the pursuit of science. I remember a
conversation I had with Bukharin in Moscow in 1935. Though he was heading
toward his fall and execution three years later, he was still a leading theoretician of
the Communist party. When I asked him about the pursuit of pure science in
Soviet Russia, he said that pure science was a morbid symptom of a class society;
under socialism the conception of science pursued for its own sake would
disappear, for the interests of scientists would spontaneously turn to problems of
the current Five-Year-Plan.

I was struck by the fact that this denial of the very existence of independent scientific thought came from a socialist theory which derived its tremendous persuasive power from its claim to scientific certainty. The scientific outlook appeared to have produced a mechanical conception of man and history in which there was no place for science itself. This conception denied altogether any intrinsic power to thought and thus denied also any grounds for claiming freedom of thought.

I saw also that this self-immolation of the mind was actuated by powerful moral motives. The mechanical course of history was to bring universal justice. Scientific skepticism would trust only material necessity for achieving universal brotherhood. Skepticism and utopianism had thus fused into a new skeptical fanaticism.

It seemed to me then that our whole civilization was pervaded by the dissonance of an extreme critical lucidity and an intense moral conscience, and that this combination had generated both our tight-lipped modern revolutions and the tormented self-doubt of modern man outside revolutionary movement. So I resolved to inquire into the roots of this condition.

My search has led me to a novel idea of human knowledge from which a harmonious view of thought and existence, rooted in the universe, seems to emerge.

I shall reconsider human knowledge by starting from the fact that *we can know more than we can tell.* This fact seems obvious enough; but it is not easy to say exactly what it means. Take an example. We know a person's face, and can recognize it among a thousand, indeed among a million. Yet we usually cannot tell how we recognize a face we know. So most of this knowledge cannot be put into words. But the police have recently introduced a method by which we can communicate much of this knowledge. They have made a large collection of pictures showing a variety of noses, mouths, and other features. From these the witness selects the particulars of the face he knows, and the pieces can then be put together to form a reasonably good likeness of the face. This may suggest that we can communicate, after all, our knowledge of a physiognomy, provided we are given adequate means for expressing ourselves. But the application of the police method does not change the fact that previous to it we did know more than we could tell at the time. Moreover, we can use the police method only by knowing how to match the features we remember with those in the collection, and we cannot tell how we do this. This very act of communication displays a knowledge that we cannot tell.

There are many other instances of the recognition of a characteristic physiognomy—some commonplace, others more technical—which have the same structure as the identification of a person. We recognize the moods of the human face, without being able to tell, except quite vaguely, by what signs we know it. At the universities great efforts are spent in practical classes to teach students to identify cases of diseases and specimens of rocks, of plants and animals. All descriptive sciences study physiognomies that cannot be fully described in words, nor even in pictures.

But can it not be argued, once more, that the possibility of teaching these

[handwritten margin notes: recognize a person by his physical appearance police investigative tactic used to place features on a face to get the total identity / moods students see a demonstration of appearance objects exterior but the identification is when he uses his intellect]

appearances by practical exercises proves that we can tell our knowledge of them? The answer is that we can do so only by relying on the pupil's intelligent co-operation for catching the meaning of the demonstration. Indeed, any definition of a word denoting an external thing must ultimately rely on pointing at such a thing. This naming-cum-pointing is called "an ostensive definition"; and this philosophic expression conceals a gap to be bridged by an intelligent effort on the part of the person to whom we want to tell what the word means. Our message had left something behind that we could not tell, and its reception must rely on it that the person addressed will discover that which we have not been able to communicate.

Gestalt psychology has demonstrated that we may know a physiognomy by integrating our awareness of its particulars without being able to identify these particulars, and my analysis of knowledge is closely linked to this discovery of Gestalt psychology. But I shall attend to aspects of Gestalt which have been hitherto neglected. Gestalt psychology has assumed that perception of a physiognomy takes place through the spontaneous equilibration of its particulars impressed on the retina or on the brain. However, I am looking at Gestalt, on the contrary, as the outcome of an active shaping of experience performed in the pursuit of knowledge. This shaping or integrating I hold to be the great and indispensable tacit power by which all knowledge is discovered and, once discovered, is held to be true.

The structure of Gestalt is then recast into a logic of tacit thought, and this changes the range and perspective of the whole subject. The highest forms of integration loom largest now. These are manifested in the tacit power of scientific and artistic genius. The art of the expert diagnostician may be listed next, as a somewhat impoverished form of discovery, and we may put in the same class the performance of skills, whether artistic, athletic, or technical. We have here examples of knowing, both of a more intellectual and more practical kind; both the "wissen" and "können" of the Germans, or the "knowing what" and the "knowing how" of Gilbert Ryle. These two aspects of knowing have a similar structure and neither is ever present without the other. This is particularly clear in the art of diagnosing, which intimately combines skillful testing with expert observation. I shall always speak of "knowing," therefore, to cover both practical and theoretical knowledge. We can, accordingly, interpret the use of tools, of probes, and of pointers as further instances of the art of knowing, and may add to our list also the denotative use of language, as a kind of verbal pointing.

Perception, on which Gestalt psychology centered its attention, now appears as the most impoverished form of tacit knowing. As such it will be shown to form the bridge between the higher creative power of man and the bodily processes which are prominent in the operations of perception.

Some recent psychological experiments have shown in isolation the principal mechanism by which knowledge is tacitly acquired. Many of you have heard of these experiments as revealing the diabolical machinery of hidden persuasion. Actually, they are but elementary demonstrations of the faculty by which we apprehend the relation between two events, both of which we know, but only one of which we can tell.

Following the example set by Lazarus and McCleary in 1949, psychologists call the exercise of this faculty a process of "subception."[1] These authors presented a person with a large number of nonsense syllables, and after showing certain of the syllables, they administered an electric shock. Presently the person showed symptoms of anticipating the shock at the sight of "shock syllables"; yet, on questioning, he could not identify them. He had come to know when to expect a shock, but he could not tell what made him expect it. He had acquired a knowledge similar to that which we have when we know a person by signs which we cannot tell.

Another variant of this phenomenon was demonstrated by Eriksen and Kuethe in 1958.[2] They exposed a person to a shock whenever he happened to utter associations to certain "shock words." Presently, the person learned to forestall the shock by avoiding the utterance of such associations, but, on questioning, it

[handwritten margin notes: when a person said nonsense syllables they shocked them had the knowledge to avoid saying those words when a person got shock words person learned to forestall the utterance of such associations]

[1]Lazarus, R. S., and McCleary, R. A., *Journal of Personality* (Vol. 18, 1949), p. 191, and *Psychological Review* (Vol. 58, 1951), p. 113. These results were called in question by Eriksen, C. W., *Psychological Review* (Vol. 63, 1956), p. 74 and defended by Lazarus, *Psychological Review* (Vol. 63, 1956), p. 343. But in a later paper surveying the whole field—*Psychological Review* (Vol. 67, 1960), p. 279—Eriksen confirmed the experiments of Lazarus and McCleary, and accepted them as evidence of subception.

I am relying on subception only as a confirmation of tacit knowing in an elementary form, capable of quantitative experimental desmonstration. For me it is the mechanism underlying the formation of Gestalt, from which I first derived my conception of tacit knowing in *Personal Knowledge*. Strangely enough, the connection of subception with Gestalt has been hardly noticed by psychologists in the course of their controversies on the validity of subception. I could find only one place alluding to it, in a paper by Klein, George S., "On Subliminal Activation," *Journal of Nervous Mental Disorders* (Vol. 128, 1959), pp 293–301. He observes: "It requires no experimental demonstration to say confidently that we are not aware of all the stimuli which we use in behavior."

I have said already basically in *Personal Knowledge* and have continued to emphasize since then, that it is a mistake to identify subsidiary awareness with unconscious awareness, or with the Jamesian fringe of awareness. What makes an awareness subsidiary is the *function it fulfills;* it can have any degree of consciousness, so long as it functions as a clue to the object of our focal attention. Klein supports this by saying that subliminal activation is but a special case of *transient or incidental stimuli* of all kinds. It is not the subliminal status that matters but "the meanings and properties [a stimulus] acquires at the periphery of thought and action."

Eriksen and Kuethe, whose observation of not consciously identified avoidance I have quoted as a kind of subception, have called this avoidance a defense mechanism, thus affiliating it to Freudian conceptions. This practice is widespread and has caused *Psychological Abstracts* to divide the subject matter into subception and defense mechanism.

Yet another fragmentation of this matter occurred by taking due notice of Otto Potzl's observations going back to 1917. A survey of his work and of that of his direct successors has appeared in *Psychological Issues* (Vol. II, No. 3, 1960) under the title "Preconscious Stimulation in Dreams, Associations, and Images" by Otto Potzl, Rudolf Allers, and Jacob Teler, International Universities Press, New York 11, N.Y. An introduction to this monograph by Charles Fisher links these observations to recent studies and notes the present uncertainty about the status of stimuli of which we become conscious only in terms of their contribution to subsequent experience. "The matter needs to be settled," writes Fisher on p. 33, "because the issue of subliminality has important implications for theories of perception."

I believe that this matter has actually much wider implications and must be generally subsumed under the logical categories of tacit knowing.

[2]Eriksen, C. W., and Kuethe, J. L., "Avoidance Conditioning of Verbal Behavior Without Awareness: A Paradigm of Repression," *Journal of Abnormal and Social Psychology* (Vol. 53, 1956), pp. 203–09.

appeared that he did not know he was doing this. Here the subject got to know a practical operation, but could not tell how he worked it. This kind of subception has the structure of a skill, for a skill combines elementary muscular acts which are not identifiable, according to relations that we cannot define.

These experiments show most clearly what is meant by saying that one can know more than one can tell. For the experimental arrangement wards off the suspicion of self-contradiction, which is not easy to dispel when anyone speaks of things he knows and cannot tell. This is prevented here by the division of roles between the subject and the observer. The experimenter observes that another person has a certain knowledge that he cannot tell, and so no one speaks of a knowledge he himself has and cannot tell.

We may carry forward, then, the following result. In both experiments that I have cited, subception was induced by electric shock. In the first series the subject was shocked after being shown certain nonsense syllables, and he learned to expect this event. In the second series he learned to suppress the uttering of certain associations, which would evoke the shock. In both cases the shock-producing particulars remained tacit. The subject could not identify them, yet he relied on his awareness of them for anticipating the electric shock.

Here we see the basic structure of tacit knowing. It always involves two things, or two kinds of things. We may call them the two terms of tacit knowing. In the experiments the shock syllables and shock associations formed the first term, and the electric shock which followed them was the second term. After the subject had learned to connect these two terms, the sight of the shock syllables evoked the expectation of a shock and the utterance of the shock associations was suppressed in order to avoid shock. Why did this connection remain tacit? It would seem that this was due to the fact that the subject was riveting his attention on the electric shock. He was relying on his awareness of the shock-producing particulars only in their bearing on the electric shock. We may say that he learned to rely on his awareness of these particulars for the purpose of attending to the electric shock.

Here we have the basic definition of the logical relation between the first and second term of a tacit knowledge. It combines two kinds of knowing. We know the electric shock, forming the second term, by attending to it, and hence the subject is *specifiably* known. But we know the shock-producing particulars only by relying on our own awareness of them for attending to something else, namely the electric shock, and hence our knowledge of them remains *tacit*. This is how we come to know these particulars, without becoming able to identify them. Such is the *functional relation* between the two terms of tacit knowing: *we know the first term only by relying on our awareness of it for attending to the second.*

In his book on freedom of the will, Austin Farrar has spoken at one point of *disattending from* certain things for attending *to* others. I shall adopt a variant of this usage by saying that in an act of tacit knowing we *attend from* something for attending *to* something else; namely, *from* the first term *to* the second term of the tacit relation. In many ways the first term of this relation will prove to be nearer to us, the second further away from us. Using the language of anatomy, we may call the first term *proximal*, and the second term *distal*. It is the proximal term, then, of which we have a knowledge that we may not be able to tell.

In the case of a human physiognomy, I would now say that we rely on our awareness of its features for attending to the characteristic appearance of a face. We are attending *from* the features *to* the face, and thus may be unable to specify the features. And I would say, likewise, that we are relying on our awareness of a combination of muscular acts for attending to the performance of a skill. We are attending *from* these elementary movements *to* the achievement of their joint purpose, and hence are usually unable to specify these elementary acts. We may call this the *functional structure* of tacit knowing.

But we may ask: does not the *appearance* of the experimental setting—composed of the nonsense syllables and the electric shocks—undergo some change when we learn to anticipate a shock at the sight of certain syllables? It does, and in a very subtle way. The expectation of a shock, which at first had been vague and unceasing, now becomes sharply fluctuating; it suddenly rises at some moments and drops between them. So we may say that even though we do not learn to recognize the shock syllables as distinct from other syllables, we do become aware of facing a shock syllable in terms of the apprehension it evokes in us. In other words, we are aware of seeing these syllables in terms of that on which we are focusing our attention, which is the probability of an electric shock. Applying this to the case of a physiognomy, we may say that we are aware of its features in terms of the physiognomy to which we are attending. In the exercise of a skill, we are aware of its several muscular moves in terms of the performance to which our attention is directed. We may say, in general, that we are aware of the proximal term of an act of tacit knowing in the appearance of its distal term; we are aware of that *from* which we are attending *to* another thing, in the *appearance* of that thing. We may call this the *phenomenal structure* of tacit knowing.

But there is a significance in the relation of the two terms of tacit knowing which combines its functional and phenomenal aspects. When the sight of certain syllables makes us expect an electric shock, we may say that they *signify* the approach of a shock. This is their *meaning* to us. We could say, therefore, that when shock syllables arouse an apprehension in us, without our being able to identify the syllables which arouse it, we know these syllables only in terms of their meaning. It is their meaning to which our attention is directed. It is in terms of their meaning that they enter into the appearance of that *to* which we are attending *from* them.

We could say, in this sense, that a characteristic physiognomy is the meaning of its features; which is, in fact, what we do say when a physiognomy expresses a particular mood. To identify a physiognomy would then amount to relying on our awareness of its features for attending to their joint meaning. This may sound far-fetched, because the meaning of the features is observed at the same spot where the features are situated, and hence it is difficult to separate mentally the features from their meaning. Yet, the fact remains that the two are distinct, since we may know a physiognomy without being able to specify its particulars.

To see more clearly the separation of a meaning from that which has this meaning, we may take the example of the use of a probe to explore a cavern, or the way a blind man feels his way by tapping with a stick. For here the separation of the two is wide, and we can also observe here the process by which this separation gradually takes place. Anyone using a probe for the first time will feel its impact against his fingers and palm. But as we learn to use a probe, or to use a stick for feeling our way, our awareness of its impact on our hand is transformed into a sense of its point touching the objects we are exploring. This is how an interpretative effort transposes meaningless feelings into meaningful ones, and places these at some distance from the original feeling. We become aware of the feelings in our hand in terms of their meaning located at the tip of the probe or stick to which we are attending. This is so also when we use a tool. We are attending to the meaning of its impact on our hands in terms of its effect on the things to which we are applying it. We may call this the *semantic aspect* of tacit knowing. All meaning tends to be displaced *away from ourselves*, and that is in fact my justification for using the terms "proximal" and "distal" to describe the first and second terms of tacit knowing.

From the three aspects of tacit knowing that I have defined so far—the functional, the phenomenal, and the semantic—we can deduce a fourth aspect; which tells us what tacit knowing is a knowledge of. This will represent its *ontological* aspect. Since tacit knowing establishes a meaningful relation between two terms, we may identify it with the *understanding* of the comprehensive entity which these two terms jointly constitute. Thus the proximal term represents the *particulars* of this entity, and we can say, accordingly, that we comprehend the entity by relying on our awareness of its particulars for attending to their joint meaning.

This analysis can be applied with interesting results to the case of visual perception. Physiologists long ago established that the way we see an object is determined by our awareness of certain efforts inside our body, efforts which we cannot feel in themselves. We are aware of these things going on inside our body in terms of the position, size, shape, and motion of an object, to which we are attending. In other words we are attending *from* these internal processes *to* the qualities of things outside. These qualities are what those internal processes *mean* to us. The transposition of bodily experiences into the perception of things outside may now appear, therefore, as an instance of the transposition of meaning away from us, which we have found to be present to some extent in all tacit knowing.

But it may be said that the feelings transposed by perception differ from those transposed by the use of tools or probes, by being hardly noticeable in themselves previous to their transposition. An answer to this—or at least part of an answer to it—is to be found in experiments extending subception to subliminal stimuli. Hefferline and collaborators have observed that when spontaneous muscular twitches, unfelt by the subject—but observable externally by a million-fold amplification of their action currents—were followed by the cessation of an unpleasant noise, the subject responded by increasing the frequency of the twitches and thus silencing the noise much of the time.[3] Tacit knowing is seen to

[3]Hefferline, Ralph F., Keenan, Brian, and Harford, Richard A., "Escape and Avoidance Conditioning in Human Subjects Without Their Observation of the Response," *Science* (Vol. 130, November 1959), pp. 1338–39. Herfferline, Ralph F., and Keenan, Brian, "Amplitude-Induction Gradient of a Small Human Operant in an Escape-Avoidance Situation," *Journal of the Experimental Analysis of Behavior* (Vol. 4, January 1961), pp. 41–43. Hefferline, Ralph F., and Perera, Thomas B., "Proprioceptive Discrimination of a Covert Operant Without Its Observation by the Subject," *Science* (Vol. 139, March 1963), pp. 834–35. Hefferline, Ralph F., and Keenan, Brian, "Amplitude-Induction Gradient of a Small Scale (Covert) Operant," *Journal of the Experimental Analysis of Behavior* (Vol. 6, July 1963), pp. 307–15. See

operate here on an internal action that we are quite incapable of controlling or even feeling in itself. We become aware of our operation of it only in the silencing of a noise. This experimental result seems closely analogous to the process by which we become aware of subliminal processes inside our body in the perception of objects outside.

This view of perception, that it is an instance of the transposition of feelings which we found in the use of probes and in the process of subception, is borne out by the fact that the capacity to see external objects must be acquired, like the use of probes and the feats of subception, by a process of learning which can be laborious.

Modern philosophers have argued that perception does not involve projection, since we are not previously aware of the internal processes which we are supposed to have projected into the qualities of things perceived. But we have now established that projection of this very kind is present in various instances of tacit knowing. Moreover, the fact that we do not originally sense the internal processes in themselves now appears irrelevant. We may venture, therefore, to extend the scope of tacit knowing to include neural traces in the cortex of the nervous system. This would place events going on inside our brain on the same footing as the subliminal twitches operated by Hefferline's subjects.[4]

This brings us to the point at which I hinted when I first mentioned perception as an instance of tacit knowing. I said that by elucidating the way our bodily processes participate in our perceptions we will throw light on the bodily roots of all thought, including man's highest creative powers. Let me show this now.

Our body is the ultimate instrument of all our external knowledge, whether intellectual or practical. In all our waking moments we are *relying* on our awareness of contacts of our body with things outside for *attending* to these things. Our own body is the only thing in the world which we normally never experience as an object, but experience always in terms of the world to which we are attending from our body. It is by making this intelligent use of our body that we feel it to be our body, and not a thing outside.

I have described how we learn to feel the end of a tool or a probe hitting things outside. We may regard this as the transformation of the tool or probe into a sentient extension of our body, as Samuel Butler has said. But our awareness of our body for attending to things outside it suggests a wider generalization of the feeling we have of our body. Whenever we use certain things for attending *from*

---

also general conclusions in Hefferline, Ralph F., "Learning Theory and Clinical Psychology—An Eventual Symbiosis?" from *Experimental Foundations of Clinical Psychology*, ed. Arthur J. Bachrach (1962).

Note also that numerous Russian observations, reported by Razran, G., "The Observable Unconscious and the Inferable Conscious," *Psychological Review* (Vol. 68, 1961), p. 81, have established the conditioning of intestinal stimuli, having a similar covert character as Hefferline's muscular twitches.

[4] Such a hypothesis does not explain how perceived sights, or any other state of consciousness, arise in conjunction with neural processes. It merely applies the principle that wherever some process in our body gives rise to consciousness in us, our tacit knowing of the process will make sense of it in terms of an experience to which we are attending.

them to other things, in the way in which we always use our own body, these
things change their appearance. They appear to us now in terms of the entities to
which we are attending *from* them, just as we feel our own body in terms of the
things outside to which we are attending *from* our body. In this sense we can say
that when we make a thing function as the proximal term of tacit knowing, we
incorporate it in our body—or extend our body to include it—so that we come to
dwell in it.

The full range of this generalization can only be hinted at here. Indications of
its scope may be seen by recalling that, at the turn of the last century, German
thinkers postulated that indwelling, or empathy, is the proper means of knowing
man and the humanities. I am referring particularly to Dilthey[5] and Lipps.[6]
Dilthey taught that the mind of a person can be understood only by reliving its
workings; and Lipps represented aesthetic appreciation as an entering into a work
of art and thus dwelling in the mind of its creator. I think that Dilthey and Lipps
described here a striking form of tacit knowing as applied to the understanding of
man and of works of art, and that they were right in saying that this could be
achieved only by indwelling. But my analysis of tacit knowing shows that they
were mistaken in asserting that this sharply distinguished the humanities from the
natural sciences. Indwelling, as derived from the structure of tacit knowing, is a
far more precisely defined act than is empathy, and it underlies all observations,
including all those described previously as indwelling.

We meet with another indication of the wide functions of indwelling when we
find acceptance to moral teachings described as their *interiorization*. To interiorize
is to identify ourselves with the teachings in question, by making them function as
the proximal term of a tacit moral knowledge, as applied in practice. This establishes the tacit framework for our moral acts and judgments. And we can trace this
kind of indwelling to logically similar acts in the practice of science. To rely on a
theory for understanding nature is to interiorize it. For we are attending from the
theory to things seen in its light, and are aware of the theory, while thus using it,
in terms of the spectacle that it serves to explain. This is why mathematical theory
can be learned only by practicing its application: its true knowledge lies in our
ability to use it.

The identification of tacit knowing with indwelling involves a shift of
emphasis in our conception of tacit knowing. We had envisaged tacit knowing in
the first place as a way to know more than we can tell. We identified the two terms
of tacit knowing, the proximal and the distal, and recognized the way we attend
from the first *to* the second, thus achieving an integration of particulars to a
coherent entity to which we are attending. Since we were not attending to the
particulars in themselves, we could not identify them: but if we now regard the
integration of particulars as an interiorization, it takes on a more positive
character. It now becomes a means of making certain things function as the
proximal terms of tacit knowing, so that instead of observing them in themselves,
we may be aware of them in their bearing on the comprehensive entity which they

[5]Dilthey, W., *Gesammelte Schriften* (Vol. VII, Leipzig and Berlin, 1914–36), pp. 213–16; [Translation by
H. A. Hodges, *Wilhelm Dilthey* (New York, Oxford University Press, 1944), pp. 121–24].
[6]Lipps, T., *Asthetik* (Hamburg, 1903).

constitute. It brings home to us that it is not by looking at things, but by dwelling in them, that we understand their joint meaning.

We can see now how an unbridled lucidity can destroy our understanding of complex matters. Scrutinize closely the particulars of a comprehensive entity and their meaning is effaced, our conception of the entity is destroyed. Such cases are well known. Repeat a word several times, attending carefully to the motion of your tongue and lips, and to the sound you make, and soon the word will sound hollow and eventually lose its meaning. By concentrating attention on his fingers, a pianist can temporarily paralyze his movement. We can make ourselves lose sight of a pattern or physiognomy by examining its several parts under sufficient magnification.

Admittedly, the destruction can be made good by interiorizing the particulars once more. The word uttered again its proper context, the pianist's fingers used again with his mind on his music, the features of a physiognomy and the details of a pattern glanced at once more from a distance: they all come to life and recover their meaning and their comprehensive relationship.

But it is important to note that this recovery never brings back the original meaning. It may improve on it. Motion studies, which tend to paralyze a skill, will improve it when followed by practice. The meticulous dismembering of a text, which can kill its appreciation, can also supply material for a much deeper understanding of it. In these cases, the detailing of particulars, which by itself would destroy meaning, serves as a guide to their subsequent integration and thus establishes a more secure and more accurate meaning of them.

But the damage done by the specification of particulars may be irremediable. Meticulous detailing may obscure beyond recall a subject like history, literature, or philosophy. Speaking more generally, the belief that, since particulars are more tangible, their knowledge offers a true conception of things is fundamentally mistaken.

Of course, tacit reintegration of particulars is not the only way to recover their meaning, destroyed by focusing our attention on them. The destructive analysis of a comprehensive entity can be counteracted in many cases by explicitly stating the relation between its particulars. Where such explicit integration is feasible, it goes far beyond the range of tacit integration. Take the case of a machine. One can learn to use it skillfully, without knowing exactly how it works. But the engineer's understanding of its construction and operation goes much deeper. We possess a practical knowledge of our own body, but the physiologist's theoretical knowledge of it is far more revealing. The formal rules of prosody may deepen our understanding of so delicate a thing as a poem.

But my examples show clearly that, in general, an explicit integration cannot replace its tacit counterpart. The skill of a driver cannot be replaced by a thorough schooling in the theory of the motorcar; the knowledge I have of my own body differs altogether from the knowledge of its physiology; and the rules of rhyming and prosody do not tell me what a poem told me, without any knowledge of its rules.

We are approaching here a crucial question. The declared aim of modern science is to establish a strictly detached, objective knowledge. Any falling short of this ideal is accepted only as a temporary imperfection, which we must aim at eliminating. But suppose that tacit thought forms an indispensable part of all knowledge, then the ideal of eliminating all personal elements of knowledge would, in effect, aim at the destruction of all knowledge. The ideal of exact science would turn out to be fundamentally misleading and possibly a source of devastating fallacies.

I think I can show that the process of formalizing all knowledge to the exclusion of any tacit knowing is self-defeating. For, in order that we may formalize the relations that constitute a comprehensive entity, for example, the relations that constitute a frog, this entity, i.e., the frog, must be first identified informally by tacit knowing; and, indeed, the meaning of a mathematical theory of the frog lies in its continued bearing on this still tacitly known frog. Moreover, the act of bringing a mathematical theory to bear on its subject is itself a tacit integration of the kind we have recognized in the use of a denotative word for designating its object. And we have seen also that a true knowledge of a theory can be established only after it has been interiorized and extensively used to interpret experience. Therefore: a mathematical theory can be constructed only by relying on *prior* tacit knowing and can function as a theory only *within* an act of tacit knowing, which consists in our attending *from* it to the previously established experience on which it bears. Thus the ideal of a comprehensive mathematical theory of experience which would eliminate all tacit knowing is proved to be self-contradictory and logically unsound.

But I must not rest my case on such an abstract argument. Let me finish this lecture, therefore, by presenting you with a most striking concrete example of an experience that cannot possibly be represented by an exact theory. It is an experience within science itself: the experience of seeing a problem, as a scientist sees it in his pursuit of discovery.

It is a commonplace that all research must start from a problem. Research can be successful only if the problem is good; it can be original only if the problem is original. But how can one see a problem, any problem, let alone a good and original problem? For to see a problem is to see something that is hidden. It is to have an intimation of the coherence of hitherto not comprehended particulars. The problem is good if this intimation is true; it is original if no one else can see the possibilities of the comprehension that we are anticipating. To see a problem that will lead to a great discovery is not just to see something hidden, but to see something of which the rest of humanity cannot have even an inkling. All this is a commonplace; we take it for granted, without noticing the clash of self-contradiction entailed in it. Yet Plato has pointed out this contradiction in the *Meno*. He says that to search for the solution of a problem is an absurdity; for either you know what you are looking for, and then there is no problem; or you do not know what you are looking for, and then you cannot expect to find anything.

The solution which Plato offered for this paradox was that all discovery is a remembering of past lives. This explanation has hardly ever been accepted, but neither has any other solution been offered for avoiding the contradiction. So we are faced with the fact that, for two thousand years and more, humanity has progressed through the efforts of people solving difficult problems, while all the time it could be shown that to do this was either meaningless or impossible. We have here the classical case of Poe's *Purloined Letter*, of the momentous document lying casually in front of everybody, and hence overlooked by all. For the *Meno* shows conclusively that if all knowledge is explicit, i.e., capable of being clearly stated, then we cannot know a problem or look for its solution. And the *Meno* also shows, therefore, that if problems nevertheless exist, and discoveries can be made by solving them, we can know things, and important things, that we cannot tell.

The kind of tacit knowledge that solves the paradox of the *Meno* consists in the intimation of something hidden, which we may yet discover. There exists another important manifestation of these mental powers. We are often told that great scientific discoveries are marked by their fruitfulness; and this is true. But how can we recognize truth by its fruitfulness? Can we recognize that a statement is true by appreciating the wealth of its yet undiscovered consequences? This would of course be nonsensical, if we had to know explicitly what was yet undiscovered. But it makes sense if we admit that we can have a tacit foreknowledge of yet undiscovered things. This is indeed the kind of foreknowledge the Copernicans must have meant to affirm when they passionately maintained, against heavy pressure, during one hundred and forty years before Newton proved the point, that the heliocentric theory was not merely a convenient way of computing the paths of planets, but was really true.

It appears, then, that to know that a statement is true is to know more than we can tell and that hence, when a discovery solves a problem, it is itself fraught with further intimations of an indeterminate range, and that furthermore, when we accept the discovery as true, we commit ourselves to a belief in all these as yet undisclosed, perhaps as yet unthinkable, consequences.

Since we have no explicit knowledge of these unknown things, there can also be no explicit justification of a scientific truth. But as we can know a problem, and feel sure that it is pointing to something hidden behind it, we can be aware also of the hidden implications of a scientific discovery, and feel confident that they will prove right. We feel sure of this, because in contemplating the discovery we are looking at it not only in itself but, more significantly, as a clue to a reality of which it is a manifestation. The pursuit of discovery is conducted from the start in these terms; all the time we are guided by sensing the presence of a hidden reality toward which our clues are pointing; and the discovery which terminates and satisfies this pursuit is still sustained by the same vision. It claims to have made contact with reality: a reality which, being real, may yet reveal itself to future eyes in an indefinite range of unexpected manifestations.

We have here reached our main conclusions. Tacit knowing is shown to account (1) for a valid knowledge of a problem, (2) for the scientist's capacity to pursue it, guided by his sense of approaching its solution, and (3) for a valid anticipation of the yet indeterminate implications of the discovery arrived at in the end.

Such indeterminate commitments are necessarily involved in any act of knowing based on indwelling. For such an act relies on interiorizing particulars to which we are not attending and which, therefore, we may not be able to specify, and relies further on our attending from these unspecifiable particulars to a comprehensive entity connecting them in a way we cannot define. This kind of knowing solves the paradox of the *Meno* by making it possible for us to know something so indeterminate as a problem or a hunch, but when the use of this faculty turns out to be an indispensable element of all knowing, we are forced to conclude that all knowledge is of the same kind as the knowledge of a problem.

This is in fact our result. We must conclude that the paradigmatic case of scientific knowledge, in which all the faculties that are necessary for finding and holding scientific knowledge are fully developed, is the knowledge of an approaching discovery.

To hold such knowledge is an act deeply committed to the conviction that there is something there to be discovered. It is personal, in the sense of involving the personality of him who holds it, and also in the sense of being, as a rule, solitary; but here is no trace in it of self-indulgence. The discoverer is filled with a compelling sense of responsibility for the pursuit of a hidden truth, which demands his services for revealing it. His act of knowing exercises a personal judgment in relating evidence to an external reality, an aspect of which he is seeking to apprehend.

The anticipation of discovery, like discovery itself, may turn out to be a delusion. But it is futile to seek for strictly impersonal criteria of its validity, as positivistic philosophies of science have been trying to do for the past eighty years or so. To accept the pursuit of science as a reasonable and successful enterprise is to share the kind of commitments on which scientists enter by undertaking this enterprise. You cannot formalize the act of commitment, for you cannot express your commitment non-committally. To attempt this is to exercise the kind of lucidity which destroys its subject matter. Hence the failure of the positivist movement in the philosophy of science. The difficulty is to find a stable alternative to its ideal of objectivity. This is indeed the task for which the theory of tacit knowing should prepare us.

ERVING GOFFMAN *(b.1922)*

In recent years Erving Goffman has made several significant contributions to the psychology and sociology of face-to-face encounters. In his studies of social institutions, from mental asylums to the simple handshake, Goffman has unlocked the codes we use to communicate more than we say. Though he does not make explicit mention of Polanyi's ideas, Goffman's chief concern in this essay (from The Presentation of Self in Everyday Life, *1959) is to show how we use our tacit knowledge in our face-to-face encounters with others. Using the metaphor of theater and stage he argues that we create ourselves through the progressive refinement of our performances. Just as a performer cannot completely articulate all the methods he or she uses for projecting a character through gestures and inflections, so our knowledge of our performances is only tacit. Further, because we value honesty and sincerity we have a stake in letting that knowledge remain tacit. We do not even want to know that we know how to perform. Goffman cuts through this self-imposed veil of illusion and in the process exposes an interesting dialectic of appearance and reality: really to be a certain sort of person in a social context entails that one appear to be that sort of person, otherwise that being is lost on others and they cannot assist in the social construction of one's self. Yet the success of the appearance partly hinges on socially defined rules for what it takes to be that sort of person. Here we have a specific case of what we dubbed earlier the "onion theory of reality": reality does not lie beneath appearances, rather it is the progressive construction of the totality of appearances. Without an appreciation of this metaphysical point the reader runs the risk of rejecting Goffman's analysis as a rationale for a very simple form of dishonesty. Try to read Goffman's analysis as an account of the dynamics of those rich situations when, together with a few friends in comfortable surroundings, you are aware of a tremendous amount of communication but perhaps unsure of precisely what is happening.*

How Others Know Me

When an individual enters the presence of others, they commonly seek to acquire information about him or to bring into play information about him already possessed. They will be interested in his general socio-economic status, his conception of self, his attitude toward them, his competence, his trustworthiness, etc. Although some of this information seems to be sought almost as an end in itself, there are usually quite practical reasons for acquiring it. Information about the individual helps to define the situation, enabling others to know in advance what he will expect of them and what they may expect of him. Informed in these ways, the others will know how best to act in order to call forth a desired response from him.

For those present, many sources of information become accessible and many carriers (or "sign-vehicles") become available for conveying this information. If unacquainted with the individual, observers can glean clues from his conduct and appearance which allow them to apply their previous experience with individuals roughly similar to the one before them or, more important, to apply untested stereotypes to him. They can also assume from past experience that only individuals of a particular kind are likely to be found in a given social setting. They can rely on what the individual says about himself or on documentary evidence he provides as to who and what he is. If they know, or know of, the individual by virtue of experience prior to the interaction, they can rely on assumptions as to the persistence and generality of psychological traits as a means of predicting his present and future behavior.

However, during the period in which the individual is in the immediate presence of the others, few events may occur which directly provide the others with the conclusive information they will need if they are to direct wisely their own activity. Many crucial facts lie beyond the time and place of interaction or lie concealed within it. For example, the "true" or "real" attitudes, beliefs, and emotions of the individual can be ascertained only indirectly, through his avowals or through what appears to be involuntary expressive behavior. Similarly, if the individual offers the others a product or service, they will often find that during the interaction there will be no time and place immediately available for eating the pudding that the proof can be found in. They will be forced to accept some events as conventional or natural signs of something not directly available to the senses. In Ichheiser's terms,[1] the individual will have to act so that he intentionally or unintentionally *expresses* himself, and the others will in turn have to be *impressed* in some way by him.

The expressiveness of the individual (and therefore his capacity to give impressions) appears to involve two radically different kinds of sign activity: the expression that he *gives*, and the expression that he *gives off*. The first involves verbal symbols or their substitutes which he uses admittedly and solely to convey the information that he and the others are known to attach to these symbols. This is communication in the traditional and narrow sense. The second involves a wide range of action that others can treat as symptomatic of the actor, the expectation being that the action was performed for reasons other than the information conveyed in this way. As we shall have to see, this distinction has an only initial validity. The individual does of course intentionally convey misinformation by means of both of these types of communication, the first involving deceit, the second feigning.

Taking communication in both its narrow and broad sense, one finds that when the individual is in the immediate presence of others, his activity will have a promissory character. The others are likely to find that they must accept the individual on faith, offering him a just return while he is present before them in exchange for something whose true value will not be established until after he has left their presence. (Of course, the others also live by inference in their dealings with the physical world, but it is only in the world of social interaction that the objects about which they make inferences will purposely facilitate and hinder this inferential process.) The security that they justifiably feel in making inferences about the individual will vary, of course, depending on such factors as the amount of information they already possess about him, but no amount of such past evidence can entirely obviate the necessity of acting on the basis of inferences. As William I. Thomas suggested:

> It is also highly important for us to realize that we do not as a matter of fact lead our lives, make our decisions, and reach our goals in everyday life either statistically or scientifically. We live by inference. I am, let us say, your guest. You do not know, you cannot determine scientifically, that I will not steal your money or your spoons. But inferentially I will not, and inferentially you have me as a guest.[2]

---

[1]Gustav Ichheiser, "Misunderstandings in Human Relations," Supplement to *The American Journal of Sociology*, LV (September, 1949), pp. 6–7.

[2]Quoted in E. H. Volkart, editor, *Social Behavior and Personality*, Contributions of W. I. Thomas to Theory and Social Research (New York: Social Science Research Council, 1951), p. 5.

Let us now turn from the others to the point of view of the individual who presents himself before them. He may wish them to think highly of him, or to think that he thinks highly of them, or to perceive how in fact he feels toward them, or to obtain no clear-cut impression; he may wish to ensure sufficient harmony so that the interaction can be sustained, or to defraud, get rid of, confuse, mislead, antagonize, or insult them. Regardless of the particular objective which the individual has in mind and of his motive for having this objective, it will be in his interests to control the conduct of the others, especially their responsive treatment of him.[3] This control is achieved largely by influencing the definition of the situation which the others come to formulate, and he can influence this definition by expressing himself in such a way as to give them the kind of impression that will lead them to act voluntarily in accordance with his own plan. Thus, when an individual appears in the presence of others, there will usually be some reason for him to mobilize his activity so that it will convey an impression to others which it is in his interests to convey. Since a girl's dormitory mates will glean evidence of her popularity from the calls she receives on the phone, we can suspect that some girls will arrange for calls to be made, and Willard Waller's finding can be anticipated:

> It has been reported by many observers that a girl who is called to the telephone in the dormitories will often allow herself to be called several times, in order to give all the other girls ample opportunity to hear her paged.[4]

Of the two kinds of communication—expressions given and expressions given off—this report will be primarily concerned with the latter, with the more theatrical and contextual kind, the non-verbal, presumably unintentional kind, whether this communication be purposely engineered or not. As an example of what we must try to examine, I would like to cite at length a novelistic incident in which Preedy, a vacationing Englishman, makes his first appearance on the beach of his summer hotel in Spain:

> But in any case he took care to avoid catching anyone's eye. First of all, he had to make it clear to those potential companions of his holiday that they were of no concern to him whatsoever. He stared through them, round them, over them—eyes lost in space. The beach might have been empty. If by chance a ball was thrown his way, he looked surprised; then let a smile of amusement lighten his face (Kindly Preedy), looked round dazed to see that there *were* people on the beach, tossed it back with a

[3]Here I owe much to an unpublished paper by Tom Burns of the University of Edinburgh. He presents the argument that in all interaction a basic underlying theme is the desire of each participant to guide and control the responses made by the others present. A similar argument has been advanced by Jay Haley in a recent unpublished paper, but in regard to a special kind of control, that having to do with defining the nature of the relationship of those involved in the interaction.

[4]Willard Waller, "The Rating and Dating Complex," *American Sociological Review*, II, p. 730.

smile to himself and not a smile *at* the people, and then resumed carelessly his nonchalant survey of space.

But it was time to institute a little parade, the parade of the Ideal Preedy. By devious handlings he gave any who wanted to look a chance to see the title of his book—a Spanish translation of Homer, classic thus, but not daring, cosmopolitan too—and then gathered together his beachwrap and bag into a neat sand-resistant pile (Methodical and Sensible Preedy), rose slowly to stretch at ease his huge frame (Big-Cat Preedy), and tossed aside his sandals (Carefree Preedy, after all).

The marriage of Preedy and the sea! There were alternative rituals. The first involved the stroll that turns into a run and a dive straight into the water, thereafter smoothing into a strong splashless crawl towards the horizon. But of course not really to the horizon. Quite suddenly he would turn on to his back and thrash great white splashes with his legs, somehow thus showing that he could have swum further had he wanted to, and then would stand up a quarter out of water for all to see who it was.

The alternative course was simpler, it avoided the cold-water shock and it avoided the risk of appearing too high-spirited. The point was to appear to be so used to the sea, the Mediterranean, and this particular beach, that one might as well be in the sea as out of it. It involved a slow stroll down and into the edge of the water—not even noticing his toes were wet, land and water all the same to *him!*—with his eyes up at the sky gravely surveying portents, invisible to others, of the weather (Local Fisherman Preedy).[5]

The novelist means us to see that Preedy is improperly concerned with the extensive impressions he feels his sheer bodily action is giving off to those around him. We can malign Preedy further by assuming that he has acted merely in order to give a particular impression, that this is a false impression, and that the others present receive either no impression at all, or, worse still, the impression that Preedy is affectedly trying to cause them to receive this particular impression. But the important point for us here is that the kind of impression Preedy thinks he is making is in fact the kind impression that others correctly and incorrectly glean from someone in their midst.

I have said that when an individual appears before others his actions will influence the definition of the situation which they come to have. Sometimes the individual will act in a thoroughly calculating manner, expressing himself in a given way solely in order to give the kind of impression to others that is likely to evoke from them a specific response he is concerned to obtain. Sometimes the individual will be calculating in his activity but be relatively unaware that this is the case. Sometimes he will intentionally and consciously express himself in a particular way, but chiefly because the tradition of his group or social status require this kind of expression and not because of any particular response (other than vague acceptance or approval) that is likely to be evoked from those impressed by the expression. Sometimes the traditions of an individual's role will lead him to give a well-designed impression of a particular kind and yet he may be

[5]William Sansom, *A Contest of Ladies* (London: Hogarth, 1956) pp. 230–32.

neither consciously nor unconsciously disposed to create such an impression. The others, in their turn, may be suitably impressed by the individual's efforts to convey something, or may misunderstand the situation and come to conclusions that are warranted neither by the individual's intent nor by the facts. In any case, in so far as the others act *as if* the individual had conveyed a particular impression, we may take a functional or pragmatic view and say that the individual has "effectively" projected a given definition of the situation and "effectively" fostered the understanding that a given state of affairs obtains....

Reality and Contrivance

In our own Anglo-American culture there seems to be two common-sense models according to which we formulate our conceptions of behavior: the real, sincere, or honest performance; and the false one that thorough fabricators assemble for us, whether meant to be taken unseriously, as in the work of stage actors, or seriously, as in the work of confidence men. We tend to see real performances as something not purposely put together at all, being an unintentional product of the individual's unself-conscious response to the facts in his situation. And contrived performances we tend to see as something painstakingly pasted together, one false item on another, since there is no reality to which the items of behavior could be a direct response. It will be necessary to see now that these dichotomous conceptions are by way of being the ideology of honest performers, providing strength to the show they put on, but a poor analysis of it.

First, let it be said that there are many individuals who sincerely believe that the definition of the situation they habitually project is the real reality. In this report I do not mean to question their proportion in the population but rather the structural relation of their sincerity to the performances they offer. If a performance is to come off, the witnesses by and large must be able to believe that the performers are sincere. This is the structural place of sincerity in the drama of events. Performers may be sincere—or be insincere but sincerely convinced of their own sincerity—but this kind of affection for one's part is not necessary for its convincing performance. There are not many French cooks who are really Russian spies, and perhaps there are not many women who play the part of wife to one man and mistress to another; but these duplicities do occur, often being sustained successfully for long periods of time. This suggests that while persons usually are what they appear to be, such appearances could still have been managed. There is, then, a statistical relation between appearances and reality, not an intrinsic or necessary one. In fact, given the unanticipated threats that play upon a performance, and given the need (later to be discussed) to maintain solidarity with one's fellow performers and some distance from the witnesses, we find that a rigid incapacity to depart from one's inward view of reality may at times endanger one's performance. Some performances are carried off successfully with complete dishonesty, others with complete honesty; but for performances in general neither of these extremes is essential and neither, perhaps, is dramaturgically advisable.

The implication here is that an honest, sincere, serious performance is less firmly connected with the solid world than one might first assume. And this implication will be strengthened if we look again at the distance usually placed between quite honest performances and quite contrived ones. In this connection take, for example, the remarkable phenomenon of stage acting. It does take deep skill, long training, and psychological capacity to become a good stage actor. But this fact should not blind us to another one: that almost anyone can quickly learn a script well enough to give a charitable audience some sense of realness in what is being contrived before them. And it seems this is so because ordinary social intercourse is itself put together as a scene is put together, by the exchange of dramatically inflated actions, counteractions, and terminating replies. Scripts even in the hands of unpracticed players can come to life because life itself is a dramatically enacted thing. All the world is not, of course, a stage, but the crucial ways in which it isn't are not easy to specify.

The recent use of "psychodrama" as a therapeutic technique illustrates a further point in this regard. In these psychiatrically staged scenes patients not only act out parts with some effectiveness, but employ no script in doing so. Their own past is available to them in a form which allows them to stage a recapitulation of it. Apparently a part once played honestly and in earnest leaves the performer in a position to contrive a showing of it later. Further, the parts that significant others played to him in the past also seem to be available, allowing him to switch from being the person that he was to being the persons that others were for him. This capacity to switch enacted roles when obliged to do so could have been predicted; everyone apparently can do it. For in learning to perform our parts in real life we guide our own productions by not too consciously maintaining an incipient familiarity with the routine of those to whom we will address ourselves. And when we come to be able properly to manage a real routine we are able to do this in part because of "anticipatory socialization,"[6] having already been schooled in the reality that is just coming to be real for us.

When the individual does move into a new position in society and obtains a new part to perform, he is not likely to be told in full detail how to conduct himself, nor will the facts of his new situation press sufficiently on him from the start to determine his conduct without his further giving thought to it. Ordinarily he will be given only a few cues, hints, and stage directions, and it will be assumed that he already has in his repertoire a large number of bits and pieces of performances that will be required in the new setting. The individual will already have a fair idea of what modesty, deference, or righteous indignation looks like, and can make a pass at playing these bits when necessary. He may even be able to play out the part of a hypnotic subject[7] or commit a "compulsive" crime[8] on the basis of models for these activities that he is already familiar with.

A theatrical performance or a staged confidence game requires a thorough

---

[6]See R. K. Merton, *Social Theory and Social Structure* (Glencoe: The Free Press, revised and enlarged edition, 1957), p. 265 ff.

[7]This view of hypnosis is neatly presented by T. R. Sarbin, "Contributions to Role-Taking Theory. I: Hypnotic Behavior," *Psychological Review*, 57, pp. 255–70.

[8]See D. R. Cressey, "The Differential Association Theory and Compulsive Crimes," *Journal of Criminal Law, Criminology and Police Science*, 45, pp. 29–40.

scripting of the spoken content of the routine; but the vast part involving "expression given off" is often determined by meager stage directions. It is expected that the performer of illusions will already know a good deal about how to manage his voice, his face, and his body, although he—as well as any person who directs him—may find it difficult indeed to provide a detailed verbal statement of this kind of knowledge. And in this, of course, we approach the situation of the straightforward man in the street. Socialization may not so much involve a learning of the many specific details of a single concrete part—often there could not be enough time or energy for this. What does seem to be required of the individual is that he learn enough pieces of expression to be able to "fill in" and manage, more or less, any part that he is likely to be given. The legitimate performances of everyday life are not "acted" or "put on" in the sense that the performer knows in advance just what he is going to do, and does this solely because of the effect it is likely to have. The expressions it is felt he is giving off will be especially "inaccessible" to him.[9] But as in the case of less legitimate performers, the incapacity of the ordinary individual to formulate in advance the movements of his eyes and body does not mean that he will not express himself through these devices in a way that is dramatized and pre-formed in his repertoire of actions. In short, we all act better than we know how.

When we watch a television wrestler gouge, foul, and snarl at his opponent we are quite ready to see that, in spite of the dust, he is, and knows he is, merely playing at being the "heavy," and that in another match he may be given the other role, that of clean-cut wrestler, and perform this with equal verve and proficiency. We seem less ready to see, however, that while such details as the number and character of the falls may be fixed beforehand, the details of the expressions and movements used do not come from a script but from command of an idiom, a command that is exercised from moment to moment with little calculation or forethought.

In reading of persons in the West Indies who become the "horse" or the one possessed of a voodoo spirit,[10] it is enlightening to learn that the person possessed will be able to provide a correct portrayal of the god that has entered him because of "the knowledge and memories accumulated in a life spent visiting congregations of the cult,"[11] that the person possessed will be in just the right social relation to those who are watching; that possession occurs at just the right moment in the ceremonial undertakings, the possessed one carrying out his ritual obligations to the point of participating in a kind of skit with persons possessed at the time with other spirits. But in learning this, it is important to see that this contextual structuring of the horse's role still allows participants in the cult to believe that possession is a real thing and that persons are possessed at random by gods whom they cannot select.

[9]This concept derives from T. R. Sarbin, "Role Theory," in Gardner Lindzey, *Handbook of Social Psychology* (Cambridge: Addison-Wesley, 1954), Vol. 1, pp. 235–36.
[10]See, for example, Alfred Métraux, "Dramatic Elements in Ritual Possession," *Diogenes*, 11, pp. 18–36.
[11]*Ibid.*, p. 24.

And when we observe a young American middle-class girl playing dumb for the benefit of her boy friend, we are ready to point to items of guile and contrivance in her behavior. But like herself and her boy friend, we accept as an unperformed fact that this perfomer *is* a young American middle-class girl. But surely here we neglect the greater part of the performance. It is commonplace to say that differenct social groupings express in different ways such attributes as age, sex, territory, and class status, and that in each case these bare attributes are elaborated by means of a distinctive complex cultural configuration of proper ways of conducting oneself. To *be* a given kind of person, then, is not merely to possess the required attributes, but also to sustain the standards of conduct and appearance that one's social grouping attaches thereto. The unthinking ease with which performers consistently carry off such standard-maintaining routines does not deny that a performance has occurred, merely that the participants have been aware of it.

A status, a position, a social place is not a material thing, to be possessed and then displayed; it is a pattern of appropriate conduct, coherent, embellished, and well articulated. Performed with ease or clumsiness, awareness or not, guile or good faith, it is none the less something that must be enacted and portrayed, something that must be realized. Sartre, here, provides a good illustration:

> Let us consider this waiter in the café. His movement is quick and forward, a little too precise, a little too rapid. He comes toward the patrons with a step a little too quick. He bends forward a little too eagerly; his voice, his eyes express an interest a little too solicitous for the order of the customer. Finally there he returns, trying to imitate in his walk the inflexible stiffness of some kind of automaton while carrying his tray with the recklessness of a tightrope-walker by putting it in a perpetually unstable, perpetually broken equilibrium which he perpetually re-establishes by a light movement of the arm and hand. All his behavior seems to us a game. He applies himself to changing his movements as if they were mechanisms, the one regulating the other; his gestures and even his voice seem to be mechanisms; he gives himself the quickness and pitiless rapidity of things. He is playing, he is amusing himself. But what is he playing? We need not watch long before we can explain it: he is playing at being a waiter in a café. There is nothing there to surprise us. The game is a kind of marking out and investigation. The child plays with his body in order to explore it, to take inventory of it; the waiter in the café plays with his condition in order to *realize* it. This obligation is not different from that which is imposed on all tradesmen. Their condition is wholly one of ceremony. The public demands of them that they realize it as a ceremony; there is the dance of the grocer, of the tailor, of the auctioneer, by which they endeavor to persuade their clientele that they are nothing but a grocer, an auctioneer, a tailor. A grocer who dreams is offensive to the buyer, because such a grocer is not wholly a grocer. Society demands that he limit himself to his function as a grocer, just as the soldier at attention makes himself into a soldier-thing with a direct regard which does not see at all, which is not longer meant to see, since it is the rule and not the interest of the moment which determines the point he must fix his eyes on (the sight "fixed at

ten paces"). There are indeed many precautions to imprison a man in what he is, as if we lived in perpetual fear that he might escape from it, that he might break away and suddenly elude his condition.[12] ...

The Role of Expression Is Conveying Impressions of Self

Perhaps a moral note can be permitted at the end. In this report the expressive component of social life has been treated as a source of impressions given to or taken by others. Impression, in turn, has been treated as a source of information about unapparent facts and as a means by which the recipients can guide their response to the informant without having to wait for the full consequences of the informant's actions to be felt. Expression, then, has been treated in terms of the communicative role it plays during social interaction and not, for example, in terms of consummatory or tension-release function it might have for the expresser.[13]

Underlying all social interaction there seems to be a fundamental dialectic. When one individual enters the presence of others he will want to discover the facts of the situation. Were he to possess this information, he could know, and make allowances for, what will come to happen and he could give the others present as much of their due as is consistent with his enlightened self-interest. To uncover fully the factual nature of the situation, it would be necessary for the individual to know all the relevant social data about the others. It would also be necessary for the individual to know the actual outcome or end product of the activity of the others during the interaction, as well as their innermost feelings concerning him. Full information of this order is rarely available; in its absence, the individual tends to employ substitutes—cues, tests, hints, expressive gestures, status symbols, etc.—as predictive devices. In short, since the reality that the individual is concerned with is unperceivable at the moment, appearances must be relied upon in its stead. And, paradoxically, the more the individual is concerned with the reality that is not available to perception, the more he must concentrate his attention on appearances.

The individual tends to treat the others present on the basis of the impression they give now about the past and the future. It is here that communicative acts are translated into moral ones. The impressions that the others give tend to be treated as claims and promises they have implicitly made, and claims and promises tend to have a moral character. In his mind the individual says: "I am using these impressions of you as a way of checking up on you and your activity, and you ought not to lead me astray." The peculiar thing about this is that the individual tends to take this stand even though he expects the others to be unconscious of many of their expressive behaviors and even though he may expect to exploit the others on the basis of the information he gleans about them. Since the sources of impression used by the observing individual involve a multitude of standards

---

[12]Sartre, *Being and Nothingness*, translated by Hazel E. Barnes (New York: Philosophical Library, 1956), p. 59.

[13]A recent treatment of this kind may be found in Talcott Parsons, Robert F. Bales, and Edward A. Shils, *Working Papers in the Theory of Action* (Glencoe, Ill.: The Free Press, 1953), Chap. II, "The Theory of Symbolism in Relation to Action."

pertaining to politeness and decorum, pertaining both to social intercourse and task-performance, we can appreciate afresh how daily life is enmeshed in moral lines of discrimination.

Let us shift now to the point of view of the others. If they are to be gentlemanly, and play the individual's game, they will give little conscious heed to the fact that impressions are being formed about them but rather act without guile or contrivance, enabling the individual to receive valid impressions about them and their efforts. And if they happen to give thought to the fact that they are being observed, they will not allow this to influence them unduly, content in the belief that the individual will obtain a correct impression and give them their due because of it. Should they be concerned with influencing the treatment that the individual gives them, and this is properly to be expected, then a gentlemanly means will be available to them. They need only guide their action in the present so that its future consequences will be the kind that would lead a just individual to treat them now in a way they want to be treated; once this is done, they have only to rely on the perceptiveness and justness of the individual who observes them.

Sometimes those who are observed do, of course, employ these proper means of influencing the way in which the observer treats them. But there is another way, a shorter and more efficient way, in which the observed can influence the observer. Instead of allowing an impression of their activity to arise as an incidental by-product of their activity, they can reorient their frame of reference and devote their efforts to the creation of desired impressions. Instead of attempting to achieve certain ends by acceptable means, they can attempt to achieve the impression that they are achieving certain ends by acceptable means. It is always possible to manipulate the impression the observer uses as a substitute for reality because a sign for the presence of a thing, not being that thing, can be employed in the absence of it. The observer's need to rely on representations of things itself creates the possibility of misrepresentation.

There are many sets of persons who feel they could not stay in business, whatever their business, if they limited themselves to the gentlemanly means of influencing the individual who observes them. At some point or other in the round of their activity they feel it is necessary to band together and directly manipulate the impression that they give. The observed become a performing team and the observers become the audience. Actions which appear to be done on objects become gestures addressed to the audience. The round of activity becomes dramatized.

We come now to the basic dialectic. In their capacity as performers, individuals will be concerned with maintaining the impression that they are living up to the many standards by which they and their products are judged. Because these standards are so numerous and so pervasive, the individuals who are performers dwell more than we might think in a moral world. But, *qua* performers, individuals are concerned not with the moral issue of realizing these standards, but with the amoral issue of engineering a convincing impression that these standards are being realized. Our activity, then, is largely concerned with moral matters, but as performers we do not have a moral concern with them. As performers we are merchants of morality. Our day is given over to intimate contact with the goods we display and our minds are filled with intimate understandings of them; but it may well be that the more attention we give to these goods, then the more distant we feel from them and from those who are believing enough to buy them. To use a different imagery, the very obligation and profitability of appearing always in a steady moral light, of being a socialized character, forces one to be the sort of person who is practiced in the ways of the stage.

Staging and the Self

The general notion that we make a presentation of ourselves to others is hardly novel; what ought to be stressed in conclusion is that the very structure of the self can be seen in terms of how we arrange for such performances in our Anglo-American society.

In this report, the individual was divided by implication into two basic parts: he was viewed as a *performer*, a harried fabricator of impressions involved in the all-too-human task of staging a performance; he was viewed as a *character*, a figure, typically a fine one, whose spirit, strength, and other sterling qualities the performance was designed to evoke. The attributes of a performer and the attributes of a character are of a different order, quite basically so, yet both sets have their meaning in terms of the show that must go on.

First, character. In our society the character one performs and one's self are somewhat equated, and this self-as-character is usually seen as something housed within the body of its possessor, especially the upper parts thereof, being a nodule, somehow, in the psychobiology of personality. I suggest that this view is an implied part of what we are all trying to present, but provides, just because of this, a bad analysis of the presentation. In this report the performed self was seen as some kind of image, usually creditable, which the individual on stage and in character effectively attempts to induce others to hold in regard to him. While this image is entertained *concerning* the individual, so that a self is imputed to him, this self itself does not derive from its possessor, but from the whole scene of his action, being generated by that attribute of local events which renders them interpretable by witnesses. A correctly staged and performed scene leads the audience to impute a self to a performed character, but this imputation—this self—is a *product* of a scene that comes off, and is not a *cause* of it. The self, then, as a performed character, is not an organic thing that has a specific location, whose fundamental fate is to be born, to mature, and to die; it is a dramatic effect arising diffusely from a scene that is presented, and the characteristic issue, the crucial concern, is whether it will be credited or discredited.

In analyzing the self then we are drawn from its possessor, from the person who will profit or lose most by it, for he and his body merely provide the peg on which something of collaborative manufacture will be hung for a time. And the means for producing and maintaining selves do not reside inside the peg; in fact these means are often bolted down in social establishments. There will be a back region with its tools for shaping the body, and a front region with its fixed props.

There will be a team of persons whose activity on stage in conjunction with available props will constitute the scene from which the performed character's self will emerge, and another team, the audience, whose interpretive activity will be necessary for this emergence. The self is a product of all of these arrangements, and in all of its parts bears the marks of this genesis.

The whole machinery of self-production is cumbersome, of course, and sometimes breaks down, exposing its separate components: back region control; team collusion; audience tact; and so forth. But, well oiled, impressions will flow from it fast enough to put us in the grips of one of our types of reality—the performance will come off and the firm self accorded each performed character will appear to emanate intrinsically from its performer.

Let us turn now from the individual as character performed to the individual as performer. He has a capacity to learn, this being exercised in the task of training for a part. He is given to having fantasies and dreams, some that pleasurably unfold a triumphant performance, others full of anxiety and dread that nervously deal with vital discreditings in a public front region. He often manifests a gregarious desire for teammates and audiences, a tactful considerateness for their concerns; and he has a capacity for deeply felt shame, leading him to minimize the chances he takes of exposure.

These attributes of the individual *qua* performer are not merely a depicted effect of particular performances; they are psychobiological in nature, and yet they seem to arise out of intimate interaction with the contingencies of staging performances.

And now a final comment. In developing the conceptual framework employed in this report, some language of the stage was used. I spoke of performers and audiences; of routines and parts; of performances coming off or falling flat; of cues, stage settings and backstage; of dramaturgical needs, dramaturgical skills, and dramaturgical strategies. Now it should be admitted that this attempt to press a mere analogy so far was in part a rhetoric and a maneuver.

The claim that all the world's a stage is sufficiently commonplace for readers to be familiar with its limitations and tolerant of its presentation, knowing that at any time they will easily be able to demonstrate to themselves that it is not to be taken too seriously. An action staged in a theater is a relatively contrived illusion and an admitted one; unlike ordinary life, nothing real or actual can happen to the performed characters—although at another level of course something real and actual can happen to the reputation of performers *qua* professionals whose everyday job is to put on theatrical performances.

And so here the language and mask of the stage will be dropped. Scaffolds, after all, are to build other things with, and should be erected with an eye to taking them down. This report is not concerned with aspects of theater that creep into everyday life. It is concerned with the structure of social encounters—the structure of those entities in social life that come into being whenever persons enter one another's immediate physical presence. The key factor in this structure is the maintenance of a single definition of the situation, this definition having to be expressed, and this expression sustained in the face of a multitude of potential disruptions.

A character staged in a theater is not in some ways real, nor does it have the same kind of real consequences as does the thoroughly contrived character performed by a confidence man; but the *successful* staging of either of these types of false figures involves use of *real* techniques—the same techniques by which everyday persons sustain their real social situations. Those who conduct face to face interaction on a theater's stage must meet the key requirement of real situations; they must expressively sustain a definition of the situation: but this they do in circumstances that have facilitated their developing an apt terminology for the interactional tasks that all of us share.

GEORGE HERBERT MEAD *(1863–1931)*

G. H. Mead stands among the giants of social psychology. His book, Mind, Self & Society *(1934), from which the following selection is drawn, brings philosophy to the study of psyche and society. Mead argues that selfhood arises from a social process. When Mead states, "In so far as the conversation of gestures can become part of conduct in the direction and control of experience, then a self can arise," we can assume that this conversation of gestures is very much the sort of thing Polanyi and Goffman describe in the previous selections. Of particular interest in this selection is Mead's distinction between the self as subjective consciousness and the self as "a certain sort of structural process" in conduct. The first sense is closely related to Descartes' cogito. Selfhood in the second sense arises when one learns the intersubjective conversation of gestures, and structures one's own behavior according to the socially shared code. In short, the self is not only a thinker but an agent as well. To Descartes' proposition, "I think, therefore I am," we must add "I act, therefore I am." Since the meaning of my act is largely defined by social convention—think of the possible meanings of raising your hand—the self that is defined by those acts is also socially defined.*

The Social Origins of the Self

The process out of which the self arises is a social process which implies interaction of individuals in the group, implies the pre-existence of the group.[1] It implies also certain co-operative activities in which the different members of the group are involved. It implies, further, that out of this process there may in turn develop a more elaborate organization than that out of which the self has arisen,

---

[1] The relation of individual organisms to the social whole of which they are members is analogous to the relation of the individual cells of a multi-cellular organism to the organism as a whole.

and that the selves may be the organs, the essential parts at least, of this more elaborate social organization within which these selves arise and exist. Thus, there is a social process out of which selves arise and within which further differentiation, further evolution, further organization, take place.

It has been the tendency of psychology to deal with the self as a more or less isolated and independent element, a sort of entity that could conceivably exist by itself. It is possible that there might be a single self in the universe if we start off by identifying the self with a certain feeling-consciousness. If we speak of this feeling as objective, then we can think of that self as existing by itself. We can think of a separate physical body existing by itself, we can assume that it has these feelings or conscious states in question, and so we can set up that sort of a self in thought as existing simply by itself.

Then there is another use of "consciousness" with which we have been particularly occupied, denoting that which we term thinking or reflective intelligence, a use of consciousness which always has, implicitly at least, the reference to an "I" in it. This use of consciousness has no necessary connection with the other; it is an entirely different conception. One usage has to do with a certain mechanism, a certain way in which an organism acts. If an organism is endowed with sense organs then there are objects in its environment, and among those objects will be parts of its own body.[2] It is true that if the organism did not have a retina and a central nervous system there would not be any objects of vision. For such objects to exist there have to be certain physiological conditions, but these objects are not in themselves necessarily related to a self. When we reach a self we reach a certain sort of conduct, a certain type of social process which involves the interaction of different individuals and yet implies individuals engaged in some sort of co-operative activity. In that process a self, as such, can arise.

We want to distinguish the self as a certain sort of structural process in the conduct of the form, from what we term consciousness of objects that are experienced. The two have no necessary relationship. The aching tooth is a very important element. We have to pay attention to it. It is identified in a certain sense with the self in order that we may control that sort of experience. Occasionally we have experiences which we say belong to the atmosphere. The whole world seems to be depressed, the sky is dark, the weather is unpleasant, values that we are interested in are sinking. We do not necessarily identify such a situation with the self; we simply feel a certain atmosphere about us. We come to remember that we are subject to such sorts of depression, and find that kind of an experience in our past. And then we get some sort of relief, we take aspirin, or we take a rest, and the

_____

[2]Our constructive selection of our environment is what we term "consciousness," in the first sense of the term. The organism does not project sensuous qualities—colors, for example—into the environment to which it responds; but it endows this environment with such qualities, in a sense similar to that in which an ox endows grass with the quality of being food, or in which—speaking more generally—the relation between biological organisms and certain environmental contents give rise to food objects. If there were no organisms with particular sense organs there would be no environment, in the proper or usual sense of the term. An organism constructs (in the selective sense) its environment; and consciousness often refers to the character of the environment in so far as it is determined or constructively selected by our human organisms, and depends upon the relationship between the former (as thus selected or constructed) and the latter.

result is that the world changes its character. There are other experiences which we may at all times identify with selves. We can distinguish, I think, very clearly between certain types of experience, which we call subjective because we alone have access to them, and that experience which we call reflective.

It is true that reflection taken by itself is something to which we alone have access. One thinks out his own demonstration of a proposition, we will say in Euclid, and the thinking is something that takes place within his own conduct. For the time being it is a demonstration which exists only in his thought. Then he publishes it and it becomes common property. For the time being it was accessible only to him. There are other contents of this sort, such as memory images and the play of the imagination, which are accessible only to the individual. There is a common character that belongs to these types of objects which we generally identify with consciousness and this process which we call that of thinking, in that both are, at least in certain phases, accessible only to the individual. But, as I have said, the two sets of phenomena stand on entirely different levels. This common feature of accessibility does not necessarily give them the same metaphysical status. I do not now want to discuss metaphysical problems, but I do want to insist that the self has a sort of structure that arises in social conduct that is entirely distinguishable from this so-called subjective experience of these particular sets of objects to which the organism alone has access—the common character of privacy of access does not fuse them together.

The self to which we have been referring arises when the conversation of gestures is taken over into the conduct of the individual form. When this conversation of gestures can be taken over into the individual's conduct so that the attitude of the other forms can affect the organism, and the organism can reply with its corresponding gesture and thus arouse the attitude of the other in its own process, then a self arises. Even the bare conversation of gestures that can be carried out in lower forms is to be explained by the fact that this conversation of gestures has an intelligent function. Even there it is a part of social process. If it is taken over into the conduct of the individual it not only maintains that function but acquires still greater capacity. If I can take the attitude of a friend with whom I am going to carry on a discussion, in taking that attitude I can apply it to myself and reply as he replies, and I can have things in very much better shape than if I had not employed that conversation of gestures in my own conduct. The same is true of him. It is good for both to think out the situation in advance. Each individual has to take also the attitude of the community, the generalized attitude. He has to be ready to act with reference to his own conditions just as any individual in the community would act.

One of the greatest advances in the development of the community arises when this reaction of the community on the individual takes on what we call an institutional form. What we mean by that is that the whole community acts toward the individual under certain circumstances in an identical way. It makes no difference, over against a person who is stealing your property, whether it is Tom, Dick, or Harry. There is an identical response on the part of the whole community under these conditions. We call that the formation of the institution.

There is one other matter which I wish briefly to refer to now. The only way in which we can react against the disapproval of the entire community is by setting up a higher sort of community which in a certain sense outvotes the one we find. A person may reach a point of going against the whole world about him; he may stand out by himself over against it. But to do that he has to speak with the voice of reason to himself. He has to comprehend the voices of the past and of the future. That is the only way in which the self can get a voice which is more than the voice of the community. As a rule we assume that this general voice of the community is identical with the larger community of the past and the future; we assume that an organized custom represents what we call morality. The things one cannot do are those which everybody would condemn. If we take the attitude of the community over against our own responses, that is a true statement, but we must not forget this other capacity, that of replying to the community and insisting on the gesture of the community changing. We can reform the order of things; we can insist on making the community standards better standards. We are not simply bound by the community. We are engaged in a conversation in which what we say is listened to by the community and its response is one which is affected by what we have to say. This is especially true in critical situations. A man rises up and defends himself for what he does; he has his "day in court"; he can present his views. He can perhaps change the attitude of the community toward himself. The process of conversation is one in which the individual has not only the right but the duty of talking to the community of which he is a part, and bringing about those changes which take place through the interaction of individuals. That is the way, of course, in which society gets ahead, by just such interactions as those in which some person thinks a thing out. We are continually changing our social system in some respects, and we are able to do that intelligently because we can think.

Such is the reflective process within which a self arises; and what I have been trying to do is to distinguish this kind of consciousness from consciousness as a set of characters determined by the accessibility to the organism of certain sorts of objects. It is true that our thinking is also, while it is just thinking, accessible only to the organism. But that common character of being accessible only to the organism does not make either thought or the self something which we are to identify with a group of objects which simply are accessible. We cannot identify the self with what is commonly called consciousness, that is, with the private or subjective thereness of the characters of objects.

There is, of course, a current distinction between consciousness and self-consciousness: consciousness answering to certain experiences such as those of pain or pleasure, self-consciousness referring to a recognition of appearance of a self as an object. It is, however, very generally assumed that these other conscious contents carry with them also a self-consciousness—that a pain is always somebody's pain, and that if there were not this reference to some individual it would not be pain. There is a very definite element of truth in this, but it is far from the whole story. The pain does have to belong to an individual; it has to be your pain if it is going to belong to you. Pain can belong to anybody, but if it did belong to everybody it would be comparatively unimportant. I suppose it is conceivable that under an anesthetic what takes place is the dissociation of experiences so that the suffering, so to speak, is no longer your suffering. We have illustrations of that, short of the anesthetic dissociation, in an experience of a disagreeable thing which loses its power over us because we give our attention to something else. If we can get, so to speak, outside of the thing, dissociating it from the eye that is regarding it, we may find that it has lost a great deal of its unendurable character. The unendurableness of pain is a reaction against it. If you can actually keep yourself from reacting against suffering you get rid of a certain content in the suffering itself. What takes place in effect is that it ceases to be your pain. You simply regard it objectively. Such is the point of view we are continually impressing on a person when he is apt to be swept away by emotion. In that case what we get rid of is not the offense itself, but the reaction against the offense. The objective character of the judge is that of a person who is neutral, who can simply stand outside of a situation and assess it. If we can get that judicial attitude in regard to the offenses of a person against ourselves, we reach the point where we do not resent them but understand them, we get the situation where to understand is to forgive. We remove much of experience outside of our own self by this attitude. The distinction and natural attitude against another is a resentment of an offense, but we now have in a certain sense passed beyond that self and become a self with other attitudes. There is a certain technique, then, to which we subject ourselves in enduring suffering or any emotional situation, and which consists in partially separating one's self from the experience so that it is no longer the experience of the individual in question.

If, now, we could separate the experience entirely, so that we should not remember it, so that we should not have to take it up continually into the self from day to day, from moment to moment, then it would not exist any longer so far as we are concerned. If we had no memory which identifies experiences with the self, then they would certainly disappear so far as their relation to the self is concerned, and yet they might continue as sensuous or sensible experiences without being taken up into a self. That sort of a situation is presented in the pathological case of a multiple personality in which an individual loses the memory of a certain phase of his existence. Everything connected with that phase of his existence is gone and he becomes a different personality. The past has a reality whether in the experience or not, but here it is not identified with the self—it does not go to make up the self. We take an attitude of that sort, for example, with reference to others when a person has committed some sort of an offense which leads to a statement of the situation, an admission, and perhaps regret, and then is dropped. A person who forgives but does not forget is an unpleasant companion; what goes with forgiving is forgetting, getting rid of the memory of it.

There are many illustrations which can be brought up of the loose relationship of given contents to a self in defense of our recognition of them as having a certain value outside of the self. At the least, it must be granted that we can approach the point where something which we recognize as a content is less and less essential to the self, is held off from the present self, and no longer has the value for that self which it had for the former self. Extreme cases seem to support the view that a certain portion of such contents can be entirely cut of from the self. While in some sense it is there ready to appear under specific conditions, for the time being it is dissociated and does not get in above the threshold of our self-consciousness.

Self-consciousness, on the other hand, is definitely organized about the social individual, and that, as we have seen, is not simply because one is in a social group and affected by others and affects them, but because (and this is a point I have been emphasizing) his own experience as a self is one which he takes over from his action upon others. He becomes a self in so far as he can take the attitude of another and act toward himself as others act. In so far as the conversation of gestures can become part of conduct in the direction and control of experience, then a self can arise. It is the social process of influencing others in a social act and then taking the attitude of the others aroused by the stimulus, and then reacting in turn to this response, which constitutes a self.

Our bodies are parts of our environment; and it is possible for the individual to experience and be conscious of his body, and of bodily sensations, without being conscious or aware of himself—without, in other words, taking the attitude of the other toward himself. According to the social theory of consciousness, what we mean by consciousness is that peculiar character and aspect of the environment of individual human experience which is due to human society, a society of other individual selves who take the attitude of the other toward themselves. The physiological conception or theory of consciousness is by itself inadequate; it requires supplementation from the socio-psychological point of view. The taking or feeling of the attitude of the other toward yourself is what constitutes self-consciousness, and not mere organic sensations of which the individual is aware and which he experiences. Until the rise of his self-consciousness in the process of social experience, the individual experiences his body—its feelings and sensations —merely as an immediate part of his environment, not as his own, not in terms of self-consciousness. The self and self-consciousness have first to arise, and then these experiences can be identified peculiarly with the self, or appropriated by the self; to enter, so to speak, into this heritage of experience, the self has first to develop within the social process in which this heritage is involved.

Through self-consciousness the individual organism enters in some sense into its own environmental field; its own body becomes a part of the set of environmental stimuli to which it responds or reacts. Apart from the context of the social process at its higher levels—those at which it involves conscious communication, conscious conversations of gestures, among the individual organisms interacting with it—the individual organism does not set itself as a whole over against its environment; it does not as a whole become an object to itself (and hence is not self-conscious); it is not as a whole a stimulus to which it reacts. On the contrary, it responds only to parts or separate aspects of itself, and regards them, not as parts or aspects of itself at all, but simply as parts or aspects of its environment in general. Only within the social process at its higher levels, only in terms of the more developed forms of the social environment or social situation, does the total individual organism become an object to itself, and hence self-conscious; in the social process at its lower, non-conscious levels, and also in the merely psychophysiological environment or situation which is logically antecedent to and presupposed by the social process of experience and behavior, it does not thus become an object to itself. In such experience or behavior as may be called self-conscious, we act and react particularly with reference to ourselves, though also with reference to other individuals; and to be self-conscious is essentially to become an object to one's self in virtue of one's social relations to other individuals.

Emphasis should be laid on the central position of thinking when considering the nature of the self. Self-consciousness, rather than affective experience with its motor accompaniments, provides the core and primary structure of the self, which is thus essentially a cognitive rather than an emotional phenomenon. The thinking or intellectual process—the internalization and inner dramatization, by the individual, of the external conversation of significant gestures which constitutes his chief mode of interaction with other individuals belonging to the same society—is the earliest experiential phase in the genesis and development of the self. Cooley and James, it is true, endeavor to find the basis of the self in reflexive affective experiences, i.e., experiences involving "self-feeling"; but the theory that the nature of the self is to be found in such experiences does not account for the origin of the self, or of the self-feeling which is supposed to characterize such experiences. The individual need not take the attitudes of others toward himself in these experiences, since these experiences merely in themselves do not necessitate his doing so, and unless he does so, he cannot develop a self; and he will not do so in these experiences unless his self has already originated otherwise, namely, in the way we have been describing. The essence of the self, as we have said, is cognitive: it lies in the internalized conversation of gestures which constitutes thinking, or in terms of which thought or reflection proceeds. And hence the origin and foundations of the self, like those of thinking, are social.

4/From Family to Society

introduction:
patriarchy in microcosm
and macrocosm

Though Plato's *Republic* presents itself most obviously as a tract in utopian political philosophy, its picture of justice in the state is meant to serve as a large-scale model of justice in the individual. Throughout the *Republic* and the *Timaeus* Plato develops an interlocking metaphorical structure linking the self, the state, and the cosmos. The present section looks at a single link in that metaphorical chain. In moving from self-creation to social and political philosophy, it is helpful to locate these issues in their microcosmic form, namely, the family. Patriarchy, or father rule, has its biological roots in the family. Because the family has often been taken as the rudimentary model of social and political organization, its sexual structure is significant. The family is not just any small group; it is a biological unit joining old and young, male and female. To the extent that the male dominates the family, patriarchy seems to be the appropriate form of political organization.

But patriarchy is under fire, both from the women's liberation movement and from the many third-world movements seeking independence from cultural and economic domination. Not surprisingly, the political and sexual assault on patriarchy comes when there is much talk of the "decline of the family." Some seek alternatives to restrictive monogamy; and the communal movement testifies to a quest for alternative forms of microcosmic social organization. How are we to understand these transformations in our culture? How are we to understand these transformations in ourselves? Social scientists of the mass media are fond of unearthing single, clearly definable causes: the cultural revolution is the result of drugs, or of the industrial and technological revolution that takes children out of the home, or of the decline and death of the great Father in the sky, God. But understanding these issues adequately depends no more on locating a single cause than understanding personal identity depended on locating a single substance at the core of the self. A philosophical approach requires a comprehensive, totalizing understanding, which sees how the various dimensions of patriarchy both influence and reflect the other dimensions. While it may be clear that historically patriarchy is on the decline, the meaning of that decline will not be clear until we have reflected on all its ramifications, political, social, sexual, and personal.

ARISTOTLE *(384?–323 B.C.)*

Aristotle was associated with the Academy of Plato for some twenty years. After Plato's death in 347, Aristotle served for a time as tutor to Alexander, eventually to become The Great. Aristotle's thoughts on politics have had considerable influence. With most of his work translated from Greek into Latin by the twelfth and thirteenth centuries—sometimes by way of Arabic—Aristotle's words have been heard by many. They have, in themselves and in Benjamin Jowett's stately translation, the ring of centuries.

In the following passage from the Politics, *Aristotle bases his theory of the state on an argument from nature. Later, Rousseau will consider the state as a human artifact. Aristotle's attempt to derive the state from nature leads him to stress the importance of biological origins. His organic perspective also leads to an explicit and eloquent rejection of individualism. For Aristotle, human beings are* by nature *political. Any withdrawal of the individual from the social context can only appear as a kind of amputation of a part from the organic whole that gives it life.*

Politics

Book I

Every state is a community of some kind, and every community is established with a view to some good; for mankind always act in order to obtain that which they think good. But, if all communities aim at some good, the state or political community, which is the highest of all, and which embraces all the rest, aims at good in a greater degree than any other, and at the highest good.

Some people think that the qualifications of a statesman, king, householder, and master are the same, and that they differ, not in kind, but only in the number of their subjects. For example, the ruler over a few is called a master; over more, the manager of a household; over a still larger number, a statesman or king, as if there were no difference between a great household and a small state. The distinction which is made between the king and the statesman is as follows: When the government is personal, the ruler is a king; when, according to the rules of the political science, the citizens rule and are ruled in turn, then he is called a statesman.

But all this is a mistake; for governments differ in kind, as will be evident to any one who considers the matter according to the method which has hitherto guided us. As in other departments of science, so in politics, the compound should always be resolved into the simple elements or least parts of the whole. We must therefore look at the elements of which the state is composed, in order that we may see in what the different kinds of rule differ from one another, and whether any scientific result can be attained about each one of them.

He who thus considers things in their first growth and origin, whether a state or anything else, will obtain the clearest view of them. In the first place there must be a union of those who cannot exist without each other; namely, of male and female, that the race may continue (and this is a union which is formed, not of deliberate purpose, but because, in common with other animals and with plants, mankind have a natural desire to leave behind them an image of themselves), and of natural ruler and subject, that both may be preserved. For that which can foresee by the exercise of mind is by nature intended to be lord and master, and that which can with its body give effect to such foresight is a subject, and by nature a slave; hence master and slave have the same interest. Now nature has distinguished between the female and the slave. For she is not niggardly, like the smith who fashions the Delphian knife for many uses; she makes each thing for a single use, and every instrument is best made when intended for one and not for many uses. But among barbarians no distinction is made between women and slaves, because there is no natural ruler among them: they are a community of slaves, male and female. Wherefore the poets say—

'It is meet that Hellenes should rule over barbarians';

as if they thought that the barbarian and the slave were by nature one.

Out of these two relationships between man and woman, master and slave, the first thing to arise is the family, and Hesiod is right when he says—

'First house and wife and an ox for the plough,'

for the ox is the poor man's slave. The family is the association established by nature for the supply of men's everyday wants, and the members of it are called by Charondas 'companions of the cupboard', and by Epimenides the Cretan, 'companions of the manger.' But when several families are united, and the association aims at something more than the supply of daily needs, the first society to be formed is the village. And the most natural form of the village appears to be that of a colony from the family, composed of the children and grandchildren, who are said to be 'suckled with the same milk'. And this is the reason why Hellenic states were originally governed by kings; because the Hellenes were under royal rule before they came together, as the barbarians still are. Every family is ruled by the eldest, and therefore in the colonies of the family the kingly form of government prevailed because they were of the same blood. As Homer says:

'Each one gives law to his children and to his wives.'

For they lived dispersedly, as was the manner in ancient times. Wherefore men say that the Gods have a king, because they themselves either are or were in ancient times under the rule of a king. For they imagine, not only the forms of the Gods, but their ways of life to be like their own.

When several villages are united in a single complete community, large enough to be nearly or quite self-sufficing, the state comes into existence, originating in the bare needs of life, and continuing in existence for the sake of a good life. And therefore, if the earlier forms of society are natural, so is the state, for it is the end of them, and the nature of a thing is its end. For what each thing is when fully developed, we call its nature, whether we are speaking of a man, a horse, or a family. Besides, the final cause and end of a thing is the best, and to be self-sufficing is the end and the best.

Hence it is evident that the state is a creation of nature, and that man is by nature a political animal. And he who by nature and not by mere accident is without a state, is either a bad man or above humanity; he is like the

'Tribeless, lawless, heartless one,'

whom Homer denounces—the natural outcast is forthwith a lover of war; he may be compared to an isolated piece at draughts.

Now, that man is more of a political animal than bees or any other gregarious animals is evident. Nature, as we often say, makes nothing in vain, and man is the only animal whom she has endowed with the gift of speech. And whereas mere voice is but an indication of pleasure or pain, and is therefore found in other animals (for their nature attains to the perception of pleasure and pain and the intimation of them to one another, and no further), the power of speech is intended to set forth the expedient and inexpedient, and therefore likewise the just and the unjust. And it is a characteristic of man that he alone has any sense of good and evil, of just and unjust, and the like, and the association of living beings who have this sense makes a family and a state.

Further, the state is by nature clearly prior to the family and to the individual, since the whole is of necessity prior to the part; for example, if the whole body be destroyed, there will be no foot or hand, except in an equivocal sense, as we might speak of a stone hand; for when destroyed the hand will be no better than that. But things are defined by their working and power; and we ought not to say that they are the same when they no longer have their proper quality, but only that they have the same name. The proof that the state is a creation of nature and prior to the individual is that the individual, when isolated, is not self-sufficing; and therefore he is like a part in relation to the whole. But he who is unable to live in society, or who has no need because he is sufficient for himself, must be either a beast or a god: he is no part of a state. A social instinct is implanted in all men by nature, and yet he who first founded the state was the greatest of benefactors. For man, when perfected, is the best of animals, but, when separated from law and justice, he is the worst of all; since armed injustice is the more dangerous, and he is equipped at birth with arms, meant to be used by intelligence and virtue, which he may use for the worst ends. Wherefore, if he have not virtue, he is the most unholy and the most savage of animals, and the most full of lust and gluttony. But justice is the bond of men in states, for the administration of justice, which is the determination of what is just, is the principle of order in political society.

JOHN LOCKE *(1632–1704)*

John Locke's Two Treatises on Civil Government *(1689), played a powerful role in the centuries-long decline of patriarchy. The first treatise was written primarily to refute Sir Robert Filmer's* Patriarcha, *(published posthumously in 1680) in which Filmer argued that the state's patriarchal power derives from a divine right of sovereignty inherited from Adam. We can thank Locke for liberating many of his contemporaries from this thesis, including the founding fathers who drafted the Declaration of Independence and the Constitution. Considering Locke's influence on the minds of those men who hammered out the political structure of the United States, it is hard to overestimate his effect on our lives hundreds of years later. If we are to uncover and understand our own roots, the right place to dig is in the writings of John Locke.*

Locke both grants and limits the jurisdiction of parents over their children and he places duties upon the parent as well as the child: the parent is responsible for the child's proper care and education. While Locke carefully defines the differences separating paternal power from state power, his limits on the extent of paternal power prefigure his limits on the extent of state power. Locke saw that in neither case is power absolute. Consequently he took pains to compare and distinguish the different kinds of power. In reading the following passage, from Concerning Civil Government, Second Essay, *try to see just how far Locke's discussion of the family anticipates the limits of authority of the state over the individual and how far he attempts to dissociate and distinguish his discussion of the family from his remarks on civil government. Where absolutes have been foresworn relative differences become important.*

On Paternal Power and Civil Society

Of Paternal Power

(52)[1] It may perhaps be censured as an impertinent criticism, in a discourse of this nature, to find fault with words and names, that have obtained in the world: and yet possibly it may not be amiss to offer new ones, when the old are apt to lead men into mistakes, as this of paternal power probably has done; which seems so to place the power of parents over their children wholly in the father, as if the mother had no share in it: whereas, if we consult reason or revelation, we shall find she hath an equal title. This may give one reason to ask, whether this might not be more properly called parental power? for whatever obligation nature and the right of generation lays on children, it must certainly bind them equally to both

---

[1][Paragraph numbers correspond to the original.—J. A. O.]

concurrent causes of it. And accordingly we see the positive law of God every where joins them together, without distinction, when it commands the obedience of children: "Honour thy father and thy mother," Exod. xx. 12. "Whosoever curseth his father or his mother," Lev. xx. 9. "Ye shall fear every man his mother and his father," Lev. xix. 5. "Children, obey your parents," &c. Eph. vi. 1. is the style of the Old and New Testament.

(53) Had but this one thing been well considered, without looking any deeper into the matter, it might perhaps have kept men from running into those gross mistakes they have made, about this power of parents; which, however it might, without any great harshness, bear the name of absolute dominion, and regal authority, when under the title of paternal power it seemed appropriated to the father; would yet have founded but oddly, and in the very name shown the absurdity, if this supposed absolute power over children had been called parental; and thereby have discovered, that it belonged to the mother too; for it will but very ill serve the turn of those men, who contend so much for the absolute power and authority of the fatherhood, as they call it, that the mother should have any share in it; and it would have but ill supported the monarchy they contend for, when by the very name it appeared that that fundamental authority, from whence they would derive their government of a single person only, was not placed in one, but two persons jointly. But to let this of names pass.

(54) Though I have said above, chap. ii. "That all men by nature are equal," I cannot be supposed to understand all sorts of equality: age or virtue may give men a just precedency: excellency of parts and merit may place others above the common level: birth may subject some, and alliance or benefits others, to pay an observance to those whom nature, gratitude, or other respects, may have made it due: and yet all this conflicts with the equality, which all men are in, in respect of jurisdiction or dominion one over another; which was the equality I there spoke of, as proper to the business in hand, being that equal right, that every man hath, to his natural freedom, without being subjected to the will or authority of any other man.

(55) Children, I confess, are not born in the state of equality, though they are born to it. Their parents have a sort of rule and jurisdiction over them, when they come into the world, and for some time after; but it is but a temporary one. The bonds of this subjection are like the swaddling clothes they are wrapt up in, and supported by, in the weakness of their infancy: age and reason, as they grow up, loosen them, till at length they drop quite off, and leave a man at his own free disposal.

(56) Adam was created a perfect man, his body and mind in full possession of their strength and reason, and so was capable from the first instant of his being to provide for his own support and preservation; and govern his actions according to the dictates of the law of reason which God had implanted in him. From him the world is peopled with his descendants, who are all born infants, weak and helpless, without knowledge or understanding: but to supply the defects of this imperfect state, till the improvement of growth and age hath removed them, Adam and Eve, and after them all parents were, by the law of nature, "under an obligation to

preserve, nourish, and educate the children," they had begotten; not as their own workmanship, but the workmanship of their own maker, the Almighty, to whom they were to be accountable for them.

(57) The law, that was to govern Adam, was the same that was to govern all his posterity, the law of reason. But his offspring having another way of entrance into the world, different from him, by a natural birth, that produced them ignorant and without the use of reason, they were not presently under that law; for nobody can be under a law, which is not promulgated to him; and this law being promulgated or made known by reason only, he that is not come to the use of his reason, cannot be said to be under this law; and Adam's children being not presently as soon as born under this law of reason, were not presently free: for law, in its true notion, is not so much the limitation, as the direction of the free and intelligent agent to his proper interest, and prescribes no farther than is for the general good of those under that law: could they be happier without it, the law, as an useless thing, would of itself vanish; and that ill deserves the name of confinement which hedges us in only from bogs and precipices. So that, however it may be mistaken, the end of law is not to abolish or restrain, but to preserve and enlarge freedom: for in all the states of created beings capable of laws, "where there is no law there is no freedom;" for liberty is to be free from restraint and violence from others; which cannot be where there is not law: but freedom is not, as we are told, "a liberty for every man to do what he lists:" (for who could be free, when every other man's humour might domineer over him?) but a liberty to dispose, and order as he lists, his person, actions, possessions, and his whole property, within the allowance of those laws under which he is, and therein not to be subject to the arbitrary will of another, but freely follow his own.

(58) The power, then, that parents have over their children, arises from that duty which is incumbent on them, to take care of their offspring, during the imperfect state of childhood. To inform the mind, and govern the actions of their yet ignorant nonage, till reason shall take its place, and ease them of that trouble, is what the children want, and the parents are bound to: for God having given man an understanding to direct his actions, has allowed him a freedom of will, and liberty of acting, as properly belonging thereunto, within the bounds of that law he is under. But whilst he is in an estate, wherein he has not understanding of his own to direct his will, he is not to have any will of his own to follow: he that understands for him, must will for him too; he must prescribe to his will, and regulate his actions; but when he comes to the estate that made his father a freeman, the son is a freeman too.

(59) This holds in all the laws a man is under, whether natural or civil. Is a man under the law of nature? What made him free of that law? what gave him a free disposing of his property, according to his own will, within the compass of that law? I answer, a state of maturity, wherein he might be supposed capable to know that law, that so he might keep his actions within the bounds of it. When he has acquired that state, he is presumed to know how far that law is to be his guide, and how far he may make use of his freedom, and so comes to have it; till then, somebody else must guide him, who is presumed to know how far the law allows a liberty. If such a state of reason, such an age of discretion made him free, the same

shall make his son free too. Is a man under the law of England? What made him free of that law? that is, to have the liberty to dispose of his actions and possessions according to his own will, within the permission of that law? A capacity of knowing that law; which is supposed by that law, at the age of one and twenty years, and in some cases sooner. If this made the father free, it shall make the son free too. Till then we see the law allows the son to have no will, but he is to be guided by the will of his father or guardian, who is to understand for him. And if the father die, and fail to substitute a deputy in his trust; if he hath not provided a tutor, to govern his son, during his minority, during his want of understanding; the law takes care to do it; some other must govern him, and be a will to him, till he hath attained to a state of freedom, and his understanding be fit to take the government of his will. But after that, the father and son are equally free as much as tutor and pupil after non-age; equally subjects of the same law together, without any dominion left in the father over the life, liberty, or estate of his son....

(63) The freedom then of man, and liberty of acting according to his own will, is grounded on his having reason, which is able to instruct him in that law he is to govern himself by, and make him know how far he is left to the freedom of his own will. To turn him loose to an unrestrained liberty, before he has reason to guide him, is not the allowing him the privilege of his nature to be free; but to thrust him amongst brutes, and abandon him to a state as wretched, and as much beneath that of a man, as their's. This is that which puts the authority into the parents hands to govern the minority of their children. God hath made it their business to employ this care on their offspring, and hath placed in them suitable inclinations of tenderness and concern to temper this power, to apply it, as his wisdom designed it, to the children's good, as long as they should need to be under it.

(64) But what reason can hence advance this care of the parents due to their offspring into an absolute arbitrary dominion of the father, whose power reaches no farther than, by such a discipline as he finds most effectual, to give such strength and health to their bodies, such vigour and rectitude to their minds, as may best fit his children to be most useful to themselves and others; and, if it be necessary to his condition, to make them work, when they are able for their own subsistence. But in this power the mother too has her share with the father.

(65) Nay, this power so little belongs to the father by any peculiar right of nature, but only as he is guardian of his children, that when he quits his care of them, he loses his power over them, which goes along with their nourishment and education, to which it is inseparably annexed; and it belongs as much to the foster father of an exposed child, as to the natural father of another. So little power does the bare act of begetting give a man over his issue; if all his care ends there, and this be all the title he hath to the name and authority of a father. And what will become of this paternal power in that part of the world where one woman hath more than one husband at a time? or in those parts of America, where, when the husband and wife part, which happens frequently, the children are all left to the mother, follow her, and are wholly under her care and provision? If the father die whilst the children are young, do they not naturally every where owe the same obedience to their mother, during their minority, as to their father were he alive; and will any one say, that the mother hath a legislative power over her children?

that she can make standing rules, which shall be of perpetual obligation, by which they ought to regulate all the concerns of their property, and bound their liberty all the course of their lives? or can she enforce the observation of them with capital punishments? for this is the proper power of the magistrate, of which the father hath not so much as the shadow. His command over his children is but temporary, and reaches not their life or property: it is but a help to the weakness and imperfection of their nonage, a discipline necessary to their education: and though a father may dispose of his own possessions as he pleases, when his children are out of danger of perishing for want, yet his power extends not to the lives or goods, which either their own industry, or another's bounty has made their's; nor to their liberty neither, when they are once arrived to the infranchisement of the years of discretion. The father's empire then ceases, and can from thenceforwards no more dispose of the liberty of his son, than that of any other man: and it must be far from an absolute or perpetual jurisdiction, from which a man may withdraw himself, having licence from divine authority to "leave father and mother, and cleave to his wife."

(66) But though there be a time when a child comes to be as free from subjection to the will and command of his father, as the father himself is free from subjection to the will of any body else, and they are each under no other restraint, but that which is common to them both, whether it be the law of nature, or municipal law of their country; yet this freedom exempts not a son from that honour which he ought, by the law of God and nature, to pay his parents. God having made the parents instruments in his great design of continuing the race of mankind, and the occasions of life to their children; as he hath laid on them an obligation to nourish, preserve, and bring up their offspring; so he has laid on the children a perpetual obligation of honouring their parents, which containing in it an inward esteem and reverence to be shown by all outward expressions, ties up the child from any thing that may ever injure or affront, disturb or endanger, the happiness or life of those from whom he received his; and engages him in all actions of defence, relief, assistance and comfort of those, by whose means he entered into being, and has been made capable of any enjoyments of life: from this obligation no state, no freedom can absolve children. But this is very far from giving parents a power of command over their children, or authority to make laws and dispose as they please of their lives and liberties. It is one thing to owe honour, respect, gratitude, and assistance; another to require an absolute obedience and submission. The honour due to parents, a monarch in his throne owes his mother; and yet this lessens not his authority, nor subjects him to her government.

(67) The subjection of a minor, places in the father a temporary government, which terminates with the minority of the child: and the honour due from a child, places in the parents perpetual right to respect, reverence, support and compliance too, more or less, as the father's care, cost, and kindness in his education, have been more or less. This ends not with minority, but holds in all parts and conditions of a man's life. The want of distinguishing these two powers, *viz.* that which the father hath in the right of tuition, during minority, and the right of honour all his life, may perhaps have caused a great part of the mistakes about this

matter: for, to speak properly of them, the first of these is rather the privilege of children, and duty of parents, than any prerogative of paternal power. . . .

(69) The first part then of paternal power, or rather duty, which is education, belongs so to the father, that it terminates at a certain season; when the business of education is over, it ceases of itself, and is also alienable before: for a man may put the tuition of his son in other hands; and he that has made his son an apprentice to another, has discharged him, during that time, of a great part of his obedience both to himself and to his mother. But all the duty of honour, the other part, remains nevertheless entire to them; nothing can cancel that: it is so inseparable from them both, that the father's authority cannot dispossess the mother of this right, nor can any man discharge his son from honouring her that bore him. But both these are very far from a power to make laws, and enforcing them with penalties that may reach estate, liberty, limbs and life. The power of commanding ends with nonage; and though after that, honour and respect, support and defence, and whatsoever gratitude can oblige a man to, for the highest benefits he is naturally capable of, be always due from a son to his parents; yet all this puts no sceptre into the father's hand, no sovereign power of commanding. He has no dominion over his son's property, or actions; nor any right that his will should prescribe to his son's in all things; however it may become his son in many things, not very inconvenient to him and his family, to pay a deference to it.

(70) A man may owe honour and respect to an ancient, or wise man; defence to his child or friend; relief and support to the distressed; and gratitude to a benefactor, to such a degree, that all he has, all he can do, cannot sufficiently pay it: but all these give no authority, no right to any one, of making laws over him from whom they are owing. And it is plain, all this is due not only to the bare title of father; not only because, as has been said, it is owing to the mother too, but because these obligations to parents, and the degrees of what is required of children, may be varied by the different care and kindness, trouble and expence, which are often employed upon one child more than another.

(71) This shows the reason how it comes to pass, that parents in societies, where they themselves are subjects, retain a power over their children, and have as much right to their subjection as those who are in the state of nature. Which could not possibly be, if all political power were only paternal, and that in truth they were one and the same thing: for then, all paternal power being in the prince, the subject could naturally have none of it. But these two powers, political and paternal, are so perfectly distinct and separate, are built upon so different foundations, and given to so different ends, that every subject that is a father, has as much a paternal power over his children, as the prince has over his: and every prince, that has parents, owes them as much filial duty and obedience, as the meanest of his subjects due to their's; and cannot therefore contain any part or degree of that kind of dominion which a prince or magistrate has over his subjects. . . .

(74) To conclude then, though the father's power of commanding extends no farther than the minority of his children, and to a degree only fit for the discipline and government of that age; and though that honour and respect, and all that which the Latins called piety, which they indispensibly owe to their parents all

their life-time, and in all estates, with all that support and defence which is due to them, gives the father no power of governing, *i.e.* making laws and enacting penalties on his children; though by all this he has no dominion over the property or actions of his son: yet it is obvious to conceive how easy it was, in the first ages of the world, and in places still, where the thinness of people gives families leave to separate into unpossessed quarters, and they have room to remove or plant themselves in yet vacant habitations, for the father of the family to become the prince[2] of it; he had been a ruler from the beginning of the infancy of his children: and since without some government it would be hard for them to live together, it was likeliest it should, by the express or tacit consent of the children when they were grown up, be in the father, where it seemed without any change barely to continue; when indeed nothing more was required to it, than the permitting the father to exercise alone, in his family, that executive power of the law of nature, which every free man naturally hath, and by that permission resigning up to him a monarchical power, whilst they remained in it. But that this was not by any paternal right, but only by the consent of his children, is evident from hence, that nobody doubts, but if a stranger, whom chance or business had brought to his family, had there killed any of his children, or committed any other act, he might condemn and put him to death, or otherwise punish him, as well as any of his children: which it was impossible he should do by virtue of any paternal authority over one who was not his child, but by virtue of that executive power of the law of nature, which, as a man, he had a right to: and he alone could punish him in his family, where the respect of his children had laid by the exercise of such a power, to give way to the dignity and authority they were willing should remain in him, above the rest of his family.

(75) Thus it was easy, and almost natural for children, by a tacit, and scarce avoidable consent, to make way for the father's authority and government. They had been accustomed in their childhood to follow his direction, and to refer their little differences to him; and when they were men, who fitter to rule them? Their little properties, and less covetousness, seldom afforded greater controversies; and when any should arise, where could they have a fitter umpire than he, by whose care they had every one been sustained and brought up, and who had a tenderness for them all? It is no wonder that they made no distinction betwixt minority and full age; nor looked after one and twenty, or any other age that might make them the free disposers of themselves and fortunes, when they could have no desire to

---

[2]It is no improbable opinion therefore, which the arch-philosopher was of, "That the chief person in every household was always, as it were, a king: so when numbers of households joined themselves in civil societies together, kings were the first kind of governors amongst them, which is also, as it seemeth, the reason why the name of fathers continued still in them, who, of fathers, were made rulers; as also the ancient custom of governors to do as Melchizedeck, and being kings, to exercise the office of priests, which fathers did at the first, grew perhaps by the same occasion. Howbeit, this is not the only kind of regiment that has been received in the world. The inconveniencies of one kind have caused sundry others to be devised; so that, in a word, all public regiment, of what kind soever, seemeth evidently to have risen from the deliberate advice, consultation, and composition between men, judging it convenient and behoveful; there being no impossibility in nature considered by itself, but that man might have lived without any public regiment." (Hooker's Eccl. P. lib. i. sect. 10.)

be out of their pupilage: the government they had been under during it, continued still to be more their protection than restraint: and they could no-where find a greater security to their peace, liberties, and fortunes, than in the rule of a father.

(76) Thus the natural fathers of families by an insensible change became the politic monarchs of them too: and as they chanced to live long, and leave able and worthy heirs, for several successions, or otherwise; so they laid the foundations of hereditary, or elective kingdoms, under several constitutions and manners, according as chance, contrivance, or occasions happened to mould them. But if princes have their titles in their fathers right, and it be a sufficient proof of the natural right of fathers to political authority, because they commonly were those in whose hands we find, de facto, the exercise of government: I say, if this argument be good, it will as strongly prove, that all princes, nay princes only, ought to be priests, since it is as certain, that in the beginning, "the father of the family was priest, as that he was ruler in his own household."

Of Political or Civil Society

(77) God having made man such a creature, that in his own judgment, it was not good for him to be alone, put him under strong obligations of necessity, convenience, and inclination, to drive him into society, as well as fitted him with understanding and language to continue and enjoy it. The first society was between man and wife, which gave beginning to that between parents and children; to which, in time, that between master and servant came to be added: and though all these might, and commonly did meet together, and make up but one family, wherein the master or mistress of it had some sort of rule proper to a family; each of these, or all together, come short of political society, as we shall see, if we consider the different ends, ties, and bounds of each of these.

(78) Conjugal society is made by a voluntary compact between man and woman; and though it consist chiefly in such a communion and right in one another's bodies as is necessary to its chief end, procreation; yet it draws with it mutual support and assistance, and a communion of interests too, as necessary not only to unite their care and affection, but also necessary to their common offspring, who have a right to be nourished and maintained by them, till they are able to provide for themselves.

(79) For the end of conjunction between male and female being not barely procreation, but the continuation of the species; this conjunction betwixt male and female ought to last, even after procreation, so long as is necessary to the nourishment and support of the young ones, who are to be sustained by those that got them, till they are able to shift and provide for themselves. This rule, which the infinite wise Maker hath set to the works of his hands, we find the inferior creatures steadily obey. In those viviparous animals which feed on grass, the conjunction between male and female lasts no longer than the very act of copulation; because the teat of the dam being sufficient to nourish the young, till it be able to feed on grass, the male only begets, but concerns not himself for the female or young, to whose sustenance he can contribute nothing. But in beasts of

prey the conjunction lasts longer: because the dam not being able well to subsist herself, and nourish her numerous offspring by her own prey alone, a more laborious, as well as more dangerous way of living, than by feeding on grass; the assistance of the male is necessary to the maintenance of their common family, which cannot subsist till they are able to prey for themselves, but by the joint care of male and female. The same is to be observed in all birds, (except some domestic ones, where plenty of food excuses the cock from feeding, and taking care of the young brood) whose young needing food in the nest, the cock and hen continue mates, till the young are able to use their wing, and provide for themselves.

(80) And herein I think lies the chief, if not the only reason, "why the male and female in mankind are tied to a longer conjunction" than other creatures, viz. because the female is capable of conceiving, and de facto is commonly with child again, and brings forth to a new birth, long before the former is out of a dependency for support on his parents help, and able to shift for himself, and has. all the assistance that is due to him from his parents: whereby the father, who is bound to take care for those he hath begot, is under an obligation to continue in conjugal society with the same woman longer than other creatures, whose young being able to subsist of themselves before the time of procreation returns again, the conjugal bond dissolves of itself and they are at liberty, till Hymen at his usual anniversary season summons them again to choose new mates. Wherein one cannot but admire the wisdom of the great Creator, who having given to man foresight, and an ability to lay up for the future, as well as to supply the present necessity, hath made it necessary, that society of man and wife should be more lasting, than of male and female amongst other creatures; that so their industry might be encouraged, and their interest better united, to make provision and lay up goods for their common issue, which uncertain mixture, or easy and frequent solutions of conjugal society, would mightily disturb.

(81) But though these are ties upon mankind, which make the conjugal bonds more firm and lasting in man, than the other species of animals; yet it would give one reason to inquire, why this compact, where procreation and education are secured, and inheritance taken care for, may not be made determinable, either by consent, or at a certain time, or upon certain conditions, as well as any other voluntary compacts, there being no necessity in the nature of the thing, nor to the ends of it, that it should always be for life; I mean, to such as are under no restraint of any positive law, which ordains all such contracts to be perpetual.

(82) But the husband and wife, though they have but one common concern, yet having different understandings, will unavoidably sometimes have different wills too; it therefore being necessary that the last determination, i.e. the rule, should be placed somewhere; it naturally falls to the man's share, as the abler and stronger. But this reaching but to the things of their common interest and property, leaves the wife in the full and free possession of what by contract is her peculiar right, and gives the husband no more power over her life than she has over his; the power of the husband being so far from that of an absolute monarch, that the wife has in many cases a liberty to separate from him, where natural right or their contract allows it; whether that contract be made by themselves in the state of nature, or by the customs or laws of the country they live in; and the

children upon such separation fall to the father's or mother's lot, as such contract does determine.

(83) For all the ends of marriage being to be obtained under politic government, as well as in the state of nature, the civil magistrate doth not abridge the right or power of either naturally necessary to those ends, viz. procreation and mutual support and assistance whilst they are together; but only decides any controversy that may arise between man and wife about them. If it were otherwise, and that absolute sovereignty and power of life and death naturally belonged to the husband, and were necessary to the society between man and wife, there could be no matrimony in any of those countries where the husband is allowed no such absolute authority. But the ends of matrimony requiring no such power in the husband, the condition of conjugal society put it not in him, it being not at all necessary to that state. Conjugal society could subsist and attain its ends without it; nay, community of goods, and the power over them, mutual assistance and maintenance, and other things belonging to conjugal society, might be varied and regulated by that contract which unites man and wife in that society, as far as many consist with procreation and the bringing up of children till they could shift for themselves; nothing being necessary to any society, that is not necessary to the ends for which it is made.

(84) The society betwixt parents and children, and the distinct rights and powers belonging respectively to them, I have treated of so largely, in the foregoing chapter, that I shall not here need to say any thing of it. And I think it is plain, that it is far different from a politic society.

(85) Master and servant are names as old as history, but given to those of far different condition; for a freeman makes himself a servant to another, by selling him, for a certain time, the service he undertakes to do, in exchange for wages he is to receive; and though this commonly puts him into the family of his master, and under the ordinary discipline thereof: yet it gives the master but a temporary power over him, and no greater than what is contained in the contract between them. But there is another sort of servants, which by a peculiar name we call slaves, who being captives taken in a just war, are by the right of nature subjected to the absolute dominion and arbitrary power of their masters. These men having, as I say, forfeited their lives, and with it their liberties, and lost their estates; and being in the state of slavery, not capable of any property; cannot in that state be considered as any part of civil society; the chief end whereof is the preservation of property.

(86) Let us therefore consider a master of a family with all these subordinate relations of wife, children, servants, and slaves, united under the domestic rule of a family; which, what resemblance soever it may have in its order, offices, and number too, with a little commonwealth, yet is very far from it, both in its constitution, power, and end: or if it must be thought a monarchy, and the paterfamilias the absolute monarch in it, absolute monarchy will have but a very shattered and short power, when it is plain, by what has been said before, that the master of the family has a very distinct and differently limited power, both as to time and extent, over those several persons that are in it: for excepting the slave (and the family is as much a family, and his power as paterfamilias as great, whether there be any

slaves in his family or no) he has no legislative power of life and death over any of them, and none too but what a mistress of a family may have as well as he. And he certainly can have no absolute power over the whole family, who has but a very limited one over every individual in it. But how a family or any other society of men, differ from that which is properly political society, we shall best see by considering wherein political society itself consists.

(87) Man being born, as has been proved, with a title to perfect freedom, and uncontrolled enjoyment of all the rights and privileges of the law of nature, equally with any other man, or number of men in the world, hath by nature a power, not only to preserve his property, that is, his life, liberty, and estate, against the injuries and attempts of other men; but to judge of and punish the breaches of that law in others, as he is persuaded the offence deserves, even with death itself, in crimes where the heinousness of the fact, in his opinion, requires it. But because no political society can be, nor subsist, without having in itself the power to preserve the property, and, in order thereunto, punish the offences of all those of that society; there, and there only is political society, where every one of the members hath quitted this natural power, resigned it up into the hands of the community in all cases that excludes him not from appealing for protection to the law established by it. And thus all private judgment of every particular member being excluded, the community comes to be umpire, by settled standing rules, indifferent, and the same to all parties: and by men having authority from the community, for the execution of those rules, decides all the differences that may happen between any members of that society concerning any matter of right; and punishes those offences which any member hath committed against the society, with such penalties as the law has established: whereby it is easy to discern, who are, and who are not, in political society together. Those who are united into one body, and have a common established law and judicature to appeal to, with authority to decide controversies between them, and punish offenders, are in civil society one with another: but those who have no such common appeal, I mean on earth, are still in the state of nature, each being, where there is no other, judge for himself, and executioner: which is, as I have before showed it, the perfect state of nature.

(88) And thus the commonwealth comes by a power to set down what punishment shall belong to the several transgressions which they think worthy of it, committed amongst the members of that society, (which is the power of making laws) as well as it has the power to punish any injury done unto any of its members, by any one that is not of it, (which is the power of war and peace;) and all this for the preservation of the property of all the members of that society, as far as is possible. But though every man who has entered into civil society, and is become a member of any commonwealth, has thereby quitted his power to punish offences against the law of nature, in prosecution of his own private judgment; yet with the judgment of offences, which he has given up to the legislative in all cases, where he can appeal to the magistrate, he has given a right to the commonwealth to employ his force, for the execution of the judgments of the commonwealth, whenever he shall be called to it; which indeed are his own judgments, they being made by himself, or his representative. And herein we have the original of the

legislative and executive power of civil society, which is to judge by standing laws, how far offences are to be punished, when committed within the commonwealth; and also to determine, by occasional judgments founded on the present circumstances of the fact, how far injuries from without are to be vindicated; and in both these to employ all the force of all the members, when there shall be need.

(89) Whenever therefore any number of men are so united into one society, as to quit every one his executive power of the law of nature, and to resign it to the public, there and there only is a political, or civil society.

WILHELM REICH *(1897–1957)*

Wilhelm Reich was one of the first in this century to integrate psychoanalytic insights and political theory. During the 1920s and 1930s he wrote several books seeking a synthesis of Freudian and Marxist theory, a synthesis since made popular by Herbert Marcuse and Norman O. Brown. Time and again rejected by both the Freudian and Communist establishments for his devotion to a synthesis they both branded as theoretically impure eclecticism, Reich immigrated to the United States where his claims for psychotherapeutic cures were branded fraudulent. He was sentenced to prison, where he died in 1957. The bizarre conclusion of Reich's career detracted considerably from his influence for some time after his death, but recent years have seen a renaissance in Reichian theory and an appreciation for Reich's original contributions to the synthesis of Freud and Marx.

In the following section from his important book, The Sexual Revolution *(1945), Reich examines the apparent conflict between the demands of nature and the demands of culture. Freud, particularly in* Civilization and Its Discontents *(1930), had concluded that these opposing sets of demands were perhaps irreconcilable. The civilizing demands of culture seemed to require that the natural instincts of both sexuality and aggression be denied, or at best sublimated (redirected), so that their energies would dissipate in cultural endeavors like art and commerce. But Freud was pessimistic; he saw civilized man buying security at the price of losing happiness. When men collectively decided to "quit every one his executive power of the law of nature," as Locke put it, they gave up the right to the immediate gratification of their instinctual drives, and that, according to Freud, amounts to giving up happiness. Either individual happiness or the securities of civilization: the opposition seemed absolute in Freud's eyes. But just as Locke relativized the concept of authority, so Reich relativizes the concept of instinctual gratification and thereby discovers a way out of the apparently absolute contradiction. His way out consists in a person's ability to influence the unconscious historically. Just as a single person's life is not the playing out of an original and permanent essence but a process of self-creation, so humankind as a whole can alter the ingredients in its store of resources, both conscious and unconscious.*

The Sexual Revolution

Freud's cultural philosophical standpoint was always that culture owes its existence to instinctual repression and renunciation. The basic idea is that cultural achievements are the result of sublimated sexual energy; from this it follows logically that sexual suppression and repression are an indispensable factor in the cultural process. There is historical evidence of the incorrectness of this formulation; there are in existence highly cultured societies without any sexual suppression and a completely free sex life.

What is correct in this theory is only that sexual suppression forms the mass-psychological basis for a *certain* culture, namely, the *patriarchal authoritarian* one, in all of its forms. What is incorrect is the formulation that sexual suppression is the basis of culture in general. How did Freud arrive at this concept? Certainly not for conscious reasons of politics or Weltanschauung [world view]. On the contrary: early works such as that on "cultural sexual morals" point definitely in the direction of a criticism of culture in the sense of a sexual revolution. Freud never followed this path; on the contrary, he was adverse to any attempts in this direction and once called them "not being in the middle of the road of psychoanalysis." It was exactly my early attempts at a sex policy involving criticism of culture which led to the first serious differences of opinion between Freud and me.

In analyzing the psychic mechanisms, Freud found the unconscious filled with antisocial impulses. Everyone using the psychoanalytic method can confirm these findings. Every man has phantasies of murdering his father and of taking the father's place with his mother. In everyone, sadistic impulses, inhibited by more or less conscious guilt feelings, are found. In most women, violent impulses to castrate men, to acquire the penis, e.g., by swallowing it, can be found. The inhibition of such impulses, which continue to work in the unconscious, results not only in social adjustment, but also in all kinds of disturbances (as, for example, hysterical vomiting). The man's sadistic phantasies of hurting or piercing the woman in the sexual act lead to various kinds of impotence if they are inhibited by anxiety and guilt feelings; if they are not, they may lead to perverse activities or sex murder. Such unconscious desires as that of eating feces can be found in a great many individuals, regardless of their social class. Such psychoanalytic discoveries as that the oversolicitude of a mother for her child or of a woman for her husband corresponds to the intensity of her unconscious phantasies of murder were highly inconvenient for the ideological champions of "sacred mother love" or of the "sacrament of marriage"; nevertheless, they are correct. Such examples could be multiplied indefinitely; but let us return to our subject. These contents of the unconscious were shown to be remnants of infantile attitudes toward parents, siblings, etc. In order to exist and to fit into our culture, the children have to suppress these impulses. The price they pay for it is the acquisition of a neurosis, that is, a reduction of their ability to work and of their sexual potency.

The finding of the antisocial nature of the unconscious was correct; so was the finding of the necessity of instinctual renunciation for the purpose of adjustment to social existence. However, two facts are at variance: On the one hand, the child has to suppress its instincts in order to become capable of cultural adjustment. On the other hand, it acquires, in this very process, a neurosis which in turn makes it incapable of cultural development and adjustment and in the end makes it antisocial. In order to make natural instinctual gratification possible, one has to eliminate the repression and to liberate the instincts. This is the prerequisite of cure, although not as yet the cure itself as Freud's early statements would have it. What, then, should take the place of instinctual repression? Certainly not the repressed instincts themselves, because, according to psychoanalytic theory, that would mean the impossibility of existing in this culture.

In many places in psychoanalytic literature we find the statement that the uncovering of the unconscious, that is, the affirmation of its existence, does by no means imply an affirmation of the corresponding action. The analyst lays down a law here which applies for life as well as for the treatment session: "You are allowed and supposed to *say* what you want; but that does not mean that you also can *do* what you want."

However, the responsible analyst was—and always is—confronted with the question as to what is to happen to the previously repressed and now liberated instincts. The psychoanalytic answer was: *sublimation* and *rejection*. Since, however, only the fewest patients prove capable of sublimation to a sufficient degree, the only other way out is renunciation through rejection of the instinct. Repression comes to be replaced by rejection. This demand was justified by the following formulation: The child faced its instincts with a weak, undeveloped ego and thus had no other choice but that of repression; the adult faces his instincts with a strong, adult ego which is capable of handling the instincts by way of rejection. Though this formulation contradicts clinical experience, it became—and still is— the accepted one. This point of view also dominates psychoanalytic pedagogy, as represented, for example, by Anna Freud.

Since, according to this concept, the individual becomes capable of culture as a result of instinctual renunciation instead of repression, and since society is regarded as behaving like the individual, it follows from this concept that culture is based on instinctual renunciation.

The whole construction seems unobjectionable and enjoys the approval not only of the majority of analysts but of the representatives of an abstract concept of culture in general. This substitution of renunciation and rejection for repression seems to banish the ghost which raised its threatening head when Freud confronted the world with his early findings. These findings showed unequivocally that sexual repression makes people not only sick but also incapable of work and cultural achievement. The whole world began to rage against Freud because of the threat to morals and ethics, and reproached Freud with preaching the "living out," with threatening culture, etc. Freud's alleged antimoralism was one of the most potent weapons of his early opponents. This ghost did not begin to vanish until the theory of rejection was propounded; Freud's earlier assurance that he was affirming "culture," that his discoveries constituted no threat to it, had made little impression. This was shown by the never-ending talk about "pansexualism." Then, after the new formulation of rejection, the previous enmity was replaced by partial acceptance. For just as long as the instincts were not lived out, it did not make any difference, from a "cultural point of view," whether it was the mechanism of instinctual rejection or that of repression which played the Cerberus keeping the shadows of the underworld from emerging to the surface. One was even able to register progress: that from the unconscious repression of evil to the voluntary renunciation of instinctual gratification. Since ethics does not consist in being asexual but, on the contrary, in resisting sexual temptations, everybody could now agree with everybody. Psychoanalysis, previously condemned, had now itself become capable of culture—unfortunately by way of "renunciation of the instinct," that is, the renunciation of its own theory of the instincts.

I regret to have to destroy some illusions. The whole system contains a miscalculation which is easily demonstrable. Not by any means in the sense that the psychoanalytic findings on which these conclusions are based are incorrect. On the contrary, they are quite correct; only, they are incomplete, and many of the formulations are abstract and thus distract from the real conclusions.

Instinctual Gratification and Instinctual Renunciation

Those German psychoanalysts who attempted a "Gleichschaltung" [unified revision] of psychoanalysis tried to justify their unscientific behavior by quotations from Freud's writings. They contain, in fact, formulations which nullify the revolutionary character of clinical psychoanalytic findings and which clearly demonstrate the contradiction between the scientist and the middle-class cultural philosopher in Freud. One such quotation runs:

> It is a bad misunderstanding, explained only by ignorance, if people say that psychoanalysis expects the cure of neurotic illness from the free "living out" of sexuality. On the contrary, the making conscious of the repressed sexual desires makes possible their *control* [italics mine. W.R.], a control which could not have been achieved by the repression. It would be more correct to say that the analysis liberates the neurotic from the shackles of his sexuality.
> (Freud, *Ges. Schriften*, Bd. XI [*Collected Writings*, Vol. XI], p. 217f.)

If, for example, the 17-year-old daughter of a National Socialist dignitary suffers from hysterical attacks as a result of a repressed desire for sexual intercourse, this desire, in the psychoanalytic treatment, will be recognized, to begin with, as an incestuous desire, and will be rejected as such. So far so good. But what happens to the sexual need? According to the above-quoted formulation, the girl is "liberated" from the shackles of her sexuality. Clinically, however, it looks like this: When the girl, with the aid of the analysis, frees herself from her father, she liberates herself only from the toils of her incest wish, *but not from her sexuality as such.* Freud's formulation neglects this basic fact. The scientific dispute about the role of genitality took its origin precisely from this clinical problem; it is the central point of divergence between the sex-economic and the revised psychoanalytic formulation. Freud's formulation postulates a renunciation on the part of the girl of all sexual life. In this form, psychoanalysis is acceptable even to the Nazi dignitary and becomes, in the hands of analysts like Müller-Braunschweig, an instrument for the "breeding of the heroic human." This form of psychoanalysis, however, has nothing in common with that psychoanalysis contained in the books which Hitler had burned. The latter kind of psychoanalysis, not hide-bound by reactionary prejudice states unequivocally that the girl can get well only if she transfers the genital desires from the father to a friend with whom she satisfies them. But just this is at variance with the total Nazi ideology and inexorably brings up the whole question of the social sexual order. Because, in order to be able to live sex-economically, it is not sufficient that the girl have a free genital sexuality; she needs, in addition, an undisturbed room, proper contraceptives, a friend who is capable of love, that is, not a National Socialist with a sex-negative structure; she needs understanding parents and a sex-affirmative social atmosphere; these needs are all the greater the less she is in a financial situation which would allow her to break through the social barriers of adolescent sex life.

The replacement of sexual repression by renunciation or rejection would be a simple matter were it not for the fact that these latter mechanisms are also dependent on the economy of instinctual life. Renunciation of the instinct is possible only under definite sex-economic conditions. The same is true of sublimation. Character-analytic experience shows clearly that lasting renunciation of a pathological or antisocial impulse is possible only when the sexual economy is in order, that is, if there is no sexual stasis which provides energy for the impulse which is to be renounced. *An ordered sex-economy, however, is possible only in the presence of such sexual gratification as corresponds to any given age.* Which means that an adult can give up infantile and pathogenic desires only if he experiences full genital gratification. The perverse and neurotic modes of gratification against which society should be protected are in themselves only substitutes for genital gratification and arise only if genital gratification is disturbed or made impossible. This fact makes it clear that we cannot speak of instinctual gratification or renunciation in general. We must ask concretely: the gratification of *what* instinct, the renunciation of *what* instinct? If analytic therapy sees its job in eliminating repressions and not in preaching morals, then it can bring about the renunciation only of *one* kind of gratification; that which does not correspond to the respective age or stage of development. Thus, it will bring a girl to the renunciation of her infantile fixation to her father by nothing else but making this fixation conscious. But that does not imply a renunciation of sexual desires as such, because the sexual energy continues to urge toward discharge. While it is easy to make her give up her sexual desires for her father, she cannot be brought to renounce her sexual gratification with a boy her age except by moralistic arguments; to do this, however, is at variance with therapeutic principles and possibilities of cure. On the other hand, she can really dissolve her fixation to her father only under one condition: when her sexuality finds another, normal object and *actual gratification*. Unless this is the case, the infantile fixation is not dissolved, or there occurs a regression to other infantile instinctual goals, and the basic problem continues to exist.

The same is true of *any* case of neurotic disease. If a woman is dissatisfied in her marriage, she will unconsciously reactivate infantile sexual demands; these she can give up only if her sexuality finds another satisfactory outlet. True, the rejection of the infantile sexual desires is a prerequisite for the establishment of a normal sexuality; but the establishment of a normal sex life with actual gratification is also an indispensable prerequisite for the final relinquishing of the infantile instinctual goals. A sexual pervert or criminal, such as a sex murderer, can be cured of his pathological impulses only if he finds his way into a biologically normal sex life. The alternative, thus, is not instinctual renunciation or instinctual living out, but renunciation of *what* impulses, and gratification of *what* impulses?

In speaking abstractly of the evil nature of the repressed unconscious, one obscures the most fundamental facts not only of the therapy and prevention of the neuroses, but of education as well. Freud made the discovery that the unconscious of the neurotics—that is, the vast majority of people in our civilization—contains essentially infantile, cruel, antisocial impulses. This finding is correct. But it obscured another fact, the fact, namely, that the unconscious also contains many impulses which represent natural biological demands, such as the sexual desire of adolescents or of people tied down in an unhappy marriage. The intensity of the later infantile and antisocial impulses derives, historically and economically, from the non-gratification of these natural demands; the damned-up libidinal energy partly reinforces primitive infantile impulses, partly creates entirely new ones, mostly of an antisocial nature, such as the desire for exhibitionism or impulses to sex murder. Ethnological research shows that such impulses are absent in primitive peoples up to a definite point of economic development and begin to make their appearance only after social repression of normal love life has become an established feature.

These antisocial impulses, which result from social repression of normal sexuality and which have to be repressed because society—rightly—does not allow them to be satisfied, these impulses are considered *biological facts* by psychoanalysis. This concept is closely related to that of Hirschfeld that exhibitionism is due to special exhibitionistic hormones. This naive mechanistic biologism is so difficult to unmask because it serves a definite function in our society: that of shifting the problem from the sociological to the biological realm where nothing can be done about it.

There is such a thing as a *sociology of the unconscious* and of antisocial sexuality, that is, a social history of the unconscious impulses, with regard to their intensity as well as their contents. Not only is repression itself a sociological phenomenon, but also that which causes the repression. The study of the "partial impulses" will have to take pointers from ethnological findings such as the fact that in certain matriarchal societies there is little if any of the anal phase of libidinal development which in our society is considered a normal stage between the oral and the genital phase. This is so because in these societies the children are nursed until the third or fourth year when they immediately enter a phase of intensive genital play activities.

The psychoanalytic concept of antisocial impulses is an absolute one and thus leads to conclusions which are at variance with the facts. If, on the other hand, one realizes the *relative* character of the antisocial impulses, one arrives at basically different conclusions regarding not only psychotherapy but especially sociology and sex-economy. The anal activities of a child of one or two have nothing whatsoever to do with "social" or "antisocial." If, however, one adheres to the abstract view that these anal impulses are antisocial, one will institute a regime designed to make the child "capable of culture" as early as the 6th month of life; the later result is exactly the opposite, namely, incapacity for anal sublimation and the development of anal-neurotic disturbances. The mechanistic concept of the absolute antithesis between sexuality and culture makes even analytically trained parents take measures against infantile masturbation, at least in the form of "mild diversions." As far as I know, none of the writings of Anna Freud mention what in private conversation she admitted to be an inevitable conclusion from psychoanalytic findings: that infantile masturbation is a physiological manifestation and should *not* be inhibited. If one adheres to the concept that that which is repressed and unconscious is also antisocial, one will, for example, condemn the genital demands of the adolescent. This is substantiated by such phrases as that the "reality principle" requires the postponement of instinctual gratification.

The fact that this reality principle is *itself relative,* that it is determined by an authoritarian society and serves its purposes, this decisive fact goes carefully unmentioned; to mention this, they say, is "politics," and science has nothing to do with politics. They refuse to see the fact that not to mention it is also politics. Such attitudes have seriously endangered analytic progress; not only have they prevented the discovery of certain facts, but, more important, they have hindered the practical application of definitely established facts by misinterpreting them in terms of conservative cultural concepts. Since psychoanalysis constantly deals with the influences exerted upon the individual by society as well as with judgments as to what is healthy or sick, social or antisocial, and at the same time is unaware of the revolutionary character of its method and findings, it moves around in a tragic circle: it finds that sexual repression endangers culture and at the same time that it is a necessary prerequisite of culture.

Let us summarize the facts which psychoanalysis has overlooked and which are at variance with the psychoanalytic concept of culture:

The unconscious itself is—quantitatively as well as qualitatively—socially determined:

The giving up of infantile and antisocial impulses presupposes the gratification of the normal physiological sexual needs;

Sublimation, as the essential cultural achievement of the psychic apparatus, is possible only in the absence of sexual repression; in the adult, it applies only to the *pregenital,* but not to the *genital* impulses;

Genital gratification—the decisive sex-economic factor in the prevention of neuroses and establishment of social achievement—is at variance, in every respect, with present-day laws and with every patriarchal religion;

The elimination of sexual repression—introduced by psychoanalysis as a therapy as well as a sociologically important factor—is strictly at variance with all those cultural elements in our society which are based just on this repression.

To the extent to which psychoanalysis maintains its cultural standpoint, it does so at the expense of the very results of its own work. The conflict between the cultural concepts of the analytic investigators on the one hand and the scientific results which militate against this culture on the other hand is solved by them in favor of the patriarchal Weltanschauung. When psychoanalysis does not dare to accept the consequences of its findings, it points to the allegedly non-political (unpragmatic) character of science, while, in fact, every step of psychoanalytic theory and practice deals with political (pragmatic) issues.

If one investigates ecclesiastical, fascist and other reactionary ideologies for their unconscious content, one finds that they are essentially defense reactions. They are formed for fear of the unconscious inferno which everyone carries within himself. From this, one could deduce a justification of an ascetic morality only if the unconscious antisocial impulses were absolute and biologically given; if that were so, the political reaction would be correct, and any attempt to eliminate sexual misery would be senseless. Then, the conservative world could correctly point out that the destruction of "the higher qualities," "the central values," the "divine" and the "moral" in the human would lead to sexual and ethical chaos. This is what people mean unconsciously when they talk of "Kulturbolschewismus." The revolutionary movement—except for the sex-political wing—does not know this connection; in fact, it often finds itself on the same front with the political reaction when it comes to basic questions of sex-economy. True, it turns against sex-economic principles for different reasons than does the political reaction: it does not know these principles and their implications. It also believes in the biological and absolute nature of the antisocial impulses and consequently in the necessity of moral inhibition and regulation. It overlooks, like its opponents, the fact that the moral regulation of instinctual life creates exactly what it pretends to master: antisocial impulses.

Sex-economic investigation, on the other hand, shows that the antisocial unconscious impulses—as far as they are really antisocial and not just regarded as such by the moralists—are a result of moral regulation and will continue to exist as long as that regulation exists. Sex-economic regulation alone can eliminate the antithesis between culture and nature; with the elimination of sexual repression, the perverse and antisocial impulses will also be eliminated.

R. D. LAING (b.1927)

In several of his books Erik Erikson repeatedly returns to his thesis that great men are those who feel most deeply the contradictions plaguing their generation. Their achievement stems from their attempt to grapple with and solve the contradictions given to a generation by its particular place in history. Similarly, the way to understand Laing and his work is to look at both in terms of the contradictions and crosscurrents that beset our time: loneliness or community; common sense or a higher state of consciousness. Laing is looking for "a way out" of the contradictions, and his path takes him through many of the themes treated in this volume.

Both his personal and his theoretical approaches to the problems of the self are dominated by a view that takes the context of the self as all-important. He found it necessary to take up residency in a ward for schizophrenics before he felt he had any insight into their self-structure. Through his experiential learning, as well as through his theoretical researches, he came to see the development of the self in terms of the solutions evolved for dealing with different transactions with other people. When others exert contradictory pressures, the self can find no way out; at this point the self is in what Gregory Bateson called a "double bind." According to Laing's view, behavior labeled as schizophrenic may be seen as a rational solution to a double-bind situation. Thus schizophrenia may not be the irrational behavior pattern of an internally confused self but the rational and even predictable outcome of a nexus of contradictory influences exerted by other selves and their situations.

Laing's insights are closely tied to the philosophical tradition culminating in Sartre; with his colleague David Cooper, Laing published a book (Reason and Violence, 1964) devoted exclusively to Sartre's philosophy. (Here it is worth pointing out the connection between Laing's work and the problem of violence treated later on by Fanon and Arendt. Sartre wrote a preface to Fanon's work, and Arendt comments on both Sartre and Laing.)

Laing's latest voyages have taken him into the realms of eastern religion and mysticism. He left his psychiatric practice in England for a journey to the East so that he could, as he said, "get on with it." Where Laing's explorations will take him, who can say? Some think him mad already; no wonder, they say, he has such insights into the world of the schizophrenic. But Laing's own works force us to hear an echo to Pontius Pilate's "What is truth?" Through Laing's thought we see that "madness" may be the only "sane" reaction to the many double binds wrought by the contemporary world, and the reversal of roles indicated by the quotation marks forces us to hear the echo, "What is madness?" Laing is none too ready to let contemporary society define the distinction between madness and sanity on the basis of the socially accepted view of the distinction between reality and unreality. Laing accepts the importance of social determinants upon the self, but he finds room for criticizing the finality of the norms used by contemporary society.

The force and implications of this essay (from Politics and the Family, 1969) are staggering, and the extent to which Laing seems to despise this ordinary life is distressing. He wishes to discard the skin of the orange symbolizing the veil of illusion once he has peeled it away. And who would not prefer to bite into that tender fruit rather than peel and keep all the successive layers of an onion. But what if—just to use the Cartesian-Laingian doubt to its utmost extent—what if in that orange peel were treasures to which our haste and excitement blinded us? What then?

Or, to return to another criticism made against Descartes, how are we to know when we have peeled far enough? Laing ingeniously uncovers the ingenuity with which society covers its tracks on its path toward repression. But his analysis is so powerful, the Cartesian drill so sharp, that it becomes difficult to know when you have reached rock-bottom in the series of nested rules for doing society's bidding. The drill keeps *cutting through the bedrock it is seeking. Once you have understood Laing's analysis, once you have seen how it is possible to be under a spell without knowing it, then ask yourself, "If I were in Heaven, or in the best conceivable social setting, would it not still be both necessary and possible to impose a doubt about whether my happiness were not the product of a clever illusion?"*

Laing is at a midpoint in his writing career. It is presumptuous to make a prediction but nonetheless we may see a subtle change in Laing's future writings, if there are any (Laing warned in The Politics of Experience, *1967, that "not everyone comes back to us again"). He will not foreswear the necessity for breaking through appearances to see another reality, but his residence in that other reality will lead him to a deeper understanding of the nature and necessity of the rules he has uncovered, and then he will exhibit a greater compassion for the keepers of those rules, conscious or unconscious as they may be.*

We return to these themes at the end of the book when we meet the mystic tradition Laing has gone off to find. For now read Laing and try to break through to that 'laborious wakefulness' Descartes spoke of. But do not imagine that with such a breakthrough the path has come to an end. Do not prejudge what is there on the "other side." What if you burn your bridges and find that the "other side" was this side all along only you didn't know it? An unlikely turn of events, you say. But I answer, with Descartes and Laing, "What if . . .?" Cross the bridge, but do not burn it.

The Politics of the Family

The most common situation I encounter in families is when what *I* think is going on bears almost no resemblance to what anyone in the family experiences or thinks is happening, whether or not this coincides with common sense. Maybe no one knows what is happening. However, one thing is often clear to an outsider: there is concerted family *resistance* to discovering what is going on, and there are complicated stratagems to keep everyone in the dark, and in the dark they are in the dark.

We would know more of what is going on if we were not forbidden to do so, and forbidden to realize that we are forbidden to do so.

Between truth and lie are images and ideas we imagine and think are real, that paralyze our imagination and our thinking in our efforts to conserve them.

Each generation projects onto the next, elements derived from a product of at least three factors: what was (1) *projected* onto it by prior generations, (2) *induced* in it by prior generations, and (3) its response to this projection and induction.

If I project element x from set A onto element y of set B, and if we call the operation of projection or mapping $\emptyset$, then y is the image of x under $\emptyset$.

As we say, Johnny is the 'image' of his grandfather.

There is always a projection or a mapping of one *set* of relations onto another *set* of relations. These are relations in time as well as space. In this type of projection or mapping, the *temporal* sequence may be retained or altered.

Projection (like other operations we shall consider later) is usually unknown to the people who are involved. Different mappings go on simultaneously.

Pure projection is not enough. As images of ghostly relations under the operation of projection, we induce others, and are ourselves induced, to *embody* them: to enact, unbeknown to ourselves, a shadow play, as images of images of images . . . of the dead, who have in their turn embodied and enacted such dramas projected upon them, and induced in them, by those before them.

One way to get someone to *do* what one wants, is to give an order. To get someone to *be* what one wants him to be, or supposes he is or is afraid he is (whether or not this is what one wants), that is, to get him to embody one's projections, is another matter. In a hypnotic (or similar) context, one does not tell him what *to be*, but tells him what he is. Such *attributions*, in context, are many times more powerful than orders (or other forms of coercion or persuasion). An instruction need not be defined as an instruction. It is my impression that we receive most of our earliest and most lasting instructions in the form of attributions. We are told such and such is the case. One is, say, told one *is* a good or a bad boy or girl, not only instructed *to be* a good or bad boy or girl. One may be subject to both, but if one *is* (this or that), it is not necessary to be told to be what one has already been 'given to understand' one is. The key medium for communication of this kind is probably not verbal language. When attributions have the function of instructions or injunctions, this function may be denied, giving rise to one type of *mystification*, akin to, or identical with, hypnotic suggestion. Hypnosis may be an experimental model of a naturally occurring phenomenon in many families. In the family situation, however, the hypnotists (the parents) are already hypnotized (by their parents) and are carrying out their instructions, by bringing their children up to bring their children up . . . in such a way, which includes not realizing that one is carrying out instructions: since one instruction is not to think that one is thus instructed. This state is easily induced under hypnosis.

One may tell someone to feel something and not to remember he has been told. Simply tell him he feels it. Better still, tell a third party, in front of him, that he feels it.

Under hypnosis, he feels it; and does not know that he has been hypnotized to feel it. How much of what we ordinarily feel, is what we have all been hypnotized to feel? How much of who we are, is what we have been hypnotized to be?

Your word is my command. A relationship of one to another may be of such power that you become what I take you to be, at my glance, at my touch, at my cough. I do not need to say anything. An attribution, as I am using the term, may be kinetic, tactile, olfactory, visual. Such an attribution is equivalent to an instruction to be obeyed 'implicitly.'

So, if I hypnotize you, I do not say, 'I order you to feel cold.' I indicate it is cold. You immediately *feel* cold. I think many children begin *in* a state like this.

We indicate to them how it is: they take up their positions in the space we define. They may then choose to become a fragment of that fragment of their possibilities we indicate they are.

What we explicitly *tell* them is, I suspect, of less account.

What we indicate they are, is, in effect, an instruction for a drama: a scenario.

For example, a naughty child is a role in particular family drama. Such a drama is a continuous production. His parents tell him he *is* naughty, because he does not do what they tell him. What they tell him he *is*, is *induction*, far more potent than what they tell him to do. Thus through the attribution: 'You are naughty', they are effectively telling him *not to do* what they are ostensibly telling him to do. We are likely to find that such words as: 'You are naughty', are the least of it. One is likely to find that the child is being induced to behave as he is by tactile–kinetic–olfactory–visual signals: and that this is part of a 'secret' communications network, dissociated from the official verbal communiqués.

These signals do not tell him to be naughty; they define what he does *as* naughty. In this way, he learns that he *is* naughty, and *how* to be naughty in his particular family: it is a learned skill. Some children have a special aptitude for it.

I do not mean this is the only way a child becomes 'naughty', but it is one way.

Thus:

Not: Do what I tell you *to* do
But: You will do what I indicate you *are* doing
         You see what I say you see
Not: Be what I tell you to be
But: You are what I indicate you are.

The clinical hypnotist *knows* what he is doing; the family hypnotist almost never. A few parents have described this technique to me as a deliberate stratagem.

More often parents are themselves confused by a child who does *x*, when they tell him to *do y* and indicate he is *x*.

'I'm always trying to get him to make more friends, but he is so self-conscious. Isn't that right, dear?'

'He's so naughty. He never does what I tell him. Do you?'

'I keep telling him to be more careful, but he's so careless, aren't you?'

When such indications or attributions[1] and instructions are discrepant, the two systems A and B are evident. If there is a smooth 'normal' state of affairs, the structure is less evident, but not essentially different. Moreover, if it all seems to work, no one is likely to want to see how it works:

'He knows right from wrong himself: I've never had to tell him not to do these things.'

'He does it without me having to ask him.'

---

[1] All the media of communication may carry these quasi-hypnotic indicators (attributions). The way things are said (paralinguistics) rather than the 'content' (linguistics). The movements we use (kinesics and para kinesics). And touch, taste, smell. The most intensive systematic study of kinesics has been conducted for some years by Professor Birdwhistell of Eastern Pennsylvanian Psychiatric Institute, and his associates. No systematic data, as far as I know, has been gathered on taste and smell. At the University of Florida Professor Jourard has made a beginning of a study of our touching habits (Jourard, 1968), but so far has not carried his studies into families. Dr. Harry Wiener of New York Medical College has published a series of highly suggestive speculations on the way our social conduct may be partially controlled by external chemical messengers (ECM) or *ecto*-hormones, as we know the intricate social coordination of some insects to be, opening up a vast and hitherto almost entirely unexplored field of human studies: the relation of ecto-hormones to social behaviour in man (Wiener, 1966, 1967, 1968).

'He knows himself when he has had enough.'

The smoothly working family system is much more difficult to study than one that is in difficulties.

There are usually great resistances against the process of mapping the past onto the future coming to light, in any circumstances. If anyone in a family begins to realize he is a shadow of a puppet, he will be wise to exercise the greatest precautions as to whom he imparts this information to.

It is not 'normal' to realize such things. There are a number of psychiatric names, and a variety of treatments, for such realizations.

I consider many adults (including myself) are or have been, more or less, in a hypnotic trance, induced in early infancy: we remain in this state until—when we dead awaken, as Ibsen makes one of his characters say—we shall find that we have never lived.

Attempts to wake before our time are often punished, especially by those who love us most. Because they, bless them, are asleep. They think anyone who wakes up, or who, still asleep, realizes that what is taken to be real is a 'dream' is going crazy. Anyone in this transitional state is likely to be confused. To indicate that this confusion is a sign of illness, is a quick way to create psychosis. The person who realizes that 'this is all a nightmare' is afraid he is going crazy. A psychiatrist who professes to be a healer of souls, but who keeps people asleep, treats them for waking up, and drugs them asleep again (increasingly effectively as this field of technology sharpens its weapons), helps to drive them crazy.

The most awake people I have met are most aware of this. They are few. They are not necessarily psychotic, nor well-known intellectuals. A celebrated philosopher told me he reckons he did not awaken from this post-infancy hypnotic state till over fifty, when he had already written most of the works for which he is renowned. . . .

When I was thirteen, I had a very embarrassing experience. I shall not embarrass you by recounting it. About two minutes after it happened, I caught myself in the process of putting it out of my mind. I had already more than half forgotten it. To be more precise, I was in the process of sealing off the whole operation by forgetting that I had forgotten it. How many times I had done this before I cannot say. It may have been many times because I cannot remember many embarrassing experiences before that one, and I have no memory of such an *act* of forgetting I was forgetting before thirteen. I am sure this was not the first time I had done that trick, and not the last, but most of these occasions, so I believe, are still so effectively repressed that I have still forgotten that I have forgotten them.

This is repression. It is not a simple operation. We forget something. And forget that we have forgotten it. As far as we are subsequently concerned, there is nothing we have forgotten.

A clean-cut operation of repression achieves a *cut-off*, so that

a.   we forget X
b.   we are unaware that there is an X that we have forgotten
c.   we are unaware that we have *forgotten* X

d. and unaware that we are unaware that we have forgotten we have
    forgotten X.

Repression is the annihilation, not only *from* the memory of, but *of* the
memory of, a part of E, *together with*, the annihilation of the experience of the
operation. It is a product of at least three operations.

When we consider any actual instance of any operations, we find that it is
almost impossible to find a pure example of a single operation in isolation. This is
what we might expect. It does not mean, because a baby moves all the fingers of
one hand at once, that it has not five fingers. Denial and displacement form a
common operation product. 'It's not *my* fault. It's your fault.' Denial and displacement can equal projection.

Wish-fulfillment and idealization are varieties of operation entailing projection and denial. All projection involves some measure of denial of the range of E. I
am unhappy. I am *not* unhappy (denial). I am *not* denying that I am unhappy
(denial of denial).

I take the principal function of all these operations to be: the production and
maintenance of E that is at best desired, at least tolerated, in the family by the
family in the first place.

The operations I have alluded to are operations on one's own experience.
They are done by one person to himself or herself. But they would be unnecessary
unless the rules of the family required them: and ineffectual unless others
cooperated. Denial is demanded by the others: it is part of a *transpersonal system of
collusion*, whereby we comply with the others, and they comply with us. For
instance, one requires collusion to play 'Happy Families'. Individually, I am
unhappy. I deny I am to *myself*; I deny I am denying anything to *myself* and to the
others. They must do the same. I must collude with their denial and collusion, and
they must collude with mine.

> So we are a happy family and we have no
> secrets from one another.
> *If* we are unhappy/we have to keep it a secret/
> and we are unhappy that we have to keep it a secret
> and unhappy *that* we have to keep secret/the fact/that we
> *have* to keep it a secret
> and that we *are* keeping all that secret.
> But since we are a happy family you can see
> this difficulty does not arise.

Repression of much infant sexuality is sanctioned, the act of repression is itself
denied, and repression, its sanction, and the denial of repression, are denied.
Nothing has happened. 'I don't know what you're talking about.' For instance,
who ever heard of a good boy, and a normal man, *ever*, having wanted to suck his
father's penis? It is quite normal, at one time, to have wanted to suck his mother's
breast. However, it is on the whole best not to connect mother's breast and girl
friend's breast, or, if one is a woman, woman's breast with boy friend's genitals. It

is safest, on the whole, to keep these sets of relations in separate partitions (splitting), and *repress*, to be even more on the safe side, *all infantile desires* in case they were too 'perverse', since they antedate partitioning and repression, etc., *and* to deny the existence of any such operations of partitioning and repression, and to deny this denial. The product arrived at is the outcome of many rules without which it could not be generated or maintained, but to admit the rules would be to admit what the rules and operations are attempting to render nonexistent.

One is expected to be capable of passion, once married, but not to have experienced too much passion (let alone acted upon it) too much before. If this is too difficult, one has to pretend first not to feel the passion one really feels, then, to pretend to passion one does *not* really feel, and to pretend that certain passionate upsurges of resentment, hatred, envy, are unreal, or don't happen, or are something else. This requires false realizations, false de-realizations, and a cover-story (rationalization). After this almost complete holocaust of one's experience on the altar of conformity, one is liable to feel somewhat empty, but one can try to fill one's emptiness up with money, consumer goods, position, respect, admirations, envy of one's fellows for their business, professional, social success. These together with a repertoire of distractions, permitted or compulsory, serve to distract one from one's own distraction: and if one finds oneself overworked, under too great a strain, there are perfectly approved additional lines of defence, concoctions to taste of, narcotics, stimulants, sedatives, tranquillizers to depress one further so that one does not know how depressed one is and to help one to over-eat and over-sleep. And there are lines of defence beyond *that*, to electro-shocks, to the (almost) final solution of simply removing sections of the offending body, especially the central nervous system. This last solution is necessary, however, only if the *normal social* lobotomy does not work, and chemical lobotomy has also failed.

I can think of no way of generating a 'normal' product from the stuff of our original selves except in some such way: once we arrive at our matrix of distinctions, we have rules for combining and partitioning them into sets and subsets. The 'normal' product requires that these operations themselves are denied. We like the food served up elegantly before us: we do not want to know about the animal factories, the slaughterhouses, and what goes on in the kitchen. Our own cities are our own animal factories; families, schools, churches are the slaughter-houses of our children; colleges and other places are the kitchens. As adults in marriages and business, we eat the product....

If my view is right, we at this moment may not know we have *rules against knowing about certain rules.*

Some of you sense that you have rules about rules, but perhaps have never thought about it in these terms.

Some of you are clear this far. You will have to bear with me, for a little, before I get to where you are at, if I can.

I want to talk about the rules that we cannot talk about—just enough to convince any of you who are not sure what I am talking about that this is a very important issue, which I cannot talk about more directly.

There is a law against murder. We can talk about murder, and about the law about murder.

There is a law against incest. We can talk about the law against incest, rather more freely than we can talk about incest: commonly there is a rule against talking about incest, in front of the children especially: but not an absolute rule against talking about whether or not there is a law against incest.

It used to be obvious to many (including Lévy-Bruhl) that when incest does not happen it is because there is a 'natural' revulsion against it. To many, it may now seem equally obvious that it does not occur more frequently because there are rules against it.

Many people used to be scandalized by this view, for it seems to imply that, if there were not such rules, people might do what was prohibited. Many people felt, and some no doubt still do, that to admit that there were rules against incest would be to admit that parents and children, and brothers and sisters, might *want* to have sexual relations with each other. Why should there be a rule against what no one 'naturally' wants to do? Freud's view was that what people think they 'naturally' don't want to do *may* be a product of repression, and other operations, at the behest of rules against even thinking much less doing it. The desire, even the thought, *and* the rule against the desire or thought, are all eliminated from our awareness, so that the product of these operations on oneself is a 'normal' state of awareness, whereby one is unaware of the desire, the thought *and* the rules, and the operations.

One tends to assume that every negative rule (such as that against incest) implies a prior desire, impulse, propensity, instinct, tendency to do it. Don't do that, implies that one would be inclined to if not forbidden.

There is treasure at the bottom of the tree. You will find it. Only remember not to think of a white monkey. The moment you do, the treasure will be lost to you forever. (A favourite story of Francis Huxley.)

We can, by direct experiment, verify that some negative injunctions have a paradoxical effect, to induce one to do what one has been told not to, *especially if one did not,* and does not, in fact, wish to.

'I would never have thought of it until I was told that I must not.'

Negative rules may themselves generate actions they prohibit. If you want people not to do something they are not doing, do not forbid it. There is a better chance that I will not think what I have not yet thought, if you do not tell me *not* to.

In this last minute, I have not been trying to establish whether or not incest is ruled out by social rules or natural laws, or both. I have wished only to demonstrate that there is not a rule against talking *about* whether or not there are such rules or such a natural law.

A family has a rule that little Johnny should not think filthy thoughts. Little Johnny is a good boy: he does not have to be told not to think filthy thoughts. They never have *taught* him *not* to think filthy thoughts. He never has.

So, according to the family, and even little Johnny, there is no rule against filthy thoughts, because there is no need to have a rule against what never happens. Moreover, we do not talk in the family about a rule against filthy thoughts, because since there are no filthy thoughts, and no rule against them, there is no need to talk about this dreary, abstract, irrelevant, or even vaguely filthy subject. There is no rule against talking about nonexistent talk about a nonexistent rule about something that is nonexistent.

Perhaps no one outside such a family rule system could knowingly embrace it—

Rule A: Don't. Rule A1: Rule A does not exist. Rule A2: Rule A1 does not exist.

This type of ruling applies only to some rules. One can talk about certain rules (when one can cross the street). But there are others that one cannot talk about without breaking the rule that one should not talk about them.

If you obey these rules, you will not know that they exist. There is no rule against talking about putting one's finger into one's own mouth, one's brother's, sister's, mother's, father's, anyone's mouth. No rule against *talking* about putting one's finger into the custard pie, though there *is* a rule about putting one's finger into the custard pie. No rule against recognizing the rule: don't put your finger into the fire. Why not? Because you will burn yourself. There is no rule against *talking* about it and giving reasons for it.

But I may say, I have never put my finger into a number of ... (unmentionable) places.[2] What places? I can't mention them. Why not? When one cannot talk about a rule about which one cannot talk, we have reached a limit to what we can talk about.

I have thought about the problem of how not to think a thought one is not supposed to think. I cannot think of any way to do so except, in some peculiar way, to 'think' what one must not think in order to ensure that one does not think it.

'Of course', it never would even occur to a perfectly brainwashed person to think certain unmentionably filthy thoughts. Such cleanliness, however, requires constant vigilance: vigilance against what? The answer is strictly unthinkable. To have clean memories, reveries, desires, dreams, imagination, one must keep clean company, and guard all senses against pollution. If one only overhears someone else talking filthy, one has been polluted. Even if one can forget one ever heard it, right away. But one has to remember to continue to forget and remember to remember to avoid that person in the future.

Many such rules about rules apply to what parts of whose body can be 'thought' of in relation to whom.

Rules apply to what kinds of sensations one is supposed to have where and when in one's own body, in relation to whom.

What are the funny places where funny feelings go on? Where do they come from? Where do they go to?

One seeks to avoid painful feelings, but there are many pleasurable feelings many people are forbidden to experience, imagine, remember, dream about, and they are definitley forbidden to talk about the fact that they are forbidden to talk about them. This is easy if one has already obeyed the injunction not even to 'think' of what I can possibly be talking about.

One has then got to the position in which one cannot think *that* one cannot

---

[2]'Unmentionable' only in relation to what cannot be related to it (my finger) in this particular context.

think about what one cannot think about because there is a rule against thinking about X, and a rule against thinking that there is a rule against thinking that one must *not* think about *not* thinking about certain things.

If some thoughts cannot be thought: and among the thoughts that cannot be thought is the thought that there are certain thoughts that cannot be thought, including the aforementioned thought, then: he who had complied with this calculus of antithoughts will not be aware he is not aware that he is obeying a rule not to think that he is obeying a rule not to think about X. So he is not aware of X and not aware that he is not aware of the rule against being not aware of X. By obeying a rule not to realize he is obeying a rule, he will deny that there is any rule he is obeying.

When one does no more than scratch the surface of the structure of one of the varieties of Western 'conscience', one must marvel at its ingenuity. It must constitute one of the biggest knots in which man has ever tied himself. One of its many peculiar features is that the more tied in the knot, the less aware are we that we are tied in it.

Anyone fully caught in the full anticalculus of this kind cannot possibly avoid being bad in order to be good. In order to comply with the rules, rules have to be broken. Even if one could wash out one's brain three times a day, part of one's self must be aware of what one is not supposed to know in order to assure the continuance of those paradoxical states of multiplex ignorance, spun in the paradoxical spiral that the more we comply with the law, the more we break the law: the more righteous we become the deeper in sin: our *righteousness* is as filthy rags.

transition:
authority and the individual

The title of John Stewart Mill's essay, "Of the Limits to the Authority of Society over the Individual" (1859), nicely states the problem that liberal democratic political theory hopes to solve. Theorists within that tradition, from Locke and Mill on through David Riesman, presuppose a picture of the individual as the basic unit from which various social systems may or may not be built and in terms of which various social systems are to be judged. Whether or not the "state of nature" ever actually existed (and a sympathetic reading of Locke, Hobbes, Rousseau, and others allows them to use the concept of a state of nature as a theoretical construct rather than as a description of unknown past ages), the role played by the state of nature in political philosophy shows that it implies a theory of the individual according to which the self is *not* constituted by a social context. The self is ontologically self-sufficient. The self *is,* as a human self, whether in society or in the state of nature. But the ontological self-sufficiency of the self does not imply a factual self-sufficiency: the individual in the state of nature may be a fully developed human self, but he may not last very long. As Hobbes put it, life in the state of nature is "solitary, poor, nasty, brutish, and short." Hence each separate and struggling Robinson Crusoe concludes that he'd be better off in his struggle with nature and other men if he joined others. As Locke describes: "Whenever therefore any number of men are so united into one society, as to quit every one his executive power of the law of nature, and to resign it to the public, there and there only is a political, or civil society." The individual pays a price: he quits his executive power of the law of nature. He cannot kill and plunder in civil society as he killed and plundered in the state of nature. The question of political theory then becomes how high a price must the individual pay, or, "the limits to the authority of society over the individual."

Political science may be regarded as the science of calculating the various degrees of security that can be bought for various prices—a scientific cost analysis in the market of freedom and authority, as it were. But political philosophy is concerned with a more radical analysis, not in the sense of being leftist or revolutionary, but radical in going to the roots of the problem (*radix:* "root"). While political science may entertain different answers to Mill's question, political philosophy will entertain different questions. Is the formulation of the question correct? Are there "individuals" in the sense presupposed by the liberal democratic tradition, or is the sense of individuality rather a result of a high state of social organization, specialization, and hence individuation? If the primordial individual suffers the same fate as the underlying subject did, that is, if the "individual" presupposed by liberal political theory turns out to be a "ghost in the machine" (Ryle), the question of political theory will have to be reformulated.

The following essays presuppose, implicitly or explicitly, different theories of the individual, and a proper reading should examine those different presuppositions rather than assume that each author answers Mill's question differently.

PLATO *(428–347 B.C.)*

Plato sees the individual as fostered by the state, though his argument does not imply that the individual can never oppose the state. Even though Socrates refused to oppose the state's laws by agreeing to escape from prison, the Crito *finds Socrates in prison as a result of his perpetual questioning of the authority of certain individuals and institutions in ancient Athens. The apparent conflict between the antiauthoritarian tenor of the* Apology *and the argument for subservience in the* Crito *might lead us to convict Plato of self-contradiction were we not aware of his subtle powers of thought and writing. Though Plato taught the importance of generalized absolutes, such as beauty, justice, and virtue, he saw how wrong it can be to seek absolute answers to specific questions, such as, "Does the state have a legitimate authority over the individual?" His answer is neither an unequivocal yes nor an unequivocal no. Does that mean he equivocates? I think not.*

Careful Plato scholarship has shown that the seemingly incidental opening lines of many of the dialogues do more than provide a dramatic introduction to the scene. In his manifold vision Plato was able to see each event many times over in all its varied significances. And he expected the same of his careful readers. Consequently he often used the first few lines to introduce the central themes of a dialogue. Take a moment now to read the opening exchanges and then think about them as saying more than might first appear. Then, if you can tear yourself away from the dialogue, return to the rest of these introductory remarks.

At a crucial point in the argument Socrates states a major premise, that a man ought to do what he admits to be right, whatever harmful consequences might befall him, and he asks, "But if this is true, what is the application?" Socrates then considers the implicit contract he has with the state of Athens by his having lived within her walls and derived benefits from her people and laws. But throughout his discussion of his debt to Athens we want to know, is his argument so strong that it would forbid any and all civil disobedience? Carefully read, the dialogue answers no, but neither does it give absolute justification for civil disobedience. The leading premises dictate that we not harm others, even where we have been unjustly treated. The application of that premise is a difficult matter, however. One almost always does greater harm in breaking the laws than in keeping them. Indeed, it is because the greatest harm usually comes from breaking the laws that the argument of the Crito *is so strong. But sometimes the laws are wrong. Plato could certainly imagine times when keeping the laws would do the greater harm. But it is hard to know just when those times are. Even if we possess standards of justice, applying them is a difficult business depending on the details of the historical matters at hand. Rather than give an absolute answer to the specific question of the authority of the state over the individual, Plato's* Crito *makes an important and appropriately strong argument for the authority of the state, combined with a subtler discourse on the applicability of absolute principles. There might just be a time for civil disobedience. Socrates wishes to know, "What is the exact time?"*

Crito

Persons of the Dialogue: SOCRATES   CRITO

Scene: The Prison of Socrates

SOCRATES.   [43][1] Why have you come at this hour, Crito? it must be quite early?

CRITO.   Yes, certainly.

SOCRATES.   What is the exact time?

CRITO.   The dawn is about to break.

SOCRATES.   I wonder that the keeper of the prison let you in.

CRITO.   He knows me, because I often come, Socrates; moreover, I have done him a kindness.

SOCRATES.   And are you only just arrived?

CRITO.   No, I came some time ago.

SOCRATES.   Then why did you sit and say nothing, instead of at once awakening me?

CRITO.   Awaken you, Socrates? Certainly not! I wish I were not myself so sleepless and full of sorrow. I have been watching with amazement your peaceful slumbers; and I deliberately refrained from awaking you, because I wished time to pass for you as happily as might be. Often before during the course of your life I have thought you fortunate in your disposition; but never did I see anything like the easy, tranquil manner in which you bear this calamity.

SOCRATES.   Why, Crito, when a man has reached my age he ought not to be repining at the approach of death.

CRITO.   And yet other old men find themselves in similar misfortunes, and age does not prevent them from repining.

SOCRATES.   That is true. But you do not say why you come so early.

CRITO.   I come to bring you a painful message; not, as I believe, to yourself, but painful and grievous to all of us who are your friends, and most grievous of all to me.

SOCRATES.   What? Has the ship come from Delos, on the arrival of which I am to die?

CRITO.   No, the ship has not actually arrived, but she will probably be here today, as persons who have come from Sunium tell me that they left her there; and therefore tomorrow, Socrates, must be the last day of your life.

SOCRATES.   Very well, Crito; if such is the will of God, I am willing; but my belief is that there will be delay of a day.

CRITO.   [44] Why do you think so?

SOCRATES.   I will tell you. I am to die on the day after the arrival of the ship.

---

[1][The numbers in brackets refer to the pages of the Stephanus edition of the Greek text of Plato's works. Scholarly editions in all languages bear these numbers, making it easy to go from one edition or translation to another.—J. A. O.]

CRITO.   Yes; that is what the authorities say.

SOCRATES.   But I do not think that the ship will be here until tomorrow; this I infer from a vision which I had last night, or rather only just now, when you fortunately allowed me to sleep.

CRITO.   And what was the nature of the vision?

SOCRATES.   There appeared to me the likeness of a woman, fair and comely, clothed in bright raiment, who called to me and said: "O Socrates, 'The third day hence to fertile Phthia shalt thou come.'[2]"

CRITO.   What a singular dream, Socrates!

SOCRATES.   There can be no doubt about the meaning, Crito, I think.

CRITO.   Yes; the meaning is only too clear. But, oh! my beloved Socrates, let me entreat you once more to take my advice and escape. For if you die I shall not only lose a friend who can never be replaced, but there is another evil: people who do not know you and me will believe that I might have saved you if I had been willing to spend money, but that I did not care. Now, can there be a worse disgrace than this—that I should be thought to value money more than the life of a friend? For the many will not be persuaded that I wanted you to escape, and that you refused.

SOCRATES.   But why, my dear Crito, should we care about the opinion of the many? The best men, and they are the only persons who are worth considering, will think of these things truly as they occurred.

CRITO.   But you see, Socrates, that the opinion of the many must be regarded, for what is now happening shows of itself that they can do the greatest evil to anyone who has lost their good opinion.

SOCRATES.   I only wish it were so, Crito, and that the many could do the greatest evil; for then they would also be able to do the greatest good—and what a fine thing this would be! But in reality they can do neither; for they cannot make a man either wise or foolish, and they do not care what they make of him.

CRITO.   Well, I will not dispute with you; but please to tell me, Socrates, whether you are not acting out of regard to me and your other friends: are you not afraid that if you escape from prison we may get into trouble with the informers for having stolen you away, and lose either the whole or a great part of our [45] property; or that even a worse evil may happen to us? Now, if you fear on our account, be at ease; for in order to save you, we ought surely to run this, or even a greater risk; be persuaded, then, and do as I say.

SOCRATES.   Yes, Crito, that is one fear which you mention, but by no means the only one.

CRITO.   Fear not—there are persons who are willing to get you out of prison at no great cost; and as for the informers, you know that they are far from being exorbitant in their demands—a little money will satisfy them. My means, which are certainly ample, are at your service, and if out of regard for my interests you have a scruple about spending my money, here are strangers who will give you the use of theirs; and one of them, Simmias the Theban, has brought a large sum for this very purpose; and Cebes and many others are prepared to spend their money

[2]Homer, *Il.* ix. 363.

in helping you to escape. I say, therefore, do not shirk the effort on our account, and do not say, as you did in the court, that you will have difficulty in knowing what to do with yourself anywhere else. For men will love you in other places to which you may go and not in Athens only; there are friends of mine in Thessaly, if you like to go to them, who will value and protect you, and no Thessalian will give you any trouble. Nor can I think that you are at all justified, Socrates, in betraying your own life when you might be saved; in acting thus you are working to bring on yourself the very fate which your enemies would and did work to bring on you, your own destruction. And further I should say that you are deserting your own children; for you might bring them up and educate them; instead of which you go away and leave them, and they will have to take their chance; and if they do not meet with the usual fate of orphans, there will be small thanks to you. No man should bring children into the world who is unwilling to persevere to the end in their nurture and education. But you appear to be choosing the easier part, not the better and manlier, which would have been more becoming in one who professes to care for virtue in all his life, like yourself. And indeed, I am ashamed not only of you, but of us who are your friends, when I reflect that the whole business may be attributed entirely to our want of courage. The trial need never have come on, or might have been managed differently; and this last opportunity will seem (crowning futility of it all) to have escaped us through our own incompetence and cowardice, who might [46] have saved you if we had been good for anything, and you might have saved yourself; for there was no difficulty at all. See now, Socrates, how discreditable as well as disastrous are the consequences, both to us and you. Make up your mind then, or rather have your mind already made up, for the time of deliberation is over, and there is only one thing to be done, which must be done this very night, and if we delay at all will be no longer practicable or possible; I beseech you therefore, Socrates, be persuaded by me, and do not say me nay.

SOCRATES.   Dear Crito, your zeal is invaluable, if a right one; but if wrong, the greater the zeal the greater the danger; and therefore we ought to consider whether I shall or shall not do as you say. For I am and always have been one of those natures who must be guided by reason, whatever the reason may be which upon reflection appears to me to be the best; and now that this chance has befallen me, I cannot repudiate my own doctrines, which seem to me as sound as ever: the principles which I have hitherto honoured and revered I still honour, and unless we can at once find other and better principles, I am certain not to agree with you; no, not even if the power of the multitude could let loose upon us many more imprisonments, confiscations, deaths, frightening us like children with hobgoblin terrors. What will be the fairest way of considering the question? Shall I return to your old argument about the opinions of men?—we were saying that some of them are to be regarded, and others not. Now were we right in maintaining this before I was condemned? And has the argument which was once good now proved to be talk for the sake of talking—mere childish nonsense? That is what I want to consider with your help, Crito:—whether, under my present circumstances, the argument will appear to me in any way different or not; and whether we shall dismiss or accept it. That argument, which, as I believe, is maintained by many persons of authority, was to the effect, as I was saying, that the opinions of some men are to be regarded, and of other men not to be regarded. Now you, Crito, are not going to die tomorrow—at least, there is no [47] human probability of this— and therefore you are disinterested and not liable to be deceived by the circumstances in which you are placed. Tell me then, I beg you, whether I am right in saying that some opinions, and the opinions of some men only, are to be valued, and that others are to be disregarded. Is not this true?

CRITO.   Certainly.

SOCRATES.   The good opinions are to be regarded, and not the bad?

CRITO.   Yes.

SOCRATES.   And the opinions of the wise are good, and the opinions of the unwise are evil?

CRITO.   Certainly.

SOCRATES.   And what was said about another matter? Does the pupil who devotes himself to the practice of gymnastics attend to the praise and blame and opinion of any and every man, or of one man only—his physician or trainer, whoever he may be?

CRITO.   Of one man only.

SOCRATES.   And he ought to fear the censure and welcome the praise of that one only, and not of the many?

CRITO.   Clearly so.

SOCRATES.   And he ought to act and train, and eat and drink in the way which seems good to his single master who has understanding, rather than according to the opinion of all other men put together?

CRITO.   True.

SOCRATES.   And if he disobeys and disregards the opinion and approval of the one, and regards the opinion of the many who have no understanding, will he not suffer evil?

CRITO.   Certainly he will.

SOCRATES.   And what will the evil be, whither tending and what affecting, in the disobedient person?

CRITO.   Clearly, affecting the body; that is what is ruined by the evil.

SOCRATES.   Very good; and is not this true, Crito, of other things which we need not separately enumerate? In questions of just and unjust, fair and foul, good and evil, which are the subjects of our present consultation, ought we to follow the opinion of the many and to fear them; or the opinion of the one man who has understanding? ought we not to fear and reverence him more than all the rest of the world, and if we desert him shall we not corrupt and outrage that principle in us which may be assumed to be improved by justice and deteriorated by injustice? —there is such a principle?

CRITO.   Certainly there is, Socrates.

SOCRATES.   Take a parallel instance:—if, acting against the advice of those who have understanding, we ruin that which is improved by health and is corrupted by disease, would life be worth having? And that which has been corrupted is—the body?

CRITO.   Yes.

SOCRATES. Is our life worth living, with an evil and corrupted body?

CRITO. Certainly not.

SOCRATES. And will it be worth living, if that higher part of man be corrupted which is improved by justice and depraved by injustice? Do we suppose that principle, whatever it may be in [48] man, which has to do with justice and injustice, to be inferior to the body?

CRITO. Certainly not.

SOCRATES. More honourable than the body?

CRITO. Far more.

SOCRATES. Then, my friend, we must not particularly regard what the many say of us: but what he, the one man who has understanding of just and unjust, will say, and what the truth will say. And therefore you begin in error when you advise that we should regard the opinion of the many about just and unjust, good and evil, honourable and dishonourable.—'Well,' someone will say, 'but the many can kill us.'

CRITO. That will clearly be the answer, Socrates; you are right there.

SOCRATES. But still, my excellent friend, I find that the old argument is unshaken as ever. And I should like to know whether I may say the same of another proposition—that not life, but a good life, is to be chiefly valued?

CRITO. Yes, that also remains unshaken.

SOCRATES. And a good life is equivalent to a just and honourable one—that holds also?

CRITO. Yes, it does.

SOCRATES. From these premises I proceed to argue the question whether it is or is not right for me to try and escape without the consent of the Athenians: and if it is clearly right, then I will make the attempt; but if not, I will abstain. The other considerations which you mention, of money and loss of character and the duty of educating one's children, are, I fear, only the doctrines of the multitude, who would restore people to life, if they were able, as thoughtlessly as they put them to death—and with as little reason. But now, since the argument has carried us thus far, the only question which remains to be considered is, whether we shall do rightly, I by escaping and you by helping me, and by paying the agents of my escape in money and thanks; or whether in reality we shall not do rightly; and if the latter, then death or any other calamity which may ensue on my remaining quietly here must not be allowed to enter into the calculation.

CRITO. I think that you are right, Socrates; how then shall we proceed?

SOCRATES. Let us consider the matter together, and do you either refute me if you can, and I will be convinced; or else cease, my friend, from repeating to me that I ought to escape against the wishes of the Athenians: for I am very eager that what I do should be done with your approval. And now please [49] to consider my first position, and try how you can best answer me.

CRITO. I will.

SOCRATES. Are we to say that we are never intentionally to do wrong, or that in one way we ought and in another way we ought not to do wrong, or is doing wrong always evil and dishonourable, as has already been often acknowledged by us? Are all the admissions we have made within these last few days to be thrown over? And have we, at our age, been earnestly discoursing with one another all our life long only to discover that we are no better than children? Or, in spite of the opinion of the many, and in spite of all consequences whether for the better or the worse, shall we insist on the truth of what was then said, that injustice is always an evil and dishonour to him who acts unjustly? Shall we say so or not?

CRITO.   Yes.

SOCRATES.   Then we must do no wrong?

CRITO.   Certainly not.

SOCRATES.   Nor when injured injure in return, as the many imagine; for we must injure no one at all?

CRITO.   Clearly not.

SOCRATES.   Again, Crito, may we do evil?

CRITO.   Surely not, Socrates.

SOCRATES.   And what of doing evil in return for evil, which is the morality of the many—is that just or not?

CRITO.   Not just.

SOCRATES.   For doing evil to another is the same as injuring him?

CRITO.   Very true.

SOCRATES.   Then we ought not to retaliate or render evil for evil to anyone, whatever evil we may have suffered from him. But I would have you consider, Crito, whether you really mean what you are saying. For this opinion has never been held, and never will be held, by any considerable number of persons; and those who are agreed and those who are not agreed upon this point have no common ground, and can only despise one another when they see how widely they differ. Tell me, then, whether you agree with and assent to my first principle, that neither injury nor retaliation nor warding off evil by evil is ever right. And shall that be the premiss of our argument? Or do you decline and dissent from this? For so I have ever thought, and continue to think; but, if you are of another opinion, let me hear what you have to say. If, however, you remain of the same mind as formerly, I will proceed to the next step.

CRITO.   You may proceed, for I have not changed my mind.

SOCRATES.   Then I will go on to the next point, which may be put in the form of a question:—Ought a man to do what he admits to be right, or ought he to betray the right?

CRITO.   He ought to do what he thinks right.

SOCRATES.   But if this is true, what is the application? In leaving [50] the prison against the will of the Athenians, do I wrong any? or rather do I not wrong those whom I ought least to wrong? Do I not desert the principles which were acknowledged by us to be just—what do you say?

CRITO.   I cannot answer your question, Socrates; for I do not understand it.

SOCRATES.   Then consider the matter in this way:—Imagine that I am about to run away (you may call the proceeding by any name which you like), and the laws and the state appear to me and interrogate me: 'Tell us, Socrates,' they say; 'what are you about? are you not going by an act of yours to bring us to ruin—the laws, and the whole state, as far as in you lies? Do you imagine that a state can subsist and not be overthrown, in which the decisions of law have no power, but are set aside and trampled upon by individuals?' What will be our answer, Crito, to these and the like words? Anyone, and especially a rhetorician, will have a good deal to say against the subversion of the law which requires a sentence to be carried out. Shall we reply, 'Yes; but the state has injured us and given an unjust sentence.' Suppose we say that?

CRITO.   Very good, Socrates.

SOCRATES.   'And was that our agreement with you?' the law would answer; 'or were you to abide by the sentence of the state?' And if we were to express our astonishment at their words, the law would probably add: 'Answer, Socrates, instead of opening your eyes—you are in the habit of asking and answering questions. Tell us,—What complaint have you to make against us which justifies you in attempting to ruin us and the state? In the first place did we not bring you into existence? Your father married your mother by our aid and begat you. Say whether you have any objection to urge against those of us who regulate marriage?' None, I should reply. 'Or against those of us who after birth regulate the nurture and education of children, in which you also were trained? Were not the laws, which have the charge of education, right in commanding your father to train you in music and gymnastic?' Right, I should reply. 'Well then, since you were brought into the world and nurtured and educated by us, can you deny in the first place that you are our child and slave, as your fathers were before you? And if this is true you cannot suppose that you are on equal terms with us in matters of right and wrong, or think that you have a right to do to us what we are doing to you. Would you have any right to strike or revile or do any other evil to your father or your master, if you had one, because you have [51] been struck or reviled by him, or received some other evil at his hands?—you would not say this? And because we think right to destroy you, do you think that you have any right to destroy us in return, and your country as far as in you lies? Will you, O professor of true virtue, pretend that you are justified in this? Has a philosopher like you failed to discover that our country is more precious and higher and holier far than mother or father or any ancestor, and more to be regarded in the eyes of the gods and of men of understanding? also to be soothed and gently and reverently entreated when angry, even more than a father, and either to be persuaded, or if not persuaded, to be obeyed? And when we are punished by her, whether with imprisonment or stripes, the punishment is to be endured in silence; and if she lead us to wounds or death in battle, thither we follow as is right; neither may anyone yield or retreat or leave his rank, but whether in battle or in a court of law, or in any other place, he must do what his city and his country order him; or he must change their view of what is just: and if he may do no violence to his father or mother, much less may he do violence to his country.' What answer shall we make to this, Crito? Do the laws speak truly, or do they not?

CRITO.   I think that they do.

SOCRATES.   Then the laws will say: 'Consider, Socrates, if we are speaking truly that in your present attempt you are going to do us a wrong. For, having brought you into the world, and nurtured and educated you, and given you and every other citizen a share in every good which we had to give, we further proclaim to any Athenian by the liberty which we allow him, that if he does not like us, the laws, when he had become of age and has seen the ways of the city, and made our acquaintance, he may go where he pleases and take his goods with him. None of us laws will forbid him or interfere with anyone who does not like us and the city, and who wants to emigrate to a colony or to any other city; he may go where he likes, with his property. But he who has experience of the manner in which we order justice and administer the state, and still remains, has by so doing entered into an implied contract that he will do as we command him. And he who disobeys us is, as we maintain, thrice wrong; first, because in disobeying us he is disobeying his parents; secondly, because we are the authors of his education; thirdly, because having made an agreement with us that he will duly obey our commands, he neither obeys them nor convinces us that our [52] commands are unjust; although we do not roughly require unquestioning obedience, but give him the alternative of obeying or convincing us;—that is what we offer, and he does neither.

'These are the sort of accusations to which, as we were saying, you, Socrates, will be exposed if you accomplish your intentions; you, above all other Athenians.' Suppose now I ask, why I rather than anybody else? no doubt they will justly retort upon me that I above all other Athenians have acknowledged the agreement. 'There is clear proof,' they will say, 'Socrates, that we and the city were not displeasing to you. Of all Athenians you have been the most constant resident in the city, which, as you never leave, you may be supposed to love. For you never went out of the city either to see the games, except once when you went to the Isthmus, or to any other place unless when you were on military service; nor did you travel as other men do. Nor had you any curiosity to know other states or their laws: your affections did not go beyond us and our state; we were your special favourites, and you acquiesced in our government of you; and here in this city you begat your children, which is a proof of your satisfaction. Moreover, you might in the course of the trial, if you had liked, have fixed the penalty at banishment; you might then have done with the state's assent what you are now setting out to do without it. But you pretended that you preferred death to exile, and that you were not unwilling to die. And now you have forgotton these fine sentiments, and pay no respect to us the laws, of whom you are the destroyer; and are doing what only a miserable slave would do, running away and turning your back upon the compacts and agreements of your citizenship which you made with us. And first of all answer this very question: Are we right in saying that you agreed to live under our government in deed, and not in word only? Is that true or not?' How shall we answer, Crito? Must we not assent?

CRITO. We cannot help it, Socrates.

SOCRATES. Then will they not say: 'You, Socrates, are breaking the covenants and agreements which you made with us at your leisure, not under any compulsion or deception or in enforced haste, but after you have had seventy years to think of them, during which time you were at liberty to leave the city, if we were not to your mind or if our covenants appeared to you to be unfair. You had your choice, and might have gone either to Lacedaemon or Crete, both which states are often praised by you for their good government, or to some other Hellenic or [53] foreign state. Whereas you, above all other Athenians, seemed to be so fond of the state, and obviously therefore of us her laws (for who would care about a state without its laws?), that you never stirred out of her; the halt, the blind, the maimed were not more stationary in her than you were. And now you refuse to abide by your agreements. Not so, Socrates, if you will take our advice; do not make yourself ridiculous by leaving the city.

'For just consider, if you transgress and err in this sort of way, what good will you do either to yourself or to your friends? That your friends will be in danger of being driven into exile and deprived of citizenship, or of losing their property, is tolerably certain; and you yourself, if you fly to one of the neighboring cities, as, for example, Thebes or Megara, both of which are well governed, will come to them as an enemy of their government and all patriotic citizens will look askance at you as a subverter of the laws, and you will confirm in the minds of the judges the justice of their own condemnation of you. For he who is a corrupter of the laws is more than likely to be a corrupter of the young and foolish portion of mankind. Will you then flee from well-ordered cities and virtuous men? and is existence worth having on these terms? Or will you go to them without shame, and talk to them, saying—what will you say to them? What you say here about virtue and justice and institutions and laws being the best things among men? Would that be decent of Socrates? Surely not. But if you go away from well-governed states to Crito's friends in Thessaly, where there is great disorder and licence, they will be charmed to hear the tale of your escape from prison, set off with ludicrous particulars of the manner in which you were wrapped in goatskin or some other disguise, and metamorphosed as the manner is of runaways; but will there be no one to remind you that in your old age, when little time is left to you, you were not ashamed to violate the most sacred laws from a greedy desire of life? Perhaps not, if you keep them in a good temper; but if they are out of temper you will hear many degrading things. You will live, but how?—fawning upon all men, and the servant of all men; and doing what?—faring sumptuously in Thessaly, having gone abroad in order that you may get a dinner. And where will be your fine sentiments about justice [54] and virtue? Say that you wish to live for the sake of your children—you want to bring them up and educate them—will you take them into Thessaly and deprive them of Athenian citizenship? Is this the benefit which you will confer upon them? Or are you under the impression that they will be better cared for and educated here if you are still alive, although absent from them; for your friends will take care of them? Do you fancy that if you have left Athens for Thessaly they will take care of them, but if you have left it for the other world that they will not take care of them? Nay; but if they who call themselves friends are good for anything, they will—to be sure they will.

'Listen, then Socrates, to us who have brought you up. Think not of life and children first, and of justice afterwards, but of justice first, that you may so vindicate yourself before the princes of the world below. For neither will you nor any that belong to you be happier or holier or juster in this life, or happier in another, if you do as Crito bids. Now you depart, if it must be so, in innocence, a sufferer and not a doer of evil; a victim, not of the laws but of men. But if you leave the city, basely returning evil for evil and injury for injury, breaking the covenants and agreements which you have made with us, and wronging those whom you ought least of all to wrong, that is to say, yourself, your friends, your country, and us, we shall be angry with you while you live, and our brethren, the laws in the world below, will give you no friendly welcome; for they will know that you have done your best to destroy us. Listen, then, to us and not to Crito.'

This, dear Crito, is the voice which I seem to hear murmuring in my ears, like the sounds of the flute in the ears of the mystic; that voice, I say, is humming in my ears, and prevents me from hearing any other. Be assured, then, that anything more which you say to shake this my faith will be said in vain. Yet speak, if you have anything to say.

CRITO.   I have nothing to say.

SOCRATES.   It is enough then, Crito. Let us fulfill the will of God, and follow whither He leads.

JOHN STUART MILL *(1806–1873)*

In his essay On Liberty, *written in 1859, John Stuart Mill makes as strong a case for political individualism as can be made. Not altogether unlike his fellow Britisher a century later, R. D. Laing, Mill argues against society's meddling in affairs that are properly personal. He endorses a charitable interpretation of the contemporary slogan, "Do your own thing." And his discourse on the particular example of prohibition of alcoholic drinks will likely be heralded as a precursor to a philosophical defense for decriminalizing marijuana.*

But before we are swept away with enthusiasm for Mill's noble defense of the rights of the individual, let us recall the price paid for individualism of the sort that Mill espouses. We have good reasons for wondering whether Mill is right when he says of the freely acting individual, "All errors which he is likely to commit against advice and warning are far outweighed by the evil of allowing others to constrain him to what they deem his good." Mill is not here speaking of dangers to others but of dangers to the individual. And Mill is not simply wrong, even if other considerations tip the balance away from individualism (note Mill's use of the term "outweighed"). Nor is he simply right, because, as the metaphor of the scale indicates, we are dealing here with a question of varying degrees. Mill describes real ills liable to befall the society with insufficient respect for the dignity of the individual, and his case must be heard and understood if we are to weigh the question of individualism today.

Of the Limits to the Authority of Society Over the Individual

What, then, is the rightful limit to the sovereignty of the individual over himself? Where does the authority of society begin? How much of human life should be assigned to individuality, and how much to society?

Each will receive its proper share, if each has that which more particularly concerns it. To individuality should belong the part of life in which it is chiefly the individual that is interested; to society, the part which chiefly interests society.

Though society is not founded on a contract, and though no good purpose is answered by inventing a contract in order to deduce social obligations from it, everyone who receives the protection of society owes a return for the benefit, and the fact of living in society renders it indispensable that each should be bound to observe a certain line of conduct towards the rest. This conduct consists, *first*, in not injuring the interests of one another; or rather certain interests, which, either by express legal provision or by tacit understanding, ought to be considered as rights; and *secondly*, in each person's bearing his share (to be fixed on some equitable principle) of the labors and sacrifices incurred for defending the society or its members from injury and molestation. These conditions society is justified in enforcing, at all costs to those who endeavor to withhold fulfillment. Nor is this all that society may do. The acts of an individual may be hurtful to others, or wanting in due consideration for their welfare, without going to the length of violating any of their constituted rights. The offender may then be justly punished by opinion, though not by law. As soon as any part of a person's conduct affects prejudicially the interests of others, society has jurisdiction over it, and the question whether the general welfare will or will not be promoted by interfering with it, becomes open to discussion. But there is no room for entertaining any such question when a person's conduct affects the interests of no persons besides himself, or need not affect them unless they like (all the persons concerned being of full age, and the ordinary amount of understanding). In all such cases, there should be perfect freedom, legal and social, to do the action and stand the consequences.

It would be a great misunderstanding of this doctrine to suppose that it is one of selfish indifference, which pretends that human beings have no business with each other's conduct in life, and that they should not concern themselves about the well-doing or well-being of one another, unless their own interest is involved. Instead of any diminution, there is need of a great increase of disinterested exertion to promote the good of others. But disinterested benevolence can find other instruments to persuade people to their good than whips and scourges, either of the literal or the metaphorical sort. I am the last person to undervalue the self-regarding virtues: they are only second in importance, if even second, to the social. It is equally the business of education to cultivate both. But even education works by conviction and persuasion as well as by compulsion, and it is by the former only that, when the period of education is passed, the self-regarding virtues should be inculcated. Human beings owe to each other help to distinguish the better from the worse, and encouragement to choose the former and avoid the latter. They should be forever stimulating each other to increased exercise of their higher faculties, and increased direction of their feelings and aims towards wise instead of foolish, elevating instead of degrading, objects and contemplations. But neither one person, nor any number of persons, is warranted in saying to another human creature of ripe years, that he shall not do with his life for his own benefit what he chooses to do with it. He is the person most interested in his own well-being: the interest which any other person, except in cases of strong personal attachment, can have in it, is trifling, compared with that which he himself has; the interest which society has in him individually (except as to his conduct to others) is fractional, and altogether indirect; while with respect to his own feelings and circumstances, the most ordinary man or woman has means of knowledge immeasurably surpassing those that can be possessed by anyone else. The interference of society to overrule his judgment and purposes in what only regards himself must be grounded on general presumptions; which may be altogether wrong, and even if right, are as likely as not to be misapplied to individual cases, by persons no better acquainted with the circumstances of such cases than those are who look at them merely from without. In this department, therefore, of human affairs, individuality has its proper field of action. In the conduct of human beings towards one another it is necessary that general rules should for the most part be observed, in order that people may know what they have to expect; but in each person's own concerns his individual spontaneity is entitled to free exercise. Considerations to aid his judgment, exhortations to strengthen his will, may be offered to him, even obtruded on him, by others: but he himself is the final judge. All errors which he is likely to commit against advice and warning are far outweighed by the evil of allowing others to constrain him to what they deem his good.

I do not mean that the feelings with which a person is regarded by others ought to be in any way affected by his self-regarding qualities or deficiencies. This is neither possible nor desirable. If he is eminent in any of the qualities which conduce to his own good, he is, so far, a proper object of admiration. He is so much the nearer to the ideal perfection of human nature. If he is grossly deficient in those qualities, a sentiment the opposite of admiration will follow. There is a degree of folly, and a degree of what may be called (though the phrase is not unobjectionable) lowness or depravation of taste, which, though it cannot justify doing harm to the person who manifests it, renders him necessarily and properly a subject of distaste, or, in extreme cases, even of contempt: a person could not have the opposite qualities in due strength without entertaining these feelings. Though doing no wrong to anyone, a person may so act as to compel us to judge him, and feel to him, as a fool, or as a being of an inferior order; and since this judgment and feeling are a fact which he would prefer to avoid, it is doing him a service to warn him of it beforehand, as of any other disagreeable consequence to which he exposes himself. It would be well, indeed, if this good office were much more freely rendered than the common notions of politeness at present permit, and if one person could honestly point out to another that he thinks him in fault, without being considered unmannerly or presuming. We have a right, also, in various ways, to act upon our unfavorable opinion of anyone, not to the oppression of his individuality, but in the exercise of ours. We are not bound, for example, to seek his society; we have a right to avoid it (though not to parade the avoidance), for we have a right to choose the society most acceptable to us. We have a right, and it may be our duty, to caution others against him, if we think his example or conversation likely to have a pernicious effect on those with whom he associates. We may give others a preference over him in optional good offices, except those which tend to his improvement. In these various modes a person may suffer very severe penalties at the hands of others for faults which directly concern only himself; but he suffers these penalties only in so far as they are the natural and, as it were, the spontaneous consequences of the faults themselves, not because they are purposely inflicted on him for the sake of punishment. A person who shows rashness, obstinacy, self-conceit—who cannot live within moderate means—who cannot restrain himself from hurtful indulgences—who pursues animal pleasures at the expense of those of feeling and intellect—must expect to be lowered in the opinion of others, and to have a less share of their favorable sentiments; but of this he has no right to complain, unless he has merited their favor by special excellence in his social relations, and has thus established a title to their good offices, which is not affected by his demerits towards himself.

What I contend for is, that the inconveniences which are strictly inseparable from the unfavorable judgment of others, are the only ones to which a person should ever be subjected for that portion of his conduct and character which concerns his own good, but which does not affect the interest of others in their relations with him. Acts injurious to others require a totally different treatment. Encroachment on their rights; infliction on them of any loss or damage not justified by his own rights; falsehood or duplicity in dealing with them; unfair or ungenerous use of advantages over them; even selfish abstinence from defending them against injury—these are fit objects of moral reprobation, and, in grave cases, of moral retribution and punishment. And not only these acts, but the dispositions which lead to them, are properly immoral, and fit subjects of disapprobation which may rise to abhorrence. Cruelty of disposition; malice and ill-nature; that most antisocial and odious of all passions, envy; dissimulation and insincerity, irascibility on insufficient cause, and resentment disproportioned to the provocation; the love of domineering over others; the desire to engross more than one's share of advantages (the $\pi\lambda\epsilon o\nu\epsilon\xi\iota\alpha$ [greediness, arrogance] of the Greeks); the pride which derives gratification from the abasement of others; the egotism which thinks self and its concerns more important than everything else, and decides all doubtful questions in its own favor;—these are moral vices, and constitute a bad and odious moral character: unlike the self-regarding faults previously mentioned, which are not properly immoralities, and to whatever pitch they may be carried, do not constitute wickedness. They may be proofs of any amount of folly, or want of personal dignity and self-respect; but they are only a subject of moral reprobation when they involve a breach of duty to others, for whose sake the individual is bound to have care for himself. What are called duties to ourselves are not socially obligatory, unless circumstances render them at the same time duties to others. The term 'duty to oneself,' when it means anything more than prudence, means self-respect or self-development, and for none of these is anyone accountable to his fellow-creatures, because for none of them is it for the good of mankind that he be held accountable to them.

The distinction between the loss of consideration which a person may rightly incur by defect of prudence or of personal dignity, and the reprobation which is due to him for an offense against the rights of others, is not a merely nominal distinction. It makes a vast difference both in our feelings and in our conduct towards him whether he displeases us in things in which we think we have a right to control him, or in things in which we know that we have not. If he displeases us, we may express our distaste, and we may stand aloof from a person as well as from a thing that displeases us; but we shall not therefore feel called on to make his life uncomfortable. We shall reflect that he already bears, or will bear, the whole penalty of his error; if he spoils his life by mismanagement, we shall not, for that reason, desire to spoil it still further: instead of wishing to punish him, we shall rather endeavor to alleviate his punishment, by showing him how he may avoid or cure the evils his conduct tends to bring upon him. He may be to us an object of pity, perhaps of dislike, but not of anger or resentment; we shall not treat him like an enemy of society: the worst we shall think ourselves justified in doing is leaving him to himself, if we do not interfere benevolently by showing interest or concern for him. It is far otherwise if he has infringed the rules necessary for the protection of his fellow-creatures, individually or collectively. The evil consequences of his acts do not then fall on himself, but on others; and society, as the protector of all its members, must retaliate on him; must inflict pain on him for the express purpose of punishment, and must take care that it be sufficiently severe. In the one case, he is an offender at our bar, and we are called on not only to sit in judgment on him, but, in one shape or another, to execute our own sentence: in the other case, it is not our part to inflict any suffering on him, except what may incidentally follow from our using the same liberty in the regulation of our own affairs, which we allow to him in his.

The distinction here pointed out between the part of a person's life which concerns only himself, and that which concerns others, many persons will refuse to admit. How (it may be asked) can any part of the conduct of a member of society be a matter of indifference to the other members? No person is an entirely isolated being; it is impossible for a person to do anything seriously or permanently hurtful to himself, without mischief reaching at least to his near connections, and often far beyond them. If he injures his property, he does harm to those who directly or indirectly derived support from it, and usually diminishes, by a greater or less amount, the general resources of the community. If he deteriorates his bodily or mental faculties, he not only brings evil upon all who depended on him for any portion of their happiness, but disqualifies himself for rendering the services which he owes to his fellow-creatures generally; perhaps becomes a burden on their affection or benevolence; and if such conduct were very frequent, hardly an offense that is committed would detract more from the general sum of good. Finally, if by his vices or follies a person does no direct harm to others, he is nevertheless (it may be said) injurious by his example, and ought to be compelled to control himself, for the sake of those whom the sight or knowledge of his conduct might corrupt or mislead.

And even (it will be added) if the consequences of misconduct could be confined to the vicious or thoughtless individual, ought society to abandon to their own guidance those who are manifestly unfit for it? If protection against themselves is confessedly due to children and persons under age, is not society equally bound to afford it to persons of mature years who are equally incapable of self-government? If gambling, or drunkenness, or incontinence, or idleness, or uncleanliness, are as injurious to happiness, and as great a hindrance to improvement, as many or most of the acts prohibited by law, why (it may be asked) should not law, so far as is consistent with practicability and social convenience, endeavor to repress these also? And as a supplement to the unavoidable imperfections of law, ought not opinion at least to organize a powerful police against these vices, and visit rigidly with social penalties those who are known to practice them? There is no question here (it may be said) about restricting individuality, or impeding the trial of new and original experiments in living. The only things it is sought to prevent are things which have been tried and condemned from the beginning of the world until now; things which experience has shown not to be useful or suitable to any person's individuality. There must be some length of time and amount of experience after which a moral or prudential truth may be regarded as established: and it is merely desired to prevent generation after generation from falling over the same precipice which has been fatal to their predecessors.

I fully admit that the mischief which a person does to himself may seriously affect, both through their sympathies and their interests, those nearly connected with him and, in a minor degree, society at large. When, by conduct of this sort, a person is led to violate a distinct and assignable obligation to any other person or persons, the case is taken out of the self-regarding class, and becomes amenable to moral disapprobation in the proper sense of the term. If, for example, a man, through intemperance or extravagance, becomes unable to pay his debts, or, having undertaken the moral responsibility of a family, becomes from the same cause incapable of supporting or educating them, he is deservedly reprobated, and might be justly punished; but it is for the breach of duty to his family or creditors, not for the extravagance. If the resources which ought to have been devoted to them, had been diverted from them for the most prudent investment, the moral culpability would have been the same. George Barnwell murdered his uncle to get money for his mistress, but if he had done it to set himself up in business, he would equally have been hanged. Again, in the frequent case of a man who causes grief to his family by addiction to bad habits, he deserves reproach for his unkindness or ingratitude; but so he may for cultivating habits not in themselves vicious, if they are painful to those with whom he passes his life, or who from personal ties are dependent on him for their comfort. Whoever fails in the consideration generally due to the interests and feelings of others, not being compelled by some more imperative duty, or justified by allowable self-preference, is a subject of moral disapprobation for that failure, but not for the cause of it, nor for the errors, merely personal to himself, which may have remotely led to it. In like manner, when a person disables himself, by conduct purely self-regarding, from the performance of some definite duty incumbent on him to the public, he is guilty of a social offense. No person ought to be punished simply for being drunk; but a soldier or a policeman should be punished for being drunk on duty. Whenever, in short, there is a definite damage, or a definite risk of damage, either to an individual or to the public, the case is taken out of the province of liberty, and placed in that of morality or law.

But with regard to the merely contingent, or, as it may be called, constructive injury which a person causes to society, by conduct which neither violates any specific duty to the public, nor occasions perceptible hurt to any assignable individual except himself, the inconvenience is one which society can afford to bear, for the sake of the greater good of human freedom. If grown persons are to be punished for not taking proper care of themselves, I would rather it were for their own sake, than under pretense of preventing them from impairing their capacity of rendering to society benefits which society does not pretend it has a right to exact. But I cannot consent to argue the point as if society had no means of bringing its weaker members up to its ordinary standard of rational conduct, except waiting till they do something irrational, and then punishing them, legally or morally, for it. Society has had absolute power over them during all the early portion of their existence: it has had the whole period of childhood and nonage in which to try whether it could make them capable of rational conduct in life. The existing generation is master both of the training and the entire circumstances of the generation to come; it cannot indeed make them perfectly wise and good, because it is itself so lamentably deficient in goodness and wisdom; and its best efforts are not always, in individual cases, its most successful ones; but it is perfectly well able to make the rising generation, as a whole, as good as, and a little better than, itself. If society lets any considerable number of its members grow up mere children, incapable of being acted on by rational consideration of distant motives, society has itself to blame for the consequences. Armed not only with all the powers of education, but with the ascendency which the authority of a received opinion always exercises over the minds who are least fitted to judge for themselves; and aided by the *natural* penalties which cannot be prevented from falling on those who incur the distaste or the contempt of those who know them; let not society pretend that it needs, besides all this, the power to issue commands and enforce obedience in the personal concerns of individuals, in which, on all principles of justice and policy, the decision ought to rest with those who are to abide the consequences. Nor is there anything which tends more to discredit and frustrate the better means of influencing conduct than a resort to the worse. If there be among those whom it is attempted to coerce into prudence or temperance any of the material of which vigorous and independent characters are made, they will infallibly rebel against the yoke. No such person will ever feel that others have a right to control him in his concerns, such as they have to prevent him from injuring them in theirs; and it easily comes to be considered a mark of spirit and courage to fly in the face of such usurped authority, and do with ostentation the exact opposite of what it enjoins; as in the fashion of grossness which succeeded, in the time of Charles II, to the fanatical moral intolerance of the Puritans. With respect to what is said of the necessity of protecting society from the bad example set to others by the vicious or the self-indulgent, it is true that bad example may have a pernicious effect, especially the example of doing wrong to others with impunity to the wrong-doer. But we are now speaking of conduct which, while it does no wrong to others, is supposed to do great harm to the agent himself: and I do not see how those who believe this can think otherwise than that the example, on the whole, must be more salutary than hurtful; since, if it displays the misconduct, it displays also the painful or degrading consequences which, if the conduct is justly censured, must be supposed to be in all or most cases attendant on it.

But the strongest of all the arguments against the interference of the public with purely personal conduct is that, when it does interfere, the odds are that it interferes wrongly, and in the wrong place. On questions of social morality, of duty to others, the opinion of the public, that is, of an overruling majority, though often wrong, is likely to be still oftener right; because on such questions they are only required to judge of their own interests; of the manner in which some mode of conduct, if allowed to be practiced, would affect themselves. But the opinion of a similar majority, imposed as a law on the minority, on questions of self-regarding conduct is quite as likely to be wrong as right; for in these cases public opinion means, at the best, some people's opinion of what is good or bad for other people; while very often it does not even mean that; the public, with the most perfect indifference, passing over the pleasure or convenience of those whose conduct they censure, and considering only their own preference. There are many who consider as an injury to themselves any conduct which they have a distaste for, and resent it as an outrage to their feelings; as a religious bigot, when charged with disregarding the religious feelings of others, has been known to retort that they disregard his feelings, by persisting in their abominable worship or creed. But there is no parity between the feeling of a person for his own opinion, and the feeling of another who is offended at his holding it; no more than between the desire of a thief to take a purse, and the desire of the right owner to keep it. And a person's taste is as much his own peculiar concern as his opinion or his purse. It is easy for anyone to imagine an ideal public which leaves the freedom and choice of individuals in all uncertain matters undisturbed, and only requires them to abstain from modes of conduct which universal experience has condemned. But where has there been seen a public which set any such limit to its censorship? or when does the public trouble itself about universal experience? In its interferences with personal conduct it is seldom thinking of anything but the enormity of acting or feeling differently from itself; and this standard of judgment, thinly disguised, is held up to mankind as the dictate of religion and philosophy, by nine-tenths of all moralists and speculative writers. These teach that things are right because they are right; because we feel them to be so. They tell us to search in our own minds and hearts for laws of conduct binding on ourselves and on all others. What can the poor public do but apply these instructions, and make their own personal feelings of good and evil, if they are tolerably unanimous in them, obligatory on all the world?

The evil here pointed out is not one which exists only in theory; and it may perhaps be expected that I should specify the instances in which the public of this age and country improperly invests it own preferences with the character of moral laws. I am not writing an essay on the aberrations of existing moral feeling. That is too weighty a subject to be discussed parenthetically, and by way of illustration. Yet examples are necessary to show that the principle I maintain is of serious and practical moment, and that I am not endeavoring to erect a barrier against imaginary evils. And it is not difficult to show, by abundant instances, that to extend the bounds of what may be called moral police, until it encroaches on the most unquestionably legitimate liberty of the individual, is one of the most universal of all human propensities.

As a first instance, consider the antipathies which men cherish on no better grounds than that persons whose religious opinions are different from theirs do not practice their religious observances, especially their religious abstinences. To cite a rather trivial example, nothing in the creed or practice of Christian does more to envenom the hatred of Mohammedans against them than the fact of their eating pork. There are few acts which Christians and Europeans regard with more unaffected disgust than Mussulmans regard this particular mode of satisfying hunger. It is, in the first place, an offense against their religion; but this circumstance by no means explains either the degree or the kind of their repugnance; for wine also is forbidden by their religion and to partake of it is by all Mussulmans accounted wrong, but not disgusting. Their aversion to the flesh of the "unclean beast" is, on the contrary, of that peculiar character, resembling an instinctive antipathy, which the idea of uncleanness, when once it thoroughly sinks into the feelings, seems always to excite even in those whose personal habits are anything but scrupulously cleanly, and of which the sentiment of religious impurity, so intense in the Hindoos, is a remarkable example. Suppose now that in a people, of whom the majority were Mussulmans, that majority should insist upon not permitting pork to be eaten within the limits of the country. This would be nothing new in Mohammedan countries.* Would it be a legitimate exercise of the moral authority of public opinion? and if not, why not? The practice is really revolting to such a public. They also sincerely think that it is forbidden and abhorred by the Deity. Neither could the prohibition be censured as religious persecution. It might be religious in its origin, but it would not be persecution for religion, since nobody's religion makes it a duty to eat pork. The only tenable ground of condemnation would be that with the personal tastes and self-regarding concerns of individuals the public has no business to interfere.

---

*The case of the Bombay Parsees is a curious instance in point. When this industrious and enterprising tribe, the descendants of the Persian fire-worshipers, flying from their native country before the Caliphs, arrived in Western India, they were admitted to toleration by the Hindoo sovereigns, on condition of not eating beef. When those regions afterwards fell under the dominion of Mohammedan conquerors, the Parsees obtained from them a continuance of indulgence, on condition of refraining from pork. What was at first obedience to authority became a second nature, and the Parsees to this day abstain both from beef and pork. Though not required by their religion, the double abstinence has had time to grow into a custom of their tribe; and custom, in the East, is a religion.

To come somewhat nearer home: the majority of Spaniards consider it a gross impiety, offensive in the highest degree to the Supreme Being, to worship him in any other manner than the Roman Catholic; and no other public worship is lawful on Spanish soil. The people of all Southern Europe look upon a married clergy as not only irreligious, but unchaste, indecent, gross, disgusting. What do Protestants think of these perfectly sincere feelings, and of the attempt to enforce them against non-Catholics? Yet, if mankind are justified in interfering with each other's liberty in things which do not concern the interests of others, on what principle is it possible consistently to exclude these cases? or who can blame people for desiring to suppress what they regard as a scandal in the sight of God and man? No stronger case can be shown for prohibiting anything which is regarded as a personal immorality, than is made out for suppressing these practices in the eyes of those who regard them as impieties; and unless we are willing to adopt the logic of persecutors, and to say that we may persecute others because we are right, and that they must not persecute us because they are wrong, we must beware of admitting a principle of which we should resent as a gross injustice the application to ourselves.

The preceding instances may be objected to, although unreasonably, as drawn from contingencies impossible among us: opinion, in this country, not being likely to enforce abstinence from meats, or to interfere with people for worshiping, and for either marrying or not marrying, according to their creed or inclination. The next example, however, shall be taken from an interference with liberty which we have by no means passed all danger of.

Wherever the Puritans have been sufficiently powerful, as in New England, and in Great Britain at the time of the Commonwealth, they have endeavored, with considerable success, to put down all public, and nearly all private amusements: especially music, dancing, public games, or other assemblages for purposes of diversion, and the theater. There are still in this country large bodies of persons by whose notions of morality and religion these recreations are condemned; and those persons belonging chiefly to the middle class, who are the ascendant power in the present social and political condition of the kingdom, it is by no means impossible that persons of these sentiments may at some time or other command a majority in Parliament. How will the remaining portion of the community like to have the amusements that shall be permitted to them regulated by the religious and moral sentiments of the stricter Calvinists and Methodists? Would they not, with considerable peremptoriness, desire these intrusively pious members of society to mind their own business? This is precisely what should be said to every government and every public, who have the pretension that no person shall enjoy any pleasure which they think wrong. But if the principle of the pretension be admitted, not one can reasonably object to its being acted on in the sense of the majority, or other preponderating power in the country; and all persons must be ready to conform to the idea of a Christian commonwealth, as understood by the early settlers in New England, if a religious profession similar to theirs should ever succeed in regaining its lost ground, as religions supposed to be declining have so often been known to do.

To imagine another contingency, perhaps more likely to be realized than the one last mentioned. There is confessedly a strong tendency in the modern world towards a democratic constitution of society, accompanied or not by popular political institutions. It is affirmed that in the country where this tendency is most completely realized—where both society and the government are most democratic —the United States—the feeling of the majority, to whom any appearance of a more showy or costly style of living than they can hope to rival is disagreeable, operates as a tolerably effectual sumptuary law, and that in many parts of the Union it is really difficult for a person possessing a very large income to find any mode of spending it which will not incur popular disapprobation. Though such statements as these are doubtless much exaggerated as a representation of existing facts, the state of things they describe is not only a conceivable and possible, but a probable result of democratic feeling, combined with the notion that the public has a right to a veto on the manner in which individuals shall spend their incomes. We have only further to suppose a considerable diffusion of Socialist opinions, and it may become infamous in the eyes of the majority to possess more property than some very small amount, or any income not earned by manual labor. Opinions similar in principle to these already prevail widely among the artisan class, and weigh oppressively on those who are amenable to the opinion chiefly of that class, namely, its own members. It is known that the bad workmen who form the majority of the operatives in many branches of industry, are decidedly of opinion that bad workmen ought to receive the same wages as good, and that no one ought to be allowed, through piecework or otherwise, to earn by superior skill or industry more than others can without it. And they employ a moral police, which occasionally becomes a physical one, to deter skillful workmen from receiving, and employers from giving, a larger remuneration for a more useful service. If the public have any jurisdiction over private concerns, I cannot see that these people are in fault, or that any individual's particular public can be blamed for asserting the same authority over his individual conduct which the general public asserts over people in general.

But, without dwelling upon supposititious cases, there are, in our own day, gross usurpations upon the liberty of private life actually practiced, and still greater ones threatened with some expectation of success, and opinions pro-pounded which assert an unlimited right in the public not only to prohibit by law everything which it thinks wrong, but, in order to get at what it thinks wrong, to prohibit a number of things which it admits to be innocent.

Under the name of preventing intemperance, the people of one English colony, and of nearly half the United States, have been interdicted by law from making any use whatever of fermented drinks, except for medical purposes: for prohibition of their sale is in fact, as it is intended to be, prohibition of their use. And though the impracticability of executing the law has caused its repeal in several of the States which had adopted it, including the one from which it derives its name, an attempt has notwithstanding been commenced, and is prosecuted with considerable zeal by many of the professed philanthropists, to agitate for a similar law in this country. The association, or "Alliance" as it terms itself, which has been formed for this purpose, has acquired some notoriety through the publicity given to a correspondence between its secretary and one of the very few English public men who hold that a politician's opinions ought to be founded on principles. Lord Stanley's share in this correspondence is calculated to strengthen the hopes already built on him, by those who know how rare such qualities as are manifested in some of his public appearances unhappily are among those who figure in political life. The organ of the Alliance, who would "deeply deplore the recognition of any principle which could be wrested to justify bigotry and persecution," undertakes to point out the "broad and impassable barrier" which divides such principles from those of the association. "All matters relating to thought, opinion, conscience, appear to me," he says "to be without the sphere of legislation; all pertaining to social act, habit, relation, subject only to a discretionary power vested in the State itself, and not in the individual, to be within it." No mention is made of a third class, different from either of these, viz., acts and habits which are not social, but individual; although it is to this class, surely, that the act of drinking fermented liquors belongs. Selling fermented liquors, however, is trading, and trading is a social act. But the infringement complained of is not on the liberty of the seller, but on that of the buyer and consumer; since the State might just as well forbid him to drink wine as purposely make it impossible for him to obtain it. The secretary, however, says, "I claim, as a citizen, a right to legislate whenever my social rights are invaded by the social act of another." And now for the definition of these 'social rights.' "If anything invades my social rights, certainly the traffic in strong drink does. It destroys my primary right of security, by constantly creating and stimulating social disorder. It invades my right of equality, by deriving a profit from the creation of a misery I am taxed to support. It impedes my right to free moral and intellectual development, by surrounding my path with dangers, and by weakening and demoralizing society, from which I have a right to claim mutual aid and intercourse." A theory of 'social rights' the like of which probably never before found its way into distinct language: being nothing short of this—that it is the absolute social right of every individual, that every other individual shall act in every respect exactly as he ought; that whosoever fails thereof in the smallest particular violates my social right, and entitles me to demand from the legislature the removal of the grievance. So monstrous a principle is far more dangerous than any single interference with liberty; there is no violation of liberty which it would not justify; it acknowledges no right to any freedom whatever, except perhaps to that of holding opinions in secret, without ever disclosing them: for, the moment an opinion which I consider noxious passes anyone's lips, it invades all the 'social rights' attributed to me by the Alliance. The doctrine ascribes to all mankind a vested interest in each other's moral, intellectual, and even physical perfection, to be defined by each claimant according to his own standard.

Another important example of illegitimate interference with the rightful liberty of the individual, not simply threatened, but long since carried into triumphant effect, is Sabbatarian legislation. Without doubt, abstinence on one day in the week, so far as the exigencies of life permit, from the usual daily occupation, though in no respect religiously binding on any except Jews, is a highly beneficial custom. And inasmuch as this custom cannot be observed without a general consent to that effect among the industrious classes, therefore, in so far as some persons by working may impose the same necessity on others, it may be allowable and right that the law should guarantee to each the observance by others of the custom, by suspending the greater operations of industry on a particular day. But this justification, grounded on the direct interest which others have in each individual's observance of the practice, does not apply to the self-chosen occupations in which a person may think fit to employ his leisure; nor does it hold good, in the smallest degree, for legal restrictions on amusements. It is true that the amusement of some is the day's work of others; but the pleasure, not to say the useful recreation, of many, is worth the labor of a few, provided the occupation is freely chosen, and can be freely resigned. The operatives are perfectly right in thinking that if all worked on Sunday, seven days' work would have to be given for six days' wages; but so long as the great mass of employments are suspended, the small number who for the enjoyment of others must still work, obtain a proportional increase of earnings; and they are not obliged to follow those occupations if they prefer leisure to emolument. If a further remedy is sought, it might be found in the establishment by custom of a holiday on some other day of the week for those particular classes of persons. The only ground, therefore, on which restrictions on Sunday amusements can be defended, must be that they are religiously wrong; a motive of legislation which can never be too earnestly protested against. *"Deorum injuriae Diis curae."* It remains to be proved that society or any of its officers holds a commission from on high to avenge any supposed offense to Omnipotence, which is not also a wrong to our fellow-creatures. The notion that it is one man's duty that another should be religious, was the foundation of all the religious persecutions ever perpetrated, and, if admitted, would fully justify them. Though the feeling which breaks out in the repeated attempts to stop railways traveling on Sunday, in the resistance to the opening of museums, and the like, has not the cruelty of the old persecutors, the state of mind indicated by it is fundamentally the same. It is a determination not to tolerate others in doing what is permitted by their religion, because it is not permitted by the persecutor's religion. It is a belief that God not only abominates the act of the misbeliever, but will not hold us guiltless if we leave him unmolested.

I cannot refrain from adding to these examples of the little account commonly made of human liberty, the language of downright persecution which breaks out from the press of this country whenever it feels called on to notice the remarkable phenomenon of Mormonism. Much might be said on the unexpected and instructive fact that an alleged new revelation, and a religion founded on it, the product of palpable imposture, not even supported by the *prestige* of extraordinary qualities in its founder, is believed by hundreds of thousands, and has been made the foundation of a society, in the age of newspapers, railways, and the electric telegraph. What here concerns us is, that this religion, like other and better religions, has its martyrs: that its prophet and founder was, for his teaching, put to death by a mob; that others of its adherents lost their lives by the same lawless violence; that they were forcibly expelled, in a body, from the country in which they first grew up; while, now that they have been chased into a solitary recess in the midst of a desert, many in this country openly declare that it would be right (only that it is not convenient) to send an expedition against them, and compel them by force to conform to the opinions of other people. The article of the Mormonite doctrine which is the chief provocative to the antipathy which thus breaks through the ordinary restraints of religious tolerance, is its sanction of polygamy; which, though permitted to Mohammedans, and Hindoos, and Chinese, seems to excite unquenchable animosity when practiced by persons who speak English and profess to be a kind of Christians. No one has a deeper disapprobation than I have of this Mormon institution; both for other reasons, and because, far from being in any way countenanced by the principle of liberty, it is a direct infraction of that principle, being a mere riveting of the chains of one half of the community, and an emancipation of the other from reciprocity of obligation towards them. Still, it must be remembered that this relation is as much voluntary on the part of the women concerned in it, and who may be deemed the sufferers by it, as is the case with any other form of the marriage institution; and however surprising this fact may appear, it has its explanation in the common ideas and customs of the world, which teaching women to think marriage the one thing needful, make it intelligible that many a woman should prefer being one of several wives, to not being a wife at all. Other countries are not asked to recognize such unions, or release any portion of their inhabitants from their own laws on the score of Mormonite opinions. But when the dissentients have conceded to the hostile sentiments of others far more than could justly be demanded; when they have left the countries to which their doctrines were unacceptable, and established themselves in a remote corner of the earth, which they have been the first to render habitable to human beings; it is difficult to see on what principles but those of tyranny they can be prevented from living there under what laws they please, provided they commit no aggression on other nations, and allow perfect freedom of departure to those who are dissatisfied with their ways. A recent writer, in some respects of considerable merit, proposes (to use his own words) not a crusade, but a *civilisade*, against this polygamous community, to put an end to what seems to him a retrograde step in civilization. It also appears so to me, but I am not aware that any community has a right to force another to be civilized. So long as the sufferers by the bad law do not invoke assistance from other communities, I cannot admit that persons entirely unconnected with them ought to step in and require that a condition of things with which all who are directly interested appear to be satisfied, should be put an end to because it is a scandal to persons some thousands of miles distant, who have no part or concern in it. Let them send missionaries, if they please, to preach against it; and let them, by any fair means (of which silencing the teachers is not one), oppose the progress of similar doctrines among their own people. If civilization has got the better of barbarism when barbarism had the world to itself, it is too much to profess to be afraid lest barbarism, after having been fairly got under, should revive and conquer civilization. A civilization that can thus succumb to its vanquished enemy, must first have become so degenerate, that neither its appointed priests and teachers, nor anybody else, has the capacity, or will take the trouble, to stand up for it. If this be so, the sooner such a civilization receives notice to quit the better. It can only go on from bad to worse, until destroyed and regenerated (like the Western Empire) by energetic barbarians.

KARL MARX *(1818–1883)*

Karl Marx's philosophy rejects the individualism found in the writing of Locke and Mill. Yet unlike the Stalinist practices carried out under his name, Marx himself did not wish to sacrifice the individual to the interests of the state. Indeed, he diagnoses the ills suffered by alienated individuals when the state functions improperly. Marx's essay, from The Economic and Philosophic Manuscripts of 1844, *prompts us to ask whether individualism is not itself a social product of alienation. If, as Mead and others have shown, the origin of the self is truly social, then perhaps it is only a sick society that individuates the self so thoroughly that the self forgets its origins and fancies itself utterly autonomous. How could this happen?*

One of the basic Marxian insights can be explicated in terms of a dialectic of means and ends: people use their agreements with one another and their development of technology in order to better the lot of each and every individual. The political-economic machinery is first conceived as a tool to further the ends of people. But as the political-economic machinery undergoes historical development, it may reach a point at which, like the Frankenstein monster, it runs amok. Though the economic rampage is less dramatically visible than Frankenstein's, especially if you are shielded from poverty, the effects are similar: what was first conceived as a tool for the ends of humankind transforms itself into an autonomous force that turns on man and often uses men as its own tools. Man comes to serve the machine rather than the reverse. In this subservient state people naturally become alienated.

Marx details four forms of alienation: the individual's alienation from nature, from himself, from his species being, and from other men. Marx's analysis of alienation from species being (Gattungswesen) is perhaps the most difficult to understand, yet it is most important as Marx's reply to individualism. The other three forms of alienation can be understood and experienced within the context of individualism, but from that starting point the very idea of species being sounds somewhat obscure if not mystical. The concept of species being is an alternative to individualism. Marx is talking about feeling oneself a part of a whole rather than an atomic unit standing against the whole, or even joined to the whole by some artificial contract. This sense of being part of a whole is very important to Marx's argument, and his analysis of the third form of alienation is also an analysis of why we may find his argument difficult to comprehend. The following paragraph contains a closer explication to which you may want to return if Marx's text remains obscure.

Marx develops the third form of alienation from the first two: "In estranging from man (1) nature, and (2) himself, his own active functions, his life-activity, estranged labour estranges the species from man. It turns for him the life of the species into a means of individual life." The concept of species being has its origins in the theology of Ludwig Feuerbach and the social philosophy of Moses Hess. Feuerbach used the idea in arguing that religion is the result of man's projection of his own perfections upon another being he chooses to call God; because no single man represents all human perfections, the collective projection is the species being of man. Hess, on the other hand, argued the specifically social connotations of the concept of species being: to be truly human, man must see himself not as an isolated individual but as a collaborator in a common task of working together in a productive community. Marx combines the ideas of Feuerbach and Hess: "First it [estranged labour] estranges the life of the species and individual life, and secondly it makes individual life in its abstract form [as isolated and atomic] the purpose of the life of the species, likewise in its abstract and estranged from [namely, as a mere totality or aggregate of those atoms]." The first point derives from Feuerbach's analysis of man's separation of the life of the species from individual life through the projection of man's species being upon God; the second from Hess' social analysis of the concept of species being. The two strands of the concept correspond to their immediate genesis from the first two aspects of alienation: man's alienation from nature corresponds to the spiritualization of man in religion, to which Feuerbach objected; second, man's alienation from himself turns out to be his failure to attain that social existence which, Hess and Marx both say, constitutes the true essence of man. To the extent that man is trapped in estranged labor, he is no better than an animal who works only to satisfy his own, immediate, individual needs. In a nonalienated society, however, men should be able to realize their species being in two senses. First, they will work together in "the working up of the objective world," a sensuous, concrete process that marks man's return from the alienation of a religion that worships a transcendent God. Second, the process of working up inorganic nature differs from animal effort in that each member of the community sees his effort as serving the conscious ends of the whole community. Finally, the two points with their two sets of two origins attain a uniquely Marxian synthesis in the idea: "Through and because of this production, nature appears as his work and his reality. The object of labour is, therefore, the objectification of man's species life: for he duplicates himself not only, as in consciousness, intellectually, but also actively, in reality, and therefore he contemplates himself in a world that he has created."

Marx saw man as potentially inhabiting a world of his own creation, a world from which he would not be alienated, a world in which he and his products would constitute a historical dialectic of human self-creation and self-expression. For Marx the historical development of social relations meant the historical development of man, for, as he put it in his theses on Feuerbach, "the human essence is no abstraction inherent in each single individual. In its reality it is the ensemble of social relations." This historicist view of man is analogous to the existentialist philosophy of the individual man as self-creative. But for Marx the creative subject must be humankind and not individual man. It is just this view of humankind as historically creative that underlies such ideas as Wilhelm Reich's theory of the historical development of the human unconscious.

On Alienation

We have proceeded from the premises of political economy. We have accepted its language and its laws. We presupposed private property, the separation of labour, capital and land, and of wages, profit of capital and rent of land—likewise division of labour, competition, the concept of exchange-value, etc. On the basis of political economy itself, in its own words, we have shown that the worker sinks to the level of a commodity and becomes indeed the most wretched of commodities; that the wretchedness of the worker is in inverse proportion to the power and magnitude of his production; that the necessary result of competition is the accumulation of capital in a few hands, and thus the restoration of monopoly in a more terrible form; that finally the distinction between capitalist and land-rentier, like that between the tiller of the soil and the factory-worker, disappears and that the whole of society must fall apart into the two classes—the property-*owners* and the propertiless *workers*.

Political economy proceeds from the fact of private property, but it does not explain it to us. It expresses in general, abstract formulae the *material* process through which private property actually passes, and these formulae it then takes for *laws*. It does not *comprehend* these laws—i.e., it does not demonstrate how they arise from the very nature of private property. Political economy does not disclose the source of the division between labour and capital, and between capital and land. When, for example, it defines the relationship of wages to profit, it takes the interest of the capitalists to be the ultimate cause; i.e., it takes for granted what it is supposed to evolve. Similarly, competition comes in everywhere. It is explained from external circumstances. As to how far these external and apparently fortuitous circumstances are but the expression of a necessary course of development, political economy teaches us nothing. We have seen how, to it, exchange itself appears to be a fortuitous fact. The only wheels which political economy sets in motion are *avarice* and the *war amongst the avaricious—competition*.

Precisely because political economy does not grasp the connections within the movement, it was possible to counterpose, for instance, the doctrine of competition to the doctrine of monopoly, the doctrine of craft-liberty to the doctrine of the corporation, the doctrine of the division of landed property to the doctrine of the big estate—for competition, craft-liberty and the division of landed property were explained and comprehended only as fortuitous, premeditated and violent consequences of monopoly, the corporation, and feudal property, not as their necessary, inevitable and natural consequences.

Now, therefore, we have to grasp the essential connection between private property, avarice, and the separation of labour, capital and landed property; between exchange and competition, value and the devaluation of men, monopoly and competition, etc.; the connection between this whole estrangement and the *money*-system.

Do not let us go back to a fictitious primordial condition as the political economist does, when he tries to explain. Such a primordial condition explains nothing. He merely pushes the question away into a grey nebulous distance. He assumes in the form of fact, of an event, what he is supposed to deduce—namely, the necessary relationship between two things—between, for example, division of labour and exchange. Theology in the same way explains the origin of evil by the fall of man: that is, it assumes as a fact, in historical form, what has to be explained.

We proceed from an *actual* economic fact.

The worker becomes all the poorer the more wealth he produces, the more his production increases in power and range. The worker becomes an ever cheaper commodity the more commodities he creates. With the *increasing value* of the world of things proceeds in direct proportion the *devaluation* of the world of men. Labour produces not only commodities: it produces itself and the worker as a *commodity*—and does so in the proportion in which it produces commodities generally.

This fact expresses merely that the object which labour produces—labour's product—confronts it as *something alien*, as a *power independent* of the producer. The product of labour is labour which has been congealed in an object, which has become material: it is the *objectification* of labour. Labour's realisation is its objectification. In the conditions dealt with by political economy this realisation of labour appears as *loss of reality* for the workers; objectification as *loss of the object* and *object-bondage;* appropriation as *estrangement,* as *alienation.*[1]

So much does labour's realisation appear as loss of reality that the worker loses reality to the point of starving to death. So much does objectification appear as loss of the object that the worker is robbed of the objects most necessary not only for his life but for his work. Indeed, labour itself becomes an object which he can get hold of only with the greatest effort and with the most irregular interruptions. So much does the appropriation of the object appear as estrangement that the more objects the worker produces the fewer can he possess and the more he falls under the dominion of his product, capital.

All these consequences are contained in the definition that the worker is related to the *product of his labour* as to an *alien* object. For on this premise it is clear that the more the worker spends himself, the more powerful the alien objective world becomes which he creates over-against himself, the poorer he himself—his inner world—becomes, the less belongs to him as his own. It is the same in religion. The more man puts into God, the less he retains in himself. The worker puts his life into the object; but now his life no longer belongs to him but to the object. Hence, the greater this activity, the greater is the worker's lack of objects. Whatever the product of his labour is, he is not. Therefore the greater this product, the less is he himself. The *alienation* of the worker in his product means not only that his labour becomes an object, an *external* existence, but that it exists *outside him,* independently, as something alien to him, and that it becomes a power on its own confronting him; it means that the life which he has conferred on the object confronts him as something hostile and alien.

---

[1] [Marx uses two terms, *Entfremdung* and *Entausserung,* both of which are often translated simply as "alienation." The present translation has the merit of distinguishing between the two, translating *Entfremdung* quite literally as "estrangement" and *Entausserung* as "alienation."—J. A. O.]

Let us now look more closely at the *objectification,* at the production of the worker; and therein at the *estrangement,* the *loss* of the object, his product.

The worker can create nothing without *nature,* without the *sensuous external world.* It is the material on which his labour is manifested, in which it is active, from which and by means of which it produces.

But just as nature provides labour with the *means of life* in the sense that labour cannot *live* without objects on which to operate, on the other hand, it also provides the *means of life* in the more restricted sense—i.e., the means for the physical subsistence of the *worker* himself.

Thus the more the worker by his labour *appropriates* the external world, sensuous nature, the more he deprives himself of *means of life* in the double respect: first, that the sensuous external world more and more ceases to be an object belonging to his labour—to be his labour's *means of life;* and secondly, that it more and more ceases to be *means of life* in the immediate sense, means for the physical subsistence of the worker.

Thus in this double respect the worker becomes a slave of his object, first, in that he receives an *object of labour,* i.e., in that he receives *work;* and secondly, in that he receives *means of subsistence.* Therefore, it enables him to exist, first, as a *worker;* and, second, as a *physical subject.* The extremity of this bondage is that it is only as a *worker* that he continues to maintain himself as a *physical subject,* and that it is only as a *physical subject* that he is a *worker.*

(The laws of political economy express the estrangement of the worker in his object thus: the more the worker produces, the less he has to consume; the more values he creates, the more valueless, the more unworthy he becomes; the better formed his product, the more deformed becomes the worker; the more civilised his object, the more barbarous becomes the worker; the mightier labour becomes, the more powerless becomes the worker; the more ingenious labour becomes, the duller becomes the worker and the more he becomes nature's bondsman).

Political economy conceals the estrangement inherent in the nature of labour by not considering the direct relationship between the worker (labour) *and production.* It is true that labour produces for the rich wonderful things—but for the worker it produces privation. It produces palaces—but for the worker, hovels. It produces beauty—but for the worker, deformity. It replaces labour by machines—but some of the workers it throws back to a barbarous type of labour, and the other workers it turns into machines. It produces intelligence—but for the worker idiocy, cretinism.

The direct relationship of labour to its produce is the relationship of the worker to the objects of his production. The relationship of the man of means to the objects of production and to production itself is only a *consequence* of this first relationship —and confirms it. We shall consider this other aspect later.

When we ask, then, what is the essential relationship of labour we are asking about the relationship of the *worker* to production.

Till now we have been considering the estrangement, the alienation of the worker only in one of its aspects, i.e., the worker's *relationship to the products of his labour.* But the estrangement is manifested not only in the result but in the *act of production*—within the *producing activity* itself. How would the worker come to face the product of his activity as a stranger, were it not that in the very act of production he was estranging himself from himself? The product is after all but the summary of the activity, of production. If then the product of labour is alienation, production itself must be active alienation, the alienation of activity, the activity of alienation. In the estrangement of the object of labour is merely summarised the estrangement, the alienation, in the activity of labour itself.

What, then, constitutes the alienation of labour?

First, the fact that labour is *external* to the worker, i.e., it does not belong to his essential being; that in his work, therefore, he does not affirm himself but denies himself, does not feel content but unhappy, does not develop freely his physical and mental energy but mortifies his body and ruins his mind. The worker therefore only feels himself outside his work, and in his work feels outside himself. He is at home when he is not working, and when he is working he is not at home. His labour is therefore not voluntary, but coerced; it is *forced labour.* It is therefore not the satisfaction of a need; it is merely a *means* to satisfy needs external to it. Its alien character emerges clearly in the fact that as soon as no physical or other compulsion exists, labour is shunned like the plague. External labour, labour in which man alienates himself, is a labour of self-sacrifice, of mortification. Lastly, the external character of labour for the worker appears in the fact that it is not his own, but someone else's, that it does not belong to him, that in it he belongs, not to himself, but to another. Just as in religion the spontaneous activity of the human imagination, of the human brain and the human heart, operates independently of the individual—that is, operates on him as an alien, divine or diabolical activity—in the same way the worker's activity is not his spontaneous activity. It belongs to another; it is the loss of his self.

As a result, therefore, man (the worker) no longer feels himself to be freely active in any but his animal functions—eating, drinking, procreating, or at most in his dwelling and in dressing-up, etc.; and in his human functions he no longer feels himself to be anything but an animal. What is animal becomes human and what is human becomes animal.

Certainly eating, drinking, procreating, etc., are also genuinely human functions. But in the abstraction which separates them from the sphere of all other human activity and turns them into sole and ultimate ends, they are animal.

We have considered the act of estranging practical human activity, labour, in two of its aspects. (1) The relation of the worker to the *product of labour* as an alien object exercising power over him. This relation is at the same time the relation to the sensuous external world, to the objects of nature as an alien world antagonistically opposed to him. (2) The relation of labour to the *act of production* within the *labour* process. This relation is the relation of the worker to his own activity as an alien activity not belonging to him; it is activity as suffering, strength as weakness, begetting as emasculating, the worker's *own* physical and mental energy, his personal life or what is life other than activity—as an activity which is turned against him, neither depends on nor belongs to him. Here we have *self-estrangement,* as we had previously the estrangement of the *thing.*

We have yet a third aspect of *estranged labour* to deduce from the two already considered.

Man is a species being, not only because in practice and in theory he adopts the species as his object (his own as well as those of other things), but—and this is only another way of expressing it—but also because he treats himself as the actual, living species; because he treats himself as a *universal* and therefore a free being.

The life of the species, both in man and in animals, consists physically in the fact that man (like the animal) lives on inorganic nature; and the more universal man is compared with an animal, the more universal is the sphere of inorganic nature on which he lives. Just as plants, animals, stones, the air, light, etc., constitute a part of human consciousness in the realm of theory, partly as objects of natural science, partly as objects of art—his spiritual inorganic nature, spiritual nourishment which he must first prepare to make it palatable and digestible—so too in the realm of practice they constitute a part of human life and human activity. Physically man lives only on these products of nature, whether they appear in the form of food, heating, clothes, a dwelling, or whatever it may be. The universality of man is in practice manifested precisely in the universality which makes all nature his *inorganic* body—both insamuch as nature is (1) his direct means of life, and (2) the material, the object, and the instrument of his life-activity. Nature is man's *inorganic body*—nature, that is, in so far as it is not itself the human body. Man *lives* on nature—means that nature is his *body*, with which he must remain in continuous intercourse if he is not to die. That man's physical and spiritual life is linked to nature means simply that nature is linked to itself, for man is a part of nature.

In estranging from man (1) nature, and (2) himself, his own active functions, his life-activity, estranged labour estranges the *species* from man. It turns for him the *life of the species* into a means of individual life. First it estranges the life of the species and individual life, and secondly it makes individual life in its abstract form the purpose of the life of the species, likewise in its abstract and estranged form.

For in the first place labour, *life-activity, productive life* itself, appears to man merely as a *means* of satisfying a need—the need to maintain the physical existence. Yet the productive life is the life of the species. It is life-engendering life. The whole character of a species—its species character—is contained in the character of its life-activity; and free, conscious activity is man's species character. Life itself appears only as a *means to life.*

The animal is immediately identical with its life-activity. It does not distinguish itself from it. It is *its life-activity.* Man makes his life-activity itself the object of his will and of his consciousness. He has conscious life-activity. It is not a determination with which he directly merges. Conscious life-activity directly distinguishes man from animal life-activity. It is just because of this that he is a species being. Or it is only because he is a species being that he is a Conscious Being, i.e., that his own life is an object for him. Only because of that is his activity free activity. Estranged labour reverses this relationship, so that it is just because man is a conscious being that he makes his life-activity, his *essential* being, a mere means to his *existence.*

In creating an *objective world* by his practical activity, in *working-up* inorganic nature, man proves himself a conscious species being, i.e., as a being that treats the species as its own essential being, or that treats itself as a species being. Admittedly animals also produce. They build themselves nests, dwellings, like bees, beavers, ants, etc. But an animal only produces what it immediately needs for itself or its young. It produces one-sidedly, whilst man produces universally. It produces only under the dominion of immediate physical need, whilst man produces even when he is free from physical need and only truly produces in freedom therefrom. An animal produces only itself, whilst man reproduces the whole of nature. An animal's product belongs immediately to its physical body, whilst man freely confronts his product. An animal forms things in accordance with the standard and the need of the species to which it belongs, whilst man knows how to produce in accordance with the standard of every species, and knows how to apply everywhere the inherent standard to the object. Man therefore also forms things in accordance with the laws of beauty.

It is just in the working-up of the objective world, therefore, that man first really proves himself to be a *species being*. This production is his active species life. Through and because of this production, nature appears as *his* work and his reality. The object of labour is, therefore, the *objectification of man's species life:* for he duplicates himself not only, as in consciousness, intellectually, but also actively, in reality, and therefore he contemplates himself in a world that he has created. In tearing away from man the object of his production, therefore, estranged labour tears from him his *species life,* his real species objectivity, and transforms his advantage over animals into the disadvantage that his inorganic body, nature, is taken from him.

Similarly, in degrading spontaneous activity, free activity, to a means, estranged labour makes man's species life a means to his physical existence.

The consciousness which man has of his species is thus transformed by estrangement in such a way that species life becomes for him a means.

Estranged labour turns thus:

(3) *Man's species being,* both nature and his spiritual species property, into a being *alien* to him, into a *means* to his *individual existence*. It estranges man's own body from him, as it does external nature and his spiritual essence, his *human* being.

(4) An immediate consequence of the fact that man is estranged from the product of his labour, from his life-activity, from his species being is the *estrangement of man* from *man*. If a man is confronted by himself, he is confronted by the *other* man. What applies to a man's relation to his work, to the product of his labour and to himself, also holds of a man's relation to the other man, and to the other man's labour and object of labour.

In fact, the proposition that man's species nature is estranged from him means that one man is estranged from the other, as each of them is from man's essential nature.[2]

[2]Species nature (and earlier species being)—*Gattungswesen:* man's essential nature—*menschlichen Wesen.*

The following short passages from Feuerbach's *Essence of Christianity* may help readers to understand the ideological background to this part of Marx's thought, and, incidentally, to see how

The estrangement of man, and in fact every relationship in which man stands to himself, is first realised and expressed in the relationship in which a man stands to other men.

Hence within the relationship of estranged labour each man views the other in accordance with the standard and the position in which he finds himself as a worker.

We took our departure from a fact of political economy—the estrangement of the worker and his production. We have formulated the concept of this fact—*estranged, alienated* labour. We have analysed this concept—hence analysing merely a fact of political economy.

Let us now see, further, how in real life the concept of estranged, alienated labour must express and present itself.

If the product of labour is alien to me, if it confronts me as an alien power, to whom, then, does it belong?

If my own activity does not belong to me, if it is an alien, a coerced activity, to whom, then, does it belong?

To a being *other* than me.

Who is this being?

The *gods?* To be sure, in the earliest times the principal production (for example, the building of temples, etc., in Egypt, India and Mexico) appears to be in the service of the gods, and the product belongs to the gods. However, the gods on their own were never the lords of labour. No more was *nature*. And what a contradiction it would be if, the more man subjugated nature by his labour and the

---

Marx accepted but infused with new content concepts made current by Feuerbach as well as by Hegel and the political economists:

"What is this essential difference between man and the brute? . . . Consciousness—but consciousness in the strict sense; for the consciousness implied in the feeling of self as an individual in discrimination by the senses, in the perception and even judgment of outward things according to definite sensible signs, cannot be denied to the brutes. Consciousness in the strictest sense is present only in a being to whom his species, his essential nature, is an object of thought. The brute is indeed conscious of himself as an individual—and he has accordingly the feeling of self as the common centre of successive sensations—but not as a species. . . . In practical life we have to do with individuals; in science, with species. . . . But only a being to whom his own species, his own nature, is an object of thought, can make the essential nature of other things or beings an object of thought. . . . The brute has only a simple, man a twofold life; in the brute, the inner life is one with the outer. Man has both an inner and an outer life. The inner life of man is the life which has relation to his species—to his general, as distinguished from his individual nature. . . . The brute can exercise no function which has relation to its species without another individual external to itself; but man can perform the functions of thought and speech, which strictly imply such a relation, apart from another individual. . . . Man is in fact at once I and Thou; he can put himself in the place of another, for this reason, that to him his species, his essential nature, and not merely his individuality, is an object of thought. . . . An object to which a subject essentially, necessarily relates, is nothing else than this subject's own, but objective nature. . . .

"The relation of the sun to the earth is, therefore, at the same time a relation of the earth to itself, or to its own nature, for the measure of the size and of the intensity of light which the sun possesses as the object of the earth, is the measure of the distance, which determines the peculiar nature of the earth. . . . In the object which he contemplates, therefore, man becomes acquainted with himself. . . . The power of the object over him is therefore the power of his own nature."

(*The Essence of Christianity*, by Ludwig Feuerbach, translated from the second German edition by Marian Evans, London, 1854, pp. 1-5.)—*Ed.*

more the miracles of the gods were rendered superfluous by the miracles of industry, the more man were to renounce the joy of production and the enjoyment of the produce in favour of these powers.

The *alien* being, to whom labour and the produce of labour belongs, in whose service labour is done and for whose benefit the produce of labour is provided, can only be *man* himself.

If the product of labour does not belong to the worker, if it confronts him as an alien power, this can only be because it belongs to some *other man than the worker.* If the worker's activity is a torment to him, to another it must be *delight* and his life's joy. Not the gods, not nature, but only man himself can be this alien power over man.

We must bear in mind the above-stated proposition that man's relation to himself only becomes *objective* and *real* for him through his relation to the other man. Thus, if the product of his labour, his labor *objectified,* is for him an *alien,* hostile, powerful object independent of him, then his position towards it is such that someone else is master of this object, someone who is alien, hostile, powerful, and independent of him. If his own activity is to him an unfree activity, then he is treating it as activity performed in the service, under the dominion, the coercion and the yoke of another man.

Every self-estrangement of man from himself and from nature appears in the relation in which he places himself and nature to men other than and differentiated from himself. For this reason religious self-estrangement necessarily appears in the relationship of the layman to the priests, or again to a mediator, etc., since we are here dealing with the intellectual world. In the real practical world self-estrangement can only become manifest through the real practical relationship to other men. The medium through which estrangement takes place is itself *practical.* Thus through estranged labour man not only engenders his relationship to the object and to the act of production as to powers that are alien and hostile to him; he also engenders the relationship in which other men stand to his production and to his product, and the relationship in which he stands to these other men. Just as he begets his own production as the loss of his reality, as his punishment; just as he begets his own product as a loss, as a product not belonging to him; so he begets the dominion of the one who does not produce over production and over the product. Just as he estranges from himself his own activity, so he confers to the stranger activity which is not his own.

Till now we have only considered this relationship from the standpoint of the worker and later we shall be considering it also from the standpoint of the non-worker.

Through *estranged, alienated labour,* then, the worker produces the relationship to this labour of a man alien to labour and standing outside it. The relationship of the worker to labour engenders the relation to it of the capitalist, or whatever one chooses to call the master of labour. *Private property* is thus the product, the result, the necessary consequence, of *alienated labour,* of the external relation of the worker to nature and to himself.

Private property thus results by analysis from the concept of *alienated labour*—i.e., of *alienated man*, of estranged labour, of estranged life, of *estranged* man.

True, it is as a result of the *movement of private property* that we have obtained the concept of *alienated labour (of alienated life)* from political economy. But on analysis of this concept it becomes clear that though private property appears to be the source, the cause of alienated labour, it is really its consequence, just as the gods *in the beginning* are not the cause but the effect of man's intellectual confusion. Later this relationship becomes reciprocal.

Only at the very culmination of the development of private property does this, its secret, re-emerge, namely, that on the one hand it is the *product* of alienated labour, and that secondly it is the *means* by which labour alienates itself, the *realisation of this alienation.*

This exposition immediately sheds light on various hitherto unsolved conflicts.

(1) Political economy starts from labour as the real soul of production; yet to labour it gives nothing, and to private property everything. From this contradiction Proudhon has concluded in favour of labour and against private property. We understand, however, that this apparent contradiction is the contradiction of *estranged labour* with itself, and that political economy has merely formulated the laws of estranged labour.

We also understand, therefore, that *wages* and *private property* are identical: where the product, the object of labour pays for labour itself, the wage is but a necessary consequence of labour's estrangement, for after all in the wage of labour, labour does not appear as an end in itself but as the servant of the wage. We shall develop this point later, and meanwhile will only deduce some conclusions.

A *forcing-up of wages* (disregarding all other difficulties, including the fact that it would be by force, too, that the higher wages, being an anomaly, could be maintained) would therefore be nothing but *better payment for the slave,* and would not conquer either for the worker or for labour their human status and dignity.

Indeed, even the *equality of wages* demanded by Proudhon only transforms the relationship of the present-day worker to his labour into the relationship of all men to labour. Society is then conceived as an abstract capitalist.

Wages are a direct consequence of estranged labour, and estranged labour is the direct cause of private property. The downfall of the one aspect must therefore mean the downfall of the other.

(2) From the relationship of estranged labour to private property it further follows that the emancipation of society from private property, etc., from servitude, is expressed in the *political* form of the *emancipation of the workers;* not that *their* emancipation alone was at stake but because the emancipation of the workers contains universal human emancipation—and it contains this, because the whole of human servitude is involved in the relation of the worker to production, and every relation of servitude is but a modification and consequence of this relation.

Just as we have found the concept of *private property* from the concept of *estranged, alienated labour* by *analysis,* in the same way every *category* of political economy can be evolved with the help of these two factors; and we shall find again in each category, e.g., trade, competition, capital, money, only a *definite* and *developed expression* of the first foundations.

Before considering this configuration, however, let us try to solve two problems.

(1) To define the general *nature of private property*, as it has arisen as a result of estranged labour, in its relation to *truly human, social property.*

(2) We have accepted the *estrangement of labour*, its *alienation*, as a fact, and we have analysed this fact. How, we now ask, does *man* come to *alienate*, to estrange, *his labour?* How is this estrangement rooted in the nature of human development? We have already gone a long way to the solution of this problem by *transforming* the question as to the *origin of private property* into the question as to the relation of *alienated labour* to the course of humanity's development. For when one speaks of *private property*, one thinks of being concerned with something external to man. When one speaks of labour, one is directly concerned with man himself. This new formulation of the question already contains its solution.

As to (1): The general nature of private property and its relation to truly human property.

Alienated labour has resolved itself for us into two elements which mutually condition one another, or which are but different expressions of one and the same relationship. *Appropriation* appears as *estrangement*, as *alienation*; and *alienation* appears as *appropriation, estrangement* as true *enfranchisement.*

We have considered the one side— *alienated* labour—in relation to the *worker* himself, i.e., the *relation of alienated labour to itself.* The *property-relation of the non-worker to the worker and to labour* we have found as the product, the necessary outcome of this relation of alienated labour. *Private property*, as the material, summary expression of alienated labour, embraces both relations—the *relation of the worker to work, to the product of his labour and to the non-worker*, and the relation of the *non-worker to the worker and to the product of his labour.*

Having seen that in relation to the worker who *appropriates* nature by means of his labour, this appropriation appears as estrangement, his own spontaneous activity as activity for another and as activity of another, vitality as a sacrifice of life, production of the object as loss of the object to an alien power, to an *alien* person—we shall now consider the relation to the worker, to labour and its object of this person who is *alien* to labour and the worker.

First it has to be noticed, that everything which appears in the worker as an *activity of alienation, of estrangement*, appears in the non-worker as a *state of alienation, of estrangement.*

Secondly, that the worker's *real, practical attitude* in production and to the product (as a state of mind) appears in the non-worker confronting him as a *theoretical* attitude.

Thirdly, the non-worker does everything against the worker which the worker does against himself; but he does not do against himself what he does against the worker.

Let us look more closely at these three relations.[3]

---

[3]At this point the first manuscript breaks off unfinished.—*Ed.*

5/Politics and the Environment

introduction:
the origins of politics

If selfhood is essentially social, does it follow that politics is a necessary part of the human condition? Aristotle described man as a political animal. Is politics therefore part of human nature? Is the political order part of the natural order? Or is politics the product of human invention? The following essays revolve around the question of the artificiality of politics. Rather than relying on natural law as a guide in the development of political institutions, the authors presented in this section see human will and intellect at work in the political order. The state is a human invention.

At least two problems arise from the nonnaturalness of the state. First, if the authority of political leaders does not derive from natural law, then it would seem that the will to regard authority as legitimate could just as easily turn around and withdraw its offer of legitimacy. Anarchy is a kind of vote of no confidence in the political process, a willed refusal to be governed. If politics is a matter of human choice, then anarchism, the lack of political order, is a perpetual possibility.

Second, if politics is, as Hobbes suggests, a contrivance for overcoming the savage brutality of uncivilized nature, then politics becomes a kind of struggle to subdue nature. If nature will not provide the pattern for politics, if biological paternity is not the blueprint for patriarchal authority in politics, then nature may begin to look like the enemy. In the theological tradition, the natural is sometimes dismissed as the sinful; nature is opposed to grace. A nonnatural politics may conspire with theology to cast nature in the role of the devil. Whether God or man carries the burden of subduing nature, human behavior that follows from such beliefs will tend to abuse the physical environment.

The ecological perspective asks us to attend to our interactions with the biosphere—the totality of life on this planet. In the politics of recent years the environmental movement has been a powerful force. By focusing our attention on the consequences of human acts—the depletion of natural resources, the pollution of our waterways and the air we breathe—the environmental movement forces us to reconsider the relationship between politics and nature. Whether or not there is some natural law that might determine a rightful role for authority in human affairs, the nonnaturalness of political institutions cannot serve as an excuse for ecologically disastrous attempts to conquer nature.

Ecology and anarchy are both issues for political philosophy because ecology and anarchy provide alternative approaches to the problem of defining the relationship between humanity and its environment. Just because nature offers no ultimate justification for political authority, an anarchistic denial of all authority need not follow. Once we accept human responsibility for political institutions, then we are free to forge any form of contract from democracy to despotism. Anarchy is no more natural than monarchy once we have cut the bond between nature and politics.

To state the general issue once again: the essays in this section take as their point of departure the idea that politics is more a matter of human choice than a fixed feature of nature. Once we give up the attempt to base politics on some absolute foundation independent of human will, then there is a temptation to say that anything goes—from anarchy to assaults on the environment. Anarchism and ecology raise issues that test the limits of the modern attempt to liberate politics from a dependency on the natural order.

THOMAS HOBBES *(1588–1679)*

In the first lines of his Introduction to Leviathan *(1666), Hobbes casts into question the distinction between the artificial and the natural: "Nature, the art whereby God hath made and governs the world, is by the art of man, as in many other things, so in this also imitated, that it can make an artificial animal." Hobbes suggests that, just as man is an artifice of nature, so "by art is created that great* Leviathan *called* Commonwealth, *or* State . . . *which is but an artificial man; though of greater stature and strength than the natural, for whose protection and defense it was intended; and in which the sovereignty is an artificial soul. . . . "*

Rather than fault Hobbes for contradicting himself in calling man both natural and artificial, consider his reasons for treating the distinction between nature and art somewhat differently from his Aristotelian predecessors. Instead of dividing the cosmos into two realms—a mental realm of creative artifice and a physical realm of nature— Hobbes insisted on seeing continuity in the cosmos. He objected to the dualistic belief that mind and body are radically distinct entities. Instead he regarded human artifice as part of nature, not something somehow outside nature: "For what is the heart but a spring; and the nerves, but so many strings, and the joints, but so many wheels, giving motion to the whole body, such as was intended by the artificer?"

Though he calls man "that rational and most excellent work of nature," Hobbes's view of nature is still so materialistic, so mechanistic, that to him humanity seems more animal-like than divine. Hence he regards uncivilized man as a beast whose motives are more selfish than social.

In considering the question of human nature—whether human beings are naturally social or naturally solitary beasts who need the authority of a sovereign to keep them from destroying one another—it is worth recalling that "the state of nature" is itself a theoretical invention. In the following selection, Hobbes reasons back to an original, natural condition from the situation of war, in which a social compact, once made, is then removed. Writers as early as Giambattista Vico (1668–1744) accused Hobbes of supposing that the solitary savages of the state of nature would have needed the sophistication of philosophers in order to be able to contrive the artifice of sovereignty needed for their civilizing.

Are we addressing a kind of chicken and egg problem? Which came first, civil society or the solitary individual with selfish motives? In fairness to Hobbes, notice that he admits there may have "never been any time wherein particular men were in a condition of war one against another." The question at issue is not the actual historical origins of the State. Instead, the priority in question has more to do with essence than with temporal origin. What is deepest in human nature, whether or not it appears first? For Hobbes, the answer is unflattering.

The State of Nature

*Of the Natural Condition of Mankind as Concerning Their Felicity,
and Misery*

Nature hath made men so equal, in the faculties of the body and mind; as
that, though there be found one man sometimes manifestly stronger in body or of
quicker mind than another, yet when all is reckoned together, the difference
between man and man is not so considerable, as that one man can thereupon claim
to himself any benefit, to which another may not pretend as well as he. For as to
the strength of body, the weakest has strength enough to kill the strongest, either
be secret machination, or by confederacy with others that are in the same danger
with himself.

And as to the faculties of the mind—setting aside the arts grounded upon
words, and especially that skill of proceeding upon general and infallible rules,
called science; which very few have, and but in few things; as being not a native
faculty, born with us; nor attained, as prudence, while we look after somewhat
else—I find yet a greater equality amongst men, than that of strength. For
prudence is but experience, which equal time equally bestows on all men, in those
things they equally apply themselves unto. That which may perhaps make such
equality incredible, is but a vain conceit of one's own wisdom, which almost all
men think they have in a greater degree than the vulgar; that is, than all men but
themselves, and a few others, whom by fame, or for concurring with themselves,
they approve. For such is the nature of men, that howsoever they may acknowledge many others to be more witty, or more eloquent, or more learned, yet they
will hardly believe there be many so wise as themselves; for they see their own wit
at hand, and other men's at a distance. But this proveth rather that men are in that
point equal, than unequal. For there is not ordinarily a greater sign of the equal
distribution of anything, than that every man is contented with his share.

From this equality of ability, ariseth equality of hope in the attaining of our
ends. And therefore if any two men desire the same thing, which nevertheless they
cannot both enjoy, they become enemies; and in the way to their end, which is
principally their own conservation, and sometimes their delectation only, endeavor to destroy, or subdue one another. And from hence it comes to pass that
where an invader hath no more to fear than another man's single power; if one
plant, sow, build, or possess a convenient seat, others may probably be expected to
come prepared with forces united, to dispossess and deprive him, not only of the
fruit of his labor, but also of his life or liberty. And the invader again is in the like
danger of another.

And from this diffidence of one another, there is no way for any man to
secure himself so reasonable as anticipation; that is, by force or wiles to master the
persons of all men he can, so long, till he see no other power great enough to
endanger him: and this is no more than his own conservation requireth, and is
generally allowed. Also because there be some, that taking pleasure in contemplat-

ing their own power in the acts of conquest, which they pursue farther than their security requires; if others, that otherwise would be glad to be at ease within modest bounds, should not by invasion increase their power, they would not be able long time, by standing only on their defense, to subsist. And by consequence, such augmentation of dominion over men being necessary to a man's conservation, it ought to be allowed him.

Again, men have no pleasure, but on the contrary a great deal of grief, in keeping company, where there is no power able to overawe them all. For every man looketh that his companion should value him at the same rate he sets upon himself; and upon all signs of contempt, or undervaluing, naturally endeavors, as far as he dares (which amongst them that have no common power to keep them in quiet, is far enough to make them destroy each other), to extort a greater value from his contemners by damage, and from others by the example.

So that in the nature of man, we find three principal causes of quarrel. First, competition; second, diffidence; thirdly, glory.

The first maketh men invade for gain; the second, for safety; and the third, for reputation. The first use violence to make themselves masters of other men's persons, wives, children, and cattle; the second, to defend them; the third, for trifles, as a word, a smile, a different opinion, and any other sign of undervalue, either direct in their persons, or by reflection in their kindred, their friends, their nation, their profession, or their name.

Hereby it is manifest that during the time men live without a common power to keep them all in awe, they are in that condition which is called war; and such a war as is of every man against every man. For *war* consisteth not in battle only, or the act of fighting, but in a tract of time wherein the will to contend by battle is sufficiently known, and therefore the notion of *time* is to be considered in the nature of war, as it is in the nature of weather. For as the nature of foul weather lieth not in a shower or two of rain, but in an inclination thereto of many days together; so the nature of war consisteth not in actual fighting, but in the known disposition thereto, during all the time there is no assurance to the contrary. All other time is *peace*.

Whatsoever therefore is consequent to a time of war, where every man is enemy to every man; the same is consequent to the time, wherein men live without other security than what their own strength and their own invention shall furnish them withal. In such condition there is no place for industry, because the fruit thereof is uncertain: and consequently no culture of the earth; no navigation, nor use of the commodities that may be imported by sea; no commodious building; no instruments of moving, and removing, such things as require much force; no knowledge of the face of the earth; no account of time; no arts; no letters; no society; and which is worst of all, continual fear, and danger of violent death; and the life of man, solitary, poor, nasty, brutish, and short.

It may seem strange to some man that has not well weighed these things, that nature should thus dissociate, and render men apt to invade and destroy one another; and he may therefore, not trusting to this inference, made from the passions, desire perhaps to have the same confirmed by experience. Let him therefore consider with himself, when taking a journey, he arms himself and seeks to go well accompanied; when going to sleep, he locks his doors; when even in his house he locks his chests; and this when he knows there be laws, and public officers, armed, to revenge all injuries shall be done him: what opinion he has of his fellow-subjects, when he rides armed; of his fellow-citizens, when he locks his doors; and of his children, and servants, when he locks his chests. Does he not there as much accuse mankind by his actions, as I do by my words? But neither of us accuse man's nature in it. The desires, and other passions of man, are in themselves no sin. No more are the actions that proceed from those passions, till they know a law that forbids them: which till laws be made they cannot know; nor can any law be made, till they have agreed upon the person that shall make it.

It may peradventure be thought, there was never such a time nor condition of war as this; and I believe it was never generally so, over all the world: but there are many places where they live so now. For the savage people in many places of America, except the government of small families, the concord whereof dependeth on natural lust, have no government at all; and live at this day in that brutish manner, as I said before. Howsoever, it may be perceived what manner of life there would be, where there were no common power to fear; by the manner of life which men that have formerly lived under a peaceful government, use to degenerate into in a civil war.

But though there had never been any time wherein particular men were in a condition of war one against another; yet in all times, kings, and persons of sovereign authority, because of their independency, are in continual jealousies, and in the state and posture of gladiators; having their weapons pointing, and their eyes fixed on· one another; that is, their forts, garrisons, and guns upon the frontiers of their kingdoms; and continual spies upon their neighbors; which is a posture of war. But because they uphold thereby the industry of their subjects, there does not follow from it that misery which accompanies the liberty of particular men.

To this war of every man against every man, this also is consequent: *that nothing can be unjust.* The notions of right and wrong, justice and injustice, have there no place. Where there is no common power, there is no law; where no law, no injustice. Force and fraud are in war the two cardinal virtues. Justice and injustice are none of the faculties neither of the body nor mind. If they were, they might be in a man that were alone in the world, as well as his senses and passions. They are qualities that relate to men in society, not in solitude. It is consequent also to the same condition, that there be no propriety, no dominion, no *mine* and *thine* distinct; but only that to be every man's, that he can get; and for so long as he can keep it. And thus much for the ill condition which man by mere nature is actually placed in; though with a possibility to come out of it, consisting partly in the passions, partly in his reason.

The passion that incline men to peace are fear of death, desire of such things as are necessary to commodious living, and a hope by their industry to obtain them. And reason suggesteth convenient articles of peace, upon which men may be drawn to agreement.

JEAN-JACQUES ROUSSEAU *(1712–1778)*

Where conservatives tend to hark back to Hobbes as the grandfather of right-wing requests for law and order, liberals count Rousseau among the earlier authors in their lineage. The difference lies in their respective theories of human nature. Those theories in turn relate back to their different uses of "the state of nature."

For Rousseau, the state of nature presents a more inviting face than the life that is "solitary, poor, nasty, brutish, and short." Rousseau has often been accused of romanticizing the "noble savage." But his intention is hardly to advocate a return to some mythical paradise. More important than their differences over whether humanity is originally, essentially, or basically noble or brutish, Rousseau differs from Hobbes in his estimate of the extent to which man can change his nature. However we began, what may we become?

For Rousseau, human nature is malleable, perhaps even perfectible. The state is not only the institution that chained those who were born free, the state is also the medium for an education to a citizenship that would make civilized people far freer than savages. Thus Rousseau opposes natural freedom for the sake of social freedom and even goes so far as to maintain that "anyone who refuses to obey the general will shall be compelled to do so by the whole body. This means nothing else than that he shall be forced to be free."

If Hobbes is ever ready to remind us of an ineradicable animality lurking beneath the surface of the most civilized societies, Rousseau is equally ready to respond with reminders of our potential for a freer, better society.

The Social Contract

BOOK 1

Introductory Note

I wish to inquire whether, taking men as they are and laws as they can be made, it is possible to establish some just and certain rule of administration in civil affairs. In this investigation I shall always strive to reconcile what right permits with what interest prescribes, so that justice and utility may not be severed.

I enter upon this inquiry without demonstrating the importance of my subject. I shall be asked whether I am a prince or a legislator that I write on politics. I reply that I am not; and that it is for this very reason that I write on politics. If I were a prince or a legislator, I should not waste my time in saying what ought to be done; I should do it or remain silent.

Having been born a citizen of a free State, and a member of the sovereign body, however feeble an influence my voice may have in public affairs, the right to vote upon them is sufficient to impose on me the duty of informing myself about them; and I feel happy, whenever I meditate on governments, always to discover in my researches new reasons for loving that of my own country.

CHAPTER 1

Subject of the First Book

Man is born free, and everywhere he is in chains. Many a one believes himself the master of others, and yet he is a greater slave than they. How has this change come about? I do not know. What can render it legitimate? I believe that I can settle this question.

If I consider only force and the results that proceed from it, I should say that so long as a people is compelled to obey and does obey, it does well; but that, so soon as it can shake off the yoke and does shake it off, it does better; for, if men recover their freedom by virtue of the same right by which it was taken away, either they are justified in resuming it, or there was no justification for depriving them of it. But the social order is a sacred right which serves as a foundation for all others. This right, however, does not come from nature. It is therefore based on conventions. The question is to know what these conventions are. Before coming to that, I must establish what I have just laid down.

CHAPTER 2

Primitive Societies

The earliest of all societies, and the only natural one, is the family; yet children remain attached to their father only so long as they have need of him for their own preservation. As soon as this need ceases, the natural bond is dissolved. The children being freed from the obedience which they owed to their father, and the father from the cares which he owed to his children, become equally independent. If they remain united, it is no longer naturally but voluntarily; and the family itself is kept together only by convention.

This common liberty is a consequence of man's nature. His first law is to attend to his own preservation, his first cares are those which he owes to himself; and as soon as he comes to years of discretion, being sole judge of the means adapted for his own preservation, he becomes his own master.

The family is, then, if you will, the primitive model of political societies; the chief is the analogue of the father, while the people represent the children; and all, being born free and equal, alienate their liberty only for their own advantage. The whole difference is that, in the family, the father's love for his children repays him for the care that he bestows upon them; while, in the State, the pleasure of ruling makes up for the chief's lack of love for his people.

Grotius denies that all human authority is established for the benefit of the governed, and he cites slavery as an instance. His invariable mode of reasoning is to establish right by fact. A juster method might be employed, but none more favorable to tyrants.

It is doubtful, then, according to Grotius, whether the human race belongs to a hundred men, or whether these hundred men belong to the human race; and he appears throughout his book to incline to the former opinion, which is also that of Hobbes. In this way we have mankind divided like herds of cattle, each of which has a master, who looks after it in order to devour it.

Just as a herdsman is superior in nature to his herd, so chiefs, who are the herdsmen of men, are superior in nature to their people. Thus, according to Philo's account, the Emperor Caligula reasoned, inferring truly enough from this analogy that kings are gods, or that men are brutes.

The reasoning of Caligula is tantamount to that of Hobbes and Grotius. Aristotle, before them all, had likewise said that men are not naturally equal, but that some are born for slavery and others for dominion.

Aristotle was right, but he mistook the effect for the cause. Every man born in slavery is born for slavery; nothing is more certain. Slaves lose everything in their bonds, even the desire to escape from them; they love their servitude as the companions of Ulysses loved their brutishness. If, then, there are slaves by nature, it is because there have been slaves contrary to nature. The first slaves were made such by force; their cowardice kept them in bondage.

I have said nothing about King Adam nor about Emperor Noah, the father of three great monarchs who shared the universe, like the children of Saturn with whom they are supposed to be identical. I hope that my moderation will give satisfaction; for, as I am a direct descendant of one of these princes, and perhaps of the eldest branch, how do I know whether, by examination of titles, I might not find myself the lawful king of the human race? Be that as it may, it cannot be denied that Adam was sovereign of the world, as Robinson was of his island, so long as he was its sole inhabitant; and it was an agreeable feature of that empire that the monarch, secure on his throne, had nothing to fear from rebellions, or wars, or conspirators.

CHAPTER 3

The Right of the Strongest

The strongest man is never strong enough to be always master, unless he transforms his power into right, and obedience into duty. Hence the right of the strongest—a right apparently assumed in irony, and really established in principle. But will this phrase never be explained to us? Force is a physical power; I do not see what morality can result from its effects. To yield to force is an act of necessity, not of will; it is at most an act of prudence. In what sense can it be a duty?

Let us assume for a moment this pretended right. I say that nothing results from it but inexplicable nonsense; for if force constitutes right, the effect changes with the cause, and any force which overcomes the first succeeds to its rights. As soon as men can disobey with impunity, they may do so legitimately; and since the strongest is always in the right, the only thing is to act in such a way that one may be the strongest. But what sort of right is it that perishes when force ceases? If it is necessary to obey by compulsion, there is no need to obey from duty; and if men are no longer forced to obey, obligation is at an end. We see then, that this word RIGHT adds nothing to force; it here means nothing at all.

Obey the powers that be. If that means, Yield to force, the precept is good but superfluous; I reply that it will never be violated. All power comes from God, I admit; but every disease comes from him too; does it follow that we are prohibited from calling in a physician? If a brigand should surprise me in the recesses of a wood, am I bound not only to give up my purse when forced, but am I also morally bound to do so when I might conceal it? For, in effect, the pistol which he holds is a superior force.

Let us agree, then, that might does not make right, and that we are bound to obey none but lawful authorities. Thus my original question ever recurs.

CHAPTER 4

Slavery

Since no man has any natural authority over his fellowmen, and since force is not the source of right, conventions remain as the basis of all lawful authority among men.

If an individual, says Grotius, can alienate his liberty and become the slave of a master, why should not a whole people be able to alienate theirs, and become subject to a king? In this there are many equivocal terms requiring explanation; but let us confine ourselves to the word *alienate*. To alienate is to give or sell. Now, a man who becomes another's slave does not give himself; he sells himself at the very least for his subsistence. But why does a nation sell itself? So far from a king supplying his subjects with their subsistence, he draws his from them; and, according to Rabelais, a king does not live on a little. Do subjects, then, give up their persons on condition that their property also shall be taken? I do not see what is left for them to keep.

It will be said that the despot secures to his subjects civil peace. Be it so; but what do they gain by that, if the wars which his ambition brings upon them, together with his insatiable greed and the vexations of his administration, harass them more than their own dissensions would? What do they gain by it if this tranquillity is itself one of their miseries? Men live tranquilly also in dungeons; is that enough to make them contented there? The Greeks confined in the cave of the Cyclops lived peacefully until their turn came to be devoured.

To say that a man gives himself for nothing is to say what is absurd and inconceivable; such an act is illegitimate and invalid, for the simple reason that he who performs it is not in his right mind. To say the same thing of a whole nation is to suppose a nation of fools; and madness does not confer rights.

Even if each person could alienate himself, he could not alienate his children; they are born free men; their liberty belongs to them, and no one has a right to dispose of it except themselves. Before they have come to years of discretion, the father can, in their name, stipulate conditions for their preservation and welfare, but not surrender them irrevocably and unconditionally; for such a gift is contrary to the ends of nature, and exceeds the rights of paternity. In order, then, that an arbitrary government might be legitimate, it would be necessary that the people in each generation should have the option of accepting or rejecting it; but in that case such a government would no longer be arbitrary.

To renounce one's liberty is to renounce one's quality as a man, the rights and also the duties of humanity. For him who renounces everything there is no possible compensation. Such a renunciation is incompatible with man's nature, for to take away all freedom from his will is to take away all morality from his actions. In short, a convention which stipulates absolute authority on the one side and unlimited obedience on the other is vain and contradictory. Is it not clear that we are under no obligations whatsoever toward a man from whom we have a right to demand everything? And does not this single condition, without equivalent, without exchange, involve the nullity of the act? For what right would my slave have against me, since all that he has belongs to me? His rights being mine, this right of me against myself is a meaningless phrase.

Grotius and others derive from war another origin for the pretended right of slavery. The victor having, according to them, the right of slaying the vanquished, the latter may purchase his life at the cost of his freedom; an agreement so much the more legitimate that it turns to the advantage of both.

But it is manifest that this pretended right of slaying the vanquished in no way results from the state of war. Men are not naturally enemies, if only for the reason that, living in their primitive independence, they have no mutual relations sufficiently durable to constitute a state of peace or a state of war. It is the relation of things and not of men which constitutes war; and since the state of war cannot arise from simple personal relations, but only from real relations, private war— war between man and man—cannot exist either in the state of nature, where there is no settled ownership, or in the social state where everything is under the authority of the laws.

Private combats, duels and encounters are acts which do not constitute a state of war; and with regard to the private wars authorized by the Establishments of Louis IX, king of France, and suspended by the Peace of God, they were abuses of the feudal government, an absurd system, if ever there was one, contrary both to the principles of natural right and to all sound government.

War, then, is not a relation between man and man, but a relation between State and State, in which individuals are enemies only by accident, not as men, nor even as citizens, but as soldiers; not as members of the fatherland, but as its defenders. In short, each State can have as enemies only other States and not individual men, inasmuch as it is impossible to fix any true relation between things of different kinds.

This principle is also conformable to the established maxims of all ages and to the invariable practice of all civilized nations. Declarations of war are not so much warnings to the powers as to their subjects. The foreigner, whether king, or nation, or private person, that robs, slays, or detains subjects without declaring war against the government, is not an enemy, but a brigand. Even in open war, a just prince, while he rightly takes possession of all that belongs to the State in an enemy's country, respects the person and property of individuals; he respects the rights on which his own are based. The aim of war being the destruction of the hostile State, we have a right to slay its defenders so long as they have arms in their hands; but as soon as they lay them down and surrender, ceasing to be enemies or instruments of the enemy, they become again simply men, and no one has any further right over their lives. Sometimes it is possible to destroy the State without killing a single one of its members; but war confers no right except what is necessary to its end. These are not the principles of Grotius; they are not based on the authority of poets, but are derived from the nature of things, and are founded on reason.

With regard to the right of conquest, it has no other foundation than the law of the strongest. If war does not confer on the victor the right of slaying the vanquished, this right, which he does not possess, cannot be the foundation of a right to enslave them. If we have a right to slay an enemy only when it is impossible to enslave him, the right to enslave him is not derived from the right to kill him; it is, therefore, an iniquitous bargain to make him purchase his life, over which the victor has no right, at the cost of his liberty. In establishing the right of life and death upon the right of slavery, and the right of slavery upon the right of life and death, is it not manifest that one falls into a vicious circle?

Even if we grant this terrible right of killing everybody, I say that a slave made in war, or a conquered nation, is under no obligation at all to a master, except to obey him so far as compelled. In taking an equivalent for his life the victor has conferred no favor on the slave; instead of killing him unprofitably, he has destroyed him for his own advantage. Far, then, from having acquired over him any authority in addition to that of force, the state of war subsists between them as before, their relation even is the effect of it; and the exercise of the rights of war supposes that there is no treaty of peace. They have made a convention. Be it so; but this convention, far from terminating the state of war, supposes its continuance.

Thus, in whatever way we regard things, the right of slavery is invalid, not only because it is illegitimate, but because it is absurd and meaningless. These terms, *slavery* and *right*, are contradictory and mutually exclusive. Whether addressed by a man to a man, or by a man to a nation, such a speech as this will always be equally foolish: "I make an agreement with you wholly at your expense and wholly for my benefit, and I shall observe it as long as I please, while you also shall observe it as long as I please."

CHAPTER 5

That It Is Always Necessary to Go Back to a First Convention

If I should concede all that I have so far refuted, those who favor despotism would be no farther advanced. There will always be a great difference between subduing a multitude and ruling a society. When isolated men, however numerous they may be, are subjected one after another to a single person, this seems to me only a case of master and slaves, not of a nation and its chief; they form, if you will, an aggregation, but not an association, for they have neither public property nor a body politic. Such a man, had he enslaved half the world, is never anything but an individual; his interests, separated from that of the rest, is never anything but a private interest. If he dies, his empire after him is left disconnected and disunited, as an oak dissolves and becomes a heap of ashes after the fire has consumed it.

A nation, says Grotius, can give itself to a king. According to Grotius, then, a nation is a nation before it gives itself to a king. This gift itself is a civil act, and presupposes a public resolution. Consequently, before examining the act by which a nation elects a king, it would be proper to examine the act by which a nation becomes a nation; for this act, being necessarily anterior to the other, is the real foundation of the society.

In fact, if there were no anterior convention, where, unless the election were unanimous, would be the obligation upon the minority to submit to the decision of the majority? And whence do the hundred who desire a master derive the right to vote on behalf of ten who do not desire one? The law of the plurality of votes is itself established by convention, and presupposes unanimity once at least.

CHAPTER 6

The Social Pact

I assume that men have reached a point at which the obstacles that endanger their preservation in the state of nature overcome by their resistance the forces which each individual can exert with a view to maintaining himself in that state. Then this primitive condition cannot longer subsist, and the human race would perish unless it changed its mode of existence.

Now as men cannot create any new forces, but only combine and direct those that exist, they have no other means of self-preservation than to form by aggregation a sum of forces which may overcome the resistance, to put them in action by a single motive power, and to make them work in concert.

This sum of forces can be produced only by the combination of many; but the strength and freedom of each man being the chief instruments of his preservation, how can he pledge them without injuring himself, and without neglecting the cares which he owes to himself? This difficulty, applied to my subject, may be expressed in these terms:

"To find a form of association which may defend and protect with the whole force of the community the person and property of every associate, and by means of which, coalescing with all, may nevertheless obey only himself, and remain as free as before." Such is the fundamental problem of which the social contract furnishes the solution.

The clauses of this contract are so determined by the nature of the act that the slightest modification would render them vain and ineffectual; so that, although they have never perhaps been formally enunciated, they are everywhere the same, everywhere tacitly admitted and recognized, until, the social pact being violated, each man regains his original rights and recovers his natural liberty while losing the conventional liberty for which he renounced it.

These clauses, rightly understood, are reducible to one only, viz, the total alienation to the whole community of each associate with all his rights; for, in the first place, since each gives himself up entirely, the conditions are equal for all; and, the conditions being equal for all, no one has any interest in making them burdensome to others.

Further, the alienation being made without reserve, the union is as perfect as it can be, and an individual associate can no longer claim anything; for, if any rights were left to individuals, since there would be no common superior who could judge between them and the public, each, being on some point his own judge, would soon claim to be so on all; the state of nature would still subsist, and the association would necessarily become tyrannical or useless.

In short, each giving himself to all, gives himself to nobody; and as there is not one associate over whom we do not acquire the same rights which we concede to him over ourselves, we gain the equivalent of all that we lose, and more power to preserve what we have.

If, then, we set aside what is not of the essence of the social contract, we shall find that it is reducible to the following terms: "Each of us puts in common his person and his whole power under the supreme direction of the general will; and in return we receive every member as an indivisible part of the whole."

Forthwith, instead of the individual personalities of all the contracting parties, this act of association produces a moral and collective body, which is composed of as many members as the assembly has voices, and which receives from this same act its unity, its common self *(moi)*, its life, and its will. This public person, which is thus formed by the union of all the individual members, formerly took the name of *city*, and now takes that of *republic* or *body politic*, which is called by its members *State* when it is passive, *sovereign* when it is active, *power* when it is compared to similar bodies. With regard to the associates, they take collectively the name of *people*, and are called individually *citizens*, as participating in the sovereign power, and *subjects*, as subjected to the laws of the State. But these terms are often confused and are mistaken one for another; it is sufficient to know how to distinguish them when they are used with complete precision.

CHAPTER 7

The Sovereign

We see from this formula that the act of association contains a reciprocal engagement between the public and individuals, and that every individual, contracting so to speak with himself, is engaged in a double relation, viz, as a member of the sovereign toward individuals, and as a member of the State toward the sovereign. But we cannot apply here the maxim of civil law that no one is bound by engagements made with himself; for there is a great difference between being bound to oneself and to a whole of which one forms part.

We must further observe that the public resolution which can bind all subjects to the sovereign in consequence of the two different relations under which each of them is regarded cannot, for a contrary reason, bind the sovereign to itself; and that accordingly it is contrary to the nature of the body politic for the sovereign to impose on itself a law which it cannot transgress. As it can only be considered under one and the same relation, it is in the position of an individual contracting with himself; whence we see that there is not, nor can be, any kind of fundamental law binding upon the body of the people, not even the social contract. This does not imply that such a body cannot perfectly well enter into engagements with others in what does not derogate from this contract; for, with regard to foreigners, it becomes a simple being, an individual.

But the body politic or sovereign, deriving its existence only from the sanctity of the contract, can never bind itself, even to others, in anything that derogates from the original act, such as alienation of some portion of itself, or submission to another sovereign. To violate the act by which it exists would be to annihilate itself; and what is nothing produces nothing.

So soon as the multitude is thus united in one body, it is impossible to injure one of the members without attacking the body, still less to injure the body without the members feeling the effects. Thus duty and interest alike oblige the two contracting parties to give mutual assistance; and the men themselves should seek to combine in this twofold relationship all the advantages which are attendant on it.

Now, the sovereign, being formed only of the individuals that compose it, neither has nor can have any interest contrary to theirs; consequently the sovereign power needs no guarantee toward its subjects, because it is impossible that the body should wish to injure all its members; and we shall see hereafter that it can injure no one as an individual. The sovereign, for the simple reason that it is so, is always everything that it ought to be.

But this is not the case as regards the relation of subjects to the sovereign, which, notwithstanding the common interest, would have no security for the performance of their engagements, unless it found means to ensure their fidelity.

Indeed, every individual may, as a man, have a particular will contrary to, or divergent from, the general will which he has as a citizen; his private interest may prompt him quite differently from the common interest; his absolute and naturally independent existence may make him regard what he owes to the common cause as a gratuitous contribution, the loss of which will be less harmful to others than the payment of it will be burdensome to him; and, regarding the moral person that constitutes the State as an imaginary being because it is not a man, he would be willing to enjoy the rights of a citizen without being willing to fulfil the duties of a subject. The progress of such injustice would bring about the ruin of the body politic.

In order, then, that the social pact may not be a vain formulary, it tacitly includes this engagement, which can alone give force to the others, that whoever refuses to obey the general will shall be constrained to do so by the whole body; which means nothing else than that he shall be forced to be free; for such is the condition which, uniting every citizen to his native land, guarantees him from all personal dependence, a condition that insures the control and working of the political machine, and alone renders legitimate civil engagements, which, without it, would be absurd and tyrannical, and subject to the most enormous abuses.

CHAPTER 8

The Civil State

The passage from the state of nature to the civil state produces in man a very remarkable change, by substituting in his conduct justice for instinct, and by giving his actions the moral quality that they previously lacked. It is only when the voice of duty succeeds physical impulse, and law succeeds appetite, that man, who till then had regarded only himself, sees that he is obliged to act on other principles, and to consult his reason before listening to his inclinations. Although, in this state, he is deprived of many advantages that he derives from nature, he acquires equally great ones in return; his faculties are exercised and developed; his ideas are expanded; his feelings are ennobled; his whole soul is exalted to such a degree that, if the abuses of this new condition did not often degrade him below that from which he has emerged, he ought to bless without ceasing the happy moment that released him from it for ever, and transformed him from a stupid and ignorant animal into an intelligent being and a man.

Let us reduce this whole balance to terms easy to compare. What man loses by the social contract is his natural liberty and an unlimited right to anything which tempts him and which he is able to attain: what he gains is civil liberty and property in all that he possesses. In order that we may not be mistaken about these compensations, we must clearly distinguish natural liberty, which is limited only by the powers of the individual, from civil liberty, which is limited by the general will; and possession, which is nothing but the result of force or the right of first occupancy, from property, which can be based only on a positive title.

Besides the preceding, we might add to the acquisitions of the civil state moral freedom, which alone renders man truly master of himself; for the impulse of mere appetite is slavery, while obedience to a self-prescribed law is liberty. But I have already said too much on this head, and the philosophical meaning of the term LIBERTY does not belong to my present subject.

CHAPTER 9

Real Property

Every member of the community at the moment of its formation gives himself up to it, just as he actually is, himself and all his powers, of which the property that he possesses forms part. By this act, possession does not change its nature when it changes hands, and become property in those of the sovereign; but, as the powers of the State *(cité)* are incomparably greater than those of an individual, public possession is also, in fact, more secure and more irrevocable, without being more legitimate, at least in respect of foreigners; for the State, with regard to its members, is owner of all their property by the social contract, which, in the State, serves as the basis of all rights; but with regard to other powers, it is owner only by the right of first occupancy which it derives from individuals.

The right of first occupancy, although more real than that of the strongest, becomes a true right only after the establishment of that of property. Every man has by nature a right to all that is necessary to him; but the positive act which makes him proprietor of certain property excludes him from all the residue. His portion having been allotted, he ought to confine himself to it, and he has no further right to the undivided property. That is why the right of first occupancy, so weak in the state of nature, is respected by every member of a State. In this right men regard not so much what belongs to others as what does not belong to themselves.

In order to legalize the right of first occupancy over any domain whatsoever, the following conditions are, in general, necessary: first, the land must not yet be inhabited by any one; secondly, a man must occupy only the area required for his subsistence; thirdly, he must take possession of it, not by an empty ceremony, but by labor and cultivation, the only mark of ownership which, in default of legal title, ought to be respected by others.

Indeed, if we accord the right of first occupancy to necessity and labor, do we not extend it as far as it can go? Is it impossible to assign limits to this right? Will the mere setting foot on common ground be sufficient to give an immediate claim to the ownership of it? Will the power of driving away other men from it for a moment suffice to deprive them for ever of the right of returning to it? How can a man or a people take possession of an immense territory and rob the whole human race of it except by a punishable usurpation, since other men are deprived of the place of residence and the sustenance which nature gives to them in common. When Nuñez Balboa on the seashore took possession of the Pacific Ocean and of the whole of South America in the name of the crown of Castile, was this sufficient to dispossess all the inhabitants, and exclude from it all the princes in the world? On this supposition such ceremonies might have been multiplied vainly enough; and the Catholic king in his cabinet might, by a single stroke, have taken possession of the whole world, only cutting off afterward from his empire what was previously occupied by other princes.

We perceive how the lands of individuals, united and contiguous, become public territory, and how the right of sovereignty, extending itself from the subjects to the land which they occupy, becomes at once real and personal; which places the possessors in greater dependence, and makes their own powers a guarantee for their fidelity—an advantage which ancient monarchs do not appear to have clearly perceived, for, calling themselves only kings of the Persians or Scythians or Macedonians, they seem to have regarded themselves as chiefs of men rather than as owners of countries. Monarchs of to-day call themselves more cleverly kings of France, Spain, England, etc.; in thus holding the land they are quite sure of holding its inhabitants.

The peculiarity of this alienation is that the community, in receiving the property of individuals, so far from robbing them of it, only assures them lawful possession, and changes usurpation into true right, enjoyment into ownership. Also, the possessors being considered as depositaries of the public property, and their rights being respected by all the members of the State, as well as maintained by all its power against foreigners, they have, as it were, by a transfer advantageous to the public and still more to themselves, acquired all that they have given up—a paradox which is easily explained by distinguishing between the rights which the sovereign and the proprietor have over the same property, as we shall see hereafter.

It may also happen that men begin to unite before they possess anything, and that afterward occupying territory sufficient for all, they enjoy it in common, or share it among themselves, either equally or in proportions fixed by the sovereign. In whatever way this acquisition is made, the right which every individual has over his own property is always subordinate to the right which the community has over all; otherwise there would be no stability in the social union, and no real force in the exercise of sovereignty.

I shall close this chapter and this book with a remark which ought to serve as a basis for the whole social system; it is that instead of destroying natural equality, the fundamental pact, on the contrary, substitutes a moral and lawful equality for the physical inequality which nature imposed upon men, so that, although unequal in strength or intellect, they all become equal by convention and legal right.

transition:
community and
the new anarchism

In answer to the traditional problem of liberal political theory—the limits to the authority of society over the individual—the traditional anarchist answers: "Society has no authority over me." This is essentially Robert Paul Wolff's argument in his book *In Defense of Anarchism* (1970). Faced with the traditional problem of political theory, he honestly and unabashedly confesses that he is unable to find any valid and persuasive argument justifying the authority claimed for the state. Consequently, the individual is left as both the alpha and omega of social theory. The old anarchy is the kingdom of the unrestrained individual, free of social contracts binding him to a particular form of government. The old anarchism is an essentially individualistic response to the problem of political philosophy.

But a new anarchism is now emerging. Some of today's anarchists take an approach that bypasses traditional political theory by starting from different premises and a different question. The new anarchism is not individualistic but communal or tribal (note Gary Snyder's title, "Why Tribe"). Consequently the new anarchists are not interested in how the *individual* relates to the state, for the new anarchists are not political theorists, but people already living a "tribal" existence. To find out why they live as they do we need to go outside political theory for the determinants of their life style. This is not to say that the anarchic life style will not have influences on political realities which must be analyzed from the perspective of political theory. But the new anarchism functions as a *cause* in the political matrix rather than as a *result* of a line of argument in political theory. Traditional anarchist literature saw anarchism as a result and tried to show why it would be desirable. I wish to distinguish a newer approach that simply takes anarchistic life styles as a fact and then seeks to explore the origins and significance of that fact.

The origins of the new anarchism can be seen in a peculiar twist on the traditional problem of political theory: where the problem once was to see how an individual could preserve himself from "the state of nature" by joining with other individuals, now the problem is to see how groups can preserve themselves from their ancestors' success at fleeing the state of nature. Humankind inserted technology and political organization between itself and nature; the new anarchists are trying to protect themselves from technology and the dominant forms of political organization. Where liberal political theory saw individuals using technology to carve out livable spaces in an alien natural environment, the new anarchism is looking for ways that groups can carve out livable spaces in an alien technological-political environment. This does not mean that the new anarchists intend to forswear technology any more than political-technological individuals forswore nature: they used rivers to drive their mills and natural resources to stoke their fires, just as anarchists use technological know-how to carve out spaces free from the ills of technology.

Analyzing the genesis of contemporary anarchism as arising from classical political and technological solutions, we might conclude that the basic insight underlying the new anarchism is just this: as makers of our own history, we continually risk subjugating ourselves to the solutions of previous problems. First the problem was nature with all its infelicities, but that problem was solved through political organization and technology. Now the problem is precisely the political organization and technology that constituted the solution to the previous problem. This sort of historical analysis of the new anarchism suggests that there might never be an eternal solution to the "problem of political theory." As makers of our own history, we guarantee that our problems keep changing. The guarantee is reflected in the anarchist's preference for the primacy of *practice* to theory, and that preference goes a long way toward accounting for the general lack of first-rank political theorists in the anarchist tradition, a lack that Benjamin Barber takes as diminishing the credibility of anarchists.

While the old anarchist may be a political theorist who believes that a radically individualistic answer to the problem of politics offers the key to the solution of man's ills, the new anarchist does not believe that *any* political answer is a key. The new anarchists are philosophically interesting for the radicalism of their nonanswer to the political question. Rather than proffer an answer, they undermine the question. They may be living as anarchists because of religious views rather than political convictions. (Here Snyder's writings are most indicative.) The new anarchists are thus political atheists: they simply do not believe in the reality of political power. They see national (but not local) politics as essentially mythical: Washington as Mount Olympus, elections as tribal rites without any discernible efficacy. However meticulously one performs the rites, life goes on much as before, whether it be too little rain or too little peace.

Such views will arouse indignation, the same indignation aroused by religious heresies when everybody believed in God and the Church. Hence the title of "political atheist" for the new anarchist. The new anarchist is not a political theorist among other political theorists any more than Nietzsche was a theologian among theologians. But just as Nietzsche brought the radicalism of philosophical critique to the questions theologians were dealing with, so the new anarchists, by their deeds as much as their words, bring the radicalism of philosophical critique into the domain of political theory.

MARTIN BUBER *(1878–1965)*

Martin Buber, one of the foremost religious philosophers in the twentieth century, was no stranger to social and political issues. At the time he was writing his book Paths in Utopia, *completed in 1945, the term 'anarchism' still suffered under the connotation of violence; it was known more as a tactic than a political philosophy. Anarchists were considered renegades who, instead of participating in party strategies, preferred to promote their political causes, whatever they might be, by acts of individual terror and violence. Consequently, Buber was careful not to refer to his political philosophy as anarchism, but his main subjects—the ideas of men like Proudhon, Kropotkin, and Landauer—are generally recognized to be central to the old anarchist tradition.*

Yet Buber's essay, from Paths in Utopia, *anticipates quite remarkably many of the tenets of the new anarchism, and in a philosophically respectable way. He sees that the problem of the individual and society is not an either-or question but, as he says, "a question of the right line of demarcation that has to be drawn ever anew." His call for a decentralization of politics is not the cry of a political conservative, as is clear from his declaration "in favor of a rebirth of the commune." Of course it is difficult these days to know just what is politically "conservative" ever since Paul Goodman, an old-time radical who was active in the contemporary scene, described himself as a radical conservative. Many of our current labels are not only confusing but even damaging to the extent that they lead us to think in either-or terms. Where a false dichotomy is the only dichotomy with a label, both sides may be wrong. Sometimes one needs to cut across old distinctions with new distinctions. As was suggested in the transition to the epistemology of interpersonal perception, the distinction between subjective relativism and absolutism inhibits our thinking of an objective relativism. There, as in the present case, careful thought requires an analysis of both sides of an easily labeled dichotomy. We needn't abandon relativism in our haste to escape the chaos of subjectivism—why throw out the baby with the bath water? Here too we want to avoid locating anarchism on one side of the false distinction between radicalism and conservatism. Just as we can be objective relativists, and Paul Goodman can be a radical conservative, so the anarchist may fall into none of the neatly labeled camps generated by the usual partisan disputes.*

Utopian Communities

In the Midst of Crisis

For the last three decades we have felt that we were living in the initial phases of the greatest crisis humanity has ever known. It grows increasingly clear to us that the tremendous happenings of the past years, too, can be understood only as symptoms of this crisis. It is not merely the crisis of one economic and social system being superseded by another, more or less ready to take its place; rather all systems, old and new, are equally involved in the crisis. What is in question, therefore, is nothing less than man's whole existence in the world.

Ages ago, far beyond our calculation, this creature "Man" set out on his journey; from the point of view of Nature a well-nigh incomprehensible anomaly; from the point of view of the spirit an incarnation hardly less incomprehensible, perhaps unique; from the point of view of both a being whose very essence it was to be threatened with disaster every instant, both from within and without, exposed to deeper and deeper crises. During the ages of his early journey man has multiplied what he likes to call his "power over Nature" in increasingly rapid tempo, and he has borne what he likes to call the "creations of his spirit" from triumph to triumph. But at the same time he has felt more and more profoundly, as one crisis succeeded another, how fragile all his glories are; and in moments of clairvoyance he has come to realize that in spite of everything he likes to call "progress" he is not travelling along the high-road at all, but is picking his precarious way along a narrow ledge between two abysses. The graver the crisis becomes the more earnest and consciously responsible is the knowledge demanded of us; for although what is demanded is a deed, only that deed which is born of knowledge will help to overcome the crisis. In a time of great crisis it is not enough to look back to the immediate past in order to bring the enigma of the present nearer to solution: we have to bring the stage of the journey we have now reached face to face with its beginnings, so far as we can picture them.

The essential thing among all those things which once helped man to emerge from Nature and, notwithstanding his feebleness as a natural being, to assert himself—more essential even than the making of a "technical" world out of things expressly formed for the purpose—was this: that he banded together with his own kind for protection and hunting, food gathering and work; and did so in such a way that from the very beginning and thereafter to an increasing degree he faced the others as more or less independent entities and communicated with them as such, addressing and being addressed by them in that manner. This creation of a "social" world out of persons at once mutually dependent and independent differed in kind from all similar undertakings on the part of animals, just as the technical work of man differed in kind from all the animals' works. Apes, too, make use of some stick they happen to have found, as a lever, a digging-tool or a weapon; but that is an affair of chance only: they cannot conceive and produce a tool as an object constituted so and not otherwise and having an existence of its own. And again, many of the insects live in societies built up on a strict division of labour; but it is just this division of labour that governs absolutely their relations with one another; they are all as it were tools; only, their own society is the thing that makes use of them for its "instinctive" purposes; there is no improvisation, no degree, however modest, of mutual independence, no possibility of "free" regard for one another, and thus no person-to-person relationship. Just as the specific technical creations of man mean the conferring of independence on things, so his specific social creation means the conferring of independence on beings of his own kind. It is in the light of this specifically human idiosyncrasy that we have to interpret man's journey with all its ups and downs, and so also the point we have reached on this journey, our great and particular crisis.

In the evolution of mankind hitherto this, then, is the line that predominates: the forming and re-forming of communities on the basis of growing personal independence, their mutual recognition and collaboration on that basis. The two most important steps that the man of early times took on the road to human society can be established with some certainty. The first is that inside the individual clan each individual, through an extremely primitive form of division of labour, was recognized and utilized in his special capacity, so that the clan increasingly took on the character of an ever-renewed association of persons each the vehicle of a different function. The second is that different clans would, under certain conditions, band together in quest of food and for campaigns, and consolidated their mutual help as customs and laws that took firmer and firmer root; so that as once between individuals, so now between communities people discerned and acknowledged differences of nature and function. Wherever genuine human society has since developed it has always been on this same basis of functional autonomy, mutual recognition and mutual responsibility, whether individual or collective. Power-centres of various kinds have split off, organizing and guaranteeing the common order and security of all; but to the political sphere in the stricter sense, the State with its police-system and its bureaucracy, there was always opposed the organic, functionally organized society as such, a great society built up of various societies, the great society in which men lived and worked, competed with one another and helped one another; and in each of the big and little societies composing it, in each of these communes and communities the individual human being, despite all the difficulties and conflicts, felt himself at home as once in the clan, felt himself approved and affirmed in his functional independence and responsibility.

All this changed more and more as the centralistic political principle subordinated the de-centralistic social principle. The crucial thing here was not that the State, particularly in its more or less totalitarian forms, weakened and gradually displaced the free associations, but that the political principle with all its centralistic features percolated into the associations themselves, modifying their structure and their whole inner life, and thus politicized society to an ever-increasing extent. Society's assimilation in the State was accelerated by the fact that, as a result of modern industrial development and its ordered chaos, involving the struggle of all against all for access to raw materials and for a larger share of the world-market, there grew up, in place of the old struggles between States, struggles between whole societies. The individual society, feeling itself threatened not only by its neighbours' lust for aggression but also by things in general, knew no way of salvation save in complete submission to the principle of centralized power; and, in the democratic forms of society no less than in its totalitarian forms, it made this its guiding principle. Everywhere the only thing of importance was the minute organization of power, the unquestioning observance of slogans, the saturation of the whole of society with the real or supposed interests of the State. Concurrently with this there is an internal development. In the monstrous confusion of modern life, only thinly disguised by the reliable functioning of the economic and State-apparatus, the individual clings desperately to the collectivity. The little society in which he was embedded cannot help him; only the great collectivities, so he thinks, can do that, and he is all too willing to let himself be deprived of personal responsibility: he only wants to obey. And the most valuable of all goods—the life between man and man—gets lost in the process; the autonomous relationships become meaningless, personal relationships wither; and the very spirit of man hires itself out as a functionary. The personal human being ceases to be the living member of a social body and becomes a cog in the "collective" machine. Just as his degenerate technology is causing man to lose the feel of good work and proportion, so the degrading social life he leads is causing him to lose the feel of community— just when he is so full of the illusion of living in perfect devotion to his community.

A crisis of this kind cannot be overcome by struggling back to an earlier stage of the journey, but only by trying to master the problems as they are, without minimizing them. There is no going back for us, we have to go through with it. But we shall only get through if we know *where* we want to go.

We must begin, obviously, with the establishment of a vital peace which will deprive the political principle of it supremacy over the social principle. And this primary objective cannot in its turn be reached by any devices of political organ- ization, but only by the resolute will of all peoples to cultivate the territories and raw materials of our planet and govern its inhabitants, *together*. At this point, however, we are threatened by a danger greater than all the previous ones: the danger of a gigantic centralization of power covering the whole planet and devour- ing all free community. Everything depends on not handing the work of planetary management over to the political principle.

Common management is only possible as socialistic management. But if the fatal question for contemporary man is: Can he or can he not decide in favour of, and educate himself up to, a common socialistic economy? then the propriety of the question lies in an inquiry into Socialism itself: what sort of Socialism is it to be, under whose aegis the common economy of man is to come about, if at all?

The ambiguity of the terms we are employing is greater here than anywhere else. People say, for instance, that Socialism is the passing of the control of the means of production out of the hands of the entrepreneurs into the hands of the collectivity; but again, it all depends on what you mean by "collectivity." If it is what we generally call the "State," that is to say, an institution in which a virtually unorganized mass allows its affairs to be conducted by "representation," as they call it, then the chief change in a socialistic society will be this: that the workers will feel themselves represented by the holders of power. But what is representation? Does not the worst defect of modern society lie precisely in everybody letting himself be represented *ad libitum?* And in a "socialistic" society will there not, on top of this passive political representation, be added a passive economic representation, so that, with everybody letting himself be represented by everybody else, we reach a state of practically unlimited representation and hence, ultimately, the reign of practically unlimited centralist accumulation of power? But the more a human group lets itself be represented in the management of its common affairs, and the more it lets itself be represented from outside, the less communal life there is in it and the more impoverished it becomes as a community. For community—not the primitive sort, but the sort possible and appropriate to modern man—declares itself primarily in the common and active management of what it has in common, and without this it cannot exist.

The primary aspiration of all history is a genuine community of human beings—genuine because it is *community all through.* A community that failed to base itself on the actual and communal life of big and little groups living and working together, and on their mutual relationships, would be fictitious and counterfeit. Hence everything depends on whether the collectivity into whose hands the control of the means of production passes will facilitate and promote in its very structure and in all its institutions the genuine common life of the various groups composing it—on whether, in fact, these groups themselves become proper foci of the productive process; therefore on whether the masses are so organized in their separate organizations (the various "communities") as to be as powerful as the common economy of man permits; therefore on whether centralist representation only goes as far as the new order of things absolutely demands. The fatal question does not take the form of a fundamental Either-Or: it is only a question of the right line of demarcation that has to be drawn ever anew—the thousandfold system of demarcation between the spheres which must of necessity be centralized and those which can operate in freedom; between the degree of government and the degree of autonomy; between the law of unity and the claims of community. The unwearying scrutiny of conditions in terms of the claims of community, as something continually exposed to the depredations of centralist power—the *custody of the true boundaries*, ever changing in accordance with changing historical circumstances: such would be the task of humanity's spiritual conscience, a Supreme Court unexampled in kind, the right true representation of a living idea. A new incarnation is waiting here for Plato's "custodians."

Representation of an idea, I say: not of a rigid principle but of a living form that wants to be shaped in the daily stuff of this earth. Community should not be made into a principle; it, too, should always satisfy a situation rather than an abstraction. The realization of community, like the realization of any idea, cannot occur once and for all time: always it must be the moment's answer to the moment's question, and nothing more.

In the interests of its vital meaning, therefore, the idea of community must be guarded against all contamination by sentimentality or emotionalism. Community is never a mere attitude of mind, and if it is *feeling* it is an inner disposition that is felt. Community is the inner disposition or constitution of a life in common, which knows and embraces in itself hard "calculation," adverse "chance," the sudden access of "anxiety." It is community of tribulation and only because of that community of spirit; community of toil and only because of that community of salvation. Even those communities which call the spirit their master and salvation their Promised Land, the "religious" communities, are community only if they serve their lord and master in the midst of simple, unexalted, unselected reality, a reality not so much chosen by them as sent to them just as it is; they are community only if they prepare the way to the Promised Land through the thickets of this pathless hour. True, it is not "works" that count, but the work of faith does. A community of faith truly exists only when it is a community of work.

The real essence of community is to be found in the fact—manifest or otherwise—that it has a centre. The real beginning of a community is when its members have a common relation to the centre overriding all other relations: the circle is described by the radii, not by the points along its circumference. And the originality of the centre cannot be discerned unless it is discerned as being transpicuous to the light of something divine. All this is true; but the more earthly, the more creaturely, the more attached the centre is, the truer and more transpicuous it will be. This is where the "social" element comes in. Not as something separate, but as the all-pervading realm where man stands the test; and it is here that the truth of the centre is proved. The early Christians were not content with the community that existed alongside or even above the world, and they went into the desert so as to have no more community save with God and no more disturbing world. But it was shown them that God does not wish man to be alone with him; and above the holy impotence of the hermit there rose the Brotherhood. Finally, going beyond St. Benedict, St. Francis entered into alliance with all creatures.

Yet a community need not be "founded." Wherever historical destiny had brought a group of men together in a common fold, there was room for the growth of a genuine community; and there was no need of an altar to the city deity in the midst when the citizens knew they were united round—and by—the Nameless. A living togetherness, constantly renewing itself, was already there, and all that needed strengthening was the immediacy of relationships. In the happiest instances common affairs were deliberated and decided not through representatives but in gatherings in the marketplace; and the unity that was felt in public permeated all personal contacts. The danger of seclusion might hang over the community, but the communal spirit banished it; for here this spirit flourished as nowhere else and broke windows for itself in the narrow walls, with a large view of people, mankind and the world.

All this, I may be told, has gone irrevocably and for ever. The modern city has no agora and the modern man has no time for negotiations of which his elected representatives can very well relieve him. The pressure of numbers and the forms of organization have destroyed any real togetherness. Work forges other personal links than does leisure, sport again others than politics, the day is cleanly divided and the soul too. These links are material ones; though we follow our common interests and tendencies together, we have no use for "immediacy." The collectivity is not a warm, friendly gathering but a great link-up of economic and political forces inimical to the play of romantic fancies, only understandable in terms of quantity, expressing itself in actions and effects—a thing which the individual has to belong to with no intimacies of any kind but all the time conscious of his energetic contribution. Any "unions" that resist the inevitable trend of events must disappear. There is still the family, of course, which, as a domestic community, seems to demand and guarantee a modicum of communal life; but it too will either emerge from the crisis in which it is involved, as an association for a common purpose, or else it will perish.

Faced with this medley of correct premises and absurd conclusions I declare in favour of a rebirth of the commune. A rebirth—not a bringing back. It cannot in fact be brought back, although I sometimes think that every touch of helpful neighbourliness in the apartment-house, every wave of warmer comradeship in the lulls and "knock-offs" that occur even in the most perfectly "rationalized" factory, means an addition to the world's community-content; and although a rightly constituted village commune sometimes strikes me as being a more real thing than a parliament; but it cannot be brought back. Yet whether a rebirth of the commune will ensue from the "water and spirit" of the social transformation that is imminent—on this, it seems to me, hangs the whole fate of the human race. An organic commonwealth—and only such commonwealths can join together to form a shapely and articulated race of men—will never build itself up out of individuals but only out of small and ever smaller communities: a nation is a community to the degree that it is a community of communities. If the family does not emerge from the crisis which to-day has all the appearance of a disintegration, purified and renewed, then the State will be nothing more than a machine stoked with the bodies of generations of men. The community that would be capable of such a renewal exists only as a residue. If I speak of its rebirth I am not thinking of a permanent world-situation but an altered one. By the new communes—they might equally well be called the new Co-operatives—I mean the subjects of a changed economy: the collectives into whose hands the control of the means of production is to pass. Once again, everything depends on whether they will be ready.

Just how much economic and political autonomy—for they will of necessity be economic and political units at once—will have to be conceded to them is a technical question that must be asked and answered over and over again; but asked and answered beyond the technical level, in the knowledge that the internal authority of a community hangs together with its external authority. The relationship between centralism and decentralization is a problem which, as we have seen, cannot be approached in principle, but, like everything to do with the relationship between idea and reality, only with great spiritual tact, with the constant and tireless weighing and measuring of the right proportion between them. Centralization—but only so much as is indispensable in the given conditions of time and place. And if the authorities responsible for the drawing and re-drawing of lines of demarcation keep an alert conscience, the relations between the base and the apex of the power-pyramid will be very different from what they are now, even in States that call themselves Communist, i.e. struggling for community. There will have to be a system of representation, too, in the sort of social pattern I have in mind; but it will not, as now, be composed of the pseudorepresentatives of amorphous masses of electors but of representatives well tested in the life and work of the communes. The represented will not, as they are to-day, be bound to their representatives by some windy abstraction, by the mere phraseology of a party-programme, but concretely, through common action and common experience.

The essential thing, however, is that the process of community-building shall run all through the relations of the communes with one another. Only a community of communities merits the title of Commonwealth.

The picture I have hastily sketched will doubtless be laid among the documents of "Utopian Socialism" until the storm turns them up again. Just as I do not believe in Marx's "gestation" of the new form, so I do not believe either in Bakunin's virgin-birth from the womb of Revolution. But I do believe in the meeting of idea and fate in the creative hour.

GARY SNYDER *(b. 1930)*

Gary Snyder is a poet. Yet his short and elegant statement is included for several reasons. First, Snyder shows the nonpolitical origins and intentions of a certain type of anarchism. Second, his gentle voice speaks its own reply to the charges Benjamin Barber raises in the essay from his Superman and Common Men. *Snyder, in a selection from* Earth House Hold *(1969), offers only a description of the tribe, no manifesto. He apparently accepts the idea that this movement may always remain on the margins of society, yet he shows none of the arrogance of elitism. No one will be kept out of the tribe. You may simply take it or leave it; it's up to you. Third, note his interest in the question, "What is Consciousness?" Philosophy can help here.*

Fourth, and finally, his incredibly compact statement: the tribe "has recognized that for one to 'follow the grain' it is necessary to look exhaustively into the negative and demonic potentials of the Unconscious, and by recognizing these powers—symbolically acting them out—one releases himself from these forces. By this profound exorcism and ritual drama, the Great Subculture destroys the one credible claim of Church and State to a necessary function." Though exorcism may sound like a ridiculous solution to today's problems, the Unconscious as a phenomenon is a well-entrenched feature of modern scientific psychology. We cannot afford to ignore it, as Reich among others recognizes. If you are intrigued by Snyder's references to the symbolic quest for the potentials of the Unconscious, you might want to read C. G. Jung. Some of his writings are not easy, and it is especially difficult to find a short statement introducing his work; hence the absence of Jung from this anthology. But if you are willing to attempt a longer piece, Jung's autobiography, Memories, Dreams and Reflections, *is an ideal introduction to his thought.*

Why Tribe

We use the term Tribe because it suggests the type of new society now emerging within the industrial nations. In America of course the word has associations with the American Indians, which we like. This new subculture is in fact more similar to that ancient and successful tribe, the European Gypsies—a group without nation or territory which maintains its own values, its language and religion, no matter what country it may be in.

The Tribe proposes a totally different style: based on community houses, villages and ashrams; tribe-run farms or workshops or companies; large open families; pilgrimages and wanderings from center to center. A synthesis of Gandhian "village anarchism" and I.W.W. syndicalism. Interesting visionary pamphlets along these lines were written several years ago by Gandhians Richard Gregg and Appa Patwardhan. The Tribe proposes personal responsibilities rather than abstract centralized government, taxes and advertising-agency-plus-Mafia type international brainwashing corporations.

In the United States and Europe the Tribe has evolved gradually over the last fifty years—since the end of World War I—in response to the increasing insanity of the modern nations. As the number of alienated intellectuals, creative types and general social misfits grew, they came to recognize each other by various minute signals. Much of this energy was channeled into Communism in the thirties and early forties. All the anarchists and left-deviationists—and many Trotskyites— were tribesmen at heart. After World War II, another generation looked at Communist rhetoric with a fresh eye and saw that within the Communist governments (and states of mind) there are too many of the same things as are wrong with "capitalism"—too much anger and murder. The suspicion grew that perhaps the whole Western Tradition, of which Marxism is but a (Millennial Protestant) part, is off the track. This led many people to study other major civilizations— India and China—to see what they could learn.

It's an easy step from the dialectic of Marx and Hegel to an interest in the dialectic of early Taoism, the *I Ching*, and the yin-yang theories. From Taoism it is another easy step to the philosophies and mythologies of India—vast, touching the deepest areas of the mind, and with a view of the ultimate nature of the universe which is almost identical with the most sophisticated thought in modern physics—that truth, whatever it is, which is called "The Dharma."

Next comes a concern with deepening one's understanding in an experiential way: abstract philosophical understanding is simply not enough. At this point many, myself included, found in the Buddha-Dharma a practical method for clearing one's mind of the trivia, prejudices and false values that our conditioning had laid on us—and more important, an approach to the basic problem of how to penetrate to the deepest non-self Self. Today we have many who are exploring the Ways of Zen, Vajrayāna, Yoga, Shamanism, Psychedelics. The Buddha-Dharma is a long, gentle, human dialog—2,500 years of quiet conversation—on the nature of human nature and the eternal Dharma—and practical methods of realization.

In the course of these studies it became evident that the "truth" in Buddhism and Hinduism is not dependent in any sense on Indian or Chinese culture; and that "India" and "China"—as societies—are as burdensome to human beings as any others; perhaps more so. It became clear that "Hinduism" and "Buddhism" as social institutions had long been accomplices of the State in burdening and binding people, rather than serving to liberate them. Just like the other Great Religions.

At this point, looking once more quite closely at history both East and West, some of us noticed the similarities in certain small but influential heretical and esoteric movements. These schools of thought and practice were usually suppressed, or diluted and made harmless, in whatever society they appeared. Peasant witchcraft in Europe, Tantrism in Bengal, Quakers in England, Tachikawa-ryú in Japan, Ch'an in China. These are all outcroppings of the Great Subculture which runs underground all through history. This is the tradition that runs without break from Paleo-Siberian Shamanism and Magdalenian cave-painting; through megaliths and Mysteries, astronomers, ritualists, alchemists and Albigensians; gnostics and vagantes, right down to Golden Gate Park.

The Great Subculture has been attached in part to the official religions but is different in that it transmits a community style of life, with an ecstatically positive vision of spiritual and physical love; and is opposed for very fundamental reasons to the Civilization Establishment.

It has taught that man's natural being is to be trusted and followed; that we need not look to a model or rule imposed from outside in searching for the center; and that in following the grain, one is being truly "moral." It has recognized that for one to "follow the grain" it is necessary to look exhaustively into the negative and demonic potentials of the Unconscious, and by recognizing these powers—symbolically acting them out—one releases himself from these forces. By this profound exorcism and ritual drama, the Great Subculture destroys the one credible claim of Church and State to a necessary function.

All this is subversive to civilization: for civilization is built on hierarchy and specialization. A ruling class, to survive, must propose a Law: a law to work must have a hook into the social psyche—and the most effective way to achieve this is to make people doubt their natural worth and instincts, especially sexual. To make "human nature" suspect is also to make Nature—the wilderness—the adversary. Hence the ecological crisis of today.

We came, therefore, (and with many Western thinkers before us) to suspect that civilization may be overvalued. Before anyone says "This is ridiculous, we all know civilization is a necessary thing," let him read some cultural anthropology. Take a look at the lives of South African Bushmen, Micronesian navigators, the Indians of California; the researches of Claude Lévi-Strauss. Everything we have thought about man's welfare needs to be rethought. The tribe, it seems, is the newest development in the Great Subculture. We have almost unintentionally linked ourselves to a transmission of gnosis, a potential social order, and techniques of enlightenment, surviving from prehistoric times.

The most advanced developments of modern science and technology have come to support some of these views. Consequently the modern Tribesman, rather than being old-fashioned in his criticism of civilization, is the most relevant type in contemporary society. Nationalism, warfare, heavy industry and consumership, are already outdated and useless. The next great step of mankind is to step into the nature of his own mind—the real question is "just what is consciousness?"—and we must make the most intelligent and creative use of science in exploring these questions. The man of wide international experience, much learning and leisure—luxurious product of our long and sophisticated history—may with good reason wish to live simply, with few tools and minimal clothes, close to nature.

The Revolution has ceased to be an ideological concern. Instead, people are trying it out right now—communism in small communities, new family organization. A million people in America and another million in England and Europe. A vast underground in Russia, which will come out in the open four or five years hence, is now biding. How do they recognize each other? Not always by beards, long hair, bare feet or beads. The signal is a bright and tender look; calmness and gentleness, freshness and ease of manner. Men, women and children—all of whom together hope to follow the timeless path of love and wisdom, in affectionate company with the sky, winds, clouds, trees, waters, animals and grasses—this is the tribe.

BENJAMIN BARBER *(b. 1939)*

A crucial question for the viability of anarchism is the breadth and popularity of its principles. Barber addresses himself to the question of why anarchism has never gained great popularity. He places part of the blame on its unsuccessful popularizers. The anarchist, he claims, is "a proselytizing aristocrat who, possessed by a noblesse oblige of the apocalyptic, is driven to share his own transfiguration with the people. He is an egalitarian elitist dedicated to the notion that all men can be made superior."

While Barber presents enough evidence to show that his case surely applies to some anarchists, a real question remains as to whether it applies equally well to all anarchists. Specifically, we want to know whether it applies to Martin Buber and Gary Snyder, whose gentle voices seem inappropriate targets for Barber's attack. Is there a new anarchism, and if so, has Barber appreciated its difference from the old? For example, his first piece of evidence has backfired. He cites James Joll as acknowledging in 1964 in The Anarchists *that the movement Joll is writing about has failed and "no longer exists as a significant historical force." Yet in 1971, Joll and David Apter edited a book of essays entitled* Anarchism Today, *and Joll ended the book with this sentence: "At least, as the essays in this volume clearly show, the international experience of the past few years has proven that, in one form or another, anarchism is, in the second half of the twentieth century, still very much a living tradition." More recently Harvard philosopher Robert Nozick has attracted attention (and a National Book Award) for his* Anarchy, State, and Utopia *(1974). Finally, the narcissistic withdrawal from society described by Wolfe and the growing libertarian movement in electoral politics, both feed on and nourish an anarchistic tradition that seems alive and well in the eighties.*

Barber's essay includes an interesting argument showing why certain forms of anarchism are bound to be unsuccessful. He speaks of the anarchists' penchant for standing the naturalistic fallacy on its head. The so-called naturalistic fallacy is to claim that things ought *to be as they* are; *for example, an extreme form would be the old idea that if we were meant to fly, we would have wings; since we do not have wings, "by nature" we ought not to fly. Barber is saying that anarchists reverse the naturalistic fallacy when they see humanity only as it ought to be and not as it is.*

Who is correct? It seems to me that the new anarchists are correct about what humanity could *be. They share with Rousseau a vivid sense of humanity's possibilities.*

But the call for political action depends for its cogency on the claim that enough people already conform to the anarchist vision. Otherwise, as Barber suggests, premature and abortive movements end only in reaction—a more repressive, less liberated existence.

Poetry and Revolution:
The Anarchist as Reactionary

> There, where the state ceaseth—pray look thither my brethren! Do you not see it, the rainbow and the bridges of the Superman?
>
> Nietzsche, *Thus Spake Zarathustra*

> Now all bonds are burst that bound me.
> Now my flag shall wave around me.
> Though none follow where I lead.
>
> Ibsen, *Brand*

Anarchism is dead. Certification papers can be found in any number of recent histories and biographies.[1] Nevertheless, anarchism lives: in the banners and slogans of the French Student Movement, in New York townhouse laboratories where amateur chemists forge weapons of terror at the risk of their lives, in the syncretic vision of the anti-authoritarian young Left, and in the street theater and comic braggadocio of the Yippies.

The typologies which have been manufactured to divide anarchists into individualists and collectivists, rationalists and irrationalists, pacifists and terrorists, nationalists and humanists, or progressives and Luddites may suffice in the dissection of anarchism's historical corpse, but they leave the more practical mysteries of the movement unresolved and thus are remarkably unhelpful in dealing with the minuscule anarchist renaissance which has attended the birth of the 1970's.

To comprehend anarchism as a historical force and as a potentially significant contemporary movement requires the focusing of attention on a different order of questions. Why has anarchism been a movement of poets rather than first-order philosophers? Of saints rather than social scientists? Of exemplary rebels rather than successful revolutionaries? Of theatrical eccentrics rather than systematic reformers? Of legends rather than accomplishments? Peruse the list of notables: Godwin, Shelley, Proudhon, Stirner, Tolstoy, Courbet, Kropotkin, Bakunin, Nechayev, Pissaro, Ravachol, Sorel, Cafiero, Makhno, Seurat, Durruti—aristocrats, dilettantes, visionaries, adventurers, literati, poets, and madmen. Where are the circumspect philosophers? The careful students of the social system? The dedicated representatives of the public will? The Hobbeses, the Webers, the Castros of anarchism are nowhere to be found.

---

[1]In *The Anarchists* (Boston, 1964), James Joll devotes the greater part of his introduction to a defense of why he is writing the history of a movement which has failed and no longer exists as a significant historical force.

But this is not the only puzzle. The anarchists are not only a strange breed of revolutionaries, they are a tribe of failures. Their failure lies less in their inability to liberate any sizable collectivity of men from the tyranny of authority than in their inability to attract any significant number of men to their peculiar vision of liberation. The question is not so much why they failed to vanquish the exploiters as why they failed to move the exploited. Where nationalism, liberal democracy, syndicalism (unionism), and Marxism succeeded, anarchism failed. Alone among nineteenth-century movements for change, it won no permanent victories, secured no trustworthy allies, and attracted no large-scale support. Only in Spain in the 1930's did it enjoy a brief encounter with success. But Spanish anarcho-syndicalism, deeply enmeshed in union organization, military planning, and peasant communalism, was an anomaly whose features are not easily reconciled with anarchism elsewhere. And even in Spain, the movement finally failed—even less able to contend with Communism than with Fascism.

These two puzzles—the peculiarities of anarchism's leaders, its failure to secure a mass following—fit together to form a picture which raises fundamental questions about the viability of anarchism as a philosophy of revolution. If there is any unity at all to be found among the anarchists it is in their common antipathy to political order (whether established or disestablished)and their concomitant dedication not merely to the eventual achievement of radical alternatives, but to the necessity for a revolutionary (though not always violent or cataclysmic) overthrow of present order to reach their goals. Anarchism is, then, a doctrine of revolution, and anarchists are always rebels (whatever else they may be).

It is critical that anarchism be defined as a doctrine of action rather than as a passive metaphysic, because it is in the problems raised by revolutionary strategy and tactics that the beginnings of an answer to our questions are to be found.

The anarchists have never satisfactorily reconciled their multiple and disparate visions of man and society as they conceive them following the revolutionary overthrow of authority with the actual requisites of successful revolutionary activity. Although they have often propounded the inseparability of means and ends—as, for example, in Bakunin's rejection of central organization and political action in the First International[2]—they have never managed to translate the doctrine into a consistent and effective instrument of revolution. Deterred by their fierce sense of mission from adopting a posture of utopian isolationism that would permit them to depict alternative futures without taking responsibility for developing the strategies required for their realization,[3] they nevertheless have not been able to bring themselves to treat strategy in terms divorced from utopia. Not even those among them possessed of a Godwinean mildness can be labeled gradualist, but neither can the most impatient and venomous be called a master strategist. For the inseparability of means and ends makes compromise a sin; and

[2]For a sharply critical discussion of the controversy from Marx's position see Engels's *Letter to T. Cuno* dated January 24, 1872 in Marx/Engels, *Selected Works*, II (Moscow, 1951).

[3]I have in mind the utopias of such thinkers as Plato or More or Swift, which were not intended to be taken as doctrinaire programs for revolutionary action.

though they are not content to be mere "visionary utopians"[4] they are equally unwilling to accommodate themselves to the realities upon which successful revolutions depend. As Andrew Hacker has written, "quite clearly anarchists wish to have it all ways at once."[5] The purity of utopia but the impact of revolution. And so, hanging somewhere between the ideal and the real, between their vision for the future and their aspirations for the present, the anarchists end by treating the men upon whom they wish to foist a revolution as figments of their own utopian ideals. Utopia becomes an operations' plan, men as they actually exist are treated as if they had already become that which the revolution aspires to make them. Bound by convention and shackled by authority, men are nonetheless entreated to behave like Shelley's Prometheus Unbound:

> Sceptreless, free, uncircumscribed—but man:
> Equal, unclassed, tribeless, and nationless,
> Exempt from awe, worship, degree, the king
> Over himself . . .

Through a confluence of their visionary utopianism and their proselytizing zeal, the anarchists manage to stand the naturalistic fallacy on its head: not that natural man, as he is, is what he ought to be; but that utopian man, as the anarchist conceives he ought to be, is in fact what man is—the evidence of history and psychology notwithstanding. The realists mistake a limited but empirical portrait of man as he can be described under specified circumstances for man as he ought to be. The anarchist mistakes man as he ought to be in the ideal unauthoritarian society, for man as he is in actual authoritarian societies. Prince Kropotkin thus constructs an ingenious argument to demonstrate that natural selection favors cooperation (mutualism) rather than competition, at least within discrete species.[6] While Huxley and the Social Darwinists try to read a normative lesson on competition *out* of the empirical data assembled by Darwin, Kropotkin tries to read a normative lesson on cooperation *into* those same data, as annotated by his own Siberian research. Similarly, while for Hobbes the laws of justice are but artifices of man and the laws of nature but a codification of how men attuned to their own interest must behave in the state of nature, for Proudhon "the system of the laws of justice is the same as the system of the laws of the world, and they are present in the human soul not only as ideas or concepts but as emotions or feelings."[7] Once again, the difference is between reading laws, *a posteriori*, out of actual behavior, and thus justifying imperatives with naturalistic descriptions, and reading laws

---

[4]As Paul Avrich misleadingly calls them in his *The Russian Anarchists* (Princeton, 1967), p. 253.

[5]"Anarchism," *International Encyclopedia of Social Sciences* (New York, 1968).

[6]"Happily enough, competition is not the rule either in the animal world or in mankind. It is limited among animals to exceptional periods, and natural selection finds better fields for its activity. Better conditions are created by the *elimination of competition* by means of mutual aid and support. . . . 'Don't compete!' . . . That is the tendency of nature, not always realized in full, but always present." P. Kropotkin, *Mutual Aid: A Factor of Evolution* (New York, 1904), p. 74.

[7]Pierre-Joseph Proudhon, *Selected Writings* (New York, 1969), p. 230.

rooted in *a priori* reasoning into actual men, thus creating a "real" man at variance with observable behavior patterns.

In light of these observations, it can be no surprise that the anarchist sees the real verichrome world in strange, monochrome hues. It is a world of infinite mutability, a world without power where the limits of revolution are circumscribed only by the rebel's imagination, where the liberation of the masses becomes an impassioned exercise in exhortation. The communist-anarchist Senex warns his individualist comrades that "political sovereignty can be attenuated but cannot be conjured out of existence by a revolutionary fiat,"[8] but most anarchists remain, in Paul Avrich's characterization, neither "able or even willing to come to terms with the inescapable realities of political power."[9] The anarchist revolutionary camp is thus strewn with rhetoric, a living theater of intentional deceptions. (The blurring of the distinction between illusion and reality, which is the special virtue of theater, is remarkably well suited to the anarchist's collapse of the distinction between utopian possibilities and revolutionary realities.) Political strategy with its endless subtleties, its stultifying caveats, is abandoned in favor of "propaganda by the deed" (*le propagande par la fait*) which turns out, however, to consist neither in suasive propaganda nor in relevant political deeds but in a species of spectacular terror that, except for the bloodshed, might easily be taken as vaudeville. Bombs and slogans become interchangeable props in an interminable theatric. The more gentle anarchists—like Dostoyevsky's *Idiot*—live not only as saints in the world but as if they lived in a world of saints.[10] And among the violent, enthusiasm is confused with success, zeal with victory. In the manner that Bakunin once fantasized about a host of international, conspiratorial anarchist societies bringing Europe to the brink of cataclysm, Jerry Rubin today fantasizes about hordes of "niggers, and longhair scum invading white middle-class homes, fucking on the living room floor, crashing on the chandeliers, spewing sperm on the Jesus pictures, breaking the furniture and smashing Sunday school napalm-blood Amerika forever."[11] Both Bakunin and Rubin confound iconoclasm with revolution. Rubin wants to "outrage Amerika until the bourgeoisie dies of apoplexy,"[12] but systems of power, not being susceptible to coronaries, have not been known to expire and collapse in the face of profanity. In fact, underlying the profanity of the Yippies and the iconoclastic rhetoric of nihilistic anarchists like Nechayev is a profound innocence about what moves men and regimes to action.

[8]Senex, "Decentralization and Socialism," *Vanguard*, IV, no. 4 (July, 1938), p. 10. Lenin makes the same argument: "The majority of anarchists think and write about the future without understanding the present." Cited by L. Schapiro, *The Origin of the Communist Autocracy* (New York, 1955), p. 182.
[9]Avrich, loc. cit.
[10]A telling difference between white radicals and black militants is the realism with which the blacks size up their opponents; Julius Lester notes that the enemies of the nineteenth-century abolitionist Garrison "were thieves and murderers, not candidates for sainthood." *Look Out Whitey! Black Power's Gon' Get Your Mama* (New York, 1969), p. 41.
[11]Jerry Rubin, *Do It!* (New York, 1970), p. 111.
[12]*Ibid.*, p. 112. The metamorphosis of politics into theatrics is reflected in popular journals that increasingly treat "political" events in their theater sections. "Is Abbie Hoffman the Will Shakespeare of the 1970's?" asks a recent Sunday *New York Times* theater columnist (October 11, 1970). (He isn't.)

In their naiveté, the anarchists are blind to the truly profane element in politics—the struggle for power among ambitious and competitive interest-oriented beings. Marx speaks of the profane in this sense when he berates Proudhon for missing the "profane origin and the profane history of the categories which he deifies."[13]

For all the anarchists' profanity, their view of actual men is wildly romanticized. Hunger, greed, ambition, avarice, the will to power, to glory, to honor, and to security which have played some role in all traditional ethnologies find no place in the anarchist portrait of man. Max Stirner, the turgid, darkly romantic early nineteenth-century anarchist, may appear as an irrationalist, but his argument for the disenthrallment of Ego is neither an invitation to the exploiters to widen their dominion nor a justification of crass, animal competition. It is a selective call to men to respond to the *unique* in themselves, to throw off the constraints with which society and religion have affected to contain their real selves. Stirner despises the mind—that same reason upon which the eighteenth-century English rationalist Godwin relies for the salvation of man—but his ultimate enemy is Godwin's enemy too: the hierachy of authority, the dominion of constraint. But where for Godwin dominion and hierarchy are products of ignorance, for Stirner they are products of reason: "Hierarchy is the dominion of thought, the dominion of mind."[14] Both seek autonomy and individuality; they differ only in where they think to have discovered them: Godwin, in the rational mind, Stirner in the unbridled Ego.[15]

Whether the thrust is toward puritanical constraint (as in Godwin or Proudhon) or toward psychic liberation (as in Stirner, Nietzsche, or the Yippies), the anarchist vision does not encompass the mundane species of placid, compromising men who for the most part inhabit the globe. Anarchists of every variety have forever gone among the people as prophets, with Zarathustra's proverb "Man is Something to be Surpassed" on their lips.[16] Reaching downward toward the primitive or upward toward the sublime, they have remained strangers to the middle regions where men live out their daily lives. They have been aggressors rather than interlocutors, proselytizers not listeners. The distinction between politics and ethics, between collective revolution and personal conversion, has escaped them in the search for what Emma Goldman (an American anarchist of the early part of the century) called a *"fundamental transvaluation of values."*[17] The anarchist becomes a "great TEACHER of the NEW ETHICS."[18]

---

[13]Marx, *Letter to P. V. Annekov,* Appendix to *The Poverty of Philosophy* (New York, 1963), p. 192. I do not mean to make a brief for the realist view of politics, which suggests that power is *all* there is to politics.

[14]Max Stirner, *The Ego and His Own* (New York, 1907), p. 95.

[15]Stirner's "Ego" is every bit as vague and indeterminate as the humanist's "man" which Stirner criticizes as "not a person, but an ideal, a spook."(*Ibid.,* p. 101.) It is in fact the particular device of his inverted naturalism noted above. Stirner's naturalism is assailed by Marx in *The German Ideology.*

[16]Friedrich Nietzsche, *Thus Spake Zarathustra,* in *The Philosophy of Nietzsche* (New York: Modern Library), p. 36.

[17]Emma Goldman, "My Further Disillusionment in Russia," in L. I. Krimerman and L. Perry, eds., *Patterns of Anarchy* (Garden City, N.Y., 1966), p. 111. (Emphasis in original.) The use of Nietzsche's phrase "transvaluation of values" (*Umwertung aller Werte*) is of course no mere coincidence.

[18]*Ibid.,* p. 113. (Emphasis in original.)

No revolutionaries can compromise with their enemies and survive, but the anarchists are unwilling to compromise with their followers. They expect men to endure a physical hunger in the struggle to quench a spiritual thirst. "I think," advises Tolstoy, "that the efforts of those who wish to improve our social life should be directed towards the liberation of themselves."[19] The enemy is within, not without, and so the anarchist posture must be one of unceasing exhortation: "Surpass Thyselves!" Like the preacher Brand in Ibsen's most austere play, the anarchist is driven by a fervent passion, both holy and profane, to lead the people out of the Egypt of their unseeing, apathetic lives into a promised land of redemptive liberation:

> Come thou, young man—fresh and free—
> Let a life-breeze lighten thee
> From this dim vault's clinging dust.
> Conquer with me! For thou must
> One day waken, one day rise,
> Nobly break with compromise;—
> Up, and fly the evil days,
> Fly the maze of middle ways,
> Strike the foreman full and fair,
> Battle to the death declare.

The revolution becomes a taking of vows;[20] not a promise to the people that they shall receive but a demand that they sacrifice; not rest to their bodies but spiritual travail and the searing transfiguration of their souls. Eventual salvation, but apocalypse and purgatory first.[21]

The cleansing by fire advocated by the violent anarchists seems intended not only to purge the enemy but to sanctify the revolutionary masses as well: "It is to violence," cries Sorel, "that Socialism owes those high ethical values by means of which it brings *salvation* to the modern world."[22] "The revolutionist is a doomed man," prophesies Nechayev in the bleak opening paragraph of his grim *Revolutionary Catechism:* "He has no personal interests, no affairs, sentiments, attachments, property, not even a name of his own. Everything in him is absorbed by one exclusive interest, one thought, one passion—the revolution."[23] Like Brand,

---

[19]Cited by George Woodcock, *Anarchism: A History of Libertarian Ideas and Movements* (New York, 1962), p. 225.

[20]Gandhi, though an anarchist more in spirit than in practice, exacted from the followers of his program of discipline vows of Truthfulness, Nonviolence, Celibacy, Control of the Palate, Nonthieving, and Nonpossession, among others.

[21]The peasants of Andalusia who tried to establish village communes on the ascetic blueprint of the anarchist leader Durruti experienced a period of trial and torment rather than liberation, and Durruti's success in the Spanish Civil War—like Makhno's in the Bolshevik campaigns against the White Forces, in which his anarchist units participated—was due primarily to his military prowess. For an account of an anarchist commune during the Spanish Civil War see Franz Borkenau, *The Spanish Cockpit* (London, 1937).

[22]Georges Sorel, *Reflections on Violence* (New York, 1950), p. 249. (Emphasis in original.) Sorel's language is typically anarchistic in its messianic tone.

[23]Cited by Philip Pomper, *The Russian Revolutionary Intelligentsia* (New York, 1970), p. 95.

Nechayev can promise only a crown of thorns; his way is hard, his dedication total. The man of the middle regions can look on in awe, but can he follow? Anarchism speaks no simple dialect; it rants, in the language of the possessed, of redemption through nihilism, rebirth through sacrifice.[24] It commences mildly enough with the ascetic rationalism of a Godwin asking only that men contain their passion and "propagate their species, not because a certain sensible pleasure is annexed to this action, but because it is right that the species should be propagated," and that the "manner in which they exercise this function . . . be regulated by the dictates of reason and duty."[25] It culminates in Nechayev's renunciation of everything save the revolution: "Surpass Thyselves O Men!"

But revolutions, though they may require renunciation, are fired by the spirit of appropriation. They may produce that "intoxication" which Stirner saw as essential to their success,[26] but they are produced by desperation and sustained by the foresight of the lifting of burdens. George Woodcock praises the more saintly anarchists for calling "on us to stand on our own moral feet like a generation of princes,"[27] but the revolutionary masses are not princes in search of Grace; they are mere men, hungry and oppressed, in search of subsistence, security, and perhaps a modicum of individual autonomy (liberty).

The anarchist remains, however, a proselytizing aristocrat who, possessed by a *noblesse oblige* of the apocalyptic, is driven to share his own transfiguration with the people. He is an egalitarian elitist dedicated to the notion that all men can be made superior. Like the artist, he perceives a larger world; like the prophet, a more enriching plain of experience; like the utopian, a more humane form of community. But unlike these visionaries, he is an impatient social activist, a driving revolutionary who would embody his perceptions in the real world, *now*. He is the *Uebermensch* [overman] of the underdogs. . . .

In his *Anarchism and Socialism*, the Russian Marxist Plekhanov draws a biased but suggestive picture of the relationship between the anarchist's ideals, his hatred of compromise, and his acquiescence to terror:

> Whenever the proletariat makes an attempt to somewhat ameliorate its economic position, "large-hearted people," vowing they love the proletariat most tenderly, rush in from all points of the compass . . . put spokes in the wheel of the movement, do their utmost to prove the movement is useless. . . . When the proletariat takes no notice of this, and pursues its "immediate economic" aims undisturbed . . . the same "large-hearted people" re-appear upon the scene armed with bombs. . . .
>
> An Anarchist will have nothing to do with "parliamentarism," since it only lulls the people to sleep . . . [no] "reforms," since reforms

---

[24]Dostoyevsky's novel about the nihilist-anarchist movement in the early part of the nineteenth century is titled *The Possessed*.

[25]William Godwin, *An Enquiry Concerning Political Justice*, 2 vols. (Philadelphia, 1796), vol. 2, Book VIII, chap. 6.

[26]"For every [revolutionary] effort arrives at reaction when it come to discreet reflection, and storms forward in the original action only so long as it is an *intoxication*." *Op. cit.*, p. 144.

[27]Woodcock, *op. cit.*, p. 476.

are but so many compromises with the possessing classes. He wants a revolution, a "full, complete, immediate and immediately economic" revolution. To attain this end he arms himself with a saucepan full of explosive materials and throws it amongst the public in a theatre or a cafe.

Plekhanov's conclusion is overblown, but it helps to explain why the reactionary right has found such succor in certain anarchist traditions:

Thus, in the name of revolution, the Anarchists serve the cause of reaction; in the name of morality they approve the most immoral acts; in the name of liberty they trample underfoot all the rights of their fellows.

The ambivalence of anarchism toward the people as a revolutionary collective is compounded by the historical circumstances in which the nineteenth-century movement sprang up. The philosophical core of anarchism consists of a rejection of all authority—particularly those oppressive forms of authority which manifested themselves in a statist coercion. Yet by the nineteenth century, the more tyrannical and arbitrary forms of statist authority had already been deposed by liberal and democratic theory—in theory if not in fact. The very concept of legitimacy had been articulated precisely to discriminate between acceptable and unacceptable varieties of authority. Though initially grounded in natural law reasoning, it had by the nineteenth century come to be seen as a function of consent—either explicitly (majoritarianism) or implicitly (the social contract). Though liberals were careful to limit the sphere of action of legitimate authority, they concurred in the general recognition that authority was a prerequisite of civilized life and that justifications for authority were necessary. Rousseau and Kant further solidified the notion of legitimate authority by exploring the relationship between individual autonomy and obedience to law.

The upshot of these developments in political philosophy was that anarchist theory—already disposed against the pliant, yielding masses by its aristocratic temper—found itself face to face not with the abstract notion of authority but with the concrete democratic justification of legitimacy. Of the traditional arguments for authority, only the one rooted in consent survived and flourished into the nineteenth century. Godwin had clearly perceived this at the end of the eighteenth century. "The Voice of the People is not . . . 'the voice of Truth and of God,'" he warns; "consent cannot convert right into wrong."[28] Proudhon was, by the beginning of the nineteenth, to be far more blunt: "Universal Suffrage is the Counterrevolution" became a lasting slogan of the movement.

The anarchists saw, much more clearly than liberals like Tocqueville and Mill (who shared their elitism), that authority blessed by numbers was far less tractable than authority consecrated by papal benediction and upheld by royalty. The more stentorian the voice, the more numerous the people, the more dangerous the enemy! Max Stirner cautioned:

[28]*Op. cit.*, Book II, chap. 5.

The monarch in the person of the "royal master" has been a paltry monarch compared with the new monarch, the "sovereign nation." This *monarchy* was a thousand times severer, stricter, and more consistent. Against the new monarch there was no longer any right, any privilege at all; how limited the "absolute king" of the *ancient regime* looks in comparison! The revolution effected the transformation of *limited monarchy* into *absolute monarchy.*[29]

Finally, anarchist theory has no choice but to reject the entire mode of discourse by which degrees and kinds of justice and injustice are distinguished in the political realm; it must reject political theory itself in favor of poetry and revelation. Like Herbert Read, it can see nothing to choose between fascism and democracy, between a Hitler and a Churchill.[30] Indeed like Read, it must view the "incursions of democracy [as] far more dangerous because they are far more deceitful."[31] And so the contemporary anarchist not only sees nothing in the choice between Humphrey and Nixon (it is not at all clear that there is anything in this choice), but also sees nothing in the choice between Wallace and Julian Bond. They are all tainted, all politicians playing the power game whether for or against the people.

Robert Paul Wolff represents the philosophical extreme of the rejection of political discourse: "On the basis of a lengthy reflection upon the concept of *de jure* legitimate authority," he relates with characteristic understatement, "I have come to the conclusion that philosophical anarchism is true. That is to say, I believe that there is not, and there could not be, a state that has a right to command and whose subjects have a binding obligation to obey."[32] If authority is to be sent into exile, it is legitimacy that must be banished. The temperamental predilection of the anarchists for elitism thus finds its philosophical analog in the need to rebut the claims not simply of democratic theory, but of political theory generally. At the same time, anarchist arguments combating democracy confirm the anarchist's temperamental disdain for the people and seem to justify his refusal to articulate revolutionary goals appropriate to the practical needs of men.

Our questions then answer themselves—for the answers are in the asking; the puzzle is solved. Anarchism has attracted no social scientists because its concerns are not with social realities; it has intrigued no first order philosophers because it is riddled with paradox, stranded between its lust for revolution and its penchant for utopia. It has attracted no followers because it has had leaders who would lead where men cannot or will not follow. It disdains the men it would liberate. At the crucial moment it prefers its own visions to their needs.

In the anarchist hierarchy of values, it is the primacy of the aesthetic that is

[29]*Op. cit.*, p. 132.

[30]"I am concerned to show that from a certain point of view there is nothing to choose between fascism and democracy." Herbert Read, *To Hell with Culture* (New York, 1964), p. 49. Also see p. 46.

[31]*Ibid.*, p. 49.

[32]"On Violence," *Journal of Philosophy*, LXVI, no. 19 (1969), p. 607. See also his *In Defense of Anarchism* (New York, 1970) in which he elaborates his assault on classical democratic theory....

most evident. The anarchist poet Laurent Tailhade speaks at least a little for all anarchists when he writes, "What matter the victims provided the gesture is beautiful?" Anarchism is a movement of the imagination—real men, mundane needs, come second.

The lesson for the contemporary anarchist ripple—it hardly qualifies as a movement—is obvious enough. Those who would save society must first face some difficult choices. They must choose between the solipsistic imagination and the realities of exploitation and human misery; between the theatrics of grand tragedy and the dull desperate plight of uninteresting prisoners of poverty, ignorance, and mediocrity; between pristine ideals and the possibilities of actual change. Not all good things mix: ultimately, they may have to choose between poetry and revolution.

transition:
politics and ecology

In recent years the management of scarce resources has become one of the chief problems facing the polity. The two essays that follow take fundamentally different approaches to the problem. The first asks why we have so mismanaged our relationship with nature and points out the dangers of an attitude of mastery over nature. The second asks what we must do to avoid further trouble and warns that totalitarian dictatorship may be the only politics capable of managing increasingly scarce resources. In short, one mastery leads to another. An attitude of rapacious mastery over nature necessitates a mastery over men and women.

In part six we will turn to relationships between men and women. Throughout history, attitudes toward women have often paralleled attitudes toward nature. Mastery over mother nature goes hand in hand with mastery over the feminine. The following two essays on ecology therefore look forward to the next part's essays on feminism. In both cases the issue is liberation from a misplaced mastery.

The essays on ecology also refer to the fundamental issues of politics raised in earlier discussions. If the state is not natural but artificial, then why can't we choose to minimize political restraints on behavior? Anarchists like Gary Snyder would have us live close to nature, in harmony with her laws rather than man's. To Murray Bookchin, in his *Post-Scarcity Anarchism* (1971), the state seemed unnecessary in an age when there appeared to be more than enough natural resources to go around. Then came the Arab oil embargo of 1973. The rising price of oil since that time seems to have vitiated the conditions of Bookchin's anarchistic arguments. When we confront the scarcity of nonrenewable fossil fuels, anarchism looks like a luxury we can ill afford.

Yet the verdict of history has yet to be heard. Even within the environmental movement—and within feminism—two different attitudes are manifest. One insists that a new mastery is the answer to our problems: political institutions must master our untutored inclinations to exploit both women and the natural environment. The Equal Rights Amendment and requirements for Environmental Impact Statements both reflect an effort to legislate a new chapter in human history. Another attitude would suggest in opposition to the first that legislating human nature is a new version of the old attempt to master and manipulate the natural environment. While in favor of feminism and dedicated to the preservation of a healthy natural environment, the second attitude would resist the use of politics to master human nature.

These days it is easy to be in favor of feminism and the natural environment. Yet the task of philosophy, ever since Socrates, has been to question confident assertions. It is not a matter of returning to old certitudes like male supremacy or our natural mastery over nature. Instead, a genuinely philosophical approach to ecology and feminism will probe beneath the new certitudes to see where old habits of thought lie hidden and unrecognized. The Socratic endeavor requires us to question whether we have truly overcome male chauvinism as long as we preserve a human chauvinism over nature. Or, if we accept the historical development of politics and technology as part of our human condition, then how can we revert to a romance with mother nature as a premise for feminism?

These are difficult questions. I pose them as a way of adding depth and context to the issues debated in the following essays. Much more is at stake in our relationship to nature than immediately meets the unreflective eye.

GREGORY BATESON *(b. 1904–1980)*

With the publication of his book, Mind and Nature, *in 1979, Gregory Bateson received the widespread attention he has long deserved. The son of William Bateson, a leading British biologist, Gregory Bateson trained in anthropology and has been a contributor to such diverse fields as cybernetic information theory and psychiatry. He is recognized by many as one of the most inventive thinkers of this century. R. D. Laing, represented earlier by* The Politics of the Family, *has been heavily influenced by Bateson.*

Throughout his working career, whether researching dolphins, exploring evolutionary theory, or studying the dynamics of families, Bateson's thinking constantly revolves around the theme central to this anthology, namely, the interrelationships between the microcosm and the macrocosm, the part and the whole, self and world. Two propositions pertaining to social theory as well as to ecology occur again and again in his writing. The first is that the unit of survival is never a single organism, not even a single species, but always species-plus-environment. Relationships of interdependence permit neither the individual nor a species to survive apart from the environment that sustains it. Bateson's second recurrent idea is that learning theory, epistemology and evolutionary theory all face similar problems, since the evolution of a species depends on its learning to adapt by genetic change to its environment. Genetic adaptation, whether by selection or mutation, is learning writ large, a macrocosmic mirror for the microcosmic learning processes of an individual. Both processes of adaptation involve processes of trial and error. Both depend on the coding of information—in the genetic material for evolution, in the brain for learning. We know little about the physiology of memory or the coding mechanisms in DNA. Yet our ignorance of the relevant physiology need not keep us from learning more about the logical structures of both the macrocosmic and microcosmic contexts through a process of mutual comparison of problems and their solutions.

The following testimony before a Senate Committee in Hawaii offers a succinct summary of some of Bateson's ideas on ecology. As important as the content of Bateson's remarks, the form and structure of his thinking is worth particular note. The diagram he draws to describe the feedback relationships between population, hubris, and technology could as well describe the relationships between, say, political, psychological, and theological forms of patriarchy. Bateson's mode of thinking is anything but reductionist. Rather than reducing politics to psychology, or psychology to physiology, Bateson would have us see patterns of mutually reinforcing relationships that pervade different dimensions of experience.

The Roots of Ecological Crisis*

Summary: Other testimony has been presented regarding bills to deal with particular problems of pollution and environmental degradation in Hawaii. It is hoped that the proposed Office of Environmental Quality Control and the Environmental Center at the University of Hawaii will go beyond this *ad hoc* approach and will study the more basic causes of the current rash of environmental troubles.

The present testimony argues that these basic causes lie in the *combined* action of (*a*) technological advance; (*b*) population increase; and (*c*) conventional (but wrong) ideas about the nature of man and his relation to the environment.

It is concluded that the next five to ten years will be a period like the Federalist period in United States history in which the whole philosophy of government, education, and technology must be debated.

We submit:

(1) That all *ad hoc* measures leave uncorrected the deeper causes of the trouble and, worse, usually permit those causes to grow stronger and become compounded. In medicine, to relieve the symptoms without curing the disease is wise and sufficient *if and only if* either the disease is surely terminal *or* will cure itself.

The history of DDT illustrates the fundamental fallacy of *ad hoc* measures. When it was invented and first put to use, it was itself an *ad hoc* measure. It was discovered in 1939 that the stuff was an insecticide (and the discoverer got a Nobel Prize). Insecticides were "needed" (*a*) to increase agricultural products; and (*b*) to save people, especially troops overseas, from malaria. In other words, DDT was a symptomatic cure for troubles connected with the increase of population.

By 1950, it was known to scientists that DDT was seriously toxic to many other animals (Rachel Carson's popular book *Silent Spring* was published in 1962).

But in the meanwhile, (*a*) there was a vast industrial commitment to DDT manufacture; (*b*) the insects at which DDT was directed were becoming immune; (*c*) the animals which normally ate those insects were being exterminated; (*d*) the population of the world was permitted by DDT to increase.

In other words, the world became *addicted* to what was once an *ad hoc* measure and is now known to be a major danger. Finally in 1970, we begin to prohibit or control this danger. And we still do not know, for example, whether the human species on its present diet can surely survive the DDT which is already circulating in the world and will be there for the next twenty years even if its use is immediately and totally discontinued.

---

*This document was testimony on behalf of the University of Hawaii, Committee on Ecology and Man, presented in March, 1970, before a Committee of the State Senate of Hawaii, in favor of a bill (S.B. 1132). This bill proposed the setting up of an Office of Environmental Quality Control in Government and an Environmental Center in the University of Hawaii. The bill was passed.

It is now reasonably certain (since the discovery of significant amounts of DDT in the penguins of Antarctica) that *all* the fish-eating birds as well as the land-going carnivorous birds and those which formerly ate insect pests are doomed. It is probable that all the carnivorous fish[1] will soon contain too much DDT for human consumption and may themselves become extinct. It is possible that the earthworms, at least in forests and other sprayed areas, will vanish—with what effect upon the forests is anybody's guess. The plankton of the high seas (upon which the entire planetary ecology depends) is believed to be still unaffected.

That is the story of one blind application of an *ad hoc* measure; and the story can be repeated for a dozen other inventions.

(2) That the proposed combination of agencies in State Government and in the University should address itself to diagnosing, understanding and, if possible, suggesting remedies for the wider processes of social and environmental degradation in the world and should attempt to define Hawaii's policy in view of these processes.

(3) That *all* of the many current threats to man's survival are traceable to three root causes:

(*a*) technological progress

(*b*) population increase

(*c*) certain errors in the thinking and attitudes of Occidental culture. Our "values" are wrong.

We believe that all three of these fundamental factors are necessary conditions for the destruction of our world. In other words, we *optimistically* believe that the correction of any *one* of them would save us.

(4) That these fundamental factors certainly interact. The increase of population spurs technological progress and creates that anxiety which sets us against our environment as an enemy; while technology both facilitates increase in population and reinforces our arrogance, or "hubris," vis-à-vis the natural environment.

The attached diagram illustrates the interconnections. It will be noted that in this diagram each corner is clockwise, denoting that each is by itself a self-promoting (or, as the scientists say, "autocatalytic") phenomenon: the bigger the population, the faster it grows; the more technology we have, the faster the rate of new invention; and the more we believe in our "power" over an enemy environment, the more "power" we seem to have and the more spiteful the environment seems to be.

Similarly the pairs of corners are clockwise connected to make three self-promoting subsystems.

The problem facing the world and Hawaii is simply how to introduce some anticlockwise processes into this system.

How to do this should be a major problem for the proposed State Office of Environmental Quality Control and the University Environmental Center.

---

[1]Ironically, it turns out that fish will probably become poisonous as carriers of mercury rather than DDT. [*G.B. 1971*]

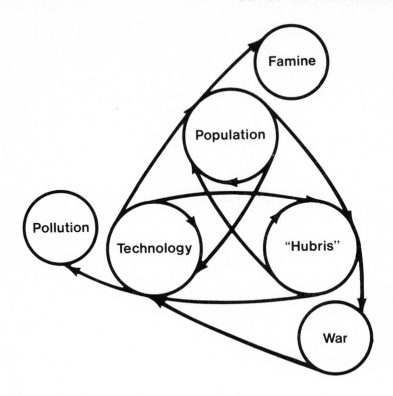

The Dynamics of Ecological Crisis

Adapted from p. 491 in *Steps to an Ecology of the Mind* by Gregory Bateson (T. Y. Crowell Co.). Copyright © 1972 by Harper & Row, Publishers, Inc. Reprinted by permission of the publisher.

It appears, at present, that the only possible entry point for reversal of the process is the conventional attitudes toward the environment.

(5) That further technological progress cannot now be prevented but that it can possibly be steered in appropriate directions, to be explored by the proposed offices.

(6) That the population explosion is the single most important problem facing the world today. As long as population continues to increase, we must expect the continuous creation of new threats to survival, perhaps at a rate of one per year, until we reach the ultimate condition of famine (which Hawaii is in no position to face). We offer no solution here to the population explosion, but we note that every solution which we can imagine is made difficult or impossible by the thinking and attitudes of Occidental culture.

(7) That the very first requirement for ecological stability is a balance between the rates of birth and death. For better or for worse, we have tampered

with the death rate, especially by controlling the major epidemic diseases and the death of infants. Always, in any living (*i.e.*, ecological) system, every increasing imbalance will generate its own limiting factors as side effects of the increasing imbalance. In the present instance, we begin to know some of Nature's ways of correcting the imbalance—smog, pollution, DDT poisoning, industrial wastes, famine, atomic fallout, and war. *But the imbalance has gone so far that we cannot trust Nature not to overcorrect.*

(8) That the ideas which dominate our civilization at the present time date in their most virulent form from the Industrial Revolution. They may be summarized as:

(a) It's us *against* the environment.

(b) It's us *against* other men.

(c) It's the individual (or the individual company, or the individual nation) that matters.

(d) We *can* have unilateral control over the environment and must strive for that control.

(e) We live within an infinitely expanding "frontier."

(f) Economic determinism is common sense.

(g) Technology will do it for us.

We submit that these ideas are simply proved *false* by the great but ultimately destructive achievements of our technology in the last 150 years. Likewise they appear to be false under modern ecological theory. *The creature that wins against its environment destroys itself.*

(9) That other attitudes and premises—other systems of human "values"— have governed man's relation to his environment and his fellow man in other civilizations and at other times. Notably, the ancient Hawaiian civilization and the Hawaiians of today are unconcerned about Occidental "hubris." In other words, our way is not the only possible human way. *It is conceivably changeable.*

(10) That change in our thinking has already begun—among scientists and philosophers, and among young people. But it is not only long-haired professors and long-haired youth who are changing their ways of thought. There are also many thousands of businessmen and even legislators who *wish* they could change but feel that it would be unsafe or not "common sense" to do so. The changes will continue as inevitably as technological progress.

(11) That these changes in thought will impact upon our government, economic structure, educational philosophy, and military stance because the old premises are deeply built into all these sides of our society.

(12) That nobody can predict what new patterns will emerge from these drastic changes. We hope that the period of change may be characterized by wisdom, rather than by either violence or the fear of violence. Indeed, the ultimate goal of this bill is to make such a transition possible.

13) We conclude that the next five to ten years will be a period comparable to the Federalist period in United States history. New philosophies of government, education, and technology must be debated both inside the government and in the public press, and especially among leading citizens. The University of Hawaii and the State Government could take a lead in these debates.

WILLIAM OPHULS *(b. 1934)*

The concluding essay of part five, from William Ophuls' Ecology and the Politics of Scarcity (1977), rounds out the discussion begun in part four. Ophuls mentions Aristotle, Locke, Plato, and Marx; and his argument revolves around sustained discussions of Hobbes and Rousseau. The central issue returns us to Mill's concern, the limits to the authority of society over the individual, only now the burden of proof is turned the other way: the limits of individual liberty in a society faced with ecological scarcity. Ophuls argues that much of our philosophical heritage presupposes an open frontier as the condition for individualism. Now that we see our ecology as a closed system with depletable natural resources, we confront a political context not so distant from Hobbes' state of nature, "the return of scarcity portends the revival of age-old political evils, for our descendents if not for ourselves. In short, the golden age of individualism, liberty, and democracy is all but over."

Ophuls offers a superb summation of the issues presented in previous readings. Yet I find his argument profoundly disturbing. He takes us out of the frying pan of ecological catastrophe only to dangle us perilously close to the fire of authoritarian, perhaps even paternalistic, politics. While I heartily agree with parts of his argument— his account of the dangers of self-serving individualism—I can't help thinking that there is something very dangerous about surrendering too much liberty for the sake of better management of the ecology. If we surrender human freedom for human survival, will the survivors remain fully human?

Ophuls argues persuasively that we cannot rely on a "technological fix" as a substitute for limited natural resources. We may make some technological breakthroughs in the coming years, but a reliance on technology has a political price: society's dependence on a technological elite. But to what extent does Ophuls relegate us to a comparable dependence on a political elite to manage in times of ecological scarcity? For surely the science of ecology can be every bit as esoteric as technology.

In the end I want to play Rousseau to Ophuls' Hobbes. Rather than presuming a selfish individualism as the last word on human nature, I would like to hope that precisely the novelty of our ecological crisis might be an occasion for the rapid education of the human species to its collective interdependence. Some of the following essays on education, aesthetics, and spirituality point to possible substitutes for the political coercion Ophuls envisages. Meanwhile we might recall, as Ophuls reminds us of the political dimensions of our ecological crisis, that the Chinese character for crisis is composed of two figures, one for danger, and one for opportunity. As Ophuls himself suggests in his closing sentence, "the crisis of ecological scarcity might actually be turned into a grand opportunity to build a more humane post-industrial society."

The Politics of Scarcity

The Political Evils of Scarcity

...Scarcity is the source of original political sin: resources that are scantier than human wants have to be allocated by governments, for otherwise, naked conflict would result. In the words of philosopher Thomas Hobbes in *Leviathan* (1651, p. 107), the life of man in an anarchic "state of nature" is "solitary, poor, nasty, brutish, and short"; to prevent the perpetual struggle for power in a war of all against all, there must be a civil authority capable of keeping the peace by regulating property and other scarce goods. Scarcity thus makes politics inescapable.

Presumably, the establishment of a truly just civil authority would completely eliminate all the political problems that arise from scarcity. With all assured of a fair share of goods, social harmony would replace strife, and men would enjoy long and happy lives of peaceful cooperation. Unfortunately, this has never happened. Although they have certainly mitigated some of the worst aspects of the anarchic state of nature (especially the total insecurity that prevails in the war of all against all), civilized polities have always institutionalized a large measure of inequality, oppression, and conflict. Thus, in addition to being the source of original political sin, scarcity is also the root of political evil.

The reason is quite simple. For most of recorded history, societies have existed at the ecological margin, or very close to it. An equal division of income and wealth, therefore, would condemn all to a life of shared poverty. Not unnaturally, the tendency has been for political institutions to further impoverish the masses by a fractional amount so as to create a surplus enabling a small elite to enjoy the fruits of civilized life. Indeed, until recently energy has been so scarce that serfdom and slavery have been the norm—justifiably so, says Aristotle in his *Politics*, for otherwise genuine civilization would be impossible. Except for a few relatively brief periods when for some reason the burden of scarcity was temporarily lifted, inequality, oppression, and conflict have been very prominent features of political life, merely waxing and waning slightly according to the character of the rulers and other ephemeral factors.

Our own era has been the longest and certainly the most important exception. During roughly the last 450 years, the carrying capacity of the globe (and especially of the highly developed nations) has been markedly expanded, and several centuries of relative abundance have completely transformed the face of the earth and made our societies and our civilization what they are today—relatively open, egalitarian, libertarian, and conflict-free.

The Great Frontier

The causes of the four-century-long economic boom we have enjoyed are readily apparent: the European discovery and exploitation of the New World, Oceania, and other founts of virgin resources (for example, Persian Gulf oil); the take-off and rapid-growth phases of science-based, energy-intensive technology;

and the existence of vast reservoirs of "free" ecological goods like air and water to absorb the consequences of exploiting the new resources with the new technology. However, the first cause is clearly the most important.

Before the discovery of the New World, the population of Europe pressed hard on its means of subsistence; as a result, European societies were politically, economically, and socially closed. But with the opening up of a "Great Frontier" in the New World, Europe suddenly faced a seemingly limitless panorama of ecological riches—the area of land available for cultivation was suddenly multiplied about five times; vast stands of high-grade timber, a scarce commodity in Europe, stretched as far as the eye could see; gold and silver were there for the taking, and rich lodes of other metals lay ready for exploitation; the introduction of the potato and other new food crops from the New World boosted European agricultural production so sharply that the population doubled between 1750 and 1850. This bonanza of found wealth lifted the yoke of ecological scarcity and, coincidentally, created all the peculiar institutions and values characteristic of modern civilization—democracy, freedom, and individualism.*

Indeed, the existence of such ecological abundance is an indispensible premise of the libertarian doctrines of John Locke and Adam Smith, the two thinkers whose works epitomize the modern bourgeois views of political economy upon which all the institutions of open societies are based. For example, Locke (1690, paras. 27–29) justifies the institution of property by saying that it derives from the mixture of a man's labor with the original commons of nature. But he continually emphasizes that for one man to make part of what is the common heritage of mankind his own property does not work to the disadvantage of other men. Why? Because "there was still enough and as good left; and more than the yet unprovided could use" (para. 33). His argument on property by appropriation is shot through with references to the wilderness of the New World, which only needed to be occupied and cultivated to be turned into property for any man who desired it. Locke's justification of original property and the natural right of a man to appropriate it from nature thus rests on cornucopian assumptions: there is always more left; society can therefore be libertarian.

The economics of Adam Smith rests on a similar vision of ecological abundance. In fact, Smith is even more optimistic than Locke, for he stresses that the opportunity to become a man of property (and therefore to enjoy the benefits of liberty) now lies more in trade and industry than in agriculture, which is potentially limited by the availability of arable land. Indeed, says Smith, under prevailing conditions, simply striking off all the mercantilist shackles on economic development and permitting a free-for-all, laissez-faire system of wealth-getting to operate instead would generate "opulence," which would in turn liberate men from the social and political restrictions of feudalism. Smith's *The Wealth of*

---

*Of course, the idea of individualism antedated the discovery of the New World, but until then it had had little opportunity for concrete expression. However, once the boom permitted it to be expressed, individualism became the basis for almost all the most characteristic features of modernity: self-rule in democracy, self-enrichment in industrial capitalism, self-salvation in Protestantism.

Nations (1776) is therefore a manifesto for the attainment of political liberty through the economic exploitation of the found wealth of the Great Frontier.

The liberal ideas of Locke and Smith have not gone unchallenged, but with very few exceptions, liberals, conservatives, socialists, communists, and other modern ideologists have taken abundance for granted and assumed the necessity of further growth. They have disagreed only about how to produce enough wealth to satisfy the demands of hedonistic, materialistic "economic" men and about what constitutes a just division of the spoils. Karl Marx was even more utopian than either Locke or Smith, for he envisioned the eventual abolition of scarcity; he merely insisted that, on grounds of social justice, the march of progress be centrally directed by the state in the interest of those whose labor actually produced the goods.

But the boom is now over. The found wealth of the Great Frontier has been all but exhausted; technology is no real substitute, for it is merely a means of manipulating *what is already there* rather than a way of creating genuinely new resources on the scale of the Great Frontier. (Moreover, technology is encountering limits of its own.) Thus, a scarcity at least as intense as that prevailing in the pre-modern era, however different it may be in important respects, is about to replace abundance, and this will necessarily undercut the material conditions that have created and sustained current ideas, institutions, and practices. Once relative abundance and wealth of opportunity are no longer available to mitigate the harsh political dynamics of scarcity, the pressures favoring greater inequality, oppression, and conflict will build up, so that the return of scarcity portends the revival of age-old political evils, for our descendants if not for ourselves. In short, the golden age of individualism, liberty, and democracy is all but over. In many important respects, we shall be obliged to return to something resembling the pre-modern, closed polity. This conclusion will be reinforced by a more detailed exploration of the political problem of controlling the competitive overexploitation of resources that has produced the ecological crisis.

The Tragedy of the Commons

It has been known since ancient times that resources held or used in common tend to be abused. As Aristotle said, "What is common to the greatest number gets the least amount of care" (Barker 1962, p. 44). However, the dynamic underlying such abuse was first suggested by a little-known Malthusian of the early 19th century, William Forster Lloyd (cited in Hardin 1969, p. 29), who wondered why the cattle on a common pasture were "so puny and stunted" and the common itself "bare-worn." He found that such an outcome was almost inevitable.

Men seeking gain naturally desire to increase the size of their herds. Since the commons is finite, the day must come when the total number of cattle reaches the carrying capacity; the addition of more cattle will cause the pasture to deteriorate and eventually destroy the resource on which the herdsmen depend. Yet, even knowing this to be the case, it is still in the rational self-interest of each herdsman to keep adding animals to his herd. Each reasons that his personal gain from adding animals outweighs his proportionate share of the damage done to the commons, for the damage is done to the commons as a whole and is thus partitioned among all the users. Worse, even if he is inclined to self-restraint, an individual herdsman justifiably fears that others may not be. They will increase their herds and gain thereby, while he will have to suffer equally the resulting damage. Competitive overexploitation of the commons is the inevitable result.

The same dynamic of competitive overexploitation applies to any "common-property resource," the economist's term for resources held or used in common. A classic illustration is the oil pool. Unless one person or organization controls the rights to exploit an oil pool or the owners of the rights can agree on a scheme of rational exploitation, it is in the interest of each to extract oil from the common pool as fast as he possibly can; in fact, failure to do so exposes the individual owner to the risk that others will not leave him his fair share. Thus, in the early boom days of the American oil industry, drillers competed with each other to sink as many wells as possible on their properties. The result was economic and political chaos, soon remedied by the establishment of state control boards that surveyed the pools and then allotted each owner a quota of production for each acre of oil-bearing land. Oil was thereby transformed from a common property resource to private property, and exploitation proceeded thereafter in a largely rational and conflict-free manner.

The dynamic of the commons is particularly stark in the case of oil, for one person's gains are another's losses. But even resources that could be exploited cooperatively to give a sustained yield in perpetuity are subject to the same dynamic. Fisheries are a prime example. At first, there was abundance enough for all to exploit the resource freely. Conflicts occurred, but their impact was local. Fishing a little farther away or improving techniques were alternatives to fighting over the limited resources in a particular area. However, in time even the vastness of the ocean began to be more or less fully exploited, and people responded just as they did in the early days of the oil business. Some nations attempted to privatize parts of the fishing common, so that all the benefits of the fishery would flow to their nationals. Thus fishing "wars" and other political conflicts over marine resources are now very common. Others responded by increasing the scale and technical virtuosity of their fishing operations, just as early oil drillers would sink dozens of wells on a tiny piece of land. Technological progress in the fishing industry has produced gigantic floating factories, which use ultramodern techniques to catch fish and can or freeze them on the spot, thus eliminating the time wasted by traditional methods in returning to port. The result, as one might have predicted, has been relentless competitive overexploitation and an alarming general decline in fish stocks.

Pollution also exemplifies the self-destructive logic of the commons, for it simply reverses the dynamic of competitive overexploitation without altering its nature: the cost to me of controlling my emissions is so much larger than my proportionate share of the environmental damage they cause that it will always be rational for me to pollute if I can get away with it. In short, it profits me to harm the public. (It does not pay me to benefit the public either; see Box 1.)

BOX 1. THE PUBLIC-GOODS PROBLEM

The public-goods problem is the obverse of the commons problem. Just as the rational individual gains by harming fellow members of the common, he loses by benefiting them with a public or collective good. At best, he gets only a small return on his investment; at worst, he is economically punished. For example, the good husbandman cannot survive in a market economy; if he maintains his soil while his neighbors mine theirs for maximum yields, sooner or later he must either abandon farming or become a subsistence farmer outside the market. He cannot afford to benefit posterity except at great personal sacrifice. Similarly, although a socially responsible plant owner might wish to control the pollution emanating from his plant, if he does it at his own expense whatever his competitors do, then he is at a competitive disadvantage. Thus the tragedy of the commons, in which the culprit gets all the benefits from transgressing the limits of the commons, but succeeds in relegating most of the costs to others, is turned around. One who tries to benefit the common good soon discovers that, while he pays all the costs, the other members of the community reap virtually all the benefits.

Of course, a producer could try to persuade consumers to pay premium prices for his products as a reward for his virtue. But he would be unlikely to find many buyers for products that, however "virtuous," were no better than the cheaper ones of his competitors. Another conceivable solution would be for the manufacturer who intended to control pollution to take up a collection from all those affected. After all, if his pollution is harmful to them, they should be willing to pay something to reduce or eliminate it. However, even if the considerable practical difficulties of organizing such a scheme were overcome it would almost certainly fail, for people are unlikely to contribute voluntarily to pollution reduction or the production of any other kind of public good in optimal amounts. The reason is simple: it is entirely rational for individuals to try to make others pay most or all of the costs of a public good that benefits everyone equally; thus the good is never available in optimal quantity under market conditions. For example, no government can subsist on voluntary tax payments; if external defense, internal order, rules for economic competition, public health, education, and other public goods are to be produced in quantities that are rationally desirable for the society, then taxes must be compulsory on all its members. Similarly, if ecological public goods like clean air and water or pleasant landscapes are to be provided in reasonable amounts, it will be only as a result of collective decisions. Thus, just as for the tragedy of the commons, the answer to the public-goods problem is authoritative political action.

Unfortunately, virtually all ecological resources—airsheds, watersheds, the land, the oceans, the atmosphere, biological cycles, the biosphere itself—are common property resources. For example, the smoke from factories or the exhaust gases from automobiles cannot be confined so that their noxious effects harm only those who produce them. They harm all in the common airshed. Even most resources that seem to be private property are in fact part of the ecological commons. The timberman who cuts down a whole stand of trees in order to maximize his profits contributes to flooding, siltation, and the decline of water quality in his watershed; if enough timbermen cut down enough trees, even climate may be altered, as has occurred many times in the past. Now that the carrying capacity of the biosphere has been approached, if not exceeded, we are in serious danger of destroying all ecological resources by competitive overexploitation. Thus the metaphor of the commons is not merely an assertion of man's ultimate dependence on the ecological life-support systems of the planet, but an accurate description of the current human predicament.

In short, resources that once were so abundant they were freely available to all have now become ecologically scarce. Unless they are somehow regulated and protected in the common interest, the inevitable outcome will be the mutual ecological ruin that the human ecologist Garrett Hardin (1968) has called "the tragedy of the commons." We need the same kind of social rules and political controls, but much more widely applied, that have traditionally governed the use of grazing lands and other commons in the past (although these controls have not always been sufficiently strong to avert partial or even total destruction of a resource).

A Hobbesian Solution?

Beyond telling us that the answer to the tragedy is "mutual coercion, mutually agreed upon by the majority of the people affected"—by which he means social restraint, not naked force—Hardin avoids political prescription. However, he does suggest that unrestrained exercise of our liberties does not bring us real freedom: "Individuals locked into the logic of the commons are free only to bring on universal ruin; once they see the necessity of mutual coercion, they become free to pursue other goals"; by recognizing the necessity to abandon many natural freedoms we now believe we possess, we avoid tragedy and "preserve and nurture other and more precious freedoms." There are obvious dangers in a regime of "mutual coercion," but without restraints on individuals, the collective selfishness and irresponsibility produced by the logic of the commons will destroy the spaceship, so that any sacrifice of freedom by the crew members is clearly the lesser evil. After all, says Hardin, "injustice is preferable to total ruin," so that "an alternative to the commons need not be perfectly just to be preferable" (Hardin 1968, pp. 1247–1248).

Hardin's implicit political theory is in all important respects identical to that of Thomas Hobbes in *Leviathan* (1651). Hardin's "logic of the commons" is simply a special version of the general political dynamic of Hobbes' "state of nature." Hobbes says that where men desire goods scarcer than their wants, they are likely to fall to fighting. They each know individually that all would be better off if they abstained from fighting and found some way of equitably sharing the desired goods. However, they also realize that they cannot alter the dynamics of the situation by their own behavior. In the absence of a civil authority to keep the peace, personal pacifism merely makes them a prey to others. Unless all can be persuaded or forced to lay down their arms simultaneously, nothing can prevent the war of all against all. The crucial problem in the state of nature is thus to make it safe for men to be reasonable, rather than merely "rational," so that they can share peacefully what the environment has to offer. Hobbes' solution was the erection by a majority of a sovereign power that would constrain all men to be reasonable and peaceful—that is, Hardin's "mutual coercion, mutually agreed upon by the majority of the people affected."*

In the tragedy of the commons, the dilemma is not as stark as it is in the state of nature—political order is not at stake—but it is in many ways much more insidious, for even without evil propensities on the part of any person or group the tragedy will occur. In the case of the village common the actors can hardly avoid noticing the causal relationship between their acts and the deterioration of the commons, but in most cases of competitive overexploitation individuals are not even aware of the damage that their acts are causing; even if they are aware their own responsibility seems infinitesimally dilute. Thus, to bring about the tragedy of the commons it is not necessary that men be bad, only that they not be actively good—that is, not altruistic enough to limit their own behavior when their fellows will not regularly perform acts of public generosity. That people are in fact not this altruistic is confirmed daily by behavior any one of us sees around him (and see Schelling 1971).

A perfect illustration of the insidiousness of the tragedy of the commons in operation is the situation of the inhabitants of Los Angeles vis-a-vis the automobile:

> Every person who lives in this basin knows that for twenty-five years he has been living through a disaster. We have all watched it happen, have participated in it with full knowledge just as men and women once went knowingly and willingly into the "dark Satanic mills." The smog is the result of ten million individual pursuits of private gratification. But there is absolutely nothing that any individual can do to stop its spread. Each Angeleno is totally powerless to end what he hates. An individual act of renunciation is now nearly impossible, and, in any case, would be meaningless unless everyone else did the same thing. But he has no way of getting everyone else to do it. He does not even have any way to talk about such a course. He does not know how or where he would do it or what language he would use [Carney 1972, pp. 28–29].

As this example clearly shows, the essence of the tragedy of the commons is that one's own contribution to the problem (assuming that one is even aware of it) seems infinitesimally small, while the disadvantages of self-denial loom very large; self-restraint therefore appears to be both unprofitable and ultimately futile unless one can be certain of universal concurrence. Thus we are being destroyed ecologically not so much by the evil acts of selfish men as by the everyday acts of

---

*For a fuller discussion of the virtual identity of analyses and prescriptions in Hardin and Hobbes, see Ophuls 1973.

ordinary men whose behavior is dominated, usually unconsciously, by the remorseless self-destructive logic of the commons.

The tragedy of the commons also exemplifies the political problem that agitated the eighteenth-century French political philosopher Jean-Jacques Rousseau, who made a crucial distinction between the "general will" and the "will of all." The former is what reasonable men, leaving aside their self-interest and having the community's interests at heart, would regard as the right and proper course of action; the latter is the mere addition of the particular wills of the individuals forming the polity, based not on a conception of the common good, but only on what serves their own self-interest. The tragedy of the commons is simply a particularly vicious instance of the way in which the "will of all" falls short of the true common interest. In essence, Rousseau's answer to this crucial problem in *The Social Contract* is not much different from Hobbes': man must be "forced to be free"—that is, protected from the consequences of his own selfishness and shortsightedness by being made obedient to the common good or "general will," which represents his real self-interest. Rousseau thus wants political institutions that will make men virtuous.

It therefore appears that if under conditions of ecological scarcity individuals rationally pursue their material self-interest unrestrained by a common authority that upholds the common interest, the eventual result is bound to be common environmental ruin. In that case, we must have political institutions that preserve the ecological common good from destruction by unrestrained human acts. The problem that the environmental crisis forces us to confront is, in fact, at the core of political philosophy: how to protect or advance the interests of the collectivity, when the individuals that make it up (or enough of them to create a problem) behave (or are impelled to behave) in a selfish, greedy, and quarrelsome fashion. The only solution is a sufficient measure of coercion (see Box 2). Following Hobbes, a certain minimum level of ecological order or peace must be established; following Rousseau, a certain minimum level of ecological virtue must be imposed by our political institutions.

It hardly need be said that these conclusions about the tragedy of the commons radically challenge fundamental American and Western values. Under conditions of ecological scarcity the individual, possessing an inalienable right to pursue happiness as he defines it and exercising his liberty in a basically laissez-faire system, will inevitably produce the ruin of the commons. Accordingly, the individualistic basis of society, the concept of inalienable rights, the purely self-defined pursuit of happiness, liberty as maximum freedom of action, and laissez faire itself all become problematic, requiring major modification or perhaps even abandonment if we wish to avert inexorable environmental degradation and eventual extinction as a civilization. Certainly, democracy as we know it cannot conceivably survive.

This is an extreme conclusion, but it seems to follow from the extremity of the ecological predicament industrial man has created for himself. Even Hobbes' severest critics concede that he is most cogent when stark political choices are faced, for self-interest moderated by self-restraint may not be workable when extreme conditions prevail. Thus theorists have long analyzed international rela-

BOX 2. COERCION

The word "coercion" has a nasty fascist ring to it. However, politics is a means of taming and legitimating power, not dispensing with it. Any form of state power is coercive. A classic example is taxation, which is nowhere voluntary, for as the theory of public goods (see Box 1) tells us, the state would starve if it were. Assuming a reasonable degree of consensus and legitimacy, coercion means no more than a state-imposed structure of incentives and disincentives that is designed to achieve the common interest. Even Locke's libertarian political theory does not proscribe coercion—if the common interest is threatened, the sovereign must do whatever is necessary to protect it. Nevertheless, unlike Hobbes, Locke does try to set up inviolable spheres of private rights that the sovereign may not invade and also demands that power be continually beholden to consent of the governed. The difference between Hobbes and Locke on the matter of coercion is one of degree, with Locke demanding more formal guarantees of limits on the sovereign's power than Hobbes believes are workable. In short, coercion is not some evil specter resurrected from an odious past. It is an inextricable part of politics, and the problem is how best to tame it and bend it to the common interest.

Some aspire to do away with power politics and state coercion entirely by making men so virtuous that they will automatically do what is in the common interest. In fact, this is precisely what Rousseau proposes: small, self-sufficient, frugal, intimate communities inculcating civic virtue so thoroughly that citizens become the "general will" incarnate. However, this merely changes the locus of coercion from outside to inside—the job of law enforcement is handed over to the internal police force of the superego—and many liberals (for example, Popper 1966) would argue that this kind of ideological or psychological coercion is far worse than overt controls on behavior. Nevertheless, political education cannot be done away with entirely, for without a reasonable degree of consensus and legitimacy no regime can long endure. Thus it is again a question of balance. Hobbes and Rousseau, for example, would both agree that law enforcement and political education must be combined, however much they might disagree on the fitting proportion of each.

In sum, political coercion in some form is inevitable. Failing to confront openly the issues it raises is likely to have the same effect repression has on the individual psyche—the repressed force returns in an unhealthy form. By contrast, if we face up to coercion full political awareness will dispel its seeming nastiness, and we shall be able to tame it and make it a pillar of the common interest. (Box 3 suggests a way of taming Leviathan....)

tions in Hobbesian terms, because the state of nature mirrors the state of armed peace existing between competing nation-states owing obedience to no higher power. Also, when social or natural disaster leads to a breakdown in the ordered patterns of society that ordinarily restrain men, even the most libertarian governments have never hesitated to impose martial law as the only alternative to anarchy. Therefore, if nuclear holocaust rather than mere war, or anarchy rather than a moderate level of disorder, or destruction of the biosphere rather than mere loss of amenity is the issue, the extremity of Hobbes' analysis fits reality, and it becomes difficult to avoid his conclusions. Similarly, although Rousseau's ultimate aim was the creation of a democratic polity, he recognized that strong sovereign power (a "Legislator" in Rousseau's language) may be necessary in certain circumstances, most especially if the bad habits of a politically "corrupt" people must be fundamentally reformed.

Altruism Is Not Enough

Some hope or assert that attitudinal change will bring about major changes in individual behavior sufficient to save a democratic, laissez-faire system from ecological ruin. However, except in very small and tightly knit social groups, education or the inculcation of rigid social norms is not sure proof against the logic of the commons. It seems to be simply not true that, once they are aware of the general gravity of the situation, men will naturally moderate their demands on the environment. A number of studies have shown that even the individuals who are presumably the most knowledgeable and concerned about population growth evince little willingness to restrain their own reproductive behavior (Attah 1973; Barnett 1971; Eisner et al. 1970). How much can we expect of the ordinary citizen? The problem is that, in order to forestall the logic of the commons, people in overwhelming numbers must be prepared to do positive good whether or not cooperation is universal; and in a political culture that conceives of the common interest as being no more than the sum of our individual interests it seems unlikely that we can prudently count on much help from unsupported altruism (this is not to say that people cannot be educated to be ecologically more responsible than they are at present).

In any event, even the most altruistic individual cannot behave responsibly without full knowledge of the consequences of his acts—and this is not available to him. If even the experts fiercely debate the pros and cons of nuclear power or the effects of a particular chemical on the ozone layer, using highly abstruse analytical techniques or complex computer programs that only the specialists can fully understand, how is the ordinary citizen to know what the facts are? An additional problem is time. High rates of change and exponential growth are accompanied by a serious lag in public understanding. For example, it seems to take two to four generations for the ideas at the frontier of science to filter down even to the informed public. We have still not completely digested Darwin, much less Einstein and quantum mechanics. How reasonable is it to expect from the public at large a sophisticated ecological understanding any time soon, especially since the academic, business, professional, and political elites who constitute the so-called attentive and informed public show little sign of having understood, much less embraced, the ecological world view?

Others pin their hopes for a solution not on individual conscience, but on the development of a collective conscience in the form of a world view or religion that would see man as the partner of nature rather than its antagonist. This will undoubtedly be essential for our survival in the long term, since without basic popular support even the most repressive regime could hardly hope to succeed in protecting the environment for long. However, mere changes in world view are not likely to be sufficient. Political and social arrangements that implement values are indispensable for turning ideals into actuality. For example, despite a basic world view that was profoundly respectful of nature, the Chinese have severely abused and degraded their environment throughout their very long history—more, ironically, than the pre-modern Europeans, who lacked a philosophy expressive of the same kind of natural harmony. Thus Chinese ideals were no proof against the urgency of human desires that drives the tragic logic of the commons. The further irony is that a reversal of this trend is now taking place under a Communist government, whose philosophy is the very antithesis of the traditional values embodied in Taoism and Buddhism, but which has a strong sense of the common interest and the will and the ability to carry it out.*

It appears therefore that individual conscience and the right kind of cultural attitudes are not by themselves sufficient to overcome the short-term calculations of utility that lead men to degrade their environment. Real altruism and genuine concern for posterity may not be entirely absent, but they are not present in sufficient strength to avert the tragedy. Only a government possessing great powers to regulate individual behavior in the ecological common interest can deal effectively with the tragedy of the commons.

To recapitulate, the tragic logic of the commons is sustained by three premises: a limited commons; cattle that need ample grazing room to prevent the commons from becoming "bare-worn"; and rational, self-seeking herdsmen. If any one of these premises is removed, the tragedy is averted. As we have already seen, the Great Frontier in fact effectively removed the first premise for nearly 400 years. It was precisely this that allowed John Locke, whose political argument is essentially the same as that of Hobbes in every particular except scarcity in the state of nature, to be basically libertarian where Hobbes is basically authoritarian. Thanks to the Great Frontier, Locke and Smith found that there was sufficient abundance in the state of nature that a Hobbesian war of all against all was unlikely; every man could take away some kind of prize, and competition would be socially constructive rather than destructive, with the "invisible hand" producing the greatest good for the society as a whole. Thus government was required only to keep the game honest—a mere referee, needing only modest powers and minimal

---

*Some (for example, Reich 1971) would protest that our age is different and that a genuinely new consciousness is emerging. This view cannot simply be brushed aside, for substantial value changes are clearly occurring in some segments of American society, and out of this essentially religious ferment great things may come. For example, the "back to the land" movement has been much ridiculed, but its symbolic reaffirmation of our ties to the earth has already had a far from negligible impact on the larger society. Nevertheless, that these new values will become universal in the future appears to be essentially a matter of faith at this point. Moreover, since past hopes for the emergence of a "new man" have been rudely treated by history, it is difficult to be optimistic.

institutional machinery—and individuals could be left alone to pursue happiness as they defined it without hindrance by society or the state. The frontier is gone now, and we have encountered the limits of the commons. However, the physical disappearance of the frontier was for a long time mitigated by technology, which allowed us to graze more cows on the same acreage of pasture. Now we have reached the limits of technology: the cows are standing almost shoulder to shoulder and the manure is piling up faster than the commons can absorb it. All that remains is to alter the rational, self-seeking behavior of the individuals and groups using the commons. This must be done by collective means, for the dynamic of the tragedy of the commons is so powerful that individuals are virtually powerless to extricate themselves unaided from its remorseless working. We must indeed be "forced to be free" by our political institutions.

Legislating Temperance

That we must give our political authorities great powers to regulate many of our daily actions is a profoundly distasteful thought. We tend to see political systems without our kind of political and economic liberties as "totalitarian," a word that brings to mind all the evil features of past dictatorships. However, even Hobbes, no matter how firm his conviction of the necessity of absolutism, certainly did not have Stalinesque tyranny in mind. Hobbes makes clear that order in the commonwealth is not the goal, but the means without which the fruits of civilization cannot be enjoyed: the sovereign power is to procure the "safety of the people. . . . But by safety here is not meant a bare preservation but also all other contentments of life which every man by lawful industry, without danger or hurt to the commonwealth, shall acquire to himself" (Hobbes 1651, p. 262). And it is part of the task of the sovereign power actively to promote these "contentments of life" among its subjects. Furthermore, Hobbes will not countenance tyranny. The sovereign power must rule lawfully, give a full explanation of its acts to its subjects, and heed their legitimate desires. Through wise laws and education, the subjects will learn moral restraint. Also, the sovereign power is not to be a dictator regulating every action of the citizen: it does not "bind the people from all voluntary actions" but only guides them with laws which Hobbes likens to "hedges . . . set not to stop travelers, but to keep them in their ways" (p. 272). Thus many different styles of rule and of life are compatible with his basic analysis.

Similarly, Hardin makes it clear that the problem is to "legislate temperance," not to institute iron discipline. He acknowledges that this may require the use of administrative law, with the consequent risk of abuse of power by the administrators. However, he believes that the application of his formula of "mutual coercion, mutually agreed upon by the majority of the people affected" would be an adequate defense against bureaucratic tyranny, for we would be *democratically coercing ourselves* to behave responsibly (Hardin 1968, p. 1247).

The question of political will is therefore crucial. Given a basic willingness to restrain individual self-seeking and legislate social temperance, social devices acceptable to reasonable men and suited to a government of laws could readily be

found to serve as the "hedges" that will keep us on the path of the steady state.*
For example, law professor Christopher Stone (1974) proposes giving natural
objects, such as trees, mountains, rivers, and lakes, legal rights (comparable to
those now enjoyed by corporations) that could be enforced in court.

However, although the socioeconomic machinery needs to enforce a steady-
state political economy need not involve dictatorial control over our everyday
lives, it will indeed encroach upon our freedom of action, *for any social device that
is effective as a hedge will necessarily prevent us from doing things we are now free to
do or make us do things we now prefer not to do.* It could hardly be otherwise: if we
can safely squeeze no more cattle onto the commons, then we herdsmen must be
satisfied either with the herds we now possess or, more likely, with the lesser
number of cattle that the commons can tolerate ecologically over the long term.
The solution to the tragedy of the commons in the present circumstances requires
a willingness to accept less, perhaps much less, than we now get from the
commons. No technical devices will save us. In order to be able mutually to agree
on the restraints we wish to apply to ourselves, we must give up the exercise of
rights we now enjoy, and bind ourselves to perform public duties in the common
interest. The only alternative to this kind of self-coercion is the coercion of
nature, or perhaps of an iron regime that will compel our consent to living life
with less.

Technology's Faustian Bargain

Given this unpalatable conclusion, the seductive appeal of technological
optimism is apparent: if adjusting human demands to the available ecological
resources will entail a greater degree of political authority, then let us by all means
press on with the attempt to surmount the limits to growth technologically. Thus,
to the extent that the technologist concedes the necessity of a steady state, he aims
at a "maximum-feasible" steady state of technological superabundance in which
we will use our alleged mastery of inexhaustible energy resources to evade
ecological constraints, instead of learning to live frugally on flow resources like
solar energy.† As we have seen, the barriers to success in such an enterprise are
enormous, but for the sake of argument, let us put aside all questions of practicality and ask instead what would be the political consequences of implementing
these kinds of technological solutions to ecological scarcity.

Alvin Weinberg, who was for many years director of the Atomic Energy

---

*Merely increasing the power of the state is not enough. And contrary to the opinion of many, mere
socialism is not a real solution to the tragedy of the commons. That is, giving the state ownership of the
means of production is not very useful if the state is committed to economic expansion, for the same
ecologically destructive dynamic operates within a socialist economic bureaucracy as in the capitalist
marketplace (see Heilbroner 1974 on this point).
†In reality, a maximum-feasible steady state is a virtual contradiction in terms, for squeezing the maximum
out of nature runs contrary to basic ecological principles. Only a life lived *comfortably* within the circle of
natural interdependence merits the designation "steady state." But the technological optimists custom-
arily talk as if there were a possible model of the steady state other than the maximum-feasible one.

Commission's Oak Ridge National Laboratory, has been a leading spokesman for the technological fix, especially nuclear power. Indeed, he has castigated environmentalists for proposing "social fixes" to ecological problems; he argues that technological solutions are "more humane" because they do not "disrupt the economy and . . . cause the human suffering that such disruption would entail" (Weinberg 1972b). Yet Weinberg himself admits that the specific technological solution he proposes comes with a truly monstrous social fix firmly attached! Because nuclear wastes will have to be kept under virtually perpetual surveillance and because nuclear technology places the most exacting demands on our engineering and management capabilities,

> We nuclear people have made a Faustian bargain with society. On the one hand, we offer . . . an inexhaustible source of energy [the breeder reactor]. . . . But the price that we demand of society for this magical energy is both a vigilance and a longevity of our social institutions that we are quite unaccustomed to [Weinberg 1972a, p. 33].

Part of the price is politically ominous:

> In a sense, what started out as a technological fix for the energy-environment impasse—clean, inexhaustible, and fairly cheap nuclear power—involves social fixes as well: the creation of a permanent cadre or priesthood of responsible technologists who will guard the reactors and the wastes so as to assure their continued safety over millennia [Weinberg 1973, p. 43].

Expanding on the "priesthood" theme, Weinberg tells us that, because "our commitment to nuclear energy is assumed to last in perpetuity," we will need "a *permanent* cadre of experts that will retain its continuity over immensely long times [but this] hardly seems feasible if the cadre is a national body," for "no government has lasted continuously for 1,000 years." What kind of organization does possess the requisite continuity?

> Only the Catholic Church has survived more or less continuously for 2,000 years or so. . . . The Catholic Church is the best example of [the International Authority] I have in mind: a *central authority* that *proclaims* and to a degree *enforces* doctrine, maintains its own long-term social stability, and has connections to every country's own Catholic Church [cited in Speth et al. 1974, emphasis added].

In proposing such a technological "priesthood," Weinberg appears to be a true heir of the French utopian social philosopher Claude Henri Saint-Simon (1760–1825), one of the earliest prophets of technocracy, who believed that it was man's mission to transcend nature with technology. Distressed by the disruptive social effects of technology within a bourgeois, laissez-faire political economy, Saint-Simon aspired to create a stable, organic civilization like that of the Middle Ages, but with Science as its religion. To this end he proposed the creation, on the model of the Catholic Church, of a scientific priesthood that would both dispense political justice and promote the economic wealth of society. Saint-Simon stressed the necessity for authority based on scientific expertise, social planning, the subordination of the individual to the needs of society as determined by the experts, and the integration of society and technology—all themes that emerge in the writings of modern technological visionaries.

By whatever name it comes to be called, technocratic government is the likely price of Weinberg's Faustian bargain. Naturally, it will not be formally voted in, but will emerge in a series of small but fateful steps as we follow what seems to be the line of least resistance through our environmental problems. Indeed, critics are already alarmed by the civil-rights implications of the safeguards proposed by the Atomic Energy Commission in its draft environmental-impact statement on plutonium recycling; these include the establishment of a federal police force for the protection of plutonium plants and shipments, the extension of current military security-clearance procedures to include all the civilians who might have access to plutonium, and generally increased police powers to cope with the security requirements of a plutonium-based power economy (Speth et al. 1974). In sum, there may be no way to assure the social stability—indeed, the near-perfect social institutions—necessary for an era of nuclear power except with an engineered society under the direction of a technocratic priesthood.

A Pact with the Devil?

It is not nuclear technology alone that offers a pact with a devil who will in the end claim our political souls. Few technological optimists are as candid as Weinberg about the political implications of the solutions they propose, but technocracy has been looming on the horizon for some time. Harrison Brown, a scientist who foresaw most of today's ecological concerns two decades ago, predicted that the instability of industrial society would become greater as development proceeded; this and other organizational requirements would create a necessity for ever greater social control, so that "it is difficult to see how the achievement of stability and the maintenance of individual liberty can be made compatible" (Brown 1954, p. 255). Buckminster Fuller, one of the most visionary of the supertechnologists, states plainly that those who run "Spaceship Earth" cannot afford to make "concessions to the non-synergetic thinking (therefore the ignorantly conditioned reflexes) of the least well advised of the potential mass customers [that is, the average citizen]" (Fuller 1968, p. 367). Numerous other writers of varying persuasions see the same trend: more technology means greater complexity and greater need for knowledge and technical expertise; the average citizen will not be able to make a constructive contribution to decision making, so that "experts" and "authorities" will perforce rule; moreover, since accidents cannot be permitted, much less individual behavior that deviates from the technological imperatives, the grip of planning and social control will of necessity become more and more complete (Bell 1973; Chamberlin 1970; Heilbroner 1974).

Thus, the question at hand is not whether technology gradually turns man into a machine. Although this may indeed become truer as technological civilization grows, it is not an essential point in the present argument.* The danger in the Faustian bargain lies rather in the mounting complexity of technology along with the staggering problems of managing the response to ecological scarcity, for these will require us to depend on a special class of experts in charge of our survival and well-being—a "priesthood of responsible technologists."

Democracy versus Elite Rule: The Issue of Competence

One of the key philosophical supports of democracy is the assumption that people do not differ greatly in competence; for if they do, effective government may require the sacrifice of political equality and majority rule. Indeed, under certain circumstances democracy *must* give way to elite rule; as the eminent political scientist and democratic theorist Robert Dahl points out, in a political association whose members "differ *crucially* in their competence, such as a hospital or a passenger ship, a reasonable man will want the most competent people to have authority over the matters on which they are most competent" (Dahl 1970, p. 58, emphasis added). In other words, the more closely one's situation resembles a perilous sea voyage, the stronger the rationale for placing power and authority in the hands of the few who know how to run the ship.

Ecological scarcity appears to have created precisely such a situation. Critical decisions must be made. Although it is true that most of them are "transscientific" in that they can only be made politically by prudent men, at least the basic scientific elements of the problems must be understood reasonably well before an informed political decision is possible. However, the average man has neither the time to inform himself nor the requisite background for understanding such complex technical problems. Moreover, he may simply not be intelligent enough to grasp the issues, much less the important features of the problems. Indeed, it is apparent that even highly attentive and competent specialists do not always understand the problems fully. Even when they do (or claim to do), they can almost always be found on both sides of any major question of public policy. (The dispute over nuclear-reactor safety is a prime example, with Nobelists lining up both for and against nuclear power.) Thus, even assuming that the politicians and people understand the issue well enough to ask the right questions, which experts should they listen to? Can they understand what the experts are saying? If we grant that the people in their majority probably will not understand and are therefore not competent to decide such issues, is it very likely that the political leaders they select will themselves be competent enough to deal with these issues? And even if they are, how can these leaders make authoritative decisions that impose heavy present costs or that violate popular expectations for the sake of

---

*However, a key point in the general cultural critque of technology is germane to the current discussion: those who defend technology as socially benign do not always seem to grasp the crucial distinction made by Jacques Ellul (1967; see also Illich 1973) between "tools," which are relatively neutral instruments that can be used by individuals as they wish, and "technique," which imposes certain behavior on men (nuclear power is an egregious example).

future advantages revealed to them only as special knowledge derived from complicated analysis, perhaps even as the Delphic pronouncements of a computer?

Such questions about the viability of democratic politics in a supertechnological age propel us toward the political thought of Plato. In *The Republic,* the fountainhead of all Western political philosophy, Plato argued that the polity was like a ship sailing dangerous waters. It therefore needed to be commanded by the most competent pilots; to allow the crew, ignorant of the art of navigation, to participate in running the vessel would be to invite shipwreck. Thus the polity would have to be run by an elite class of guardians, who would themselves be guided by the cream of this elite—the philosopher-kings. As the quotation from Dahl suggests, to the extent that Plato's analogy of the ship of state approximates reality his political prescriptions are difficult to evade, which is precisely why, from Aristotle on, those who have favored democratic rather than oligarchic politics have concerned themselves with keeping the political community small enough and simple enough so that elite rule would not be necessary for social survival. The emerging large, highly-developed, complex technological civilization operating at or very near the ecological margin apears to fit Plato's premises more and more closely, foreshadowing the necessity of rule by a class of Platonic guardians, the "priesthood of responsible technologists" who alone know how to run the spaceship.

Such a development has always been implicit in technology, as the ideas of Saint-Simon suggest. It is simply that its necessity has become overwhelmingly manifest in a crowded world living close to the ecological limits, for only the most exquisite care will avert the collapse of the technological Leviathan we are well on the way to creating. C. S. Lewis observed that "What we call Man's power over Nature turns out to be a power exercised by some men over other men with Nature as its instrument" (Lewis 1965, p. 69), and it appears that the greater the technological power, the more absolute the political power that must be yielded up to some men by the others. Thus we must ask ourselves if continued technological growth will not merely serve to replace the so-called tyranny of nature with a potentially even more odious tyranny of men. Why indeed should we deliver ourselves over to a "priesthood of responsible technologists" who are merely technical experts and mainly lack the excellence of character and deep philosophical understanding that Plato insists his guardians must possess in order to justify their rule? In fact, why accept the rule of even a genuinely Platonic elite possessed of both wisdom and expertise, when all history teaches us that the abilities, foresight, and goodwill of mortal men are limited and imperfect? The technological response to ecological scarcity thus raises profound political issues, in particular one of the most ancient and difficult political dilemmas—*quis custodiet ipsos custodes?* or "Who will watch the guardians themselves?"

Technology and the Path to a Brave New World

Modern man has used technology along with energy to try to transcend nature. We have seen that it cannot be done; nature is not to be transcended by a biological organism that depends on it. Worse, the attempt to do so will have momentous political and social consequences. Far from protecting us from painful and disruptive social changes, as the technological optimist is wont to claim, continued technological growth is likely to force such changes on us. We are, in fact, in the process of making the Faustian bargain without ever having consciously decided to do so. As a result, we appear to be traveling down the road to total domination by technique and the machine, to the "Brave New World" that Aldous Huxley (1932) warned was the logical end point of a hedonistic, high-technology civilization.*

Technology may not be inherently evil, but it does have side effects and it does exact a social price. Moreover, in the hands of less than perfect human beings, technology can never be neutral, as its proponents too often claim; it can only be used for good or evil. Thus technological fixes are dangerous surrogates for political decisions. There is no escape from politics. As a consequence of ecological scarcity, major ethical, political, economic and social changes are inevitable whatever we do. The choice is between change that happens to us as a "side effect" of ever more stringent technological imperatives and change that is deliberately selected to accord with our values.

Unfortunately, at this point even total renunciation of technology as dangerous to our democratic health would not avoid all the political dilemmas described above. During the transition to any form of steady state one can envisage it would be imperative to use physical resources as efficiently as possible, and this probably would mean greater centralization and expert control in the short term, even if the long-term goal is a technologically simple, decentralized society favorable to a democratic politics.

Even beyond the transition period, whether a steady-state society can be democratic (as we understand it) is at least questionable. A society cannot persist as a genuine democracy unless the people in their majority understand technology and ecology well enough to make responsible decisions; and although the technology of a frugal steady state should be more accessible to the common man's understanding than our own current brand is, the same may not be true of the ecological knowledge upon which the steady-state society will have to be based. Intuition and common sense alone are of little help in understanding the counterintuitive complexity of the human ecosystem—and nowhere else can a little knowledge be so dangerous. Thus, although not intrinsically mysterious, ecology is esoteric in the sense that only those whose talents and training have equipped them to be the "specialists in the general" are likely to possess the kind of competence that would satisfy Dahl's "reasonable man." The ecologically complex steady-state society may therefore require, if not a class of ecological guardians, then at least a class of ecological mandarins who possess the esoteric knowledge needed to run it well. Thus, whatever its level of material affluence, the steady-state society will not only be more authoritarian and less democratic than the industrial societies of today—the necessity to cope with the tragedy of the

*All the techniques of social control and biological manipulation forecast in Huxley's dystopian novel are being invented today in our laboratories (Cohen 1973; Delgado 1969; Holden 1973; Kass 1971, 1972; Skinner 1971); well before these developments, Huxley (1958) was himself appalled to discover that much of what he had imagined as taking place six or seven hundred years in the future was coming true within his own lifetime.

commons would alone ensure that—but it will also in all likelihood be much more oligarchic as well, with only those possessing the ecological and other competencies necessary to make prudent decisions allowed full participation in the political process.

Hard Political Realities and a New Paradigm

To sum up, scarcity in general erodes the material basis for the relatively benign individualistic and democratic politics characteristic of the modern industrial era; ecological scarcity in particular seems to engender overwhelming pressures toward political systems that are frankly authoritarian by current standards, for there seems to be no other way to check competitive over-exploitation of resources and to assure competent direction of a complex society's affairs in accord with steady-state imperatives. Leviathan may be mitigated, but not evaded (see Box 3).

BOX 3. TAMING LEVIATHAN: MACRO-CONSTRAINTS AND MICRO-FREEDOMS

The only escape from the political dilemma of ecological scarcity—authoritative rule or ecological ruin—is indicated in the Epigraph: if men exercise sufficient self-control of their passions, the fetters of external authority become unnecessary. Unfortunately, political history suggests that the level of moral restraint and altruism to be expected from the members of large, complex, mass societies is limited at best. These virtues are even less likely to be found in industrial civilization, for its citizens have been brought up to believe that satisfying their hedonistic wants is not only legitimate, but positively virtuous. Besides, in complicated and highly interdependent societies, even the most willing citizen would not know how to be ecologically virtuous without a large amount of central direction and coordination. In other words, unless we return to face-to-face, simple, decentralized, small-community living—which may be a desirable long-term goal but hardly a short-term possibility—we are stuck with the problem of making authority palatable and protecting ourselves against those who would abuse their ecological guardianship.

Traditional political theory has proposed many answers to this problem. However, one basic principle stands out: if self-restraint is inadequate, macro-constraints are vastly to be preferred to micro-constraints, for the psychological differences between them are crucial. That is, limitations on our freedom that are indirect, remote, and impersonal are preferable to those that are direct, proximate, and personal; in the former case, the limitations become an almost invisible part of "the way things are," instead of obvious impositions. For example, modern man *feels* generally free despite his nearly total submission to such powerful but faceless forces as technological change and the marketplace; the feudal peasant, by contrast, was so bound up in a web of direct personal obligations that he felt much less free, even though this web of obligations may have been in important respects less tyrannical in practice than the impersonal forces to which modern man is obliged to submit. Putting the matter more abstractly, the contemporary political philosopher Isaiah Berlin (1969) has defined freedom as the number of doors open to a man, how open they are, and upon what prospects they open. All other things being equal, then, the widest number of meaningful options brings the maximum of freedom; macro-freedom is the sum of the micro-freedoms available to us. Since the destruction of the commons leaves us with few meaningful options, some of the doors now available to us must be partly or even completely closed, but if we wish to preserve a sense of freedom, then this should be done in ways that limit the micro-freedoms or close the doors of daily life as little as possible.

Thus an effective way of making authority acceptable is the application of macro-constraints encouraging the behavior necessary to maintain a steady-state society but leaving the individual with a relative abundance of micro-freedoms that, when added up, give him an overall sense of freedom. . . .

Ecological scarcity thus forces us to confront once again, perhaps in a particularly acute form, the hard realities and cruel dilemmas of classical politics, from which four centuries of abnormal abundance have shielded us. As a result, we shall have to reexamine fundamental political questions in the light of ecology and construct a new steady-state paradigm of politics based on ecological premises instead of on the individualistic, hedonistic, materialistic, and anthropocentric premises of bourgeois "social contract" theory (see Box 4). The alternative is to let the shape of the steady-state paradigm be decided for us by accepting the outcome of current trends toward technocracy.

BOX 4. THE ECOLOGICAL CONTRACT

The Great Frontier and the Industrial Revolution unleashed forces that eventually destroyed the medieval political synthesis, which was based generally on the Heaven-ordained hierarchy of the "great chain of being" and specifically on the "divine right of kings." Changing economic conditions gradually transferred de facto political power from monarchs, priests, and nobles to the enterprising middle classes. Although at first the bourgeois acquiesced in continued autocratic rule and aristocratic patronage, he eventually tired of supporting what he came to see as unproductive social parasites; he overthrew the ancien régime and embarked on democratic self-rule, the only form of government that could be intellectually and practically reconciled with his new sense of individualism. Such major transfers of power must be theoretically and morally legitimated, and the "social contract" theory of government was devised to fulfill this need.

In essence, the theory of the social contract says that individuals are not part of a pre-existing hierarchy to which they must unquestioningly adapt, but free to decide how they wish to be ruled. It is thus primarily concerned with how free and equal individuals (starting from an anarchic "state of nature") can come together to erect political institutions that will preserve their individual rights to the fullest extent, yet also promote the social harmony they need to enjoy these rights in peace. Ironically, the device of the social contract was used by Hobbes to provide secular support for monarchy, starting from the individualistic, hedonistic, and materialistic premises of the bourgeois world view. However, as it was later developed by Locke and Rousseau, the social contract became the foundation for popular sovereignty and liberal democracy (even Marxism has very deep roots in Rousseau's thought). The untrammeled individual was now king.

As a product of a the Great Frontier, the theory of the social contract is fundamentally cornucopian: nature's abundance being endless and inexhaustible, one has only to solve the problem of achieving social harmony through a just division of the spoils. Nature is thus external to politics. But these cornucopian premises have become as anomalous in an age of ecological scarcity as the divine right of kings was in the era of the Great Frontier and the Industrial Revolution. Ecology and politics are now inseparable; out of prudent self-restraint, if for no other reason, a valid political theory of the steady state will be obliged to give the same weight to ecological harmony as to social harmony. Thus, just as it was the task of the seventeenth- and eighteenth-century political philosophers to create the social-contract theory of government to take account of the new socioeconomic conditions and justify the political ascent of the bourgeois class, so it will be the duty of the next generation of philosophers to create an "ecological contract" theory promoting harmony not just between men, but also between man and nature.

Given current political values, this may not seem like much of a choice. However, the one certain thing is that current values and institutions will not be able to endure unchanged. Moreover, the latitude of choice is wider than might be suspected; indeed, the crisis of ecological scarcity might actually be turned into a grand opportunity to build a more humane post-industrial society.

Notes

Attah, Ernest B.
1973   "Racial Aspects of Zero Population Growth," *Science* 180:1143–1151.
Barker, Ernst, trans.
1962   *The Politics of Aristotle* (New York: Oxford).
Barnett, Larry D.
1971   "Zero Population Growth, Inc." *BioScience* 21:759–765.
Bell, Daniel
1973   *The Coming of Post-Industrial Society: A Venture in Social Forecasting* (New York: Basic Books).
Berlin, Isaiah
1969   *Four Essays on Liberty* (New York: Oxford).
Brown, Harrison
1954   *The Challenge of Man's Future* (New York: Viking).
Buchanan, James
1969   *The Demand and Supply of Public Goods* (Chicago: Rand McNally).
Burch, William R., Jr.
1971   *Daydreams and Nightmares: A Sociological Essay on the American Environment* (New York: Harper and Row).
Butler, Samuel
1872   *Erewhon* (New York: Signet, 1960).
Callahan, Daniel J.
1973   *The Tyranny of Survival: and Other Pathologies of Civilized Life* (New York: Macmillan).
Carney, Francis
1972   "Schlockology," *New York Review of Books,* June 1, pp. 26–29.
Chamberlin, Neil W.
1970   *Beyond Malthus: Population and Power* (New York: Basic Books).
Christy, Francis T., Jr., and Anthony Scott
1965   *The Common Wealth in Ocean Fisheries* (Baltimore: Johns Hopkins).
Cohen, David
1973   "Chemical Castration," *New Scientist* 57:525–526.
Cornford, Francis M., trans.
1945   *The Republic of Plato* (New York: Oxford).
Crowe, Beryl L.
1969   "The Tragedy of the Commons Revisited," *Science* 166:1103–1107.
Dahl, Robert A.
1970   *After the Revolution?: Authority in a Good Society* (New Haven: Yale).
Delgado, Jose Manuel R.
1969   *Physical Control of the Mind: Toward a Psychocivilized Society* (New York: Harper and Row).
Eisner, Thomas, Ari van Tienhaven, and Frank Rosenblatt
1970   "Population Control, Sterilization, and Ignorance," *Science* 167:337.
Ellul, Jacques
1967   *The Technological Society* (rev.; New York: Knopf).
Fife, Daniel
1971   "Killing the Goose," *Environment* 13(3):20–27 [the logic of the commons].
Forster, E. M.
1928   *The Eternal Moment* (New York: Harcourt, Brace).
Fuller, R. Buckminster
1968   "An Operating Manual for Spaceship Earth" in *Environment and Change: The Next Fifty Years,* ed. William R. Ewald, Jr. (Bloomington: Indiana).
1969   "Vertical Is to Live, Horizontal Is to Die," *American Scholar* 39(1):27–47.
Geesaman, Donald P., and Dean E. Abrahamson
1974   "The Dilemma of Fission Power," *Bulletin of the Atomic Scientists* 30(9):37–41 [the extreme security measures a nuclear power economy will require].

Haefele, Edwin T., ed.
    1975   *The Governance of Common Property Resources* (Baltimore: Johns Hopkins).
Hardin, Garrett
    1968   "The Tragedy of the Commons," *Science* 162:1243–1248.
    1972   *Exploring New Ethics for Survival* (New York: Viking).
———, ed.
    1969   *Population, Evolution, and Birth Control: A Collage of Controversial Ideas* (2nd ed.: San Francisco: W. H. Freeman and Co.).
Heilbroner, Robert L.
    1974   *An Inquiry into the Human Prospect* (New York: Norton).
Hobbes, Thomas
    1651   *Leviathan, or the Matter, Form and Power of a Commonwealth, ecclesiastical and civil*, ed. H. W. Schneider (Indianapolis: Bobbs-Merrill, 1958).
Holden, Constance
    1973   "Psychosurgery: Legitimate Therapy or Laundered Lobotomy?" *Science* 179:1109–1114.
Huxley, Aldous L.
    1932   *Brave New World* (New York: Modern Library, 1956).
    1958   *Brave New World Revisited* (New York: Harper).
Illich, Ivan
    1973   *Tools for Conviviality* (New York: Harper and Row).
Kahn, Alfred E.
    1966   "The Tyranny of Small Decisions: Market Failures, Imperfections, and the Limits of Economics," *Kyklos* (I):23–47 [the logic of the commons].
Kahn, Herman, and Anthony J. Wiener
    1968   "Faustian Powers and Human Choice: Some Twenty-First Century Technological and Economic Issues" in *Environment and Choice*, ed. William R. Ewald, Jr. (Bloomington: Indiana), pp. 101–131.
Kass, Leon R.
    1971   "The New Biology: What Price Relieving Man's Estate?" *Science* 174:779–788.
    1972   "Making Babies—The New Biology and the 'Old' Morality," *Public Interest* 26:18–56.
Lewis, C. S.
    1965   *The Abolition of Man* (New York: Macmillan).
Locke, John
    1690   *Second Treatise*, in *Two Treatises of Government*, ed. Peter Laslett (New York: New American Library, 1965).
McDermott, John
    1969   "Technology: The Opiate of the Intellectuals," *New York Review of Books*, July 31, pp. 25–35.
Michael, Donald N.
    1970   *The Unprepared Society: Planning for a Precarious Future* (New York: Harper and Row).
Morrison, Denton E., Kenneth E. Hornback, and W. Keith Warner
    1974   *Environment: A Bibliography of Social Science and Related Literature* (Washington: GPO).
    1975   *Energy: A Bibliography of Social Science and Related Literature* (New York: Garland).
Myers, Norman
    1975   "The Whaling Controversy," *American Scientist* 63:448–455 [an excellent case study of the kinds of pressures that promote overexploitation].
Odell, Rice
    1975   "How Will We React to an Age of Scarcity?" *Conservation Foundation Letter*, January [a review of many different opinions].
Olson, Mancur, Jr.
    1968   *The Logic of Collective Action: Public Goods and the Theory of Groups* (New York: Schocken).
———, and Hans Landsberg, eds.
    1973   *The No-Growth Society* (New York: Norton).
Ophuls, William
    1973   "Leviathan or Oblivion?" in *Toward a Steady-State Economy*, ed. Herman E. Daly (San Francisco: W. H. Freeman and Co.), pp. 215–230.

Orwell, George
    1963   *Nineteen Eighty-Four: Text, Sources, Criticism,* ed. Irving Howe (New York: Harcourt, Brace
            and World).
Pirages, Dennis C., and Paul R. Ehrlich
    1974   *Ark II: Social Response to Environmental Imperatives* (San Francisco: W. H. Freeman and
            Company).
Popper, Karl R.
    1966   *The Open Society and Its Enemies* (2 vols, 5th ed., rev.; Princeton University Press).
Reich, Charles A.
    1971   *The Greening of America* (New York: Random House).
Rousseau, Jean-Jacques
    1762   *The Social Contract,* ed. Charles Frankel (New York: Hafner, 1947).
Russett, Bruce M., and John D. Sullivan
    1971   "Collective Goods and International Organization," *International Organization* 25:845–865.
Schelling, Thomas C.
    1971   "On the Ecology of Micromotives," *Public Interest* 25:61–98.
Skinner, B. F.
    1971   *Beyond Freedom and Dignity* (New York: Knopf).
Smith, Adam
    1776   *An Inquiry into the Nature and Causes of the Wealth of Nations,* ed. Edwin Cannan (New York:
            Modern Library, 1937).
Speth, J. Gustave, Arthur R. Tamplin, and Thomas B. Cochran
    1974   "Plutonium Recycle: The Fateful Step." *Bulletin of the Atomic Scientists* 30(9):15–22.
Stillman, Peter G.
    1975   "The Tragedy of the Commons: A Re-Analysis," *Alternatives* 4(2):12–15.
Stone, Christopher D.
    1974   *Should Trees Have Standing?: Toward Legal Rights for Natural Objects* (Los Altos, Calif.:
            William Kaufmann).
Susskind, Charles
    1973   *Understanding Technology* (Baltimore: Johns Hopkins).
Tuan, Yi-Fu
    1970   "Our Treatment of the Environment in Ideal and Actuality," *American Scientist* 58:244–249
            [the Chinese and their environment through history].
Wade, Nicholas
    1974   "Sahelian Drought: No Victory for Western Aid," *Science* 185:234–237 [how an aid program
            destroyed the traditional controls on a common—with catastrophic results].
Webb, Walter Prescott
    1952   *The Great Frontier* (Boston: Houghton Mifflin).
Weinberg, Alvin M.
    1972a   "Social Institutions and Nuclear Energy," *Science* 177:27–34.
    1972b   Review of John Holdren and Philip Herrera, *Energy: A Crisis in Power,* in *American Scientist*
            60:775–776.
    1973   "Technology and Ecology—Is There a Need for Confrontation?" *BioScience* 23:41–46.
White, Lynn, Jr.
    1967   "The Historical Roots of Our Ecologic Crisis," *Science* 155:1203–1207.
Wilkinson, Richard G.
    1973   *Poverty and Progress: An Ecological Perspective on Economic Development* (New York: Praeger).
Willrich, Mason
    1975   "Terrorists Keep Out!: The Problem of Safeguarding Nuclear Materials in a World of
            Malfunctioning People," *Bulletin of the Atomic Scientists* 31(5):12–16.
Wynne-Edwards, V. C.
    1970   "Self-Regulatory Systems in Populations of Animals," in *The Subversive Science,* ed. Paul
            Shepard and Daniel McKinley (Boston: Houghton Mifflin), pp. 99–111 [valuable biological
            perspective on the tragedy of the commons].

6/Ethics

introduction: dialectics of oppression and liberation

Part of the new politics has been the proliferation of liberation fronts. Third World and women's liberation movements are not unconnected. They do not form a conspiracy; they do not hold secret meetings to coordinate strategy and ideology. But the roughly simultaneous emergence of these movements suggests that even in their ideological variety and geographical distance from each other they nevertheless share a common origin in the history that spawned them, and consequently they share some common problems, at least at a formal level.

In recent decades many different groups of people have banded together (albeit in different bands) to say, "No, absolutely not! We will not have it go on any more the way it is now." The various liberation movements all seemed to come of age at once, following a latent period in the fifties. They all decided to have done with patriarchy, whether it be the paternalism of the United States represented in the Shah's regime in Iran, or the paternalism of an outright colonial power like Portugal in Angola, or the paternalism of resident whites in South Africa descended from those proud British who were ready to "carry the white man's burden," or the paternalism of the male sex toward the female sex.

In citing paternalism as a common issue I hardly intend to claim that all oppressors act like fathers, or that all fathers are oppressors. The accusation of paternalism usually implies that someone is demanding the prerogatives of fatherhood in an inappropriate context or without accepting its obligations. Locke emphasized the duties that attend the privileges of fatherhood, but even accepting those duties elicits the accusation of paternalism where the claim to fatherhood is inappropriate. Despite the inappropriateness of the claim, however, that the oppressed experience their oppression as paternalism suggests that they are fighting some of the same battles fought by children against parents. Once again this is not to demean liberation movements as childish; we are only exploring the analogy between the struggle of the oppressed and the struggle of growth. The keys to the analogy are the concepts of *internalization, identification,* and *dynamic development.* After seeing the meaning of these concepts in the context of the family, we shall test their validity in the very different context of liberation struggles.

Freud describes a son as wavering back and forth between wishing to be like his father in every way and harboring animosity toward his father, occasioned partly by knowing that, unlike his father, he cannot possess his mother. A son becomes who he is partially by internalizing his father's values, yet he cannot identify completely, as the ancient taboo against incest with the mother symbolizes. So man born of woman is to a certain extent unlike other living things, which reproduce true to type. A son cannot be exactly like his father. Yet the son's differentiation, his success in consolidating his own identity, does not consist merely in opposition or negation. Instead, Freud unfolds a dynamic development of identification and rejection: "the great task of detaching himself from his parents" is not a one-shot operation but a series of interactions including "reconciling himself with his father if he has remained antagonistic to him, or in freeing himself from his domination if, in the reaction to the infantile revolt, he has lapsed into subservience to him."[1]

The more one has internalized from and identified with a paternal power, the more the pain of liberation is a function of how much one is trying to cut away from a part of oneself. Liberation is not simply the good guys wresting control from the bad guys. It often represents an internal struggle, difficult precisely because we are fighting a part of ourselves. I am who I am partly through the process of identification with my father. When I detach myself from my father, as I must do, I detach myself from part of myself; and that part of myself may not like it. Hence the perpetual fear of "Uncle Tomism" in the liberation movements. Some people seem happy, like Uncle Tom, with their subservience to a paternalistic master. And those people are a threat to every liberationist, because the liberationist knows the extent to which he or she too shares some of the same feelings. How could it be otherwise? We are who we are partly as a result of the paternalism we are in the midst of rejecting, even if the effort of rejection makes us temporarily blind to those similarities.

Another formal feature shared by aptly named liberation *movements* is their developmental character. We can hardly overlook the various stages of liberation movements, for example, from the militant rejection and rioting, through accommodating schemes of blacks and whites working together, to nonmilitant black separatist movements, and so on. A similar dynamic attends the women's liberation movement, though in both movements claims to a strict linearity of stages must by tempered by the confusing evidence of different people in different stages at the same time. Yet it seems safe to say that individuals do tend to recapitulate historical movements in their attempts to come to terms with the liberation struggle.

To summarize: first, the struggle is often with a real part of ourselves, since we were partially created by that from which we now wish liberation. Second, the task of liberation is a dynamic process involving a dialectical development of rejection and identification. These two ideas fit together with many of the ideas developed in earlier

---

[1]Sigmund Freud, *Complete Introductory Lectures on Psychoanalysis,* ed. and trans. James Strachey, Standard Edition 16, 1917 (New York: W. W. Norton, 1966), p. 337.

essays: the process of identification is encouraged by all the subtleties discussed by Goffman, Polanyi, Mead, and Laing. Through various kinds of attribution, positive reinforcement, applause, and so on, our parents and our peers aid in the constitution of the self and its identity. Further, the existentialist, historicist view of the self as a process of development argues even more strongly than Freud ever did that we are what we become.

If we combine the formal features of the dialectics of liberation with the developmental ideas just mentioned, we get the following picture. Assuming that one feels the necessity of saying no to some forces of oppression, one must then acknowledge that the forces are not all without; many are within. The external enemy is the more oppressive the more it can condition the oppressed to accept a negative self-image. But then the more oppressive a force is, the more it has placed the enemy within. If racism were not effective at making oppressed races think poorly of themselves then racism would not be so oppressive. But a large part of racism in the United States is the subtle reinforcement of a negative self-image. Hence the importance of "black is beautiful" as a stage in the dialectic. If sexism were not effective at making women feel inferior, then sexism would not really be very oppressive. But cultural reinforcement does make women feel that the sexist claims are true. Consequently—and here is the import of historicism—oppression has an uncanny way of generating its own "truth": if you convince people in subtle and deepseated ways that they are lazy or stupid, chances are that the attribution may stick, not because they *are* (essentially) lazy or stupid, but because people are capable of *becoming* any number of things with enough social reinforcement. With a certain "coming of age" a person or a people may somehow become aware of other possibilities. Perhaps I might become different from what I have become. I may in fact come to despise what I have become, and I may blame others for making me become what I have become. But one point remains distressingly clear from the arguments combined so far: I will get nowhere in becoming something else until I acknowledge how much I am, at least for now, what I have become up to now. I say "distressingly clear" because it is much easier to believe that the righteousness of a liberation front derives from the simple mistakenness of the current enemy, as if sexists and racists and nationalists were simply wrong and had to be shown the error of their ways. Like a child struggling for his or her identity, each movement must struggle with its identification with the oppressor. The struggle is difficult because it arouses self-doubt: what I am fighting is in me, perhaps even to the extent that the form of my struggle is dictated by what has been done to me; perhaps it is even silly to imagine that I could ever fight my way out if the fight itself is part of my conditioning—if, for example, I'm only proving them true when they say I am surly and rebellious. Around and around it goes: the awareness of the reality of identification engenders a distrust in one's ability to detach oneself from the parents, and the distrust itself gets blamed on the parents, from whom one then wants detachment all the more. It is easier to ignore the reality of identification. But to view the dialectics of liberation philosophically requires that we put aside the doctrinaire mongering of simple slogans that locate the entire problem in someone else's consciousness and actions. The quest for self-knowledge requires an uncovering of our own racism and sexism toward ourselves. In short, we need a little consciousness raising.

ARTHUR SCHOPENHAUER *(1788–1860)*

    Arthur Schopenhauer was a pessimist, yet his thought is so full of paradox that sometimes it reflects an irrepressible hope. A fundamental tenet of his philosophy is that life, even the examined life, is fundamentally not worth living. Life is a series of sorrows, or, less sentimentally and more in Schopenhauer's style, an unpleasant chore of balancing occasional peace against the heavier weights of boredom and pain. Yet the energy of his writing belies the ascetic resignation that should follow from his pessimism.

    A taste for paradox complements the sources of his thought. By his own declaration Schopenhauer acknowledged that his philosophy contains very little that is new. Rather, it grew from a synthesis of Kant's philosophy and the long tradition of Indian philosophy, going back to the Vedanta scriptures of about 2500–2000 B.C. Kant's claim that we know appearances rather than things in themselves is interpreted by Schopenhauer in terms of the Indian doctrine of maya, or illusion. We live most of our lives in a world of illusion; the best we can do is deny the reality of the illusion, which amounts to denying what most people regard as life. Hence the implication of ascetic withdrawal and indifference that pervades much of Schopenhauer's writing. Yet his very indifference sometimes gives him the clarity of one who has no stake in the matter, no interests to protect. Schopenhauer is free of the need to bolster his picture of reality with convenient, optimistic truths, because he has already resigned himself to the possibility that each inquiry will demonstrate anew the intolerability of life. And that very resignation sometimes allows him, more than others, to penetrate to the truths that set one free. Sometimes his pessimism colors the objects of his inquiry, but often it merely removes the rosy glasses that keep others from seeing true colors. Reading Schopenhauer presents the difficult task of deciding whether his pessimism allows a perspective on the truth or gets in the way of the truth. His essay on women, from Parerga und Paralipomena *(1851, translated here by Thomas Bailey Saunders), is a case in point.*

    Schopenhauer demolishes women. He is the ultimate "male chauvinist pig." He accuses women of being deficient in intellect and the arts. According to him, they are somewhere between children and fully developed men. They are experts only in such things as dissimulation and child rearing; they are not to be trusted with important matters like handling property or capital; and so on. In suggesting that Schopenhauer's essay be taken even the least bit seriously the point is that we are all male chauvinists by our very birth into modern western civilization. Most women are male chauvinists, even those champions of women's rights—those who claim that there are no important differences between men and women. They have been brainwashed with the idea that to be fully human is to be like a man, so they deny that they are in any significant way different from men, and to deny differences is to limit chances of their proper evaluation.

    Schopenhauer's essay is helpful in trying to ferret out the realities of our chauvinism, for we cannot help admitting that on many points his words ring true: there are women who are as Schopenhauer describes them. If we refuse to accept this fact we can hardly begin to liberate ourselves, for how can you liberate yourself from what is unac-knowledged? Only when we recognize that things are as bad as Schopenhauer says they are can we know the realities well enough to change them.

I hardly endorse everything Schopenhauer has to say. I find it necessary to distinguish between the descriptive and the evaluative in his essay. After accurately describing some differences between men and women, he unjustifiably values everything masculine and devalues everything feminine. But we can learn from his descriptions without agreeing with his evaluations. Simply to deny the differences he describes is to agree with his evaluations: if you insist that men and women are equally suited to both child rearing and high finance, and do so in order to gain jobs for women in "more important posts," then chances are you think economics is to be valued more than child rearing. But that is a male chauvinist evaluation. Am I claiming that women are better suited to rear children and that this natural endowment should be honored above their desires to do other things such as pursue careers? No. I am not arguing that everything is as it ought to be in some sort of natural scheme of alloted endowments or essences. Aside from biological considerations, women have been socially conditioned to their affinity with children. But we must not lose sight of the reality of this social condition-ing. Many women are as Schopenhauer describes them, not by nature, but because they are believed to be that way, and this widely held belief has its historical influence on social reality. We cannot change that reality until we acknowledge that it is indeed reality.

Read Schopenhauer's essay carefully. Try to distinguish the truly male chauvinist evaluations from the descriptions his pessimism allows him to acknowledge. And finally, try to be pessimistically honest about the depths of your own chauvinism. This is consciousness raising.

On Women

Schiller's poem in honour of women, *Würde der Frauen*, is the result of much careful thought, and it appeals to the reader by its antithetic style and its use of contrast; but as an expression of the true praise which should be accorded to them, it is, I think, inferior to these few words of Jouy's: *Without women the beginning of our life would be helpless; the middle, devoid of pleasure; and the end, of consolation.* The same thing is more feelingly expressed by Byron in *Sardanapalus:*—

> The very first
> Of human life must spring from women's breast,
> Your first small words are taught you from her lips,
> Your first tears quench'd by her, and your last sighs
> Too often breathed out in a woman's hearing,
> When men have shrunk from the ignoble care
> Of watching the last hour of him who led them.
> (Act I. Scene 2)

These two passages indicate the right standpoint for the appreciation of women.

You need only look at the way in which she is formed to see that woman is not meant to undergo great labour, whether of the mind or of the body. She pays the debt of life not by what she does but by what she suffers; by the pains of childbearing and care for the child, and by submission to her husband, to whom she should be a patient and cheering companion. The keenest sorrows and joys are not for her, nor is she called upon to display a great deal of strength. The current of her life should be more gentle, peaceful and trivial than man's, without being essentially happier or unhappier.

Women are directly fitted for acting as the nurses and teachers of our early childhood by the fact that they are themselves childish, frivolous and short-sighted; in a word, they are big children all their life long—a kind of intermediate stage between the child and the full-grown man, who is man in the strict sense of the word. See how a girl will fondle a child for days together, dance with it and sing to it; and then think what a man, with the best will in the world, could do if he were put in her place.

With young girls Nature seems to have had in view what, in the language of the drama, is called a *coup de théâtre.* For a few years she dowers them with a wealth of beauty and is lavish in her gift of charm, at the expense of the rest of their life, in order that during those years they may capture the fantasy of some man to such a degree that he is hurried into undertaking the honourable care of them, in some form or other, as long as they live—a step for which there would not appear to be any sufficient warranty if reason only directed his thoughts. Accordingly Nature has equipped woman, as she does all her creatures, with the weapons and implements requisite for the safeguarding of her existence, and for just as long as it is necessary for her to have them. Here, as elsewhere, Nature proceeds with her usual economy; for just as the female ant, after fecundation, loses her wings, which are then superfluous, nay, actually a danger to the business of breeding; so, after giving birth to one or two children, a woman generally loses her beauty; probably, indeed, for similar reasons.

And so we find that young girls, in their hearts, look upon domestic affairs or work of any kind as of secondary importance, if not actually as a mere jest. The only business that really claims their earnest attention is love, making conquests, and everything connected with this—dress, dancing, and so on.

The nobler and more perfect a thing is, the later and slower it is in arriving at maturity. A man reaches the maturity of his reasoning powers and mental faculties hardly before the age of twenty-eight; a woman, at eighteen. And then, too, in the case of woman, it is only reason of a sort—very niggard in its dimensions. That is why women remain children their whole life long; never seeing anything but what is quite close to them, cleaving to the present moment, taking appearance for reality, and preferring trifles to matters of the first importance. For it is by virtue of his reasoning faculty that man does not live in the present only, like the brute, but looks about him and considers the past and the future; and this is the origin of prudence, as well as of that care and anxiety which so many people exhibit. Both the advantages and the disadvantages which this involves, are shared in by the woman to a smaller extent because of her weaker power of reasoning. She may, in fact, be described as intellectually shortsighted, because, while she has an intuitive understanding of what lies quite close to her, her field of vision is narrow and does not reach to what is remote: so that things which are absent or past or to come have much less effect upon women than upon men. This is the reason why women are more often inclined to be extravagant, and sometimes carry their inclination to a length that borders upon madness. In their hearts women think that it is men's business to earn money and theirs to spend it—if possible during their husband's life, but, at any rate, after his death. The very fact that their husband hands them over his earnings for purposes of housekeeping strengthens them in this belief.

However many disadvantages all this may involve, there is at least this to be said in its favour: that the woman lives more in the present than the man, and that, if the present is at all tolerable, she enjoys it more eagerly. This is the source of that cheerfulness which is peculiar to woman, fitting her to amuse man in his hours of recreation, and, in case of need, to console him when he is borne down by the weight of his cares.

It is by no means a bad plan to consult women in matters of difficulty, as the Germans used to do in ancient times; for their way of looking at things is quite different from ours, chiefly in the fact that they like to take the shortest way to their goal, and, in general, manage to fix their eyes upon what lies before them; while we, as a rule, see far beyond it, just because it is in front of our noses. In cases like this, we need to be brought back to the right standpoint, so as to recover the near and simple view.

Then, again, women are decidedly more sober in their judgment than we are, so that they do not see more in things than is really there; whilst, if our passions are aroused, we are apt to see things in an exaggerated way, or imagine what does not exist.

The weakness of their reasoning faculty also explains why it is that women show more sympathy for the unfortunate than men do, and so treat them with more kindness and interest; and why it is that, on the contrary, they are inferior to men in point of justice, and less honourable and conscientious. For it is just because their reasoning power is weak that present circumstances have such a hold over them, and those concrete things which lie directly before their eyes exercise a power which is seldom counteracted to any extent by abstract principles of thought, by fixed rules of conduct, firm resolutions, or, in general, by consideration for the past and the future, or regard for what is absent and remote. Accordingly, they possess the first and main elements that go to make a virtuous character, but they are deficient in those secondary qualities which are often a necessary instrument in the formation of it.

Hence it will be found that the fundamental fault of the female character is that it has *no sense of justice*. This is mainly due to the fact, already mentioned, that women are defective in the powers of reasoning and deliberation; but it is also traceable to the position which Nature has assigned to them as the weaker sex. They are dependent, not upon strength, but only craft; and hence their instinctive capacity for cunning, and their ineradicable tendency to say what is not true. For as lions are provided with claws and teeth, and elephants and boars with tusks, bulls with horns, and the cuttle fish with its cloud of inky fluid, so Nature has equipped woman, for her defence and protection, with the arts of dissimulation; and all the power which Nature has conferred upon man in the shape of physical strength and reason has been bestowed upon women in this form. Hence dissimulation is innate in woman, and almost as much a quality of the stupid as of the clever. It is as natural for them to make use of it on every occasion as it is for those animals to employ their means of defence when they are attacked; they have a feeling that in doing so they are only within their rights. Therefore a woman who is perfectly truthful and not given to dissimulation is perhaps an impossibility, and for this very reason they are so quick at seeing through dissimulation in others that it is not a wise thing to attempt it with them. But this fundamental defect which I have stated, with all that it entails, gives rise to falsity, faithlessness, treachery, ingratitude, and so on. Perjury in a court of justice is more often committed by women than by men. It may, indeed, be generally questioned whether women ought to be sworn at all. From time to time one finds repeated cases everywhere of ladies, who want for nothing, taking things from shopcounters when no one is looking and making off with them.

Nature has appointed that the propagation of the species shall be the business of men who are young, strong and handsome; so that the race may not degenerate. This is the firm will and purpose of Nature in regard to the species, and it finds its expression in the passions of women. There is no law that is older or more powerful than this. Woe, then, to the man who sets up claims and interests that will conflict with it; whatever he may say and do, they will be unmercifully crushed at the first serious encounter. For the innate rule that governs women's conduct, though it is secret and unformulated, nay, unconscious in its workings, is this: *We are justified in deceiving those who think they have acquired rights over the species by paying little attention to the individual, that is, to us. The constitution and, therefore, the welfare of the species have been placed in our hands and committed to our care, through the control we obtain over the next generation, which proceeds from us; let us discharge our duties conscientiously.* But women have no abstract knowledge of this leading principle; they are conscious of it only as a concrete fact; and they have no other method of giving expression to it than the way in which they act when the opportunity arrives. And then their conscience does not trouble them so much as we fancy; for in the darkest recesses of their heart they are aware that, in committing a breach of their duty towards the individual, they have all the better fulfilled their duty towards the species, which is infinitely greater.

And since women exist in the main solely for the propagation of the species, and are not destined for anything else, they live, as a rule, more for the species than for the individual, and in their hearts take the affairs of the species more seriously than those of the individual. This gives their whole life and being a certain levity; the general bent of their character is in a direction fundamentally different from that of man; and it is this which produces that discord in married life which is so frequent, and almost the normal state.

The natural feeling between men is mere indifference, but between women it is actual enmity. The reason of this is that trade-jealousy which, in the case of men, does not go beyond the confines of their own particular pursuit but with women embraces the whole sex; since they have only one kind of business. Even when they meet in the street women look at one another like Guelphs and Ghibellines. And it is a patent fact that when two women make first acquaintance with each other they behave with more constraint and dissimulation than two men would show in a like case; and hence it is that an exchange of compliments between two women is a much more ridiculous proceeding than between two men. Further, whilst a man will, as a general rule, always preserve a certain amount of consideration and humanity in speaking to others, even to those who are in a very inferior position, it is intolerable to see how proudly and disdainfully a fine lady will generally behave towards one who is in a lower social rank (I do not mean a woman who is in her service), whenever she speaks to her. The reason of this may be that, with women, differences of rank are much more precarious than with us; because, while a hundred considerations carry weight in our case, in theirs there is only one, namely, with which man they have found favour; as also that they stand in much nearer relations with one another than men do, in consequence of the one-sided nature of their calling. This makes them endeavour to lay stress upon differences of rank.

It is only the man whose intellect is clouded by his sexual impulses that could give the name of *the fair sex* to that undersized, narrow-shouldered, broad-hipped, and short-legged race: for the whole beauty of the sex is bound up with this impulse. Instead of calling them beautiful, there would be more warrant for describing women as the unaesthetic sex. Neither for music, nor for poetry, nor for fine art, have they really and truly any sense or susceptibility; it is a mere mockery if they make a pretence of it in order to assist their endeavour to please. Hence, as a result of this, they are incapable of taking a *purely objective interest* in anything; and the reason of it seems to me to be as follows. A man tries to acquire *direct* mastery over things, either by understanding them or by forcing them to do his will. But a woman is always and everywhere reduced to obtaining this mastery *indirectly*, namely through a man; and whatever direct mastery she may have is entirely confined to him. And so it lies in woman's nature to look upon everything only as a means for conquering man; and if she takes an interest in anything else it is simulated—a mere roundabout way of gaining her ends by coquetry and feigning what she does not feel. Hence even Rousseau declared: *Women have, in general, no love of any art; they have no proper knowledge of any; and they have no genius.*[1]

No one who sees at all below the surface can have failed to remark the same thing. You need only observe the kind of attention women bestow upon a concert, an opera, or a play—the childish simplicity, for example, with which they keep on chattering during the finest passages in the greatest masterpieces. If it is true that the Greeks excluded women from their theatres, they were quite right in what they did; at any rate you would have been able to hear what was said upon the stage. In our day, besides, or in lieu of saying, *Let a woman keep silence in the church*, it would be much to the point to say, *Let a woman keep silence in the theatre*. This might, perhaps, be put up in big letters on the curtain.

And you cannot expect anything else of a woman if you consider that the

[1]Lettre à d'Alembert. Note xx.

most distinguished intellects among the whole sex have never managed to produce a single achievement in the fine arts that is really great, genuine, and original; or given to the world any work of permanent value in any sphere. This is most strikingly shown in regard to painting, where mastery of technique is at least as much within their power as within ours—and hence they are diligent in cultivating it; but still, they have not a single great painting to boast of, just because they are deficient in that objectivity of mind which is so directly indispensable in painting. They never get beyond a subjective point of view. It is quite in keeping with this that ordinary women have no real susceptibility for art at all; for Nature proceeds in strict sequence—*non facit saltum*. The case is not altered by particular and partial exceptions; taken as a whole, women are, and remain, thorough-going philistines, and quite incurable. Hence, with that absurd arrangement which allows them to share the rank and title of their husbands, they are a constant stimulus to his ignoble ambitions. And, further, it is just because they are philistines that modern society, where they take the lead and set the tone, is in such a bad way. Napoleon's saying—that *women have no rank*—should be adopted as the right standpoint in determining their position in society; and as regards their other qualities Chamfort makes the very true remark:

> They are made to trade with our own weaknesses and our follies, but not with our reason. The sympathies that exist between them and men are skin-deep only, and do not touch the mind or the feelings or the character.

They form the *sexus sequior*—the second sex, inferior in every respect to the first; their infirmities should be treated with consideration; but to show them great reverence is extremely ridiculous, and lowers us in their eyes. When Nature made two divisions of the human race, she did not draw the line exactly through the middle. These divisions are polar and opposed to each other, it is true; but the difference between them is not qualitative merely, it is also quantitative.

This is just the view which the ancients took of woman, and the view which people in the East take now; and their judgment as to her proper position is much more correct than ours, with our old French notions of gallantry and our preposterous system of reverence—that highest product of Teutonico-Christian stupidity. These notions have served only to make women more arrogant and overbearing; so that one is occasionally reminded of the holy apes in Benares, who in the consciousness of their sanctity and inviolable position think they can do exactly as they please.

But in the West the woman, and especially the *lady*, finds herself in a false position; for woman, rightly called by the ancients *sexus sequior*, is by no means fit to be the object of our honour and veneration, or to hold her head higher than man and be on equal terms with him. The consequences of this false position are sufficiently obvious. Accordingly it would be a very desirable thing if this Number Two of the human race were in Europe also relegated to her natural place, and an end put to that lady-nuisance, which not only moves all Asia to laughter but would have been ridiculed by Greece and Rome as well. It is impossible to calculate the good effects which such a change would bring about in our social, civil and political arrangements. There would be no necessity for the Salic law: it would be a superfluous truism. In Europe the *lady*, strictly so-called, is a being who should not exist at all; she should be either a housewife or a girl who hopes to become one; and she should be brought up, not to be arrogant, but to be thrifty and submissive. It is just because there are such people as *ladies* in Europe that the women of the lower classes, that is to say, the great majority of the sex, are much more unhappy than they are in the East. And even Lord Byron says:

> Thought of the state of women under the ancient Greeks—convenient enough. Present state, a remnant of the barbarism of the chivalric and the feudal ages—artificial and unnatural. They ought to mind home— and be well fed and clothed—but not mixed in society. Well educated, too, in religion—but to read neither poetry nor politics—nothing but books of piety and cookery. Music—drawing—dancing—also a little gardening and ploughing now and then. I have seen them mending the roads in Epirus with good success. Why not, as well as haymaking and milking?

The laws of marriage prevailing in Europe consider the woman as the equivalent of the man—start, that is to say, from a wrong position. In our part of the world where monogamy is the rule, to marry means to halve one's rights and double one's duties. Now when the laws gave women equal rights with man, they ought to have also endowed her with a masculine intellect. But the fact is that, just in proportion as the honours and privileges which the laws accord to women exceed the amount which Nature gives, there is a diminution in the number of women who really participate in these privileges; and all the remainder are deprived of their natural rights by just so much as is given to the others over and above their share. For the institution of monogamy, and the laws of marriage which it entails, bestow upon the woman an unnatural position of privilege, by considering her throughout as the full equivalent of the man, which is by no means the case; and seeing this men who are shrewd and prudent very often scruple to make so great a sacrifice and to acquiesce in so unfair an arrangement.

Moreover, the bestowal of unnatural rights upon women has imposed upon them unnatural duties, and nevertheless a breach of these duties makes them unhappy. Let me explain. A man may often think that his social or financial position will suffer if he marries, unless he makes some brilliant alliance. His desire will then be to win a woman of his own choice under conditions other than those of marriage, such as will secure her position and that of the children. However fair, reasonable, fit and proper these conditions may be, if the woman consents by foregoing that undue amount of privilege which marriage alone can bestow, she to some extent loses her honour, because marriage is the basis of civic society; and she will lead an unhappy life, since human nature is so constituted that we pay an attention to the opinion of other people which is out of all proportion to its value. On the other hand, if she does not consent, she runs the risk either of having to be given in marriage to a man whom she does not like, or of being landed high and dry as an old maid; for the period during which she has a chance of being settled for life is very short. And in view of this aspect of the institution of monogamy, Thomasius' profoundly learned treatise *On Concubinage* is well worth reading; for it shows that, amongst all nations and in all ages, down to the Lutheran Reformation, concubinage was permitted; nay, that it was an institution which was to a certain extent actually recognised by law, and attended with no dishonour. It was only the Lutheran Reformation that degraded it from this position. It was seen to be a further justification for the marriage of the clergy; and then, after that, the Catholic Church did not dare to remain behind-hand in the matter.

The first love of a mother for her child is, with the lower animals as with men, of a purely *instinctive* character, and so it ceases when the child is no longer in a physically helpless condition. After that, the first love should give way to one that is based on habit and reason; but this often fails to make its appearance, especially where the mother did not love the father. The love of a father for his child is of a different order, and more likely to last; because it has its foundation in the fact that in the child he recognises his own inner self; that is to say, his love for it is metaphysical in its origin.

In almost all nations, whether of the ancient or the modern world, even amongst the Hottentots, property is inherited by the male descendants alone; it is only in Europe that a departure has taken place; but not amongst the nobility, however. That the property which has cost men long years of toil and effort, and been won with so much difficulty, should afterwards come into the hands of women, who then, in their lack of reason, squander it in a short time, or otherwise fool it away, is a grievance and a wrong, as serious as it is common, which should be prevented by limiting the right of women to inherit. In my opinion the best arrangement would be that by which women, whether widows or daughters, should never receive anything beyond the interest for life on property secured by mortgage, and in no case the property itself, or the capital, except where all male descendants fail. The people who make money are men, not women; and it follows from this that women are neither justified in having unconditional possession of it, nor fit persons to be entrusted with its administration. When wealth, in any true sense of the word, that is to say, funds, houses or land, is to go to them as an inheritance, they should never be allowed the free disposition of it. In their case a guardian should always be appointed; and hence they should never be given the free control of their own children, wherever it can be avoided. The vanity of women, even though it should not prove to be greater than that of men, has this much danger in it that it takes an entirely material direction. They are vain, I mean, of their personal beauty, and then of finery, show and magnificence. That is just why they are so much in their element in society. It is this, too, which makes them so inclined to be extravagant, all the more as their reasoning power is low. But with men vanity often takes the direction of non-material advantages, such as intellect, learning, courage.

That woman is by nature meant to obey may be seen by the fact that every woman who is placed in the unnatural position of complete independence, imme-diately attaches herself to some man, by whom she allows herself to be guided and ruled. It is because she needs a lord and master. If she is young, it will be a lover; if she is old, a priest.

GERMAINE GREER (b. 1939)

Among the many manifestoes of the women's liberation movement Germaine Greer's The Female Eunuch *(1970) is one of the best, partly because it is least like a manifesto. Greer feels* and *thinks. She does not simplify for the sake of polemics. She does not argue a simple sameness of men and women. Instead she acknowledges descriptive differences and then attacks the chauvinist evaluations of those differences. Inferiority does not follow from difference. Indeed, Greer's essay links together with many of the essays in this volume in a way that suggests a superiority of traditionally "female" virtues. Faced with the claim that men often possess stronger egos, she challenges their tenacity to a rigid sense of identity. Here support can be found in Ryle, Hume, and Bergson. She explicitly invokes an erotic sense of reality, in which a connectedness with one's environment would replace a rigid, atomic individualism. The very characteristics for which women have often been chided turn out to be the traits that would characterize the wise man as his picture emerges from many of the essays in this volume. For example, 'women's intuition' turns out to be no more than an openness and sensitivity to the riches of communication discussed by Laing, Goffman, and Polanyi. And the political attack on patriarchy is hardly irrelevant to women's liberation. In short, at least half the essays in this volume have a direct bearing on Greer's "Womanpower."*

Womanpower

The failure of specially designed tests to reveal any specifically sexual difference in intellectual capacity between males and females is irrelevant as far as those who challenge women's fitness for certain responsibilities and work are concerned. They think that the tests reflect more upon the testers and the method of testing than they do upon male and female. Dr. Leavis believed that he could identify a woman writer by her style, even though necessarily all that she wrote must have been a parody of some man's superior achievement. After all, there was not much wrong with Virginia Woolf except that she was a woman. It could be argued that the tests were specially contoured in an attempt to counteract the effect of sexual conditioning, while real women in the real world are continually conditioned. No adjustment of our theoretical opinion of their basic capacity can alter the nature of their achievement. Men complain that they cannot handle women, that arguments with women must be avoided at all costs because they always get the last word mostly by foul means. How "like a woman" they sigh, and all agree. The detection of sex in mind is not only the privilege of the most eminent literary pundits from Dr. Leavis to Norman Mailer,[1] it extends to the lowest levels of illiteracy—the schoolboy muttering about "bloody girls." Because the difference is so wholeheartedly believed in, it is also experienced. As a conviction it becomes a motive for behavior and a continuing cause of the phenomenon itself. It is not to be put aside by rational means. There is of course no reason why women should limit themselves to logic: we might perversely decide to *exploit* the Ovarian Theory of Mind.[2]

One of the fullest statements of the theory of the female soul was set out in *Sex and Character,* a remarkably rigorous and committed book by a mere boy, Otto Weininger, who committed suicide some years after its publication. His brilliant, neurotic life can be taken as an illustration of what dimorphism must eventually accomplish. By disintegrating human nature and building boundaries between

---

Women tend to make their emotions perform the functions they exist to serve, and hence remain mentally much healthier than men.

Ashley Montagu,
The Natural Superiority of Women, 1953

---

warring halves, Weininger condemned himself to perversion, guilt, and early death. He began by identifying women with the body, with unconscious sexuality, and thereafter with passive animalism. As a rational male he condemned such a bestial element. "No men who think really deeply about women retain a high opinion of them; men either despise women or they have never thought seriously about them."[3]

Like Freud, with whom he had much more in common, he thought of women as castrated by nature; because he thought so highly of the penis he thought women did too:

An absolute nude female figure in life leaves an impression of something wanting, an incompleteness which is incompatible with beauty...[4]
The qualities that appeal to a woman are the signs of a developed sexuality; those that repel her are the qualities of the higher mind. Woman is essentially a phallus worshipper...[5]

Weininger thought the dimorphism of the sexes right through, and discovered that, given such a polarity, men could have no real communion with women, only a highly compromised shared hypocrisy. Valerie Solanas performed the same exercise for women, and found that men covet all that women are, seeking

---

[1]See Mary Ellman, *Thinking About Women* (New York, 1968), *passim.* Mailer explains his concept of the novel as the Great Bitch and how women cannot be said to get a piece of her in "Some Children of the Goddess," *Cannibals and Christians* (New York, 1966).
[2]The term is culled from Cynthia Ozick, "The Demise of the Dancing Dog," *Motive,* March–April 1969.
[3]Otto Weininger, *Sex and Character* (London, 1906), p. 236.
[4]*Ibid.,* p. 241.
[5]*Ibid.,* p. 250.

degradation and effeminization at their hands.[6] She retaliated by shooting Andy Warhol in the chest. Weininger more honestly made his attempt upon himself and succeeded. Just as Solanas despises men as they present themselves to be and in their failure to live up to their own stereotype, Weininger despises women both because their image is passive and animalistic, and because they are not genuinely so. Their pretense is brought about by the exigency of the sexual situation which they exploit, hence the duplicity and mendacity which characterize all their actions. Because woman lives vicariously she need take no moral responsibility for her behavior: because she has no responsibility she has no morality and no ego. Because of the lack of ego and the variety of roles that women manipulate, they have no identity, as one may guess from their willingness to give up their names. Woman is never genuine at any period of her life.[7]

Political and civic equality of the sexes implies moral equality. It implies the perfectly appalling logical consequence that the morals of women shall in future be the same as those of respectable Christian Victorian man—at best. That, of course, means the total collapse of Christian morality.

Robert Briffault, *Sin and Sex*, 1931, p. 132

The most chastening reflection is that Weininger was simply describing what he saw in female behavior around him. He could not see that these deformities were what women would one day clamor to be freed from. As far as he could see, women were like that and he did not know what came first, their condition or their character. He assumed that it must have been the latter, because he could not explain their condition any other way.

All the moral deficiencies Weininger detected masqueraded in Victorian society as virtues. Weininger is to be credited with describing them properly. Nevertheless his concepts of ego, identity, logic and morality were formed from observation of this same undesirable status quo, and women today might well find that what Weininger describes as defects might be in fact *freedoms* which they might do well to promote. For example:

With women thinking and feeling are identical, for man they are in opposition. The woman has many of her mental experiences as henids (undifferentiated perceptions) whilst in man these have passed through a process of clarification.[8]

[6]Valerie Solanas, *The S.C.U.M. Manifesto* (New York, 1968), p. 73.

[7]Weininger (*op. cit.*), p. 274. The claim that deceitfulness is a secondary sexual characteristic of the female mind has been made by many observers, including feminists like Mary Wollstonecraft who saw it as an essential consequence of female degradation and B. L. Hutchins, *Conflicting Ideals: Two Sides of the Woman Question* (London, 1913), "Girls have been brought up on intensely insincere ideals" (p. 30).

[8]Weininger (*op cit.*), p. 100. The assumptions that women perceive differently from men, are subjective rather than men and so on, despite the failure of testing to indicate any justification for them, are taken on trust by psychologists who deal with femininity. Deutsch luxuriates in extolling the value of women's subjective, intuitive perception as the desirable complement to male objectivity and mental aggression.

"Definitio est negatio." We might argue that clarification is tantamount to falsification: if you want to know what happened in a particular situation you would be better off asking someone who had perceived the whole and remembered all of it, not just some extrapolated clarification. How sad it is for men to have feeling and thought in opposition! Eliot argued that the seventeenth century had seen a dissociation of sensibility, so that intelligence no longer served as a direct index of the intensity of feeling but rather undermined it.[9] Can it be that women have survived the process which debilitated the rest of male-dominated western culture? If we can make anything of such a seductive possibility, we must reflect that most educated women have simply been admitted to the masculine academic culture, and have lost their power to perceive in henids. According to Antonin Artaud, Anaïs Nin might have survived even that:

> I brought many people, men and women, to see the beautiful canvas, but it is the first time I ever saw artistic emotion make a human being palpitate like love. Your senses trembled and I realized that the mind and body are formidably linked in you, because such a pure spiritual could unleash such a powerful storm in your organism. But in that universal marriage it is the mind that lords over the body and dominates it, and it must end up by dominating it in every way. I feel that there is a world of things in you that are begging to be born should it find its exorcist.[10]

Most of this is nonsense. We might expect the inventor of the theater of cruelty to see the phenomenon of unified sensibility and spend a paragraph trying to prove the domination of the mind to the point of implying that she needed an exorcist! Artaud's manicheism prevented him from seeing that the stimulus of the painting was sensual in the first instance. All that happened was that Nin responded with both mind and body to a sensible and intelligent stimulus. The painting was one and her response was equally integrated.

If women retain their experience in their original unclassified form they may escape the great limitation of scientific thought, which was pointed out by A. N. Whitehead in *Adventures of Ideas.*

> In the study of ideas it is necessary to remember that insistence on hard-headed clarity issues from sentimental feeling, as it were a mist, cloaking the complexities of fact. Insistence on clarity at all costs is based on sheer superstition as to the mode in which human intelligence functions. Our reasonings grasp at straws for premises and float on gossamers for deductions.[11]

[9]T. S. Eliot, "The Metaphysical Poets," *Selected Essays* (New York, 1950).

[10]Antonin Artaud, "Letters to Anais Nin," translated by Mary Beach, *International Times*, No. 16. Letter of June 14 or 15, 1933.

[11]This quotation appears in Marshall McLuhan, *The Medium Is the Massage* (New York, 1967), ascribed to A. N. Whitehead, and a book called *Adventures in Ideas*. I cannot recall seeing it in *Adventures of Ideas* but it does catch the drift of much that Whitehead did say, e.g., "The Anatomy of Some Scientific Ideas," in *The Organisation of Thought* (London, 1917), pp. 134–90 *passim*, or *Science and the Modern World* (Cambridge, 1927), Chap. V, "The Romantic Reaction" (pp. 93–118), *passim*, or indeed *Adventures of Ideas* (Cambridge, 1933), pp. 150–1, 173, 184–5.

At a banal level this functioning difference in male and female thought is easily demonstrated: we have only to think of Father mocking Mother for keeping the salt in a box marked Sago, or the frequently celebrated female intuition, which is after all only a faculty for observing tiny insignificant aspects of behavior and forming an empirical conclusion which cannot be syllogistically examined. Now that most information is not disseminated in argumentative form on the printed page, but is assimilated in various nonverbal ways from visual and aural media, clarification and the virtues of disputation are more and more clearly seen to be simply alternative ways of knowing and not the only or the principal ones. The take-over by computers of much vertical thinking has placed more and more emphasis on the creative propensities of human thought. The sudden increase in political passion in the last decade, especially among the generation which has absorbed most of its education in this undifferentiated form, bears witness to a reintegration of thought and feeling happening on a wide scale. In the circumstances any such peculiarity of the female mind could well become a strength.

Unfortunately my own arguments have all the faults of an insufficient regard for logic and none of its strengths, the penalty after all for a Cartesian education. So much for privilege. Here I am, a Negro who cannot do the lindyhop or sing the Blues! Nowadays education itself is changing so that creative thought does not decline with the inculcation of mental disciplines, which are now not taught as ends but simply as means to other ends. Unfortunately, the chief result of the change so far seems to be the reluctance of children to study science, but eventually science itself will become a complete study.

Weininger has more serious charges though:

A woman cannot grasp that one must act from principle; as she has no continuity she does not experience the necessity for logical support of her mental processes... she may be regarded as "logically insane."[12]

It is true that women often refuse to argue logically. In many cases they simply do not know how to, and men may dazzle them with a little pompous sophistry. In some cases they are intimidated and upset before rationalization begins. But it is also true that in most situations logic is simply rationalization of an infralogical aim. Women know this; even the best educated of them know that arguments with their menfolk are disguised realpolitik. It is not a contest of mental agility with the right as the victor's spoils, but a contest of wills. The rules of logical discourse are no more relevant than the Marquess of Queensberry's are to a pub brawl. Female hardheadedness rejects the misguided masculine notion that men are rational animals. Male logic can only deal with simple issues: women, because they are passive and condemned to observe and react rather than initiate, are more aware of complexity. Men have been forced to suppress their receptivity, in the interests of domination. One of the possible advantages of infantilization of women is that they might after all become, in the words of Lao-Tse, "a channel drawing all the world towards it" so that they "will not be severed from the eternal

[12]Weininger (op. cit.), p. 149.

virtue" and "can return again to the state of infancy."[13] If only the state of women were infancy, and not what we have reduced infancy itself to, new possibilities might be closer to realization than they seem. When Schopenhauer described the state of women as *moral infancy*, he was reflecting not only his prejudice against women, but also against babies. The failure of women to take logic seriously has serious consequences for their morality. Freud adds the gloss to Weininger's text:

> I cannot evade the notion (though I hesitate to give it expression) that for women the level of what is ethically normal is different from what it is in men. Their superego is never so inexorable, so impersonal, so independent of its emotional origins as we require it to be in men. Character-traits which critics of every epoch have brought up against women—that they show less sense of justice than men, that they are less ready to submit to the great exigencies of life, that they are more often influenced in their judgements by their feelings of affection or hostility —all these would be amply accounted for in the modification of the formation of their superego.... We must not allow ourselves to be deflected from such conclusions by the denial of the feminists, who are anxious to force us to regard the two sexes as completely equal in position and worth.[14]

The circularity of this utterance is quite scary. After all, are the sexes equal in position and worth or not? What is position? What is worth? He promises to explain unsubstantiated deficiencies in the female character by an unsubstantiated modification in an unsubstantiated entity, the superego: if physiology is destiny Freud is anxious to invent a physiology of the mind. If judgment had not been separated from feeling so unnaturally in the Nazi officers presumably they would not have carried out orders so crisply. What kind of criticism is it to say that women are less stoical than men? After two world wars stoicism seems to have outlived its value. If women have been denied moral responsibility by male "justice" and dubbed angels while they were treated with contempt, it is likely that they will have formed their own conclusions about the monstrous superego and illusory morality of men. Protestant Europe has set for itself an unattainable morality of integrity in defiance of heavenly mercy, the unaided conscience bowed by full and unending responsibility for all actions, despite the partiality of knowledge and infirmity of will which characterize human action. Freud saw the results in his own community but he could not postulate an alternative to guilt and neurosis. The chief mainstay of such religion is the capacity of the ego to continue repression. Women may be bad at keeping up the cycle of the organism punishing itself, but that too may be an advantage which involves less delusion than its opposite.

The feeling of identity in all circumstances is quite wanting in the true woman, because her memory, even if exceptionally good, is devoid of

---

[13]J. Needham, *Science and Civilisation in China* (Cambridge, 1954), Vol. II, p. 58.
[14]S. Freud, *Some Psychic Consequences of the Anatomical Distinction Between the Sexes*, Complete Works, Vol. XIX, pp. 257–8.

continuity... women, if they look back on their earlier lives, never
understand themselves.[15]

My colleague Nathan Leites, Ph.D., has concluded after a review of the
literature that the term "identity" has little use other than as a fancy
dress in which to disguise vagueness, ambiguity, tautologies, lack of
clinical data, and poverty of explanation.

Robert Stoller, *Sex and Gender*, 1968, p. x

On Weininger's evidence the ego is ersatz, consisting of the memory of the
self which exists at any particular time. He remarks with horror that if you ask a
woman about herself, she understands it to be her body. She does not seek to
define herself by asserting her image of her merit, her behavior. Man has a
temporal notion of identity, which is falsifiable, woman a simple spatial one. "Here
you are," said the white buttons Yoko Ono gave away at her exhibition. It seems
important after all. Perhaps woman, like the child, retains some power of connecting freely with external reality. Weininger seemed to think so. "The absolute
female has no ego."[16]

The primal act of the human ego is a negative one—not to accept reality,
specifically the separation of the child's body from the mother's body
...this negative posture blossoms into negation of self (repression) and
negation of the environment (aggression).[17]

What a blossoming! If women had no ego, if they had no sense of separation
from the rest of the world, no repression and no regression, how nice that would
be! What need would there be of justice if everyone felt no aggression but infinite
compassion! Of course I am taking advantage of the masters of psychology,
bending and selecting their words like this, but what else can they be for? We
cannot allow them to define what must be or change would be impossible.
Whitehead and Needham looked forward to a new kind of knowledge which would
correct the insanity of pure intelligence, "a science based on an erotic sense of
reality, rather than an aggressive dominating attitude to reality."[18] If wisdom
might not be incompatible with a low sense of ego, then charity seems in the
mystical definitions of it to be dependent upon such a corrosion of separateness:
the greatest myth of Christianity is that of the mystical body.

To heal is to make whole, as in wholesome; to make one again; to unify
or reunify; this is Eros in action. Eros is the instinct that makes for
union, or unification, and Thanatos, the death instinct, is the instinct
that makes for separation or division.[19]

---

[15]Weininger (*op. cit*), p. 146.
[16]*Ibid.*, p. 186.
[17]Norman O. Brown, *Life Against Death*.
[18]*Ibid.*, p. 276.
[19]Norman O. Brown, *Love's Body* (New York, 1966), p. 80.

Weininger's disgust for Eros and his devotion to Thanatos drive him to state women's comprehensiveness more fully. Believing him we might think we have been saved already:

> This sense of continuity with the rest of mankind is a sexual character of the female, and displays itself in the desire to touch, to be in contact with the object of her pity; the mode in which her tenderness expresses itself is a kind of animal sense of contact. It shows an absence of that sharp line that separates one real personality from another.[20]

Poor Weininger finally cut himself off altogether in a last act of fealty to death. The immorality of individualism is obvious in an age when loneliness is the most pernicious disease of our overcrowed metropolises. The results of parceling families in tiny slivers living in self-contained dwellings have defaced our cities and created innumerable problems of circulation and cohabitation. The sense of separateness is vainly counteracted by the pressure for conformity without community. In most of the big cities of the world the streets are dangerous to walk upon. Woman's oceanic feeling for the race has little opportunity for expression; it is grotesquely transmogrified in organized works of charity, where her genius for touching and soothing has dwindled into symbolic attitudinizing. Weininger's repugnance for animal contact is still universal among the northern races. Even crushed against his brother in the Tube the average Englishman pretends desperately that he is alone. Psychoanalysis, the most obscenely intimate contact of all, is not hallowed by any physical contact. Latterly, special classes form in church halls in arty suburbs, so that men and women can recover their sense of reassurance by touch. Too late for Weininger.

The intellectual pressure to make the whole world whole again has come from mystics like Lao-Tse, scientists like Whitehead and Needham and Merleau-Ponty, and as brilliant speculation from Norman O. Brown, Herbert Marcuse, Borges. Their words were not specifically addressed to women, because all of them felt that the polarity of the sexes was the basic alienation of man from himself, but none of them would reject the idea that their words were a special encouragement to women to undertake the work of saving mankind. Perhaps my treatment of their

---

Might the cleavage betweeen the subjective and objective have been badly made; might the opposition between a universe of science—entirely outside of self—and a universe of consciousness—defined by the total presence of self to self—be untenable? And if realistic analysis fails will biology find its method in an ideal analysis of the psychomathematical type, in Spinozistic intellection? Or might not value and signification be intrinsic determinations of the organism which could only be acessible to a new mode of "comprehension"?

Maurice Merleau-Ponty,
The Structure of Behaviour, p. 10

---

[20]Weininger (*op. cit.*), p. 198.

highly sophisticated arguments has been brutal, but reverence before authority has never accomplished much in the way of changing things. In inventing a new mythology one must plunder all sources, letting the situation into which the ideas fall serve as their crucible. Most of the defects pointed out by critics of women are simply the results of their having been sheltered from the subtler and more effective types of enculturation which their society lavished upon its male leaders. The strengths they have are of sheer ignorance.

> Dominant ideas need not always be so obvious for them to exert just as powerful an organizing influence on the way a person thinks and approaches a problem. Old and adequate ideas, like old and adequate cities, come to polarize everything around them. All organization is based on them, all things are referred to them. Minor alterations can be made on the outskirts, but it is impossible to change the whole structure radically and very difficult to shift the center of organization to a different place.[21]

Facing this problem, Edward de Bono devised a series of exercises to develop the faculty he called lateral thinking. Lateral thought is the kind which produces ideas and inventions, rather than demonstrable solutions to specific problems. It is the kind of problem-solving which would not get you good marks for method in an examination, and is nevertheless right. It cannot be duplicated by a computer, which only has to learn what it is fed and a method to deal with it. In fact lateral thinking is a one-dimensional analogue of the child's modes of thought. A woman might claim to retain some of the child's faculties, although very limited and diffused, simply because she has not been encouraged to learn methods of thought and develop a disciplined mind. As long as education remains largely induction, ignorance will retain these advantages over learning and it is time that women impudently put them to work.

The prevailing criticism of the female soul can best be explained by the male battle to repress certain faculties in their own mental functioning. Women possessed in abundance those qualities which civilized men strove to repress in themselves, just as children and savages did. The value of such criticism is in the degree to which it reveals the severity of the contouring of the ideal personality, that is to say, male criticism of the female mind is revealing only of the male

---

For a Tear is an Intellectual thing,
And a Sigh is the Sword of an Angel King,
And the bitter groan of a Martyr's woe
Is an Arrow from the Almightie's Bow.
                                                     Blake, *Jerusalem*, pl. 52

---

[21]Edward De Bono, *New Think: The Use of Lateral Thinking in the Generation of New Ideas* (New York, 1968); *cf.* A. N. Whitehead, *An Introduction to Mathematics* (London, 1911), p. 138, and William James, *Same Problems in Philosophy*, Chap. X.

himself. Men in our culture crippled themselves by setting up an impossible standard of integrity: women were not given the chance to fool themselves in this way. Women have been charged with deviousness and duplicity since the dawn of civilization so they have never been able to pretend that their masks were anything but masks. It is a slender case but perhaps it does mean that women have always been in closer contact with reality than men: it would seem to be the just recompense for being deprived of idealism.

If women understand by emancipation the adoption of the masculine role then we are lost indeed. If women can supply no counterbalance to the blindness of male drive the aggressive society will run to its lunatic extremes at ever-escalating speed. Who will safeguard the despised animal faculties of compassion, empathy, innocence and sensuality? What will hold us back from Weininger's fate? Most women who have arrived at positions of power in a men's world have done so by adopting masculine methods which are not incompatible with the masquerade of femininity. They still exploit the sado-masochistic hook-up of the sexes, in which "we have only the choice of being hammer or anvil."[22] Wanda wore feminine clothes to add poignancy to her torture of Gregor, just as Mrs. Castle made sure that she looked attractive when she went to berate the workers as a criminal and irresponsible element in society. It is up to women to develop a form of genuine womanpower against which the Omnipotent Administrator in frilly knickers cannot prevail.

There is much to suggest that when human beings acquired the powers of conscious attention and rational thought they became so fascinated with these new tools that they forgot all else, like chickens hypnotized with their beaks to a chalk line. Our total sensitivity became identified with these partial functions so that we lost the ability to feel nature from the inside, and more, to feel the seamless unity of ourselves and the world. Our philosophy of action falls into the alternatives of voluntarism and determinism, because we have no sense of the wholeness of the endless knot and of the identity of its actions and ours.

A. E. Watts, *Nature, Man and Woman*, 1958, p. 12

Womanpower means the self-determination of women, and that means that all the baggage of paternalistic society will have to be thrown overboard. Woman must have room and scope to devise a morality which does not disqualify her from excellence, and a psychology which does not condemn her to the status of a spiritual cripple. The penalties for such delinquency may be terrible for she must explore the dark without any guide. It may seem at first that she merely exchanges one mode of suffering for another, one neurosis for another. But she may at last claim to have made a definite choice which is the first prerequisite of moral action. She may never herself see the ultimate goal, for the fabric of society is not unraveled in a single lifetime, but she may state it as her belief and find hope in it.

[22]Leopold Von Sacher-Masoch, *Venus in Furs* (London, 1969), p. 160.

> The great renewal of the world will perhaps consist in this, that man and maid, freed from all false feeling and aversion, will seek each other not as opposites, but as brother and sister, as neighbours, and will come together as human beings.[23]

[23]Rainer Maria Rilke, *Letters to a Young Poet* (Edinburgh, 1945), p. 23.

JUDITH JARVIS THOMSON *(b. 1929)*

Women are both blessed and cursed with the burden of childbearing. Not all pregnancies are chosen. Sometimes women terminate pregnancies with abortion. For many years abortion was regarded as equivalent to murder. Feminists, both male and female, beg to differ. They argue for a woman's right to choose for herself or with her mate whether she must bear an unwanted child. Others respond that the unborn fetus has a right to life. How, then, to resolve the conflicting rights of a pregnant woman and her unborn fetus? Some try to dodge the conflict by arguing that the fetus is not yet a person and therefore has no rights. In the following essay, published in the inaugural issue of the journal Philosophy and Public Affairs, *Judith Jarvis Thomson spurns this easy way out. She grants, for the sake of argument, the personhood of the unborn fetus, then examines the status of the conflicting claims. Though she affirms some arguments and refutes others, she concludes, "I am inclined to think it a merit of my account precisely that it does* not *give a general yes or a general no." By grappling with specific conditions and extenuating circumstances, Thomson shows why there is little room for simplistic generalities where genuine moral issues are at stake.*

A Defense of Abortion[1]

Most opposition to abortion relies on the premise that the fetus is a human being, a person, from the moment of conception. The premise is argued for, but, as I think, not well. Take, for example, the most common argument. We are asked to notice that the development of a human being from conception through birth into childhood is continuous; then it is said that to draw a line, to choose a point in this development and say "before this point the thing is not a person, after this point it is a person" is to make an arbitrary choice, a choice for which in the nature of things no good reason can be given. It is concluded that the fetus is, or anyway that we had better say it is, a person from the moment of conception. But this

[1]I am very much indebted to James Thomson for discussion, criticism, and many helpful suggestions.

conclusion does not follow. Similar things might be said about the development of an acorn into an oak tree, and it does not follow that acorns are oak trees, or that we had better say they are. Arguments of this form are sometimes called "slippery slope arguments"—the phrase is perhaps self-explanatory—and it is dismaying that opponents of abortion rely on them so heavily and uncritically.

I am inclined to agree, however, that the prospects for "drawing a line" in the development of the fetus look dim. I am inclined to think also that we shall probably have to agree that the fetus has already become a human person well before birth. Indeed, it comes as a surprise when one first learns how early in its life it begins to acquire human characteristics. By the tenth week, for example, it already has a face, arms and legs, fingers and toes; it has internal organs, and brain activity is detectable.[2] On the other hand, I think that the premise is false, that the fetus is not a person from the moment of conception. A newly fertilized ovum, a newly implanted clump of cells, is no more a person than an acorn is an oak tree. But I shall not discuss any of this. For it seems to me to be of great interest to ask what happens if, for the sake of argument, we allow the premise. How, precisely, are we supposed to get from there to the conclusion that abortion is morally impermissible? Opponents of abortion commonly spend most of their time establishing that the fetus is a person, and hardly any time explaining the step from there to the impermissibility of abortion. Perhaps they think the step too simple and obvious to require much comment. Or perhaps instead they are simply being economical in argument. Many of those who defend abortion rely on the premise that the fetus is not a person, but only a bit of tissue that will become a person at birth; and why pay out more arguments than you have to? Whatever the explanation, I suggest that the step they take is neither easy nor obvious, that it calls for closer examination than it is commonly given, and that when we do give it this closer examination we shall feel inclined to reject it.

I propose, then, that we grant that the fetus is a person from the moment of conception. How does the argument go from here? Something like this, I take it. Every person has a right to life. So the fetus has a right to life. No doubt the mother has a right to decide what shall happen in and to her body; everyone would grant that. But surely a person's right to life is stronger and more stringent than the mother's right to decide what happens in and to her body, and so outweighs it. So the fetus may not be killed; an abortion may not be performed.

It sounds plausible. But now let me ask you to imagine this. You wake up in the morning and find yourself back to back in bed with an unconscious violinist. A famous unconscious violinist. He has been found to have a fatal kidney ailment, and the Society of Music Lovers has canvassed all the available medical records and found that you alone have the right blood type to help. They have therefore kidnapped you, and last night the violinist's circulatory system was plugged into yours, so that your kidneys can be used to extract poisons from his blood as well as

[2]Daniel Callahan, *Abortion: Law, Choice and Morality* (New York, 1970), p. 373. This book gives a fascinating survey of the available information on abortion. The Jewish tradition is surveyed in David M. Feldman, *Birth Control in Jewish Law* (New York, 1968), Part 5, the Catholic tradition in John T. Noonan, Jr., "An Almost Absolute Value in History," in *The Morality of Abortion*, ed. John T. Noonan, Jr. (Cambridge, Mass., 1970).

your own. The director of the hospital now tells you, "Look, we're sorry the Society of Music Lovers did this to you—we would never have permitted it if we had known. But still, they did it, and the violinist now is plugged into you. To unplug you would be to kill him. But never mind, it's only for nine months. By then he will have recovered from his ailment, and can safely be unplugged from you." Is it morally incumbent on you to accede to this situation? No doubt it would be very nice of you if you did, a great kindness. But do you *have* to accede to it? What if it were not nine months, but nine years? Or longer still? What if the director of the hospital says, "Tough luck, I agree, but you've now got to stay in bed, with the violinist plugged into you, for the rest of your life. Because remember this. All persons have a right to life, and violinists are persons. Granted you have a right to decide what happens in and to your body, but a person's right to life outweighs your right to decide what happens in and to your body. So you cannot ever be unplugged from him." I imagine you would regard this as outrageous, which suggests that something really is wrong with that plausible-sounding argument I mentioned a moment ago.

In this case, of course, you were kidnapped; you didn't volunteer for the operation that plugged the violinist into your kidneys. Can those who oppose abortion on the ground I mentioned make an exception for a pregnancy due to rape? Certainly. They can say that persons have a right to life only if they didn't come into existence because of rape; or they can say that all persons have a right to life, but that some have less of a right to life than others, in particular, that those who came into existence because of rape have less. But these statements have a rather unpleasant sound. Surely the question of whether you have a right to life at all, or how much of it you have, shouldn't turn on the question of whether or not you are the product of a rape. And in fact the people who oppose abortion on the ground I mentioned do not make this distinction, and hence do not make an exception in case of rape.

Nor do they make an exception for a case in which the mother has to spend the nine months of her pregnancy in bed. They would agree that would be a great pity, and hard on the mother; but all the same, all persons have a right to life, the fetus is a person, and so on. I suspect, in fact, that they would not make an exception for a case in which, miraculously enough, the pregnancy went on for nine years, or even the rest of the mother's life.

Some won't even make an exception for a case in which continuation of the pregnancy is likely to shorten the mother's life; they regard abortion as impermissible even to save the mother's life. Such cases are nowadays very rare, and many opponents of abortion do not accept this extreme view. All the same, it is a good place to begin: a number of points of interest come out in respect to it.

1. Let us call the view that abortion is impermissible even to save the mother's life "the extreme view." I want to suggest first that it does not issue from the argument I mentioned earlier without the addition of some fairly powerful premises. Suppose a woman has become pregnant, and now learns that she has a cardiac condition such that she will die if she carries the baby to term. What may be done for her? The fetus, being a person, has a right to life, but as the mother is a person too, so has she a right to life. Presumably they have an equal right to life.

How is it supposed to come out that an abortion may not be performed? If mother and child have an equal right to life, shouldn't we perhaps flip a coin? Or should we add to the mother's right to life her right to decide what happens in and to her body, which everybody seems to be ready to grant—the sum of her rights now outweighing the fetus' right to life?

The most familiar argument here is the following. We are told that performing the abortion would be directly killing[3] the child, whereas doing nothing would not be killing the mother, but only letting her die. Moreover, in killing the child, one would be killing an innocent person, for the child has committed no crime, and is not aiming at his mother's death. And then there are a variety of ways in which this might be continued. (1) But as directly killing an innocent person is always and absolutely impermissible, an abortion may not be performed. Or, (2) as directly killing an innocent person is murder, and is always and absolutely impermissible, an abortion may not be performed.[4] Or, (3) as one's duty to refrain from directly killing an innocent person is more stringent than one's duty to keep a person from dying, an abortion may not be performed. Or, (4) if one's only options are directly killing an innocent person or letting a person die, one must prefer letting the person die, and thus an abortion may not be performed.[5]

Some people seem to have thought that these are not further premises which must be added if the conclusion is to be reached, but that they follow from the very fact that an innocent person has a right to life.[6] But this seems to me to be a mistake, and perhaps the simplest way to show this is to bring out that while we must certainly grant that innocent persons have a right to life, the theses in (1) through (4) are all false. Take (2), for example. If directly killing an innocent person is murder, and thus is impermissible, then the mother's directly killing the innocent person inside her is murder, and thus impermissible. But it cannot seriously be thought to be murder if the mother performs an abortion on herself to save her life. It cannot seriously be said that she *must* refrain, that she *must* sit

---

[3]The term "direct" in the arguments I refer to is a technical one. Roughly, what is meant by "direct killing" is either killing as an end in itself, or killing as a means to some end, for example, the end of saving someone else's life. See note 6, below, for an example of its use.

[4]Cf. *Encyclical Letter of Pope Pius XI on Christian Marriage*, St. Paul Editions (Boston, n.d.), p. 32: "however much we may pity the mother whose health and even life is gravely imperiled in the performance of the duty allotted to her by nature, nevertheless what could ever be a sufficient reason for excusing in any way the direct murder of the innocent? This is precisely what we are dealing with here." Noonan (*The Morality of Abortion*, p. 43) reads this as follows: "What cause can ever avail to excuse in any way the direct killing of the innocent? For it is a question of that."

[5]The thesis in (4) is in an interesting way weaker than those in (1), (2), and (3): they rule out abortion even in cases in which both mother *and* child will die if the abortion is not performed. By contrast, one who held the view expressed in (4) could consistently say that one needn't prefer letting two persons die to killing one.

[6]Cf. the following passage from Pius XII, *Address to the Italian Catholic Society of Midwives:* "The baby in the maternal breast has the right to life immediately from God.—Hence there is no man, no human authority, no science, no medical, eugenic, social, economic or moral 'indication' which can establish or grant a valid juridical ground for a direct deliberate disposition of an innocent human life, that is a disposition which looks to its destruction either as an end or as a means to another end perhaps in itself not illicit.—The baby, still not born, is a man in the same degree and for the same reason as the mother" (quoted in Noonan, *The Morality of Abortion*, p. 45).

passively by and wait for her death. Let us look again at the case of you and the violinist. There you are, in bed with the violinist, and the director of the hospital says to you, "It's all most distressing, and I deeply sympathize, but you see this is putting an additional strain on your kidneys, and you'll be dead within the month. But you *have* to stay where you are all the same. Because unplugging you would be directly killing an innocent violinist, and that's murder, and that's impermissible." If anything in the world is true, it is that you do not commit murder, you do not do what is impermissible, if you reach around to your back and unplug yourself from that violinist to save your life.

The main focus of attention in writings on abortion has been on what a third party may or may not do in answer to a request from a woman for an abortion. This is in a way understandable. Things being as they are, there isn't much a woman can safely do to abort herself. So the question asked is what a third party may do, and what the mother may do, if it is mentioned at all, is deduced, almost as an afterthought, from what it is concluded that third parties may do. But it seems to me that to treat the matter in this way is to refuse to grant to the mother that very status of person which is so firmly insisted on for the fetus. For we cannot simply read off what a person may do from what a third party may do. Suppose you find yourself trapped in a tiny house with a growing child. I mean a very tiny house, and a rapidly growing child—you are already up against the wall of the house and in a few minutes you'll be crushed to death. The child on the other hand won't be crushed to death; if nothing is done to stop him from growing he'll be hurt, but in the end he'll simply burst open the house and walk out a free man. Now I could well understand it if a bystander were to say, "There's nothing we can do for you. We cannot choose between your life and his, we cannot be the ones to decide who is to live, we cannot intervene." But it cannot be concluded that you too can do nothing, that you cannot attack it to save your life. However innocent the child may be, you do not have to wait passively while it crushes you to death. Perhaps a pregnant woman is vaguely felt to have the status of house, to which we don't allow the right of self-defense. But if the woman houses the child, it should be remembered that she is a person who houses it.

I should perhaps stop to say explicitly that I am not claiming that people have a right to do anything whatever to save their lives. I think, rather, that there are drastic limits to the right of self-defense. If someone threatens you with death unless you torture someone else to death, I think you have not the right, even to save your life, to do so. But the case under consideration here is very different. In our case there are only two people involved, one whose life is threatened, and one who threatens it. Both are innocent: the one who is threatened is not threatened because of any fault, the one who threatens does not threaten because of any fault. For this reason we may feel that we bystanders cannot intervene. But the person threatened can.

In sum, a woman surely can defend her life against the threat to it posed by the unborn child, even if doing so involves its death. And this shows not merely that the theses in (1) through (4) are false; it shows also that the extreme view of abortion is false, and so we need not canvass any other possible ways of arriving at it from the argument I mentioned at the outset.

2. The extreme view could of course be weakened to say that while abortion is permissible to save the mother's life, it may not be performed by a third party, but only by the mother herself. But this cannot be right either. For what we have to keep in mind is that the mother and the unborn child are not like two tenants in a small house which has, by an unfortunate mistake, been rented to both: the mother *owns* the house. The fact that she does adds to the offensiveness of deducing that the mother can do nothing from the supposition that third parties can do nothing. But it does more than this: it casts a bright light on the supposition that third parties can do nothing. Certainly it lets us see that a third party who says "I cannot choose between you" is fooling himself if he thinks this is impartiality. If Jones has found and fastened on a certain coat, which he needs to keep him from freezing, but which Smith also needs to keep him from freezing, then it is not impartiality that says "I cannot choose between you" when Smith owns the coat. Women have said again and again "This body is *my* body!" and they have reason to feel angry, reason to feel that it has been like shouting into the wind. Smith, after all, is hardly likely to bless us if we say to him, "Of course it's your coat, anybody would grant that it is. But no one may choose between you and Jones who is to have it."

We should really ask what it is that says "no one may choose" in the face of the fact that the body that houses the child is the mother's body. It may be simply a failure to appreciate this fact. But it may be something more interesting, namely the sense that one has a right to refuse to lay hands on people, even where it would be just and fair to do so, even where justice seems to require that somebody do so. Thus justice might call for somebody to get Smith's coat back from Jones, and yet you have a right to refuse to be the one to lay hands on Jones, a right to refuse to do physical violence to him. This, I think, must be granted. But then what should be said is not "no one may choose," but only "*I* cannot choose," and indeed not even this, but "*I* will not *act*," leaving it open that somebody else can or should, and in particular that anyone in a position of authority, with the job of securing people's rights, both can and should. So this is no difficulty. I have not been arguing that any given third party must accede to the mother's request that he perform an abortion to save her life, but only that he may.

I suppose that in some views of human life the mother's body is only on loan to her, the loan not being one which gives her any prior claim to it. One who held this view might well think it impartiality to say "I cannot choose." But I shall simply ignore this possibility. My own view is that if a human being has any just, prior claim to anything at all, he has a just, prior claim to his own body. And perhaps this needn't be argued for here anyway, since, as I mentioned, the arguments against abortion we are looking at do grant that the woman has a right to decide what happens in and to her body.

But although they do grant it, I have tried to show that they do not take seriously what is done in granting it. I suggest the same thing will reappear even more clearly when we turn away from cases in which the mother's life is at stake, and attend, as I propose we now do, to the vastly more common cases in which a woman wants an abortion for some less weighty reason than preserving her own life.

3. Where the mother's life is not at stake, the argument I mentioned at the outset seems to have a much stronger pull. "Everyone has a right to life, so the unborn person has a right to life." And isn't the child's right to life weightier than anything other than the mother's own right to life, which she might put forward as ground for an abortion?

This argument treats the right to life as if it were unproblematic. It is not, and this seems to me to be precisely the source of the mistake.

For we should now, at long last, ask what it comes to, to have a right of life. In some views having a right to life includes having a right to be given at least the bare minimum one needs for continued life. But suppose that what in fact *is* the bare minimum a man needs for continued life is something he has no right at all to be given? If I am sick unto death, and the only thing that will save my life is the touch of Henry Fonda's cool hand on my fevered brow, then all the same, I have no right to be given the touch of Henry Fonda's cool hand on my fevered brow. It would be frightfully nice of him to fly in from the West Coast to provide it. It would be less nice, though no doubt well meant, if my friends flew out to the West Coast and carried Henry Fonda back with them. But I have no right at all against anybody that he should do this for me. Or again, to return to the story I told earlier, the fact that for continued life that violinist needs the continued use of your kidneys does not establish that he has a right to be given the continued use of your kidneys. He certainly has no right against you that *you* should give him continued use of your kidneys. For nobody has any right to use your kidneys unless you give him such a right; and nobody has the right against you that you shall give him this right—if you do allow him to go on using your kidneys, this is a kindness on your part, and not something he can claim from you as his due. Nor has he any right against anybody else that *they* should give him continued use of your kidneys. Certainly he had no right against the Society of Music Lovers that they should plug him into you in the first place. And if you now start to unplug yourself, having learned that you will otherwise have to spend nine years in bed with him, there is nobody in the world who must try to prevent you, in order to see to it that he is given something he has a right to be given.

Some people are rather stricter about the right to life. In their view, it does not include the right to be given anything, but amounts to, and only to, the right not to be killed by anybody. But here a related difficulty arises. If everybody is to refrain from killing that violinist, then everybody must refrain from doing a great many different sorts of things. Everybody must refrain from slitting his throat, everybody must refrain from shooting him—and everybody must refrain from unplugging you from him. But does he have a right against everybody that they shall refrain from unplugging you from him? To refrain from doing this is to allow him to continue to use your kidneys. It could be argued that he has a right against us that *we* should allow him to continue to use your kidneys. That is, while he had no right against us that we should give him the use of your kidneys, it might be argued that he anyway has a right against us that we shall not now intervene and deprive him of the use of your kidneys. I shall come back to third-party interventions later. But certainly the violinist has no right against you that *you* shall allow him to continue to use your kidneys. As I said, if you do allow him to use them, it is a kindness on your part, and not something you owe him.

The difficulty I point to here is not peculiar to the right to life. It reappears in connection with all the other natural rights; and it is something which an adequate account of rights must deal with. For present purposes it is enough just to draw attention to it. But I would stress that I am not arguing that people do not have a right to life—quite to the contrary, it seems to me that the primary control we must place on the acceptability of an account of rights is that it should turn out in that account to be a truth that all persons have a right to life. I am arguing only that having a right to life does not guarantee having either a right to be given the use of or a right to be allowed continued use of another person's body—even if one needs it for life itself. So the right to life will not serve the opponents of abortion in the very simple and clear way in which they seem to have thought it would.

4. There is another way to bring out the difficulty. In the most ordinary sort of case, to deprive someone of what he has a right to is to treat him unjustly. Suppose a boy and his small brother are jointly given a box of chocolates for Christmas. If the older boy takes the box and refuses to give his brother any of the chocolates, he is unjust to him, for the brother has been given a right to half of them. But suppose that, having learned that otherwise it means nine years in bed with that violinist, you unplug yourself from him. You surely are not being unjust to him, for you gave him no right to use your kidneys, and no one else can have given him any such right. But we have to notice that in unplugging yourself, you are killing him; and violinists, like everybody else, have a right to life, and thus in the view we were considering just now, the right not to be killed. So here you do what he supposedly has a right you shall not do, but you do not act unjustly to him in doing it.

The emendation which may be made at this point is this: the right to life consists not in the right not to be killed, but rather in the right not to be killed unjustly. This runs a risk of circularity, but never mind: it would enable us to square the fact that the violinist has a right to life with the fact that you do not act unjustly toward him in unplugging yourself, thereby killing him. For if you do not kill him unjustly, you do not violate his right to life, and so it is no wonder you do him no injustice.

But if this emendation is accepted, the gap in the argument against abortion stares us plainly in the face: it is by no means enough to show that the fetus is a person, and to remind us that all persons have a right to life—we need to be shown also that killing the fetus violates its right to life, i.e., that abortion is unjust killing. And is it?

I suppose we may take it as a datum that in a case of pregnancy due to rape the mother has not given the unborn person a right to the use of her body for food and shelter. Indeed, in what pregnancy could it be supposed that the mother has given the unborn person such a right? It is not as if there were unborn persons drifting about the world, to whom a woman who wants a child says "I invite you in."

But it might be argued that there are other ways one can have acquired a right to the use of another person's body than by having been invited to use it by that person. Suppose a woman voluntarily indulges in intercourse, knowing of the chance it will issue in pregnancy, and then she does become pregnant; is she not in part responsible for the presence, in fact the very existence, of the unborn person inside her? No doubt she did not invite it in. But doesn't her partial responsibility for its being there itself give it a right to the use of her body?[7] If so, then her aborting it would be more like the boy's taking away the chocolates, and less like your unplugging yourself from the violinist—doing so would be depriving it of what it does have a right to, and thus would be doing it an injustice.

And then, too, it might be asked whether or not she can kill it even to save her own life: If she voluntarily called it into existence, how can she now kill it, even in self-defense?

The first thing to be said about this is that it is something new. Opponents of abortion have been so concerned to make out the independence of the fetus, in order to establish that it has a right to life, just as its mother does, that they have tended to overlook the possible support they might gain from making out that the fetus is *dependent* on the mother, in order to establish that she has a special kind of responsibility for it, a responsibility that gives it rights against her which are not possessed by any independent person—such as an ailing violinist who is a stranger to her.

On the other hand, this argument would give the unborn person a right to its mother's body only if her pregnancy resulted from a voluntary act, undertaken in full knowledge of the chance a pregnancy might result from it. It would leave out entirely the unborn person whose existence is due to rape. Pending the availability of some further argument, then, we would be left with the conclusion that unborn persons whose existence is due to rape have no right to the use of their mothers' bodies, and thus that aborting them is not depriving them of anything they have a right to and hence is not unjust killing.

And we should also notice that it is not at all plain that this argument really does go even as far as it purports to. For there are cases and cases, and the details make a difference. If the room is stuffy, and I therefore open a window to air it, and a burglar climbs in, it would be absurd to say, "Ah, now he can stay, she's given him a right to the use of her house—for she is partially responsible for his presence there, having voluntarily done what enabled him to get in, in full knowledge that there are such things as burglars, and that burglars burgle." It would be still more absurd to say this if I had had bars installed outside my windows, precisely to prevent burglars from getting in, and a burglar got in only because of a defect in the bars. It remains equally absurd if we imagine it is not a burglar who climbs in, but an innocent person who blunders or falls in. Again, suppose it were like this: people-seeds drift about in the air like pollen, and if you open your windows, one may drift in and take root in your carpets or upholstery. You don't want children, so you fix up your windows with fine mesh screens, the very best you can buy. As can happen, however, and on very, very rare occasions does happen, one of the screens is defective; and a seed drifts in and takes root. Does the person-plant who now develops have a right to the use of your house?

---

[7]The need for a discussion of this argument was brought home to me by members of the Society for Ethical and Legal Philosophy, to whom this paper was originally presented.

Surely not—despite the fact that you voluntarily opened your windows, you knowingly kept carpets and upholstered furniture, and you knew that screens were sometimes defective. Someone may argue that you are responsible for its rooting, that it does have a right to your house, because after all you *could* have lived out your life with bare floors and furniture, or with sealed windows and doors. But this won't do—for by the same token anyone can avoid a pregnancy due to rape by having a hysterectomy, or anyway by never leaving home without a (reliable!) army.

It seems to me that the argument we are looking at can establish at most that there are *some* cases in which the unborn person has a right to the use of its mother's body, and therefore *some* cases in which abortion is unjust killing. There is room for much discussion and argument as to precisely which, if any. But I think we should sidestep this issue and leave it open, for at any rate the argument certainly does not establish that all abortion is unjust killing.

5. There is room for yet another argument here, however. We surely must all grant that there may be cases in which it would be morally indecent to detach a person from your body at the cost of his life. Suppose you learn that what the violinist needs is not nine years of your life, but only one hour: all you need do to save his life is to spend one hour in that bed with him. Suppose also that letting him use your kidneys for that one hour would not affect your health in the slightest. Admittedly you were kidnapped. Admittedly you did not give anyone permission to plug him into you. Nevertheless it seems to me plain you *ought* to allow him to use your kidneys for that hour—it would be indecent to refuse.

Again, suppose pregnancy lasted only an hour, and constituted no threat to life or health. And suppose that a woman becomes pregnant as a result of rape. Admittedly she did not voluntarily do anything to bring about the existence of a child. Admittedly she did nothing at all which would give the unborn person a right to the use of her body. All the same it might well be said, as in the newly emended violinist story, that she *ought* to allow it to remain for that hour—that it would be indecent in her to refuse.

Now some people are inclined to use the term "right" in such a way that it follows from the fact that you ought to allow a person to use your body for the hour he needs, that he has a right to use your body for the hour he needs, even though he has not been given that right by any person or act. They may say that it follows also that if you refuse, you act unjustly toward him. This use of the term is perhaps so common that it cannot be called wrong; nevertheless it seems to me to be an unfortunate loosening of what we would do better to keep a tight rein on. Suppose that box of chocolates I mentioned earlier had not been given to both boys jointly, but was given only to the older boy. There he sits, stolidly eating his way through the box, his small brother watching enviously. Here we are likely to say "You ought not to be so mean. You ought to give your brother some of those chocolates." My own view is that it just does not follow from the truth of this that the brother has any right to any of the chocolates. If the boy refuses to give his brother any, he is greedy, stingy, callous—but not unjust. I suppose that the people I have in mind will say it does follow that the brother has a right to some of the chocolates, and thus that the boy does act unjustly if he refuses to give his brother any. But the effect of saying this is to obscure what we should keep distinct, namely the difference between the boy's refusal in this case and the boy's refusal in the earlier case, in which the box was given to both boys jointly, and in which the small brother thus had what was from any point of view clear title to half.

A further objection to so using the term "right" that from the fact that A ought to do a thing for B, it follows that B has a right against A that A do it for him, is that it is going to make the question of whether or not a man has a right to a thing turn on how easy it is to provide him with it; and this seems not merely unfortunate, but morally unacceptable. Take the case of Henry Fonda again. I said earlier that I had no right to the touch of his cool hand on my fevered brow, even though I needed it to save my life. I said it would be frightfully nice of him to fly in from the West Coast to provide me with it, but that I had no right against him that he should do so. But suppose he isn't on the West Coast. Suppose he has only to walk across the room, place a hand briefly on my brow—and lo, my life is saved. Then surely he ought to do it, it would be indecent to refuse. Is it to be said "Ah, well, it follows that in this case she has a right to the touch of his hand on her brow, and so it would be an injustice in him to refuse"? So that I have a right to it when it is easy for him to provide it, though no right when it's hard? It's rather a shocking idea that anyone's rights should fade away and disappear as it gets harder and harder to accord them to him.

So my own view is that even though you ought to let the violinist use your kidneys for the one hour he needs, we should not conclude that he has a right to do so—we should say that if you refuse, you are like the boy who owns all the chocolates and will give none away, self-centered and callous, indecent in fact, but not unjust. And similarly, that even supposing a case in which a woman pregnant due to rape ought to allow the unborn person to use her body for the hour he needs, we should not conclude that he has a right to do so; we should conclude that she is self-centered, callous, indecent, but not unjust, if she refuses. The complaints are no less grave; they are just different. However, there is no need to insist on this point. If anyone does wish to deduce "he has a right" from "you ought," then all the same he must surely grant that there are cases in which it is not morally required of you that you allow the violinist to use your kidneys, and in which he does not have a right to use them, and in which you do not do him an injustice if you refuse. And so also for mother and unborn child. Except in such cases as the unborn person has a right to demand it—and we were leaving open the possibility that there may be such cases—nobody is morally *required* to make large sacrifices, of health, of all other interests and concerns, of all other duties and commitments, for nine years, or even for nine months, in order to keep another person alive.

6. We have in fact to distinguish between two kinds of Samaritan: the Good Samaritan and what we might call the Minimally Decent Samaritan. The story of the Good Samaritan, you will remember, goes like this:

> A certain man went down from Jerusalem to Jericho, and fell among thieves, which stripped him of his raiment, and wounded him, and departed, leaving him half dead.

And by chance there came down a certain priest that way; and when he saw him, he passed by on the other side.

And likewise a Levite, when he was at the place, came and looked on him, and passed by on the other side.

But a certain Samaritan, as he journeyed, came where he was; and when he saw him he had compassion on him.

And went to him, and bound up his wounds, pouring in oil and wine, and set him on his own beast, and brought him to an inn, and took care of him.

And on the morrow, when he departed, he took out two pence, and gave them to the host, and said unto him, "Take care of him; and whatsoever thou spendest more, when I come again, I will repay thee."

(Luke 10:30–35)

The Good Samaritan went out of his way, at some cost to himself, to help one in need of it. We are not told what the options were, that is, whether or not the priest and the Levite could have helped by doing less than the Good Samaritan did, but assuming they could have, then the fact they did nothing at all shows they were not even Minimally Decent Samaritans, not because they were not Samaritans, but because they were not even minimally decent.

These things are a matter of degree, of course, but there is a difference, and it comes out perhaps most clearly in the story of Kitty Genovese, who, as you will remember, was murdered while thirty-eight people watched or listened, and did nothing at all to help her. A Good Samaritan would have rushed out to give direct assistance against the murderer. Or perhaps we had better allow that it would have been a Splendid Samaritan who did this, on the ground that it would have involved a risk of death for himself. But the thirty-eight not only did not do this, they did not even trouble to pick up a phone to call the police. Minimally Decent Samaritanism would call for doing at least that, and their not having done it was monstrous.

After telling the story of the Good Samaritan, Jesus said "Go, and do thou likewise." Perhaps he meant that we are morally required to act as the Good Samaritan did. Perhaps he was urging people to do more than is morally required of them. At all events it seems plain that it was not morally required of any of the thirty-eight that he rush out to give direct assistance at the risk of his own life, and that it is not morally required of anyone that he give long stretches of his life— nine years or nine months—to sustaining the life of a person who has no special right (we were leaving open the possibility of this) to demand it.

Indeed, with one rather striking class of exceptions, no one in any country in the world is *legally* required to do anywhere near as much as this for anyone else. The class of exceptions is obvious. My main concern here is not the state of the law in respect of abortion, but it is worth drawing attention to the fact that in no state in this country is any man compelled by law to be even a Minimally Decent Samaritan to any person; there is no law under which charges could be brought against the thirty-eight who stood by while Kitty Genovese died. By contrast, in most states in this country women are compelled by law to be not merely Minimally Decent Samaritans, but Good Samaritans to unborn persons inside them. This doesn't by itself settle anything one way or the other, because it may well be argued that there should be laws in this country—as there are in many European countries—compelling at least Minimally Decent Samaritanism.[8] But it does show that there is a gross injustice in the existing state of the law. And it shows also that the groups currently working against liberalization of abortion laws, in fact working toward having it declared unconstitutional for a state to permit abortion, had better start working for the adoption of Good Samaritan laws generally, or earn the charge that they are acting in bad faith.

I should think, myself, that Minimally Decent Samaritan laws would be one thing, Good Samaritan laws quite another, and in fact highly improper. But we are not here concerned with the law. What we should ask is not whether anybody should be compelled by law to be a Good Samaritan, but whether we must accede to a situation in which somebody is being compelled—by nature, perhaps—to be a Good Samaritan. We have, in other words, to look now at third-party interventions. I have been arguing that no person is morally required to make large sacrifices to sustain the life of another who has no right to demand them, and this even where the sacrifices do not include life itself; we are not morally required to be Good Samaritans or anyway Very Good Samaritans to one another. But what if a man cannot extricate himself from such a situation? What if he appeals to us to extricate him? It seems to me plain that there are cases in which we can, cases in which a Good Samaritan would extricate him. There you are, you were kidnapped, and nine years in bed with that violinist lie ahead of you. You have your own life to lead. You are sorry, but you simply cannot see giving up so much of your life to the sustaining of his. You cannot extricate yourself, and ask us to do so. I should have thought that—in light of his having no right to the use of your body—it was obvious that we do not have to accede to your being forced to give up so much. We can do what you ask. There is no injustice to the violinist in our doing so.

7. Following the lead of the opponents of abortion, I have throughout been speaking of the fetus merely as a person, and what I have been asking is whether or not the argument we began with, which proceeds only from the fetus' being a person, really does establish its conclusion. I have argued that it does not.

But of course there are arguments and arguments, and it may be said that I have simply fastened on the wrong one. It may be said that what is important is not merely the fact that the fetus is a person, but that it is a person for whom the woman has a special kind of responsibility issuing from the fact that she is its mother. And it might be argued that all my analogies are therefore irrelevant—for you do not have that special kind of responsibility for that violinist, Henry Fonda does not have that special kind of responsibility for me. And our attention might be drawn to the fact that men and women both *are* compelled by law to provide support for their children.

I have in effect dealt (briefly) with this argument in section 4 above; but a (still briefer) recapitulation now may be in order. Surely we do not have any such "special responsibility" for a person unless we have assumed it, explicitly or implicitly. If a set of parents do not try to prevent pregnancy, do not obtain an

---

[8]For a discussion of the difficulties involved, and a survey of the European experience with such laws, see *The Good Samaritan and the Law,* ed. James M. Ratcliffe (New York, 1966).

abortion, and then at the time of birth of the child do not put it out for adoption, but rather take it home with them, then they have assumed responsibility for it, they have given it rights, and they cannot *now* withdraw support from it at the cost of its life because they now find it difficult to go on providing for it. But if they have taken all reasonable precautions against having a child, they do not simply by virtue of their biological relationship to the child who comes into existence have a special responsibility for it. They may wish to assume responsibility for it, or they may not wish to. And I am suggesting that if assuming responsibility for it would require large sacrifices, then they may refuse. A Good Samaritan would not refuse—or anyway, a Splendid Samaritan, if the sacrifices that had to be made were enormous. But then so would a Good Samaritan assume responsibility for that violinist; so would Henry Fonda, if he is a Good Samaritan, fly in from the West Coast and assume responsibility for me.

8. My argument will be found unsatisfactory on two counts by many of those who want to regard abortion as morally permissible. First, while I do argue that abortion is not impermissible, I do not argue that it is always permissible. There may well be cases in which carrying the child to term requires only Minimally Decent Samaritanism of the mother, and this is a standard we must not fall below. I am inclined to think it a merit of my account precisely that it does *not* give a general yes or a general no. It allows for and supports our sense that, for example, a sick and desperately frightened fourteen-year-old schoolgirl, pregnant due to rape, may *of course* choose abortion, and that any law which rules this out is an insane law. And it also allows for and supports our sense that in other cases resort to abortion is even positively indecent. It would be indecent in the woman to request an abortion, and indecent in a doctor to perform it, if she is in her seventh month, and wants the abortion just to avoid the nuisance of postponing a trip abroad. The very fact that the arguments I have been drawing attention to treat all cases of abortion, or even all cases of abortion in which the mother's life is not at stake, as morally on a par ought to have made them suspect at the outset.

Secondly, while I am arguing for the permissibility of abortion in some cases, I am not arguing for the right to secure the death of the unborn child. It is easy to confuse these two things in that up to a certain point in the life of the fetus it is not able to survive outside the mother's body; hence removing it from her body guarantees its death. But they are importantly different. I have argued that you are not morally required to spend nine months in bed, sustaining the life of that violinist; but to say this is by no means to say that if, when you unplug yourself, there is a miracle and he survives, you then have a right to turn around and slit his throat. You may detach yourself even if this costs him his life; you have no right to be guaranteed his death, by some other means, if unplugging yourself does not kill him. There are some people who will feel dissatisfied by this feature of my argument. A woman may be utterly devastated by the thought of a child, a bit of herself, put out for adoption and never seen or heard of again. She may therefore want not merely that the child be detached from her, but more, that it die. Some opponents of abortion are inclined to regard this as beneath contempt—thereby showing insensitivity to what is surely a powerful source of despair. All the same, I agree that the desire for the child's death is not one which anybody may gratify, should it turn out to be possible to detach the child alive.

At this place, however, it should be remembered that we have only been pretending throughout that the fetus is a human being from the moment of conception. A very early abortion is surely not the killing of a person, and so is not dealt with by anything I have said here.

DANIEL CALLAHAN *(b. 1930)*

In his role as director of the Institute of Society, Ethics and the Life Sciences, philosopher Daniel Callahan plays a major role in the increasingly discussed field of medical ethics. In the following selection from Abortion: Law, Choice and Morality *(1970), Callahan stresses the sense in which an abortion decision requires not only an attention to arguments, but also an act of choice on the part of the individual woman involved. The difference between Callahan's approach and Thomson's does not reduce to a simple matter of one being* for *abortion and the other* against. *Both appreciate the complexity of the issue. Yet I get the sense that for Thomson the complexity of a particular case is like a problem in long division: if one works hard enough at it, there is a right answer in particular cases, even if there is no general rule justifying or condemning all abortions. For Callahan, on the other hand, the most important point is to preserve the tension of conflicting values. Callahan is closer to an existentialist view for which life is sometimes incalculably and irresolvably tragic. His point is not so much to aid us in coming up with "the right answer" as to remind us that, if we are to remain fully human, we must sometimes entertain the possibility that our problems are nothing at all like long division. Sometimes we are condemned to hard choices between one evil and another. No series of arguments will preserve our innocence. Moral seriousness then requires responsibility for the* choices we make, *which is something more than an acknowledgment of the* conclusions we draw.

Abortion and Moral Seriousness

The strength of pluralistic societies lies in the personal freedom they afford individuals. One is free to choose among religious, philosophical, ideological and political creeds; or one can create one's own highly personal, idiosyncratic moral code and view of the universe. Increasingly, the individual is free to ignore the morals, manners and mores of society. The only limitations are upon those actions which seem to present clear and present dangers to the common good, and even there the range of prohibited actions is diminishing as more and more choices are left to personal and private decisions. I have contended that, apart from some regulatory laws, abortion decisions should be left, finally, up to the women themselves. Whatever one may think of the morality of abortion, it cannot be established that it poses a clear and present danger to the common good. Thus society does not have the right decisively to interpose itself between a woman and the abortion she wants. It can only intervene where it can be shown that some of its own interests are at stake *qua* society. Regulatory laws of a minimal kind therefore seem in order, since in a variety of ways already mentioned society will be affected by the number, kind and quality of legal abortions. In short, with a few important stipulations, what I have been urging is tantamount to saying that abortion decisions should be private decisions. It is to accept, in principle, the contention of those who believe that, in a free, pluralistic society, the woman should be allowed to make her own moral choice on abortion and be allowed to implement that choice.

But pluralistic societies also lay a few traps for the unwary. It is not a large psychological step from saying that individuals should be left free to make up their own minds on some crucial moral issues (of which abortion is one) to an adoption of the view that one personal decision is as good as another, that any decision is a good one as long as it is honest or sincere, that a free decision equals a correct decision. However short the psychological step, the logical gap is very large. An absence of cant, hypocrisy and coercion may prepare the way for good personal decisions. But that is only to clean the room, and something must then be put in it. The hazard is that, once cleaned, it will be filled with capriciousness, sentimentality, a thinly disguised conformity to the reigning moral taste, or strongly felt but inadequately analyzed moral opinions. This is a particular danger in affluent pluralistic societies, heavily dominated by popular tastes, communication media and the absence of shared values. Philosophically, the view that all values are equally good and all private moral choices on a par is all but dead; but it still has a strong life at the popular level, where there is a tendency to act as if, once personal freedom is legally and socially achieved, moral questions cease to exist.

A considerable quantity of literature exists in the field of ethics concerned with such problems as subjective and objective values, the meaning and use of ethical principles and moral rules, the role of intentionality. That literature need not be reviewed here. But it is directly to the point to observe that a particular failing of the abortion-on-request literature is that it persistently scants the moral problem of how a woman, if granted the desired legal freedom to make her own decision about abortion, should go about making that decision. Up to a point, this deficiency is understandable. The immediate tactical problem has been to get the laws changed or repealed; that has been the burden of the public struggle, which has concentrated on statutes and legislators rather than on the moral contents and problems of personal decision-making. It is reasonable and legitimate to say that a woman should be left free to make the decision in the light of her own personal values; that is, I believe, the best legal solution. But it leaves totally untouched the question of how, once freedom is achieved, she ought to go about the personal business of forming a coherent, rational, sensitive moral perspective and opinion on abortion. After freedom, what then? Society may have no right to demand that a woman give it good reasons why she should have an abortion before permitting it. But this does not entail that the woman should not, as a morally responsible person, have good reasons to justify her desires or acts in her own eyes.

This is only to say that a solution of the legal problem is not the same as a solution to the moral problem. That the moral struggle is transferred from the public to the private sphere should not be taken to mean that the moral problem has been solved; only its public aspect, under a permissive law or a repeal of all laws, has been dealt with. The personal problem will remain.

Some women will be part of a religious group or ethical tradition which they freely choose and which can offer them something, possibly very much, in the way of helpful moral insight consistent with that tradition. The obvious course in that instance is for them to turn to their tradition to see what it has to offer them on the particular problem of abortion. But what of those who have no tradition to repair to or those who find their tradition wanting on this problem? One way or another, they will have to find some way of developing a set of ethical principles and moral rules to help them act responsibly, to justify their own conduct in their own eyes. To press the problem to a finer point, what ought they to think about as they try to work out their own views on abortion?

Only a few suggestions will be made here, taking the form of arguing for an ethic of personal responsibility which tries, in the process of decision-making, to make itself aware of a number of things. The biological evidence should be considered, just as the problem of methodology must be considered; the philosophical assumptions implicit in different uses of the word "human" need to be considered; a philosophical theory of biological analysis is required; the social consequences of different kinds of analyses and different meanings of the word "human" should be thought through; consistency of meaning and use should be sought to avoid *ad hoc* and arbitrary solutions.

It is my own conviction that the "developmental school" offers the most helpful and illuminating approach to the problem of the beginning of human life, avoiding, on the one hand, a too narrow genetic criterion of human life and, on the other, a too broad and socially dangerous social definition of the "human." Yet the kinds of problems which appear in any attempt to decide upon the beginning of life suggest that no one position can be either proved or disproved from biological evidence alone. It becomes a question of trying to do justice to the evidence while, at the same time, realizing that how the evidence is approached and used will be a function of one's way of looking at reality, one's moral policy, the values and rights one believes need balancing, and the type of questions one thinks need to be asked. At the very least, however, the genetic evidence for the uniqueness of zygotes and embryos (a uniqueness of a different kind than that of the uniqueness of sperm and ova), their potentiality for development into a human person, their early development of human characteristics, their genetic and organic distinctness from the organism of the mother, appear to rule out a treatment even of zygotes, much less the more developed stages of the conceptus, as mere pieces of "tissue," of no human significance or value. The "tissue" theory of the significance of the conceptus can only be made plausible by a systematic disregard of the biological evidence. Moreover, though one may conclude that a conceptus is only potential human life, in the process of continually actualizing its potential through growth and development, a respect for the sanctity of life, with its bias in favor even of undeveloped life, is enough to make the taking of such life a moral problem. There is a choice to be made and it is a moral choice. In the near future, it is likely that some kind of simple, safe abortifacient drug will be developed, which either prevents implantation or destroys the conceptus before it can develop. It will be tempting then to think that the moral dilemma has vanished, but I do not believe it will have.

It is possible to imagine a huge number of situations where a woman could, in good and sensitive conscience, choose abortion as a moral solution to her personal or social difficulties. But, at the very least, the bounds of morality are overstepped when either through a systematic intellectual negligence or a willful choosing of that moral solution most personally convenient, personal choice is deliberately made easy and problem-free. Yet it seems to me that a pressure in that direction is a growing part of the ethos of technological societies; it is easily possible to find people to reassure us that we need have no scruples about the way we act, whether the issue is war, the suppression of rebellion and revolution, discrimination against minorities or the use of technolocial advances. Pluralism makes possible the achieving of freer, more subtle moral thinking; but it is a possibility constantly endangered by cultural pressures which would simplify or dissolve moral doubts and anguish.

The question of abortion "indications" returns at the level of personal choice. I have contended that the advent of permissive laws should not mean a cessation of efforts to explore the problem of "indications." When a woman asks herself, as she ought, whether her reasons for wanting an abortion are sound reasons—which presumes abortion is a serious enough moral issue to warrant the need to provide oneself with good reasons for choosing it—she will be asking herself about justifiable indications. Thus, transposed from the legal to the personal level, the kinds of concerns adumbrated in the earlier chapters on indications remain fully pertinent. It was argued in those chapters that, with the possible exception of exceedingly rare instances of a direct threat to the physical life of the mother, one cannot speak of general categories of abortion indications as *necessitating* an abortion. In a number of circumstances, abortion may be a wise and justifiable solution to a distressed pregnancy. But when the language of necessity is used, the implication is that no other conceivable alternative is available. It may be granted, willingly enough, that some set of practical circumstances in some (possibly very many) concrete cases may indicate that abortion is the only feasible option open. But these cases cannot readily be determined in advance, and, for that reason, it is necessary to say that no formal indication as such (e.g., a psychiatric indication) entails a necessary, predetermined choice in favor of abortion.

The word "indication" remains the best word, suggesting that a number of given circumstances will bring the possibility or desirability of abortion to the fore. But to escalate the concept of an indication into that of a required procedure is to go too far. Abortion is one way to solve the problem of an unwanted or hazardous pregnancy (physically, psychologically, economically or socially), but it is rarely the only way, at least in affluent societies (I would be considerably less certain about making the same statement about poor societies). Even in the most extreme cases—rape, incest, psychosis, for instance—alternatives will usually be available and different choices, open. It is not necessarily the end of every woman's chance for a happy, meaningful life to bear an illegitimate child. It is not necessarily the automatic destruction of a family to have a seriously defective child born into it. It is not necessarily the ruination of every family living in overcrowded housing to have still another child. It is not inevitable that every immature woman would become even more so if she bore a child or another child. It is not inevitable that a gravely handicapped child can hope for nothing from life. It is not inevitable that every unwanted child is doomed to misery. It is not written in the essence of things, as a fixed law of human nature, that a woman cannot come to accept, love and be a good mother to a child who was initially unwanted. Nor is it a fixed law that she could not come to cherish a grossly deformed child. Naturally, these are only generalizations. The point is only that human beings are as a rule flexible, capable of doing more than they sometimes think they can, able to surmount serious dangers and challenges, able to grow and mature, able to transform inauspicious beginnings into satisfactory conclusions. Everything in life, even in procreative and family life, is not fixed in advance; the future is never wholly unalterable.

Yet the problem of personal question-asking must be pushed a step farther. The way the questions are answered will be very much determined by a woman's way of looking at herself and at life. A woman who has decided, as a personal moral policy, that nothing should be allowed to stand in the way of her own happiness, goals and self-interest will have no trouble solving the moral problem. For her, an unwanted pregnancy will, by definition, be a pregnancy to be terminated. But only by a Pickwickian use of words could this form of reasoning be called moral. It would preclude any need to consult the opinion of others, any need to examine the validity of one's own viewpoint, any need to, for instance, ask when human life begins, any need to interrogate oneself in any way, intellectually or morally; will and desire would be king.

Assuming, however, that most women would seek a broader ethical horizon than that of their exclusively personal self-interest, what might they think about when faced with an abortion decision? A respect for the sanctity of human life should, I believe, incline them toward a general and strong bias against abortion. Abortion is an act of killing, the violent, direct destruction of potential human life, already in the process of development. That fact should not be disguised, or glossed over by euphemism and circumlocution. It is not the destruction of a human person—for at no stage of its development does the conceptus fulfill the definition of a person, which implies a developed capacity for reasoning, willing, desiring and relating to others—but it is the destruction of an important and valuable form of human life. Its value and its potentiality are not dependent upon the attitude of the woman toward it; it grows by its own biological dynamism and has a genetic and morphological potential distinct from that of the woman. It has its own distinctive and individual future. If contraception and abortion are both seen as forms of birth limitation, they are distinctly different acts; the former precludes the possibility of a conceptus being formed, while the latter stops a conceptus already in existence from developing. The bias implied by the principle of the sanctity of human life is toward the protection of all forms of human life, especially, in ordinary circumstances, the protection of the right to life. That right should be accorded even to doubtful life; its existence should not be wholly dependent upon the personal self-interest of the woman.

Yet she has her own rights as well, and her own set of responsibilities to those around her; that is why she may have to choose abortion. In extreme situations of overpopulation, she may also have a responsibility for the survival of the species or of a people. In many circumstances, then, a decision in favor of abortion—one which overrides the right to life of the potential human being she carries within —can be a responsible moral decision, worthy neither of the condemnation of others nor of self-condemnation. But the bias of the principle of the sanctity of life is against a routine, unthinking employment of abortion; it bends over backwards not to take life and gives the benefit of the doubt to life. It does not seek to diminish the range of responsibility toward life—potential or actual—but to extend it. It does not seek the narrowest definition of life, but the widest and the richest. It is mindful of individual possibility, on the one hand, and of a destructive human tendency, on the other, to exclude from the category of "the human" or deny rights to those beings whose existence is or could prove burdensome to others.

The language used to describe abortion will have an important bearing on the sensitivities and imagination of those women who must make abortion decisions. Abortion can be talked about in the language of medical technology and technique —as, say, "a therapeutic procedure involving the emptying of the uterine contents." That language is neutral, clinical, unemotional. Or abortion can be talked about in the emotive language of relieving woman from suffering, or meeting the need for freedom among women, or saving the nation from a devastating overpopulation. Both kinds of language have their place, for abortion has more than one result and meaning and abortion can legitimately be talked about in more than one way. What is objectionable is a conscious manipulation of language to incite an irrational emotional response, to allay doubts or to mislead the imagination. Particularly misleading is one commonly employed mixture of rhetorical modes by advocates of abortion on request. That is the use of a detached, clinical language to describe the actual operation itself combined with an emotive rhetoric to evoke the personal and social goods which an abortion can bring about. Thus, when every effort is made to suggest that emotion and feeling are perfectly appropriate to describe the social and personal goals of abortion, but that a clinical language only is appropriate when the actual technique and medical objective of an abortion is described, then the moral imagination is being misled.

Any human act can be described in impersonal, technological language, just as any act can be described in emotive language. What is wanted is an equity in the language. It is fair enough and to the point to say that in many circumstances abortion will save a woman's health or her family. It only becomes misleading when the act itself, as distinguished from its therapeutic goal, is talked about in an entirely different way. For, abortion is not just an "emptying of the uterine contents." It is also an act of killing; there will be no abortion unless the conceptus is killed (or its further existence made impossible, which amounts to the same thing). If it is appropriate to evoke the imagination and elicit sympathy for those women in a distressed pregnancy who could be helped by abortion, it is no less appropriate to evoke the imagination about what actually occurs in an abortion "procedure."

Imagination should also come into play at another point. It is often argued by proponents of abortion that there is no need for a woman ever to take any chances in a distressed pregnancy, particularly in the instance of an otherwise healthy woman who, if she has an abortion on one occasion, could simply get pregnant again on another, more auspicious occasion. This might be termed the "replace-ment theory" of abortion indications: since fetus "x" can be replaced by fetus "y," then there is no reason why a woman should have any scruples about such a replacement. This way of conceiving the choices effectively dissolves them; it becomes important only to know whether a woman can get pregnant again when she wants to. But this strategy can be employed only at the price of convincing oneself that there is no difference whatever among embryos and fetuses, that they all have exactly the same potentiality. But even the sketchiest knowledge of the genetic uniqueness of each conceptus (save in the instance of monozygotic twins), and thus the different genetic potentialities of each, should raise doubts on that point. Yet, having said that, I would not want to deny that the possibility of a further pregnancy could have an important bearing on the moral reasoning of a woman whose present pregnancy was threatening. If, out of a sense of responsibil-ity toward her present children or her present life situation, a woman decided that an abortion was the wisest, most moral course, then the possibility that she could become pregnant later, when these responsibilities would be less pressing, would be a pertinent consideration.

The goal of these remarks is to keep alive in the consciences of women who have an abortion choice a moral tension; and it is to hope that they will be willing to bear the pain and the uncertainty of having to make a moral choice. It is the automatic, unthinking and unimaginative personal solution of abortion questions which women themselves should be extremely wary of, either for or against an abortion. A woman can, with little trouble, find both people and books to reassure her that there is no problem about abortion at all; or people and books to convince her that she would be a moral monster if she chose abortion. A woman can choose in advance the views she will listen to and thus have her predispositions con-firmed. Yet a willingness to keep alive a moral tension, and to be wary of precipi-tous solutions, presupposes two things. First, that the woman herself wants to do what is right, realizing that what is right may not always be that which is most convenient, most easy or most immediately apt to solve a pressing problem. It is simply not the case that what one wants to do, or would like to do, or is predisposed to do is necessarily the right thing to do. A willingness seriously to entertain that moral perception—which, of course, does not in itself imply a decision for or against an abortion—is one sign of moral seriousness.

Second, moral seriousness presupposes one is concerned with the protection and furthering of life. This means that, out of respect for human life, one bends over backwards not to eliminate human life, not to desensitize oneself to the meaning and value of potential life, not to seek definitions of the "human" which serve one's self-interest only. A desire to respect human life in all of its forms means, therefore, that one voluntarily imposes upon oneself a pressure against the taking of life; that one demands of oneself serious reasons for doing so, even in the case of a very early embryo; that one use not only the mind but also the imagination when a decision is being made; that one seeks not to evade the moral issues but to face them; that one searches out the alternatives and conscientiously entertains them before turning to abortion. A bias in favor of the sanctity of human life in all of its forms would include a bias against abortion on the part of women; it would be the last rather than the first choice when unwanted pregnancies occurred. It would be an act to be avoided if at all possible.

A bias of this kind, voluntarily imposed by a woman upon herself, would not trap her; for it is also part of a respect for the dignity of life to leave the way open for an abortion when other reasonable choices are not available. For she also has duties toward herself, her family and her society. There can be good reasons for taking the life even of a very late fetus; once that also is seen and seen as a counterpoise in particular cases to the general bias against the taking of potential life, the way is open to choose abortion. The bias of the moral policy implies the need for moral rules which seek to preserve life. But, as a policy which leaves room for choice—rather than entailing a fixed set of rules—it is open to flexible interpretation when the circumstances point to the wisdom of taking exception to the normal ordering of the rules in particular cases. Yet, in that case, one is not genuinely taking exception to the rules. More accurately, one would be deciding that, for the preservation or furtherance of other values or rights—species-rights, person-rights—a choice in favor of abortion would be serving the sanctity of life. That there would be, in that case, conflict between rights, with one set of rights set aside (reluctantly) to serve another set, goes without saying. A subversion of the principle occurs when it is made out that there is no conflict and thus nothing to decide.

transition:
violence and liberation

As if individual instances of abortion were not tragic enough, what are we to say when the lives and customs of whole peoples are extinguished? Should they fight back? Does one violence deserve another? As if the question of abortion were not difficult enough, I now suggest considering abortion as a species of violence and then juxtaposing the violence of abortion against the violence of liberation.

Perhaps this joining of issues is unfair. Perhaps there is no logical relationship between the violence of revolution and the violence of abortion. But in the introduction to these six essays I suggested a similarity between the plights of several liberation movements. Both racism and male chauvinism involve processes of internalization of a sense of impotence on the part of the oppressed. Fanon will argue that certain forms of violence are the necessary therapy for regaining a sense of power and autonomy. Likewise, some women have argued that the choice for abortion amounts to a reclaiming of a sense of power over their own bodies and lives. Whether or not a pregnant woman actually chooses to abort, the right to make that choice seems to be a condition for her autonomous personhood.

I will not pretend to resolve these difficult issues with a few glib sentences. Instead I would only add that a sense of moral integrity demands a certain consistency of reasoning in realms we often keep apart. For example, we cannot condemn technology in general for its contribution to pollution, then applaud its application to, say, recorded music. Similarly, violence is an option in many different contexts—from professional sports to abortion to revolution. If we appreciate both the similarities and the differences among contexts, then we might come to see that violence in itself is not as obviously immoral as we might have thought. Rather, a specific context determines an act of violence as immoral. But why some contexts and not others? A close comparison of different contexts might contribute to an answer. Try to consider the cogency of some of the arguments in the following two essays as they reflect on the issue of abortion.

FRANTZ FANON *(1925–1961)*

Black thinkers are divided on whether color is skin deep or deeper—that is, does color make no difference or a difference that blacks and whites alike should esteem rather than disvalue. For those who see the differences to be valued, many of the issues discussed in relation to women are equally important concerning blacks: if we reject the dominant character traits of the white male as exclusively defining what it is to be a human, then what are the dominant black character traits that add to the rich plurality of ways to be human?

But stressing differences, even where they are esteemed, runs the risk of justifying injustices. Despite differences in ways of being human, men, women, blacks, whites, Indians, and Aryans all share a common humanity and deserve equality from any of man's laws. Fanon's Wretched of the Earth *(1963) chronicles the results of a systematic denial of basic human equality.*

Despite his importance to Third World liberation movements, Fanon's insights into revolution do not derive from the political practice that informs the writings of revolutionaries like Che Guevara. Fanon is a psychoanalyst. From his clinical practice, particularly with patients who suffered the horrors of the Algerian struggle with French colonial rule, he discovered ways that oppression works through the capacity of the oppressed to internalize the values of the oppressors. Or to recall an earlier formulation, Fanon explored the identification *of part of the oppressed personality with the attributions and reinforcements encouraged by the oppressor. Fanon sees this process as being so thorough that violence may be required to break the spell of identification. Greer's closing paragraph suggests that "all the baggage of paternalistic society will have to be thrown overboard." Though Greer does not draw out the implications of the violence of her metaphor, Fanon is concerned precisely with throwing out the baggage of paternalistic society and is explicit about the violence of the metaphor. He sees violence as a purgatory a colonialized people may have to pass through before they can achieve a fresh sense of their own identity, distinct from internalized colonial values.*

The pain of apocalypse is a general theme in the dialectics of oppression and liberation. Recall yet once again Plato's description of the person forced to turn his eyes away from the images on the cave wall. And think again of the formal similarities running through all the dialectics of liberation: just as it is possible to extrapolate from the women's movement to the importance of esteeming differences in fighting racist evaluations of color differences, so reflect on how the blacks' struggle for basic human equality before the law may shed light on women's liberation. What violence may women have to perpetrate to free themselves from the yoke of their own identification with male chauvinist values? Fanon's reflections do not extol violence as either a legitimate or even a successful means of vanquishing an external enemy. His argument, based as it is on the dynamics of internalization and identification, has far more to do with the role of violence in regard to the enemy within.

Violence and Liberation

The settler makes history and is conscious of making it. And because he constantly refers to the history of his mother country, he clearly indicates that he himself is the extension of that mother country. Thus the history which he writes is not the history of the country which he plunders but the history of his own nation in regard to all that she skims off, all that she violates and starves.

The immobility to which the native is condemned can only be called in question if the native decides to put an end to the history of colonization—the history of pillage—and to bring into existence the history of the nation—the history of decolonization.

A world divided into compartments, a motionless, Manicheistic world, a world of statues: the statue of the general who carried out the conquest, the statue of the engineer who built the bridge; a world which is sure of itself, which crushes with its stones the backs flayed by whips: this is the colonial world. The native is a being hemmed in; apartheid is simply one form of the division into compartments of the colonial world. The first thing which the native learns is to stay in his place, and not to go beyond certain limits. This is why the dreams of the native are always of muscular prowess; his dreams are of action and of aggression. I dream I am jumping, swimming, running, climbing; I dream that I burst out laughing, that I span a river in one stride, or that I am followed by a flood of motorcars which never catch up with me. During the period of colonization, the native never stops achieving his freedom from nine in the evening until six in the morning.

The colonized man will first manifest this aggressiveness which has been deposited in his bones against his own people. This is the period when the niggers beat each other up, and the police and magistrates do not know which way to turn when faced with the astonishing waves of crime in North Africa. We shall see later how this phenomenon should be judged. When the native is confronted with the colonial order of things, he finds he is in a state of permanent tension. The settler's world is a hostile world, which spurns the native, but at the same time it is a world of which he is envious. We have seen that the native never ceases to dream of putting himself in the place of the settler—not of becoming the settler but of substituting himself for the settler. This hostile world, ponderous and aggressive because it fends off the colonized masses with all the harshness it is capable of, represents not merely a hell from which the swiftest flight possible is desirable, but also a paradise close at hand which is guarded by terrible watchdogs.

The native is always on the alert, for since he can only make out with difficulty the many symbols of the colonial world, he is never sure whether or not he has crossed the frontier. Confronted with a world ruled by the settler, the native is always presumed guilty. But the native's guilt is never a guilt which he accepts; it is rather a kind of curse, a sort of sword of Damocles, for, in his innermost spirit, the native admits no accusation. He is overpowered but not tamed; he is treated as an inferior but he is not convinced of his inferiority. He is patiently waiting until the settler is off his guard to fly at him. The native's muscles are always tensed. You can't say that he is terrorized, or even apprehensive. He is in fact ready at a moment's notice to exchange the role of the quarry for that of the hunter. The native is an oppressed person whose permanent dream is to become the persecutor. The symbols of social order—the police, the bugle calls in the barracks, military parades and the waving flags—are at one and the same time inhibitory and stimulating: for they do not convey the message "Don't dare to budge"; rather, they cry out "Get ready to attack." And, in fact, if the native had any tendency to fall asleep and to forget, the settler's hauteur and the settler's anxiety to test the strength of the colonial system would remind him at every turn that the great showdown cannot be put off indefinitely. That impulse to take the settler's place implies a tonicity of muscles the whole time; and in fact we know that in certain emotional conditions the presence of an obstacle accentuates the tendency toward motion.

The settler-native relationship is a mass relationship. The settler pits brute force against the weight of numbers. He is an exhibitionist. His preoccupation with security makes him remind the native out loud that there he alone is master. The settler keeps alive in the native an anger which he deprives of outlet; the native is trapped in the tight links of the chains of colonialism. But we have seen that inwardly the settler can only achieve a pseudo petrification. The native's muscular tension finds outlet regularly in bloodthirsty explosions—in tribal warfare, in feuds between septs, and in quarrels between individuals.

Where individuals are concerned, a positive negation of common sense is evident. While the settler or the policeman has the right the livelong day to strike the native, to insult him and to make him crawl to them, you will see the native reaching for his knife at the slightest hostile or aggressive glance cast on him by another native; for the last resort of the native is to defend his personality vis-à-vis his brother. Tribal feuds only serve to perpetuate old grudges buried deep in the memory. By throwing himself with all his force into the vendetta, the native tries to persuade himself that colonialism does not exist, that everything is going on as before, that history continues. Here on the level of communal organizations we clearly discern the well-known behavior patterns of avoidance. It is as if plunging into a fraternal blood bath allowed them to ignore the obstacle, and to put off till later the choice, nevertheless inevitable, which opens up the question of armed resistance to colonialism. Thus collective autodestruction in a very concrete form is one of the ways in which the native's muscular tension is set free. All these patterns of conduct are those of the death reflex when faced with danger, a suicidal behavior which proves to the settler (whose existence and domination is by them all the more justified) that these men are reasonable human beings. In the same way the native manages to by-pass the settler. A belief in fatality removes all blame from the oppressor; the cause of misfortunes and of poverty is attributed to God: He is Fate. In this way the individual accepts the disintegration ordained by God, bows down before the settler and his lot, and by a kind of interior restabilization acquires a stony calm.

Meanwhile, however, life goes on, and the native will strengthen the inhibitions which contain his aggressiveness by drawing on the terrifying myths which are so frequently found in underdeveloped communities. There are maleficent spirits which intervene every time a step is taken in the wrong direction, leopard-men, serpent-men, six-legged dogs, zombies—a whole series of tiny animals or giants which create around the native a world of prohibitions, of barriers and of inhibitions far more terrifying than the world of the settler. This magical super-structure which permeates native society fulfills certain well-defined functions in the dynamism of the libido. One of the characteristics of underdeveloped societies is in fact that the libido is first and foremost the concern of a group, or of the family. The feature of communities whereby a man who dreams that he has sexual relations with a woman other than his own must confess it in public and pay a fine in kind or in working days to the injured husband or family is fully described by ethnologists. We may note in passing that this proves that the so-called prehistoric societies attach great importance to the unconscious.

The atmosphere of myth and magic frightens me and so takes on an un-doubted reality. By terrifying me, it integrates me in the traditions and the history of my district or of my tribe, and at the same time it reassures me, it gives me a status, as it were an identification paper. In underdeveloped countries the occult sphere is a sphere belonging to the community which is entirely under magical jurisdiction. By entangling myself in this inextricable network where actions are repeated with crystalline inevitability, I find the everlasting world which belongs to me, and the perenniality which is thereby affirmed of the world belonging to us. Believe me, the zombies are more terrifying than the settlers; and in consequence the problem is no longer that of keeping oneself right with the colonial world and its barbed-wire entanglements, but of considering three times before urinating, spitting, or going out into the night.

The supernatural magical powers reveal themselves as essentially personal; the settler's powers are infinitely shrunken, stamped with their alien origin. We no longer really need to fight against them since what counts is the frightening enemy created by myths. We preceive that all is settled by a permanent confrontation on the phantasmic plane.

It has always happened in the struggle for freedom that such a people, formerly lost in an imaginary maze, a prey to unspeakable terrors yet happy to lose themselves in a dreamlike torment, such a people becomes unhinged, re-organizes itself, and in blood and tears gives birth to very real and immediate action. Feeding the *moudjahidines*,[1] posting sentinels, coming to the help of families which lack the bare necessities, or taking the place of a husband who has been killed or imprisoned: such are the concrete tasks to which the people is called during the struggle for freedom.

In the colonial world, the emotional sensitivity of the native is kept on the surface of his skin like an open sore which flinches from the caustic agent; and the psyche shrinks back, obliterates itself and finds outlet in muscular demonstrations which have caused certain very wise men to say that the native is a hysterical type. This sensitive emotionalism, watched by invisible keepers who are however in unbroken contact with the core of the personality, will find its fulfillment through eroticism in the driving forces behind the crisis' dissolution.

On another level we see the native's emotional sensibility exhausting itself in

[1]Highly-trained soldiers who are completely dedicated to the Moslem cause.—*Trans.*

dances which are more or less ecstatic. This is why any study of the colonial world should take into consideration the phenomena of the dance and of possession. The native's relaxation takes precisely the form of a muscular orgy in which the most acute aggressivity and the most impelling violence are canalized, transformed, and conjured away. The circle of the dance is a permissive circle: it protects and permits. At certain times on certain days, men and women come together at a given place, and there, under the solemn eye of the tribe, fling themselves into a seemingly unorganized pantomime, which is in reality extremely systematic, in which by various means—shakes of the head, bending of the spinal column, throwing of the whole body backward—may be deciphered as in an open book the huge effort of a community to exorcise itself, to liberate itself, to explain itself. There are no limits—inside the circle. The hillock up which you have toiled as if to be nearer to the moon; the river bank down which you slip as if to show the connection between the dance and ablutions, cleansing and purification—these are sacred places. There are no limits—for in reality your purpose in coming together is to allow the accumulated libido, the hampered aggressivity, to dissolve as in a volcanic eruption. Symbolical killings, fantastic rides, imaginary mass murders—all must be brought out. The evil humors are undammed, and flow away with a din as of molten lava.

One step further and you are completely possessed. In fact, these are actually organized séances of possession and exorcism; they include vampirism, possession by djinns, by zombies, and by Legba, the famous god of the voodoo. This disintegrating of the personality, this splitting and dissolution, all this fulfills a primordial function in the organism of the colonial world. When they set out, the men and women were impatient, stamping their feet in a state of nervous excitement; when they return, peace has been restored to the village; it is once more calm and unmoved.

During the struggle for freedom, a marked alienation from these practices is observed. The native's back is to the wall, the knife is at his throat (or, more precisely, the electrode at his genitals): he will have no more call for his fancies. After centuries of unreality, after having wallowed in the most outlandish phantoms, at long last the native, gun in hand, stands face to face with the only forces which contend for his life—the forces of colonialism. And the youth of a colonized country, growing up in an atmosphere of shot and fire, may well make a mock of, and does not hesitate to pour scorn upon the zombies of his ancestors, the horses with two heads, the dead who rise again, and the djinns who rush into your body while you yawn. The native discovers reality and transforms it into the pattern of his customs, into the practice of violence and into his plan for freedom.

We have seen that this same violence, though kept very much on the surface all through the colonial period, yet turns in the void. We have also seen that it is canalized by the emotional outlets of dance and possession by spirits; we have seen how it is exhausted in fratricidal combats. Now the problem is to lay hold of this violence which is changing direction. When formerly it was appeased by myths and exercised its talents in finding fresh ways of committing mass suicide, now new conditions will make possible a completely new line of action. . . .

But let us return to that atmosphere of violence, that violence which is just under the skin. We have seen that in its process toward maturity many leads are attached to it, to control it and show it the way out. Yet in spite of the metamorphoses which the colonial regime imposes upon it in the way of tribal or regional quarrels, that violence makes its way forward, and the native identifies his enemy and recognizes all his misfortunes, throwing all the exacerbated might of his hate and anger into this new channel. But how do we pass from the atmosphere of violence to violence in action? What makes the lid blow off? There is first of all the fact that this development does not leave the settler's blissful existence intact. The settler who "understands" the natives is made aware by several straws in the wind showing that something is afoot. "Good" natives become scarce; silence falls when the oppressor approaches; sometimes looks are black, and attitudes and remarks openly aggressive. The nationalist parties are astir, they hold a great many meetings, the police are increased and reinforcements of soldiers are brought in. The settlers, above all the farmers isolated on their land, are the first to become alarmed. They call for energetic measures.

The authorities do in fact take some spectacular measures. They arrest one or two leaders, they organize military parades and maneuvers, and air force displays. But the demonstrations and warlike exercises, the smell of gunpowder which now fills the atmosphere, these things do not make the people draw back. Those bayonets and cannonades only serve to reinforce their aggressiveness. The atmosphere becomes dramatic, and everyone wishes to show that he is ready for anything. And it is in these circumstances that the guns go off by themselves, for nerves are jangled, fear reigns and everyone is trigger-happy. A single commonplace incident is enough to start the machine-gunning: Sétif in Algeria, the Central Quarries in Morocco, Moramanga in Madagascar.

The repressions, far from calling a halt to the forward rush of national consciousness, urge it on. Mass slaughter in the colonies at a certain stage of the embryonic development of consciousness increases that consciousness, for the hecatombs are an indication that between oppressors and oppressed everything can be solved by force. It must be remarked here that the political parties have not called for armed insurrection, and have made no preparations for such an insurrection. All these repressive measures, all those actions which are a result of fear are not within the leaders' intentions: they are overtaken by events. At this moment, then, colonialism may decide to arrest the nationalist leaders. But today the governments of colonized countries know very well that it is extremely dangerous to deprive the masses of their leaders; for then the people, unbridled, fling themselves into *jacqueries*, mutinies, and "brutish murders." The masses give free rein to their "bloodthirsty instincts" and force colonialism to free their leaders, to whom falls the difficult task of bringing them back to order. The colonized people, who have spontaneously brought their violence to the colossal task of destroying the colonial system, will very soon find themselves with the barren, inert slogan "Release X or Y."[2] Then colonialism will release these men, and hold discussions with them. The time for dancing in the streets has come.

[2]It may happen that the arrested leader is in fact the authentic mouthpiece of the colonized masses. In this case colonialism will make use of his period of detention to try to launch new leaders.

In certain circumstances, the party political machine may remain intact. But as a result of the colonialist repression and of the spontaneous reaction of the people the parties find themselves out-distanced by their militants. The violence of the masses is vigorously pitted against the military forces of the occupying power, and the situation deteriorates and comes to a head. Those leaders who are free remain, therefore, on the touchline. They have suddenly become useless, with their bureaucracy and their reasonable demands; yet we see them, far removed from events, attempting the crowning imposture—that of "speaking in the name of the silenced nation." As a general rule, colonialism welcomes this godsend with open arms, transforms these "blind mouths" into spokesmen, and in two minutes endows them with independence, on condition that they restore order.

So we see that all parties are aware of the power of such violence and that the question is not always to reply to it by a greater violence, but rather to see how to relax the tension.

What is the real nature of this violence? We have seen that it is the intuition of the colonized masses that their liberation must, and can only, be achieved by force. By what spiritual aberration do these men, without technique, starving and enfeebled, confronted with the military and economic might of the occupation, come to believe that violence alone will free them? How can they hope to triumph?

It is because violence (and this is the disgraceful thing) may constitute, in so far as it forms part of its system, the slogan of a political party. The leaders may call on the people to enter upon an armed struggle. This problematical question has to be thought over. When militarist Germany decides to settle its frontier disputes by force, we are not in the least surprised; but when the people of Angola, for example, decide to take up arms, when the Algerian people reject all means which are not violent, these are proofs that something has happened or is happening at this very moment. The colonized races, those slaves of modern times, are impatient. They know that this apparent folly alone can put them out of reach of colonial oppression. A new type of relations is established in the world. The underdeveloped peoples try to break their chains, and the extraordinary thing is that they succeed. It could be argued that in these days of sputniks it is ridiculous to die of hunger; but for the colonized masses the argument is more down-to-earth. The truth is that there is no colonial power today which is capable of adopting the only form of contest which has a chance of succeeding, namely, the prolonged establishment of large forces of occupation.

HANNAH ARENDT *(1906-1975)*

For decades Hannah Arendt was one of the finest philosophically trained minds in the field of social commentary and contemporary history, as her books The Origins of Totalitarianism; Eichmann in Jerusalem; *and particularly* The Human Condition *show. During her final years she taught advanced seminars at both The New School for Social Research in New York City and at the University of Chicago.*

In the following essay, a slightly altered version of a lecture she delivered at Yale and then published in the New York Review of Books, *Arendt notes the changed climate of current reflections on violence, referring explicitly to Fanon and to Sartre's introduction to Fanon's book. She then draws a series of important distinctions among the concepts of violence, power, force, strength, and authority. Violence, she argues, is not the necessary means to power but quite the contrary of power. Violence is used as a last resort where power is lacking. Because power and violence are contraries, however, violence cannot lead to power; it can lead only to the destruction of power.*

On Violence

The more dubious and uncertain an instrument violence has become in international relations, the more it has gained in reputation and appeal in domestic affairs, specifically in the matter of revolution. The strong Marxist rhetoric of the New Left coincides with the steady growth of the entirely non-Marxian conviction, proclaimed by Mao Tse-tung, that "Power grows out of the barrel of a gun." To be sure, Marx was aware of the role of violence in history, but this role was to him secondary; not violence but the contradictions inherent in the old society brought about its end. The emergence of a new society was preceded, but not caused, by violent outbreaks, which he likened to the labor pangs that precede, but of course do not cause, the event of organic birth. In the same vein he regarded the state as an instrument of violence in the command of the ruling class; but the actual power of the ruling class did not consist of or rely on violence. It was defined by the role the ruling class played in society, or, more exactly, by its role in the process of production. It has often been noticed, and sometimes deplored, that the revolutionary Left under the influence of Marx's teachings ruled out the use of violent means; the "dictatorship of the proletariat"—openly repressive in Marx's writings —came after the revolution and was meant, like the Roman dictatorship, to last a strictly limited period. Political assassination, except for a few acts of individual terror perpetrated by small groups of anarchists, was mostly the prerogative of the Right, while organized armed uprisings remained the specialty of the military. The Left remained convinced "that all conspiracies are not only useless but harmful. They [knew] only too well that the revolutions are not made intentionally and arbitrarily, but that they were always and everywhere the necessary result of circumstances entirely independent of the will and guidance of particular parties and whole classes."[1]

On the level of theory there were a few exceptions. Georges Sorel, who at the beginning of the century tried to combine Marxism with Bergson's philosophy of life—the result, though on a much lower level of sophistication, is oddly similar to Sartre's current amalgamation of existentialism and Marxism—thought of class struggle in military terms; yet he ended by proposing nothing more violent than the famous myth of the general strike, a form of action which we today would think of as belonging rather to the arsenal of nonviolent politics. Fifty years ago even this modest proposal earned him the reputation of being a fascist, notwithstanding his enthusiastic approval of Lenin and the Russian Revolution. Sartre, who in his preface to Fanon's *The Wretched of the Earth* goes much farther in his glorification of violence than Sorel in his famous *Reflections on Violence*—farther than Fanon himself, whose argument he wishes to bring to its conclusion—still mentions "Sorel's fascist utterances." This shows to what extent Sartre is unaware of his basic disagreement with Marx on the question of violence, especially when he states that "irrepressible violence . . . is man recreating himself," that it is through "mad fury" that "the wretched of the earth" can "become men." These notions are all the more remarkable because the idea of man creating himself is strictly in the tradition of Hegelian and Marxian thinking; it is the very basis of all leftist humanism. But according to Hegel man "produces" himself through thought,[2] whereas for Marx, who turned Hegel's "idealism" upside down, it was labor, the human form of metabolism with nature, that fulfilled this function. And though one may argue that all notions of man creating himself have in common a rebellion against the very factuality of the human condition—nothing is more obvious than that man, whether as member of the species or as an individual, does *not* owe his existence to himself—and that therefore what Sartre, Marx, and Hegel have in common is more relevant than the particular activities through which this non-fact should presumably have come about, still it cannot be denied that a gulf separates the essentially peaceful activities of thinking and laboring from all deeds of violence. "To shoot down a European is to kill two birds with one stone . . . there remain a dead man and a free man," says Sartre in his preface. This is a sentence Marx could never have written.

I quoted Sartre in order to show that this new shift toward violence in the thinking of revolutionaries can remain unnoticed even by one of their most representative and articulate spokesmen, and it is all the more noteworthy for evidently not being an abstract notion in the history of ideas. (If one turns the "idealistic" *concept* of thought upside down, one might arrive at the "materialistic" *concept* of labor; one will never arrive at the notion of violence.) No doubt all

---

[1] I owe this early remark of Engels, in a manuscript of 1847, to Jacob Barion, *Hegel und die marxistische Staatslehre*, Bonn, 1963.

[2] It is quite suggestive that Hegel speaks in this context of *"Sichselbstproduzieren."* See *Vorlesungen über die Geschichte der Philosophie*, ed. Hoffmeister, p. 114, Leipzig, 1938.

this has a logic of its own, but it is one springing from experience, and this experience was utterly unknown to any generation before.

The pathos and the *élan* of the New Left, their credibility, as it were, are closely connected with the weird suicidal development of modern weapons; this is the first generation to grow up under the shadow of the atom bomb. They inherited from their parents' generation the experience of a massive intrusion of criminal violence into politics: they learned in high school and in college about concentration and extermination camps, about genocide and torture,[3] about the wholesale slaughter of civilians in war without which modern military operations are no longer possible even if restricted to "conventional" weapons. Their first reaction was a revulsion against every form of violence, an almost matter-of-course espousal of a politics of nonviolence. The very great successes of this movement, especially in the field of civil rights, were followed by the resistance movement against the war in Vietnam, which has remained an important factor in determining the climate of opinion in this country. But it is no secret that things have changed since then, that the adherents of nonviolence are on the defensive, and it would be futile to say that only the "extremists" are yielding to a glorification of violence and have discovered—like Fanon's Algerian peasants—that "only violence pays."[4]

It is, I think, a rather sad reflection on the present state of political science that our terminology does not distinguish among such key words as "power," "strength," "force," "authority," and, finally, "violence"—all of which refer to distinct, different phenomena and would hardly exist unless they did. (In the words of d'Entrèves, "might, power, authority: these are all words to whose exact implications no great weight is attached in current speech; even the greatest thinkers sometimes use them at random. Yet it is fair to presume that they refer to different properties, and their meaning should therefore be carefully assessed and examined.... The correct use of these words is a question not only of logical grammar, but of historical perspective.")[5] To use them as synonyms not only indicates a certain deafness to linguistic meanings, which would be serious enough, but it has also resulted in a kind of blindness to the realities they correspond to. In such a situation it is always tempting to introduce new definitions, but—though I

[3]Noam Chomsky rightly notices among the motives for open rebellion the refusal "to take one's place alongside the 'good German' we have all learned to despise." *American Power and the New Mandarins* (New York, 1969), p. 368.
[4]Frantz Fanon, *The Wretched of the Earth* (1961), Grove Press edition, 1968, p. 61. I am using this work because of its great influence on the present student generation. Fanon himself, however, is much more doubtful about violence than his admirers. It seems that only the book's first chapter, "Concerning Violence," has been widely read. Fanon knows of the "unmixed and total brutality [which], if not immediately combatted, invariably leads to the defeat of the movement within a few weeks" (p. 147).
For the recent escalation of violence in the student movement, see the instructive series "Gewalt" in the German news magazine *Der Spiegel* (February 10, 1969 ff.), and the series "Mit dem Latein am Ende" (Nos. 26 and 27, 1969).
[5]P. D'Entrèves, *The Notion of the State, An Introduction to Political Theory* (Oxford, 1967), p. 7. Cf. also p. 171, where, discussing the exact meaning of the words "nation" and "nationality," he rightly insists that "the only competent guides in the jungle of so many different meanings are the linguists and the historians. It is to them that we must turn for help." And in distinguishing authority and power, he turns to Cicero's *potestas in populo, auctoritas in senatu.*

shall briefly yield to temptation—what is involved is not simply a matter of careless speech. Behind the apparent confusion is a firm conviction in whose light all distinctions would be, at best, of minor importance: the conviction that the most crucial political issue is, and always has been, the question of Who rules Whom? Power, strength, force, authority, violence—these are but words to indicate the means by which man rules over man; they are held to be synonyms because they have the same function. It is only after one ceases to reduce public affairs to the business of dominion that the original data in the realm of human affairs will appear, or, rather, reappear, in their authentic diversity.

These data, in our context, may be enumerated as follows:

Power corresponds to the human ability not just to act but to act in concert. Power is never the property of an individual; it belongs to a group and remains in existence only so long as the group keeps together. When we say of somebody that he is "in power" we actually refer to his being empowered by a certain number of people to act in their name. The moment the group, from which the power originated to begin with (*potestas in populo*, without a people or group there is no power), disappears, "his power" also vanishes. In current usage, when we speak of a "powerful man" or a "powerful personality," we already use the word "power" metaphorically; what we refer to without metaphor is "strength."

Strength unequivocally designates something in the singular, an individual entity; it is the property inherent in an object or person and belongs to its character, which may prove itself in relation to other things or persons, but is essentially independent of them. The strength of even the strongest individual can always be overpowered by the many, who often will combine for no other purpose than to ruin strength precisely because of its peculiar independence. The almost instinctive hostility of the many toward the one has always, from Plato to Nietzsche, been ascribed to resentment, to the envy of the weak for the strong, but this psychological interpretation misses the point. It is in the nature of a group and its power to turn against independence, the property of individual strength.

Force, which we often use in daily speech as a synonym for violence, especially if violence serves as a means of coercion, should be reserved, in terminological language, for the "forces of nature" or the "force of circumstances" *(la force des choses)*, that is, to indicate the energy released by physical or social movements.

Authority, relating to the most elusive of these phenomena and therefore, as a term, most frequently abused,[6] can be vested in persons—there is such a thing as personal authority, as, for instance, in the relation between parent and child, between teacher and pupil—or it can be vested in offices, as, for instance, in the Roman senate *(auctoritas in senatu)* or in the hierarchical offices of the Church (a priest can grant valid absolution even though he is drunk). Its hallmark is unquestioning recognition by those who are asked to obey; neither coercion nor

---

[6]There is such a thing as authoritarian government, but it certainly has nothing in common with tyranny, dictatorship, or totalitarian rule. For a discussion of the historical background and political significance of the term, see my "What is Authority?" in *Between Past and Future: Exercises in Political Thought*, New York, 1968, and Part I of Karl-Heinz Lubke's valuable study, *Auctoritas bei Augustin*, Stuttgart, 1968, with extensive bibliography.

persuasion is needed. (A father can lose his authority either by beating his child or by starting to argue with him, that is, either by behaving to him like a tyrant or by treating him as an equal.) To remain in authority requires respect for the person or the office. The greatest enemy of authority, therefore, is contempt, and the surest way to undermine it is laughter.[7]

Violence, finally, as I have said, is distinguished by its instrumental character. Phenomenologically, it is close to strength, since the implements of violence, like all other tools, are designed and used for the purpose of multiplying natural strength until, in the last stage of their development, they can substitute for it.

It is perhaps not superfluous to add that these distinctions, though by no means arbitrary, hardly ever correspond to watertight compartments in the real world, from which nevertheless they are drawn. Thus institutionalized power in organized communities often appears in the guise of authority, demanding instant, unquestioning recognition; no society could function without it. (A small, and still isolated, incident in New York shows what can happen if authentic authority in social relations has broken down to the point where it cannot work any longer even in its derivative, purely functional form. A minor mishap in the subway system—the doors on a train failed to operate—turned into a serious shutdown on the line lasting four hours and involving more than fifty thousand passengers, because when the transit authorities asked the passengers to leave the defective train, they simply refused.)[8] Moreover, nothing, as we shall see, is more common than the combination of violence and power, nothing less frequent than to find them in their pure and therefore extreme form. From this, it does not follow that authority, power, and violence are all the same.

Still it must be admitted that it is particularly tempting to think of power in terms of command and obedience, and hence to equate power with violence, in a discussion of what actually is only one of power's special cases—namely, the power of government. Since in foreign relations as well as domestic affairs violence appears as a last resort to keep the power structure intact against individual challengers—the foreign enemy, the native criminal—it looks indeed as though violence were the prerequisite of power and power nothing but a façade,

---

[7]Wolin and Schaar, in "Berkeley: The Battle of People's Park" (*New York Review of Books*, June 19, 1969), are entirely right: "The rules are being broken because University authorities, administrators and faculty alike, have lost the respect of many of the students." They then conclude, "When authority leaves, power enters." This too is true, but, I am afraid, not quite in the sense they meant it. What entered first at Berkeley was student power, obviously the strongest power on every campus simply because of the students' superior numbers. It was in order to break this power that authorities resorted to violence, and it is precisely because the university is essentially an institution based on authority, and therefore in need of respect, that it finds it so difficult to deal with power in nonviolent terms. The university today calls upon the police for protection exactly as the Catholic church used to do before the separation of state and church forced it to rely on authority alone. It is perhaps more than an oddity that the severest crisis of the church as an institution should coincide with the severest crisis in the history of the university, the only secular institution still based on authority. Both may indeed be ascribed to "the progressing explosion of the atom 'obedience' whose stability was allegedly eternal," as Heinrich Böll remarked of the crisis in the churches. See "Es wird immer später," in *Antwort an Sacharow*, Zürich, 1969.

[8]See the New York *Times*, January 4, 1969, pp. 1 and 29.

the velvet glove which either conceals the iron hand or will turn out to belong to a paper tiger. On closer inspection, though, this notion loses much of its plausibility. For our purpose, the gap between theory and reality is perhaps best illustrated by the phenomenon of revolution.

Since the beginning of the century theoreticians of revolution have told us that the chances of revolution have significantly decreased in proportion to the increased destructive capacities of weapons at the unique disposition of governments.[9] The history of the last seventy years, with its extraordinary record of successful and unsuccessful revolutions, tells a different story. Were people mad who even tried against such overwhelming odds? And, leaving out instances of full success, how can even a temporary success be explained? The fact is that the gap between state-owned means of violence and what people can muster by themselves —from beer bottles to Molotov cocktails and guns—has always been so enormous that technical improvements make hardly any difference. Textbook instructions on "how to make a revolution" in a step-by-step progression from dissent to conspiracy, from resistance to armed uprising, are all based on the mistaken notion that revolutions are "made." In a contest of violence against violence the superiority of the government has always been absolute; but this superiority lasts only as long as the power structure of the government is intact—that is, as long as commands are obeyed and the army or police forces are prepared to use their weapons. When this is no longer the case, the situation changes abruptly. Not only is the rebellion not put down, but the arms themselves change hands—sometimes, as in the Hungarian revolution, within a few hours. (We should know about such things after all these years of futile fighting in Vietnam, where for a long time, before getting massive Russian aid, the National Liberation Front fought us with weapons that were made in the United States.) Only after this has happened, when the disintegration of the government in power has permitted the rebels to arm themselves, can one speak of an "armed uprising," which often does not take place at all or occurs when it is no longer necessary. Where commands are no longer obeyed, the means of violence are of no use; and the question of this obedience is not decided by the command-obedience relation but by opinion, and, of course, by the number of those who share it. Everything depends on the power behind the violence. The sudden dramatic breakdown of power that ushers in revolutions reveals in a flash how civil obedience—to laws, to rulers, to institutions—is but the outward manifestation of support and consent.

[9]Thus Franz Borkenau, reflecting on the defeat of the Spanish revolution, states: "In this tremendous contrast with previous revolutions one fact is reflected. Before these latter years, counter-revolution usually depended upon the support of reactionary powers, which were technically and intellectually inferior to the forces of revolution. This has changed with the advent of fascism. Now, every revolution is likely meet the attack of the most modern, most efficient, most ruthless machinery yet in existence. It means that the age of revolutions free to evolve according to their own laws is over." This was written more than thirty years ago (*The Spanish Cockpit*, London, 1937; Ann Arbor, 1963, pp. 288–289) and is now quoted with approval by Chomsky (*op. cit.*, p. 310). He believes that American and French intervention in the civil war in Vietnam proves Borkenau's prediction accurate, "with substitution of 'liberal imperialism' for fascism.'" I think that this example is rather apt to prove the opposite.

Where power has disintegrated, revolutions are possible but not necessary. We know of many instances when utterly impotent regimes were permitted to continue in existence for long periods of time—either because there was no one to test their strength and reveal their weakness or because they were lucky enough not to be engaged in war and suffer defeat. Disintegration often becomes manifest only in direct confrontation; and even then, when power is already in the street, some group of men prepared for such an eventuality is needed to pick it up and assume responsibility. We have recently witnessed how it did not take more than the relatively harmless, essentially nonviolent French students' rebellion to reveal the vulnerability of the whole political system, which rapidly disintegrated before the astonished eyes of the young rebels. Unknowingly they had tested it; they intended only to challenge the ossified university system, and down came the system of governmental power, together with that of the huge party bureaucracies —"une sorte de désintegration de toutes les hiérarchies."[10] It was a textbook case of a revolutionary situation[11] that did not develop into a revolution because there was nobody, least of all the students, prepared to seize power and the responsibility that goes with it. Nobody except, of course, de Gaulle. Nothing was more characteristic of the seriousness of the situation than his appeal to the army, his journey to see Massu and the generals in Germany, a walk to Canossa, if there ever was one, in view of what had happened only a few years before. But what he sought and received was support, not obedience, and the means were not commands but concessions. If commands had been enough, he would never have had to leave Paris.

No government exclusively based on the means of violence has ever existed. Even the totalitarian ruler, whose chief instrument of rule is torture, needs a power basis—the secret police and its net of informers. Only the development of robot soldiers, which, as previously mentioned, would eliminate the human completely and, conceivably, permit one man with a push button to destroy whomever he pleased, could change this fundamental ascendancy of power over violence. Even the most despotic domination we know of, the rule of master over slaves, who always outnumbered him, did not rest on superior means of coercion as such, but on a superior organization of power—that is, on the organized solidarity of the masters.[12] Single men without others to support them never have enough power to use violence successfully. Hence, in domestic affairs, violence functions as the last resort of power against criminals or rebels—that is, against single individuals who, as it were, refuse to be overpowered by the consensus of the majority. And as for actual warfare, we have seen in Vietnam, how an

[10]Raymond Aron, *La Revolution Introuvable*, 1968, p. 41.

[11]Stephen Spender, in *The Year of the Young Rebels* (New York, 1969), p. 56, disagrees: "What was so much more apparent than the revolutionary situation [was] the nonrevolutionary one." It may be "difficult to think of a revolution taking place when . . . everyone looks particularly good humoured," but this is what usually happens in the beginning of revolutions—during the early great ecstasy of fraternity.

[12]In ancient Greece, such an organization of power was the polis, whose chief merit, according to Xenophon, was that it permitted the "citizens to act as bodyguards to one another against slaves and criminals so that none of the citizens may die a violent death." (*Hiero*, IV, 3.)

enormous superiority in the means of violence can become helpless if confronted with an ill-equipped but well-organized opponent who is much more powerful. This lesson, to be sure, was there to be learned from the history of guerrilla warfare, which is at least as old as the defeat in Spain of Napoleon's still-unvanquished army.

To switch for a moment to conceptual language: Power is indeed of the essence of all government, but violence is not. Violence is by nature instrumental; like all means, it always stands in need of guidance and justification through the end it pursues. And what needs justification by something else cannot be the essence of anything. The end of war—end taken in its twofold meaning—is peace or victory; but to the question And what is the end of peace? there is no answer. Peace is an absolute, even though in recorded history periods of warfare have nearly always outlasted periods of peace. Power is in the same category; it is, as they say, "an end in itself." (This, of course, is not to deny that governments pursue policies and employ their power to achieve prescribed goals. But the power structure itself precedes and outlasts all aims, so that power, far from being the means to an end, is actually the very condition enabling a group of people to think and act in terms of the means-end category.) And since government is essentially organized and institutionalized power, the current question What is the end of government? does not make much sense either. The answer will be either question-begging—to enable men to live together—or dangerously utopian—to promote happiness or to realize a classless society or some other nonpolitical ideal, which if tried out in earnest cannot but end in some kind of tyranny.

Power needs no justification, being inherent in the very existence of political communities; what it does need is legitimacy. The common treatment of these two words as synonyms is no less misleading and confusing than the current equation of obedience and support. Power springs up whenever people get together and act in concert, but it derives its legitimacy from the initial getting together rather than from any action that then may follow. Legitimacy, when challenged, bases itself on an appeal to the past, while justification relates to an end that lies in the future. Violence can be justifiable, but it never will be legitimate. Its justification loses in plausibility the farther its intended end recedes into the future. No one questions the use of violence in self-defense, because the danger is not only clear but also present, and the end justifying the means is immediate.

Power and violence, though they are distinct phenomena, usually appear together. Wherever they are combined, power, we have found, is the primary and predominant factor. The situation, however, is entirely different when we deal with them in their pure states—as, for instance, with foreign invasion and occupation. We saw that the current equation of violence with power rests on government's being understood as domination of man over man by means of violence. If a foreign conqueror is confronted by an impotent government and by a nation unused to the exercise of political power, it is easy for him to achieve such domination. In all other cases the difficulties are great indeed, and the occupying invader will try immediately to establish Quisling governments, that is, to find a native power base to support his dominion. The head-on clash between Russian tanks and the entirely nonviolent resistance of the Czechoslovak people is a textbook case of a confrontation between violence and power in their pure states. But while domination in such an instance is difficult to achieve, it is not impossible. Violence, we must remember, does not depend on numbers or opinions, but on implements, and the implements of violence, as I mentioned before, like all other tools, increase and multiply human strength. Those who oppose violence with mere power will soon find that they are confronted not by men but by men's artifacts, whose inhumanity and destructive effectiveness increase in proportion to the distance separating the opponents. Violence can always destroy power; out of the barrel of a gun grows the most effective command, resulting in the most instant and perfect obedience. What never can grow out of it is power.

In a head-on clash between violence and power, the outcome is hardly in doubt. If Gandhi's enormously powerful and successful strategy of nonviolent resistance had met with a different enemy—Stalin's Russia, Hitler's Germany, even prewar Japan, instead of England—the outcome would not have been decolonization, but massacre and submission. However, England in India and France in Algeria had good reasons for their restraint. Rule by sheer violence comes into play where power is being lost; it is precisely the shrinking power of the Russian government, internally and externally, that became manifest in its "solution" of the Czechoslovak problem—just as it was the shrinking power of European imperialism that became manifest in the alternative between decolonization and massacre. To substitute violence for power can bring victory, but the price is very high; for it is not only paid by the vanquished, it is also paid by the victor in terms of his own power. This is especially true when the victor happens to enjoy domestically the blessings of constitutional government. Henry Steele Commager is entirely right: "If we subvert world order and destroy world peace we must inevitably subvert and destroy our own political institutions first."[13] The much-feared boomerang effect of the "government of subject races" (Lord Cromer) on the home government during the imperialist era meant that rule by violence in faraway lands would end by affecting the government of England, that the last "subject race" would be the English themselves. The recent gas attack on the campus at Berkeley, where not just tear gas but also another gas, "outlawed by the Geneva Convention and used by the Army to flush out guerrillas in Vietnam," was laid down while gas-masked Guardsmen stopped anybody and everybody "from fleeing the gassed area," is an excellent example of this "backlash" phenomenon. It has often been said that impotence breeds violence, and psychologically this is quite true, at least of persons possessing natural strength, moral or physical. Politically speaking, the point is that loss of power becomes a temptation to substitute violence for power—in 1968 during the Democratic convention in Chicago we could watch this process on television—and that violence itself results in impotence. Where violence is no longer backed and restrained by power, the well-known reversal in reckoning with means and ends has taken place. The means, the means of destruction, now determine the end—with the consequence that the end will be the destruction of all power.

[13]"Can We Limit Presidential Power?" in *The New Republic*, April 6, 1968.

Nowhere is the self-defeating factor in the victory of violence over power more evident than in the use of terror to maintain domination, about whose weird successes and eventual failures we know perhaps more than any generation before us. Terror is not the same as violence; it is, rather, the form of government that comes into being when violence, having destroyed all power, does not abdicate but, on the contrary, remains in full control. It has often been noticed that the effectiveness of terror depends almost entirely on the degree of social atomization. Every kind of organized opposition must disappear before the full force of terror can be let loose. This atomization—an outrageously pale, academic word for the horror it implies—is maintained and intensified through the ubiquity of the informer, who can be literally omnipresent because he no longer is merely a professional agent in the pay of the police but potentially every person one comes into contact with. How such a fully developed police state is established and how it works—or, rather, how nothing works where it holds sway—can now be learned in Aleksandr I. Solzhenitsyn's *The First Circle*, which will probably remain one of the masterpieces of twentieth-century literature and certainly contains the best documentation on Stalin's regime in existence. The decisive difference between totalitarian domination, based on terror, and tyrannies and dictatorships, established by violence, is that the former turns not only against its enemies but against its friends and supporters as well, being afraid of all power, even the power of its friends. The climax of terror is reached when the police state begins to devour its own children, when yesterday's executioner becomes today's victim. And this is also the moment when power disappears entirely. There exist now a great many plausible explanations for the de-Stalinization of Russia—none, I believe, so compelling as the realization by the Stalinist functionaries themselves that a continuation of the regime would lead, not to an insurrection, against which terror is indeed the best safeguard, but to paralysis of the whole country.

To sum up: politically speaking, it is insufficient to say that power and violence are not the same. Power and violence are opposites; where the one rules absolutely, the other is absent. Violence appears where power is in jeopardy, but left to its own course it ends in power's disappearance. This implies that it is not correct to think of the opposite of violence as nonviolence; to speak of nonviolent power is actually redundant. Violence can destroy power; it is utterly incapable of creating it. Hegel's and Marx's great trust in the dialectial "power of negation," by virtue of which opposites do not destroy but smoothly develop into each other because contradictions promote and do not paralyze development, rests on a much older philosophical prejudice: that evil is no more than a privative *modus* of the good, that good can come out of evil; that, in short, evil is but a temporary manifestation of a still-hidden good. Such time-honored opinions have become dangerous. They are shared by many who have never heard of Hegel or Marx, for the simple reason that they inspire hope and dispel fear—a treacherous hope used to dispel legitimate fear. By this, I do not mean to equate violence with evil; I only want to stress that violence cannot be derived from its opposite, which is power, and that in order to understand it for what it is, we shall have to examine its roots and nature.

7/Tradition and Upheaval: Esthetics and Education

introduction:
education and society

Before I introduce the next two authors, let us examine the general trend of the argument uniting the preceding essays with the five that follow. We are moving around a curve that is continuous with the previous section on liberation, through the related issues of student power and pedagogy, to the actual anatomy of the classroom situation where the quality of the immediate experience is important. Freire emphasizes the importance of the teacher-student relationship, Dewey notes the unfortunate loss of physicality and concreteness in many classrooms, and Leonard, with explicit reference to Dewey, takes a close look at the esthetics of the classroom. Leonard wants to make us aware of the felt quality, the texture, the potential beauty of the classroom experience. He talks about it much as one talks about the experience of a work of art—which brings us to esthetics as the philosophy of art. Plato and Breton talk about art, but each, in his separate way, leads the discussion of esthetics back to politics so that the curve of topical progression recrosses itself.

The essays naturally lend themselves to this arrangement because the so-called branches of philosophy are not in fact separable or separate. Rubrics like 'esthetics,' 'education,' 'politics' tend to make us think we are dealing with clearly distinguishable species of the genus philosophy. Rather than thinking in terms of the 'branches' of philosophy—a natural metaphor that corresponds well to the logical separateness of species in a "tree" of genus-species distinctions—we would do better to regard philosophy as an even more organic whole that can be dissected only at the risk of death. Each part of the organism is in a living relationship with every other, and a sense of their connectedness is as important as a knowledge of each part. Let us move now from politics and education to education and esthetics, from there to esthetics and art, and thence to art and politics.

Ever since Plato, thinkers have drawn on the analogy between the dynamics of the self and the structure of the state. The same idea finds application in speaking of *repression* of parts of the self and political *repression* of classes of people deemed less than equal. This analogy has been played out in the arena of education. The New

Politics—the slightly anarchistic politics that finds the meaning of politics elsewhere than in elections and parliamentary procedures—the politics that has grown visibly on the campus, I shall refer to from now on as metapolitics. The educational reform movement has gone through many changes, and many of them correspond to the dialectics of oppression and liberation. For example, we hear less nowadays about "student power" than in the 1960's when it was a goal conceived according to the old politics. People still believed in hierarchic structures, and the point was to get some "student representatives" high in the hierarchy. To the extent that the hierarchies remain, that kind of infiltration may still be necessary, but more and more students are simply fed up with playing the hierarchies game. How can you build a community of equals if the rules and structure of the game dictate from the outset that some must be on top and some on the bottom? Who cares if you win when you are playing a game where winning means losing the goal you started with?

Whether you "win" or "lose," activism in the old political context just keeps the competitive, hierarchic context going. So students look around for modes of political behavior unlike the traditional and visible student activism.

A large part of nonactivist action has taken the form of community organizing: food co-ops, health clinics, crisis centers, and so on, but even these manifestations are too visible to serve as the best evidence of metapolitical consciousness on campus. What I am talking about is the all-but-invisible shared awareness of political realities, the tacit agreements among so many students about where they stand with respect to the "system." Not that these agreements are all that clear; often they lie precisely in the quality of doubt about both the dominant political order and those who oppose it with confident militancy. This, then, is a particularly apt time for the pursuit of philosophy. Now seems to be the time when students wish to gain their own awareness of their situation in a social-educational-political order, an awareness that can be shared among a vast majority rather than bought from the few political heavyweights who always seemed at the hub of the action during the really political stages of the student movement. In my own experience I can recall the contradiction between the fact of leadership by a few and an explicit awareness that we were seeking broad-based, participatory, nonhierarchic modes of organization and action. There was the active vanguard whose task it was to rouse the apathetic masses, yet all the majority had to do was listen to the *content* of what the few were saying in order to see that the *form*—many listening to a few—was inappropriate to the goal. The few were talking about participatory democracy and community, but in a most nonparticipatory, noncommunal manner.

But many got the message. They may have resisted pressure to man the barricades in militant activism, but they got the message about alternative styles of social organization and education. And now they want to learn more, understand more, so they can build a truly broadbased, participatory, metapolitical culture. And the campus can be used to gain that understanding. Naturally there will be regressions and exceptions; surely not everyone is already completely self-conscious and knows precisely what is happening. My intention is to acknowledge a confusion and ambivalence, a latent period in the dialectic when things are not as clear as when one extreme dominates. I am trying to clarify the fact of confusion and openness.

The following essays help clarify the confusion. Though they hardly represent anything like the full range of issues in the philosophy of education, they at least show how some of them relate to other circles of self-awareness. Much of the confusion about what is going on in education derives from the fact that we fail to make those connections. Just as our schools are in many cases physically separated from the community, so we tend to separate family life from education and education from society. But these separations are to some extent artificial, however expedient they may sometimes be. If we think about education from the perspective of the home or the society, we achieve insights that rarely surface in the classroom where education is supposed to be happening. But those insights, those connections that constitute the web of self-awareness, *can* surface in the classroom, especially where there is a philosophical inquiry into fundamentals.

For instance, Why education? A simple question, but one that is rarely asked except perhaps in the less radical form of, Why education for me? Why go to college? Actually these questions seem radical when they are first confronted. If we have always assumed that going to college is the thing to do, it is radical to wonder *why* it is the thing to do. Parents say you go to college to get an education, but that leads us again to, Why education? For the individual the answer may have to do with getting a better job. But why do we demand so much education of those who usually do not use much of their classroom training in their jobs anyway? We could probably dole out the jobs and get just as much done without using the vast clearinghouse of higher education. What other reasons might there be for the major role that education plays in modern society?

To be most blunt—a bluntness that will be refined in a dialectical development of this initially extreme view—perhaps education is central to modern society not to increase people's self-awareness but rather to decrease it in favor of a social awareness. This is, perhaps the role of education is to socialize people in the negative sense of regimenting them into a manipulable order. Of course, I take this view to be just one moment, one extreme, in the dialectic. If this book increases your self-awareness, and if you are reading it in the context of the educational system, then the negative charge cannot be entirely true. We will then want to distinguish between good education and bad education, rather than speak of the function of education in general. The next two essays speak about good education and bad education in relation to social systems.

PAOLO FREIRE *(b. 1921)*

Among those who have been thinking, writing, and reading about educational reform in recent years, one of the most talked-about books has been Paolo Freire's Pedagogy of the Oppressed *(1970). Though Freire's experience has been mostly in South America, what he has to say is frequently applicable to our own educational framework. In the following essay—Chapter 2 from his book—Freire opposes what he calls the "banking" concept of education to the "problem posing" concept of education. In the former the students are passive receptacles for knowledge possessed initially only by the teacher. In the latter the teacher-student relationship is infused with the dynamism of a group of human beings inquiring together into the problems posed by their ever changing historical situation.*

Freire's ideas relate to the rest of this book, both in their form and their content. The contemporary situation is the starting point of Self *and* World, *and the here and now of self-knowledge is the stated goal for each reader. The form of the book follows the historical and personal quest for consciousness. The contents include some of the sources that are also central to Freire's picture of man as dynamic, changing, and historical. Yet an essay like Freire's makes me realize that even this book could be used in a classroom that follows the banking concept of education, could be regarded (mistakenly) as a body of information to be deposited in the student's mind. Freire's essay cannot help but raise the issue of the teacher-student relationship in the classes where this book is used. For those who have not yet looked at the teacher-student relationship, for those to whom the following essay may sound like a condemnation, a few words of special introduction may be helpful.*

It is never too late to withdraw from the banking concept of education. Let us pose, right now, a problem to students and teachers alike: say you read the following essay and find you are participating in what Freire regards as the stultifying banking-concept classroom. Both students and *teachers face this problem, and the first step in solving the problem is to see that they do indeed face it* together *and not against each other, that they get beyond blaming the other side for keeping the bank functioning as a bank. Students blame teachers for subjecting them to hours of deposits to be held in storage until the exam. Teachers blame students for not participating, for asking to be entertained and regaled with riches of information. The problem is our problem. We all come to the classroom programmed by years of banking education, and it is not easy to change. The story is the same in rural high schools and the most elite colleges. Many of the students at universities are there precisely because their talents at banking got them through the rigorous admissions competition. If the university teacher ceases to make the deposits, they get upset; they are not getting the goods they paid for.*

Both teachers and students are victimized by a tradition manifested in the following education study: Kindergarten teachers were asked what they conceived their job to be. What were they doing for their children? Most answered that they were preparing them for first grade. The first grade teachers by and large said they were preparing their children for second grade. Grammar school teachers prepare their students for high school. High school teachers prepare their students for college. Many college professors tend to favor those students they can train for graduate school in their fields of expertise. And finally, graduate schools train their students to be teachers. The circle is so tight that once again it remains possible to traverse the entire circle without ever asking, Why education? The teacher who receives a classroom of students trained in this circle will not have an easy time breaking out of it, and sooner or later may stop trying, however noble his or her first intentions. After all, who can put up with all the anxiety produced when a whole classroom of students suddenly, perhaps for the first time, feels the pain of being wrenched away from the images on the wall of the cave? It is much easier to become an expert on the images, a narrator for the story everyone is used to hearing. Students often like best the teachers most talented at tying them to the images on the wall of the cave; and many of us like to be liked.

The problem is not easy. To liberate the teacher-student relationship from the shackles of past programming requires ongoing and cumulative interaction. The first attempts usually fail. I remember when I had just finished graduate school I was determined to avoid the banking concept; I would learn from my students. But my concept of learning was dominated by the way I learned in graduate school. Consequently, I found myself disappointed and resentful that my students were not teaching me anything, since, of course, they were not teaching me the way my teachers in graduate school had. So then I started teaching, and lo and behold, as I got feedback on what I had to say, I began to learn—a very obscure process that took several years to unravel, and the end of the ball of twine is hardly in sight.

Perhaps these special introductory remarks are unnecessary. I make them in hopes that mutual understanding and compassion might take the place of animosity or disrespect. The problem of teacher-student relationships is always our problem, and it is one of the most difficult that a problem-posing education can pose.

The Pedagogy of the Oppressed

A careful analysis of the teacher-student relationship at any level, inside or outside the school, reveals its fundamentally *narrative* character. This relationship involves a narrating Subject (the teacher) and patient, listening objects (the students). The contents, whether values or empirical dimensions of reality, tend in the process of being narrated to become lifeless and petrified. Education is suffering from narration sickness.

The teacher talks about reality as if it were motionless, static, compartmentalized, and predictable. Or else he expounds on a topic completely alien to the existential experience of the students. His task is to "fill" the students with the contents of his narration—contents which are detached from reality, disconnected from the totality that engendered them and could give them significance. Words are emptied of their concreteness and become a hollow, alienated, and alienating verbosity.

The outstanding characteristic of this narrative education, then, is the sonority of words, not their transforming power. "Four times four is sixteen; the capital of Pará is Belém." The student records, memorizes, and repeats these phrases without perceiving what four times four really means, or realizing the true significance of "capital" in the affirmation "the capital of Pará is Belém," that is, what Belém means for Pará and what Pará means for Brazil.

Narration (with the teacher as narrator) leads the students to memorize mechanically the narrated content. Worse yet, it turns them into "containers," into "receptacles" to be "filled" by the teacher. The more completely he fills the receptacles, the better a teacher he is. The more meekly the receptacles permit themselves to be filled, the better students they are.

Education thus becomes an act of depositing, in which the students are the depositories and the teacher is the depositor. Instead of communicating, the teacher issues communiqués and makes deposits which the students patiently receive, memorize, and repeat. This is the "banking" concept of education, in which the scope of action allowed to the students extends only as far as receiving, filing, and storing the deposits. They do, it is true, have the opportunity to become collectors or cataloguers of the things they store. But in the last analysis, it is men themselves who are filed away through the lack of creativity, transformation, and knowledge in this (at best) misguided system. For apart from inquiry, apart from the praxis, men cannot be truly human. Knowledge emerges only through invention and re-invention, through the restless, impatient, continuing, hopeful inquiry men pursue in the world, with the world, and with each other.

In the banking concept of education, knowledge is a gift bestowed by those who consider themselves knowledgeable upon those whom they consider to know nothing. Projecting an absolute ignorance onto others, a characteristic of the ideology of oppression, negates education and knowledge as processes of inquiry. The teacher presents himself to his students as their necessary opposite; by considering their ignorance absolute, he justifies his own existence. The students, alienated like the slave in the Hegelian dialectic, accept their ignorance as justifying the teacher's existence—but, unlike the slave, they never discover that they educate the teacher.

The *raison d'être* of libertarian education, on the other hand, lies in its drive towards reconciliation. Education must begin with the solution of the teacher-student contradiction, by reconciling the poles of the contradiction so that both are simultaneously teachers *and* students.

This solution is not (nor can it be) found in the banking concept. On the contrary, banking education maintains and even stimulates the contradiction through the following attitudes and practices, which mirror oppressive society as a whole:

a. the teacher teaches and the students are taught;
b. the teacher knows everything and the students know nothing;
c. the teacher thinks and the students are thought about;
d. the teacher talks and the students listen—meekly;
e. the teacher disciplines and the students are disciplined;
f. the teacher chooses and enforces his choice, and the students comply;
g. the teacher acts and the students have the illusion of acting through the action of the teacher;

    h. the teacher chooses the program content, and the students (who were not consulted) adapt to it;

    i. the teacher confuses the authority of knowledge with his own professional authority, which he sets in opposition to the freedom of the students;

    j. the teacher is the Subject of the learning process, while the pupils are mere objects.

It is not surprising that the banking concept of education regards men as adaptable, manageable beings. The more students work at storing the deposits entrusted to them, the less they develop the critical consciousness which would result from their intervention in the world as transformers of that world. The more completely they accept the passive role imposed on them, the more they tend simply to adapt to the world as it is and to the fragmented view of reality deposited in them.

The capability of banking education to minimize or annul the students' creative power and to stimulate their credulity serves the interests of the oppressors, who care neither to have the world revealed nor to see it transformed. The oppressors use their "humanitarianism" to preserve a profitable situation. Thus they react almost instinctively against any experiment in education which stimulates the critical faculties and is not content with a partial view of reality but always seeks out the ties which link one point to another and one problem to another.

Indeed, the interests of the oppressors lie in "changing the consciousness of the oppressed, not the situation which oppresses them";[1] for the more the oppressed can be led to adapt to that situation, the more easily they can be dominated. To achieve this end, the oppressors use the banking concept of education in conjunction with a paternalistic social action apparatus, within which the oppressed receive the euphemistic title of "welfare recipients." They are treated as individual cases, as marginal men who deviate from the general configuration of a "good, organized, and just" society. The oppressed are regarded as the pathology of the healthy society, which must therefore adjust these "incompetent and lazy" folk to its own patterns by changing their mentality. These marginals need to be "integrated," "incorporated" into the healthy society that they have "forsaken."

The truth is, however, that the oppressed are not "marginals," are not men living "outside" society. They have always been "inside"—inside the structure which made them "beings for others." The solution is not to "integrate" them into the structure of oppression, but to transform that structure so that they can become "beings for themselves." Such transformation, of course, would undermine the oppressors' purposes; hence their utilization of the banking concept of education to avoid the threat of student *conscientização* [the deepening awareness of social, political, and economic contradictions inherent in one's own situation].

The banking approach to adult education, for example, will never propose to students that they critically consider reality. It will deal instead with such vital

[1]Simone de Beauvoir, *La Pensée de Droite, Aujourd'hui* (Paris); ST, *El Pensamiento político de la Derecha* (Buenos Aires, 1963), p. 34

questions as whether Roger gave green grass to the goat, and insist upon the importance of learning that, on the contrary, Roger gave green grass to the rabbit. The "humanism" of the banking approach masks the effort to turn men into automatons—the very negation of their ontological vocation to be more fully human.

Those who use the banking approach, knowingly or unknowingly (for there are innumerable well-intentioned bank-clerk teachers who do not realize that they are serving only to dehumanize), fail to perceive that the deposits themselves contain contradictions about reality. But, sooner or later, these contradictions may lead formerly passive students to turn against their domestication and the attempt to domesticate reality. They may discover through existential experience that their present way of life is irreconcilable with their vocation to become fully human. They may perceive through their relations with reality that reality is really a *process*, undergoing constant transformation. If men are searchers and their ontological vocation is humanization, sooner or later they may perceive the contradiction in which banking education seeks to maintain them, and then engage themselves in the struggle for their liberation.

But the humanist, revolutionary educator cannot wait for this possibility to materialize. From the outset, his efforts must coincide with those of the students to engage in critical thinking and the quest for mutual humanization. His efforts must be imbued with a profound trust in men and their creative power. To achieve this, he must be a partner of the students in his relations with them.

The banking concept does not admit to such partnership—and necessarily so. To resolve the teacher-student contradiction, to exchange the role of depositor, prescriber, domesticator, for the role of student among students would be to undermine the power of oppression and serve the cause of liberation.

Implicit in the banking concept is the assumption of a dichotomy between man and the world: man is merely *in* the world, not *with* the world or with others; man is spectator, not re-creator. In this view, man is not a conscious being (*corpo consciente*); he is rather the possessor of *a* consciousness: an empty "mind" passively open to the reception of deposits of reality from the world outside. For example, my desk, my books, my coffee cup, all the objects before me—as bits of the world which surrounds me—would be "inside" me, exactly as I am inside my study right now. This view makes no distinction between being accessible to consciousness and entering consciousness. The distinction, however, is essential: the objects which surround me are simply accessible to my consciousness, not located within it. I am aware of them, but they are not inside me.

It follows logically from the banking notion of consciousness that the educator's role is to regulate the way the world "enters into" the students. His task is to organize a process which already occurs spontaneously, to "fill" the students by making deposits of information which he considers to constitute true knowledge.[2] And since men "receive" the world as passive entities, education should make them more passive still, and adapt them to the world. The educated man is the

---

[2]This concept corresponds to what Sartre calls the "digestive" or "nutritive" concept of education, in which knowledge is "fed" by the teacher to the students to "fill them out." See Jean-Paul Sartre, "Une idée fondamentale de la phénoménologie de Husserl: L'intentionalité," *Situations I* (Paris, 1947).

adapted man, because he is better fit for the world. Translated into practice, this concept is well suited to the purposes of the oppressors, whose tranquility rests on how well men fit the world the oppressors have created, and how little they question it.

The more completely the majority adapt to the purposes which the dominant minority prescribe for them (thereby depriving them of the right to their own purposes), the more easily the minority can continue to prescribe. The theory and practice of banking education serve this end quite efficiently. Verbalistic lessons, reading requirements,[3] the methods for evaluating "knowledge," the distance between the teacher and the taught, the criteria for promotion: everything in this ready-to-wear approach serves to obviate thinking.

The bank-clerk educator does not realize that there is no true security in his hypertrophied role, that one must seek to live *with* others in solidarity. One cannot impose oneself, nor even merely co-exist with one's students. Solidarity requires true communication, and the concept by which such an educator is guided fears and proscribes communication.

Yet only through communication can human life hold meaning. The teacher's thinking is authenticated only by the authenticity of the students' thinking. The teacher cannot think for his students, nor can he impose his thought on them. Authentic thinking, thinking that is concerned about *reality*, does not take place in ivory tower isolation, but only in communication. If it is true that thought has meaning only when generated by action upon the world, the subordination of students to teachers becomes impossible.

Because banking education begins with a false understanding of men as objects, it cannot promote the development of what Fromm calls "biophily," but instead produces its opposite: "necrophily."

> While life is characterized by growth in a structured, functional manner, the necrophilous person loves all that does not grow, all that is mechanical. The necrophilous person is driven by the desire to transform the organic into the inorganic, to approach life mechanically, as if all living persons were things. . . . Memory, rather than experience; having, rather than being, is what counts. The necrophilous person can relate to an object—a flower or a person—only if he possesses it; hence a threat to his possession is a threat to himself; if he loses possession he loses contact with the world. . . . He loves control, and in the act of controlling he kills life.[4]

Oppression—overwhelming control—is necrophilic; it is nourished by love of death, not life. The banking concept of education, which serves the interests of oppression, is also necrophilic. Based on a mechanistic, static, naturalistic, spatialized view of consciousness, it transforms students into receiving objects. It attempts to control thinking and action, leads men to adjust to the world, and inhibits their creative power.

---

[3]For example, some professors specify in their reading lists that a book should be read from pages 10 to 15—and do this to "help" their students!

[4]Erich Fromm, *The Heart of Man* (New York, 1966), p. 41.

When their efforts to act responsibly are frustrated, when they find themselves unable to use their faculties, men suffer. "This suffering due to impotence is rooted in the very fact that the human equilibrium has been disturbed."[5] But the inability to act which causes men's anguish also causes them to reject their impotence, by attempting

> ...to restore [their] capacity to act. But can [they], and how? One way is to submit to and identify with a person or group having power. By this symbolic participation in another person's life, [men have] the illusion of acting, when in reality [they] only submit to and become a part of those who act.[6]

Populist manifestations perhaps best exemplify this type of behavior by the oppressed, who, by identifying with charismatic leaders, come to feel that they themselves are active and effective. The rebellion they express as they emerge in the historical process is motivated by that desire to act effectively. The dominant elites consider the remedy to be more domination and repression, carried out in the name of freedom, order, and social peace (that is, the peace of the elites). Thus they can condemn—logically, from their point of view—"the violence of a strike by workers and [can] call upon the state in the same breath to use violence in putting down the strike."[7]

Education as the exercise of domination stimulates the credulity of students, with the ideological intent (often not perceived by educators) of indoctrinating them to adapt to the world of oppression. This accusation is not made in the naive hope that the dominant elites will thereby simply abandon the practice. Its objective is to call the attention of true humanists to the fact that they cannot use banking educational methods in the pursuit of liberation, for they would only negate that very pursuit. Nor may a revolutionary society inherit these methods from an oppressor society. The revolutionary society which practices banking education is either misguided or mistrusting of men. In either event, it is threatened by the specter of reaction.

Unfortunately, those who espouse the cause of liberation are themselves surrounded and influenced by the climate which generates the banking concept, and often do not perceive its true significance or its dehumanizing power. Paradoxically, then, they utilize this same instrument of alienation in what they consider an effort to liberate. Indeed, some "revolutionaries" brand as "innocents," "dreamers," or even "reactionaries" those who would challenge this educational practice. But one does not liberate men by alienating them. Authentic liberation—the process of humanization—is not another deposit to be made in men. Liberation is a praxis: the action and reflection of men upon their world in order to transform it. Those truly committed to the cause of liberation can accept neither the mechanistic concept of consciousness as an empty vessel to be filled, nor the use of banking methods of domination (propaganda, slogans—deposits) in the name of liberation.

[5]*Ibid.*, p. 31.
[6]*Ibid.*
[7]Reinhold Niebuhr, *Moral Man and Immoral Society* (New York, 1960), p. 130.

Those truly committed to liberation must reject the banking concept in its entirety, adopting instead a concept of men as conscious beings, and consciousness as consciousness intent upon the world. They must abandon the educational goal of deposit-making and replace it with the posing of the problems of men in their relations with the world. "Problem-posing" education, responding to the essence of consciousness—*intentionality*—rejects communiqués and embodies communication. It epitomizes the special characteristic of consciousness: being *conscious of*, not only as intent on objects but as turned in upon itself in a Jasperian "split"— consciousness as consciousness *of* consciousness.

Liberating education consists in acts of cognition, not transferrals of information. It is a learning situation in which the cognizable object (far from being the end of the cognitive act) intermediates the cognitive actors—teacher on the one hand and students on the other. Accordingly, the practice of problem-posing education entails at the outset that the teacher-student contradiction be resolved. Dialogical relations—indispensable to the capacity of cognitive actors to cooperate in perceiving the same cognizable object—are otherwise impossible.

Indeed, problem-posing education, which breaks with the vertical patterns characteristic of banking education, can fulfill its function as the practice of freedom only if it can overcome the above contradiction. Through dialogue, the teacher-of-the-students and the students-of-the-teacher cease to exist and a new term emerges: teacher-student with students-teachers. The teacher is no longer merely the-one-who-teaches, but one who is himself taught in dialogue with the students, who in turn while being taught also teach. They become jointly responsible for a process in which all grow. In this process, arguments based on "authority" are no longer valid; in order to function, authority must be *on the side of* freedom, not *against* it. Here, no one teaches another, nor is anyone self-taught. Men teach each other, mediated by the world, by the cognizable objects which in banking education are "owned" by the teacher.

The banking concept (with its tendency to dichotomize everything) distinguishes two stages in the action of the educator. During the first, he cognizes a cognizable object while he prepares his lessons in his study or his laboratory; during the second, he expounds to his students about that object. The students are not called upon to know, but to memorize the contents narrated by the teacher. Nor do the students practice any act of cognition, since the object towards which the act should be directed is the property of the teacher rather than a medium evoking the critical reflection of both teacher and students. Hence in the name of the "preservation of culture and knowledge" we have a system which achieves neither true knowledge nor true culture.

The problem-posing method does not dichotomize the activity of the teacher-student: he is not "cognitive" at one point and "narrative" at another. He is always "cognitive," whether preparing a project or engaging in dialogue with the students. He does not regard cognizable objects as his private property, but as the object of reflection by himself and the students. In this way, the problem-posing educator constantly re-forms his reflections in the reflection of the students. The students—no longer docile listeners—are now critical co-investigators in dialogue with the teacher. The teacher presents the material to the students for their consideration, and re-considers his earlier considerations as the students express their own. The role of the problem-posing educator is to create, together with the students, the conditions under which knowledge at the level of the *doxa* [opinion] is superseded by true knowledge, at the level of the *logos* [science].

Whereas banking education anesthetizes and inhibits creative power, problem-posing education involves a constant unveiling of reality. The former attempts to maintain the *submersion* of consciousness; the latter strives for the *emergence* of consciousness and *critical intervention* in reality.

Students, as they are increasingly posed with problems relating to themselves in the world and with the world, will feel increasingly challenged and obliged to respond to that challenge. Because they apprehend the challenge as interrelated to other problems within a total context, not as a theoretical question, the resulting comprehension tends to be increasingly critical and thus constantly less alienated. Their response to the challenge evokes new challenges, followed by new understandings; and gradually the students come to regard themselves as committed.

Education as the practice of freedom—as opposed to education as the practice of domination—denies that man is abstract, isolated, independent, and unattached to the world; it also denies that the world exists as a reality apart from men. Authentic reflection considers neither abstract man nor the world without men, but men in their relations with the world. In these relations consciousness and world are simultaneous: consciousness neither precedes the world nor follows it.

La conscience et le monde sont dormés d'un même coup: extérieur par essence
à la conscience, le monde est, par essence relatif a elle.[8]

In one of our culture circles in Chile, the group was discussing (based on a codification) the anthropological concept of culture. In the midst of the discussion, a peasant who by banking standards was completely ignorant said: "Now I see that without man there is no world." When the educator responded: "Let's say, for the sake of argument, that all the men on earth were to die, but that the earth itself remained, together with trees, birds, animals, rivers, seas, the stars... wouldn't all this be a world?" "Oh no," the peasant replied emphatically. "There would be no one to say: 'This is a world'."

The peasant wished to express the idea that there would be lacking the consciousness of the world which necessarily implies the world of consciousness. *I* cannot exist without a *not-I*. In turn, the *not-I* depends on that existence. The world which brings consciousness into existence becomes the world *of* that consciousness. Hence, the previously cited affirmation of Sartre: *"La conscience et le monde sont dormés d'un même coup."*

As men, simultaneously reflecting on themselves and on the world, increase the scope of their perception, they begin to direct their observations towards previously inconspicuous phenomena:

In perception properly so-called, as an explicit awareness [*Gewahren*], I am turned towards the object, to the paper, for instance. I apprehend it as being this here and now. The apprehension is a singling out, every object having a background in experience. Around and about the paper

8Sartre, *op. cit.*, p. 32.

lie books, pencils, ink-well, and so forth, and these in a certain sense are also "perceived", perceptually there, in the "field of intuition"; but whilst I was turned towards the paper there was no turning in their direction, not any apprehending of them, not even in a secondary sense. They appeared and yet were not singled out, were not posited on their own account. Every perception of a thing has such a zone of background intuitions or background awareness, if "intuiting" already includes the state of being turned towards, and this also is a "conscious experience", or more briefly a "consciousness of" all indeed that in point of fact lies in the co-perceived objective background.[9]

That which had existed objectively but had not been perceived in its deeper implications (if indeed it was perceived at all) begins to "stand out," assuming the character of a problem and therefore of challenge. Thus, men begin to single out elements from their "background awarenesses" and to reflect upon them. These elements are now objects of men's consideration and, as such, objects of their action and cognition.

In problem-posing education, men develop their power to perceive critically *the way they exist* in the world *with which* and *in which* they find themselves; they come to see the world not as a static reality, but as a reality in process, in transformation. Although the dialectical relations of men with the world exist independently of how these relations are perceived (or whether or not they are perceived at all), it is also true that the form of action men adopt is to a large extent a function of how they perceive themselves in the world. Hence, the teacher-student and the students-teachers reflect simultaneously on themselves and the world without dichotomizing this reflection from action, and thus establish an authentic form of thought and action.

Once again, the two educational concepts and practices under analysis come into conflict. Banking education (for obvious reasons) attempts, by mythicizing reality, to conceal certain facts which explain the way men exist in the world; problem-posing education sets itself the task of demythologizing. Banking education resists dialogue; problem-posing education regards dialogue as indispensable to the act of cognition which unveils reality. Banking education treats students as objects of assistance; problem-posing education makes them critical thinkers. Banking education inhibits creativity and domesticates (although it cannot completely destroy) the *intentionality* of consciousness by isolating consciousness from the world, thereby denying men their ontological and historical vocation of becoming more fully human. Problem-posing education bases itself on creativity and stimulates true reflection and action upon reality, thereby responding to the vocation of men as beings who are authentic only when engaged in inquiry and creative transformation. In sum: banking theory and practice, as immobilizing and fixating forces, fail to acknowledge men as historical beings; problem-posing theory and practice take man's historicity as their starting point.

Problem-posing education affirms men as beings in the process of *becoming*— as unfinished, uncompleted beings in and with a likewise unfinished reality.

[9]Edmund Husserl, *Ideas—General Introduction to Pure Phenomenology* (London, 1969), pp. 105–106.

Indeed, in contrast to other animals who are unfinished, but not historical, men know themselves to be unfinished; they are aware of their incompletion. In this incompletion and this awareness lie the very roots of education as an exclusively human manifestation. The unfinished character of men and the transformational character of reality necessitate that education be an ongoing activity.

Education is thus constantly remade in the praxis. In order to *be,* it must *become.* Its "duration" (in the Bergsonian meaning of the word) is found in the interplay of the opposites *permanence* and *change.* The banking method emphasizes permanence and becomes reactionary; problem-posing education—which accepts neither a "well-behaved" present nor a predetermined future—roots itself in the dynamic present and becomes revolutionary.

Problem-posing education is revolutionary futurity. Hence it is prophetic (and, as such, hopeful). Hence, it corresponds to the historical nature of man. Hence, it affirms men as beings who transcend themselves, who move forward and look ahead, for whom immobility represents a fatal threat, for whom looking at the past must only be a means of understanding more clearly what and who they are so that they can more wisely build the future. Hence, it identifies with the movement which engages men as beings aware of their incompletion—an historical movement which has its point of departure, its Subjects and its objective.

The point of departure of the movement lies in men themselves. But since men do not exist apart from the world, apart from reality, the movement must begin with the men-world relationship. Accordingly, the point of departure must always be with men in the "here and now," which constitutes the situation within which they are submerged, from which they emerge, and in which they intervene. Only by starting from this situation—which determines their perception of it— can they begin to move. To do this authentically they must perceive their state not as fated and unalterable, but merely as limiting—and therefore challenging.

Whereas the banking method directly or indirectly reinforces men's fatalistic perception of their situation, the problem-posing method presents this very situation to them as a problem. As the situation becomes the object of their cognition, the naïve or magical perception which produced their fatalism gives way to perception which is able to perceive itself even as it perceives reality, and can thus be critically objective about that reality.

A deepened consciousness of their situation leads men to apprehend that situation as an historical reality susceptible of transformation. Resignation gives way to the drive for transformation and inquiry, over which men feel themselves to be in control. If men, as historical beings necessarily engaged with other men in a movement of inquiry, did not control that movement, it would be (and is) a violation of men's humanity. Any situation in which some men prevent others from engaging in the process of inquiry is one of violence. The means used are not important; to alienate men from their own decision-making is to change them into objects.

This movement of inquiry must be directed towards humanization—man's historical vocation. The pursuit of full humanity, however, cannot be carried out in isolation or individualism, but only in fellowship and solidarity; therefore it cannot unfold in the antagonistic relations between oppressors and oppressed. No one can be authentically human while he prevents others from being so. Attempting *to be more* human, individualistically, leads to *having more,* egotistically: a form of dehumanization. Not that it is not fundamental *to have* in order *to be* human. Precisely because it *is* necessary, some men's *having* must not be allowed to constitute an obstacle to other's *having,* must not consolidate the power of the former to crush the latter.

Problem-posing education, as a humanist and liberating praxis, posits as fundamental that men subjected to domination must fight for their emancipation. To that end, it enables teachers and students to become Subjects of the educational process by overcoming authoritarianism and an alienating intellectualism; it also enables men to overcome their false perception of reality. The world—no longer something to be described with deceptive words—becomes the object of that transforming action by men which results in their humanization.

Problem-posing education does not and cannot serve the interests of the oppressor. No oppressive order could permit the oppressed to begin to question: Why? While only a revolutionary society can carry out this education in systematic terms, the revolutionary leaders need not take full power before they can employ the method. In the revolutionary process, the leaders cannot utilize the banking method as an interim measure, justified on grounds of expediency, with the intention of *later* behaving in a genuinely revolutionary fashion. They must be revolutionary—that is to say, dialogical—from the outset.

JOHN DEWEY *(1859–1952)*

Much of John Dewey's inquiry revolved around experience *as a central category. In this he was like William James (1842–1910), and both were known as pragmatists, along with the third member of the triumvirate of American pragmatism, Charles Sanders Peirce (1839–1914). Pragmatist philosophy is characterized by the double role of experience: first, as the source of the real-life problem that gives rise to an inquiry, and second, as the ultimate court of appeals for the solution to any intellectual problem. The pragmatists were not inclined to begin an inquiry for inquiry's sake as more scholastic-minded philosophers might. Nor were they inclined to settle on a solution that was elegant in theory but lacked any conceivable validation in practice. Experience was the key, both at the beginning and end of inquiry. Dewey quite agrees with Freire in the value of problem-posing education situated in current historical experience. He further agrees that a repressive stratification in a class society inhibits the aims of education. But Dewey's perspective on the inhibitions induced by class society is different from Freire's and, I think, nicely complementary. Dewey regrets the ills of stratification from the side of the oppressor rather than the oppressed. He does not say so explicitly, but you can read the following chapter from* Democracy and Education *(1916) as arguing that the way the oppressors educate their heirs dehumanizes them by distancing them*

*from the full range of experience. Because stratification defines a labor class and a
leisure class, and different educational tracks are intended to reproduce that stratification, each class is excluded from some of the experiences needed to render education
whole and appropriately human. But Dewey's main concern seems to be the nonexperi-
ential, overintellectual education awarded to the leisure class.*

*Dewey's contributions to the philosophy of education are immense. Aside from
several books that have profoundly influenced American education, his personal
influence and energy contributed to countless experiments in educational reform. Dewey
carries the influence of social stratification into personal stratification among the parts
of the self, and his insights anticipate a good deal of contemporary thinking in social
psychology. Dewey's respect for the body, for a full integration of all the parts of a fully
human self, make him as contemporary now as he was when he was writing over fifty
years ago.*

Labor and Leisure

The Origin of the Opposition

The isolation of aims and values which we have been considering leads to
opposition between them. Probably the most deep-seated antithesis which has
shown itself in educational history is that between education in preparation for
useful labor and education for a life of leisure. The bare terms "useful labor" and
"leisure" confirm the statement already made that the segregation and conflict of
values are not self-inclosed, but reflect a division within social life. Were the two
functions of gaining a livelihood by work and enjoying in a cultivated way the
opportunities of leisure, distributed equally among the different members of a
community, it would not occur to any one that there was any conflict of educational agencies and aims involved. It would be self-evident that the question was
how education could contribute most effectively to both. And while it might be
found that some materials of instruction chiefly accomplished one result and
other subject matter the other, it would be evident that care must be taken to
secure as much overlapping as conditions permit; that is, the education which had
leisure more directly in view should indirectly reënforce as much as possible the
efficiency and the enjoyment of work, while that aiming at the latter should
produce habits of emotion and intellect which would procure a worthy cultivation
of leisure.

These general considerations are amply borne out by the historical development of educational philosophy. The separation of liberal education from professional and industrial education goes back to the time of the Greeks, and was
formulated expressly on the basis of a division of classes into those who had to
labor for a living and those who were relieved from this necessity. The conception
that liberal education, adapted to men in the latter class, is intrinsically higher
than the servile training given to the former class reflected the fact that one class

was free and the other servile in its social status. The servile class labored not only for its own subsistence, but also for the means which enabled the superior class to live without personally engaging in occupations taking almost all the time and not of a nature to engage or reward intelligence.

That a certain amount of labor must be engaged in goes without saying. Human beings have to live and it requires work to supply the resources of life. Even if we insist that the interests connected with getting a living are only material and hence intrinsically lower than those connected with enjoyment of time released from labor, and even if it were admitted that there is something engrossing and insubordinate in material interests which leads them to strive to usurp the place belonging to the higher ideal interests, this would not—barring the fact of socially divided classes—lead to neglect of the kind of education which trains men for the useful pursuits. It would rather lead to scrupulous care for them, so that men were trained to be efficient in them and yet to keep them in their place; education would see to it that we avoided the evil results which flow from their being allowed to flourish in obscure purlieus of neglect. Only when a division of these interests coincides with a division of an inferior and a superior social class will preparation for useful work be looked down upon with contempt as an unworthy thing: a fact which prepares one for the conclusion that the rigid identification of work with material interests, and leisure with ideal interests is itself a social product.

The educational formulations of the social situation made over two thousand years ago have been so influential and give such a clear and logical recognition of the implications of the division into laboring and leisure classes, that they deserve especial note. According to them, man occupies the highest place in the scheme of animate existence. In part, he shares the constitution and functions of plants and animals—nutritive, reproductive, motor or practical. The *distinctively* human function is reason existing for the sake of beholding the spectacle of the universe. Hence the truly human end is the fullest possible of this distinctive human prerogative. The life of observation, meditation, cogitation, and speculation pursued as an end in itself is the proper life of man. From reason moreover proceeds the proper control of the lower elements of human nature—the appetites and the active, motor, impulses. In themselves greedy, insubordinate, lovers of excess, aiming only at their own satiety, they observe moderation—the law of the mean— and serve desirable ends as they are subjected to the rule of reason.

Such is the situation as an affair of theoretical psychology and as most adequately stated by Aristotle. But this state of things is reflected in the constitution of classes of men and hence in the organization of society. Only in a comparatively small number is the function of reason capable of operating as a law of life. In the mass of people, vegetative and animal functions dominate. Their energy of intelligence is so feeble and inconstant that it is constantly overpowered by bodily appetite and passion. Such persons are not truly ends in themselves, for only reason constitutes a final end. Like plants, animals and physical tools, they are means, appliances, for the attaining of ends beyond themselves, although unlike them they have enough intelligence to exercise a certain discretion in the execution of the tasks committed to them. Thus by nature, and not merely by social convention, there are those who are slaves—that is, means for the ends of others.* The great body of artisans are in one important respect worse off than even slaves. Like the latter they are given up to the service of ends external to themselves; but since they do not enjoy the intimate association with the free superior class experienced by domestic slaves they remain on a lower plane of excellence. Moreover, women are classed with slaves and craftsmen as factors among the animate instrumentalities of production and reproduction of the means for a free or rational life.

Individually and collectively there is a gulf between merely living and living worthily. In order that one may live worthily he must first live, and so with collective society. The time and energy spent upon mere life, upon the gaining of subsistence, detracts from that available for activities that have an inherent rational meaning; they are also unfit for the latter. Means are menial, the serviceable is servile. The true life is possible only in the degree in which the physical necessities are had without effort and without attention. Hence slaves, artisans, and women are employed in furnishing the means of subsistence in order that others, those adequately equipped with intelligence, may live the life of leisurely concern with things intrinsically worth while.

To these two modes of occupation, with their distinction of servile and free activities (or "arts") correspond two types of education: the base or mechanical and the liberal or intellectual. Some persons are trained by suitable practical exercises for capacity in *doing* things, for ability to use the mechanical tools involved in turning out physical commodities and rendering personal service. This training is a mere matter of habituation and technical skill; it operates through repetition and assiduity in application, not through awakening and nurturing thought. Liberal education aims to train intelligence for its proper office: to know. The less this knowledge has to do with practical affairs, with making or producing, the more adequately it engages intelligence. So consistently does Aristotle draw the line between menial and liberal education that he puts what are now called the "fine" arts, music, painting, sculpture, in the same class with menial arts so far as their practice is concerned. They involve physical agencies, assiduity of practice, and external results. In discussing, for example, education in music he raises the question how far the young should be practiced in the playing of instruments. His answer is that such practice and proficiency may be tolerated as conduce to appreciation; that is, to understanding and enjoyment of music when played by slaves or professionals. When professional power is aimed at, music sinks from the liberal to the professional level. One might then as well teach cooking, says Aristotle. Even a liberal concern with the works of fine art depends upon the existence of a hireling class of practitioners who have subordinated the development of their own personality to attaining skill in mechanical execution. The higher the activity the more purely mental is it; the less does it have to do with physical things or with the body. The more purely mental it is, the more independent or self-sufficing is it.

These last words remind us that Aristotle again makes a distinction of

*Aristotle does not hold that the class of actual slaves and of natural slaves necessarily coincide.

superior and inferior even within those living the life of reason. For there is a distinction in ends and in free action, according as one's life is merely accompanied by reason or as it makes reason its own medium. That is to say, the free citizen who devotes himself to the public life of his community, sharing in the management of its affairs and winning personal honor and distinction, lives a life accompanied by reason. But the thinker, the man who devotes himself to scientific inquiry and philosophic speculation, works, so to speak, *in* reason, not simply *by* it. Even the activity of the citizen in his civic relations, in other words, retains some of the taint of practice, of external or merely instrumental doing. This infection is shown by the fact that civic activity and civic excellence need the help of others; one cannot engage in public life all by himself. But all needs, all desires imply, in the philosophy of Aristotle, a material factor; they involve lack, privation; they are dependent upon something beyond themselves for completion. A purely intellectual life, however, one carries on by himself, in himself; such assistance as he may derive from others is accidental, rather than intrinsic. In *knowing*, in the life of theory, reason finds its own full manifestation; knowing for the sake of knowing irrespective of any application is alone independent, or self-sufficing. Hence only the education that makes for power to know as an end in itself, without reference to the practice of even civic duties, is truly liberal or free.

The Present Situation

If the Aristotelian conception represented just Aristotle's personal view, it would be a more or less interesting historical curiosity. It could be dismissed as an illustration of the lack of sympathy or the amount of academic pedantry which may coexist with extraordinary intellectual gifts. But Aristotle simply described without confusion and without that insincerity always attendant upon mental confusion the life that was before him. That the actual social situation has greatly changed since his day there is no need to say. But in spite of these changes, in spite of the abolition of legal serfdom, and the spread of democracy, with the extension of science and of general education (in books, newspapers, travel, and general intercourse as well as in schools), there remains enough of a cleavage of society into a learned and an unlearned class, a leisure and a laboring class, to make his point of view a most enlightening one from which to criticize the separation between culture and utility in present education. Behind the intellectual and abstract distinction as it figures in pedagogical discussion, there looms a social distinction between those whose pursuits involve a minimum of self-directive thought and aesthetic appreciation, and those who are concerned more directly with things of the intelligence and with the control of the activities of others.

Aristotle was certainly permanently right when he said that "any occupation or art or study deserves to be called mechanical if it renders the body or soul or intellect of free persons unfit for the exercise and practice of excellence." The force of the statement is almost infinitely increased when we hold, as we nominally do at present, that all persons, instead of a comparatively few, are free. For when the mass of men and all women were regarded as unfree by the very nature of their bodies and minds, there was neither intellectual confusion nor moral hypocrisy in giving them only the training which fitted them for mechanical skill, irrespective of its ulterior effect upon their capacity to share in a worthy life. He was permanently right also when he went on to say that "all mercenary employments as well as those which degrade the condition of the body are mechnical, since they deprive the intellect of leisure and dignity,"—permanently right, that is, if gainful pursuits as matter of fact deprive the intellect of the conditions of its exercise and so of its dignity. If his statements are false, it is because they identify a phase of social custom with a natural necessity. But a different view of the relations of mind and matter, mind and body, intelligence and social service, is better than Aristotle's conception only if it helps render the old idea obsolete in fact—in the actual conduct of life and education.

Aristotle was permanently right in assuming the inferiority and subordination of mere skill in performance and mere accumulation of external products to understanding, sympathy of appreciation, and the free play of ideas. If there was an error, it lay in assuming the necessary separation of the two: in supposing that there is a natural divorce between efficiency in producing commodities and rendering service, and self-directive thought; between significant knowledge and practical achievement. We hardly better matters if we just correct his theoretical misapprehension, and tolerate the social state of affairs which generated and sanctioned his conception. We lose rather than gain in change from serfdom to free citizenship if the most prized result of the change is simply an increase in the mechanical efficiency of the human tools of production. So we lose rather than gain in coming to think of intelligence as an organ of control of nature through action, if we are content that an unintelligent, unfree state persists in those who engage directly in turning nature to use, and leave the intelligence which controls to be the exclusive possession of remote scientists and captains of industry. We are in a position honestly to criticize the division of life into separate functions and of society into separate classes only so far as we are free from responsibility for perpetuating the educational practices which train the many for pursuits involving mere skill in production, and the few for a knowledge that is an ornament and a cultural embellishment. In short, ability to transcend the Greek philosophy of life and education is not secured by a mere shifting about of the theoretical symbols meaning free, rational, and worthy. It is not secured by a change of sentiment regarding the dignity of labor, and the superiority of a life of service to that of an aloof self-sufficing independence. Important as these theoretical and emotional changes are, their importance consists in their being turned to account in the development of a truly democratic society, a society in which all share in useful service and all enjoy a worthy leisure. It is not a mere change in the concepts of culture—or a liberal mind—and social service which requires an education reorganization; but the educational transformation is needed to give full and explicit effect to the changes implied in social life. The increased political and economic emancipation of the "masses" has shown itself in education; it has effected the development of a common school system of education, public and free. It has destroyed the idea that learning is properly a monopoly of the few who are predestined by nature to govern social affairs. But the revolution is still incomplete. This idea still prevails that a truly cultural or liberal education cannot have anything in common, directly at least, with industrial affairs, and that the education which is fit for the masses must be a useful or practical education in a sense which opposes useful and practical to nurture of appreciation and liberation of thought.

As a consequence, our actual system is an inconsistent mixture. Certain studies and methods are retained on the supposition that they have the sanction of peculiar liberality, the chief content of the term liberal being uselessness for practical ends. This aspect is chiefly visible in what is termed the higher education —that of the college and of preparation for it. But it has filtered through into elementary education and largely controls its processes and aims. But, on the other hand, certain concessions have been made to the masses who must engage in getting a livelihood and to the increased rôle of economic activities in modern life. These concessions are exhibited in special schools and courses for the professions, for engineering, for manual training and commerce in vocational and prevocational courses; and in the spirit in which certain elementary subjects, like the three R's, are taught. The result is a system in which both "cultural" and "utilitarian" subjects exist in an inorganic composite where the former are not by dominant purpose socially serviceable and the latter not liberative of imagination or thinking power.

In the inherited situation, there is a curious intermingling, in even the same study, of concession to usefulness and a survival of traits once exclusively attributed to preparation for leisure. The "utility" element is found in the motives assigned for the study, the "liberal" element in methods of teaching. The outcome of the mixture is perhaps less satisfactory than if either principle were adhered to in its purity. The motive popularly assigned for making the studies of the first four or five years consist almost entirely of reading, spelling, writing, and arithmetic, is, for example, that ability to read, write, and figure accurately is indispensable to getting ahead. These studies are treated as mere instruments for entering upon a gainful employment or of later progress in the pursuit of learning, according as pupils do not or do remain in school. This attitude is reflected in the emphasis put upon drill and practice for the sake of gaining automatic skill. If we turn to Greek schooling, we find that from the earliest years the acquisition of skill was subordinated as much as possible to acquisition of literary content possessed of aesthetic and moral significance. Not getting a tool for subsequent use but present subject matter was the emphasized thing. Nevertheless the isolation of these studies from practical application, their reduction to purely symbolic devices, represents a survival of the idea of a liberal training divorced from utility. A thorough adoption of the idea of utility would have led to instruction which tied up the studies to situations in which they were directly needed and where they were rendered immediately and not remotely helpful. It would be hard to find a subject in the curriculum within which there are not found evil results of a compromise between the two opposed ideals. Natural science is recommended on the ground of its practical utility, but is taught as a special accomplishment in removal from application. On the other hand, music and literature are theoretically justified on the ground of their culture value and are then taught with chief emphasis upon forming technical modes of skill.

If we had less compromise and resulting confusion, if we analyzed more carefully the respective meanings of culture and utility, we might find it easier to construct a course of study which should be useful and liberal at the same time. Only superstition makes us believe that the two are necessarily hostile so that a subject is illiberal because it is useful and cultural because it is useless. It will generally be found that instruction which, in aiming at utilitarian results, sacrifices the development of imagination, the refining of taste and the deepening of intellectual insight—surely cultural values—also in the same degree renders what is learned limited in its use. Not that it makes it wholly unavailable but that its applicability is restricted to routine activities carried on under the supervision of others. Narrow modes of skill cannot be made useful beyond themselves; any mode of skill which is achieved with deepening of knowledge and perfecting of judgment is readily put to use in new situations and is under personal control. It was not the bare fact of social and economic utility which made certain activities seem servile to the Greeks but the fact that the activities directly connected with getting a livelihood were not, in their days, the expression of a trained intelligence nor carried on because of a personal appreciation of their meaning. So far as farming and the trades were rule-of-thumb occupations and so far as they were engaged in for results external to the minds of agricultural laborers and mechanics, they were illiberal—but only so far. The intellectual and social context has now changed. The elements in industry due to mere custom and routine have become subordinate in most economic callings to elements derived from scientific inquiry. The most important occupations of today represent and depend upon applied mathematics, physics, and chemistry. The area of the human world influenced by economic production and influencing consumption has been so indefinitely widened that geographical and political considerations of an almost infinitely wide scope enter in. It was natural for Plato to deprecate the learning of geometry and arithmetic for practical ends, because as matter of fact the practical uses to which they were put were few, lacking in content and mostly mercenary in quality. But as their social uses have increased and enlarged, their liberalizing or "intellectual" value and their practical value approach the same limit.

Doubtless the factor which chiefly prevents our full recognition and employment of this identification is the conditions under which so much work is still carried on. The invention of machines has extended the amount of leisure which is possible even while one is at work. It is a commonplace that the mastery of skill in the form of established habits frees the mind for a higher order of thinking. Something of the same kind is true of the introduction of mechanically automatic operations in industry. They may release the mind for thought upon other topics. But when we confine the education of those who work with their hands to a few years of schooling devoted for the most part to acquiring the use of rudimentary symbols at the expense of training in science, literature, and history, we fail to prepare the minds of workers to take advantage of this opportunity. More fundamental is the fact that the great majority of workers have no insight into the social aims of their pursuits and no direct personal interest in them. The results actually achieved are not the ends of *their* actions, but only of their employers. They do what they do, not freely and intelligently, but for the sake of the wage earned. It is this fact which makes the action illiberal, and which will make any education designed simply to give skill in such undertakings illiberal and immoral. The activity is not free because not freely participated in.

Nevertheless, there is already an opportunity for an education which, keeping in mind the larger features of work, will reconcile liberal nurture with training in social serviceableness, with ability to share efficiently and happily in occupations which are productive. And such an education will of itself tend to do away with the evils of the existing economic situation. In the degree in which men have an active concern in the ends that control their activity, their activity becomes free or voluntary and loses its externally enforced and servile quality, even though the physical aspect of behavior remain the same. In what is termed politics, democratic social organization makes provision for this direct participation in control: in the economic region, control remains external and autocratic. Hence the split between inner mental action and outer physical action of which the traditional distinction between the liberal and the utilitarian is the reflex. An education which should unify the disposition of the members of society would do much to unify society itself.

Summary

Of the segregations of educational values discussed in the last chapter, that between culture and utility is probably the most fundamental. While the distinction is often thought to be intrinsic and absolute, it is really historical and social. It originated, so far as conscious formulation is concerned, in Greece, and was based upon the fact that the truly human life was lived only by a few who subsisted upon the results of the labor of others. This fact affected the psychological doctrine of the relation of intelligence and desire, theory and practice. It was embodied in a political theory of a permanent division of human beings into those capable of a life of reason and hence having their own ends, and those capable only of desire and work, and needing to have their ends provided by others. The two distinctions, psychological and political, translated into educational terms, effected a division between a liberal education, having to do with the self-sufficing life of leisure devoted to knowing for its own sake, and a useful, practical training for mechanical occupations, devoid of intellectual and aesthetic content. While the present situation is radically diverse in theory and much changed in fact, the factors of the older historic situation still persist sufficiently to maintain the educational distinction, along with compromises which often reduce the efficacy of the educational measures. The problem of education in a democratic society is to do away with the dualism and to construct a course of studies which makes thought a guide of free practice for all and which makes leisure a reward of accepting responsibility for service, rather than a state of exemption from it.

transition:
esthetic education

Freire argues that the best education awakens students to their own interests and the systematic denial of those interests by political oppression. Dewey argues the importance of experiential immediacy in education. Both are saying that education should meet real needs rather than induce false needs. Erikson, Mead, Goffman, and Laing all agree that the socially constituted self is manipulable even to the extent of denying the reality of some of its most immediate needs. Indeed the very concept of false need becomes questionable if we regard the self as wholly constituted by its social context: whatever needs are induced, even the need for the conspicuous consumption of status symbols, may be real if society is the ultimate creator of selves and conspicuous consumption serves the ends of society as a whole. But clearly society is not the sole creator, and equally clearly many products in a waste economy do not gratify genuinely human needs. If society is not the sole creator of the self, however, how can we correct the social standards of real and false needs? What other criteria are available, and where may we find them?

Traditionally, philosophers and theologians have found it easy to contrast human creation and divine creation. If man was created in God's image, one had only to appeal to the divine image of man for a criterion of needs transcending the historical flux of human society. But modern historicist and existentialist philosophers have undermined belief in an eternal transcendent standard. Man makes himself. Herein lies the hope of modern man to solve his problems. As Reich argued, even the unconscious, that repository of man's most basic instinctual desires, is subject to historical modification. But how are we to judge whether the historical development of man's needs is for the better or for the worse? Who is to say what counts as a false need, and why?

Here esthetics comes into the picture as more than just the philosophical basis of art criticism. As the science of sensibility esthetics deals with minimally cognitive reactions to stimuli. If we withdraw connotations of eternal essence from the term 'natural,' we can say that esthetics deals with our more natural, less artificial, less societally influenced reactions. Esthetics, then, is the way out of the dilemma between accepting all of society's historical meanderings as creating true needs or appealing to an eternal standard of human nature for identifying all created needs as false. Some true needs are historically generated; some true needs—for example, the instinct for aggression—may be outgrown in human history. We need a criterion for distinguishing true from false needs, a criterion that does not define the true as the natural and the natural as the anthropologically original. Esthetics offers a way of putting us in touch with natural man who is still historical man. Esthetic education not only educates the student to the man-made products of his cultural tradition; it also quickens his sensitivity to his own felt needs for a balanced and whole human existence. Wholeness is an elusive standard when the parts of human existence keep changing with the flux of history. A fixed inventory of human capacities no more functions as a checklist for wholeness than a list of colors tells a painter when he has completed a picture. The point is not to use each of the colors or human capacities. We need an esthetic sensibility to tell us whether man's most recent creations of himself cohere in a healthy pattern of wholeness or fall apart into schizoid decadence. Esthetic sensibility becomes the arbiter of true and false needs.

GEORGE LEONARD *(b. 1931)*

Just as Freire's Pedagogy of the Oppressed *and Dewey's "Labor and Leisure"*
make us aware of the political dimensions of education, George Leonard's Education
and Ecstasy *(1968) emphasizes the esthetic dimension of education. Leonard extends*
Dewey's insights into the experience of education in its sensuous immediacy. Actually, the
word 'sensuous' does not capture the full range of experiences that qualify as ecstatic,
just as 'art' does not define the full range of experiences that qualify as esthetic. We take
the sensuous and the artistic as paradigms for the immediate experience of a very rich
joy. But, as the greatest thinkers have always known, the joy associated with art and
sensuousness can also be felt in experiencing nonartistic objects and exercising facilities
other than taste, smell, and touch.

Leonard's inroad into the importance of immediacy certainly came through the
senses. Before devoting himself to research and writing on education he helped establish
the Esalen Institute at Big Sur in California. In the inviting context of hot springs, sea,
and sunlight, Leonard and others developed the techniques of sensitivity training. For
some years now Esalen has been running workshops in the many methods of awakening
people to the immediate quality of their experience—how one feels one's body, one's
sensations, and one's emotions. While the Esalen mystique has tended to lead some of
its followers to a total and one-sided condemnation of "head-tripping," it has given
others the opportunity for discovering an immediacy that can be intellectual as well as
sensuous. Leonard even claims that "solving an elegant mathematical problem and
making love are different classes in the same order of things, sharing common ecstasy."

Some of Leonard's critics find him overoptimistic precisely to the extent that his
vision is restricted to the esthetics of education and excludes the political dimension. As
appealing and persuasive as are Leonard's descriptions of classrooms where teachers
and students alike cultivate an intense and ecstatic awareness about every aspect of their
pedagogical environment, Leonard's critics ask how the consciousness of the student can
develop such esthetic-intellectual sensitivity when the world outside the classroom insists
on bludgeoning him or her back into insensitivity. Leonard's classroom is utopian, they
claim, and cannot survive or function in the context of the present social order.

This criticism echoes an argument developed nearly two hundred years ago by
Friedrich Schiller, an amazingly talented and prolific German poet, playwright, and
philosopher. In his Letters on the Aesthetic Education of Man *(1795), Schiller spells*
out the almost paradoxical relationship between esthetics and politics in the quest for
liberation. After describing the same specialization and divisions Dewey found in
contemporary education, Schiller asks whether we can expect the state to solve the
problem of the fragmentation of man. He answers no, "for the State, as it is now
constituted, has brought about the evil; and the rationally conceived State, instead of
being able to establish this better humanity, must first be itself established by it." Yet
Schiller acknowledges, along with Leonard's critics, that the "esthetic education of
man" is a difficult enterprise in a hostile political environment. We seem to need

esthetic education to develop a better society, yet a better society seems to be a condition for the possibility of an education. Where to begin? Part of Leonard's clarity derives from his unequivocal claim that we can break into the circle of politics, education, esthetics, art, and politics at the point where education and esthetics meet.

Education and Ecstasy

There are no neutral moments, Even in those classrooms where the education some of us might hope for is impossible, a kind of shadowy, negative learning is going on. Some pupils learn how to daydream; others, how to take tests. Some learn the petty deceptions involved in cheating; others, the larger deceptions of playing the school game absolutely straight (the well-kept notebook, the right answer, the senior who majors in good grades). Most learn that the symbolic tricks their keepers attempt to teach them have little to do with their own deeper feelings or anything in the here and now. The activity that masquerades under the ancient and noble name of "education" actually seems to serve as a sort of ransom to the future, a down payment toward "getting ahead"—or at least toward not falling behind. Lifetime-earnings figures are pressed upon potential high-school dropouts. These figures seem to show that giving an acceptable interpretation of "Ode on a Grecian Urn" somehow means you will live in a better suburb and drive a bigger car. A vision of Florida retirement superimposes itself on every diagram in plane geometry. Some students refuse to pay the ransom, and you should not be surprised that these students may be what the society itself calls the "brighter" ones. (According to Dr. Louis Bright, director of research for the U.S. Office of Education, high-school dropouts in large cities where the figures are available have higher IQ's than high-school graduates.) But dropouts and graduates alike have had plenty of practice in fragmenting their lives—segregating senses from emotions from intellect, building boxes for art and abstractions, divorcing the self from the reality and the joy of the present moment. No need for obscure psychological explanations for modern man's fragmentation; that is what his schools teach.

Perhaps this has been so ever since education was first formalized. Historian Arnold Toynbee traces the disintegration of the Chinese Empire under the Ts'in and Han Dynasties as well as that of the Roman Empire, in part, to their attempts to extend formal education from the privileged minority to a wider circle. "One reason," Toynbee wrote, "was that the former privileged minority's traditional system of education was impoverished in the process of being disseminated. It degenerated into a formal education in book learning divorced from a spontaneous apprenticeship for life. . . . In fact, the art of playing with words was substituted for the art of living."

In more primitive cultures, the Polynesian, for example, education was sacramental. Every aspect of life, every act of living was related, and life's procedures were learned in a manner simultaneously more intense and more casual than would seem possible in a formal institution. All things were observed and experienced in unity. The educational institutions of Western civilization, on the other hand, have almost always been formalistic and symbolic to the extreme. When the Renaissance academies took the Roman educator Quintilian for their model, they managed to adopt his most negative and stultifying precepts, leading to purely verbal training in ancient literature—even though Quintilian's was a specialized school for orators.

Until relatively recent times, however, only a tiny proportion of the West's population ever saw the inside of an academy. (As recently as 1900, less than ten percent of American sixteen-year-olds were in school.) Education for the vast majority, though less sacramental and ecstatic, resembled that of the Polynesians. Under the tutelage of such stable institutions as the family, the farm, the village, the church and the craft guild, the ordinary young Westerner served his apprenticeship for living—limiting perhaps, but all of a piece. As for the aristocrat, he lived and learned under the sure guidance of class tradition and accepted formal education primarily as an instrument for fortifying class lines. Better than badges and plumes were Latin and Greek, maintained, under the fiction of teaching "thinking," for centuries after the world's literature was available in translation. (All attempts to prove that the study of Latin improves thinking skills have failed.) A school accent served as well as a school tie in bolstering those barriers between people which seemed so necessary in building and maintaining a militaristic, colonial empire.

The successive historical events we know as Enlightenment, the process of democratization, the Industrial Revolution and the explosive developments of consumerism and leisure weakened the prime educating institutions of the past (family, farm, village, church, guild), leaving successively more of the younger generation's total education-for-living to the schools and colleges. The young crowded into classrooms and were led away from life.

Reformers tried to stop the fragmentation. The greatest among them was John Dewey. We have at last reached a hillock in time from which we can look across a lot of pointless controversy and view this man's genius with a certain clarity and dispassion. Dewey sought a unity in life. He recognized that education is a process of living and not a preparation for future living. He believed that education is the fundamental method of social progress and reform. He provided a philosophical underpinning for the Progressive Education movement which, simply stated, saved the American public-school system by making it just flexible and forgiving enough to accommodate the children of immigrants, poor farmers and other followers of the American dream.

But Dewey did not provide educators with the hard-honed tools of true reform. Seduced by the psychology of his time, he enjoined teachers to spend more energy helping children form "images" than making them learn certain things. More disabling yet, he was fascinated with the notion of "interests" which he felt would automatically manifest themselves in children when they were *ready* to learn something. This notion, somewhat misinterpreted, led a generation of teachers to wait for children to show signs of "interest" before they moved ahead and thereby woefully to underrate their capacity for learning. Teachers found further justification for just waiting in the work of developmental psychologists who followed Dewey. These good-hearted doubters are still around with stacks of studies to show us precisely what children *cannot* do until this age or that age. Their studies becomes worthless, as we shall see in the next chapter, when children are placed in learning environments designed to let them crash through all the ceilings erected by the past. Progressive education was a useful, humane and sometimes joyful reform, but it was not the true revolution in education that the times then needed and now demand. The worst of that movement may be summed up in one sentence: It is as cruel to bore a child as to beat him.

Learning eventually involves interaction between learner and environment, and its effectiveness relates to the frequency, variety and intensity of the interaction.

For the most part, the schools have not really changed. They have neither taken up the slack left by the retreat of the past's prime educators nor significantly altered the substance and style of their teaching. The most common mode of instruction today, as in the Renaissance, has a teacher sitting or standing before a number of students in a single room, presenting them with facts and techniques of a verbal-rational nature. Our expectation of what the human animal can learn, can do, can be remains remarkably low and timorous. Our definition of education's root purpose remains shortsightedly utilitarian. Our map of the territory of learning remains antiquated: vocational training, homemaking, driving and other "fringe" subjects, themselves limiting and fragmenting, have invaded the curriculum, but are generally considered outside the central domain of "education." This domain, this venerable bastion, is still a place where people are trained to split their world into separate symbolic systems, the better to cope with and manipulate it. Such "education," suprarationalistic and analytical to the extreme, has made possible colonialism, the production line, space voyaging and the H-bomb. But it has not made people happy or whole, nor does it now offer them ways to change, deep down, in an age that cries out with the urgency of a rocket's flight, "Change or die."

All that goes on in most schools and colleges today is only a thin slice, as we shall see, of what education can become. And yet, our present institutions show a maddening inefficiency even in dealing with this thin slice. In recent years, there has been a small net gain in American students' performance in the basic subjects. But this has been accomplished only at the cost of a large increase in gross effort—more and more homework assigned under threat of more and tougher exams to force students to learn, on their own, what most of today's teachers have long since realized they cannot teach them. A visitor from another planet might conclude that our schools are hellbent on creating—in a society that offers leisure and demands creativity—a generation of joyless drudges.

There are signs the school will not succeed in this drab mission. Already, the seeds of a real change are germinating—on college campuses, in teachers' associations, in laboratories of science, in out-of-the-way places that will be discussed in later chapters. This reform would bypass entirely the patchwork remedial measures (Spanish in second grade, teachers in teams, subject matter updated) that presently pass for reform. It cuts straight to the heart of the educational enterprise, in and out of school, seeking new method, content, idiom, domain, purpose and, indeed, a new definition of education. Far from decrying and opposing an onrushing technology, it sees technology as an ally, a force that can as easily enhance as diminish the human spirit. Avoiding hard-and-fast assumptions of its own, it is rigorous in questioning some of the automatic assumptions of the past. It is a new journey. To join it, you had best leave your awe of history behind, open your mind to unfamiliar or even disreputable solutions if they are the ones that work, look upon all systems of abstractions as strictly tentative and throw out of the window every prior guideline about what human beings can accomplish.

The prospects are exhilarating, though it is becoming dangerous to write about them if only because nowadays it is so hard to stay ahead of reality. Let us assume the future will surprise us; and, so assuming, speculate only about what is already coming to pass. For example, the following prospects are in the realm of possibility:

1. Ways can be worked out to help average students learn whatever is needed of present-day subject matter in a third or less of the present time, pleasurably rather than painfully, with almost certain success. Better yet, the whole superstructure of rational-symbolic knowledge can be rearranged so that these aspects of life's possibilities can be perceived and learned as unity and diversity within change rather than fragmentation within an illusory permanence.

2. Ways can be worked out to provide a new apprenticeship for living, appropriate to a technological age of constant change. Many new types of learning having to do with crucial areas of human functioning that are now neglected or completely ignored can be made a part of the educational enterprise. Much of what will be learned tomorrow does not today have even a commonly accepted name.

3. Ways can be worked out so that almost every day will be a "teachable day," so that almost every educator can share with his students the inspired moments of learning now enjoyed by only the most rare and remarkable.

4. Education in a new and greatly broadened sense can become a lifelong pursuit for everyone. To go on learning, to go on sharing that learning with others may well be considered a purpose worthy of mankind's ever-expanding capacities.

Education, at best, is ecstatic.

If education in the coming age is to be, not just a part of life, but the main purpose of life, then education's purpose will, at last, be viewed as central. What, then, is the purpose, the goal of education? A large part of the answer may well be what men of this civilization have longest feared and most desired: *the achievement of moments of ecstasy*. Not fun, not simply pleasure as in the equation of Bentham and Mill, not the libido pleasure of Freud, but ecstasy, *ananda*, the ultimate delight.

Western civilization, for well-known historical reasons, has traditionally eschewed ecstasy as a threat to goal-oriented control of men, matter and energy—and has suffered massive human unhappiness. Other civilizations, notably that of India, have turned their best energies toward the attainment of ecstasy, while neglecting practical goals—and have suffered massive human unhappiness. Now modern science and technology seem to be preparing a situation where the successful control of practical matters and the attainment of ecstasy can safely coexist; where each reinforces the other; and, quite possibly, where neither can long exist *without* the other. Abundance and population control already are logically and technologically feasible. At the same time, cybernation, pervasive and instantaneous communication and other feedback devices of increasing speed, range and sensitivity extend and enhance man's sensory apparatus, multiplying the possibilities for understanding and ecstasy as well as for misunderstanding and destruction. The times demand that we choose delight.

Do discipline and mastery of technique stand in opposition to freedom, self-expression and the ecstatic moment? Most Western educators have acted as if they did. Strange, when there exist so many models of the marriage between the two. Take the artistic endeavor: the composer discovers that the soul of creation transcends the body of form only when form is his completely. The violinist arrives as the sublime only through utter mastery of technique. The instruments of living that are now coming into our hands—rich, responsive and diverse— require mastery. The process of mastery itself can be ecstatic, leading to delight that transcends mastery.

The new revolutionaries of education must soothe those who fear techniques no less than those who fear delight. Many a liberal educational reform has foundered on lack of specific tools for accomplishing its purposes—even if a tool may be something as simply as knowing *precisely when* to leave the learner entirely alone. Education must use its most powerful servant, technique, in teaching skills that go far beyond those which submit to academic achievement tests. Even today, as will be seen, specific, systematic ways are being worked out to help people learn to love, to feel deeply, to expand their inner selves, to create, to enter new realms of being.

What is education? The answer may be far simpler than we imagine. Matters of great moment and processes that affect our lives at the very heart are generally less obscure and mysterious than they at first appear. The travels of celestial bodies, once requiring the efforts of a pantheon of gods, now follow a few easy formulas. Chemical reactions explained by essences, vapors, phlogiston became easier to understand when reduced to a single variable: weight. Mankind's most awesome mystery, fire, once understood, could be handled by little children. Throughout history, the way to understanding, control and ecstasy has been a long, sinuous journey toward simplicity and unity.

To learn is to change. Education is a process that changes the learner.

The first part of a simple, operational definition of education calls on the educator to view his work as consequential, not theoretical or formalistic. Looking for *change* in his student (and himself) as a measure, he will discover what is important in his work and what is waste motion. Asking himself, "What has changed in the student, and me, because of this particular experience?," he may have to answer that what has changed is only the student's ability to recite a few more "facts" than he could before the session. He may find that the student has changed in wider and deeper ways. He may have to admit that the student has hardly changed at all or, if so, in a way that no one had intended. In any case, he will not ask himself the *wrong* questions ("Wasn't my presentation brilliant?" "Why are they so dumb?").

Looking for the *direction and further consequences* of the change, he will be forced to ask whether it is for the good of the student, himself and society. In doing this, the educator will discover he has to become sensitive to what is happening to the student at every moment, and thereby will become a feeling participant in the circle of learning. Viewing learning as anything that changes the learner's behavior, the educator will expand his domain a thousandfold, for he will realize that there are hardly any aspects of human life that cannot be changed, educated. He will see clearly that, if the educational enterprise limits itself to what is now ordinarily taught in classrooms, it will be pursuing failure in the coming age.

Learning involves interaction between the learner and his environment, and its effectiveness relates to the frequency, variety and intensity of the interaction.

Guided by this second part of the definition, the educator will pay far closer attention to the learning environment than ever before in education's history. The environment may be a book, a game, a programmed device, a choir, a brainwave feedback mechanism, a silent room, an interactive group of students, even a teacher—but in every case, the educator will turn his attention from mere *presentation* of the environment (a classroom lecture, for example) to the *response* of the learner. He will study and experiment with the learning process, the series of responses, at every step along the way, better to utilize the increasing capacities of environment and learner as each changes. Observing the work of what has been called "master teachers" in this light, he will find that their mysterious, unfathomable "artistry" actually comprises a heightened sensitivity to student responses plus the use of personally developed, specific, flexible techniques. The educator will work out ways to help every teacher become an "artist."

Education, at best, is ecstatic.

The first two parts of the definition need the third, which may be seen as a way of praising learning for its own sake. And yet, it goes further, for the educator of the coming age will not be vague or theoretical about this matter. As he loses his fear of delight, he will become explicit and specific in his pursuit of the ecstatic moment. At its best, its most effective, its most unfettered, the moment of learning is a moment of delight. This essential and obvious truth is demonstrated for us every day by the baby and the preschool child, by the class of the "artist" teacher, by learners of all ages interacting with new learning programs that are designed for success. When joy is absent, the effectiveness of the learning process falls and falls until the human being is operating hesitantly, grudgingly, fearfully at only a tiny fraction of his potential.

The notion that ecstasy is mainly an inward-directed experience testifies to our distrust of our own society, of the outer environment we have created for ourselves. Actually, the varieties of ecstasy are limitless, as will be seen in the coming chapters. The new educator will seek out the possibility of delight in every form of learning. He will realize that solving an elegant mathematical problem and making love are different classes in the same order of things, sharing common ecstasy. He will find that even education now considered nothing more than present drudgery for future payoff—learning the multiplication tables, for example—can become joyful when a skillfully designed learning environment (a pro-

grammed game, perhaps) makes the learning quick and easy. Indeed, the skillful
pursuit of ecstasy will make the pursuit of excellence, not for the few, but for the
many, what it never has been—successful. And yet, make no mistake about it,
excellence, as we speak of it today, will be only a byproduct of a greater unity, a
deeper delight.

PLATO *(428–347 B.C.)*

*With Plato we move to another point on the circle of politics–education–esthetics-
art–politics: the meeting of esthetics and art. Politics and education are not hard to see
in the background: the following selection, translated by Benjamin Jowett, renews the
discussion of education in the ideal state of the* Republic. *Talk of the meeting of
esthetics and art may sound redundant to some, as if esthetics were equivalent to the
philosophy of fine art. Though the term 'esthetics' is sometimes used to refer to the
philosophy of art, Kant, among others, favored its use to cover a wider range of
immediate experience.*

*I wish nevertheless to call attention to two senses of 'esthetics': not only are we
talking about the philosophy of fine art, we also include under esthetics the science of
sensibility. We want to know how we look at things other than art objects. Esthetics
might then sound very much like epistemology, but with this difference: where epistemology includes the study of knowledge of a logical, rational type (for example, mathematics and science), esthetics is more concerned with the affective dimensions of
feeling and sensation. As rough as this distinction is, to refine it any more might give
the impression that feelings are in no way rational or that cognition involves no
affective elements. The distinction between esthetics and epistemology cannot really
separate two discrete kinds of awareness, only two dimensions of the same awareness.*

*To distinguish between esthetics and the philosophy of art helps in understanding
Plato's attitude toward artists. As usual his text contains depths of meaning beneath the
surface argument. If we ignore the distinction between esthetics and the philosophy of
art and restrict ourselves to a literal reading of the surface level—if, in short, we remain
esthetically insensitive to Plato's art—we will see only an outrageous argument
condemning artists of untruth in their second-hand imitation of reality. The literal
reading compares the things of the realm of becoming (recall the divided line) to their
forms in the realm of being; as the former relate to the latter in an imitative way, so the
work of art relates to the things in the realm of becoming. The work of art stands at a
second remove from reality, and therein lies its falsity and deceptiveness. The outra-
geousness of the argument lies in the assumption that the function of art is to imitate, as
if a painter were trying to be a photographer.*

But beneath the literal level we can find more in Plato's text. That Plato could not condemn art is clear from his own artistry. What, then, did he intend as the role of art? At one crucial point in the argument he asks, "Is the man at unity with himself?" Plato cites the multiplicity of "oppositions occurring at the same moment," which cause a man to lose his bearings and act foolishly. Of the good man who suffers the misfortune of losing a son he says, "will he have no sorrow; or shall we say that although he cannot help sorrowing, he will moderate his sorrow?" From a quick reading of Plato's attack on the poets we might have concluded that he attacks them for portraying heroes with any emotion at all, as if a man's unity with himself were to be achieved at the price of eliminating all the stresses and strains of emotions. Yet here Plato praises the good man for sorrowing, so long as his sorrow is moderate, that is, appropriate to the unity and balance of his being. To sorrow not at all would be clearly inappropriate to the loss of a son.

Plato's complaint with artists is that they tend to exploit extremes for the purposes of their art, whereas the proper role for art is in the service of that moderation that brings unity to the self and to a society. (Moderation, by the way, does not mean stultifying constraint; repression is the other extreme of madness, and moderation is "in between." One can be immoderate in the pursuit of stability as well as in the pursuit of pleasure.) Opposed to those artists who exploit human extremes for their art, Plato exploits art to achieve unity and balance in his dialogues. This is a more difficult task than mimetic or imitative art, since it requires the artist, namely Plato, to know what he is talking about. The imitative artist is like the illustrator of an anatomy book who tries to copy the details of each separate muscle. The true artist is more like the doctor who uses knowledge rather than imitation to restore the functional unity of health to a diseased body; or, as Plato says in his development of the analogy between art and medicine, art should aid us in "always accustoming the soul forthwith to apply a remedy, raising up that which is sickly and fallen, banishing the cry of sorrow by the healing art."

The content of Plato's second-level argument on art* shows why he employs the art of writing on different levels. Precisely the people who tend to be most easily moved to extremes by taking seriously the literal meaning of an art work are those who penetrate only the literal level of Plato's dialogue. They need to hear that it is dangerous to trust unquestioningly the written works of poets and tragedians, however highly they may be respected. Those who already know how to question and inquire more deeply, who are less inclined to extremes of feeling, will be more likely to penetrate to a level of the dialogue that endorses appropriate feelings and the potentially healing character of art. Like Socrates, Plato's dialogues measure their words according to the needs of the interlocutor. Plato's deeper argument suggests the role of a "healing art," but different people need different treatments. Consequently the universal elixir in the artistic medium is an art that adapts itself to the needs of its audience, an art that bends to the esthetic sensibility of each reader.

*I say 'second-level' rather than deepest level argument because I make no claims that the second-level argument represents Plato's final word on art. Deeper levels of interpretation may be available to the careful reader. It may be that, like the Bible, Plato's dialogues defy final interpretation. The "reformation" in Plato scholarship sees attempts to establish orthodoxy as inconsistent with the Socratic flexibility of the Platonic text.

The Case Against Art

[595][1] Of the many excellences which I perceive in the order of our State, there is none which upon reflection pleases me better than the rule about poetry.

To what do you refer?

To the rejection of imitative poetry, which certainly ought not to be received; as I see far more clearly now that the parts of the soul have been distinguished.

What do you mean?

Speaking in confidence, for I should not like to have my words repeated to the tragedians and the rest of the imitative tribe—but I do not mind saying to you, that all poetical imitations are ruinous to the understanding of the hearers, and that the knowledge of their true nature is the only antidote to them.

Explain the purport of your remark

Well, I will tell you, although I have always from my earliest youth had an awe and love of Homer, which even now makes the words falter on my lips, for he is the great captain and teacher of the whole of that charming tragic company; but a man is not to be reverenced more than the truth, and therefore I will speak out.

Very good, he said.

Listen to me then, or rather, answer me.

Put your question.

Can you tell me what imitation is? for I really do not know.

A likely thing, then, that I should know. [596]

Why not? for the duller eye may often see a thing sooner than the keener.

Very true, he said; but in your presence, even if I had any faint notion, I could not muster courage to utter it. Will you enquire yourself?

Well then, shall we begin the enquiry in our usual manner: Whenever a number of individuals have a common name, we assume them to have also a corresponding idea or form:—do you understand me?

I do.

Let us take any common instance; there are beds and tables in the world—plenty of them, are there not?

Yes.

But there are only two ideas or forms of them—one the idea of a bed, the other of a table.

True.

And the maker of either of them makes a bed or he makes a table for our use, in accordance with the idea—that is our way of speaking in this and similar instances—but no artificer makes the ideas themselves: how could he?

Impossible.

And there is another artist,—I should like to know what you would say of him.

---

[1][The numbers in brackets refer to the pages of the Stephanus edition of the Greek text of Plato's works. Scholarly editions in all languages bear these numbers, making it easy to go from one edition or translation to another.—J. A. O.]

Who is he?

One who is the maker of all the works of all other workmen.

What an extraordinary man!

Wait a little, and there will be more reason for your saying so. For this is he who is able to make not only vessels of every kind, but plants and animals, himself and all other things—the earth and heaven, and the things which are in heaven or under the earth; he makes the gods also.

He must be a wizard and no mistake.

Oh! you are incredulous, are you? Do you mean that there is no such maker or creator, or that in one sense there might be a maker of all these things but in another not? Do you see that there is a way in which you could make them all yourself?

What way?

An easy way enough; or rather, there are many ways in which the feat might be quickly and easily accomplished, none quicker than that of turning a mirror round and round—you would soon enough make the sun and the heavens, and the earth and yourself, and other animals and plants, and all the other things of which we were just now speaking, in the mirror.

Yes, he said; but they would be appearances only.

Very good, I said, you are coming to the point now. And the painter too is, as I conceive, just such another—a creator of appearances, is he not?

Of course.

But then I suppose you will say that what he creates is untrue. And yet there is a sense in which the painter also creates a bed?

Yes, he said, but not a real bed. [597]

And what of the maker of the bed? were you not saying that he too makes, not the idea which, according to our view, is the essence of the bed, but only a particular bed?

Yes, I did.

Then if he does not make that which exists he cannot make true existence, but only some semblance of existence; and if any one were to say that the work of the maker of the bed, or of any other workman, has real existence, he could hardly be supposed to be speaking the truth.

At any rate, he replied, philosophers would say that he was not speaking the truth.

No wonder, then, that his work too is an indistinct expression of truth.

No wonder.

Suppose now that by the light of the examples just offered we enquire who this imitator is?

If you please.

Well, here are three beds: one existing in nature, which is made by God, as I think that we may say—for no one else can be the maker?

No.

There is another which is the work of the carpenter?

Yes.

And the work of the painter is a third?

Yes.

Beds, then, are of three kinds, and there are three artists who superintend them: God, the maker of the bed, and the painter?

Yes, there are three of them.

God, whether from choice or from necessity, made one bed in nature and one only; two or more such ideal beds neither ever have been nor ever will be made by God.

Why is that?

Because even if he had made but two, a third would still appear behind them which both of them would have for their idea, and that would be the ideal bed and not the two others.

Very true, he said.

God knew this, and He desired to be the real maker of a real bed, not a particular maker of a particular bed, and therefore He created a bed which is essentially and by nature one only.

So we believe.

Shall we, then, speak of Him as the natural author or maker of the bed?

Yes, he replied; inasmuch as by the natural process of creation He is the author of this and of all other things.

And what shall we say of the carpenter—is not he also the maker of the bed?

Yes.

But would you call the painter a creator and maker?

Certainly not.

Yet if he is not the maker, what is he in relation to the bed?

I think, he said, that we may fairly designate him as the imitator of that which the others make.

Good, I said; then you call him who is third in the descent from nature an imitator?

Certainly, he said.

And the tragic poet is an imitator, and therefore, like all other imitators, he is thrice removed from the king and from the truth?

That appears to be so.

Then about the imitator we are agreed. And what about the painter? [598]—I would like to know whether he may be thought to imitate that which originally exists in nature, or only the creations of artists?

The latter.

As they are or as they appear? you have still to determine this.

What do you mean?

I mean, that you may look at a bed from different points of view, obliquely or directly or from any other point of view, and the bed will appear different, but there is no difference in reality. And the same of all things.

Yes, he said, the difference is only apparent.

Now let me ask you another question: Which is the art of painting designed to be—an imitation of things as they are, or as they appear—of appearance or of reality?

Of appearance.

Then the imitator, I said, is a long way off the truth, and can do all things because he lightly touches on a small part of them, and that part an image. For example: A painter will paint a cobbler, carpenter, or any other artist, though he knows nothing of their arts; and, if he is a good artist, he may deceive children or simple persons, when he shows them his picture of a carpenter from a distance, and they will fancy that they are looking at a real carpenter.

Certainly.

And whenever any one informs us that he has found a man who knows all the arts, and all things else that anybody knows, and every single thing with a higher degree of accuracy than any other man—whoever tells us this, I think that we can only imagine him to be a simple creature who is likely to have been deceived by some wizard or actor whom he met, and whom he thought all-knowing, because he himself was unable to analyse the nature of knowledge and ignorance and imitation.

Most true.

And so, when we hear persons saying that the tragedians, and Homer, who is at their head, know all the arts and all things human, virtue as well as vice, and divine things too, for that the good poet cannot compose well unless he knows his subject, and that he who has not this knowledge can never be a poet, we ought to consider whether here also there may not be a similar illusion. Perhaps they may have come across imitators and been deceived by them; [599] they may not have remembered when they saw their works that these were but imitations thrice removed from the truth, and could easily be made without any knowledge of the truth, because they are appearances only and not realities? Or, after all, they may be in the right, and poets do really know the things about which they seem to the many to speak so well?

The question, he said, should by all means be considered.

Now do you suppose that if a person were able to make the original well as the image, he would seriously devote himself to the image-making branch? Would he allow imitation to be the ruling principle of his life, as if he had nothing higher in him?

I should say not.

The real artist, who knew what he was imitating, would be interested in realities and not in imitations; and would desire to leave as memorials of himself works many and fair; and, instead of being the author of encomiums, he would prefer to be the theme of them.

Yes, he said, that would be to him a source of much greater honour and profit.

Then, I said, we must put a question to Homer; not about medicine, or any of the arts to which his poems only incidentally refer: we are not going to ask him, or any other poet, whether he has cured patients like Asclepius, or left behind him a school of medicine such as the Asclepiads were, or whether he only talks about medicine and other arts at second-hand; but we have a right to know respecting military tactics, politics, education, which are the chiefest and noblest subjects of his poems, and we may fairly ask him about them. 'Friend Homer,' then we say to him, 'if you are only in the second remove from truth in what you say of virtue, and not in the third—not an image maker or imitator—and if you are able to discern what pursuits make men better or worse in private or public life, tell us what State was ever better governed by your help? The good order of Lacedaemon is due to Lycurgus, and many other cities great and small have been similarly benefited by others; but who says that you have been a good legislator to them and have done them any good? Italy and Sicily boast of Charondas, and there is Solon who is renowned among us; but what city has anything to say about you?' Is there any city which he might name?

I think not, said Glaucon; not even the Homerids themselves pretend that he was a legislator. [600]

Well, but is there any war on record which was carried on successfully by him, or aided by his counsels, when he was alive?

There is not.

Or is there any invention of his, applicable to the arts or to human life, such as Thales the Milesian or Anacharsis the Scythian, and other ingenious men have conceived, which is attributed to him?

There is absolutely nothing of the kind.

But, if Homer never did any public service, was he privately a guide or teacher of any? Had he in his lifetime friends who loved to associate with him, and who handed down to posterity an Homeric way of life, such as was established by Pythagoras who was so greatly beloved for his wisdom, and whose followers are to this day quite celebrated for the order which was named after him?

Nothing of the kind is recorded of him. For surely, Socrates, Creophylus, the companion of Homer, that child of flesh, whose name always makes us laugh, might be more justly ridiculed for his stupidity, if, as is said, Homer was greatly neglected by him and others in his own day when he was alive?

Yes, I replied, that is the tradition. But can you imagine, Glaucon, that if Homer had really been able to educate and improve mankind—if he had possessed knowledge and not been a mere imitator—can you imagine, I say, that he would not have had many followers, and been honoured and loved by them? Protagoras of Abdera, and Prodicus of Ceos, and a host of others, have only to whisper to their contemporaries: 'You will never be able to manage either your own house or your own State until you appoint us to be your ministers of education'—and this ingenious device of theirs has such an effect in making men love them that their companions all but carry them about on their shoulders. And is it conceivable that the contemporaries of Homer, or again of Hesiod, would have allowed either of them to go about as rhapsodists, if they had really been able to make mankind virtuous? Would they not have been as unwilling to part with them as with gold, and have compelled them to stay at home with them? Or, if the master would not stay, then the disciples would have followed him about everywhere, until they had got education enough?

Yes, Socrates, that, I think, is quite true.

Then must we not infer that all these poetical individuals, beginning with Homer, are only imitators; they copy images of virtue and the like, but the truth they never reach: The poet is like a painter who, as we have already observed, will make a likeness of a cobbler though he understands nothing of cobbling; and his picture is good enough for those who know no more than he does, and judge only by colours and figures. [601]

Quite so.

In like manner the poet with his words and phrases[2] may be said to lay on the colours of the several arts, himself understanding their nature only enough to imitate them; and other people, who are as ignorant as he is, and judge only from his words, imagine that if he speaks of cobbling, or of military tactics, or of anything else, in metre and harmony and rhythm, he speaks very well—such is the sweet influence which melody and rhythm by nature have. And I think that you must have observed again and again what a poor appearance the tales of poets make when stripped of the colours which music puts upon them, and recited in simple prose.

Yes, he said.

They are like faces which were never really beautiful, but only blooming; and now the bloom of youth has passed away from them?

Exactly.

Here is another point: The imitator or maker of the image knows nothing of true existence; he knows appearances only. Am I not right?

Yes.

Then let us have a clear understanding, and not be satisfied with half an explanation.

Proceed.

Of the painter we say that he will paint reins, and he will paint a bit?

Yes.

And the worker in leather and brass will make them?

Certainly.

But does the painter know the right form of the bit and reins? Nay, hardly even the workers in brass and leather who make them: only the horseman who knows how to use them—he knows their right form.

Most true.

And may we not say the same of all things?

What?

That there are three arts which are concerned with all things: one which uses, another which makes, a third which imitates them?

Yes.

And the excellence or beauty or truth of every structure, animate or inanimate, and of every action of man, is relative to the use for which nature or the artist has intended them. [602]

True.

Then the user of them must have the greatest experience of them, and he must indicate to the maker the good or bad qualities which develop themselves in use; for example, the flute-player will tell the flute-maker which of his flutes is satisfactory to the performer; he will tell him how he ought to make them, and the other will attend to his instructions?

[2]Or, 'with his nouns and verbs.'

Of course.

The one knows and therefore speaks with authority about the goodness and badness of flutes, while the other, confiding in him, will do what he is told by him?

True.

The instrument is the same, but about the excellence or badness of it the maker will only attain to a correct belief; and this he will gain from him who knows, by talking to him and being compelled to hear what he has to say, whereas the user will have knowledge?

True.

But will the imitator have either? Will he know from use whether or no his drawing is correct or beautiful? or will he have right opinion from being compelled to associate with another who knows and gives him instructions about what he should draw?

Neither.

Then he will no more have true opinion than he will have knowledge about the goodness or badness of his imitations?

I suppose not.

The imitative artist will be in a brilliant state of intelligence about his own creations?

Nay, very much the reverse.

And still he will go on imitating without knowing what makes a thing good or bad, and may be expected therefore to imitate only that which appears to be good to the ignorant multitude?

Just so.

Thus far then we are pretty well agreed that the imitator has no knowledge worth mentioning of what he imitates. Imitation is only a kind of play or sport, and the tragic poets, whether they write in Iambic or in Heroic verse, are imitators in the highest degree?

Very true.

And now tell me, I conjure you, has not imitation been shown by us to be concerned with that which is thrice removed from the truth?

Certainly.

And what is the faculty in man to which imitation is addressed?

What do you mean?

I will explain: The body which is large when seen near, appears small when seen at a distance?

True.

And the same object appears straight when looked at out of the water, and crooked when in the water; and the concave becomes convex, owing to the illusion about colours to which the sight is liable. Thus every sort of confusion is revealed within us; and this is that weakness of the human mind on which the art of conjuring and of deceiving by light and shadow and other ingenious devices imposes, having an effect upon us like magic.

True.

And the arts of measuring and numbering and weighing come to the rescue of the human understanding—there is the beauty of them—and the apparent greater or less, or more or heavier, no longer have the mastery over us, but give way before calculation and measure and weight?

Most true.

And this, surely, must be the work of the calculating and rational principle in the soul?

To be sure.

And when this principle measures and certifies that some things are equal, or that some are greater or less than others, there occurs an apparent contradiction?

True.

But were we not saying that such a contradiction is impossible—the same faculty cannot have contrary opinions at the same time about the same thing?

Very true. [603]

Then that part of the soul which has an opinion contrary to measure is not the same with that which has an opinion in accordance with measure?

True.

And the better part of the soul is likely to be that which trusts to measure and calculation?

Certainly.

And that which is opposed to them is one of the inferior principles of the soul?

No doubt.

This was the conclusion at which I was seeking to arrive when I said that painting or drawing, and imitation in general, when doing their own proper work, are far removed from truth, and the companions and friends and associates of a principle within us which is equally removed from reason, and that they have no true or healthy aim.

Exactly.

The imitative art is an inferior who marries an inferior, and has inferior offspring.

Very true.

And is this confined to the sight only, or does it extend to the hearing also, relating in fact to what we term poetry?

Probably the same would be true of poetry.

Do not rely, I said, on a probability derived from the analogy of painting; but let us examine further and see whether the faculty with which poetical imitation is concerned is good or bad.

By all means.

We may state the question thus:—Imitation imitates the actions of men, whether voluntary or involuntary, on which, as they imagine, a good or bad result has ensued, and they rejoice or sorrow accordingly. Is there anything more?

No, there is nothing else.

But in all this variety of circumstances is the man at unity with himself—or rather, as in the instance of sight there was confusion and opposition in his opinions about the same things, so here also is there not strife and inconsistency in his life? Though I need hardly raise the question again, for I remember that all this has been already admitted; and the soul has been acknowledged by us to be full of these and ten thousand similar oppositions occurring at the same moment?

And we were right, he said.

Yes, I said, thus far we were right; but there was an omission which must now be supplied.

What was the omission?

Were we not saying that a good man, who has the misfortune to lose his son or anything else which is most dear to him, will bear the loss with more equanimity than another?

Yes.

But will he have no sorrow, or shall we say that although he cannot help sorrowing, he will moderate his sorrow?

The latter, he said, is the truer statement. [604]

Tell me: will he be more likely to struggle and hold out against his sorrow when he is seen by his equals, or when he is alone?

It will make a great difference whether he is seen or not.

When he is by himself he will not mind saying or doing many things which he would be ashamed of any one hearing or seeing him do?

True.

There is a principle of law and reason in him which bids him resist, as well as a feeling of his misfortune which is forcing him to indulge his sorrow?

True.

But when a man is drawn in two opposite directions, to and from the same object, this, as we affirm, necessarily implies two distinct principles in him?

Certainly.

One of them is ready to follow the guidance of the law?

How do you mean?

The law would say that to be patient under suffering is best, and that we should not give way to impatience, as there is no knowing whether such things are good or evil; and nothing is gained by impatience; also, because no human thing is of serious importance, and grief stands in the way of that which at the moment is most required.

What is most required? he asked.

That we should take counsel about what has happened, and when the dice have been thrown order our affairs in the way which reason deems best; not, like children who have had a fall, keeping hold of the part struck and wasting time in setting up a howl, but always accustoming the soul forthwith to apply a remedy, raising up that which is sickly and fallen, banishing the cry of sorrow by the healing art.

Yes, he said, that is the true way of meeting the attacks of fortune.

Yes, I said; and the higher principle is ready to follow this suggestion of reason?

Clearly.

And the other principle, which inclines us to recollection of our troubles and

to lamentation, and can never have enough of them, we may call irrational,
useless, and cowardly?

Indeed, we may.

And does not the latter—I mean the rebellious principle—furnish a great
variety of materials for imitation? Whereas the wise and calm temperament, being
always nearly equable, is not easy to imitate or to appreciate when imitated,
especially at a public festival when a promiscuous crowd is assembled in a theatre.
For the feeling represented is one to which they are strangers.

Certainly. [605]

Then the imitative poet who aims at being popular is not by nature made, nor
is his art intended, to please or to affect the rational principle in the soul; but he
will prefer the passionate and fitful temper, which is easily imitated?

Clearly.

And now we may fairly take him and place him by the side of the painter, for
he is like him in two ways: first, inasmuch as his creations have an inferior degree
of truth—in this, I say, he is like him; and he is also like him in being concerned
with an inferior part of the soul; and therefore we shall be right in refusing to
admit him into a well-ordered State, because he awakens and nourishes and
strengthens the feelings and impairs the reason. As in a city when the evil are
permitted to have authority and the good are put out of the way, so in the soul of
man, as we maintain, the imitative poet implants an evil constitution, for he
indulges the irrational nature which has no discernment of greater and less, but
thinks the same thing at one time great and at another small—he is a manufacturer of images and is very far removed from the truth.

Exactly.

But we have not yet brought forward the heaviest count in our accusation:—
the power which poetry has of harming even the good (and there are very few who
are not harmed), is surely an awful thing?

Yes, certainly, if the effect is what you say.

Hear and judge: The best of us, as I conceive, when we listen to a passage of
Homer, or one of the tragedians, in which he represents some pitiful hero who is
drawling out his sorrows in a long oration, or weeping, and smiting his breast—the
best of us, you know, delight in giving way to sympathy, and are in raptures at the
excellence of the poet who stirs our feelings most.

Yes, of course I know.

But when any sorrow of our own happens to us, then you may observe that
we pride ourselves on the opposite quality—we would fain be quiet and patient;
this is the manly part, and the other which delighted us in the recitation is now
deemed to be the part of a woman.

Very true, he said.

Now can we be right in praising and admiring another who is doing that which
any one of us would abominate and be ashamed of in his own person?

No, he said, that is certainly not reasonable.

Nay, I said, quite reasonable from one point of view. [606]

What point of view?

If you consider, I said, that when in misfortune we feel a natural hunger and desire to relieve our sorrow by weeping and lamentation, and that this feeling which is kept under control in our own calamities is satisfied and delighted by the poets;—the better nature in each of us, not having been sufficiently trained by reason or habit, allows the sympathetic element to break loose because the sorrow is another's; and the spectator fancies that there can be no disgrace to himself in praising and pitying any one who comes telling him what a good man he is, and making a fuss about his troubles; he thinks that the pleasure is a gain, and why should he be supercilious and lose this and the poem too? Few persons ever reflect, as I should imagine, that from the evil of other men something of evil is communicated to themselves. And so the feeling of sorrow which has gathered strength at the sight of the misfortunes of others is with difficulty repressed in our own.

How very true!

And does not the same hold also of the ridiculous? There are jests which you would be ashamed to make yourself, and yet on the comic stage, or indeed in private, when you hear them, you are greatly amused by them, and are not at all disgusted at their unseemliness;—the case of pity is repeated;—there is a principle in human nature which is disposed to raise a laugh, and this which you once restrained by reason, because you were afraid of being thought a buffoon, is now let out again; and having stimulated the risible faculty at the theatre, you are betrayed unconsciously to yourself into playing the comic poet at home.

Quite true, he said.

And the same may be said of lust and anger and all the other affections, of desire and pain and pleasure, which are held to be inseparable from every action—in all of them poetry feeds and waters the passions instead of drying them up; she lets them rule, although they ought to be controlled, if mankind are ever to increase in happiness and virtue.

I cannot deny it.

Therefore, Glaucon, I said, whenever you meet with any of the eulogists of Homer declaring that has been the educator of Hellas, and that he is profitable for education and for the ordering of human things, and that you should take him up again and again and get to know him and regulate your whole life according to him, we may love and honour those who say these things—they are excellent people, as far as their lights extend; [607] and we are ready to acknowledge that Homer is the greatest of poets and first of tragedy writers; but we must remain firm in our conviction that hymns to the gods and praises of famous men are the only poetry which ought to be admitted into our State. For if you go beyond this and allow the honeyed muse to enter, either in epic or lyric verse, not law and the reason of mankind, which by common consent have ever been deemed best, but pleasure and pain will be the rulers in our State.

That is most true, he said.

And now since we have reverted to the subject of poetry, let this our defence serve to show the reasonableness of our former judgment in sending away out of our State an art having the tendencies which we have described; for reason constrained us. But that she may not impute to us any harshness or want of politeness, let us tell her that there is an ancient quarrel between philosophy and poetry; of which there are many proofs, such as the saying of 'the yelping hound howling at her lord,' or of one 'mighty in the vain talk of fools,' and 'the mob of sages circumventing Zeus,' and the 'subtle thinkers who are beggars after all'; and there are innumerable other signs of ancient enmity between them. Notwithstanding this, let us assure our sweet friend and the sister arts of imitation, that if she will only prove her title to exist in a well-ordered State we shall be delighted to receive her—we are very conscious of her charms; but we may not on that account betray the truth. I dare say, Glaucon, that you are as much charmed by her as I am, especially when she appears in Homer?

Yes, indeed, I am greatly charmed.

Shall I propose, then, that she be allowed to return from exile, but upon this condition only—that she make a defence of herself in lyrical or some other metre?

Certainly.

And we may further grant to those of her defenders who are lovers of poetry and yet not poets the permission to speak in prose on her behalf: let them show not only that she is pleasant but also useful to States and to human life, and we will listen in a kindly spirit; for if this can be proved we shall surely be the gainers—I mean, if there is a use in poetry as well as a delight?

transition: metaphysics and modern art

Whatever Plato may have intended at the deepest levels of his dialogues, superficial readings contributed to a Platonic-Christian tradition that some have condemned as the spirit of literalism. According to the orthodox tradition (and its legacy, common sense) inquiry and art should aim at picturing the world *as it really is,* not as it appears to be. The orthodox, common-sense view is consistent with what I have dubbed the orange theory of reality: we must penetrate and discard the rind of illusion to reach the fruit of truth. That truth, once revealed, will exhibit Cartesian clarity and a univocity or singleness of meaning that is susceptible to literal representation. In such a view—which amounts to a metaphysics—art plays at least two roles: it may assist in penetrating the rind of illusion, or it may simply amuse. Actually the two roles intertwine: art helps an audience penetrate illusion precisely to the extent that it entertains. We are not inclined to listen to someone if he bores us. Similarly, the role of art may be to render the truth more vivid by translating it into a more intense or more palatable or more entertaining message. In this orthodox or traditional view, art as a medium is in principle distinct from the literal truth or falsity of its message. Plato could complain that art was capable of a powerful transmission of false messages to the extent that it represented the realm of becoming rather than the realm of being.

To understand the upheaval in the arts it is necessary to understand that modern art reflects an upheaval in all our traditions, including orthodox Christian-Platonic metaphysics. In the context of the traditional metaphysics, esthetics consisted largely of developing criteria for judgments concerning the effectiveness with which art represented truth and beauty. Indeed, the subjective experience of beauty was taken by many as an index of the truth of what was represented through the medium of the art work. But the modern upheaval in metaphysics undercuts traditional esthetics because modern art has no final truth to represent, so how can esthetics concern itself with the truthfulness, that is, the beauty, of the representation?

But surely modern paintings represent faces or mountains or other objects, however distorted these may be by impressionism or expressionism or cubism. Surely something is represented, and the distortions are intended to make us see in a less literal, but more truthful, way. But what about abstract art and the various works of so-called antiart: empty canvases, vacant frames, perfectly silent pieces of music? A different theory is needed for these most extreme cases; it will not do to say that they remain representational and choose nothingness or silence as their object. They are, instead, commentaries on modern art itself and the nonrepresentational role it plays, an abandonment of the entire Christian-Platonic orthodoxy with its orange theory of metaphysics. Is the onion theory any more helpful? Let us review its features.

If reality is not a clear and distinct bedrock lying beneath a layer of appearances, or, to return to the culinary metaphor, a rich fruit beneath the rind of illusion; if reality is, like the onion, a totality of the layers of "illusion," or the interlocking wholeness of a multiplicity of appearances, then art has no literal truth to represent. There is no separate absolute that art may glorify above the relativities of appearance. There is an absolute, but it is not separate; it is the totality of all those relativities the traditional metaphysics discarded as the rind of illusion. But how can art represent the absolute if the absolute is the totality? To represent everything is to represent nothing. I write: 'everything.' And I have said nothing. Traditional art said *something* to the extent that it could represent a part rather than the whole, namely that part that the artist took to be truth as distinct from error. But the modern artist, to the extent that he reflects the onion theory of metaphysics, cannot reject any part of reality as being less true, less a part of the all-comprehensive absolute, than any other. Hence we find in our art museums everything from empty canvases to piles of junk.

Rather than exploiting esthetic sensibility to represent a truth distinct from appearances, modern art uses appearances to exercise the esthetic sensibility. The esthetic sensibility is important not because it opens a door to a single, literal truth but because it is uniquely suited to perceive the multiplicity of meanings exhibited in every appearance. Art as a medium then comes to be itself the message: art does not represent reality; it is symbolic of reality to the extent that everything is symbolic. Everything is a representation of a representation of a representation of ... The psychology of Oedipal development represents politics; similarly the politics of nations represents the politics of races; the politics of races represents the politics of sexes, and so on. No one explanation, psychological, political, or physical, represents the final truth.[1] Only art, to the extent that it symbolizes the multiplicity of possible interpretations, reflects the nonreductionist metaphysics of the onion theory of reality. Art does not say everything is nothing but art. Art says everything is what it is and symbolic of a lot else besides.

Art is neither a knife cutting through to the fruit of truth from which it is separated as a means to an end, nor is art itself the truth to which other ways of looking at the world must be subordinated. Despite modern art's special role in symbolizing the multiplicity of the whole, art itself is but one more layer of the onion. As such it

---

[1]While many classical theoretical systems claim to describe the fruit of the orange in a reductionistic way—that is, by saying that everything is *nothing but* economics or instinctual manifestation or matter in space and time, and consequently everything could be explained by the laws of economics, or the laws of physics—some theorists seem aware of the representative rather than the reductionistic relationships among various theories. Thus psycho-history, in the hands of someone like Erikson, is not so much an attempt to explain history in terms of psychology as it is an attempt to enrich psychology through a mutual representation with history.

represents the other layers and is represented by them. The next essay shows not only (a) the way in which the upheaval in art reflects an upheaval in the metaphysical tradition, but also (b) how modern art and modern politics mutually represent one another, that is, how each pictures the other while both reciprocally influence each other.

Traditional metaphysics and esthetics described the relationship between art and politics as either nonexistent or at best restricted to the function of propaganda. Contemporary common sense—the legacy of traditional metaphysics—generally takes the former view, that there is no important relationship between art and politics and that artists and philosophers can insist on such a relationship only in the interests of propaganda. Thus art may be removed from its normally innocuous role as entertainment or diversion and serve instead a specific political ideology. One thinks of the heavy-handed works of Soviet painting and architecture under Stalin, the mechanical representations attempting to glorify the workers' struggle. But against this "backward" art one can find artists who see a different relationship between their art and their politics, an often unconscious relationship that others have to uncover. Briefly stated, modern art serves to effect liberation rather than represent liberation. The best modern art touches viewers by liberating them from the literal, not by impressing them with a specific truth. Because this liberating effect is so largely negative, classical esthetics is baffled in its attempt to find "the meaning of modern art." Because modern art liberates its audience from the tyranny of single meanings to the multiplicity of all possible meanings, it is fundamentally mistaken to pursue the meaning of modern art. But this liberation from univocal meaning is a powerful political force, for no longer will the audience accept the idea of a single order of things. The multiplicity of meanings reflected in art corresponds to the multiplicity of stages in the Hegelian dialectic that moves Marxist revolutions; and the lack of a final order at the core of the onion corresponds to the temporalized version of multiplicity in the modern concept of permanent revolution. Just as the role of art is no longer as a means to an end, a medium separate from a message, so revolution is no longer a means to an end, but an aspect, a layer of a permanent state of becoming. Just as nonrepresentational modern art symbolizes (and is symbolized by) the multiplicity of meanings at a single moment, so the dizzying dispersion of ever newer schools in modern art symbolizes (and is symbolized by) the permanent revolution and dispersion of decentralized metapolitical forms. Permanent flux is multiplicity in time. Modern art generates the consciousness capable of this permanent flux. Rather than representing a particular order of things, modern art bewilders the critics in its capacity for propelling its audience out of the existing order and into a state of flux.

ANDRÉ BRETON *(1896–1966)*

André Breton would undoubtedly be one of the first men exiled from Plato's Republic. He was a poet and an early practitioner of French surrealism, the very title of which advertises a rejection of the realism implicit in Plato's critique of artists. Breton has no intention of representing the real according to a Platonic scheme of grades of reality and appearance at different removes from reality. He wants to deepen his audience's respect for the dimensions of experience that the Platonic tradition rejects as least real: namely, the dimensions of dream and fantasy in the underworld of the unconscious. Breton's "Manifesto" reflects a radically un-Platonic metaphysics and ontology. His entire essay leads up to the elusive last line, "Existence is elsewhere."

While parts of Breton's esthetics suggest a distance from worldly affairs, he was in fact intensely involved in political disputes. The choice of "Manifesto" for the title reflects Breton's respect for the Communist Manifesto *by Marx and Engels. As he became more and more embroiled in the turbulence of French politics, the 1924 "Manifesto of Surrealism" reprinted here was followed by a "Second Manifesto of Surrealism" in 1930 and a "Prolegomena to a Third Surrealist Manifesto or Not" in 1942. His struggles with the Communist Party, his collaborations with the anarchist Leon Trotsky, and his lasting dedication to art all reflect a political struggle: is the revolutionary trying to liberate souls from the prevailing order or shackle them to a different order?*

Manifesto of Surrealism

The mere word "freedom" is the only one that still excites me. I deem it capable of indefinitely sustaining the old human fanaticism. It doubtless satisfies my only legitimate aspiration. Among all the many misfortunes to which we are heir, it is only fair to admit that we are allowed the greatest degree of freedom of thought. It is up to us not to misuse it. To reduce the imagination to a state of slavery—even though it would mean the elimination of what is commonly called happiness—is to betray all sense of absolute justice within oneself. Imagination alone offers me some intimation of what *can be*, and this is enough to remove to some slight degree the terrible injunction; enough, too, to allow me to devote myself to it without fear of making a mistake (as though it were possible to make a bigger mistake). Where does it begin to turn bad, and where does the mind's stability cease? For the mind, is the possibility of erring not rather the contingency of good?

There remains madness, "the madness that one locks up," as it has aptly been described. That madness or another.... We all know, in fact, that the insane owe their incarceration to a tiny number of legally reprehensible acts and that, were it not for these acts their freedom (or what we see as their freedom) would not be threatened. I am willing to admit that they are, to some degree, victims of their imagination, in that it induces them not to pay attention to certain rules—outside of which the species feels itself threatened—which we are all supposed to know and respect. But their profound indifference to the way in which we judge them, and even to the various punishments meted out to them, allows us to suppose that they derive a great deal of comfort and consolation from their imagination, that they enjoy their madness sufficiently to endure the thought that its validity does not extend beyond themselves. And, indeed, hallucinations, illusions, etc., are not a source of trifling pleasure. The best controlled sensuality partakes of it, and I know that there are many evenings when I would gladly tame that pretty hand which, during the last pages of Taine's *L'Intelligence,* indulges in some curious misdeeds. I could spend my whole life prying loose the secrets of the insane. These people are honest to a fault, and their naiveté has no peer but my own. Christopher Columbus should have set out to discover America with a boatload of madmen. And note how this madness has taken shape, and endured.

It is not the fear of madness which will oblige us to leave the flag of imagination furled.

The case against the realistic attitude demands to be examined, following the case against the materialistic attitude. The latter, more poetic in fact than the former, admittedly implies on the part of man a kind of monstrous pride which, admittedly, is monstrous, but not a new and more complete decay. It should above all be viewed as a welcome reaction against certain ridiculous tendencies of spiritualism. Finally, it is not incompatible with a certain nobility of thought.

By contrast, the realistic attitude, inspired by positivism, from Saint Thomas Aquinas to Anatole France, clearly seems to me to be hostile to any intellectual or moral advancement. I loathe it, for it is made up of mediocrity, hate, and dull conceit. It is this attitude which today gives birth to these ridiculous books, these insulting plays. It constantly feeds on and derives strength from the newspapers and stultifies both science and art by assiduously flattering the lowest of tastes; clarity bordering on stupidity, a dog's life. The activity of the best minds feels the effects of it; the law of the lowest common denominator finally prevails upon them as it does upon the others. An amusing result of this state of affairs, in literature for example, is the generous supply of novels. Each person adds his personal little "observation" to the whole. As a cleansing antidote to all this, M. Paul Valéry recently suggested that an anthology be compiled in which the largest possible number of opening passages from novels be offered; the resulting insanity, he predicted, would be a source of considerable edification. The most famous authors would be included. Such a thought reflects great credit on Paul Valéry who, some time ago, speaking of novels, assured me that, so far as he was concerned, he would continue to refrain from writing: "The Marquise went out at five." But has he kept his word?

If the purely informative style, of which the sentence just quoted is a prime example, is virtually the rule rather than the exception in the novel form, it is because, in all fairness, the author's ambition is severely circumscribed. The circumstantial, needlessly specific nature of each of their notations leads me to believe that they are perpetrating a joke at my expense. I am spared not even one of the character's slightest vacillations: will he be fairhaired? what will his name be? will we first meet him during the summer? So many questions resolved once and for all, as chance directs; the only discretionary power left me is to close the book, which I am careful to do somewhere in the vicinity of the first page. And the descriptions! There is nothing to which their vacuity can be compared; they are nothing but so many superimposed images taken from some stock catalogue, which the author utilizes more and more whenever he chooses; he seizes the opportunity to slip me his postcards, he tries to make me agree with him about the clichés:

> The small room into which the young man was shown was covered with yellow wallpaper: there were geraniums in the windows, which were covered with muslin curtains; the setting sun cast a harsh light over the entire setting. . . . There was nothing special about the room. The furniture, of yellow wood, was all very old. A sofa with a tall back turned down, an oval table opposite the sofa, a dressing table and a mirror set against the pierglass, some chairs along the walls, two or three etchings of no value portraying some German girls with birds in their hands—such were the furnishings.[1]

I am in no mood to admit that the mind is interested in occupying itself with such matters, even fleetingly. It may be argued that this school-boy description has its place, and that at this juncture of the book the author has his reasons for burdening me. Nevertheless he is wasting his time, for I refuse to go into his room. Others' laziness or fatigue does not interest me. I have too unstable a notion of the continuity of life to equate or compare my moments of depression or weakness with my best moments. When one ceases to feel, I am of the opinion one should keep quiet. And I would like it understood that I am not accusing or condemning lack of originality *as such*. I am only saying that I do not take particular note of the empty moments of my life, that it may be unworthy for any man to crystallize those which seem to him to be so. I shall, with your permission, *ignore* the description of that room, and many more like it.

Not so fast, there; I'm getting into the area of psychology, a subject about which I shall be careful not to joke.

The author attacks a character and, this being settled upon, parades his hero to and fro across the world. No matter what happens, this hero, whose actions and reactions are admirably predictable, is compelled not to thwart or upset—even though he looks as though he is—the calculations of which he is the object. The currents of life can appear to lift him up, roll him over, cast him down, he will still belong to this *readymade* human type. A simple game of chess which doesn't interest me in the least—man, whoever he may be, being for me a mediocre opponent. What I cannot bear are those wretched discussions relative to such and

[1]Dostoevski, *Crime and Punishment.*

such a move, since winning or losing is not in question. And if the game is not worth the candle, if objective reason does a frightful job—as indeed it does—of serving him who calls upon it, is it not fitting and proper to avoid all contact with these categories? "Diversity is so vast that every different tone of voice, every step, cough, every wipe of the nose, every sneeze. . . ."[2] If in a cluster of grapes there are no two alike, why do you want me to describe this grape by the other, by all the others, why do you want me to make a palatable grape? Our brains are dulled by the incurable mania of wanting to make the unknown known, classifiable. The desire for analysis wins out over the sentiments.[3] The result is statements of undue length whose persuasive power is attributed solely to their strangeness and which impress the reader only by the abstract quality of their vocabulary, which moreover is ill-defined. If the general ideas that philosophy has thus far come up with as topics of discussion revealed by their very nature their definitive incursion into a broader or more general area, I would be the first to greet the news with joy. But up till now it has been nothing but idle repartee; the flashes of wit and other niceties vie in concealing from us the true thought in search of itself, instead of concentrating on obtaining successes. It seems to me that every act is its own justification, at least for the person who has been capable of committing it, that it is endowed with a radiant power which the slightest gloss is certain to diminish. Because of this gloss, it even in a sense ceases to happen. It gains nothing to be thus distinguished. Stendhal's heroes are subject to the comments and appraisals—appraisals which are more or less successful—made by that author, which add not one whit to their glory. Where we really find them again is at the point at which Stendhal has lost them.

We are still living under the reign of logic: this, of course, is what I have been driving at. But in this day and age logical methods are applicable only to solving problems of secondary interest. The absolute rationalism that is still in vogue allows us to consider only facts relating directly to our experience. Logical ends, on the contrary, escape us. It is pointless to add that experience itself has found itself increasingly circumscribed. It paces back and forth in a cage from which it is more and more difficult to make it emerge. It too learns for support on what is most immediately expedient, and it is protected by the sentinels of common sense. Under the pretense of civilization and progress, we have managed to banish from the mind everything that may rightly or wrongly be termed superstition, or fancy; forbidden is any kind of search for truth which is not in conformance with accepted practices. It was, apparently, by pure chance that a part of our mental world which we pretended not to be concerned with any longer—and, in my opinion by far the most important part—has been brought back to light. For this we must give thanks to the discoveries of Sigmund Freud. On the basis of these discoveries a current of opinion is finally forming by means of which the human explorer will be able to carry his investigations much further, authorized as he will henceforth be not to confine himself solely to the most summary realities. The

[2]Pascal.
[3]Barrès, Proust.

imagination is perhaps on the point of reasserting itself, of reclaiming its rights. If the depths of our mind contain within it strange forces capable of augmenting those on the surface, or of waging a victorious battle against them, there is every reason to seize them—first to seize them, then, if need be, to submit them to the control of our reason. The analysts themselves have everything to gain by it. But it is worth noting that no means has been designated a priori for carrying out this undertaking, that until further notice it can be construed to be the province of poets as well as scholars, and that its success is not dependent upon the more or less capricious paths that will be followed.

Freud very rightly brought his critical faculties to bear upon the dream. It is, in fact, inadmissible that this considerable portion of psychic activity (since, at least from man's birth until his death, thought offers no solution of continuity, the sum of the moments of dream, from the point of view of time, and taking into consideration only the time of pure dreaming, that is the dreams of sleep, is not inferior to the sum of the moments of reality, or, to be more precisely limiting, the moments of waking) has still today been so grossly neglected. I have always been amazed at the way an ordinary observer lends so much more credence and attaches so much more importance to waking events than to those occurring in dreams. It is because man, when he ceases to sleep, is above all the plaything of his memory, and in its normal state memory takes pleasure in weakly retracing for him the circumstances of the dream, in stripping it of any real importance, and in dismissing the only *determinant* from the point where he thinks he has left it a few hours before: this firm hope, this concern. He is under the impression of continuing something that is worthwhile. Thus the dream finds itself reduced to a mere parenthesis, as is the night. And, like the night, dreams generally contribute little to furthering our understanding. This curious state of affairs seems to me to call for certain reflections:

1. Within the limits where they operate (or are thought to operate) dreams give every evidence of being continuous and show signs of organization. Memory alone arrogates to itself the right to excerpt from dreams, to ignore the transitions, and to depict for us rather a series of dreams than the *dream itself*. By the same token, at any given moment we have only a distinct notion of realities, the coordination of which is a question of will.[4] What is worth noting is that nothing allows us to presuppose a greater dissipation of the elements of which the dream is constituted. I am sorry to have to speak about it according to a formula which in principle excludes the dream. When will we have sleeping logicians, sleeping philosophers? I would like to sleep, in order to surrender myself to the dreamers, the way I surrender myself to those who read me with eyes wide open; in order to stop imposing, in this realm, the conscious rhythm of my thought. Perhaps my

---

[4]Account must be taken of the *depth* of the dream. For the most part I retain only what I can glean from its most superficial layers. What I most enjoy contemplating about a dream is everything that sinks back below the surface in a waking state, everything I have forgotten about my activities in the course of the preceding day, dark foliage, stupid branches. In "reality," likewise, I prefer to fall.

dream last night follows that of the night before, and will be continued the next night, with an exemplary strictness. *It's quite possible*, as the saying goes. And since it has not been proved in the slightest that, in doing so, the "reality" with which I am kept busy continues to exist in the state of dream, that it does not sink back down into the immemorial, why should I not grant to dreams what I occasionally refuse reality, that is, this value of certainty in itself which, in its own time, is not open to my repudiation? Why should I not expect from the sign of the dream more than I expect from a degree of consciousness which is daily more acute? Can't the dream also be used in solving the fundamental questions of life? Are these questions the same in one case as in the other and, in the dream, do these questions already exist? Is the dream any less restrictive or punitive than the rest? I am growing old and, more than that reality to which I believe I subject myself, it is perhaps the dream, the difference with which I treat the dream, which makes me grow old.

2. Let me come back again to the waking state. I have no choice but to consider it a phenomenon of interference. Not only does the mind display, in this state, a strange tendency to lose its bearings (as evidenced by the slips and mistakes the secrets of which are just beginning to be revealed to us), but, what is more, it does not appear that, when the mind is functioning normally, it really responds to anything but the suggestions which come to it from the depths of that dark night to which I commend it. However conditioned it may be, its balance is relative. It scarcely dares express itself and, if it does, it confines itself to verifying that such and such an idea, or such and such a woman, has made an impression on it. What impression it would be hard pressed to say, by which it reveals the degree of its subjectivity, and nothing more. This idea, this woman, disturb it, they tend to make it less severe. What they do is isolate the mind for a second from its solvent and spirit it to heaven, as the beautiful precipitate it can be, that it is. When all else fails, it then calls upon chance, a divinity even more obscure than the others to whom it ascribes all its aberrations. Who can say to me that the angle by which that idea which affects it is offered, that what it likes in the eye of that woman is not precisely what links it to its dream, binds it to those fundamental facts which, through its own fault, it has lost? And if things were different, what might it be capable of? I would like to provide it with the key to this corridor.

3. The mind of the man who dreams is fully satisfied by what happens to him. The agonizing question of possibility is no longer pertinent. Kill, fly faster, love to your heart's content. And if you should die, are you not certain of reawaking among the dead? Let yourself be carried along, events will not tolerate your interference. You are nameless. The ease of everything is priceless.

What reason, I ask, a reason so much vaster than the other, makes dreams seem so natural and allows me to welcome unreservedly a welter of episodes so strange that they would confound me now as I write? And yet I can believe my eyes, my ears; this great day has arrived, this beast has spoken.

If man's awaking is harder, if it breaks the spell too abruptly, it is because he has been led to make for himself too impoverished a notion of atonement.

4. From the moment when it is subjected to a methodical examination, when, by means yet to be determined, we succeed in recording the contents of dreams in their entirety (and that presupposes a discipline of memory spanning generations; but let us nonetheless begin by noting the most salient facts), when its graph will expand with unparalleled volume and regularity, we may hope that the mysteries which really are not will give way to the great Mystery. I believe in the future resolution of these two states, dream and reality, which are seemingly so contradictory, into a kind of absolute reality, a *surreality*, if one may so speak. It is in quest of this surreality that I am going, certain not to find it but too unmindful of my death not to calculate to some slight degree the joys of its possession.

A story is told according to which Saint-Pol-Roux, in times gone by, used to have a notice posted on the door of his manor house in Camaret, every evening before he went to sleep, which read: THE POET IS WORKING.

A great deal more could be said, but in passing I merely wanted to touch upon a subject which in itself would require a very long and much more detailed discussion; I shall come back to it. At this juncture, my intention was merely to mark a point by noting the *hate of the marvelous* which rages in certain men, this absurdity beneath which they try to bury it. Let us not mince words: the marvelous is always beautiful, anything marvelous is beautiful, in fact only the marvelous is beautiful. . . .

Man proposes and disposes. He and he alone can determine whether he is completely master of himself, that is, whether he maintains the body of his desires, daily more formidable, in a state of anarchy. Poetry teaches him to. It bears within itself the perfect compensation for the miseries we endure. It can also be an organizer, if ever, as the result of a less intimate disappointment, we contemplate taking it seriously. The time is coming when it decrees the end of money and by itself will break the bread of heaven for the earth! There will still be gatherings on the public squares, and *movements* you never dared hope participate in. Farewell to absurd choices, the dreams of dark abyss, rivalries, the prolonged patience, the flight of the seasons, the artificial order of ideas, the ramp of danger, time for everything! May you only take the trouble to *practice* poetry. Is it not incumbent upon us, who are already living off it, to try and impose what we hold to be our case for further inquiry?

It matters not whether there is a certain disproportion between this defense and the illustration that will follow it. It was a question of going back to the sources of poetic imagination and, what is more, of remaining there. Not that I pretend to have done so. It requires a great deal of fortitude to try to set up one's abode in these distant regions where everything seems at first to be so awkward and difficult, all the more so if one wants to try to take someone there. Besides, one is never sure of really being there. If one is going to all that trouble, one might just as well stop off somewhere else. Be that as it may, the fact is that the way to these regions is clearly marked, and that to attain the true goal is now merely a matter of the travelers' ability to endure.

We are all more or less aware of the road traveled. I was careful to relate, in

the course of a study of the case of Robert Desnos entitled ENTRÉE DES MÉDIUMS,[5]
that I had been led to "concentrate my attention on the more or less partial
sentences which, when one is quite alone and on the verge of falling asleep,
become perceptible for the mind without its being possible to discover what
provoked them." I had then just attempted the poetic adventure with the minimum of risks, that is, my aspirations were the same as they are today but I trusted
in the slowness of formulation to keep me from useless contacts, contacts of which
I completely disapproved. This attitude involved a modesty of thought certain
vestiges of which I still retain. At the end of my life, I shall doubtless manage to
speak with great effort the way people speak, to apologize for my voice and my few
remaining gestures. The virtue of the spoken word (and the written word all the
more so) seemed to me to derive from the faculty of foreshortening in a striking
manner the exposition (since there was exposition) of a small number of facts,
poetic or other, of which I made myself the substance. I had come to the
conclusion that Rimbaud had not proceeded any differently. I was composing,
with a concern for variety that deserved better, the final poems of *Mont de piété*,
that is, I managed to extract from the blank lines of this book an incredible
advantage. These lines were the closed eye to the operations of thought that I
believed I was obliged to keep hidden from the reader. It was not deceit on my part,
but my love of shocking the reader. I had the illusion of a possible complicity,
which I had more and more difficulty giving up. I had begun to cherish words
excessively for the space they allow around them, for their tangencies with
countless other words that I did not utter. The poem BLACK FOREST derives
precisely from this state of mind. It took me six months to write it, and you may
take my word for it that I did not rest a single day. But this stemmed from the
opinion I had of myself in those days, which was high, please don't judge me too
harshly. I enjoy these stupid confessions. At that point cubist pseudopoetry was
trying to get a foothold, but it had emerged defenseless from Picasso's brain, and I
was thought to be as dull as dishwater (and still am). I had a sneaking suspicion,
moreover, that from the viewpoint of poetry I was off on the wrong road, but I
hedged my bet as best I could, defying lyricism with salvos of definitions and
formulas (the Dada phenomena were waiting in the wings, ready to come on stage)
and pretending to search for an application of poetry to advertising (I went so far
as to claim that the world would end, not with a good book but with a beautiful
advertisement for heaven or for hell).

In those days, a man at least as boring as I, Pierre Reverdy, was writing:

The image is a pure creation of the mind.
    It cannot be born from a comparison but from a juxtaposition of
two more or less distant realities.
    The more the relationship between the two juxtaposed realities is
distant and true, the stronger the image will be—the greater its emotional power and poetic reality...[6]

---

[5]See *Les Pas perdus*, published by N. R. F. [Nouvelle Revue Français]
[6]*Nord-Sud*, March 1918

These words, however sibylline for the uninitiated, were extremely revealing, and I pondered them for a long time. But the image eluded me. Reverdy's aesthetic, a completely a posteriori aesthetic, led me to mistake the effects for the causes. It was in the midst of all this that I renounced irrevocably my point of view.

One evening, therefore, before I fell asleep, I perceived, so clearly articulated that it was impossible to change a word, but nonetheless removed from the sound of any voice, a rather strange phrase which came to me without any apparent relationship to the events in which, my consciousness agrees, I was then involved, a phrase which seemed to me insistent, a phrase, if I may be so bold, *which was knocking at the window.* I took cursory note of it and prepared to move on when its organic character caught my attention. Actually, this phrase astonished me: unfortunately I cannot remember it exactly, but it was something like: "There is a man cut in two by the window," but there could be no question of ambiguity, accompanied as it was by the faint visual image[7] of a man walking cut half way up by a window perpendicular to the axis of his body. Beyond the slightest shadow of a doubt, what I saw was the simple reconstruction in space of a man leaning out a window. But this window having shifted with the man, I realized that I was dealing with an image of a fairly rare sort, and all I could think of was to incorporate it into my material for poetic construction. No sooner had I granted it this capacity than it was in fact succeeded by a whole series of phrases, with only brief pauses between them, which surprised me only slightly less and left me with the impression of their being so gratuitous that the control I had then exercised upon myself seemed to me illusory and all I could think of was putting an end to the interminable quarrel raging within me.[8]

[7] Were I a painter, this visual depiction would doubtless have become more important for me than the other. It was most certainly my previous predispositions which decided the matter. Since that day, I have had occasion to concentrate my attention voluntarily on similar apparitions, and I know that they are fully as clear as auditory phenomena. With a pencil and white sheet of paper to hand, I could easily trace their outlines. Here again it is not a matter of drawing, *but simply of tracing.* I could thus depict a tree, a wave, a musical instrument, all manner of things of which I am presently incapable of providing even the roughest sketch. I would plunge into it, convinced that I would find my way again, in a maze of lines which at first glance would seem to be going nowhere. And, upon opening my eyes, I would get the very strong impression of something "never seen." The proof of what I am saying has been provided many times by Robert Desnos: to be convinced, one has only to leaf through the pages of issue number 36 of *Feuilles libres* whch contains several of his drawings (*Romeo and Juliet, A Man Died This Morning,* etc.) which were taken by this magazine as the drawings of a madman and published as such.

[8] Knut Hamsum ascribes this sort of revelation to which I had been subjected as deriving from *hunger,* and he may not be wrong. (The fact is I did not eat every day during that period of my life). Most certainly the manifestations that he describes in these terms are clearly the same:

"The following day I awoke at an early hour. It was still dark. My eyes had been open for a long time when I heard the clock in the apartment above strike five. I wanted to go back to sleep, but I couldn't; I was wide awake and a thousand thoughts were crowding through my mind.

Suddenly a few good fragments came to mind, quite suitable to be used in a rough draft, or serialized; all of a sudden I found, quite by chance, beautiful phrases, phrases such as I had never written. I repeated them to myself slowly, word by word; they were excellent. And there were still more

Completely occupied as I still was with Freud at that time, and familiar as I was with his methods of examination which I had had some slight occasion to use on some patients during the war, I resolved to obtain from myself what we were trying to obtain from them, namely, a monologue spoken as rapidly as possible without any intervention on the part of the critical faculties, a monologue consequently unencumbered by the slightest inhibition and which was, as closely as possible, akin to *spoken thought*. It had seemed to me, and still does—the way in which the phrase about the man cut in two had come to me is an indication of it—that the speed of thought is no greater than the speed of speech, and that thought does not necessarily defy language, nor even the fast-moving pen. It was in this frame of mind that Philippe Soupault—to whom I had confided these initial conclusions—and I decided to blacken some paper, with a praiseworthy disdain for what might result from a literary point of view. The ease of execution did the rest. By the end of the first day we were able to read to ourselves some fifty or so pages obtained in this manner, and begin to compare our results. All in all, Soupault's pages and mine proved to be remarkably similar: the same overconstruction, shortcomings of a similar nature, but also, on both our parts, the illusion of an extraordinary verve, a great deal of emotion, a considerable choice of images of a quality such that we would not have been capable of preparing a single one in longhand, a very special picturesque quality and, here and there, a strong comical effect. The only difference between our two texts seemed to me to derive essentially from our respective tempers, Soupault's being less static than mine, and, if he does not mind my offering this one slight criticism, from the fact that he had made the error of putting a few words by way of titles at the top of certain pages, I suppose in a spirit of mystification. On the other hand, I must give credit where credit is due and say that he constantly and vigorously opposed any effort to retouch or correct, however slightly, any passage of this kind which seemed to me unfortunate. In this he was, to be sure, absolutely right.[9] It is, in fact, difficult to appreciate fairly the various elements present; one may even go so far as to say that it is impossible to appreciate them at a first reading. To you who write, these elements are, on the surface, *as strange to you as they are to anyone else*, and naturally you are wary of them. Poetically speaking, what strikes you about them

---

coming. I got up and picked up a pencil and some paper that were on a table behind my bed. It was as though some vein had burst within me, one word followed another, found its proper place, adapted itself to the situation, scene piled upon scene, the action unfolded, one retort after another welled up in my mind. I was enjoying myself immensely. Thoughts came to me so rapidly and continued to flow so abundantly that I lost a whole host of delicate details, because my pencil could not keep up with them, and yet I went as fast as I could, my hand in constant motion, I did not lose a minute. The sentences continued to well up within me, I was pregnant with my subject."

Apollinaire asserted that Chirico's first paintings were done under the influence of cenesthesic disorders (migraines, colics, etc.).

[9] I believe more and more in the infallibility of my thought with respect to myself, and this is too fair. Nonetheless, with this *thought-writing*, where one is at the mercy of the first outside distraction, "ebullutions" can occur. it would be inexcusable for us to pretend otherwise. By definition, thought is strong, and incapable of catching itself in error. The blame for these obvious weaknesses must be placed on suggestions that come to it from without.

above all is their *extreme degree of immediate absurdity*, the quality of this absurdity, upon closer scrutiny, being to give way to everything admissible, everything legitimate in the world: the disclosure of a certain number of properties and of facts no less objective, in the final analysis, than the others.

In homage to Guillaume Apollinaire, who had just died and who, on several occasions, seemed to us to have followed a discipline of this kind, without however having sacrificed to it any mediocre literary means, Soupault and I baptized the new mode of pure expression which we had at our disposal and which we wished to pass on to our friends, by the name of SURREALISM. I believe that there is no point today in dwelling any further on this word and that the meaning we gave it initially has generally prevailed over its Apollinarian sense. To be even fairer, we could probably have taken over the word SUPERNATURALISM employed by Gérard de Nerval in his dedication to the *Filles de feu*.[10] It appears, in fact, that Nerval possessed to a tee the spirit with which we claim a kinship, Apollinaire having possessed, on the contrary, naught but *the letter*, still imperfect, of Surrealism, having shown himself powerless to give a valid theoretical idea of it. Here are two passages by Nerval which seem to me to be extremely significant in this respect:

I am going to explain to you, my dear Dumas, the phenomenon of which you have spoken a short while ago. There are, as you know, certain storytellers who cannot invent without identifying with the characters their imagination has dreamt up. You may recall how convincingly our old friend Nodier used to tell how it had been his misfortune during the Revolution to be guillotined; one became so completely convinced of what he was saying that one began to wonder how he had managed to have his head glued back on.

...And since you have been indiscreet enough to quote one of the sonnets composed in this SUPERNATURALISTIC dream-state, as the Germans would call it, you will have to hear them all. You will find them at the end of the volume. They are hardly any more obscure than Hegel's metaphysics or Swedenborg's MEMORABILIA, and would lose their charm if they were explained, if such were possible; at least admit the worth of the expression....[11]

Those who might dispute our right to employ the term SURREALISM in the very special sense that we understand it are being extremely dishonest, for there can be no doubt that this word had no currency before we came along. Therefore, I am defining it once and for all:

SURREALISM, *n.* Psychic automatism in its pure state, by which one proposes to express—verbally, by means of the written word, or in any other manner—the actual functioning of thought. Dictated by thought, in the absence of any control exercised by reason, exempt from any aesthetic or moral concern.

[10]And also by Thomas Carlyle in *Sartor Resartus* ([Book III] Chapter VIII, "Natural Supernaturalism"), 1833–34.

[11]See also *L'Idéoréalisme* by Saint-Pol-Roux.

ENCYCLOPEDIA. *Philosophy.* Surrealism is based on the belief in the superior reality of certain forms of previously neglected associations, in the omnipotence of dream, in the disinterested play of thought. It tends to ruin once and for all all other psychic mechanisms and to substitute itself for them in solving all the principal problems of life. . . .

The theater, philosophy, science, criticism would all succeed in finding their bearings there. I hasten to add that future Surrealist techniques do not interest me.

Far more serious, in my opinion[12]—I have intimated it often enought—are the applications of Surrealism to action. To be sure, I do not believe in the prophetic nature of the Surrealist word. "It is the oracle, the things I say,"[13] Yes, *as much as I like*, but what of the oracle itself?[14] Men's piety does not fool me. The Surrealist voice that shook Cumae, Dodona, and Delphi is nothing more than the voice which dictates my less irascible speeches to me. My *time* must not be its time, why should this voice help me resolve the childish problem of my destiny? I pretend, unfortunately, to act in a world where, in order to take into account its

---

[12]Whatever reservations I may be allowed to make concerning responsibility in general and the medico-legal considerations which determine an individual's degree of responsibility—complete responsibility, irresponsiblity, limited responsibility (sic)—however, difficult it may be for me to accept the principle of any kind of responsibility, I would like to know how the first punishable offenses, the Surrealist character of which will be clearly apparent, will be *judged*. Will the accused be acquitted, or will he merely be given the benefit of the doubt because of extenuating circumstances? It's a shame that the violation of the laws governing the Press is today scarcely repressed, for if it were not we would soon see a trial of this sort: the accused has published a book which is an outrage to public decency. Several of his "most respected and honorable" fellow citizens have lodged a complaint against him, and he is also charged with slander and libel. There are also all sorts of other charges against him, such as insulting and defaming the army, inciting to murder, rape, etc. The accused, moreover, wastes no time in agreeing with the accusers in "stigmatizing" most of the ideas expressed. His only defense is claiming that he does not consider himself to be the author of his book, said book being no more and no less than a Surrealist concoction which precludes any question of merit or lack of merit on the part of the person who signs it; further, that all he has done is copy a document without offering any opinion thereon, and that he is at least as foreign to the accused text as is the presiding judge himself.

What is true for the publication of a book will also hold true for a whole host of other acts as soon as Surrealist methods begin to enjoy widespread favor. When that happens, a new morality must be substituted for the prevailing morality, the souce of all our trials and tribulations.

[13]Rimbaud.

[14]Still, STILL. . . . We must absolutely get to the bottom of this. Today, June 8, 1924, about one o'clock, the voice whispered to me: "Béthune, Béthune." What did it mean? I have never been to Béthune, and have only the vaguest notion as to where it is located on the map of France. Béthune evokes nothing for me, not even a scene from *The Three Musketeers.* I should have left for Béthune, where perhaps there was something awaiting me; that would have been too simple, really. Someone told me they had read in a book by Chesterton about a detective who, in order to find someone he is looking for in a certain city, simply scoured from roof to cellar the houses which, from the outside, seemed somehow abnormal to him, were it only in some slight detail. This system is as good as any other.

Similarly, in 1919, Soupault went into any number of impossible buildings to ask the concierge whether Philippe Soupault did in fact live there. He would not have been surprised, I suspect, by an affirmative reply. He would have gone and knocked on his door.

suggestions, I would be obliged to resort to two kinds of interpreters, one to translate its judgments for me, the other, impossible to find, to transmit to my fellow men whatever sense I could make out of them. This world, in which I endure what I endure (don't go see) this modern world, I mean, what the devil do you want me to do with it? Perhaps the Surrealist voice will be stilled, I have given up trying to keep track of those who have disappeared. I shall no longer enter into, however, briefly, the marvelous detailed description of my years and my days. I shall be like Nijinski who was taken last year to the Russian ballet and did not realize what spectacle it was he was seeing. I shall be alone, very alone within myself, indifferent to all the world's ballets. What I have done, what I have left undone, I give it to you.

And ever since I have had a great desire to show forbearance to scientific musing, however unbecoming, in the final analysis, from every point of view. Radios? Fine. Syphilis? If you like. Photography? I don't see any reason why not. The cinema? Three cheers for darkened rooms. War? Gave us a good laugh. The telephone? Hello. Youth? Charming white hair. Try to make me say thank you: "Thank you." Thank you. If the common man has a high opinion of things which properly speaking belong to the realm of the laboratory, it is because such research has resulted in the manufacture of a machine or the discovery of some serum which the man in the street views as affecting him directly. He is quite sure that they have been trying to improve his lot. I am not quite sure to what extent scholars are motivated by humanitarian aims, but it does not seem to me that this factor constitutes a very marked degree of goodness. I am, of course, referring to true scholars and not to the vulgarizers and popularizers of all sorts who take out patents. In this realm as in any other, I believe in the pure Surrealist joy of the man who, forewarned that all others before him have failed, refuses to admit defeat, sets off from whatever point he chooses, along any other path save a reasonable one, and arrives whenever he can. Such and such an image, by which he deems it opportune to indicate his progress and which may result, perhaps, in his receiving public acclaim, is to me, I must confess, a matter of complete indifference. Nor is the material with which he must perforce encumber himself; his glass tubes or my metallic feathers ... As for his method, I am willing to give it as much credit as I do mine. I have seen the inventor of the cutaneous plantar reflex at work; he manipulated his subjects without respite, it was much more than an "examination" he was employing; *it was obvious that he was following no set plan.* Here and there he formulated a remark; distantly, without nonetheless setting down his needle, while his hammer was never still. He left to others the futile task of curing patients. He was wholly consumed by and devoted to that sacred fever.

Surrealism, such as I conceive of it, asserts our complete *nonconformism* clearly enough so that there can be no question of translating it, at the trial of the real world, as evidence for the defense. It could, on the contrary, only serve to justify the complete state of distraction which we hope to achieve here below. Kant's absentmindedness regarding women, Pasteur's absentmindedness about "grapes," Curie's absentmindedness with respect to vehicles, are in this regard profoundly symptomatic. This world is only very relatively in tune with thought, and incidents of this kind are only the most obvious episodes of a war in which I am proud to be participating. Surrealism is the "invisible ray" which will one day enable us to win out over our opponents. "You are no longer trembling, carcass." This summer the roses are blue, the wood is of glass. The earth, draped in its verdant cloak, makes as little impression upon me as a ghost. It is living and ceasing to live that are imaginary solutions. Existence is elsewhere.

8/The Community of Man and Cosmos

introduction:
on relating to the divine

A good deal of philosophy of religion deals with various proofs for the existence of God and the philosophical criticism of those proofs. The philosophy is interesting, but as far as the existence of God is concerned, who cares? Blasphemy? Not so. Existence is not the issue, at least not in the sense of whether God exists the way the moon exists—as a particular entity apart from this world, accessible only to some.

Here again the fate of the underlying subject, or the "ghost in the machine," is instructive. In denying the existence of the ghost in the machine Ryle is not denying the existence of selves. Similarly, in denying the existence of God some theologians are not denying the dimension of divinity in our lives. They are simply saying that we have been relating to that divinity in the wrong way. We have been asking the wrong questions and expecting the wrong *kind* of answers. Even in talking about "God" we may be individualizing the dimension of the divine too much, just as we are inclined to simplify the many interrelated processes of the self into a single substance called the "subject." Consequently, Karl Barth, a leading twentieth-century theologian, writes that whenever we use the name "God" we are talking about the not-God. Our use of language fools us. We feel gratitude and we know how to give thanks only when we are giving thanks to someone. But that is *our* shortcoming. So in saying that the existence of God is not the point, contemporary theologians are not denying the appropriateness of the feeling of gratitude, only that we may be confused in the way we *express* our feelings.

Though a theological disinterest in the existence of God would seem to be a correlate of "death of God" theology, many modern theologians have denied that the existence of God is a central issue. As Martin Buber put it, after Auschwitz the question is not whether God exists but whether we can pray to him. Here again the question is one of the appropriate expression of our relationship to something divine.

Just as twentieth-century developments in esthetics reflect an upheaval in the Platonic-Christian metaphysical tradition, so twentieth-century theology reflects that same upheaval. If the quest for truth is no longer a quest for a reality that art can find *beneath* the veil of illusion, then theology no longer looks for a God who stands *above and apart from* worldly appearances. Just as Nietzsche anticipates Ryle's purge of the ghost in his claim that the soul is something about the body, so modern theology could claim that God is something about the world. In the language of theology this point is usually put using the terms 'immanence' and 'transcendence': the traditional, transcendent God existed beyond or apart from human experience. To say that God is immanent is to say that God pervades our experience. But the theology of immanence naturally finds it easier to talk about the divine aspect of experience and not about a God whose particularity as a "person" renders the pervasiveness of immanence difficult to conceive.

So rather than worship or thank or pray to a particular, transcendent God, modern theology tends to reflect upon the divine within experience. The so-called death of the transcendent God is not equivalent to a secularization of experience. Quite the contrary. If the transcendent God stood like a single star above the flat horizon of secular existence, the new theology might look to some like an atheism that simply banishes that star from the heavens. A more careful reading shows that the new theology replaces the old picture with a "vertical" existence stretching from the mysteries of demonology to the marvels of the sacred. The theology of immanence transfigures the horizon of secularism into a tower of sacred-profane existence. And this transfiguration has very little to do with the existence of God, except perhaps as a convenient but misleading way of talking about the sacredness of that existence.

This new way of talking about religion renders a continuity with the other issues of philosophy much more plausible. In talking about religion we are not talking about any new entities, but about a new way of seeing the same things we have been talking about all along. It almost sounds like esthetics. And certainly some of the language of the Bible suggests the appropriateness of this new way: "those who have eyes to see..." Thus the question of belief or faith becomes a question of the mode of one's relationship to experience and not one of the existence of some object that may or may not be encountered within or beyond experience. Consequently, the whole grammar of the terms 'belief' and 'faith' tends to be misleading, since we usually take belief as belief *in* something and faith as faith *in* something, where the something is just the sort of object which the theology of immanence has rejected. To use Ryle's example of a category-mistake, if you have seen all the particular buildings of a university and then ask to see the university, must you have faith in the university once you have been told you cannot see it the way you can see its buildings? To relate to the university is to relate to what goes on in its buildings. What about someone who claims to have faith in the university but never goes to classes? How is that person like many who profess belief in God?

The turn to eastern religions is consistent with the new religious spirit because Buddhism and Taoism are in general less preoccupied with God than are the western religions. The eastern religions place a greater emphasis on the self and those states of consciousness and modes of activity that put one in relation to the cosmos. Yet we could hardly accuse the eastern religions of secularism; religious experience is a central element in their path to enlightenment. What is needed is a definition of the religious that does not depend on God for its meaning. Then it will be clear that a denial of transcendent Gods is not a denial of religion.

SØREN KIERKEGAARD *(1813–1855)*

Søren Kierkegaard lived and died in Denmark, during the years 1813 to 1855, to be precise. Yet he would be the first to point out the paradox of such precision. What does such objective precision matter, measured against his contemporaneity as perhaps the first truly existentialist philosopher and his quest for an eternal happiness against which historical dates seem irrelevant? Kierkegaard's life was dominated by the most intense experiences of paradox. He broke off an engagement with a girl he loved and then suffered as he saw her quickly take another man. His writings are filled with images of paradox: the king who loves a peasant girl but knows that he cannot appear to her as the king without foredooming all hopes of a loving relationship; the mother who blackens her breast to wean the baby she cherishes. Always in the background of Kierkegaard's tortured and passionate thought looms the specter of paradox: I must, but I cannot. And this paradox is nowhere more intense than in Kierkegaard's relation to God.

Disgusted by the ease with which his contemporaries paraded into church, Kierkegaard was at pains to point out the follies of popular theology. Kierkegaard believed passionately, which to him was the only way to believe. Otherwise one was simply holding opinions about objective truths, and religion has little to do with objective truths. Kierkegaard held in contempt the calm assurances concerning the completeness of the "system" advertised by the Danish Hegelians. Against dialectical mediations of extremes, Kierkegaard demanded his readers to face radical choices—one of his most famous books is titled Either/Or.

Reading Kierkegaard is difficult. His language is perfectly intelligible—indeed he is a master stylist—but he poses alternatives that are difficult to accept, which was precisely his intention. It is hard to accept the apparent irrationalism of his leap of faith, to accept a subjectivism that, in the extreme form Kierkegaard develops it, seems a close cousin to a socially and spiritually destructive individualism. Yet I keep reading Kierkegaard and try to accommodate his insights. I sweep away his objections to the Danish Hegelians with the Hegelian reflection that Kierkegaard's thought is the next important turn in the dialectic after Hegel synthesized its progress up to the advent of Kierkegaard. Kierkegaard then becomes the subjective negation of the objective totality in Hegel's dialectic, symbolizing that part in each of us that must ask, "So what?" What is it to me, an existing individual, that all the relationships in the cosmos have been objectively drawn and understood? How do these "truths" relate to me? And then, of course, a synthesis between Kierkegaardian subjectivism and Hegelian objectivism should follow. But before we can proceed to that synthesis, Kierkegaard is there crying out, "I will not be synthesized! I will not be mediated! If you synthesize me with Hegel it cannot be me you have synthesized!" So we are thrust back into Kierkegaard's finality of objective uncertainty. And perhaps this objective uncertainty is the only legitimate synthesis. Certainly Kierkegaard is the last one to be offering us objective truths; he leaves the questions relentlessly up to the reader.

In order to do battle with Kierkegaard's demands, think about some previous essays as you read Kierkegaard. Kiekegaard's essay can help formulate a real differ-

ence between possessive individualism on the one hand and what I still think we can call an objective relativism. Here Kierkegaard's contribution is to make us see that truths must relate to the subject, even if they are relative to more than the subject. Even the most complete system of self-awareness is always seen from some perspective. If we lose sight of the perspective, the existing individual, we fall into error.

Truth Is Subjectivity

When the question of truth is raised in an objective manner, reflection is directed objectively to the truth, as an object to which the knower is related. Reflection is not focussed upon the relationship, however, but upon the question of whether it is the truth to which the knower is related. If only the object to which he is related is the truth, the subject is accounted to be in the truth. When the question of the truth is raised subjectively, reflection is directed subjectively to the nature of the individual's relationship; if only the mode of this relationship is in the truth, the individual is in the truth even if he should happen to be thus related to what is not true.[1] Let us take as an example the knowledge of God. Objectively, reflection is directed to the problem of whether this object is the true God; subjectively, reflection is directed to the question whether the individual is related to a something *in such a manner* that his relationship is in truth a God-relationship. On which side is the truth now to be found? Ah, may we not here resort to a mediation, and say: It is on neither side, but in the mediation of both? Excellently well said, provided we might have it explained how an existing individual manages to be in a state of mediation. For to be in a state of mediation is to be finished, while to exist is to become. Nor can an existing individual be in two places at the same time—he cannot be an identity of subject and object. When he is nearest to being in two places at the same time he is in passion; but passion is momentary, and passion is also the highest expression of subjectivity.

The existing individual who chooses to pursue the objective way enters upon the entire approximation-process by which it is proposed to bring God to light objectively. But this is in all eternity impossible, because God is a subject, and therefore exists only for subjectivity in inwardness. The existing individual who chooses the subjective way apprehends instantly the entire dialectical difficulty involved in having to use some time, perhaps a long time, in finding God objectively; and he feels this dialectical difficulty in all its painfulness, because every moment is wasted in which he does not have God.[2] That very instant he has

---

[1]The reader will observe that the question here is about essential truth, or about the truth which is essentially related to existence, and that it is precisely for the sake of clarifying it as inwardness or as subjectivity that this contrast is drawn.

[2]In this manner God certainly becomes a postulate, but not in the otiose manner in which this word is commonly understood. It becomes clear rather that the only way in which an existing individual comes into relation with God, is when the dialectical contradiction brings his passion to the point of despair, and helps him to embrace God with the "category of despair" (faith). Then the postulate is so far from being arbitrary that it is precisely a life-necessity. It is then not so much that God is a postulate, as that the existing individual's postulation of God is a necessity.

God, not by virtue of any objective deliberation, but by virtue of the infinite passion of inwardness. The objective inquirer, on the other hand, is not embarrassed by such dialectical difficulties as are involved in devoting an entire period of investigation to finding God—since it is possible that the inquirer may die tomorrow; and if he lives he can scarcely regard God as something to be taken along if convenient, since God is precisely that which one takes *a tout prix*, which in the understanding of passion constitutes the true inward relationship to God.

It is at this point, so difficult dialectically, that the way swings off for everyone who knows what it means to think, and to think existentially; which is something very different from sitting at a desk and writing about what one has never done, something very different from writing *de omnibus dubitandum* [doubt everything] and at the same time being as credulous existentially as the most sensuous of men. Here is where the way swings off, and the change is marked by the fact that while objective knowledge rambles comfortably on by way of the long road of approximation without being impelled by the urge of passion, subjective knowledge counts every delay a deadly peril, and the decision so infinitely important and so instantly pressing that it is as if the opportunity had already passed.

Now when the problem is to reckon up on which side there is most truth, whether on the side of one who seeks the true God objectively, and pursues the approximate truth of the God-idea; or on the side of one who, driven by the infinite passion of his need of God, feels an infinite concern for his own relationship to God in truth (and to be at one and the same time on both sides equally, is as we have noted not possible for an existing individual, but is merely the happy delusion of an imaginary I-am-I): the answer cannot be in doubt for anyone who has not been demoralized with the aid of science. If one who lives in the midst of Christendom goes up to the house of God, the house of the true God, with the true conception of God in his knowledge, and prays, but prays in a false spirit; and one who lives in an idolatrous community prays with the entire passion of the infinite, although his eyes rest upon the image of an idol: where is there most truth? The one prays in truth to God though he worships an idol; the other prays falsely to the true God, and hence worships in fact an idol.

When one man investigates objectively the problem of immortality, and another embraces an uncertainty with the passion of the infinite: where is there most truth, and who has the greater certainty? The one has entered upon a never-ending approximation, for the certainty of immortality lies precisely in the subjectivity of the individual; the other is immortal, and fights for his immortality by struggling with the uncertainty. Let us consider Socrates. Nowadays everyone dabbles in a few proofs; some have several such proofs, others fewer. But Socrates! He puts the question objectively in a problematic manner: *if* there is an immortality. He must therefore be accounted a doubter in comparison with one of our modern thinkers with the three proofs? By no means. On this "if" he risks his entire life, he has the courage to meet death, and he has with the passion of the infinite so determined the pattern of his life that it must be found acceptable—*if* there is an immortality. Is any better proof capable of being given for the immortality of the soul? But those who have the three proofs do not at all determine their lives in conformity therewith; if there is an immortality it must feel disgust over their manner of life: can any better refutation be given of the three proofs? The bit of uncertainty that Socrates had, helped him because he himself contributed the passion of the infinite; the three proofs that the others have do not profit them at all, because they are dead to spirit and enthusiasm, and their three proofs, in lieu of proving anything else, prove just this. A young girl may enjoy all the sweetness of love on the basis of what is merely a weak hope that she is beloved, because she rests everything on this weak hope; but many a wedded matron more than once subjected to the strongest expressions of love, has in so far indeed had proofs, but strangely enough has not enjoyed *quod erat demonstrandum* [that which was to be proven]. The Socratic ignorance, which Socrates held fast with the entire passion of his inwardness, was thus an expression for the principle that the eternal truth is related to an existing individual, and that this truth must therefore be a paradox for him as long as he exists; and yet it is possible that there was more truth in the Socratic ignorance as it was in him, than in the entire objective truth of the System, which flirts with what the times demand and accommodates itself to *Privatdocents*.

The objective accent falls on WHAT is said, the subjective accent on HOW it is said. The distinction holds even in the aesthetic realm, and receives definite expression in the principle that what is in itself true may in the mouth of such and such a person become untrue. In these times this distinction is particularly worthy of notice, for if we wish to express in a single sentence the difference between ancient times and our own, we should doubtless have to say: "In ancient times only an individual here and there knew the truth; now all know it, except that the inwardness of its appropriation stands in an inverse relationship to the extent of its dissemination.[3] Aesthetically the contradiction that truth becomes untruth in this or that person's mouth, is best construed comically: In the ethico-religious sphere, accent is again on the "how." But this is not to be understood as referring to demeanor, expression, or the like; rather it refers to the relationship sustained by the existing individual, in his own existence, to the content of his utterance. Objectively the interest is focussed merely on the thought-content, subjectively on the inwardness. At its maximum this inward "how" is the passion of the infinite, and the passion of the infinite is the truth. But the passion of the infinite is precisely subjectivity, and thus subjectivity becomes the truth. Objectively

---

[3]*Stages on Life's Way*, Note on p. 426. Though ordinarily not wishing an expression of opinion on the part of reviewers, I might at this point almost desire it, provided such opinions, so far from flattering me, amounted to an assertion of the daring truth that what I say is something that everybody knows, even every child, and that the cultured know infinitely much better. If it only stands fast that everyone knows it, my standpoint is in order, and I shall doubtless make shift to manage with the unity of the comic and the tragic. If there were anyone who did not know it I might perhaps be in danger of being dislodged from my position of equilibrium by the thought that I might be in a position to communicate to someone the needful preliminary knowledge. It is just this which engages my interest so much, this that the cultured are accustomed to say: that everyone knows what the highest is. This was not the case in paganism, or in Judaism, nor in the seventeen centuries of Christianity. Hail to the nineteenth century! Everyone knows it. What progress has been made since the time when only a few knew it. To make up for this, perhaps, we must assume that no one nowadays does it.

there is no infinite decisiveness, and hence it is objectively in order to annul the difference between good and evil; together with the principle of contradiction, and therewith also the infinite difference between the true and the false. Only in subjectivity is there decisiveness, to seek objectivity is to be in error. It is the passion of the infinite that is the decisive factor and not its content, for its content is precisely itself. In this manner subjectivity and the subjective "how" constitute the truth.

By the "how" which is thus subjectively accentuated precisely because the subject is an existing individual, is also subject to a dialectic with respect to time. In the passionate moment of decision, where the road swings away from objective knowledge, it seems as if the infinite decision were thereby realized. But in the same moment the existing individual finds himself in the temporal order, and the subjective "how" is transformed into a striving, a striving which receives indeed its impulse and a repeated renewal from the decisive passion of the infinite, but is nevertheless a striving.

When subjectivity is the truth, the conceptual determination of the truth must include an expression for the antithesis to objectivity, a memento of the fork in the road where the way swings off; this expression will at the same time serve as an indication of the tension of the subjective inwardness. Here is such a definition of truth: *An objective uncertainty held fast in an appropriation-process of the most passionate inwardness is the truth*, the highest truth attainable for an *existing* individual. At the point where the way swings off (and where this is cannot be specified objectively, since it is a matter of subjectivity), there objective knowledge is placed in abeyance. Thus the subject merely has, objectively, the uncertainty; but it is this which precisely increases the tension of that infinite passion which constitutes his inwardness. The truth is precisely the venture which chooses an objective uncertainty with the passion of the infinite. I contemplate the order of nature in the hope of finding God, and I see omnipotence and wisdom; but I also see much else that disturbs my mind and excites anxiety. The sum of all this is an objective uncertainty. But it is for this very reason that the inwardness becomes as intense as it is, for it embraces this objective uncertainty with the entire passion of the infinite. In the case of a mathematical proposition the objectivity is given, but for this reason the truth of such a proposition is also an indifferent truth.

But the above definition of truth is an equivalent expression for faith. Without risk there is no faith. Faith is precisely the contradiction between the infinite passion of the individual's inwardness and the objective uncertainty. If I am capable of grasping God objectively, I do not believe, but precisely because I cannot do this I must believe. If I wish to preserve myself in faith I must constantly be intent upon holding fast the objective uncertainty, so as to remain out upon the deep, over seventy thousand fathoms of water, still preserving my faith. . . .

Let us now call the untruth of the individual *Sin*. Viewed eternally he cannot be sin, nor can he be eternally presupposed as having been in sin. By coming into existence therefore (for the beginning was that subjectivity is untruth), he becomes a sinner. He is not born as a sinner in the sense that he is presupposed as being a sinner before he is born, but he is born in sin and as a sinner. This we might call *Original Sin*. But if existence has in this manner acquired a power over him, he is prevented from taking himself back into the eternal by way of recollection. If it was paradoxical to posit the eternal truth in relationship to an existing individual, it is now absolutely paradoxical to posit it in relationship to such an individual as we have here defined. But the more difficult it is made for him to take himself out of existence by way of recollection, the more profound is the inwardness that his existence may have in existence; and when it is made impossible for him, when he is held so fast in existence that the back door of recollection is forever closed to him, then his inwardness will be the most profound possible. But let us never forget that the Socratic merit was to stress the fact that the knower is an existing individual; for the more difficult the matter becomes, the greater the temptation to hasten along the easy road of speculation, away from fearful dangers and crucial decisions, to the winning of renown and honors and property, and so forth. If even Socrates understood the dubiety of taking himself speculatively out of existence back into the eternal, although no other difficulty confronted the existing individual except that he existed, and that existing was his essential task, now it is impossible. Forward he must, backward he cannot go.

Subjectivity is the truth. By virtue of the relationship subsisting between the eternal truth and the existing individual, the paradox came into being. Let us now go further, let us suppose that the eternal essential truth is itself a paradox. How does the paradox come into being? By putting the eternal essential truth into juxtaposition with existence. Hence when we posit such a conjunction within the truth itself, the truth becomes a paradox. The eternal truth has come into being in time: this is the paradox. If in accordance with the determinations just posited, the subject is prevented by sin from taking himself back into the eternal, now he need not trouble himself about this; for now the eternal essential truth is not behind him but in front of him, through its being in existence or having existed, so that if the individual does not existentially and in existence lay hold of the truth, he will never lay hold of it.

Existence can never be more sharply accentuated than by means of these determinations. The evasion by which speculative philosophy attempts to recollect itself out of existence has been made impossible. With reference to this, there is nothing for speculation to do except to arrive at an understanding of this impossibility; every speculative attempt which insists on being speculative shows *eo ipso* that it has not understood it. The individual may thrust all this away from him, and take refuge in speculation; but it is impossible first to accept it, and then to revoke it by means of speculation, since it is definitely calculated to prevent speculation.

When the eternal truth is related to an existing individual it becomes a paradox. The paradox repels in the inwardness of the existing individual, through the objective uncertainty and the corresponding Socratic ignorance. But since the paradox is not in the first instance itself paradoxical (but only in its relationship to the existing individual), it does not repel with a sufficient intensive inwardness. For without risk there is no faith, and the greater the risk the greater the faith; the more objective security the less inwardness (for inwardness is precisely subjectivity), and the less objective security the more profound the possible inwardness.

When the paradox is paradoxical in itself, it repels the individual by virtue of its absurdity, and the corresponding passion of inwardness is faith. But subjectivity, inwardness, is the truth; for otherwise we have forgotten what the merit of the Socratic position is. But there can be no stronger expression for inwardness than when the retreat out of existence into the eternal by way of recollection is impossible; and when, with truth confronting the individual as a paradox, gripped in the anguish and pain of sin, facing the tremendous risk of the objective insecurity, the individual believes. But without risk no faith, not even the Socratic form of faith, much less the form of which we here speak.

When Socrates believed that there was a God, he held fast to the objective uncertainty with the whole passion of his inwardness, and it is precisely in this contradiction and in this risk, that faith is rooted. Now it is otherwise. Instead of the objective uncertainty, there is here a certainty, namely, that objectively it is absurd; and this absurdity, held fast in the passion of inwardness, is faith. The Socratic ignorance is as a witty jest in comparison with the earnestness of facing the absurd; and the Socratic existential inwardness is as Greek light-mindedness in comparison with the grave strenuosity of faith.

What now is the absurd? The absurd is—that the eternal truth has come into being in time, that God has come into being, has been born, has grown up, and so forth, precisely like any other individual human being, quite indistinguishable from other individuals. For every assumption of immediate recognizability is pre-Socratic paganism. . . .

The immediate relationship to God is paganism, and only after the breach has taken place can there be any question of a true God-relationship. But this breach is precisely the first act of inwardness in the direction of determining the truth as inwardness. Nature is, indeed, the work of God, but only the handiwork is directly present, not God. Is not this to behave, in His relationship to the individual, like an elusive author who nowhere sets down his result in large type, or gives it to the reader beforehand in a preface? And why is God elusive? Precisely because He is the truth, and by being elusive desires to keep men from error. The observer of nature does not have a result immediately set before him, but must by himself be at pains to find it, and thereby the direct relationship is broken. But this breach is precisely the act of self-activity, the irruption of inwardness, the first determination of the truth as inwardness.

Or is not God so unnoticeable, so secretly present in His works, that a man might very well live his entire life, be married, become known and respected as citizen, father, and captain of the hunt, without ever having discovered God in His works, and without ever having received any impression of the infinitude of the ethical, because he helped himself out with what constitutes an analogy to the speculative confusion of the ethical with the historical process, in that he helped himself out by having recourse to the customs and traditions prevailing in the town where he happened to live? As a mother admonishes her child when it sets off for a party: "Now be sure to behave yourself, and do as you see the other well-behaved children do,"—so he might manage to live by conducting himself as he sees others do. He would never do anything first, and he would never have any opinion which he did not first know that others had; for this "others" would be for him the first. Upon extraordinary occasions he would behave as when at a banquet a dish is served, and one does not know how it should be eaten: he would look around until he saw how the others did it, and so forth. Such a man might perhaps know many things, perhaps even know the System by rote; he might be an inhabitant of a Christian country, and bow his head whenever the name of God was mentioned; he would perhaps also see God in nature when in company with others who saw God; he would be a pleasant society man—and yet he would have been deceived by the direct nature of his relationship to the truth, to the ethical, and to God.

If one were to delineate such a man experimentally, he would be a satire upon the human. Essentially it is the God-relationship that makes a man a man, and yet he lacked this. No one would hesitate, however, to regard him as a real man (for the absence of inwardness is not directly apparent); in reality he would constitute a sort of marionette, very deceptively imitating everything human—even to the extent of having children by his wife. At the end of his life, one would have to say that one thing had escaped him: his consciousness had taken no note of God. If God could have permitted a direct relationship, he would doubtless have taken notice. If God, for example, had taken on the figure of a very rare and tremendously large green bird, with a red beak, sitting in a tree on the mound, and perhaps even whistling in an unheard of manner—then the society man would have been able to get his eyes open, and for the first time in his life would be first.

All paganism consists in this, that God is related to man directly, as the obviously extraordinary to the astonished observer. But the spiritual relationship to God in the truth, i.e. in inwardness, is conditioned by a prior irruption of inwardness, which corresponds to the divine elusiveness that God has absolutely nothing obvious about Him, that God is so far from being obvious that He is invisible. It cannot immediately occur to anyone that He exists, although His invisibility is again His omnipresence. An omnipresent person is one that is everywhere to be seen, like a policeman, for example: how deceptive then, that an omnipresent being should be recognizable precisely by being invisible,[4] only and alone recognizable by this trait, since his visibility would annul his omnipresence. The relationship between omnipresence and invisibility is like the relation between mystery and revelation. The mystery is the expression for the fact that the revelation is a revelation in the stricter sense, so that the mystery is the only trait by which it is known; for otherwise a revelation would be something very like a policeman's omnipresence.

---

[4]To point out how deceptive the rhetorical can be, I shall here show how one might rhetorically perhaps produce an effect upon a listener, in spite of the fact that what was said was dialectically a regress. Let a pagan religious speaker say that here on earth, God's temples are really empty, but (and now begins the rhetorical) in heaven, where all is more perfect, where water is air and air is ether, there are also temples and sanctuaries for the gods, but the difference is that the gods really dwell in these temples: then we have here a dialectical regress in the proposition that God really dwells in the temple, for the fact that He does not so dwell in an expression for the spiritual relationship to the invisible. But rhetorically it produces an effect. I have as a matter of fact, had in view a definite passage by a Greek author, whom I do not, however, wish to cite.

FRIEDRICH NIETZSCHE *(1844–1900)*

Many of us, when we first read Friedrich Nietzsche, misread him. The idiosyncratic German philosopher lends himself to misinterpretation, as his use by the Nazis bears evidence. At times he sounds like a bitter old man who lashes out at whatever feelings he is incapable of having. But a more attentive reading shows Nietzsche to be a more discerning judge than the cantankerous cynic we may first take him to be. For instance, he does not condemn everything about Christianity, just most things. He distinguishes various grades of authenticity in the Christian experience. Christ comes off very well, the apostles less well, the priests poorly, and those in the pews are the butt of his worst scorn. Nietzsche favors leaders rather than followers, as in his respect for Christ despite his scouring criticisms of Christians. He does not regard Christ as the literal son of God, but he does accept the importance of the symbolism of father and son. The father, he says, symbolizes the feeling of "the transfiguration of all things," while the son symbolizes the entry into that feeling.

Nietzsche experienced the transfiguration of all things, the perfection of the world in its totality despite the wonder and disgust aroused by its parts taken separately. In the fourth part of his famous Thus Spake Zarathustra *Nietzsche includes what can only be interpreted as the record of a religious or mystic experience, which he could hardly have described so well without first-hand experience. While Nietzsche was really the first to proclaim openly the "death of God," his reason was hardly to argue that the earth was as flat as the mediocrity of enlightenment secularism. He removes "God above" in order to see man above. His world is an "order of rank," a vertical order of sacredness. And Christ is clearly one of the men above.*

The wonder is that man could so completely misread the "good news" that he would take a transfigured way of living and turn it into directions for a way of dying. Like Kierkegaard, Nietzsche is amazed at history's obscure ironies. But unlike Kierkegaard he does not see those ironies as God's way of purposely covering his tracks to produce the objective uncertainty that is the condition for faith. Nietzsche sees man's blindness simply as man's blindness. He accounts for the blindness: cowardice, lack of honesty, and a perversion of the will to power.

It is, by the way, best to interpret "the will to power" with care. The words do not mean what we usually mean when we say someone is power hungry. Nietzsche offers a psychological analysis of those who lust after power over others as if that power would somehow give them a justification for themselves they otherwise lack. The phrase "will to power" is a coathook on which Nietzsche hangs everything he values. It plays the role of an undefinable first principle in his thought. You must come to an understanding of his will to power; do not work from your own understanding of "will to power" in order to pass judgment on Nietzsche's use of the phrase, because your initial understanding could not possibly have all the connotations Nietzsche eventually attaches to this centerpole of his thought. Eventually the phrase becomes almost equivalent to a principle of life, or a "will to willing," as Martin Heidegger puts it in his two-volume study of Nietzsche's posthumously published The Will to Power.

Try to see what follows the connotation Nietzsche attaches to the "will to power" through his use of the concept. Consider also the force of Nietzsche's evaluations. He condemns Schopenhauer as a nihilist, as a nay-sayer to life. But many of Nietzsche's judgments are negative. How does the descriptive/evaluative distinction discussed in introducing Schopenhauer work out in relation to Nietzsche? Both these nineteenth-century Germans write in a polemical style and both ask and require an intense vigilance from the reader.

The Antichrist

7

Christianity is called the religion of *pity*. Pity stands opposed to the tonic emotions which heighten our vitality: it has a depressing effect. We are deprived of strength when we feel pity. The loss of strength which suffering as such inflicts on life is still further increased and multiplied by pity. Pity makes suffering contagious. Under certain circumstances, it may engender a total loss of life and vitality out of all proportion to the magnitude of the cause (as in the case of the death of the Nazarene). That is the first consideration, but there is a more important one.

Suppose we measure pity by the value of the reactions it usually produces; then its perilous nature appears in an even brighter light. Quite in general, pity crosses the law of development, which is the law of *selection*. It preserves what is ripe for destruction; it defends those who have been disinherited and condemned by life; and by the abundance of the failures of all kinds which it keeps alive, it gives life itself a gloomy and questionable aspect.

Some have dared to call pity a virtue (in every *noble* ethic it is considered a weakness); and as if this were not enough, it has been made *the* virtue, the basis and source of all virtues. To be sure—and one should always keep this in mind— this was done by a philosophy that was nihilistic and had inscribed the *negation of life* upon its shield. Schopenhauer was consistent enough: pity negates life and renders it *more deserving of negation*.

Pity is the *practice* of nihilism. To repeat: this depressive and contagious instinct crosses those instincts which aim at the preservation of life and at the enhancement of its value. It multiplies misery and conserves all that is miserable, and is thus a prime instrument of the advancement of decadence: pity persuades men to *nothingness!* Of course, one does not say "nothingness" but "beyond" or "God," or "*true* life," or Nirvana, salvation, blessedness.

This innocent rhetoric from the realm of the religious-moral idiosyncrasy appears much less innocent as soon as we realize which tendency it is that here shrouds itself in sublime words: *hostility against life*. Schopenhauer was hostile to life; therefore pity became a virtue for him.

Aristotle, as is well known, considered pity a pathological and dangerous condition, which one would be well advised to attack now and then with a purge: he understood tragedy as a purge. From the standpoint of the instinct of life, a remedy certainly seems necessary for such a pathological and dangerous accumulation of pity as is represented by the case of Schopenhauer (and unfortunately by our entire literary and artistic decadence from St. Petersburg to Paris, from Tolstoi to Wagner)—to puncture it and make it *burst*.

In our whole unhealthy modernity there is nothing more unhealthy than Christian pity. To be physicians *here*, to be inexorable *here*, to wield the scalpel *here*—that is *our* part, that is *our* love of man, that is how *we* are philosophers, we *Hyperboreans*.

8

It is necessary to say whom we consider our antithesis: it is the theologians and whatever has theologians' blood in its veins—and that includes our whole philosophy.

Whoever has seen this catastrophe at close range or, better yet, been subjected to it and almost perished of it, will no longer consider it a joking matter (the freethinking of our honorable natural scientists and physiologists is, to my mind, a joke: they lack passion in these matters, they do not suffer them as their passion and martyrdom). This poisoning is much more extensive than is generally supposed: I have found the theologians' instinctive arrogance wherever anyone today considers himself an "idealist"—wherever a right is assumed, on the basis of some higher origin, to look at reality from a superior and foreign vantage point.

The idealist, exactly like the priest, holds all the great concepts in his hand (and not only in his hand!); he plays them out with a benevolent contempt for the "understanding," the "senses," "honors," "good living," and "science"; he considers all that *beneath* him, as so many harmful and seductive forces over which "the spirit" hovers in a state of pure for-itselfness—as if humility, chastity, poverty, or, in one word, *holiness*, had not harmed life immeasurably more than any horrors or vices. The pure spirit is the pure lie.

As long as the priest is considered a *higher* type of man—this *professional* negator, slanderer, and poisoner of life—there is no answer to the question: what *is* truth? For truth has been stood on its head when the conscious advocate of nothingness and negation is accepted as the representative of "truth."

9

Against this theologians' instinct I wage war; I have found its traces everywhere. Whoever has theologians' blood in his veins, sees all things in a distorted and dishonest perspective to begin with. The pathos which develops out of this condition calls itself *faith:* closing one's eyes to oneself once and for all, lest one suffer the sight of incurable falsehood. This faulty perspective on all things is elevated into a morality, a virtue, a holiness; the good conscience is tied to faulty vision; and no *other* perspective is conceded any further value once one's own has been made sacrosanct with the names of "God," "redemption," and "eternity." I have dug up the theologians' instinct everywhere: it is the most widespread, really *subterranean,* form of falsehood found on earth.

Whatever a theologian feels to be true *must* be false: this is almost a criterion of truth. His most basic instinct of self-preservation forbids him to respect reality at any point or even to let it get a word in. Wherever the theologians' instinct extends, *value judgments* have been stood on their heads and the concepts of "true" and "false" are of necessity reversed: whatever is most harmful to life is called "true"; whatever elevates it, enhances, affirms, justifies it, and makes it triumphant, is called "false." When theologians reach out for *power* through the "conscience" of princes (*or* of peoples), we need never doubt what really happens at bottom: the will to the end, the *nihilistic* will, wants power....

15

In Christianity neither morality nor religion has even a single point of contact with reality. Nothing but imaginary *causes* ("God," "soul," "ego," "spirit," "free will"—for that matter, "unfree will"), nothing but imaginery *effects* ("sin," "redemption," "grace," "punishment," "forgiveness of sins"). Intercourse between imaginary *beings* ("God," "spirits," "souls"); an imaginary *natural* science (anthropocentric; no trace of any concept of natural causes); an imaginary *psychology* (nothing but self-misunderstandings, interpretations of agreeable or disagreeable general feelings—for example, of the states of the *nervus sympathicus* —with the aid of the sign language of the religio-moral idiosyncrasy: "repentance," "pangs of conscience," "temptation by the devil," "the presence of God"); an imaginary *teleology* ("the kingdom of God," "the Last Judgment," "eternal life").

This *world of pure fiction* is vastly inferior to the world of dreams insofar as the latter *mirrors* reality, whereas the former falsifies, devalues, and negates reality. Once the concept of "nature" had been invented as the opposite of "God," "natural" had to become a synonym of "reprehensible": this whole world of fiction is rooted in *hatred* of the natural (of reality!); it is the expression of a profound vexation at the sight of reality.

But this explains everything. Who alone has good reason to lie his way out of reality? He who suffers from it. But to suffer from reality is to be a piece of reality that has come to grief. The preponderance of feelings of displeasure over feelings of pleasure is the cause of this fictitious morality and religion; but such a preponderance provides the very formula for decadence.

16

A critique of the *Christian conception of God* forces us to the same conclusion. A people that still believes in itself retains its own god. In him it reveres the conditions which let it prevail, its virtues: it projects its pleasure in itself, its feeling of power, into a being to whom one may offer thanks. Whoever is rich wants to give of his riches; a proud people needs a god: it wants to *sacrifice*. Under such conditions, religion is a form of thankfulness. Being thankful for himself, man needs a god. Such a god must be able to help and to harm, to be friend and enemy—he is admired whether good or destructive. The *anti-natural* castration of a god, to make him a god of the good alone, would here be contrary to everything desirable. The evil god is needed no less than the good god: after all, we do not owe our own existence to tolerance and humanitarianism.

What would be the point of a god who knew nothing of wrath, revenge, envy, scorn, cunning, and violence? who had perhaps never experienced the delightful *ardeurs* of victory and annihilation? No one would understand such a god: why have him then?

To be sure, when a people is perishing, when it feels how its faith in the future and its hope of freedom are waning irrevocably, when submission begins to appear to it as the prime necessity and it becomes aware of the virtues of the subjugated as the conditions of self-preservation, then its god *has to* change too. Now he becomes a sneak, timid and modest; he counsels "peace of soul," hate-no-more, forbearance, even "love" of friend and enemy. He moralizes constantly, he crawls into the cave of every private virtue, he becomes god for everyman, he becomes a private person, a cosmopolitan.

Formerly, he represented a people, the strength of a people, everything aggressive and power-thirsty in the soul of a people; now he is merely the good god.

Indeed, there is no other alternative for gods: *either* they are the will to power, and they remain a people's gods, *or* the incapacity for power, and then they necessarily become *good....*

33

In the whole psychology of the "evangel" the concept of guilt and punishment is lacking; also the concept of reward. "Sin"—any distance separating God and man—is abolished: *precisely this is the "glad tidings."* Blessedness is not promised, it is not tied to conditions: it is the only reality—the rest is a sign with which to speak of it.

The consequence of such a state projects itself into a new practice, the genuine evangelical practice. It is not a "faith" that distinguishes the Christian: the Christian *acts*, he is distinguished by acting *differently*; by not resisting, either in words or in his heart, those who treat him ill; by making no distinction between foreigner and native, between Jew and not-Jew ("the neighbor"—really the coreligionist, the Jew); by not growing angry with anybody, by not despising anybody; by not permitting himself to be seen or involved at courts of law ("not swearing"); by not divorcing his wife under any circumstances, not even if his wife has been proved unfaithful. All of this, at bottom one principle; all of this, consequences of one instinct.

The life of the Redeemer was nothing other than *this* practice—nor was his death anything else. He no longer required any formulas, any rites for his intercourse with God—not even prayer. He broke with the whole Jewish doctrine of repentance and reconciliation; he knows that it is only in the *practice* of life that one feels "divine," "blessed," "evangelical," at all times a "child of God." Not "repentance," not "prayer for forgiveness," are the ways to God: *only the evangelical practice* leads to God, indeed it *is* "God"! What was disposed of with the evangel was the Judiasm of the concepts of "sin," "forgiveness of sin," "faith," "redemption through faith"—the whole Jewish *ecclesiastical* doctrine was negated in the "glad tidings."

The deep instinct for how one must *live*, in order to feel oneself "in heaven," to feel "eternal," while in all other behavior one decidedly does *not* feel oneself "in heaven"—this alone is the psychological reality of "redemption." A new way of life, *not* a new faith.

34

If I understand anything about this great symbolist, it is that he accepted only *inner* realities as realities, as "truths"—that he understood the rest, everything natural, temporal, spatial, historical, only as signs, as occasions for parables. The concept of "the son of man" is not a concrete person who belongs in history, something individual and unique, but an "eternal" factuality, a psychological symbol redeemed from the concept of time. The same applies once again, and in the highest sense, to the *God* of this typical symbolist, to the "kingdom of God," to the "kingdom of heaven," to the "filiation of God." Nothing is more unchristian than the *ecclesiastical crudities* of a god as a person, of a "kingdom of God" which is to come, of a "kingdom of heaven" beyond, of a "son of God" as the second person in the Trinity. All this is—forgive the expression—like a fist in the eye—oh, in what an eye!—of the evangel—a *world-historical cynicism* in the derision of symbols. But what the signs "father" and "son" refer to is obvious—not to everyone, I admit: the word "son" expresses the *entry* into the over-all feeling of the transfiguration of all things (blessedness); the word "father" expresses *this feeling itself*, the feeling of eternity, the feeling of perfection. I am ashamed to recall what the church has made of this symbolism: Has it not placed an Amphitryon story at the threshold of the Christian "faith"? And a dogma of "immaculate conception" on top of that? *But with that it has maculated conception.*

The "kingdom of heaven" is a state of the heart—not something that is to come "above the earth" or "after death." The whole concept of natural death is lacking in the evangel: death is no bridge, no transition; it is lacking because it belongs to a wholly different, merely apparent world, useful only insofar as it furnishes signs. The "hour of death" is *no* Christian concept—an "hour," time, physical life and its crises do not even exist for the teacher of the "glad tidings." The "kingdom of God" is nothing that one expects; it has no yesterday and no day after tomorrow, it will not come in "a thousand years"—it is an experience of the heart; it is everywhere, it is nowhere.

35

This "bringer of glad tidings" died as he had lived, as he had taught—*not* to "redeem men" but to show how one must live. This practice is his legacy to mankind: his behavior before the judges, before the catchpoles, before the accusers and all kinds of slander and scorn—his behavior on the *cross*. He does not resist, he does not defend his right, he takes no step which might ward off the worst; on the contrary, he *provokes* it. And he begs, he suffers, he loves *with* those, *in* those, who do him evil. *Not* to resist, *not* to be angry, *not* to hold responsible— but to resist not even the evil one—to *love* him.

36

Only we, we spirits who have *become free*, have the presuppositions for understanding something that nineteen centuries have misunderstood: that integrity which, having become instinct and passion, wages war against the "holy lie" even more than against any other lie. Previous readers were immeasurably far removed from our loving and cautious neutrality, from that discipline of the spirit which alone makes possible the unriddling of such foreign, such tender things: with impudent selfishness they always wanted only their own advantage; out of the opposite of the evangel the church was constructed.

If one were to look for signs that an ironical divinity has its fingers in the great play of the world, one would find no small support in the *tremendous question mark* called Christianity. Mankind lies on its knees before the opposite of that which was the origin, the meaning, the *right* of the evangel; in the concept of "church" it has pronounced holy precisely what the "bringer of the glad tidings" felt to be *beneath* and *behind* himself—one would look in vain for a greater example of *world-historical irony*.

transition: on believing

Whether or not the existence of God is an issue, believing or not believing remains one. Even though the star symbolizing a separate God be struck from the heavens, there remains the question of regarding the world as the flatland of secularism or the transfigured world of sacred and profane. If there is a religiousness that does not derive its meaning from a God, then a problem remains whether or not to believe that reality is indeed sacred in a sense that does not depend on divine grace. What grounds might we have for such a belief? What would be the logic for deciding such an issue? Must it be a completely subjective decision, a totally irrational leap to faith, or does it make sense to weigh the alternatives on some sort of scale?

The following two essays relate to the rightness or wrongness, reasonableness or unreasonableness, of belief in a sacred reality. A common theme in each essay is the role of evidence. Is the question one for which more evidence would be helpful in making a decision? What kind of evidence would be relevant? Or is the question of religious belief based on evidence at all?

Just as Kierkegaard unfolded the objective ambiguity of the religious question, so the following authors acknowledge the unavailability of knock-down-drag-out arguments based on incorrigible evidence. But a common theme is agreement on certain questions that *must* be decided, whether or not one has all the means at one's disposal for making a truly objective or scientific decision. To get a feel for the kind of questions these might be, including the question of religious belief, think again about self-identity. As Sartre and Erikson argued, the self is to some extent a self-creation. The logic of this self-creation is not unlike the logic of religious belief. One faces the same objective ambiguity, the same incompleteness of evidence. If it is true that I become what I do, if it is true that I need not merely play out an essence that remains unchanged from birth to death, if it is true that I do not develop from potentiality to actuality but from one actuality to another actuality to yet other actualities connected by strands of continuity and assimilation, then it is quite impossible at any particular time for me to give a thorough and convincing argument offering fully cogent objective grounds for decisions that will influence my becoming. I cannot appeal to an objectively determinate essence within me as justification for the rightness of following one path or another. In a very real sense I can only know when I get there.

To take a small-scale example, think of the major requirements in the curricula of most colleges and universities. The idea is to give you a taste of many fields of learning in your first years and then, because you cannot study everything, you pick one field to specialize in. Often you are required to choose a major after the sophomore year. Many find this an uncomfortable choice, for it seems to be so important and yet one is so ill equipped to make a choice. How can I know whether I want to major in physics when I haven't yet taken any advanced physics? If I choose physics and take the courses, I will have missed the chance to try out sociology, which happens to be another major interest. And the life of a physicist or engineer is very different from the life of, say, a social worker. The choice seems so critical and there is so little time. The method of totalization sounds like a fine technique to avoid one-sidedness in settling an intellectual question, but in living you simply cannot do everything. You cannot be a butcher, a baker, *and* a candlestick-maker. At some point you must make choices, knowing that those choices influence *who you become,* and also knowing that you lack the means for reaching certainty in making the choice. This frightful exigency, the pressures of time and our finitude, transforms the question of self-identity into an identity *crisis.* And a similar exigency attaches to the question of religious belief, for it is the world one lives in and the life one leads that are at stake in the question of religious belief.

Among approaches to pressing questions we can distinguish possible stances that feel very different on the inside but are sometimes indistinguishable to the external observer. First, there are those who are unaware of the importance of the choice. The river of life flows on and they bob like corks, floating along on currents over which they exercise no control. Second, there are those who refuse to choose without adequate grounds for a choice. But that is a choice: to remain upstream. Third are those who choose foolishly. Because objective ambiguity is so painful they hurl themselves thoughtlessly into one current or another and, like the student with no mathematical aptitude who nevertheless majors in physics because labs are fun, end up hurtling over a waterfall into the depths of disaster. (Even if you cannot get *enough* evidence to be certain, you cannot ignore what evidence you have.) Then, fourth, there are those who face a crisis, see its dimensions, struggle with a choice, follow that choice, and, looking very much like those in the first stance, go with the flow.

Suffice it to say that the high stakes and the objective ambiguity that characterize both identity crises and questions of religious belief render them similar in the logic of exigency. But the questions share more than a common form. Religious belief is part of the content of self-identity. To be a Christian or a Jew or a Muslim or a Buddhist is to maintain or commit oneself to a certain kind of life. Almost all religions speak of the new birth attending faith. The matter of religious belief is indeed the widest circle of self-awareness. When I relate myself (or fail to relate myself) to religious belief, I relate myself (or fail to relate myself) to all that is, was, and ever shall be. I experience (or do not experience) a transfiguration of self and world.

W. K. CLIFFORD (1845–1879)

W. K. Clifford was a nineteenth-century scientist-philosopher who left little of real distinction in his literary wake. Part of his essay, "The Ethics of Belief," is included here mainly to represent the position James attacks in the essay after. But Clifford is no straw man; the position he represents is formidable and must be understood lest objective ambiguity be confused with an irrational chaos offering equal lack of justification to any and all decisions. Clifford does well to point out, even if slightly melodramatically, the mishaps and tragedies that follow unnecessarily from overzealous credulity.

The Ethics of Belief

The Duty of Inquiry

A shipowner was about to send to sea an emigrant-ship. He knew that she was old, and not over-well built at the first; that she had seen many seas and climes, and often had needed repairs. Doubts had been suggested to him that possibly she was not seaworthy. These doubts preyed upon his mind, and made him unhappy; he thought that perhaps he ought to have her thoroughly overhauled and refitted, even though this should put him to great expense. Before the ship sailed, however, he succeeded in overcoming these melancholy reflections. He said to himself that she had gone safely through so many voyages and weathered so many storms that it was idle to suppose she would not come safely home from this trip also. He would put his trust in Providence, which could hardly fail to protect all these unhappy families that were leaving their fatherland to seek for better times elsewhere. He would dismiss from his mind all ungenerous suspicions about the honesty of builders and contractors. In such ways he acquired a sincere and comfortable conviction that his vessel was thoroughly safe and seaworthy; he watched her departure with a light heart, and benevolent wishes for the success of the exiles in their strange new home that was to be; and he got his insurance-money when she went down in mid-ocean and told no tales.

What shall we say of him? Surely this, that he was verily guilty of the death of those men. It is admitted that he did sincerely believe in the soundness of his ship; but the sincerity of his conviction can in no wise help him, because *he had no right to believe on such evidence as was before him.* He had acquired his belief not by honestly earning it in patient investigation, but by stifling his doubts. And although in the end he may have felt so sure about it that he could not think otherwise, yet inasmuch as he had knowingly and willingly worked himself into that frame of mind, he must be held responsible for it.

Let us alter the case a little, and suppose that the ship was not unsound after all; that she made her voyage safely, and many others after it. Will that diminish the guilt of her owner? Not one jot. When an action is once done, it is right or wrong forever; no accidental failure of its good or evil fruits can possibly alter that. The man would not have been innocent, he would only have been not found out. The question of right or wrong has to do with the origin of his belief, not the matter of it; not what it was, but how he got it; not whether it turned out to be true or false, but whether he had a right to believe on such evidence as was before him.

There was once an island in which some of the inhabitants professed a religion teaching neither the doctrine of original sin nor that of eternal punishment. A suspicion got abroad that the professors of this religion had made use of unfair means to get their doctrines taught to children. They were accused of wresting the laws of their country in such a way as to remove children from the care of their natural and legal guardians; and even of stealing them away and keeping them concealed from their friends and relations. A certain number of men formed themselves into a society for the purpose of agitating the public about this matter. They published grave accusations against individual citizens of the highest position and character, and did all in their power to injure these citizens in the exercise of their professions. So great was the noise they made, that a Commission was appointed to investigate the facts; but after the Commission had carefully inquired into all the evidence that could be got, it appeared that the accused were innocent. Not only had they been accused on insufficient evidence, but the evidence of their innocence was such as the agitators might easily have obtained, if they had attempted a fair inquiry. After these disclosures the inhabitants of that country looked upon the members of the agitating society, not only as persons whose judgment was to be distrusted, but also as no longer to be counted honorable men. For although they had sincerely and conscientiously believed in the charges they had made, yet *they had no right to believe on such evidence as was before them*. Their sincere convictions, instead of being honestly earned by patient inquiring, were stolen by listening to the voice of prejudice and passion.

Let us vary this case also, and suppose, other things remaining as before, that a still more accurate investigation proved the accused to have been really guilty. Would this make any difference in the guilt of the accusers? Clearly not; the question is not whether their belief was true or false, but whether they entertained it on wrong grounds. They would no doubt say, 'Now you see that we were right after all; next time perhaps you will believe us.' And they might be believed, but they would not thereby become honorable men. They would not be innocent, they would only be not found out. Every one of them, if he chose to examine himself *in foro conscientiae*, would know that he had acquired and nourished a belief, when he had no right to believe on such evidence as was before him; and therein he would know that he had done a wrong thing.

It may be said, however, that in both of these supposed cases it is not the belief which is judged to be wrong, but the action following upon it. The shipowner might say, 'I am perfectly certain that my ship is sound, but still I feel it

my duty to have her examined, before trusting the lives of so many people to her.'
And it might be said to the agitator, 'However convinced you were of the justice of
your cause and the truth of your convictions, you ought not to have made a public
attack upon any man's character until you had examined the evidence on both
sides with the utmost patience and care.'

In the first place, let us admit that, so far as it goes, this view of the case is
right and necessary; right, because even when a man's belief is so fixed that he
cannot think otherwise, he still has a choice in regard to the action suggested by it,
and so cannot escape the duty of investigating on the ground of the strength of his
convictions; and necessary, because those who are not yet capable of controlling
their feelings and thoughts must have a plain rule dealing with overt acts.

But this being premised as necessary, it becomes clear that it is not sufficient,
and that our previous judgment is required to supplement it. For it is not possible
so to sever the belief from the action it suggests as to condemn the one without
condemning the other. No man holding a strong belief on one side of a question, or
even wishing to hold a belief on one side, can investigate it with such fairness and
completeness as if he were really in doubt and unbiased; so that the existence of a
belief not founded on fair inquiry unfits a man for the performance of this
necessary duty.

Nor is that truly a belief at all which has not some influence upon the actions
of him who holds it. He who truly believes that which prompts him to an action
has looked upon the action to lust after it, he has committed it already in his heart.
If a belief is not realized immediately in open deeds, it is stored up for the guidance
of the future. It goes to make a part of that aggregate of beliefs which is the link
between sensation and action at every moment of all our lives, and which is so
organized and compacted together that no part of it can be isolated from the rest,
but every new addition modifies the structure of the whole. No real belief,
however trifling and fragmentary it may seem, is ever truly insignificant; it
prepares us to receive more of its like, confirms those which resembled it before,
and weakens others; and so gradually it lays a stealthy train in our inmost
thoughts, which may some day explode into overt action, and leave its stamp upon
our character forever.

And no one man's belief is in any case a private matter which concerns
himself alone. Our lives are guided by that general conception of the course of
things which has been created by society for social purposes. Our words, our
phrases, our forms and processes and modes of thought, are common property,
fashioned and perfected from age to age; an heirloom which every succeeding
generation inherits as a precious deposit and a sacred trust to be handed on to the
next one, not unchanged but enlarged and purified, with some clear marks of its
proper handiwork. Into this, for good or ill, is woven every belief of every man
who has speech of his fellows. An awful privilege, and an awful responsibility, that
we should help to create the world in which posterity will live.

In the two supposed cases which have been considered, it has been judged
wrong to believe on insufficient evidence, or to nourish belief by suppressing
doubts and avoiding investigation. The reason of this judgment is not far to seek: it

is that in both these cases the belief held by one man was of great importance to other men. But forasmuch as no belief held by one man, however seemingly trivial the belief, and however obscure the believer, is ever actually insignificant or without its effect on the fate of mankind, we have no choice but to extend our judgment to all cases of belief whatever. Belief, that sacred faculty which prompts the decisions of our will, and knits into harmonious working all the compacted energies of our being, is ours not for ourselves, but for humanity. It is rightly used on truths which have been established by long experience and waiting toil, and which have stood in the fierce light of free and fearless questioning. Then it helps to bind men together, and to strengthen and direct their common action. It is desecrated when given to unproved and unquestioned statements, for the solace and private pleasure of the believer; to add a tinsel splendor to the plain straight road of our life and display a bright mirage beyond it; or even to drown the common sorrows of our kind by a self-deception which allows them not only to cast down, but also to degrade us. Whoso would deserve well of his fellows in this matter will guard the purity of his belief with a very fanaticism of jealous care, lest at any time it should rest on an unworthy object, and catch a stain which can never be wiped away.

It is not only the leader of men, statesman, philosopher, or poet, that owes this bounden duty to mankind. Every rustic who delivers in the village alehouse his slow, infrequent sentences, may help to kill or keep alive the fatal superstitions which clog his race. Every hard-worked wife of an artisan may transmit to her children beliefs which shall knit society together, or rend it in pieces. No simplicity of mind, no obscurity of station, can escape the universal duty of questioning all that we believe.

It is true that this duty is a hard one, and the doubt which comes out of it is often a very bitter thing. It leaves us bare and powerless where we thought that we were safe and strong. To know all about anything is to know how to deal with it under all circumstances. We feel much happier and more secure when we think we know precisely what to do, no matter what happens, than when we have lost our way and do not know where to turn. And if we have supposed ourselves to know all about anything, and to be capable of doing what is fit in regard to it, we naturally do not like to find that we are really ignorant and powerless, that we have to begin again at the beginning, and try to learn what the thing is and how it is to be dealt with—if indeed anything can be learnt about it. It is the sense of power attached to a sense of knowledge that makes men desirous of believing, and afraid of doubting.

This sense of power is the highest and best of pleasures when the belief on which it is founded is a true belief, and has been fairly earned by investigation. For then we may justly feel that it is common property, and holds good for others as well as for ourselves. Then we may be glad, not that *I* have learned secrets by which I am safer and stronger, but that *we men* have got mastery over more of the world; and we shall be strong, not for ourselves, but in the name of Man and in his strength. But if the belief has been accepted on insufficient evidence, the pleasure is a stolen one. Not only does it deceive ourselves by giving us a sense of power which we do not really possess, but it is sinful, because it is stolen in defiance of our duty to mankind. That duty is to guard ourselves from such beliefs as from a pestilence, which may shortly master our own body and then spread to the rest of the town. What would be thought of one who, for the sake of a sweet fruit, should deliberately run the risk of bringing a plague upon his family and his neighbors?

And, as in other such cases, it is not the risk only which has to be considered; for a bad action is always bad at the time when it is done, no matter what happens afterward. Every time we let ourselves believe for unworthy reasons, we weaken our powers of self-control, of doubting, of judicially and fairly weighing evidence. We all suffer severely enough from the maintenance and support of false beliefs and the fatally wrong actions which they lead to, and the evil born when one such belief is entertained is great and wide. But a greater and wider evil arises when the credulous character is maintained and supported, when a habit of believing for unworthy reasons is fostered and made permanent. If I steal money from any person, there may be no harm done by the mere transfer of possession; he may not feel the loss, or it may prevent him from using the money badly. But I cannot help doing this great wrong toward Man, that I make myself dishonest. What hurts society is not that it should lose its property, but that it should become a den of thieves; for then it must cease to be society. This is why we ought not to do evil that good may come; for at any rate this great evil has come, that we have done evil and are made wicked thereby. In like manner, if I let myself believe anything on insufficient evidence, there may be no great harm done by the mere belief; it may be true after all, or I may never have occasion to exhibit it in outward acts. But I cannot help doing this great wrong toward Man, that I make myself credulous. The danger to society is not merely that it should believe wrong things, though that is great enough; but that it should become credulous, and lose the habit of testing things and inquiring into them; for then it must sink back into savagery.

The harm which is done by credulity in a man is not confined to the fostering of a credulous character in others, and consequent support of false beliefs. Habitual want of care about what I believe leads to habitual want of care in others about the truth of what is told to me. Men speak the truth to one another when each reveres the truth in his own mind and in the other's mind; but how shall my friend revere the truth in my mind when I myself am careless about it, when I believe things because I want to believe them, and because they are comforting and pleasant? Will he not learn to cry, 'Peace,' to me, when there is no peace? By such a course I shall surround myself with a thick atmosphere of falsehood and fraud, and in that I must live. It may matter little to me, in my cloud-castle of sweet illusions and darling lies; but it matters much to Man that I have made my neighbors ready to deceive. The credulous man is father to the liar and the cheat; he lives in the bosom of this his family, and it is no marvel if he should become even as they are. So closely are our duties knit together, that whoso shall keep the whole law, and yet offend in one point, he is guilty of all.

To sum up: it is wrong always, everywhere and for any one, to believe anything upon insufficient evidence.

WILLIAM JAMES *(1842–1910)*

The thesis of James's essay is clearly stated only well into the argument: "Our passional nature not only lawfully may, but must, decide an option between propositions, whenever it is a genuine option that cannot by its nature be decided on intellectual grounds; for to say, under such circumstances, 'Do not decide, but leave the question open,' is itself a decision,—just like deciding yes or no,—and is attended with the same risk of losing the truth." This quotation is not only relevant to the discussion in the last "Transition," but also shows the role played by the phrase, 'genuine option.' In the early part of the essay James takes care to define his terms, and unless one appreciates in advance the importance of his definitions, one is liable to misconstrue the scope of his argument. He is not interested in justifying a Sartrean voluntarism or a Kierkegaardian irrationalism. James is very explicit about the precise conditions under which credulity may be exercised and those under which it may not. Attend to his statements of those conditions.

Beyond its contribution to the question of belief, James's essay also adds to the ongoing debate over the nature of philosophy and its proper method. He makes a powerful case against the Cartesian quest for certainty. James's distinction between the two imperatives: "know the truth," and "avoid error," does indeed characterize two very different kinds of philosophical pursuits. The drive toward ever more technically precise exercises in linguistic analysis follows from the imperative to avoid error. But to the extent that philosophy is driven only by a fear of error its products tend to be sterile. Naturally a will to truth wholly unchecked by fear of error may issue in fantasies that are far from sterile, but also far from truth. James's distinction of kinds of philosophy is useful in reviewing other essays that touch on methodology: Descartes, Ryle, and Polanyi, as well as Clifford.

The Will to Believe

1

. . . Let us give the name of *hypothesis* to anything that may be proposed to our belief; and just as the electricians speak of live and dead wires, let us speak of any hypothesis as either *live* or *dead*. A live hypothesis is one which appeals as a real possibility to him to whom it is proposed. If I ask you to believe in the Mahdi, the notion makes no electric connection with your nature,—it refuses to scintillate with any credibility at all. As an hypothesis it is completely dead. To an Arab, however (even if he be not one of the Mahdi's followers), the hypothesis is among the mind's possibilities: it is alive. This shows that deadness and liveness in an hypothesis are not intrinsic properties, but relations to the individual thinker. They are measured by his willingness to act. The maximum of liveness in an hypothesis means willingness to act irrevocably. Practically, that means belief; but there is some believing tendency wherever there is willingness to act at all.

Next, let us call the decision between two hypotheses an *option*. Options may be of several kinds. They may be—1, *living* or *dead*; 2, *forced* or *unavoidable*; 3, *momentous* or *trivial*; and for our purposes we may call an option a *genuine* option when it is of the forced, living, and momentous kind.

1. A living option is one in which both hypotheses are live ones. If I say to you: "Be a theosophist or be a Mohammedan," it is probably a dead option, because for you neither hypothesis is likely to be alive. But if I say: "Be an agnostic or be a Christian," it is otherwise: trained as you are, each hypothesis makes some appeal, however small, to your belief.

2. Next, if I say to you: "Choose between going out with your umbrella or without it," I do not offer you a genuine option, for it is not forced. You can easily avoid it by not going out at all. Similarly, if I say, "Either love me or hate me," "Either call my theory true or call it false," your option is avoidable. You may remain indifferent to me, neither loving nor hating, and you may decline to offer any judgment as to my theory. But if I say, "Either accept this truth or go without it," I put on you a forced option, for there is no standing place outside of the alternative. Every dilemma based on a complete logical disjunction, with no possibility of not choosing, is an option of this forced kind.

3. Finally, if I were Dr. Nansen and proposed to you to join my North Pole expedition, your option would be momentous; for this would probably be your only similar opportunity, and your choice now would either exclude you from the North Pole sort of immortality altogether or put at least the chance of it into your hands. He who refuses to embrace a unique opportunity loses the prize as surely as if he tried and failed. *Per contra*, the option is trivial when the opportunity is not unique, when the stake is insignificant, or when the decision is reversible if it later prove unwise. Such trivial options abound in the scientific life. A chemist finds an hypothesis live enough to spend a year in its verification: he believes in it to that extent. But if his experiments prove inconclusive either way, he is quit for his loss of time, no vital harm being done.

It will facilitate our discussion if we keep all these distinctions well in mind.

2

The next matter to consider is the actual psychology of human opinion. When we look at certain facts, it seems as if our passional and volitional nature lay at the root of all our convictions. When we look at others, it seems as if they could do nothing when the intellect had once said its say. Let us take the latter facts up first.

Does it not seem preposterous on the very face of it to talk of our opinions being modifiable at will? Can our will either help or hinder our intellect in its perceptions of truth? Can we, by just willing it, believe that Abraham Lincoln's existence is a myth, and that the portraits of him in McClure's Magazine are all of some one else? Can we, by any effort of our will, or by any strength of wish that it were true, believe ourselves well and about when we are roaring with rheumatism in bed, or feel certain that the sum of the two one-dollar bills in our pocket must be a hundred dollars? We can *say* any of these things, but we are absolutely impotent to believe them; and of just such things is the whole fabric of the truths that we do believe in made up—matters of fact, immediate or remote, as Hume said, and relations between ideas, which are either there or not there for us if we see them so, and which if not there cannot be put there by any action of our own.

In Pascal's Thoughts there is a celebrated passage known in literature as Pascal's wager. In it he tries to force us into Christianity by reasoning as if our concern with truth resembled our concern with the stakes in a game of chance. Translated freely his words are these: You must either believe or not believe that God is—which will you do? Your human reason cannot say. A game is going on between you and the nature of things which at the day of judgment will bring out either heads or tails. Weigh what your gains and your losses would be if you should stake all you have on heads, or God's existence: if you win in such case, you gain eternal beatitude; if you lose, you lose nothing at all. If there were an infinity of chances, and only one for God in this wager, still you ought to stake your all on God; for though you surely risk a finite loss by this procedure, any finite loss is reasonable, even a certain one is reasonable, if there is but the possibility of infinite gain. Go, then, and take holy water, and have masses said; belief will come and stupefy your scruples,—*Cela vous fera croire et vous abêtira.* Why should you not? At bottom, what have you to lose?

You probably feel that when religious faith expresses itself thus, in the language of the gamingtable, it is put to its last trumps. Surely Pascal's own personal belief in masses and holy water had far other springs; and this celebrated page of his is but an argument for others, a last desperate snatch at a weapon against the hardness of the unbelieving heart. We feel that a faith in masses and holy water adopted wilfully after such a mechanical calculation would lack the inner soul of faith's reality; and if we were ourselves in the place of the Deity, we should probably take particular pleasure in cutting off believers of this pattern from their infinite reward. It is evident that unless there be some pre-existing tendency to believe in masses and holy water, the option offered to the will by Pascal is not a living option. Certainly no Turk ever took to masses and holy water on its account; and even to us Protestants these means of salvation seem such foregone impossibilities that Pascal's logic, invoked for them specifically, leaves us unmoved. As well might the Mahdi write to us, saying, "I am the Expected One whom God has created in his effulgence. You shall be infinitely happy if you confess me; otherwise you shall be cut from the light of the sun. Weigh, then, your infinite gain if I am genuine against your finite sacrifice if I am not!" His logic would be that of Pascal; but he would vainly use it on us, for the hypothesis he offers us is dead. No tendency to act on it exists in us to any degree.

The talk of believing by our volition seems, then, from one point of view, simply silly. From another point of view it is worse than silly, it is vile. When one turns to the magnificent edifice of the physical sciences, and sees how it was reared; what thousands of disinterested moral lives of men lie buried in its mere foundations; what patience and postponement, what choking down of preference, what submission to the icy laws of outer fact are wrought into its very stones and mortar; how absolutely impersonal it stands in its vast augustness,—then how besotted and contemptible seems every little sentimentalist who comes blowing his voluntary smoke-wreaths, and pretending to decide things from out of his private dream! Can we wonder if those bred in the rugged and manly school of science should feel like spewing such subjectivism out of their mouths? The whole system of loyalties which grow up in the schools of science go dead against its toleration; so that it is only natural that those who have caught the scientific fever should pass over to the opposite extreme, and write sometimes as if the incorruptibly truthful intellect ought positively to prefer bitterness and unacceptableness to the heart in its cup.

> It fortifies my soul to know
> That, though I perish, Truth is so—

sings Clough, while Huxley exclaims: "My only consolation lies in the reflection that, however bad our posterity may become, so far as they hold by the plain rule of not pretending to believe what they have no reason to believe, because it may be to their advantage so to pretend [the word 'pretend' is surely here redundant], they will not have reached the lowest depth of immorality." And that delicious *enfant terrible* Clifford writes: "Belief is desecrated when given to unproved and unquestioned statements for the solace and private pleasure of the believer.... Whoso would deserve well of his fellows in this matter will guard the purity of his belief with a very fanaticism of jealous care, lest at any time it should rest on an unworthy object, and catch a stain which can never be wiped away.... If [a] belief has been accepted on insufficient evidence [even though the belief be true, as Clifford on the same page explains] the pleasure is a stolen one.... It is sinful because it is stolen in defiance of our duty to mankind. That duty is to guard ourselves from such beliefs as from a pestilence which may shortly master our own body and then spread to the rest of the town.... It is wrong always, everywhere, and for every one, to believe anything upon insufficient evidence."

3

All this strikes one as healthy, even when expressed, as by Clifford, with somewhat too much of robustious pathos in the voice. Free-will and simple wishing do seem, in the matter of our credences, to be only fifth wheels to the coach. Yet if any one should thereupon assume that intellectual insight is what remains after wish and will and sentimental preference have taken wing, or that pure reason is what then settles our opinions, he would fly quite as directly in the teeth of the facts.

It is only our already dead hypotheses that our willing nature is unable to bring to life again. But what has made them dead for us is for the most part a previous action of our willing nature of an antagonistic kind. When I say 'willing nature,' I do not mean only such deliberate volitions as may have set up habits of belief that we cannot now escape from,—I mean all such factors of belief as fear and hope, prejudice and passion, imitation and partisanship, the circumpressure of our caste and set. As a matter of fact we find ourselves believing, we hardly know how or why. Mr. Balfour gives the name of 'authority' to all those influences, born of the intellectual climate, that make hypotheses possible or impossible for us, alive or dead. Here in this room, we all of us believe in molecules and the conservation of energy, in democracy and necessary progress, in Protestant Christianity and the duty of fighting for 'the doctrine of the immortal Monroe,' all for no reasons worthy of the name. We see into these matters with no more inner clearness, and probably with much less, than any disbeliever in them might possess. His unconventionality would probably have some grounds to show for its conclusions; but for us, not insight, but the *prestige* of the opinions, is what makes the spark shoot from them and light up our sleeping magazines of faith. Our reason is quite satisfied, in nine hundred and ninety-nine cases out of every thousand of us, if it can find a few arguments that will do to recite in case our credulity is criticised by some one else. Our faith is faith in some one else's faith, and in the greatest matters this is most the case. Our belief in truth itself, for instance, that there is a truth, and that our minds and it are made for each other,—what is it but a passionate affirmation of desire, in which our social system backs us up? We want to have a truth; we want to believe that our experiments and studies and discussions must put us in a continually better and better position towards it; and on this line we agree to fight out our thinking lives. But if a pyrrhonistic sceptic asks us *how we know* all this, can our logic find a reply? No! certainly it cannot. It is just one volition against another,—we willing to go in for life upon a trust or assumption which he, for his part, does not care to make.[1]

As a rule we disbelieve all facts and theories for which we have no use. Clifford's cosmic emotions find no use for Christian feelings. Huxley belabors the bishops because there is no use for sacerdotalism in his scheme of life. Newman, on the contrary, goes over to Romanism, and finds all sorts of reasons good for staying there, because a priestly system is for him an organic need and delight. Why do so few 'scientists' even look at the evidence for telepathy, so called? Because they think, as a leading biologist, now dead, once said to me, that even if such a thing were true, scientists ought to band together to keep it suppressed and concealed. It would undo the uniformity of Nature and all sorts of other things without which scientists cannot carry on their pursuits. But if this very man had been shown something which as a scientist he might *do* with telepathy, he might not only have examined the evidence, but even have found it good enough. This very law which the logicians would impose upon us—if I may give the name of logicians to those who would rule out our willing nature here—is based on nothing but their own natural wish to exclude all elements for which they, in their professional quality of logicians, can find no use.

Evidently, then, our non-intellectual nature does influence our convictions. There are passional tendencies and volitions which run before and others which

[1]Compare the admirable page 310 in S. H. Hodgson's "Time and Space," London, 1865.

come after belief, and it is only the latter that are too late for the fair; and they are not too late when the previous passional work has been already in their own direction. Pascal's argument, instead of being powerless, then seems a regular clincher, and is the last stroke needed to make our faith in masses and holy water complete. The state of things is evidently far from simple; and pure insight and logic, whatever they might do ideally, are not the only things that really do produce our creeds.

4

Our next duty, having recognized this mixed-up state of affairs, is to ask whether it be simply reprehensible and pathological, or whether, on the contrary, we must treat it as a normal element in making up our minds. The thesis I defend is, briefly stated, this: *Our passional nature not only lawfully may, but must, decide an option between propositions, whenever it is a genuine option that cannot by its nature be decided on intellectual grounds; for to say, under such circumstances, "Do not decide, but leave the question open," is itself a passional decision,—just like deciding yes or no,—and is attended with the same risk of losing the truth.* The thesis thus abstractly expressed will, I trust, soon become quite clear. But I must first indulge in a bit more of preliminary work.

5

It will be observed that for the purposes of this discussion we are on 'dogmatic' ground,—ground, I mean, which leaves systematic philosophical scepticism altogether out of account. The postulate that there is truth, and that it is the destiny of our minds to attain it, we are deliberately resolving to make, though the sceptic will not make it. We part company with him, therefore, absolutely, at this point. But the faith that truth exists, and that our minds can find it, may be held in two ways. We may talk of the *empiricist* way and of the *absolutist* way of believing in truth. The absolutists in this matter say that we not only can attain to knowing truth, but we can *know when* we have attained to knowing it; while the empiricists think that although we may attain it, we cannot infallibly know when. To *know* is one thing, and to know for certain *that* we know is another. One may hold to the first being possible without the second; hence the empiricists and the absolutists, although neither of them is a sceptic in the usual philosophic sense of the term, show very different degrees of dogmatism in their lives.

If we look at the history of opinions, we see that the empiricist tendency has largely prevailed in science, while in philosophy the absolutist tendency has had everything its own way. The characteristic sort of happiness, indeed, which philosophies yield has mainly consisted in the conviction felt by each successive school or system that by it bottom-certitude had been attained. "Other philosophies are collections of opinions, mostly false; *my* philosophy gives standing-ground forever,"—who does not recognize in this the key-note of every system worthy of the name? A system, to be a system at all, must come as a *closed* system, reversible in this or that detail, perchance, but in its essential features never!

Scholastic orthodoxy, to which one must always go when one wishes to find perfectly clear statement, has beautifully elaborated this absolutist conviction in a doctrine which it calls that of 'objective evidence.' ... You believe in objective evidence, and I do. Of some things we feel that we are certain: we know, and we know that we do know. There is something that gives a click inside of us, a bell that strikes twelve, when the hands of our mental clock have swept the dial and meet over the meridian hour. The greatest empiricists among us are only empiricists on reflection: when left to their instincts, they dogmatize like infallible popes. When the Cliffords tell us how sinful it is to be Christians on such 'insufficient evidence,' insufficiency is really the last thing they have in mind. For them the evidence is absolutely sufficient, only it makes the other way. They believe so completely in an anti-christian order of the universe that there is no living option; Christianity is a dead hypothesis from the start.

6

But now, since we are all such absolutists by instinct, what in our quality of students of philosophy ought we to do about the fact? Shall we espouse and indorse it? Or shall we treat it as a weakness of our nature from which we must free ourselves, if we can?

I sincerely believe that the latter course is the only one we can follow as reflective men. Objective evidence and certitude are doubtless very fine ideals to play with, but where on this moonlit and dream-visited planet are they found? I am, therefore, myself a complete empiricist so far as my theory of human knowledge goes. I live, to be sure, by the practical faith that we must go on experiencing and thinking over our experience, for only thus can our opinions grow more true; but to hold any one of them—I absolutely do not care which—as if it never could be reinterpretable or corrigible, I believe to be a tremendously mistaken attitude, and I think that the whole history of philosophy will bear me out. There is but one indefectibly certain truth, and that is the truth that pyrrhonistic scepticism itself leaves standing,—the truth that the present phenomenon of consciousness exists. That, however, is the bare starting-point of knowledge, the mere admission of a stuff to be philosophized about. The various philosophies are but so many attempts at expressing what this stuff really is. And if we repair to our libraries what disagreement do we discover! Where is a certainly true answer found? Apart from abstract propositions of comparison (such as two and two are the same as four), propositions which tell us nothing by themselves about concrete reality, we find no proposition ever regarded by any one as evidently certain that has not either been called a falsehood, or at least had its truth sincerely questioned by some one else. The transcending of the axioms of geometry, not in play but in earnest, by certain of our contemporaries (as Zöllner and Charles H. Hinton), and the rejection of the whole Aristotelian logic by the Hegelians, are striking instances in point....

But please observe, now, that when as empiricists we give up the doctrine of objective certitude, we do not thereby give up the quest or hope of truth itself. We still pin our faith on its existence, and still believe that we gain an ever better position towards it by systematically continuing to roll up experiences and think. Our great difference from the scholastic lies in the way we face. The strength of his system lies in the principles, the origin, the *terminus a quo* of his thought; for us the strength is in the outcome, the upshot, the *terminus ad quem*. Not where it comes from but where it leads to is to decide. It matters not to an empiricist from what quarter an hypothesis may come to him: he may have acquired it by fair means or by foul; passion may have whispered or accident suggested it; but if the total drift of thinking continues to confirm it, that is what he means by its being true.

7

One more point, small but important, and our preliminaries are done. There are two ways of looking at our duty in the matter of opinion,—ways entirely different, and yet ways about whose difference the theory of knowledge seems hitherto to have shown very little concern. *We must know the truth;* and *we must avoid error,*—these are our first and great commandments as would-be knowers; but they are not two ways of stating an identical commandment, they are two separable laws. Although it may indeed happen that when we believe the truth *A*, we escape as an incidental consequence from believing the falsehood *B*, it hardly ever happens that by merely disbelieving *B* we necessarily believe *A*. We may in escaping *B* fall into believing other falsehoods, *C* or *D*, just as bad as *B*, or we may escape *B* by not believing anything at all, not even *A*.

Believe truth! Shun error!—these, we see, are two materially different laws; and by choosing between them we may end by coloring differently our whole intellectual life. We may regard the chase for truth as paramount, and the avoidance of error as secondary; or we may, on the other had, treat avoidance of error as more imperative, and let truth take its chance. Clifford, in the instructive passage which I have quoted, exhorts us to the latter course. Believe nothing, he tells us, keep your mind in suspense forever, rather than by closing it on insufficient evidence incur the awful risk of believing lies. You, on the other hand, may think that the risk of being in error is a very small matter when compared with the blessings of real knowledge, and be ready to be duped many times in your investigation rather than postpone indefinitely the chance of guessing true. I myself find it impossible to go with Clifford. We must remember that these feelings of our duty about either truth or error are in any case only expressions of our passional life. Biologically considered, our minds are as ready to grind out falsehood as veracity, and he who says, "Better go without belief forever than believe a lie!" merely shows his own preponderant private horror of becoming a dupe. He may be critical of many of his desires and fears, but this fear he slavishly obeys. He cannot imagine any one questioning its binding force. For my own part, I have also a horror of being duped; but I can believe that worse things than being duped may happen to a man in this world: so Clifford's exhortation has to my ears a thoroughly fantastic sound. It is like a general informing his soldiers that it is better to keep out of battle forever than to risk a single wound. Not so are victories either over enemies or over nature gained. Our errors are surely not such awfully solemn things. In a world where we are so certain to incur them in spite of all of our caution, a certain lightness of heart seems healthier than this excessive nervousness on their behalf. At any rate, it seems the fittest thing for the empiricist philosopher.

8

And now, after all this introduction, let us go straight at our question. I have said, and now repeat it, that not only as a matter of fact do we find our passional nature influencing us in our opinions, but that there are some options between opinions in which this influence must be regarded both as an inevitable and as a lawful determinant of our choice.

I fear here that some of you my hearers will begin to scent danger, and lend an inhospitable ear. Two first steps of passion you have indeed had to admit as necessary,—we must think so as to avoid dupery, and we must think so as to gain truth; but the surest path to those ideal consummations, you will probably consider, is from now onwards to take no further passional step.

Well, of course, I agree as far as the facts will allow. Wherever the option between losing truth and gaining it is not momentous, we can throw the chance of *gaining truth* away, and at any rate save ourselves from any chance of *believing falsehood*, by not making up our minds at all till objective evidence has come. In scientific questions, this is almost always the case; and even in human affairs in general, the need of acting is seldom so urgent that a false belief to act on is better than no belief at all. Law courts, indeed, have to decide on the best evidence attainable for the moment, because a judge's duty is to make law as well as to ascertain it, and (as a learned judge once said to me) few cases are worth spending much time over: the great thing is to have them decided on *any* acceptable principle, and got out of the way. But in our dealings with objective nature we obviously are recorders, not makers, of the truth; and decisions for the mere sake of deciding promptly and getting on to the next business would be wholly out of place. Throughout the breadth of physical nature facts are what they are quite independently of us, and seldom is there any such hurry about them that the risks of being duped by believing a premature theory need be faced. The questions here are always trivial options, the hypotheses are hardly living (at any rate not living for us spectators), the choice between believing truth or falsehood is seldom forced. The attitude of sceptical balance is therefore the absolutely wise one if we would escape mistakes. What difference, indeed, does it make to most of us whether we have or have not a theory of the Röntgen rays, whether we believe or not in mind-stuff, or have a conviction about the causality of conscious states? It makes no difference. Such options are not forced on us. On every account it is better not to make them, but still keep weighing reasons *pro et contra* with an indifferent hand....

The question next arises: Are there not somewhere forced options in our speculative questions, and can we (as men who may be interested at least as much in positively gaining truth as in merely escaping dupery) always wait with impunity till the coercive evidence shall have arrived? It seems *a priori* improbable that the truth should be so nicely adjusted to our needs and powers as that. In the great boarding-house of nature, the cakes and the butter and the syrup seldom come out so even and leave the plates so clean. Indeed, we should view them with scientific suspicion if they did.

9

Moral questions immediately present themselves as questions whose solution cannot wait for sensible proof. A moral question is a question not of what sensibly exists, but of what is good, or would be good if it did exist. Science can tell us what exists; but to compare the *worths*, both of what exists and of what does not exist, we must consult not science, but what Pascal calls our heart. Science herself consults her heart when she lays it down that the infinite ascertainment of fact and correction of false belief are the supreme goods for man. Challenge the statement, and science can only repeat it oracularly, or else prove it by showing that such ascertainment and correction bring man all sorts of other goods which man's heart in turn declares. The question of having moral beliefs at all or not having them is decided by our will. Are our moral preferences true or false, or are they only odd biological phenomena, making things goods or bad for *us*, but in themselves indifferent? How can your pure intellect decide? If your heart does not *want* a world of moral reality, your head will assuredly never make you believe in one. Mephistophelian scepticism, indeed, will satisfy the head's play-instincts much better than any rigorous idealism can. Some men (even at the student age) are so naturally cool-hearted that the moralistic hypothesis never has for them any pungent life, and in their supercilious presence the hot young moralist always feels strangely ill at ease. The appearance of knowingness is on their side, of *naïveté* and gullibility on his. Yet, in the inarticulate heart of him, he clings to it that he is not a dupe, and that there is a realm in which (as Emerson says) all their wit and intellectual superiority is no better than the cunning of a fox. Moral scepticism can no more be refuted or proved by logic than intellectual scepticism can. When we stick to it that there *is* truth (be it of either kind), we do so with our whole nature, and resolve to stand or fall by the results. The sceptic with his whole nature adopts the doubting attitude; but which of us is the wiser, Omniscience only knows.

Turn now from these wide questions of good to a certain class of questions of fact, questions concerning personal relations, states of mind between one man and another. *Do you like me or not?*—for example. Whether you do or not depends, in countless instances, on whether I meet you half-way, am willing to assume that you must be like me, and show you trust and expectation. The previous faith on my part in your liking's existence is in such cases what makes your liking come. But if I stand aloof, and refuse to budge an inch until I have objective evidence, until you shall have done something apt, as the absolutists say, *ad extorquendum assensum meum*, ten to one your liking never comes. How many women's hearts are vanquished by the mere sanguine insistence of some man that they *must* love him! he will not consent to the hypothesis that they cannot. The desire for a certain kind of truth here brings about that special truth's existence; and so it is innumerable cases of other sorts. Who gains promotions, boons, appointments, but the man in whose life they are seen to play the part of live hypotheses, who discounts them, sacrifices other things for their sake before they have come, and takes risks for them in advance? His faith acts on the powers above him as a claim, and creates its own verification.

A social organism of any sort whatever, large or small, is what it is because each member proceeds to his own duty with a trust that the other members will simultaneously do theirs. Wherever a desired result is achieved by the co-operation of many independent persons, its existence as a fact is a pure consequence of the precursive faith in one another of those immediately concerned. A government, an army, a commercial system, a ship, a college, an athletic team, all exist on this condition, without which not only is nothing achieved, but nothing is even attempted. A whole train of passengers (individually brave enough) will be looted by a few highwaymen, simply because the latter can count on one another, while each passenger fears that if he makes a movement of resistance, he will be shot before any one else backs him up. If we believed that the whole carfull would rise at once with us, we should each severally rise, and train-robbing would never even be attempted. There are, then, cases where a fact cannot come at all unless a preliminary faith exists in its coming. *And where faith in a fact can help create the fact*, that would be an insane logic which should say that faith running ahead of scientific evidence is the 'lowest kind of immorality' into which a thinking being can fall. Yet such is the logic by which our scientific absolutists pretend to regulate our lives!

10

In truths dependent on our personal action, then, faith based on desire is certainly a lawful and possibly an indispensable thing.

But now, it will be said, these are all childish human cases, and have nothing to do with great cosmical matters, like the question of religious faith. Let us then pass on to that. Religions differ so much in their accidents that in discussing the religious question we must make it very generic and broad. What then do we now mean by the religious hypothesis? Science says things are; morality says some things are better than other things; and religion says essentially two things.

First, she says that the best things are the more eternal things, the overlapping things, the things in the universe that throw the last stone, so to speak, and say the final word. "Perfection is eternal,"—this phrase of Charles Secrétan seems a good way of putting this first affirmation of religion, an affirmation which obviously cannot yet be verified scientifically at all.

The second affirmation of religion is that we are better off even now if we believe her first affirmation to be true.

Now, let us consider what the logical elements of this situation are *in case the religious hypothesis in both its branches be really true.* (Of course, we must admit that possibility at the outset. If we are to discuss the question at all, it must involve a living option. If for any of you religion be a hypothesis that cannot, by any living possibility be true, then you need go no farther. I speak to the 'saving remnant' alone.) So proceeding, we see, first that religion offers itself as a *momentous* option. We are supposed to gain, even now, by our belief, and to lose by our nonbelief, a certain vital good. Secondly, religion is a *forced* option, so far as that good goes. We cannot escape the issue by remaining sceptical and waiting for more light, because, although we do avoid error in that way *if religion be untrue,* we lose the good, *if it be true,* just as certainly as if we positively chose to disbelieve. It is as if a man should hesitate indefinitely to ask a certain woman to marry him because he was not perfectly sure that she would prove an angel after he brought her home. Would he not cut himself off from that particular angel-possibility as decisively as if he went and married some one else? Scepticism, then, is not avoidance of option; it is option of a certain particular kind of risk. *Better risk loss of truth than chance of error,*—that is your faith-vetoer's exact position. He is actively playing his stake as much as the believer is; he is backing the field against the religious hypothesis, just as the believer is backing the religious hypothesis against the field. To preach scepticism to us as a duty until 'sufficient evidence' for religion be found, is tantamount therefore to telling us, when in presence of the religious hypothesis, that to yield to our fear of its being error is wiser and better than to yield to our hope that it may be true. It is not intellect against all passions, then; it is only intellect with one passion laying down its law. And by what, forsooth, is the supreme wisdom of this passion warranted? Dupery for dupery, what proof is there that dupery through hope is so much worse than dupery through fear? I, for one, can see no proof; and I simply refuse obedience to the scientist's command to imitate his kind of option, in a case where my own stake is important enough to give me the right to choose my own form of risk. If religion be true and the evidence for it be still insufficient, I do not wish, by putting your extinguisher upon my nature (which feels to me as if it had after all some business in this matter), to forfeit my sole chance in life of getting upon the winning side,—that chance depending, of course, on my willingness to run the risk of acting as if my passional need of taking the world religiously might be prophetic and right.

All this is on the supposition that it really may be prophetic and right, and that, even to us who are discussing the matter, religion is a live hypothesis which may be true. Now, to most of us religion comes in a still further way that makes a veto on our active faith even more illogical. The more perfect and more eternal aspect of the universe is represented in our religions as having personal form. The universe is no longer a mere *It* to us, but a *Thou,* if we are religious; and any relation that may be possible from person to person might be possible here. For instance, although in one sense we are passive portions of the universe, in another we show a curious autonomy, as if we were small active centres on our own account. We feel, too, as if the appeal of religion to us were made to our own active good-will, as if evidence might be forever withheld from us unless we met the hypothesis half-way. To take a trivial illustration: just as a man who in a company of gentlemen made no advances, asked a warrant for every concession, and believed no one's word without proof, would cut himself off by such churlishness from all the social rewards that a more trusting spirit would earn,—so here, one who should shut himself up in snarling logicality and try to make the gods extort his recognition willy-nilly, or not get it at all, might cut himself off forever from his only opportunity of making the gods' acquaintance. This feeling, forced on us we know not whence, that by obstinately believing that there are gods (although not to do so would be so easy both for our logic and our life) we are doing the universe the deepest service we can, seems part of the living essence of the religious hypothesis. If the hypothesis *were* true in all its parts, including this one, then pure intellectualism, with its veto on our making willing advances, would be an absurdity; and some participation of our sympathetic nature would be logically required. I, therefore, for one, cannot see my way to accepting the agnostic rules for truth-seeking, or wilfully agree to keep my willing nature out of the game. I cannot do so for this plain reason, that *a rule of thinking which would absolutely prevent me from acknowledging certain kinds of truth if those kinds of truth were really there, would be an irrational rule.* That for me is the long and short of the formal logic of the situation, no matter what the kinds of truth might materially be.

I confess I do not see how this logic can be escaped. But sad experience makes me fear that some of you may still shrink from radically saying with me, *in abstracto*, that we have the right to believe at our own risk any hypothesis that is live enough to tempt our will. I suspect, however, that if this is so, it is because you have got away from the abstract logical point of view altogether, and are thinking (perhaps without realizing it) of some particular religious hypothesis which for you is dead. The freedom to 'believe what we will' you apply to the case of some patent superstition; and the faith you think of is the faith defined by the schoolboy when he said, "Faith is when you believe something that you know ain't true." I can only repeat that this is misapprehension. *In concreto*, the freedom to believe can only cover living options which the intellect of the individual cannot by itself resolve; and living options never seem absurdities to him who has them to consider. When I look at the religious question as it really puts itself to concrete men, and when I think of all the possibilities which both practically and theoretically it involves, then this command that we shall put a stopper on our heart, instincts, and courage, and *wait*—acting of course meanwhile more or less as if religion were *not* true[2]—till doomsday, or till such time as our intellect and senses working together may have raked in evidence enough,—this command, I say, seems to me the queerest idol ever manufactured in the philosophic cave. Were we

[2]Since belief is measured by action, he who forbids us to believe religion to be true, necessarily also forbids us to act as we should if we did believe it to be true. The whole defence of religious faith hinges upon action. If the action required or inspired by the religious hypothesis is in no way different from that dictated by the naturalistic hypothesis, then religious faith is a pure superfluity, better pruned away, and controversy about its legitimacy is a piece of idle trifling, unworthy of serious minds. I myself believe, of course, that the religious hypothesis gives to the world an expression which specifically determines our reactions, and makes them in a large part unlike what they might be on a purely naturalistic scheme of belief.

scholastic absolutists, there might be more excuse. If we had an infallible intellect with its objective certitudes, we might feel ourselves disloyal to such a perfect organ of knowledge in not trusting to it exclusively, in not waiting for its releasing word. But if we are empiricists, if we believe that no bell in us tolls to let us know for certain when truth is in our grasp, then it seems a piece of idle fantasticality to preach so solemnly our duty of waiting for the bell. Indeed we *may* wait if we will,—I hope you do not think that I am denying that,—but if we do so, we do so at our peril as much as if we believed. In either case we *act*, taking our life in our hands. No one of us ought to issue vetoes to the other nor should we bandy words of abuse. We ought, on the contrary, delicately and profoundly to respect one another's mental freedom: then only shall we bring about the intellectual republic; then only shall we have that spirit of inner tolerance without which all our outer tolerance is soulless, and which is empiricism's glory; then only shall we live and let live, in speculative as well as in practical things.

transition: mysticism

Let me lengthen the title of this transition to express a ratio: religion is to mysticism as knowledge is to wisdom and as speech is to silence. Because knowledgeable speech is at issue in understanding this ratio I am naturally at a loss for unambiguous words. To meet the mystics on their own terms I resort to allegory. The following allegory is about words, and the need for allegory will be explained by the allegory.

Imagine a city. It is a city of words. Outside the city lie peaceful pastures and forests of silence. As one approaches the suburbs he finds a few houses, modest edifices of words, mere opinions compared to the larger structures that knowledge has built within the city proper. Now each of us who is a user of language, a knower of truths, or a holder of opinions resides somewhere within the confines of this city or its suburbs. The quest for knowledge leads us deeper into the heart of the city where ever newer buildings are being built. The quest for wisdom—philosophy—takes us in the opposite direction, toward the city limits, beyond which lies the silence of mysticism. This silence is neither absolute quiet nor a refusal to speak. Similarly, mysticism is not the opposite of philosophy, nor wisdom the opposite of knowledge. The silence of mysticism is like nature's silence: nondidactic sounds that are heard only when you listen, a "speech" in rhythms about the fullness of time.

Now I want to draw out the allegory by showing how it helps to answer some perennially baffling questions about the nature of philosophy, such as why philosophy makes no cumulative progress. Other fields of knowledge seem to make advances, but in philosophy we still read the ancient Greeks. What is more, one of those ancients claimed to know nothing, yet we still read about him. What did Socrates mean when he said his wisdom consisted in knowing that he was ignorant? What is the relation between philosophy and knowledge? What is the difference between wisdom and knowledge? The picture of the city of words suggests a very simple answer: The quest for knowledge takes one toward the center of the city, the love of wisdom takes one toward the periphery. Philosophy makes no cumulative advances because it builds no buildings. It does not erect any new edifices of words. Yet it uses words in new and different ways because its task is to construct a word-map showing the way out of the city of words. Philosophy must acquaint itself with each new project in urban renewal, not in order to add its own new knowledge, but to revise the map leading out of the city. Socrates was well acquainted with the knowledge of his day, but he insisted that he had no special knowledge that others lacked. He could not build any new buildings in the city of words. He could only lead others out of the city.

The picture also helps us understand two other curious phenomena about philosophy: first, Socrates' need to talk to different people in different ways, and second, the proliferation and survival of different and conflicting philosophies. Because different people reside at different places within the city of words, different paths mark the shortest routes to the periphery. Consequently Socrates will lead different people along different paths, and the history of philosophy, unlike the history of science, does not have to shut off one path in order to open another. Urban renewal requires the destruction of one building to make way for another, but philosophy is not about erecting new knowledge that will be the same for all who approach it. One philosophy shows the way out of one part of the city, another philosophy shows the way out of another.

Part of the importance of self-knowledge derives from the need to know your location in the city. You cannot use a map until you know where you are located on the map. And the lover of wisdom who has the good fortune to make his or her way out of the city must recognize that his or her way out will not necessarily serve others who start somewhere else. Here we can see a distinction between the wisdom of the artist who has access to a silence beyond knowledge, and the achievement of the philosopher who knows that it is not enough merely to have left the city. Though he too can describe the peace and beauty of the surrounding pastures, his real task is a return trip to map as many paths as he can so that others may find the beauty described so evocatively by artists—and mystics.

The relationship between philosophy and mysticism can be complementary. Contemporary attitudes often reveal an unnecessary antagonism between those pursuing philosophy and those drawn toward mysticism. Because the philosopher sees the need for words, even in the quest for a silence beyond words, he distrusts the mystic's hasty leap into paradox, irrationalism, and silence. Because the mystic truly does reside outside the city of words he sometimes talks as if words are a hindrance, an unnecessary obstruction to higher states of consciousness. The picture of the city and its surroundings suggests that the philosopher and the mystic are simply preoccupied with different parts of the same journey. The word-maps are necessary to lead the lover of wisdom to where it finally makes sense to transcend words, at which point the mystic way is necessary for further progress. But the mystic can only speak to those who have ears to hear, that is, to those who have made it to the outer limits, whether through philosophy or through accidental wanderings (grace, they used to call it). It is a mistake to imagine that one can, while residing at the middle of the city, utter a few mystic incantations and find oneself seated in pastures of eternal bliss. It is also a mistake to imagine that as you approach the edge of the city you can expect another book, another piece of knowledge, another string of words to take you from knowledge to wisdom. But who knows when he stands at the edge? How much further have you to go? The path is so constituted that you can see behind you but you cannot see ahead. The one who can help you most is one who knows where you are because he knows you and has traversed the same path before you. With the exception of Socrates, the western tradition has placed very little emphasis on the role of guru, the spiritual master whose individual insight into the student's place enables him to see where the next step should lead. We have placed our trust instead in a religion that tends to treat everyone equally. Christianity has had its beneficial side effects in promoting a spirit of egalitarianism whose democratic ideals led to a political order that is perhaps more just than the caste system in India. But Christian egalitarianism has been confused with the idea that everyone is in the "same place" so that religion can present itself much like a body of knowledge, a temple standing alongside other buildings in the heart of the city. Western religion tends to ignore the importance of differences among individual locations within the secular city. Though almost in spite of itself the church has housed many mystics and many gurus, the favored form of religious education has remained the preacher who speaks the same words to an entire congregation. Using the term "religion" to refer primarily to western religion, I therefore contrast public religion to the privacy of the mystic way just as I contrast the public, intersubjectivity of knowledge to the privacy or at least the particularity of locations on the way to wisdom. Language is the public, intersubjective medium. Its unambiguous, literal use broadcasts the same message to all. Art and allegory, on the other hand, evoke the silences between their words. Within the interstices of nonliteral speech you may hear, if you listen in your own way, a hint of the mystic silence.

DAISETZ T. SUZUKI *(1870–1966)*

Many westerners first learned of Zen Buddhism from Daisetz T. Suzuki. For years he has been writing books on Zen. I have chosen the following little-known essay partly because his other works are easily available, partly because this essay includes so many points of close relation to other themes presented in this book.

Suzuki contrasts the "outward way" and the "inward way." The inward way leads through self-knowledge to different forms of consciousness. Suzuki's description of the inward way recalls the picture just painted in the preceding transition, as well as the examination of consciousness called for by Descartes, Snyder, and Laing, among others. Suzuki's descriptions of the obscure and seemingly nonsensical sayings of the Buddhist monks also bear comparison with Breton's description of surrealist methods. Could surrealism be a western version of the Zen mondo—*the nonsensical question and answer?*

Finally, consider once again the theme of individualism and/or subjectivism. Throughout the following essays on mysticism you might keep in mind a typically paradoxical possibility within the mystic tradition: the way to transcending possessive individualism lies not in the immediate denial *of self but rather at the end of a path that leads* through *the self—the inward way.*

The Awakening of a New Consciousness in Zen

1

My position in regard to "the awakening of a new consciousness," summarily stated, is as follows:

The phrasing, "the awakening of a new consciousness" as it appears in the title of this paper, is not a happy one, because what is awakened in the Zen experience is not a "new" consciousness, but an "old" one which has been dormant ever since our loss of "innocence," to use the Biblical term. The awakening is really the re-discovery or the excavation of a long-lost treasure.[1]

---

[1] Cf. "The Ten Oxherding Pictures," IX, entitled "Returning to the Origin, Back to the Source." In the *Lankāvatara Sūtra*, reference is also made to visiting one's native town where every road is familiar. "A new consciousness" is not at all new. Hakuin (1685–1768) refers to Ganto, an ancient master of the T'ang dynasty, while Kosen (1816–1892) brings out Confucius as a witness to his *satori* experience. In Zen literature we often come across such expressions as "Back at home and quietly sitting," "Like seeing one's family in a strange town," etc.

There is in every one of us, though varied in depth and strength, an eternal longing for "something" which transcends a world of inequalities. This is a somewhat vague statement containing expressions not altogether happy. "To transcend" suggests "going beyond," "being away from," that is, a separation, a dualism. I have, however, no desire to hint that the "something" stands away from the world in which we find ourselves. And then "inequalities" may sound too political. When I chose the term I had in mind the Buddhist word *asama* which contrasts with *sama*, "equal" or "same." We may replace it by such words as "differentiation" or "individualisation" or "conditionality." I just want to point out the fact that as soon as we recognise this world to be subject to constant changes we somehow begin to feel dissatisfied with it and desire for something which is permanent, free, above sorrow, and of eternal value.

This longing is essentially religious and each religion has its own way of designating it according to its tradition. Christians may call it longing for the Kingdom of Heaven or renouncing the world for the sake of divine love or praying to be saved from eternal damnation. Buddhists may call it seeking for emancipation or freedom. Indians may understand it as wishing to discover the real self.

Whatever expressions they may use, they all show a certain feeling of discontent with the situation in which they find themselves. They may not yet know exactly how to formulate this feeling and conceptually represent it either to themselves or to others.

I specified this obscure feeling as a longing for something. In this, it may be said, I have already a preconceived idea by assuming the existence of a something for which there is a longing on our part. Instead of saying this, it might have been better to identify the feeling of dissatisfaction with such modern feelings as fear or anxiety or a sense of insecurity. But the naming is not so important. As long as the mind is upset and cannot enjoy any state of equilibrium or perfect equanimity, this is a sense of insecurity or discontent. We feel as if we were in the air and trying to find a place for landing.

But we do not know exactly where this place for landing is. The objective is an altogether unknown quantity. It can nowhere be located and the fact adds a great deal to our sense of insecurity. We must somewhere and somehow find the landing.

Two ways are open: outward and inward. The outward one may be called intellectual and objective, but the inward one cannot be called subjective or affective or conative. The "inward" is misleading, though it is difficult to desig-

---

The term "new" may be permissible from the point of view of psychology. But Zen is mainly metaphysical, and it deals with a total personality and not parts of it. Rinzai talks about "the whole being in action" (*zentai sayu*). This is the reason why in Zen beating, slapping, kicking, and other bodily activities are in evidence. Concrete experiences are valued more than mere conceptualisation. Language becomes secondary. In Zen, consciousness in its ordinary scientific sense, has no use; the whole being must come forward. The whole elephant is needed and not its parts as studied by the blind. This will be clearer later on.

nate it in any other way. For all designations are on the plane of intellection. But as we must name it somehow, let us be content for a while to call it "inward" in contrast to "outward."

Let me give you this caution here: as long as the inward way is to be understood in opposition to the outward way,—though to do otherwise is impossible because of the human inability to go beyond language as the means of communication—the inward way after all turns to be an outward way. The really inward way is when no contrast exists between the inward and the outward. This is a logical contradiction. But the full meaning of it will I hope become clearer when I finish this paper.

The essential characteristic of the outward way consists in its never-ending procession, either forward or backward, but mostly in a circular movement, and always retaining the opposition of two terms, subject and object. There is thus no finality in the outward way, hence the sense of insecurity, though security does not necessarily mean "standing still," "not moving anywhere," or "attached to something."

The inward way is the reverse of the outward way. Instead of going out endlessly and dissipating and exhausting itself, the mind turns inwardly to see what is there behind all this endless procession of things. It does not stop the movement in order to examine what is there. If it does, the movement ceases to be a movement; it turns into something else. This is what the intellect does while the inward way refuses to do so. As soon as there is any kind of bifurcation, the outward way asserts itself and the inward way no longer exists. The inward way consists in taking things as they are, in catching them in their is-ness or suchness. I would not say, "in their oneness" or "in their wholeness." These are the terms belonging to the outward way. Even to say "is-ness" or "suchness" or "thusness" or in Japanese "sono-mama" or in Chinese "chi-mo," is not, strictly speaking, the inward way. "To be" is an abstract term. It is much better to lift a finger and say nothing *about* it. The inward way in its orthodoxy generally avoids appealing to language though it never shuns it.

The inward way occasionally uses the term "one" or "all," but in this case "one" means "one that is never one," and "all" means "all that is never all." The "one" will be "a one ever becoming one" and never a closed-up "one." The "all" will be "an all ever becoming all" and never a closed-up "all." This means that in the inward way the one is an absolute one, that one is all and all is one, and further that when "the ten thousand things" are reduced to an absolute oneness which is an absolute nothingness, we have the inward way perfecting itself.

Buddhism, especially Zen Buddhism as it developed in China, is rich in expressions belonging to the inward way. In fact, it is Zen that has effected, for the first time, a deep excavation into the mine of the inward way. To illustrate my point read the following—I give just one instance:

Suigan at the end of the summer session made this declaration: "I have been talking, east and west, all this summer for my Brotherhood. See if my eye-brows are still growing."[2]

One of his disciples said, "How finely they are growing!"

Another said, "One who commits a theft feels uneasy in his heart."

A third one without saying anything simply uttered "Kwan!"[3]

It goes without saying that all these utterances of the disciples as well as of the master give us a glimpse into the scene revealed only to the inward way. They are all expressions directly bursting out of an abyss of absolute nothingness.

Now we come to the psycho-metaphysical aspect of the inward way. Buddhists call this "abyss of absolute nothingness" *kokoro* in Japanese. *Kokoro* is *hsin* in Chinese and in Sanskrit *citta*, or *sarvasattvacitta* to use the term in Aśvaghosha's *Awakening of Faith*. *Kokoro* is originally a psychological term, meaning "heart," "soul," "spirit," "mind," "thought"; it later came to denote the kernel or essence of a thing, becoming synonymous metaphysically with "substance" and ethically "sincerity," "verity," "faithfulness," etc. It is thus difficult to give one English equivalent for *kokoro*.

Out of this *kokoro* all things are produced and all things ultimately go back to it. But this must not be understood in relation to time. The *kokoro* and all things are one and yet not one; they are two and yet not two. A monk asked Chao-chou (Joshu in Japanese), "I am told that the ten thousand things all return to the One, but where does the One return to?"

Chao-chou answered, "When I was in Ching-chou, I had a robe made which weighed seven *chin*." This *mondo*[4] demonstrates eloquently the difference between the outward way and the inward way. If this sort of question was asked of the philosopher he will go on writing one book after another. But the Zen master who thoroughly knows the inward way does not stop to think and instantly gives his answer which is final, with no going-on-and-on.

The *kokoro* is not to be confused with the *Ālaya-vijñāna* of the Yogā-cāra, one of the Mahāyāna schools. The *kokoro* reveals itself only when the Ālaya is broken through. The Ālaya may be considered as corresponding to "the Unconscious" or

---

[2]An old Indian tradition states that if a man utters an untruth all his facial hair such as beard and eyebrows will fall off. Suigan has spent his summer talking about things that can never be talked about, hence his allusion to his eyebrows still growing.

[3]Language deals with concepts and therefore what cannot be conceptualised is beyond the reach of language. When language is forced, it gets crooked, which means that it becomes illogical, paradoxical, and unintelligible from the viewpoint of ordinary usage of language or by the conventional way of thinking. For instance, the waters are to flow and the bridge is to stay over them. When this is reversed the world of senses goes topsy-turvy. The flowers bloom on the ground and not on rock. Therefore, when a Zen master declares, "I plant the flowers on rock," this must sound crazy. This crookedness all issues from language being used in the way not meant for it. Zen wants to be direct and to act without a medium of any kind. Hence "Katz!" or "Kwan!" Just an ejaculation with no "sense" attached to it. Nor is it a symbol, it is the thing itself. The person is acting and not appealing to concepts. This is intelligible only from the inward way of seeing reality.

[4]"Question and answer."

to "the Collective Unconscious," but the Ālaya is more than mere Unconscious as distinguished from the Conscious, for it comprises both. The *kokoro*, however, is not the Ālaya, in which, I would say, there is still something savouring of intellection. The *kokoro* is thoroughly purged of all sorts of intellection, it is an abyss of absolute nothingness.

And yet there is something moving in the midst of the *kokoro*. From the point of view of the outward way, this will be incomprehensible, because how could "absolute nothingness" be made to "move" at all? That such a thing should actually take place is a mystery. Some may call it "the mystery of being." As if from the unfathomable depths of an abyss, the *kokoro* is stirred. The *kokoro* wants to know itself. As long as it remains in itself all is quiet: the mountain remains a mountain towering up to the sky; the river flows as a river singing its way down to the ocean. But as soon as a tiny speck of cloud appears in the blue, it in no time spreads out enveloping the whole universe, even vomiting thunders and lightnings. The *kokoro* is in all this, but human intellectuality loses sight of it and would go on bewildered and annoyed and full of fearful thoughts. The *kokoro* is lost in the maze of perplexities.

In Western terminology, the *kokoro* may be regarded as corresponding to God or Godhead. God also wants to know himself; he did not or could not remain himself eternally absorbed in meditation. Somehow he came out of his is-ness and uttered a *mantram*, "Let there be light!" and lo, the whole world leaped out into existence. From where? Nowhere! Out of nothing! Out of the Godhead! And the world is God and God is the world, and God exclaims, "It is good!"

According to Aśvaghosha, "In the midst of the *kokoro* a *nen* is spontaneously awakened." A *nen* (*nien* in Chinese, *cittakshāna* in Sanskrit) is a moment of consciousness coming to itself; it is, one might say, a consciousness rising from the unconscious, though with a certain reservation. The Sanskrit, *ekacittakshāna*, literally means "one-mind-(or thought) moment." It is a "thought-instant" or "a consciousness-unit" which constitutes consciousness like a second or a minute which is a unit-measure for time. "Spontaneously" (*kotsunen* in Japanese) describes the way a *cittakshāna* rises in the *kokoro*. God uttered his fiat just as spontaneously. When the *kokoro* is said to have raised a thought to know itself, there was no conscious intentionality in it; it just happened so—that is, spontaneously.

But what we must remember in this connection is that when we say "no intentionality" we are apt to understand it in the outward way along the intellectual line and may find it difficult to reconcile it with the idea of human consciousness. It takes a long series of discussions to make this point clear, and as it does not directly concern us here, let it pass with this remark that with God as with the *kokoro* freedom and necessity are one.

When Buddhists make reference to God, God must not be taken in the Biblical sense. When I talk about God's giving an order to light, which is recorded in the Genesis, I allude to it with the desire that our Christian readers may come to a better understanding of the Buddhist idea of the inward way. What follows, therefore, is to be understood in this spirit.

The Biblical God is recorded as having given his Name to Moses at Mount Sinai as "I am that I am." I do not of course know much about Christian or Jewish theology, but this "name," whatever its original Hebrew meaning of the word may be, seems to me of such significance that we must not put it aside as not essential to the interpretation of God-idea in the development of Christian thought. The Biblical God is always intensely personal and concretely intimate, and how did he ever come to declare himself under such a highly metaphysical designation as he did to Moses? "A highly metaphysical designation," however, is from the outward way of looking at things, while from the inward way "I am that I am" is just as "spontaneous" as the fish swimming about in the mountain stream or the fowl of the air flying across the sky. God's is-ness is my is-ness and also the cat's is-ness sleeping on her mistress' lap. This is reflected in Christ's declaration that "I am before Abraham was." In this is-ness which is not to be assumed under the category of metaphysical abstractions, I feel like recognising the fundamental oneness of all the religious experiences.

The spontaneity of is-ness, to go back to the first part of this paper, is what is revealed in the "eternal longing" for something which has vanished from the domain of the outward way of intellectualisation. The *kokoro's* wishing to know itself, or God's demanding to see "light" is, humanly expressed, no other than our longing to transcend this world of particulars. While in the world, we find ourselves too engrossed in the business of "knowing" which started when we left the garden of "innocence." We all now want "to know," "to think," "to choose," "to decide," "To be responsible," etc., with everything that follows from exercising what we call "freedom."

"Freedom" is really the term to be found in the inward way only and not in the outward way. But somehow a confusion has come into our mind and we find ourselves madly running after things which can never be attained in the domain of the outward way. The feeling of insecurity then grows out of this mad pursuit, because we are no more able to be in "the spontaneity of is-ness."

We can now see that "The awakening of a new consciousness" is not quite a happy expression. The longing is for something we have lost and not for an unknown quantity of which we have not the remotest possible idea. In fact, there is no unknown quantity in the world into which we have come to pass our time. The longing of any sort implies our previous knowledge of it, though we may be altogether ignorant of its presence in our consciousness. The longing of the kind to which I have been referring is a shadow of the original *kokoro* cast in the track of the inward way. The real object can never be taken hold of until we come back to the abode which we inadvertently quitted. "The awakening of a new consciousness" is therefore the finding ourselves back in our original abode where we lived even before our birth. This experience of home-coming and therefore of the feeling of perfect security is evinced everywhere in religious literature.

The feeling of perfect security means the security of freedom and the securing of freedom is no other than "the awakening of a new consciousness." Ordinarily, we talk of freedom too readily, mostly in the political sense, and also in the moral sense. But as long as we remain in the outward way of seeing things, we can never understand what freedom is. All forms of freedom we generally talk of are far from being freedom in its deepest sense. Most people are sadly mistaken in this respect.

That the awakening of a new consciousness is in fact being restored to one's original abode goes in Christianity with the idea of God's fatherhood. The father's "mansion" can be no other than my own home where I was born and brought up till I became willful and left it on my own account. But, really, however willful I may be I can never leave my original abode behind and wander away from it. I am always where I was born and I can never be anywhere else. It is only my imagination or illusion that I was led to believe that I was not in it. To become conscious of this fact is to awaken a new consciousnes so called. There is nothing "new" in this, it is only the recovery of what I thought I had lost; in the meantime I have been in possession of it; I have been in it; I have been carrying it all the time; no, I am it and it is I.

The Shin Buddhists are quite emphatic in asserting this idea of restoration or rather of identification. They go further and say that Amida is always pursuing us and that even when we wanted to run away from him he would never let us go, for we are held firmly in his arms. The harder we struggle to get away from him the tighter he holds us, just as the mother does to her baby who tries to assert its self-will.[5]

In Zen the idea of restoration or re-cognition may be gleaned from Yeno's reference to "the original (or primal) face" which he wanted his disciples to see. This "face" is what we have even prior to our birth. In other words, this is the face of "innocence" which we have before our eating of the fruit from the tree of knowledge. "The tree of knowledge" is the outward way of intellection. When it begins to operate, "innocence" which is the inward way hides itself and becomes invisible. Most people take the "innocence" in a moral sense, but I would interpret it symbolically. "Innocence" corresponds to Aśvaghosha's "Original (or primal) Enlightenment" in which we were or are. It has never been lost even when "knowledge" is in full operation, because without it our existence has no significance whatever and "knowledge" itself of any kind would be altogether impossible. In this sense, "the inward way" is at once inward and outward. When it is separated and considered in opposition to "the outward way" it ceases to be itself.

---

[5]It may interest you to know that there is no word in European languages, as far as I know, equivalent for the Japanese word *oya*. *Oya* is neither father nor mother, it means both and applies to either of them. *Oya* is the quality to be found in each and both of them. It has no sex; therefore, its relationship to us is not that of progenitor; it is love pure and simple, it is love personified. Cannot we say that in the Jewish and Christian conception of God as father one feels him somewhat cold, distant and critical; and further that it is for this reason that Maria with Christ-child in her arms is needed to occupy an important niche in the Christian hierarchy? In Shin, Amida as *oya-sama* has nothing to do with the business of forgiving. We simply find ourselves in his grip when a new consciousness is awakened in us. Amida is neither father nor mother, he is *oya*, he is above sex, he is love itself.

Incidentally, Zen is often criticised as not having any direct contact with the world of particulars, but the critics forget the fact that Zen has never gone out of this world and therefore that the question of contact has no sense here.

Aśvaghosha's great work on the Mahāyāna is entitled *The Awakening of Faith,* but Zen generally does not use the term. The reason is that faith implies a division and Zen is emphatic in denying it in any sense. But if it (faith) is used in its absolute sense—which is in accordance with the inward way of seeing things— faith may be regarded as another name for *satori* and is no other than the awakening of "a new consciousness" though, as I have repeatedly said, there is really nothing "new" in Zen. Whatever this may be, "the awakening of a new consciousness" is the awakening of faith in Aśvaghosha's sense, that is, in its absolute sense. Then, faith corresponds to becoming aware of "Original Enlightenment" in which we are all the time. Faith is coming back to ourselves, to our own is-ness, and has nothing to do with the so-called objective existence of God. Christians and other theists seem to be unnecessarily busy in trying to prove God as objectively existing before they believe in him. But from the Zen point of view the objectivity of God is an idle question. I would say that those who are so engrossed in the question of this sort have really no God whatever, that is, subjectively as well as objectively. As soon as they have faith, they have God. Faith is God and God is faith. To wait for an objective proof is the proof—the most decisive one—that they have no God yet. Faith comes first and then God. It is not God who gives us faith, but faith that gives us God. Have faith and it will create God. Faith is God coming to his own knowledge.[6]

When the Zen man has a *satori,* the whole universe comes along with it; or we may reverse this and say that with *satori* the whole universe sinks into nothingness. In one sense, *satori* is leaping out of an abyss of absolute nothingness, and in another sense it is going down into the abyss itself. *Satori* is, therefore, at once a total annihilation and a new creation.

A monk asked a Zen master, "Does 'this' go away with the universe when the

---

[6]Cannot I say that Christians wanted Christ and so they have him? And also that they still wanted his mother Maria and therefore they have her? Being Christ's mother, she could not stay with us on earth, so she was made to go up to Heaven. Where Heaven is, is immaterial. In our religious experience, what we in our logical way think to be the law of causation is reversed, the effect comes first and then the cause. Instead of the cause proceeding to the effect, the effect precedes the cause.

When a Shin Buddhist was asked, "Can Amida really save us?" he answered, "You are not yet saved!" Christians may have the same way of expressing their faith. They would tell us to have faith first and all other things will follow. Is it not a somewhat futile attempt on the part of the Christian theologian to try to prove the historicity of Christ and then to proceed to tell us that for this reason we must believe in him? The same thing can be said of the crucifixion and the resurrection.

One may ask: If it is faith that is needed first, why so many different expressions of it? One faith goes out to Christ, another to Krishna, and still another to Amida, and so on. Why these variations? And why the fighting among them as we actually see in history?

I do not know if my interpretation of the phenomena is sufficient, but a tentative one is that faith, as soon as it goes out to express itself, is liable to be conditioned by all accidental things it finds around it, such as history, individual temperaments, geographical formations, biological peculiarities, etc. As regards the fighting among them, this will grow less and less as we get better acquainted with all these conditional accidents. And this is one of our aims in the study of religion in all its differentiations.

latter is totally consumed by fire at the end of the kalpa?" The master answered, "Yes." When the same question was proposed to another master, he said "No." From the inward way, "Yes" and "No" are one; destruction and construction are one.

The awakening of a new consciousness is the awakening of faith, and the awakening of faith is the creating of a new universe with infinite possibilities.[7] It is a new universe, yes, but in reality an old, old universe, where beings, sentient and non-sentient, have been dreaming their dreams, each in his way, ever since "Let there be light" came to work out its destiny. Here the Biblical time has no meaning. . . .

We talk ordinarily so much of self-consciousness as if we knew all about it, but in reality we have never come to a full knowledge of what self-consciousness is. Consciousness has always been conscious of something other than itself. As to "the Self" it has never even attempted to know, because the Self cannot be conscious of itself insofar as it remains dichotomous. The Self is known only when it remains itself and yet goes out of itself. This contradiction can never be understood on the level of the outward way. It is absolutely necessary to rise above this level if the meaning of self-consciousness is to be realised to its full depths.

The awakening of a new consciousness so called, as far as the inward way of seeing into the nature of things is concerned, is no other than consciousness becoming acquainted with itself. Not that a new consciousness rises out of the Unconscious but consciousness itself turns inwardly into itself. This is the home-coming. This is the seeing of one's own "primal face" which one has even before one's birth. This is God's pronouncing his name to Moses. This is the birth of Christ in each one of our souls. This is Christ rising from death. "The Unconscious" which has been lying quietly in consciousness itself now raises its head and announces its presence through consciousness.

We humans have the very bad habit of giving a name to a certain object with a certain number of attributes and think this name exhausts the object thus designated, whereas the object itself has no idea of remaining within the limit prescribed by the name. The object lives, grows, expands, and often changes into something else than the one imprisoned within the name. We who have given the name to it imagine that the object thus named for ever remains the same, because for the practical purposes of life or for the sake of what we call logic it is convenient to retain the name all the time regardless of whatever changes that have taken place and might take place in it. We become a slave to a system of nomenclature we ourselves have invented.

This applies perfectly to our consciousness. We have given the name "consciousness" to a certain group of psychological phenomena and another name

---

[7]The statement that faith creates God may be misconstrued. What I mean is that faith discovers God and simultaneously God discovers the man. The discovery is mutual and takes place concomitantly. To use Buddhist terms, when Amida is enlightened all beings are enlightened, and when we are enlightened we realize that Amida attained his enlightenment whereby our rebirth into the Pure Land is assured. The objective interpretation betrays that the critic has not deeply delved into the matter.

"unconscious" to another group. We keep them strictly separated one from the other. A confusion will upset our thought-structure. This means that what is named "conscious" cannot be "unconscious" and vice versa. But in point of fact human psychology is a living fact and refuses to observe an arbitrary system of grouping. The conscious wants to be unconscious and the unconscious conscious. But human thinking cannot allow such a contradiction: the unconscious must remain unconscious and the conscious conscious; no such things as the unconscious conscious or the conscious unconscious must take place, because they cannot take place in the nature of things, logicians would say. If they are to happen, a time-agent must come in and make consciousness rise out of the unconscious.

But Zen's way of viewing or evaluating things differs from the outward way of intellection. Zen would not object to the possibility of an "unconscious conscious" or a "conscious unconscious." Therefore, not the awakening of a new consciousness but consciousness coming to its own unconscious.

Language is used to give a name to everything, and when an object gets a name, we begin to think that the name is the thing and adjust ourselves to a new situation which is our own creation. So much confusion arises from it. If there is one thing Zen does for modern people, it will be to awaken them from this self-imposed thralldom. A Zen master would take up a staff, and, producing it before the audience declare, "I do not call it a staff. What would you call it?" Another master would say, "Here is a staff. It has transformed itself into a dragon, and the dragon has swallowed up the whole universe. Where do you get all these mountains, lakes, and the great earth?" When I got for the first time acquainted with Zen I thought this was a logical quibble, but I now realise that there is something here far more serious, far more real, and far more significant, which can be reached only by following the inward way.

W. T. STACE (1886–1967)

The next two essays constitute a dialogue between two thinkers with fairly similar backgrounds. Both pursued a good part of their careers in England, both are scholars of Hegel, both have taught philosophy in America—Stace at Princeton and Findlay at Yale—and both have ventured into the philosophy of mysticism. To describe their controversy in Hegelian terms, it expresses a difference in identity. Their dialogue is rich and meaningful because it is built on a shared basis, a sameness in difference.

The key issue of the following debate is the extent to which mysticism has a logic. In his "Mysticism and Human Reason" (1955), Stace argues that any attempt to explain or attain the mystic experience through logic is doomed to failure. Findlay argues that there is indeed a "Logic of Mysticism." Part of their difference depends on the breadth each allows to logic, but part depends on their substantively different stances toward mysticism. The debate over the logic of mysticism relates to Kierkegaard's Christianity of paradox. Consider whether Kierkegaard would be more sympathetic to Stace or Findlay.

Mysticism and Human Reason

Anyone who is acquainted with the mystical literature of the world will know that great mystics invariably express themselves in the language of paradox and contradiction; and it is to this aspect of mysticism that I especially want to draw your attention tonight. But before I do so I would like to make a few introductory remarks about mysticism in general. Mysticism is not a regional or local phenomenon. It is universal. By this I mean that it is found in every country, in every age, in every culture, and in association with every one of the great world-religions. I do not speak here of primitive cultures and primitive religions. No doubt mysticism expresses itself in them in primitive ways. But I am only speaking about advanced cultures and advanced religions. For instance, those ancient inspired documents, the Upanishads, which go back in time from 2,500 to 3,000 years, and which are the fountainheads both of the Hindu religion and of the Vedanta philosophy, are a direct report of mystical experience. Buddhism, too, is a mystical religion throughout. It is founded upon the mystical experience of Gautama Buddha. In the East, in India, the word "mysticism" or any word corresponding to it is not generally used. It is called "enlightenment" or "illumination." But the enlightenment experience of the East is basically the same as what is called the mystical experience in the West. In the Mohammedan religion the Sufis were the great representatives of mysticism. Mysticism appears in China in connection with Taoism. The Tao is a mystical conception. Judaism produced notable mystics. The history of Christianity is rich with the names of great mystics and some of these names are household words: Meister Eckhart, Saint Teresa, St. John of the Cross, and many others. Even outside the boundaries of any institutional religion, in the ancient Greco-Roman pagan world, not attached, perhaps, to any particular religion, Plotinus was one of the supremely great mystics.

Now, of course, as between these mysticisms in the various cultures, there are certain differences. For instance, Hindu mysticism is not quite the same as Christian mysticism. But I believe that the resemblances, the common elements, the elements which are universally found in all these mysticisms, are far more striking than the differences. I should say that the differences are superficial, while the common, basic, universal elements in all mysticism are fundamental. Should you ask me: "What are those common elements which appear in mysticism in all these different cultures and religions?" I can, perhaps, very briefly, summarize them.

In the first place, the absolutely basic, fundamental characteristic of all mystical experience is that it is called "the unitary consciousness," or, as it is sometimes called, "the unifying vision." We may contrast the mystical consciousness with our ordinary, everyday, rational consciousness. Our ordinary, everyday consciousness is characterized by multiplicity. I mean that both the senses and the intellect, which constitute our everyday consciousness, are in contact with and are aware of a vast number, a plurality, a multiplicity of different things. In our ordinary consciousness we discriminate between one thing and another. But the mystical consciousness transcends all differences and all multiplicity. In it there is no multiplicity and no division of difference. "Here," says Eckhart "all is one, and one is all." He goes on to say that in that supreme vision there are "no contrasts." "Contrast" is Eckhart's word for the difference between one thing and another, for instance between yellow and green. He even goes so far as to say that in that experience there are no contrasts, i.e. differences, between grass, wood, and stone, but that all these "are one."

Closely connected with, and perhaps as a result of this characteristic of transcending all multiplicity, discrimination, and division are other characteristics common to mystical experience in all religions. It is non-sensuous, non-intellectual, and non-conceptual. And since all words except proper names stand for concepts, this means mystical experience is beyond all words, incapable of being expressed in any language; "ineffable" is the usual word. Another characteristic is that what is experienced is beyond space and beyond time. It is timeless; and timelessness is eternity. And therefore the mystical consciousness, even though it lasts only for a very short while, perhaps only a moment, is nevertheless eternal. For that moment gathers into itself all eternity. It is an eternal moment.

Another universal characteristic is that mystical consciousness is blessedness —it is the peace which passeth all understanding. One might quote at length from the utterances of great mystics in all religions to prove that these are the common characteristics. I have time for only one quotation which I choose because it happens to include most of them in a few sentences. In the Mandukya Upanishad it is written:

> It is neither inward experience nor outward experience. It is neither intellectual knowledge nor inferential knowledge. It is beyond the senses, beyond the understanding, beyond all expression. It is the pure unitary consciousness wherein awareness of the world and of multiplicity is completely obliterated. It is ineffable peace. It is the supreme good. It is the One without a second.

One other common element I must mention. The mystic everywhere, except perhaps in Buddhism, which is a rather doubtful case here, invariably feels an absolute certainty that he is in direct touch with, and not only in direct touch with, but has entered into actual union with, the Divine Being. Plotinus expressed this by saying that "the man"—the mystic, that is—"is merged with the Supreme, sunken into it, one with it." And William James in his famous book, *Varieties of Religious Experience*, has an excellent brief chapter on mysticism, and in that he uses these words:

This overcoming of all barriers between the individual and the Absolute is the great mystic achievement. In mystic states we become one with the Absolute. This is the everlasting and triumphant mystic tradition, hardly altered by differences of climate, culture, or creed. In Hinduism, in Neo-Platonism, in Sufism, in Christian mysticism, we find the same recurring note, so that there is about mystic utterances an eternal unanimity which ought to make the critic stop and think.

Now, of course, this mystical experience, basically the same in all cultures as it is, might nevertheless be nothing but a beautiful dream. It is possible that it is a purely subjective state of the mystic's own mind, and that he is under an illusion when he thinks that he is in contact with some great being objective and outside himself. The only logical argument, the only piece of evidence which can be used to show that it is more than a beautiful dream, that it does actually reveal contact with an objective, divine being is this remarkable agreement, as regards basic features, of the different mysticisms in all the cultures of the world. Of course one may be convinced by faith, or intuition, or feeling. But I am speaking here of logical argument or evidence.

Regarding this I will quote you a few words written by Professor C. D. Broad of Cambridge, England. He says this:

I am prepared to admit that although the experiences have differed considerably at different times and places, there are probably certain characteristics which are common to all of them, and which suffice to distinguish them from all other kinds of experience. In view of this, I think it more likely than not that in mystical experience men come into contact with some Reality or some aspect of Reality which they do not come into contact with in any other way.[1]

The reason I read this very guarded statement—you see, he doesn't speak of this aspect of Reality as God—the reason I read this is because Broad happens to be a very remarkable kind of witness in such a matter. He says, in the same book which I am quoting, that he has no religious beliefs. He says also that he has never had anything which could be called a mystical or even a religious experience. But he claims that he has absolutely no bias, either for religion or against it. He thus claims to be entirely impartial. His is certainly a critical mind, inclined to be skeptical, certainly not inclined to accept any moonshine. Any of my philosophical colleagues who are acquainted, as they all are, with Broad's writings, will bear out the fact that this is a correct description of Broad. You will see that the evidence which he himself quoted for supposing that mystical experience is something more than a beautiful subjective dream is precisely the unanimity, the universal character of certain basic characteristics of it.

I consider that Broad's opinion is a reasonable one, and I shall adopt it, going, however, just one little step—or is it a little step?—further than Broad. For this aspect of reality, or this reality, with which the mystic is in contact, I shall use, as

[1] *Religion, Philosophy, and Psychical Research*, pp. 172-173.

he does not, the name "God." I use this word partly because it is the word that the mystics themselves use, but also because, whatever it is, the experience possesses the kind of qualities or characteristics that we think of as divine qualities: supreme value, blessedness, supreme goodness, love, and so on. But I do not wish to be understood as saying more than I actually am saying. I mean by the word "God" only what I have just said, namely, a reality which is possessed of divine qualities. I do not wish that there should be included in the connotation of the term the many superstitions and anthropomorphic meanings which have often clustered around it.

I turn now to what is the essential subject of my lecture, the paradoxes of mysticism. There are many such paradoxes. Their general character is this: that whatever is affirmed of God must be at the same time and in one and the same breath categorically denied. Whatever is said of the Divine Being, the opposite, the contradictory, must also be said. There are many such paradoxes, but I am going to speak tonight only about one, which is perhaps the most startling of them. This may be expressed by saying that God is both being and non-being. If you like, you can say it means that God both exists and does not exist; or again that God is beyond both existence and non-existence. There is thus both a positive and negative aspect. There is the positive divine and the negative divine. As to the positive divine, it is hardly necessary for me to say much about it because it is well known to everyone. It is the content of popular religion everywhere. We begin, I suppose, by saying that God exists. "Exist" is a positive word. We go on to say that he is a mind, a spirit, a person. These, too, are positive conceptions. Finally, we say that God is love, justice, mercy, power, knowledge, wisdom, and so on. All these are positive terms. And you will recognize that statements of this kind about the Divine Being are the content of ordinary, everyday, popular religious thought. This is true not only of Christianity but, I think, of all the great religions of the world, with the possible exception of Buddhism which is often called an atheistic religion. I don't think that there is really very much disagreement between the great world religions in regard to these basic attributes of God. There may be some difference of emphasis. No doubt it is the case that in Christianity the emphasis is upon God as love. In Hinduism the emphasis is on God as bliss. In Islam perhaps the emphasis is on God as power, and so on.

If we turn now to the negative divine, we pass into a region which is not so well known. This is usually especially associated with mystical religion. It may be expressed by saying that, just as for the positive divine God is being, here God is non-being. Even more striking words than this are used by the great mystics. God is "Nothing." He is "empty." He is "the Void." He is "the bottomless abyss of nothingness." And sometimes metaphors are used. Darkness as the absence of light, and silence as the absence of sound, are negative. Therefore God is spoken of as the great darkness, the great silence.

I am going to document these statements by referring very briefly (I cannot give very much of the evidence in a short lecture) to some of the great mystic utterances in the different religions of the world. I want to show that this is universal.

To begin with Christianity: Meister Eckhart, as you know, was a great Roman

Catholic mystic of the 13th century. In one place he says: "God is as void as if he were not." Elsewhere he says: "Thou shalt worship God as he is, a non-God, a non-form, a non-person." One of his followers wrote this of him: "Wise Meister Eckhart speaks to us about Nothingness. He who does not understand this, in him has never shone the divine light." Using the metaphor of darkness, Eckhart says: "The end of all things is the hidden darkness of the eternal Godhead." He also refers on many occasions to God as "the nameless nothing." Another well-known Christian mystic, Tauler, uses the same kind of language. He, too, refers to God as "the nameless nothing." Albertus Magnus writes this: "We first deny of God all bodily and sensible attributes, and then all intelligible attributes, and lastly, that being which would place him among created things." Notice that being, existence, is here said to be the mark of created things.

Turning to Judaism we find that Jewish mystics often referred to Jehovah as "the mystical Nothing." And again, "in the depths of His nothingness" is a common phrase. One of the Hassidic mystics wrote: "There are those who worship God with their human intellects, and others whose gaze is fixed on Nothing. He who is granted this supreme experience loses the reality of his intellect, but when he returns from such contemplation to the intellect, he finds it full of divine and inflowing splendor."

Turning to Buddhism we find a rather difficult case for our exposition because it is often said that Buddhism is an atheistic religion. This is true with some reservations. It is true that you do not find the Western concept of God in Buddhism. And it therefore might be said that it is obvious that Buddhism can have neither a positive nor a negative conception of God. This, however, is really not a justifiable conclusion. I can't go into the matter in any great detail here. On the whole, the concept of Nirvana is what corresponds in Buddhism to the Christian and Jewish concept of God. Nirvana, the experience of Nirvana, is, I think, what we would recognize as the divine experience, the experience of the divine element in the world. It is not important that the word God is not used. If Nirvana corresponds to the concept of the divine, then one can say that the concept of Nirvana has both the positive and negative aspects. Positively, it is bliss unspeakable. Negatively, it is the Void. This conception of the Void which you see that Eckhart also uses, is basic to Buddhism. Ultimate reality is the Void.

I find that in Hinduism this positive-negative paradox is more fully developed, more clear than it is in Christianity, Judaism, or Buddhism. In Hinduism it may be said that this paradox has three aspects. Brahman is the name used in the Upanishads and generally in Hindu thought for the ultimate, supreme God. The first aspect of the paradox is that Brahman both has qualities and yet is without any qualities at all. On the positive side the qualities of Brahman are the usual divine qualities to which I have already referred. On the negative side he is "unqualified." This is often expressed in the Upanishads by using a string of negative terms. For example, it is said that Brahman "is soundless, formless, shapeless, intangible, tasteless, odorless, mindless." Notice this last word, "mindless." This quotation is similar in meaning to the one which I read from Albertus Magnus. First we deny all physical qualities. He is "soundless, formless, shapeless, intangible, odorless, and tasteless." Next we deny all "intelligible," i.e. psychological or spiritual attributes. He is "mindless." But the negative of the paradox, the denial of all qualities, is summed up in a very famous verse in the Upanishads. Brahman is here, as often, referred to as the Self. The verse says: "That Self is to be described as not this, not that." One of the earlier translators worded it thus: "That Self is to be described by 'No! No!'." The force of this "No! No!" is clear. Whatever attribute you suggest, whatever predicate you suggest, whatever quality you suggest, of Brahman, the answer always is "No." Is he matter? No. Is he mind? No. Is he good? No. Is he evil? No. And so throughout every word that you can possibly choose.

The second aspect of the paradox in Hinduism is that Brahman is both personal and impersonal. His personality is carried by the very word "Self." He is the Self. He is personal and as such is wise, just, good, and so on. But he is also wholly impersonal. The word "mindless" contains this implication. For a person must necessarily be a mind. Also he is specifically referred to as "the impersonal Brahman." And sometimes the word "he" and sometimes the word "it" is used of Brahman. "He" conveys the notion of personality, "it" the notion of impersonality.

The third and final aspect of the paradox in Hinduism is that Brahman is both dynamic and static. Dynamic means that he is active, static means that he is actionless. On the positive side God is dynamic. He is the creative energy of the world, the creator. Also he acts in the world, guides and controls the world. On the static side it is specifically stated in the Upanishads that he is wholly actionless.[2] And the entire paradox is summed up in the following verse from the Upanishads:

That One, though never stirring, is swifter than thought; though standing still, it overtakes those who run. It moves and it moves not.

In this phrase, "It moves and it moves not," you have the whole paradox of the dynamic and static character of God summed up in five words.

Perhaps you will say, "Well, this is just poetic language. Everybody knows that poets like pleasant sounding phrases. And they like a balance of clauses. 'It moves and it moves not' sounds very well but it is mere words." I think you are quite mistaken if you take that interpretation. This is a literal statement of the paradox of the dynamic and the static.

Now I am persuaded that this entire paradox, and particularly that of the dynamic and the static character of the divine being, is not peculiar to Hinduism but is a universal characteristic of the religious consciousness everywhere, although in Hinduism it is more explicit, more baldly stated, than in other religions. In other religions it is present but tends to be veiled. Let us look at Christianity, for example. No one will deny that the Christian God is active. He is the creator of the world; he guides and controls it. But where, you will ask me, do you find evidence that the Christian God is static, inactive? It is true that you must look under the surface to find this. It is implied, implicit rather than explicit, in the

---

[2]Rudolph Otto in his *Mysticism East and West* claims it is as a superiority of the Christian God over the Hindu, that the latter is merely static, the former dynamic. He has missed the paradox and been misled by the frequent statements that Brahman is inactive.

concept of God as *unchangeable and immutable*. The changelessness, the immuta-
bility of God, is not only a Christian idea. It is a universal intuition of the religious
consciousness found in all religions. "In him is no shadow of turning," and there
is a well-known hymn which begins with the words:

> O strength and stay upholding all creation
> Who ever dost thyself *unmoved abide*.

The last two words convey the idea of the motionless, actionless character of God.
We hardly realize when we speak of God as "immutable" and yet as the Creator of
the world that we are uttering a paradox. There is, in fact, a contradiction between
God as active and God as unchanging, because that which acts necessarily
changes—changes from that state in which the action is not done to that state in
which the action is done. Therefore, that which is wholly unchanging is also
wholly inactive. The same idea also appears in poetry. T. S. Eliot twice to my
knowledge in his poems uses the phrase, "The still point of the turning world."
The literal meaning of this is obvious. It refers to the planet, the periphery and the
outer parts of which are turning, while the axis in the middle is motionless. But
the mystical meaning is also clear. It means that this world is a world of flux and
change and becoming, but at the center of it, in the heart of things, there is
silence, stillness, motionlessness.

So much, then, for the exposition of this paradox. But the human intellect,
when it comes to a logical contradiction, necessarily attempts to get rid of it,
attempts to explain away the contradiction. It tries to show that although there is
an apparent contradiction, there is not really one. To get rid of a contradiction is
essential to the very nature of our logical and rationalistic intellect.

Mystics themselves often show this characteristic since they are rational
beings. I will give you two examples of attempts by religious thinkers to explain
this paradox of the positive and negative divine logically, to make it comprehen-
sible to the logical intellect. One logical way of getting rid of a contradiction is to
separate the contradictory predicates and to declare that they apply to two
different things. For example, if we speak of a square circle, this is a contradiction.
If I say this desk top in front of me is both square and circular, this is a
contradiction. But if I say the concept "square" applies to one thing and the
concept "circular" to something else, if I say "this thing over here is square, and
that thing over there is circular," then of course the contradiction disappears.
This method of getting rid of the contradiction of the positive and negative has
been used by mystics themselves. The great Hindu philosopher Sankara, who lived
in the eighth century A.D. and who wrote a great commentary upon the
Upanishads and endeavored to systematize the Vedanta philosophy, was very
clearly and well aware of this contradiction about which I have been speaking. He
attempted a solution by saying that there are really two Brahmans. One of them,
which he called the Higher Brahman, is void, empty, qualityless, impersonal,
actionless, negative. The other Brahman, which he calls the Lower Brahman,
carries the usual divine attributes—that is, he is the creator of the universe, he is
personal, wise, just, and so on. He is, in fact, the God of popular religion. Sankara
held, however, that the ultimate ground of the world is the Higher Brahman, and

the Lower Brahman merely issues forth from this ultimate ground as its first manifestation. Thus the contradiction is got rid of because the Higher Brahman carries the inactive, the negative character, while the Lower Brahman carries the positive attributes.

One may be quite sure that this is the wrong solution because the religious intuition is peremptory that God is one and not two, and this is especially the case in Hinduism since everywhere Brahman is spoken of as the One, and more emphatically as "the One without a second."

It is extremely instructive and interesting to see that exactly the same solution of this paradox is offered by the Christian mystic, Meister Eckhart, of course in complete independence of Sankara. Eckhart makes a distinction between God and the Godhead. It is the Godhead, according to him, which is void, empty, and negative. God has the usual positive, divine attributes. As before, one must say that this is the wrong solution. But Eckhart, in a sense, withdraws it himself. For he identifies the Godhead with God the Father, and God with God the Son. And in accordance with the doctrine of the Trinity these two are one in spite of their duality. Yet Eckhart, like Sankara, declares that it is the void Godhead which is the ultimate ground of all things.

My own belief is that all attempts to rationalize the paradox, to make it logically acceptable, are futile because the paradoxes of religion and of mysticism are irresoluble by the human intellect. My view is that they never have been, they never can be, and they never will be resolved, or made logical. That is to say, these paradoxes and contradictions are inherent in the mystical experience and cannot be got rid of by any human logic or ingenuity. This, in my opinion, is an aspect of what is sometimes called the mystery of God or the incomprehensibility of God. This mystery of God is not something which we can get rid of, something which we could understand by being a little more clever or a little more learned. It is ultimate, it is an ultimate and irremovable character of the divine. When you say that God is incomprehensible, one thing you mean is just that these contradictions break out in our intellect and cannot be resolved, no matter how clever or how good a logician you may be. And I think that this view is in the end the view of the mystics themselves, including Eckhart, in spite of his apparent attempt to explain the paradox.

In order to show that this is in fact the view of the mystics themselves in all religions, I will read to you from a Christian mystic, a Hindu, and a Buddhist. The Christian example again is Eckhart. Rudolph Otto writes that "Eckhart establishes a polar unity between rest and motion within the Godhead itself. The eternally resting Godhead is also the wheel rolling out of itself." And in Eckhart's own words: "This divine ground is a unified stillness, immovable in itself. Yet from this immobility all things are moved and receive life."

The Hindu from whom I wish to quote is Aurobindo, who died only a few years ago. There is no doubt in my mind that he himself experienced the mystical vision in full measure. He says:

Those who have thus possessed the calm within can perceive always welling out from its silence the perennial supply of the energies which work in the world.

I wish to comment on this sentence. "Those who have thus possessed the calm within" means those who have possessed mystical vision. "Can perceive always welling out from its silence"—"silence" is the motionlessness, the stillness, the inactivity of the divine. "The perennial supply of the energies which work in the world" refers to the creative activity of the divine. These creative energies are said to "well out from the silence." In other words, they issue out of the empty void. Finally, we see the paradox of the static and the dynamic directly stated as an *experience*. The word "perceive" is used. This is not an intellectual proposition, a theory, an intellectual construction, a philosophical opinion. It is a direct perception or vision of reality.

My last example is Suzuki, the well-known Zen Buddhist mystic, now teaching in New York. He writes:

> It is not the nature of "prajna" to remain in the state of "sunyata," absolutely motionless.

("Prajna" is the word for mystical intuition, while "sunyata" means the void.) So he is saying it is not the nature of mystical consciousness to remain in a state of void, absolutely motionless.

> It demands of itself that it differentiate itself unlimitedly and, at the same time, it deserves to remain in itself undifferentiated. This is why "sunyata" is said to be a reservoir of infinite possibility, and not just a state of mere emptiness. Differentiating itself and yet remaining in itself undifferentiated, it goes on eternally in the work of creation. We can say of it that it is creation out of nothing. "Sunyata" is not to be conceived statically but dynamically, or better, as at once static and dynamic.

David Hume asked ironically, "Have you ever seen a world created under your eyes—have you ever observed an act of creation of the world?" The answer is: Yes, there are men who have seen this.

I conclude that these contradictions and paradoxes are impossible of logical adjustment or resolution. What, then, should we think about the matter? Should we say that there is contradiction in the nature of God himself, in the ultimate being? Well, if we were to say that, I think that we shouldn't be saying anything very unusual or very shocking. Many people have said this or at any rate implied it. Does not the Christian doctrine of the Trinity itself imply this? What could be a greater paradox than that? And it is not to be believed that the three-in-one, the three which is one and the one which is three, could be understood or explained by a super-Einstein, or by a higher mathematics than has yet been invented. It is irremovable and an absolute paradox. Also one might quote the words of Jacob Boëhme suggesting that there is contradiction in the heart of things, in the ultimate itself. Schwegler, a distinguished German historian of philosophy, writes this:

> The main thought of Boëhme's philosophizing is this: that self-distinction, inner diremption is the essential characteristic of spirit, and,

consequently of God. God is the living spirit only if and insofar as he comprehends within himself difference from himself.

One might also perhaps quote Boëhme's well-known statement that God is both "the Eternal Yea" and "the Eternal Nay," but this perhaps might also be taken simply as a brief expression of the negative-positive paradox.

Although I do not think it would be anything seriously erroneous if we would say that there is contradiction in the Ultimate, yet I would prefer myself to use other language. I should say that the contradiction is in us, in our intellect, and not in God. This means that God is utterly and forever beyond the reach of the logical intellect or of any intellectual comprehension, and that in consequence when we try to comprehend his nature intellectually, contradictions appear in our thinking. Let me use a metaphor to express this. We speak of God as the "Infinite" and of ourselves as "finite" minds. As a matter of fact what the word "infinite" means in this connection is itself a difficult problem in the philosophy of religion. It is certain that the word "infinite," when applied to God, is not used in the same sense as when we speak of infinite time or infinite space or the infinite number series. What it does mean is a problem. I believe that it can be solved, that is to say, it is possible to give a clear meaning to the word "infinite"—different from the infinity of space and time—as the word is applied to God. However, if I am allowed to use this language of finite and infinite, my metaphor is that if you try to pour the infinite into the finite vessels which are human minds, these finite vessels split and crack, and these cracks and splits are the contradictions and paradoxes of which I have been talking. Therefore this amounts to saying that God is utterly incomprehensible, incapable of being intellectually understood. In order to make my final point I will use the word "unknowable." It means that God is, in a sense, unknowable. But we must be very careful of this. If God were absolutely unknowable, and in no sense knowable, then there could be no such thing as religion, because in some sense or other religion is the knowledge of God.

The explanation of this is that he is unknowable to *the logical intellect*, but that he can be known in direct religious or mystical experience. Perhaps this is much the same as saying that he can be known by "faith" but not by "reason." Any attempt to reach God through logic, through the conceptual, logical intellect, is doomed, comes up against an absolute barrier; but this does not mean the death of religion—it does not mean that there is no possibility of that knowledge and communion with God which religion requires. It means that the knowledge of God which is the essence of religion is not of an intellectual kind. It is rather the direct experience of the mystic himself. Or if we are not mystics, then it is whatever it is that you would call religious experience. And this experience of God—in the heart, shall we say, not any intellectual understanding or explanation—this experience of God is the essence of religion.

JOHN FINDLAY (b. 1903)

As noted in the introduction to Stace, John Findlay comes to mysticism with a background in Hegel studies. Findlay's approach to Hegel and mysticism is more thoroughly Hegelian than Stace's. As Findlay states in his comments on the role of philosophy (from Religious Studies, *1972), he conceives the task of philosophy as finding connections where none may be obvious. This was Hegel's great talent, and Findlay applies it to the phenomena of mysticism. He argues that the logic of mysticism is basically the logic of a nonatomic, unified world, that our ordinary logic is inadequate to the mystical experience only because our ordinary logic derives from a very partial type of experience of a nonunified world. Findlay opposes this atomic metaphysics of common sense to the monistic metaphysics of mysticism, and he is willing to argue that the latter is in the last analysis more true than the former, though the monistic metaphysics must also account for the experience of pluralism, disparateness, imperfection, and evil.*

Although Findlay addresses many of his remarks to Stace's Mysticism and Philosophy *(1960), Stace's views remain substantially unchanged from what they were in the 1955 address.*

The Logic of Mysticism

. . . I am calling my present lecture 'The Logic of Mysticism' because I wish to study what is admittedly a very important and widespread form or set of forms of human experience from a predominantly logical point of view. I intend, that is, to study a whole range of notions and assertions and reasonings that could be called 'mystical', and the peculiar language in which they express themselves, rather than any highly specific, greatly prized experiences which lie behind these notions and assertions. And I wish to see whether there are not peculiar rules and guiding principles governing these mystical notions and assertions, and whether it is not possible to raise questions of the well-formed and the ill-formed, of validity and invalidity, in regard to them, as we can in other fields of discourse, e.g., of discourse on probability or on morals. I am approaching mysticism in this way because there is a widespread persuasion abroad that mysticism, so far from having a peculiar logic that can be studied and evaluated, has no trace of logic in its utterances at all, that it is in fact the very antithesis of the logical, and that the experiences it embraces, and which inspire its peculiar utterances, are not even experiences of which a satisfactory verbal expression is possible. They are intrinsically ineffable experiences, as the mystics themselves often allege, while expressing them so richly and so eloquently as to demonstrate their extraordinary effability. They are also experiences whose expression delights to flout all logical rules rather than to obey them, and which accordingly admit of no logical treatment whatever. The experiences which lie behind mystical assertions are often thought, further, to be experiences of a very peculiar class of persons called mystics, people liable to trances, seizures, illuminations and unmotivated convictions: if we value them, we value them as we do clairvoyants or people gifted with extra-sensory perception, and if we do not value them, we think of them as physically and psychologically abnormal beings who must certainly not be encouraged. In neither case is there anything of profound philosophical importance in what they say, let alone anything of *logical* significance. Whereas what I want to hold is that mystical utterances reflect a very peculiar and important way of looking at things which is as definite and characteristic as any other, which, while it may override and sublate ordinary ways of looking at things, and so have an appearance of senselessness and inconsistency, none the less has its own characteristic, higher-order consistency, and I wish further to suggest that this mystical way of looking at things, so far from being the special possession of peculiar people called mystics, rather enters into the experience of most men at many times, just as views of the horizon and the open sky enter into most ordinary views of the world. At the horizon things become confused or vastly extended, parallel lines meet and so on; just so, in the mystical sectors of experience, some things behave and appear quite differently from things in the near or middle distances of experience. Some people refuse to cultivate mystical ways of looking at things, and in fact resolutely exclude them. In the same way some people never look beyond the physical situation in which they immediately find themselves. This kind of experiential and logical myopia only shows that there are many myopic people, and that some are deliberately myopic: it shows nothing about the logical or illogical character of mystical utterances and experiences. On the view to which I adhere the so-called great mystics, people like Plotinus, Jalalud'in Rumi, St Teresa and so on, are merely people who carry to the point of genius an absolutely normal, ordinary, indispensable side of human experience and attitude, just as some other people carry to the point of genius the numerical, additive way of looking at things which all men possess in some degree. There are people whose incapacity for mathematics leads them to form an aversion from the whole subject, and there are people whose incapacity for mysticism leads them to form a similar aversion, yet it does not follow that either capacity is not a form of normal human endowment, expressing itself in a peculiar type of utterance and discourse, in fact with such regularity as to merit the title of a 'logic'. Such, at least, will be the assumption on which the present lecture will proceed.

In the lecture I am about to give I have been greatly assisted by W. T. Stace's excellent book *Mysticism and Philosophy*, published in 1961.[1] This book is valuable because it deals with the essential questions which concern mysticism, and deals with them in what I consider a reasonably adequate manner. Stace starts, not by attempting to define mysticism or the mystical, which would *assume* that there was one uniform phenomenon called 'mysticism' in all the experiences and utterances that we cover by this name, but by asking whether there is not what he calls a

---

[1] [W. T. Stace, *Mysticism and Philosophy*, Philadelphia, Lippincott, 1960.—J. A. O.]

'common core' to all the experiences and utterances in question.... Stace then elaborately shows, by quoting a wealth of material, that there are immense similarities of approach in utterances called 'mystical', which stem from the most varied sources, and have few or no historical links: a Christian saint uses much the same astounding language as a Moslem devotee or a Hindu Yogi, without being aware of the wide community he exemplifies. Profound differences there certainly are between varied styles of mysticism, but the resemblances are much more striking, even oppressively so, and they are not at all like the loose family resemblance embodied in, say, the Hapsburg features or countenance. Stace arrives at the view, after considering all the material, that there is something like a uniform core to the many cases that we unhesitatingly class as instances of 'mysticism', and he further arrives at the view that this core diverges into two main specifications which he calls 'extrovertive' and 'introvertive' mysticism respectively. Of each of these varieties he gives a careful and well-documented characterisation, and he does so without claiming for it either exhaustiveness or definitory exactness, and without rejecting the possibility of isolated cases which deviate from it. Some performances and utterances may have *some* of the marks of the mystical without the others, but the marks cluster together in a great number of cases, and have moreover, a character of mutual 'belongingness' which makes such a clustering seem natural and appropriate.

Having thus pinned mysticism down as a more or less treatable, uniform phenomenon, Stace considers the question of the validity of mystical utterances: he deals with this under the heading of 'The Problem of Objective Reference'. Is mysticism, in other words, a merely personal, subjective way of looking at things, or does it really contribute to our vision of the world? I do not myself at all agree with Stace's interpretation of this question, nor with the answer he gives to it. For he practically identifies objectivity with membership of a law-governed causal system, and, while mysticism as an *attitude* may fit in with such a system, and so be 'objective', the matters it claims to reveal, that it takes a stance towards, certainly lie quite outside any such system. Mysticism does not profess to acquaint us with something like high entropy or the Aurora Borealis, and it is in this obvious sense not objective. But, since it makes no claim to be filling in a particular gap in a law-governed cosmic picture, mysticism is not, in Stace's view, subjective either. What it reveals is not hallucinatory or delusive like, say, ectoplasm or the canals on Mars. Mysticism, says Stace, is neither subjective nor objective, but trans-subjective: it is a community of attitude that many people share. Now I am not in the least satisfied with all this, for mystical moods and persons, are, above all, assertive, and they put something before us as *true*, as *real*, whether anyone thinks so or not. Mysticism is characterised throughout by the noetic quality on which William James laid such stress in his account of religious experience. If mysticism tells us nothing about the world, then it is, in a deep sense, very false indeed, since it certainly professes to tell us something about it. I certainly therefore wish to answer this question as to the validity of mysticism in a manner different from Stace, and I do not wish to assume that whatever validates a mystical utterance is also what validates a scientific utterance. The truth of mysticism may be deeper than the truth of science, and it may only be in the light of mystical truth that scientific truth is fully intelligible. But Stace has proceeded usefully in separating the question of validity from the question of phenomenological description, and in showing the peculiar difficulty of the questions 'Is mysticism true?', 'Are mystical assertions valid?'. . . .

I now wish to follow Stace's method by documenting mysticism with quotation. I could quote from the Upanishads or the Buddhist Sutras, or the Tao-teh-King or St Teresa or Ruysbroeck, etc., but, since we are all philosophers, and our purpose philosophical, I shall mainly cite from one who is as great a philosopher as he is a mystic, namely Plotinus. He certainly practised mysticism to the limit, since he achieved the uttermost ecstasy or union with the Absolute on at least four occasions, as his biographer Porphyry relates. My first quotation is from *Ennead* V, Treatise viii, paragraphs three and four, *On Intelligible Beauty;* it describes the manner of existence in the true, the intelligible world. 'For all there is heaven: earth is heaven and the sea is heaven, and so are the animals and plants and men, all heavenly things in that heaven. . . . And life is easy yonder, and truth is their parent and nurse, their substance and sustenance, and they see all things, not such as are in flux but as have true being, and they see themselves in others: for all things are transparent, and nothing is dark and resistant: everything is inwardly clear to everything and in all respects: light is made manifest to light. And each holds all within itself, and again sees all in each other thing, so that everything is everywhere, and all is all, and each all, and the glory infinite. Each of those things is great, since even the small is great, and the sun yonder is all the stars, and each star the sun, and again all the stars. One things stands forth in each, though it also displays all. . . . Each there walks, as it were, on no alien earth, but is itself always its own place; its starting-point accompanies it as it hastens aloft, and it is not one thing and its region another.'[2] In this passage we have the mystical doctrine of interpenetration, of seeing the diverse things in the world as in some deep sense one and the same. This doctrine is put forward by Meister Eckhart when he says: 'All that a man has here externally in multiplicity is intrinsically one. Here all blades of grass, wood and stone, all things are one. This is the deepest depth.' And again: 'Say, Lord, when is a man in mere understanding? I say to you, when a man sees one thing separated from another. And when is he above mere understanding? That I can tell you. When he sees all in all, then a man stands above mere understanding.'[3] I could also quote famous utterances from Mahayanist Buddhist sutras in which the same doctrine of mystical interpenetration is put forward.

I return, however, to a second quotation from Plotinus of a somewhat different tenor: it comes from *Ennead* VI, Treatise ix, paras. 5, 6, 11. 'This is the point of the rule which governs our mysteries, that they should not be divulged to outsiders: one is forbidden to reveal the divine to one who has not enjoyed the vision of it. Since seer and seen were then not twain, and the seen was united with the seer rather than seen by it, the seer retains an image of the Supreme when he remembers his union with it. He himself was the One, having no difference towards anything in himself, nor towards other things. All then was still with him,

---

[2] It is interesting to report that Leo Robertson wrote a poem on this passage.
[3] See Otto, *Mysticism, East and West*, p. 61, quoted by Stace, *loc. cit.* pp. 63-4.

no stirring, no desire was with him when he rose to that state, nor any notion nor act of thinking, nor if one may so put it, himself. But as if caught up, rapt, he has passed in quiet to an unshaken state of solitude, completely at rest, and become as it were, rest itself.' (The last phrase 'rest itself' is a typical piece of mystical syntax.) 'He no longer moves among beauties and has outstripped beauty itself, has outstripped the choir of the virtues also, and is like one who, entering an inner sanctuary, leaves behind the statues in the temple that will again be the first to greet him, as secondary spectacles, after the spectacle and the communion within, a communion not with a statue or an image, but with the thing itself. Perhaps, however, there was no spectacle there, but an approach other than sight, an ecstasy, a simplification, a surrender of self, a reaching towards contact, a peace, a contrivance of harmony that brings what is in the sanctuary into view. To look otherwise is to find nothing there.' This extraordinary passage can be paralleled by many passages from St Teresa where she speaks of a beam of light being temporarily lost in a larger light, or of the water in a bucket being temporarily lost in a larger body of water in which it is immersed. Or one can quote from the *Brihadaranyakopanishat*, VI, iii, 21, 23, 32, where it says that 'Now as a man, when embraced by a beloved wife, knows nothing that is without, nothing that is within, thus this person, when embraced by the intelligent self, knows nothing that is without, nothing that is within. . . . And when he does not see, yet he is seeing, though he does not see. For sight is inseparable from the seer, because it cannot perish. But there is then no second, nothing else different from him that he could see.' One is not operating very differently if one turns to Wittgenstein's *Tractatus:* 'The world and life are one' (5.621); 'I am my world' (5.632); 'The subject does not belong to the world, but it is a limit of the world' (5.632); 'The philosophical I is not the man, not the human body or the human soul of which psychology treats, but the metaphysical subject, the limit, not a part of the world' (5.641); 'The contemplation of the world *sub specie aeterni* is its contemplation as a limited whole. The feeling of the world as a limited whole is the mystical feeling' (6.45); 'There is certainly something ineffable: this shows itself, it is the mystical, (6.522); 'My propositions are elucidatory in this way: he who understands me finally recognises them as senseless when he has climbed out through them, on them, over them: he must so to speak throw away the ladder after he has climbed up on it' (6.54). This last proposition is paralleled by an aphorism from the founder of Zen Buddhism about throwing away a raft once it has taken one to the further shore.

I shall now consider the enumeration of the basic traits of mysticism, its 'universal core', which occurs in Stace's book. Stace, as I have said, distinguishes two varieties of mysticism, an extrovertive and an introvertive, and for the extrovertive he enumerates the following. (I rephrase his words a little.)

1. The unifying vision, expressed by the formula 'All is one'. The one is perceived in and through the multiplicity of objects.

2. The more concrete apprehension of One as an inner subjectivity, a life, a consciousness, a living presence in all things, 'Nothing is really dead'.

3. The sense of objectivity or reality: what is apprehended is absolutely real.

4. The feeling of extreme blessedness, joy, happiness, satisfaction, etc.
5. The feeling that what is apprehended is holy or sacred.
6. The feeling that what is apprehended is paradoxical.

And with reservations he adds:

7. The allegation that what is apprehended is 'ineffable'. 'Such phrases as "inexpressible", "unutterable" bespatter the writings of mystics all over the world.'

For introvertive mysticism Stace gives the same list of features, except that its first two members are different. In introvertive mysticism we have, instead of a unifying vision connected with all empirical contents and objects, 'a unifying consciousness from which all the multiplicity of sensuous or conceptual or other empirical content has been excluded, so that there remains only a void and empty unity'. Instead of the One which is All, one has, in short, the One which is Nothing. And instead of (2), the sense of a universal life and consciouness in things, one has the idea of something essentially non-spatial and non-temporal, and otherwise uninvolved. Stace here quotes from a Buddhist sutra: 'There is, monks, an unborn, not become, not made, uncompounded, and were it not, monks, for this unborn, not become, not made, uncompounded, no escape could be shown for what is born, has become, is made, is compounded.'[4]

I think Stace's account of mysticism has deep faults which reflect its method. It is an external, empirical account based on mere examination of single cases, and an attempt to find common traits which occur in them all. Its outcome is a rag-bag of empirical features, having no plain philosophical significance. Some people, it seems, like to speak in terms of an absolute unity present in all things, or utterly separate from them all, they like to say that this unity is objective or real, they feel bliss and awe in its contemplation, they like to say paradoxical things about it, they profess to find it indescribable, etc. Such people, it seems, are also liable to appear all over the world and at any point of time, like mongols or cretins, and the things they say are always remarkably uniform. But all this is a mere fact of human experience and behavior like, for example, the basic characters and the many mutations of the sexual instinct. I myself am a philosopher who is utterly uninterested in anything which is a mere matter of fact, externally observed, even if it is a fact connected with what people think and say, and I do not regard any mere decanting and classification of empirical fact as genuine philosophical investigation. Philosophy is to me the bringing forth, not the mere registration or discovery, of conceptions which are what I should call intelligible unities, whose various components hang together necessarily, or with some approach to rational necessity, and which alone can illuminate the complex windings of fact. Philosophy I regard as the overcoming of notional contingency, of the kind of loose combination of traits into a concept because such traits often occur together in actual cases, or are combined together in people's actual usage. If mysticism or the

[4]*Loc. cit.* p. 126.

mystical is to be a worthwhile theme for philosophical study, it must be a coherent, notional unit, and a coherent notional unit which is necessary for the understanding of man and the world, and so rightly reckoned as fundamental. I am not at all interested in mysticism if it is a mere natural fact, or body of natural facts, about man, or if its concept is a mere natural fact, or body of natural facts, about human language. I think there is such a thing as belongingness or mutual affinity among conceptual features which moves us to combine them into a single concept, and to use a single term more or less to cover them all, and that their analytic discoverability in the meaning or use of that term is a consequence of this affinity. And I think the business of philosophers is to make concepts more of a notional unity, involving a deeper belongingness, than do the concepts which occur in ordinary usage. Philosophical analyses that profess to concern themselves with mere facts of usage in fact do not do so. The usages they select and consider together, always have a notional unity and importance, and the concepts they use to illuminate them, even when geared to what the ordinary man thinks or says, always depart far from the ordinary man's style of thinking. The immense merit of Austin is to have shown how fantastically far ordinary usage is from philosophy, but the concepts he himself elaborates, to *deal* with ordinary usage, the illocutionary, perlocutionary, etc., suggests that philosophers like himself do well to depart far from ordinary usage. The notion of the perlocutionary, for example, is not one that ordinary speakers ever have framed or could frame.

Leaving these methodological issues aside, I proceed to sketch the mystical in what I feel to be a more satisfactory manner, and I am led to say, first of all, that mysticism is essentially a frame of mind connected with an *absolute* of some sort, meaning by an absolute an object of very peculiar type having very peculiar logical properties. By an absolute I mean something which, on the one hand, is irremoveable and necessarily existent and self-existent, which could not meaningfully be supposed absent, nor dependent for its existence on anything else, and on which all contingencies of existence, whether within or without itself, are wholly dependent, and which further has the uniqueness and singleness which goes with its absolute status. I also wish to mean by it something which shows forth absolutely *every* recognised type of excellence or value in a fashion so transcendent that it can perhaps be rather said to *be* all these types of excellence than merely to embody or exemplify them, which *is* them all of necessity and is them all *together*, and which is certainly the sole cause for their presence in any finite case or contingent manifestation. I do not doubt that you will see what I mean by saying that the features of an absolute have logical affinity, that, while it is logically significant to conceive of them apart from each other, and so to build up the notion of a quasi-absolute which has some of these traits and not others—value-free quasi-absolutes are certainly constructed by many—the features in question do belong together and do complete each other, and that what they furnish is an integrated whole, the conception of something superlative, self-explanatory and all-explanatory, which rounds off all our concepts and valuations, and provides the necessary background for all of them. The various features which Stace laboriously discovers all arise because mysticism is oriented towards an absolute: the feature of absolute unity because an absolute is necessarily single and unique, the feature of reality because an absolute can only be thought of as inescapable, necessarily existent, the emotional colouring of bliss and awe, because an absolute is thought of as embodying all values and embodying them necessarily, the features of paradoxicality and ineffability, because an absolute necessarily differs in category, we may say, from any ordinary, finite object, being necessarily self-existent while ordinary objects exist contingently and dependently, and being all excellences whereas an ordinary object cannot have one excellence without inevitably failing to have another, and so on. Many would say that what I have called an absolute is a deeply contradictory or senseless notion, since the notions of necessary existence and unsurpassable excellence are either meaningless or self-contradictory. But whether this is true or not, self-contradictory and empty notions play a vast part in human experience and attitude, and this is certainly true of man's limiting notions of absolutes. Even philosophies which repudiate absolutes in their logic, and have professedly built up radically contingent, value-free systems, generally smuggle in absolutes of some sort, matter, logical space, the totality of atomic states of affairs, etc. etc. The paradoxicality and ineffability of mystical absolutes is simply a logical consequence of their being absolutes at all: every absolute differs *toto caelo* [completely] from any ordinary, empirical existent.

The traits of absolutes we have so far mentioned would, however, be found in purely intellectual approaches of various sorts that are anything but mystical. Much orthodox theology, for instance, is concerned with the unique properties of a transcendent deity, without there being the slightest spice of mysticism in its approaches to this being. It may even be held that strict theism is essentially unmystical, and this is why mysticism is frequently condemned in a theistic period of orthodoxy. Meister Eckhart, perhaps the greatest of Christian mystical philosophers, was condemned as a heretic by John XXII, the worst of the Popes. Mysticism may in fact be said to arise when an absolute is treated with extreme seriousness, both in theoretical vision and in practice: it is the sort of absolute we get when the logic of absoluteness is pursued to its furthest limit. Above all, what characterises mysticism is a refusal to accept and use the notions of identity and diversity which the ordinary logic applies so confidently, whether in the relation of finite objects to the absolute, or of finite objects to one another. Ordinary logic assumes confidently that we can always pick out a number of separate items, a, b, c, d, e, etc., which, however much alike and intimately related, have each their own numerically distinct individuality, and can maintain it for a considerable period, during which they have absolutely no tendency to pass over into other things, or coalesce with them, or lose themselves in them. Whereas, if the uniqueness and omni-responsibility of an absolute is taken seriously, and there is not thought to be anything that is not an extension or expression of itself, then there can be no a, b, c, d, e, etc., which are not simply different names and guises of the same absolute, and which do not really differ from each other otherwise than as the morning star differs from the evening star. To take the notion of an absolute quite seriously is in fact to put the ordinary notion of diversity, and with it the ordinary notion of identity, out of action. Both can be only notions of the surface, of the first regard, which can be given an immediate, but not an ultimate, application. Mystics do not believe that the effective use of a notion in ordinary situations is sufficient to establish its ultimate legitimacy. The only sort of identity that can be ultimately admitted is one that can be stretched in varying degrees, which can come nearer and nearer to the limit of sheer diversity, otherness, without ever reaching it. We may say, if we like, that the absolute may be *alienated* from itself in different degrees in different forms or phases, and these in different degrees from one another, without ever reaching the breaking-point of sheer diversity. What we ordinarily wish to say will appear in a new form in a fully developed mystical logic, in which all absurdity will be carefully circumvented. But a mystical logic, like any other logic, takes a long time in construction, and, before it is fully developed, there will be phases in which we shall seem merely to be subverting ordinary forms of expression without putting anything effective and lucid in their place. We can understand how, plagued by the seeming absurdity of two conflicting schemes of diction, there should be a desire to say of an absolute that it has *none* of the mutually exclusive characters of its forms and phases, that it is, in some quite non-ordinary sense, wholly *other* than them, or beyond them, that it is not to be called a *thing* or an *entity*, and that it is in some very deep sense Nothing at all. Most Japanese teahouses have a symbol for the ultimate Nothingness which blessedly underlies tea-drinking like all finite objects, but it is plain that this Nothingness is only a step removed from the Everythingness and All-pervadingness of more positive mystical characterisations. Even of some of our packed thoughts it is as proper to say that they are very rich in distinct items as that they are wholly void of any distinct items at all, and such seemingly contradictory characterisations, which are certainly only analogical, are *a fortiori* no objection when applied to so remote and difficult an object as a mystical absolute.

To take this notion of an absolute seriously is further to treat the identity of everything, including oneself, with the absolute, as no mere remote intellectual conviction, but as something that ought to be capable of being realised so vividly and compellingly that it becomes a direct personal experience. Mystical experiences are not to be assimilated to queer extrasensory perceptions. They are the understandings of an identity as logically perspicuous as 'If p then p' or 'If $p.q$. then $q.p$.'. Only, while the theorems of the propositional calculus can be understood without passion, being adjusted to our normal state of alienation, the theorems of mysticism can only be understood with passion; one must oneself live through, consummate the identity which they postulate. All mysticism involves a doctrine and a practice and an experience of ecstasy, and the experiential character of mysticism is simply a consequence of the meaning of the identity it posits, an identity in which the ordinary person is taken out of his alienation, and taken up, or partially taken up, into the ultimate mystical unity.

Some of you will perhaps have been charitable enough to concede that what I have so far said may be quite all right as describing what mystics *think* is the logic of their utterances, but will none the less doubt whether there is any serious logic of this putative sort. The notion of an identity underlying plainly incompatible specifications is, they would say, a purely self-contradictory notion, especially when the absolute is not thought of as broken up into parts, and as admitting incompatible characterisations of its several parts. The notion of an identity underlying separable entities is likewise a wholly empty conception: it points to nothing and tells us nothing about anything. The notion that sheer diversity and complete independence are impossible is likewise inadmissible: they are perfectly possible, and should be recognised as such in any sound logic. And the notion of what exists of necessity is purely meaningless: necessity only connects characterisations of possible existents with one another, and existence always involves the connection of characterisations and descriptions with extralinguistic reality. A necessary existent, were it admissible, would, moreover, be there whatever were the case, like the number Two or the ideal of Chastity, and this would make its so-called existence a wholly empty, abstract case of subsistence. Only what could be absent from the world could also contribute to its content, could exist in an ordinary sense, and could exercise all those saving, illuminative virtues which mystical thinkers have always been ready to attribute to their absolute. There is, finally, no meaning in the notion of perfection, in the joint embodiment of all excellence in an unsurpassable form: it is the nature of valuable qualities to conflict with other valuable qualities, and to be such as to have no maximum, but to permit always of being surpassed.

The answer to these and to many other similar objections is difficult: all that I here have to say is that the difficulties raised are to a large extent question-begging; they rest on a metaphysic or ontology which lies securely ensconced behind the very forms of our common utterances, of our ordinary logic, and which so absolutely commits us to a certain way of regarding the world and anticipating its contents, that it seems to commit us to nothing at all. The forms of our common utterance are by no means vacuous and innocuous: though they may not *say* that the world consists of certain types and ranges of elements and no others, or that it permits of certain sorts of treatment and no others, they may be said to *imply* that this is the case, and what they imply may be open to question, it may not, on reflection, be the only nor the truest way of viewing the facts in the world. The forms of our common utterance imply the existence or the possibility of an independent array of logical subjects, *a, b, c, d, e*, etc., each capable of existing or not existing separately without others, and permitting the attribution of characters, the possession of which by one logical subject tells us nothing as to the possession of the same character by another logical subject. They also imply the presence of relations among subjects which are external and indifferent to their existence and their character. The forms of this type of utterance readily lead to the development of a metaphysical atomism even more drastic than that worked out by Wittgenstein in the *Tractatus Logicophilosophicus*, an atomism of wholly independent existences, quite contingently characterised and related. But there is nothing to prevent us from holding this metaphysic to be merely an abstract or surface way of regarding the world, completely absurd if regarded as setting forth in completeness what a world conceivably could be, unable to make sense of the rational procedures which enable us comprehensively to understand the world and the beings who share it with us, and yet presupposing these procedures in the comprehensive, *soi-disant* [so-called] intelligible view it sets forth of what is. Faced by deep reflection on what I may call the unitive aspects of our experience, we may well move towards a Spinozistic logic in which, instead of saying things about separate finite logical subjects, we say them in a somewhat transformed guise of a single logical subject *in so far* as it is expressed in this or that modification. Instead of saying that John is tall, and Paul fat, we may say that the absolute substance is tall in its Johannine aspect, fat in its Pauline one. We may then, taking into account certain deeper strands of experience, progress to Meister Eckhart's statement that this blade of grass is this wood and this stone: properly understood, this is no more illogical and no more destructive of ordinary beliefs suitably expressed, than saying that the morning star is the evening star. If certain philosophers here object that we are merely talking about ordinary facts in an extravagant and unenlightening way, we may question the whole metaphysics of hard facts indifferent to the conventions of our language, and we may say that the whole structure of the world and thinking subjects, and the structure of any world and any thinking subjects, makes certain ways of talking about the world more deeply revelatory of its being, truer to its deep structure, than others. . . .

The notion of unsurpassable, all-inclusive excellence or perfection likewise raises considerable difficulties, but these can perhaps best be met by holding, as mystical people in fact frequently hold, that the absolute does not so much *have* all excellences as *is* them all: that is, the absolute is not beautiful but beauty itself, not just but justice itself, etc. etc. In the case of the absolute, in short, the distinction of type and instance falls away: it is not a case of goodness, nor an abstract character of such cases, but it is, if you like, a character which is also a unique case, and a unique case which is also a character. I am not sure that this is not exactly what was present in the mind of Plato when he talked about the causality of the Forms and of the Form of the Good which engendered them all. If there is difficulty in the notion of a subsistent perfection, or set of subsistent perfections, there is certainly no difficulty in a mind which contemplates and desires them all, and which only contingently contemplates or desires particular instances of them, and which is so intrinsically one with what it desires and contemplates as to be rightly said to *be* them all, and to be them all in unity. I do not think it is at all difficult to conceive a profound spiritual simplicity in which all possibilities of being and goodness will be enjoyed together in a single vision, and which is such that any instantiation of such a comprehensive unity will necessarily be one-sided and partial and piecemeal, or in other words creaturely. Nor is it hard to imagine that the relation of finite instantial beings to the all-embracing seminal absolute is neither one of mere otherness nor of simple identity, but a unique variable relation of logical remoteness or alienation. It is not one of mere otherness, since it is arguably of the essence of a mystical absolute that its ideal perfections should be variously forthshadowed in actual instances, and, since each of those instances embodies an aspect, a side of its eternal essence, and can be mystically seen as embodying precisely this, but it is also not one of mere identity, since any realised instance differs categorially from a spiritual simplicity which involves thought of all realisable instances, and sorts of instances, whatever.

This is not the time nor the place to develop a complete mystical logic and mystical theology, nor do I think that more than the rudiments of it exist in such works as the *Summae* of Thomas Aquinas, or the Commentaries on the *Vedanta Sutras* of Shankaracharya and Ramanujacharya. Suffice it to say that I think that, while mysticism and its logic can be developed in an undisciplined chaotic or poetic way, in which no attempt is made to achieve genuine consistency, and contradictions are even reverenced as stigmata of higher truth, mysticism can also be developed in a manner which has complete logical viability, even if it involves many concepts strange to ordinary thought and reflection. The logic of a mystical absolute is the logic of a limiting case, and we must not expect a limiting case to behave in the same logical manner as a case which does not fall at the limit. If even in mathematics we can regard a straight line as a queer limiting case of an ellipse, we must not steer clear of similar queernesses in the construction of a viable mystical absolute. The outcome of my statement is clear: the forms of utterance that we adopt in our ultimate view of the world should not be arbitrary, but should reflect our profound reflections on what, considered most carefully, is really necessary and possible, and the fact that our ordinary, unconsidered forms of utterances have little or nothing that is mystical about them, does not prove that the forms of utterance which will survive in the deepest and most careful reflection will not be entirely mystical. It is not a question of being inconsistent or illogical, but of deciding what form one's consistency or logicality may take. Ultimately there may prove to be only one such wholly satisfactory pattern of consistency or logicality, and that a mystical one.

It is, however, one thing to remove the main sources of objection to mysticism, and quite another thing to recommend it strongly and positively. And it is here, of course, that a lot of persuasive argument is necessary, for most men at most times, and some men at all times, feel no impulse to pass beyond the sundered, dismembered, sorry world of our common experience, and see nothing but an irrelevant expression of temperament in the utterances of mystics. Even if they at times see the world in a mystical light, as involving 'something far more deeply interfused' and Wordsworthian, they are at other times no more inclined to see anything more deeply revealing in their vision than is seen in the euphoria of drunkenness, the ecstasy of sex or the dead sea dryness of jaundice. Mysticism, they think, is an attitude, deeply and widely human, which paints the world in peculiar, transcendental colours: these colours are an insubstantial pageant which reflects nothing deeply rooted in the nature of things.

To counter this line of attack, I shall first argue that mystical unity at the limit or centre of things alone guarantees that coherence and continuity at the periphery which is involved in all our basic rational enterprises. Unmystical ways of viewing the world would see it as composed of a vast number of wholly independent entities and features, and this, as is well known, raises a whole host of notional quandaries, or ontological and epistemological problems. How can we form a valid conception of the structure of all space and time from the small specimens given to us? How can we extrapolate the character and behaviour of an individual from the small segment known to us? How can we generalise from the character and behaviour of one individual to the character and behaviour of a whole infinite class of individuals, wherever it may be distributed in the infinite reaches of space and time? Why, finally, do we think experienced things will have that affinity with our minds and our concepts that will enable us to plumb their secrets? It is well known that, on a metaphysic of radical independence and atomism, all these questions admit of no satisfactory answer. Whereas, on a mystical basis, the profound fit and mutual accommodation of alienated, peripheral things is precisely what is to be expected: it is the alienated expression of a mystical unity which, however much strained to breaking point, never ceases to be real and effective.

Much the same holds if we turn to that deep understanding of the interior life of others which arguably underlies all our interpretation and prediction of other people's behaviour, all acts of communication and cooperation, and all the ethical experiences and endeavours which arise in our relations with them. It is surely clear that unmystical views have the greatest difficulty in rendering these matters intelligible. They cannot make plain why we should be clear that others feel as we do in similar circumstances, and even how we attach meaning to such a presumption. They are forced to give unsatisfactory, behaviouristic analyses of what we are so sure of, or justify our certainty in strange left-handed ways. Whereas, on a mystical basis, our understanding of others rests on the fact that they are not absolutely others, but only variously alienated forms of the same ultimate, pervasive unity, which expresses itself in the inkling, whether clear or remote, of what may be present in the experience of others. . . .

I should, however, be misrepresenting the difficulty of all that I have been saying if I did not indicate further presumptions and tasks which I think the acceptance of a mystical logic would certainly involve. A mystical system must not only explain and justify what I may call the unitive aspects of our experience, but also the patent disunity, confusion, imperfection and badness which the world at its surface exhibits. It must, to be a satisfactory logic, integrate the surface of the world with its centre, show each to be necessary to the other. This it is plain is what many mystical ways of regarding things certainly have not done, and they have accordingly become largely an empty form of words, inflated with an emotional inspiration which meaninglessly babbles of a profound unity, embodying and unifying all value, behind the job-lot which actually confronts us. There are, however, forms of mysticism which make alienation and deep-identity mutually dependent: the absolute must alienate itself in limited, instantial forms so that it may steadily reduce and overcome their alienation, and in so doing truly possess and enjoy and recognise itself. This is more or less the creed of some of the great Christian mystics, mainly Germans, who include Meister Eckhart; it is a view which also runs through the whole philosophy of Hegel, and so may fitly be called the 'Germanic Theology'. Some form of the Germanic Theology is, I think, necessary to giving a viable sense to mystical utterances. And I should go further in thinking that a fully developed working mysticism demands a developed otherwordly cosmology, in which numerous states of being are postulated which mediate between the extreme of alienation characteristic of this world and the extreme of unity characteristic of a mystical ecstasy. There must be levels of experience and being achieved either in or after this life, in which things become steadily more manageable and dreamlike, more fluid and interpenetrating, more general, more marked by personal attitude and communion, more dominated by values than things in this life, until in the end the extreme of mystical unity is reached. Competent mystics like Plotinus, Dante, Swedenborg, the Buddhists, have described such transitional states, and it is my conviction that this world and this experience only makes sense if it is linked, not only to an ultimate mystical unity, but also to the transitional states in question. Mysticism is a logical matter, but a logic is only acceptable if it finds the right sort of empirical material to fit it, and the right sort of material must include worlds and lives stricken with less dispersion and diversity than our present life.

In concluding this lecture on mysticism I shall not apologise for the way in which I have dealt with the subject, that is as a committed partisan, concerned to put on mystical phenomena a very special logical slant of my own. The subject is so vast, difficult and complex that without a strong, simplifying, personal line, one cannot hope to get anywhere among its intricacies. I believe that mysticism enters into almost everyone's attitudes, and that it is as much a universal background to experience as the open sky is to vision: to ignore it is to be drearily myopic, and to take the element of splendour and depth out of everything, and certainly out of philosophy. That element of splendour and depth is certainly present in Plato and Aristotle, in Plotinus, Aquinas, Spinoza, Hegel, and let me finally say in Wittgenstein. And there is no reason why we should let it be squeezed out of philosophy by any form of logic-chopping or minute analysis.

a final transition

So we come to the end of this group of essays called *Self and World.* What is the conclusion? Is there a conclusion? Can there be a conclusion to the question of self-knowledge when the self is intimately intertwined with its world and its world is both variable and ambiguous? Further, only the reader could write the conclusion that would articulate the reader's own self-knowledge. Nonetheless, something like a review is in order.

We began with the Good Brahmin's problems. That wealthy and well-attended man was miserable because, he claimed, "I do not know whence I came, whither I go, what I am, nor what I shall become." Most of the essays in this book bear more or less directly on the Good Brahmin's series of questions. They deal with different dimensions of self-definition. The first set of essays deals primarily with self-identity in terms of an attempt to locate the core of consciousness, the ultimate witness of experience, or the locus of free will. The later parts of the book deal with the self not as a dimensionless point of perspective or agency, but as an assemblage of dispositions, traits, behaviors, functions, beliefs—in short, in terms of its *contents* rather than its *perspective.* In this final review of issues I want to relate three ideas: first, the complementarity between viewing the self as contents and as a perspective; second, the variability of the world and how our historical existence relates to the religious quest for some kind of eternal essence; third, a review of issues as seen from the perspective of the kind of mysticism Findlay discusses where the whole and the part, world and self, are perpetually interrelated.

The quest for a core identity led from Descartes' *cogito* through Hume's and Ryle's doubts about the existence of any permanent monitor of consciousness. Often the question of self-identity has less to do with an origin of consciousness than with the achievement of personality. The issue is not the nature of the witness of experience. Instead an identity crisis, in Erikson's sense, relates to what is witnessed: the events, the acts, the choices that characterize a personality. The distinction between contents and perspective is hardly clear-cut, however. One's perspective influences the contents of consciousness; how you look at things influences what you see. The contents seen then reinforce the perspective that admitted them to consciousness. Paolo Freire's "Pedagogy of the Oppressed" offers a reminder of the way class consciousness automatically reproduces itself. Education offers an opportunity to expand one's vision beyond the restrictions of a culturally imposed identity. So too the essays by Fanon and Greer reflect on the contents of identity as they are influenced by the perspectives of race and gender. Once aware of the circular relationship between the contents and perspective of consciousness, you cannot help but have some doubts about the accuracy of your own self-knowledge. For the object of such knowledge is its subject as well. It is as if you were to measure your height by putting your own hand on your head. Isn't there some more objective way to "measure" one's self? Isn't there some absolute measure for self-knowledge to be gained from a less subjective perspective?

In an effort to reach some final, absolute answer to the question of self-identity, people sometimes ask themselves "Who am I really?" The addition of *really* predetermines the form of the answer. The addition of *really* implies the existence of some singular and deep truth beyond and behind the surfaces of illusion. This presupposed reality would be the long sought fruit beneath the rind of illusion, the true identity to be found beneath phony defenses. But such imagery, in its appealing simplicity, betrays the relational complexities of selfhood. Self-identity may not require a single core beneath or behind or within the self. The effort to gain self-knowledge by focusing purely on one's inner experience is therefore a mistake. Self-knowledge requires knowledge of one's world. To the extent that the self is not some isolated ghost in the machine but is instead to be identified with a network of relations spanning different dimensions of psychological, social, and spiritual dimensions of existence, it makes sense to see self-knowledge as requiring something more than narcissistic navel-gazing. So after leaving Descartes' *cogito* and Hume's unsuccessful search for a permanent identity at the core of experience, later essays turn away from the inward path to find the self in its relationships with a world.

Because the self is not a nucleus of personality but a network of relationships in different dimensions, the essays on family and society do not leave the question of self-knowledge. Instead they elaborate the question of self-knowledge by tracing out the self's own extensions throughout the concentric spheres of its environment: first the family, then primitive society, the state, the planet with its limited natural resources, and so on. The self identifies itself as male or female, and further as a member of some ethnic or racial group. Each of the self's identifications further defines its way of being in the world. And each of the self's identifications with parts of its world make it vulnerable to redefinition as parts of its world undergo change.

This point brings us to the second topic: the variability of the world and the relationship between historical existence and claims for eternal truths in religion. More specifically, what is one to say about the variability of religious experience? In recent decades remarkable numbers of Americans have turned toward what can only be described as a more direct experience of the sacred. Whether as born-again Christians, or as devotees of oriental teachings, many have turned from an epistemology of *belief* mediated by traditional institutions toward an epistemology of *experience*. Sociologist of religion Robert Bellah calls it a shift from sky religions toward earth religions. Whatever one calls it, a historical shift is changing the shape of relations to the purportedly eternal divine.

When posing a historical question about religious movements it is difficult to know how to begin to answer because the nature of the historical phenomenon in question presupposes eternal realities that transcend history. The historical or sociological answer is apt to conflict with the religious answer. The historical or sociological answer appeals to contingent historical situations: times are bad and people are looking for an escape; the increase in drug use tunes people in to the spiritual; the decline of western culture is being symptomized by a new planetary consciousness. But the religious response to the historical question tends to reject such answers as not giving credit to the eternal realities forming the content of religious belief. Consequently the historical question poses a paradox to religious belief just as Kierkegaard claimed. How can you ask, "Why *now*?" when the answer is supposed to come from an eternal source that transcends all particular nows? With respect to the historical Christ, Kierkegaard asked how the believer's faith in an eternal happiness can depend on an event (the crucifixion) that took place at a historical moment in time. The same question poses itself with a different reference today: How can so many pursue paths toward spiritual enlightenment when that spiritual quest seems to be so obviously based in a particular historical situation? Isn't it strange to be in possession of eternal truths if it is a historical accident that one even has access to those truths? Isn't it peculiar to base one's eternal happiness on the teachings of a Meher Baba or a Krishnamurti or a Baba Ram Dass when it is clear that if one had been born fifty years earlier one would never have heard of these men? Isn't it odd that so many can acknowledge that the consumption of a man-made drug introduced them into a consciousness that seems to transcend the petty affairs of men? These modern analogues to the historical paradox posed by Kierkegaard strike me as very difficult questions.

The mere posing of such questions may seem to suggest a critique of the religious impulse as rooted in nothing but historical-variable human needs. Whether or not we finally accept such a critique of the new mysticism, we need to be aware of its force. Now, as rarely before, the problem of the false prophet presses upon us. When so many offer salvation in so many different ways, how can one help but suspect that someone is being sold a bill of goods? Our credulity is strained. Clifford begins to make more sense when we are faced with the fanaticism of some Jesus-freaks or a band of orange-clad, headshaven Hare Krishna converts. We begin to fear the all-consuming fire of a driving irrationalism, and the voice of reason and the testaments of history provoke an uninvited anticipation of new crusades, inquisitions, and religious wars.

As has always been the case with religious movements, part of the phenomenon may cause alarm but part reflects an important coming to terms with the spiritual dimensions of human existence. To ignore that dimension is to be less than fully human; to inflate the spiritual dimension into fanaticism is to pervert the religious impulse. We cannot use a blanket criticism of the new mysticism to hide us from the difficult task of steering an even course between the two extremes of ignoring and perverting our spiritual life.

To summarize: the process of establishing identity involves both a perspective on the world and specific contents to the self-knowledge seen from that perspective. Second, some of those contents are historical and variable, even when the perspective is spiritual. Now we come to the third set of interrelated ideas in the final transition: How does the spiritual quest relate to some of the recurrent themes of this book? Consider the following seven issues:

1. The Critique of What Is Otherworldly   Nietzsche's attack on the life-denying flight into otherworldliness and a life beyond seems to me—and to Nietzsche elsewhere in his writings—less applicable to Buddhism than Christianity. True, many Christians stress the thisworldly aspects of their religion, and there are traces of escapism in the Buddhist will to nothingness and the transcending of all desires. Nevertheless, Jung's generalization is as correct as any can be: "The Christian principle which unites opposites is the *worship of God,* in Buddhism it is the *worship of the self—self development"* (*Psychological Types,* Paragraph 375).

2. The Self   The importance of beginning with the self, which has informed the entire structure of this volume, is reflected in the "inward way" of the new mysticism. Though there are false prophets who ask for subservience to the most varied doctrines, much of the new mysticism stresses the importance of finding whatever one can find within one's self.

3. Individualism   Yet the inward way leads to transcending ego rather than reinforcing it. An emphasis upon the self does not entail the selfishness of possessive individualism or the atomism of the individualist metaphysics of the self. The inward way simply takes seriously the importance of identifying the situatedness of one's perspective. Subjectivism is inescapable, certainly as long as one has not uncovered the unconscious influences of one's private provincialism. But the inward way permits a new perspective on the outer. Once we uncover the sources of our consciousness we are better able to distinguish the anatomy of appearances. We are in a better position to distinguish merely subjective bias from trans-subjective or objective truth. Consequently we are closer to joining a transpersonal, nonindividualistic spiritual community.

4. The Body   One of the sources of our consciousness is the incarnateness of consciousness. While this is clearly the message of the incarnation of Christ and the resurrection of the whole body, the perversion of this truth by the historical Church led to a denial of body-consciousness in the Christian tradition. This loss is being restored in the new mysticism with its stress on the importance of certain kinds of food and physical training in yoga, and its regard for the healthy body as both a symptom and a symbol of organic wholeness in human existence.

5. Rationalism and Expanded Awareness   Without in the least denigrating the importance of reason, Laing, Goffman, Polanyi, Leonard, Dewey, and many others agree that we have tended to define reason too narrowly in the western tradition. We have taken conscious logical processes like mathematics as the paradigm, and we have ignored the many subtleties of affective and symbolic consciousness in our attempts to define what is reasonable. We have developed what Marcuse calls an irrational rationality, which promotes the cult of efficiency at the heart of technology. The new mysticism might counter the onesidedness of rationalism without an attack on reason in general.

6. Authoritarianism   Having seen that paternalism in many of its forms has come under attack (Greer, Locke, Laing, Reich, and Fanon) we should take note of the different dynamics of authority in eastern cultures. While relations of authority are hardly absent—the spiritual guru is more blatantly authoritarian than most Protestant ministers (read servants) would ever dare be—the eastern religious teachings seem to point more toward the transcendence of authority relationships than to their preservation. Rather than replacing the father with a God, the worship of the self is aimed at the realization that one can look within rather than aloft to find the sacred.

7. Transfiguration   Seventh, and finally, we come full circle to another aspect of the thisworldliness of the new mysticism. Despite the esoteric talk of astral planes and hidden realms, a dominant theme of the new mysticism seems to reflect a transfiguration of this world rather than a flight into some other. What is at stake is an accurate picture of what this world of human experience really does contain. Is it the flatland of secularism (with or without a transcendent God above), or can we experience this world as transfigured into a sacred existence? Each of the previous six comparisons enters into a doctrine of the possibility and actuality of transfiguration: (1) an emphasis on the finality of this world; (2) the sacredness of the self; that is, (3) community of the self with the cosmos rather than its isolation in individualism; the potential richness of experience that comes with a recognition of (4) incarnate consciousness; and (5) expanded modes of awareness that transcend a onesided rationalism; and finally (6) the realization that the resources lie within and do not depend on the dispensation of some father above. This is not to say that the individual can stand up to the cosmos with a pride unbecoming so small a part of the cosmos; transcending authority does not justify a return to a rationalism in which the individual fancies his mind sufficient to master the world. All six features taken together generate a transfiguration in the seventh circle of self-awareness. The wholeness of human existence adds a sacredness to every part traversed separately. When the pattern is complete, when the method of totalization has included every appearance in its partiality, the parts together take on new meaning. Some people call it being high, others call it being enlightened, and still others call it wisdom.

Sources and Acknowledgments

The following list includes the sources of all of the selections, in order of their appearance, as well as acknowledgments. The author is grateful to those publishers and copyright holders who gave permission to reprint some of the material used in this book.

Part 1

STORY OF A GOOD BRAHMIN   From *The Portable Voltaire*, edited by Ben Ray Redman (New York: The Viking Press, 1949), pp. 436–38. Copyright 1949 by The Viking Press, Inc., © renewed 1977 by Viking Penguin Inc. Reprinted by permission of Viking Penguin Inc.

ON EGO EXTENSION AND OVERJOY   From *The Pump House Gang* by Tom Wolfe (New York: Farrar, Straus & Giroux, 1964), pp. 3–14. Copyright © 1968 by Tom Wolfe, copyright © 1966 by the World Journal Tribune Corporation, copyright © 1964, 1965, 1966 by the New York Herald Tribune, Inc.

Part 2

MEDITATIONS I AND II   From *Meditations on the First Philosophy Which the Existence of God and the Distinction Between Mind and Body Are Demonstrated* by René Descartes.

DESCARTES' MYTH   From *The Concept of Mind* by Gilbert Ryle (New York: Barnes & Noble, 1949), pp. 11–24. Copyright, 1949 by Gilbert Ryle. By permission of Harper & Row, Publishers, Inc. and Hutchinson & Co. Ltd.

ON FREE WILL   From *Augustine: Earlier Writings*, Vol. IV, The Library of Christian Classics, edited by John H. S. Burleigh (Philadelphia, Pa.: The Westminster Press, 1953), pp. 169–77. Used by permission.

FREEDOM AND SELF-CREATION   From *Being and Nothingness* by Jean-Paul Sartre (New York: Philosophical Library, 1956), pp. 38–44, 55–56, 58. Copyright © 1965 by Philosophical Library, Inc. Reprinted by permission of Philosophical Library, Inc.

ON SELF-IDENTITY   From "Of Personal Identity," Book I, Part IV, Section 6 of *The Treatise of Human Nature* by David Hume, edited by T. H. Green and T. H. Grose (London: Longmans, Green, and Co., 1886), pp. 533-43.

IDENTITY, YOUTH AND CRISIS   From *Identity, Youth and Crisis* by Erik Erikson (New York: W. W. Norton, 1968), pp. 15-19, 19-23, 31-35. Selections are reprinted with the permission of W. W. Norton & Company, Inc. Copyright © 1968 by W. W. Norton & Company, Inc.

Part 3

THE DIVIDED LINE AND THE MYTH OF THE CAVE   From *The Republic*, Books VI and VII, in *The Dialogues of Plato*, 4th ed., Vol. II, translated by Benjamin Jowett (New York: Oxford University Press, 1953), pp. 368-75, 376-83. Reprinted by permission of Oxford University Press.

LETTER TO MENOECEUS   From "Epicurus to Menoeceus," in *Epicurus, The Extant Remains*, translated by Cyril Bailey (Oxford, England: The Clarendon Press, 1926), pp. 83-93. Reprinted by permission of Oxford University Press.

METAPHYSICAL INTUITION AND THE SELF   From *The Creative Mind: Introduction to Metaphysics* by Henri Bergson (Secaucus, N.J.: Citadel Press, 1974), pp. 24-30. Copyright by Philosophical Library, Inc.

PHILOSOPHICAL ANALYSIS AND THE PROBLEM OF OTHER MINDS   From *Language, Truth and Logic* by A. J. Ayer (New York: Dover Publications, 1952), pp. 62-66, 122-30. Reprinted by permission.

HOW I KNOW OTHERS   From *The Tacit Dimension* by Michael Polanyi (Garden City, N.Y.: Doubleday & Co., 1966), pp. 3-25. Copyright © 1966 by Michael Polanyi. Reprinted by permission of Doubleday & Company, Inc.

HOW OTHERS KNOW ME   From *The Presentation of Self in Everyday Life* by Erving Goffman (Garden City, N.Y.: Doubleday & Co., 1959), pp. 1-6, 70-76, 248-55. Copyright © 1959 by Erving Goffman. Reprinted by permission of Doubleday & Company, Inc.

THE SOCIAL ORIGINS OF THE SELF   From *Mind, Self and Society* by George H. Mead, edited by Charles W. Morris (Chicago, Ill.: The University of Chicago Press, 1934), pp. 164-73. Reprinted by permission of The University of Chicago Press. Copyright 1934 by The University of Chicago.

Part 4

POLITICS   From "Politics," Book I, Chapters 1 and 2, translated by Benjamin Jowett, in *The Oxford Translation of Aristotle*, Vol. 10, edited by W. D. Ross

(Oxford, England: Clarendon Press, 1921). Reprinted by permission of Oxford University Press.

ON PATERNAL POWER AND CIVIL SOCIETY From "Concerning Civil Government," Second Essay, Chapters VI and VII, in *The Works of John Locke in Ten Volumes*, Vol. 5 (London: Bye and Law, 1801), pp. 367–82.

THE SEXUAL REVOLUTION From *The Sexual Revolution*, 4th rev. ed., by Wilhelm Reich, translated by Theodore P. Wolfe (New York: Farrar, Straus & Giroux, 1969), pp. 10–21. Reprinted with permission of Farrar, Straus & Giroux, Inc. Copyright © 1945, 1962 by Mary Boyd Higgins as trustee of the Wilhelm Reich Infant Trust Fund.

THE POLITICS OF THE FAMILY From *The Politics of the Family and Other Essays* by R. D. Laing (New York: Pantheon Books, 1969), pp. 77–82, 98–102, 111–16. Copyright © 1969–1971 by the R. D. Laing Trust. Reprinted by permission of Pantheon Books, a division of Random House, Inc.

CRITO From *Crito*, in *The Dialogues of Plato*, Vol. I, 4th ed., translated by Benjamin Jowett (New York: Oxford University Press, 1953), pp. 371–84. Reprinted by permission of Oxford University Press.

OF THE LIMITS TO THE AUTHORITY OF SOCIETY OVER THE INDIVIDUAL From *On Liberty* by John Stuart Mill, in *Dissertations and Discussions: Political, Philosophical, and Historical*, Vol. I (Boston, Mass.: William V. Spencer, 1865), pp. 211–32.

ON ALIENATION From *The Economic and Philosophic Manuscripts of 1844* by Karl Marx (Moscow: Foreign Languages Publishing House).

Part 5

THE STATE OF NATURE From *Leviathan*, Chapter XIII, in *The English Works of Thomas Hobbes*, Vol. III (London: John Bohn, 1839), pp. 110–16.

THE SOCIAL CONTRACT From *The Social Contract*, Book I, in *Ideal Empires and Republics*, edited by Charles M. Andrews (New York: M. Walter Dunne, 1901), pp. 3–20.

UTOPIAN COMMUNITIES From *Paths in Utopia* by Martin Buber, translated by R. F. C. Hull (New York: Macmillan, 1950), pp. 129–38. Reprinted by permission of The Macmillan Company and of Routledge & Kegan Paul Ltd. Copyright 1949 by Martin Buber.

WHY TRIBE From *Earth House Hold* by Gary Snyder (New York: New Directions, 1957), pp. 113–16. Copyright 1969 by Gary Snyder. Reprinted by permission of New Directions Corporation.

POETRY AND REVOLUTION: THE ANARCHIST AS REACTIONARY From *Superman and Common Men* by Benjamin R. Barber (New York: Praeger, 1971), pp. 14–25, 31–36. Reprinted by permission.

THE ROOTS OF ECOLOGICAL CRISIS   From *Steps to an Ecology of Mind* by Gregory Bateson (New York: T. Y. Crowell, 1972), pp. 488–93. Copyright © 1972 by Harper & Row, Publishers, Inc. Reprinted by permission of the publisher.

THE POLITICS OF SCARCITY   From *Ecology and the Politics of Scarcity: Prologue to a Political Theory of the Steady State* by William Ophuls (San Francisco, Cal.: W. H. Freeman, 1977), pp. 142–64. Copyright © 1977.

Part 6

ON WOMEN   From *Parerga und Paralipomena* by Arthur Schopenhauer (1857), translated by Thomas Bailey Saunders.

WOMANPOWER   From *The Female Eunuch* by Germaine Greer (New York: McGraw-Hill, 1971). Copyright © 1970, 1971 by Germaine Greer. Used with permission of McGraw-Hill Book Co.

A DEFENSE OF ABORTION   From "A Defense of Abortion" by Judith Jarvis Thompson, *Philosophy & Public Affairs* 1, No. 1 (Fall 1971). Copyright © 1971 by Princeton University Press. Reprinted by permission.

ABORTION AND MORAL SERIOUSNESS   From *Abortion: Law, Choice and Morality* by Daniel Callahan (New York: Macmillan, 1970), pp. 493–501. Reprinted with permission of Macmillan Publishing Co. Copyright © 1970 by Daniel Callahan.

VIOLENCE AND LIBERATION   From *The Wretched of the Earth* by Frantz Fanon (New York: Grove Press, 1963), pp. 51–58, 71–75. Reprinted by permission of Grove Press, Inc. Copyright © 1963 by Presence Africaine.

ON VIOLENCE   From *Crisis of the Republic* by Hannah Arendt (New York: Harcourt Brace Jovanovich, 1970), pp. 113–16, 142–55. © 1970 by Hannah Arendt. By permission of Harcourt Brace Jovanovich, Inc.

Part 7

THE PEDAGOGY OF THE OPPRESSED   From *The Pedagogy of the Oppressed* by Paolo Freire, translated by Myra Bergman Ramos (New York: Herder and Herder, 1970), pp. 27–56. Reprinted by permission.

LABOR AND LEISURE   From *Democracy and Education* by John Dewey (New York: Macmillan, 1916), pp. 250–61. Reprinted with permission of Macmillan Publishing Co., Inc. Copyright 1916 by Macmillan Publishing Co., Inc. renewed 1944 by John Dewey.

EDUCATION AND ECSTASY   From *Education and Ecstasy* by George B. Leonard (New York: Delacorte Press, 1963), pp. 10–21. Copyright © 1968 by George B. Leonard. Reprinted by permission of the publisher, Delacorte Press.

THE CASE AGAINST ART   From *The Republic*, Book X, in *The Dialogues of Plato*, 4th ed., Vol. II, translated by Benjamin Jowett (New York: Oxford University Press, 1953), pp. 468–84. Reprinted by permission of Oxford University Press.

MANIFESTO OF SURREALISM   From *Manifestoes of Surrealism* by André Breton, translated by Richard Seaver and Helen R. Lane (Ann Arbor, Mich.: The University of Michigan Press, 1972), pp. 4–14, 18–26, 44–47. Reprinted by permission.

Part 8

TRUTH IS SUBJECTIVITY   From *Concluding Unscientific Postscript* by Søren Kierkegaard, translated by David F. Swenson and Walter Lowrie (Princeton, N.J.: Princeton University Press, 1941), pp. 178–82, 186–88, 218–20. Copyright 1941 © 1969 by Princeton University Press and the American Scandinavian Foundation.

THE ANTICHRIST   From *The Portable Nietzsche*, edited and translated by Walter Kaufman (New York: Viking Press, 1954), pp. 581–83, 606–08. Copyright 1954 by The Viking Press, Inc. Reprinted by permission of The Viking Press, Inc.

THE ETHICS OF BELIEF   From *Lectures and Essays by the Late William Kingdon Clifford*, edited by Leslie Stephen and Frederick Pollock (London: Macmillan, 1879).

THE WILL TO BELIEVE   From *The Will to Believe and Other Essays* by William James (New York: Longman's Green and Co., 1897).

THE AWAKENING OF A NEW CONSCIOUSNESS IN ZEN   From "The Awakening of a New Consciousness in Zen" by Daisetz T. Suzuki, in *Eranos Jahrbuch*, Vol. XXIII, edited by Olga Fröbe-Kapteyn (Zurich, Switzerland: Rhein-Verlag, 1955), pp. 275–86, 294–96 . Reprinted by permission of Matsugaoka Bunko (The Pine Hill Library).

MYSTICISM AND HUMAN REASON   From "Mysticism and Human Reason" by W. T. Stace, Riecker Memorial Lecture Number 1, in University of Arizona Bulletin Series, Vol. XXVI, No. 3 (May 1955), pp. 9–20. Reprinted by permission.

THE LOGIC OF MYSTICISM   From *Religious Studies* by John Findlay (Cambridge, England: Cambridge University Press, 1972), pp. 145–62. Reprinted by permission.